I0755194

SWEDISH CATALOGUE

I.

STATISTICS.

By DR. ELIS SIDENBLADH,
Secretary of the Roy. Swedish Statistical Central Bureau.

INTERNATIONAL EXHIBITION, 1876.

PHILADELPHIA.

Press of HALLOWELL & COMPANY,
121 South Third Street,
PHILADELPHIA.

INTRODUCTION.

The Official Catalogue of Sweden for the International Exhibition at Vienna, in 1873, consisted of two parts, one (Schweden, Statistische Mittheilungen) was intended to give a general view of Sweden—its government, and industries; the other a more particular account of the articles exhibited. The same plan has been adopted in the preparation of the present Catalogue for the Centennial Exhibition at Philadelphia.

Part I, has, however, been thoroughly revised, and the system of classification changed so as to be in accordance with that of the Centennial Committee.

The compass of the work, the meager reports on some branches of industry, and the exhaustive contributions on others, have rendered it impossible to allot to each branch *that space* which is due to its importance.

The materials placed at my command were official reports. Contributions from government officials, scientists and specialists, whose names have been given, in all cases where it seemed necessary, in foot notes.

STOCKHOLM, Feb. 19, 1876. E. S.

INDEX.

SWEDEN.

SWEDEN AND NORWAY, (Sverige and Norge), two independent kingdoms, but under a common King, form the Scandinavian Peninsula, whose shores are washed by the waters of the Gulf of Bothnia, the Baltic, the Sound, the Kattegat, the Skager-Rack, the North Sea, the Atlantic and Arctic Oceans, and is thus completely separated from the main-land, with the exception of its north-eastern part. The length of its coast, which is indented with numerous bays and fiords, and protected from the brunt of the sea by innumerable islands and rocks, may be estimated at a little upwards of 5000 kilomètres, or about 3200 English miles, each kingdom possessing about one-half. The Scandinavian Peninsula, of which Sweden forms the eastern and southern part (58 per cent.), while Norway makes up the rest (42 per cent.), embraces an area of 761,500 square kilomètres (13,830 geographical square miles; 294,000 English square miles.)

The united kingdoms form, next to Russia, the largest State in Europe, and have a population of rather more than six millions, of which 70 per cent. belong to Sweden, and 30 per cent. to Norway.

In the following we will consider *Sweden*; its country, people, material resources, and development:—

SITUATION, AREA AND DIVISION.

Although Sweden extends northward to latitude 69° 3′ 21.1″, thus passing beyond the Arctic circle, it reaches southward to latitude 55° 20′ 18″, thus coming within the latitude of its neighboring state, Denmark, and even further south than the northern part of Prussia, where it projects northward along the eastern shore of the Baltic. The total length of Sweden, from north to south, is about 1500 kilomètres, (950 English miles), and the width from 300 to 400 kilomètres, (200 to 250 English miles.) The Observatory of Stockholm lies 18° 3′ 29.85″ east of Greenwich, or 15° 43′ 20.4″ east of Paris.

The Läns (governments or departments), are the largest administrative divisions of the country, and are so arranged in the following table that the capital and its environs come first, then those along the east coast of the country as far as the most southerly Län, Malmöhus, and thence toward the north as far as the Län of Norrbotten, which is the most northern. (Compare foregoing map.)

THE AREA OF THE KINGDOM IS DIVIDED AS FOLLOWS:

"Läns" or Governments.	Swedish Square Miles.		Square Kilomètres.	Geograph. Square Miles.	English Square Miles.
	Main Land and Isl's.	Lakes.	Total.	Total.	Total.
Town of Stockholm, Stockholm's Län	61.608	3.232	7,407.78	134.542	2,860
Uppsala - - - - - do.	44.485	1.186	5,217.78	94.767	2,015
(Nyköping, or) Södermanland's do.	54.018	5.002	6,742.86	122.466	2,603
(Linköping, or) Östergötland's do.	85.052	8.915	10,735.45	194.981	4,145
Jönköping's - - - - - do.	88.277	9.199	11,136.34	202.262	4,300
(Wexiö, or) Kronoberg's - do.	78.251	8.834	9,949.17	180.700	3,842
Kalmar - - - - - do.	95.876	4.900	11,513.36	209.109	4,445
(Wisby, or Gottland's - do.	25.059	2.424	3,139.85	57.027	1,212
(Karlskrona, or) Blekinge - do.	25.347	1.042	3,014.87	54.757	1,164
Kristianstad's - - - do.	54.841	1.991	6,492.82	117,991	2,507
(Malmö, or) Malmöhus - do.	40.989	0.881	4,783.60	86.882	1,847
(Halmstad, or) Halland's - do.	41.748	1.311	4,919.38	89.347	1,899
Göteborg's and Bohus - - do.	42.934	1.328	5,056.80	91.843	1,953
(Wenersborg, or) Elfsborg's - do.	104.269	7.902	12,815.24	232.754	4,948
(Mariestad, or) Skaraborg's - do.	71.470	3.560	8,571.95	155.687	3,310
(Karlstad, or) Wermland's - do.	133.412	14.392	16,886.16	306.692	6,520
Örebro, (or Nerike) - - do.	72.400	7.000	9,071.21	164.754	3,503
(Westerås, or) Westmanland's do.	54.948	2.836	6,601.65	119.902	2,549
(Falun, or) Kapparberg's - do.	237.681	17.117	29,109.90	528.704	11,240
(Gefle, or) Gefleborg's - - do.	155.000	14.200	19,330.59	351.089	7,464
(Hernösand, or) Wester-norrland's do.	203.700	12.000	24,643.07	447.575	9,515
(Östersund, or) Jemtland's - do.	408.000	36.000	50,725.66	921.296	19,586
(Umeå, or) Westerbotten's - do.	516.000	25.000	61,807.63	1,122.571	23,865
(Luleå, or) Norrbotten's - - do.	871.000	60.000	106,363.96	1,931.812	41.069
Lake Wener - - -	——	45.648	5,215.15	94.719	2,014
" Wetter - - -	——	16.220	1,853.09	33.656	715
" Mälar - - - -	——	10.708	1,223.36	22.219	472
" Hjelmar -	——	4.248	485.32	8.815	187
Land - - -	3,566.365	——	407,446.51	7,400.173	157,321
Water - -	——	327.076	37,367.49	678.680	14,428
Total - - -	3,893.441		444,814.00	8,078.853	171,749

N. B.—The above figures will, in all probability, be altered a little, when the computations of the area of the kingdom, which are now being made, have been completed.

The Läns frequently have two names, one which is derived from the seat of government, (all such names are placed first in the foregoing table); the other, usually from the old division of the provinces.

These Provinces, which in former times were of greater importance, as they formed little Kingdoms and maintained their own provincial laws till even later times; have now no special political significance, but inasmuch as certain provincial differences still remain, and their names are frequently used instead of the new ones, it may be proper, just here, to dwell upon them a little. The Geographic division of the Kingdom into three parts stands in intimate relation with the old provincial division. The three geographical divisions are as follows: Svealand, (the central), Götaland, (the southern), Norrland, (the northern); and though the boundaries of the Läns and the provinces do not quite correspond, the following may on the whole be stated as correct:—

Svealand has six provinces: 1. Uppland, (the Län of Uppsala, and the greater part of the Län of Stockholm, or that called Roslagen); 2. Södermanland, (the remaining part of the Län of Stockholm, or that called Södertörn, and the whole Län of Södermanland); 3. Westmanland, (the Län of Westmanland and the northern part of the Län of Örebro); 4. Nerike, (the southern part of the Län of Örebro); 5. Vermland, (the Län of Vermland); 6. Dalecarlia or Dalarne, (the Län of Kopparberg.)

Götaland has nine provinces: 1. Östergötland, (the Län of Östergötland); 2. Westergötland, (the Län of Skaraborg, and the southern part of the Län of Elfsborg); 3. Dalsland, (the northern part of the Län of Elfsborg); 4. Småland, (the Läns of Jönköping, Kronoberg and Kalmar, to which also belongs the Isle of Öland); 5. Gottland, (the Län of Gottland); 6. Blekinge, (the Län of Blekinge); 7. Scania or Skåne, (the Läns of Kristianstad and Malmöhus); 8. Halland, (the Län of Halland); 9. Bohuslän (the Län of Göteborg and Bohus.)

Norrland comprises the following provinces: 1 and 2. Gestrikland and Helsingland, (the Län of Gefleborg); 3 and 4. Medelpad and Ångermanland, (the Län of Westernorrland); 5 and 6. Jemtland and Herjedalen, (the Län of Jemtland), as also 7. Westerbotten, together with Lappland, (the Läns of Westerbotten and Norrbotten.)

Norrland is sometimes considered as extending down to the river Dal-elf, in which case Dalarne is included in that division.

Lappland, the most northern part of Sweden, bordering on Norway, has an area of 100,000 square kilomètres, (2000 geographical or 40,000 English square miles), or nearly one-quarter of the area of the Kingdom, and together with Norrland, forms more than one-half of the whole area. This vast territory is of all the Swedish provinces, the least adapted to agriculture, and if one wishes to form a true estimate of Sweden's prosperity, he must discriminate sharply between this and the rest of the Kingdom, for the difference is very great, for instance, between Skåne and Lappland; the former comparing favorably in climate, still more so in cultivation and density of population, with the most highly cultivated States of Europe—while Lappland is but sparsely populated, outside of its nomads, and agriculture, while it is to some extent in several sections, it is nowhere prosecuted as a chief branch of industry. And yet Lappland may have a bright future, for she possesses not only vast forests, but also immense mineral wealth, especially in iron, which is scarcely or not at all developed.

Ecclesiastically the Kingdom is divided into twelve **bishoprics**, which are all named after the place of residence of the bishop: 1. Uppsala, (Archbishopric), comprising the provinces of Uppland, Gestrikland and Helsingland; 2. Strengnäs, (Södermanland and Nerike); 3. Linköping, (Östergötland and part of Småland); 4. Wexiö, (the western part of Småland); 5. Kalmar, (the eastern part of Småland, together with the isle of Öland); 6. Visby, (Gottland); 7. Lund, (Skåne and Blekinge); 8. Göteborg, (Halland and Bohuslän, together with a part of Westergötland); 9. Skara, (the greater part of Westergötland); 10. Karlstad, (Vermland and Dalsland); 11. Westerås, (Westmanland and Dalarne); 12. Hernösand, (Medelpad, Ångermanland, Jemtland, Herjedalen, Westerbotten, and Lappland. For the capital, which is properly included in the archbishopric, there is a Consistory of the town of Stockholm. There is also a Court-consistory.

MOUNTAINS AND PLAINS.

Sweden is generally not so mountainous as its "Brother Kingdom," Norway, and the highest mountains are found just on the border of that country. The boundary line itself is supposed to run along a mountain chain, which is called by geographers the Kölen, though in reality there is no mountain of that name. The highest mountain in Sweden, Sulitelma, (6315 Swedish feet, or 1874.9 mètres above the level of the sea), lies in Lappland, and is the only alpine elevation in Sweden, where, as far as is known, glaciers are found, but there are other mountains in these districts, and still further south along the frontier of the kingdom, in Jemtland, and Herjedalen, with an elevation of from 4000 to 5000 feet, (1200 to 1500 mètres), whose peaks are dotted with patches of snow the whole year round. Of the more noted mountains we may here mention Åreskutan, (4958 feet or 1472 mètres), in Jemtland; Städjan, (3961 feet or 1176 mètres), in Dalarne, and those called the Westgötaberg, (Kinnekulle, Billingen, Halleberg, Hunneberg and others), the latter of which are not so remarkable for their height (not exceeding 1000 feet or 300 mètres) as for their shape and geological formation.

About eight per cent. of the area of Sweden is considered to lie upwards of 2000 feet (600 mètres) above the level of the sea. Those parts which sometimes extend beyond the tree-line, are exclusively in Norrland and Dalarne, and border upon Norway. The coast-line along the Gulf of Bothnia, and the whole of the central and southern parts of Sweden, lie, with few exceptions, lower than 800 feet (20 mètres) above the level of the sea. Of the whole area of the kingdom, a third part does not lie 300 feet (90 mètres) above the level of the sea, and it is within these lower lying districts, that the most highly cultivated parts of the country are found, as well as the largest plains, such as the Uppland, the Östgöta, the Westgöta, and the Skåne plains. With the exception of these, the plains are neither numerous nor large, for, though there are extensive tracts of land, which attain a height of only a few hundred feet above the level of the sea, these are generally intersected by numerous hills and valleys.

LAKES AND RIVERS.

Sweden, next to Finland, is the best irrigated country in Europe, as her lakes and rivers cover an area of 37,367 kilomètres, (14,428 English square miles) or 8.4 per cent. of her whole territory, while she has a sea coast of 2500 kilomèters, (1500 English miles.)

The Russian Lakes, Ladoga and Onega, are the two largest in Europe, but the Swedish Wener ranks third, having a surface of 5215 square kilomètres (2014 English square miles), and lies 148.5 feet (44.1 mètres) above the level of the sea. Of the other large lakes, the Vetter lies 297. feet (88.2 mètres), the Hjelmar 793 feet (235 mètres), while the Mälar lies only 1. foot (0.3 mètres) above the level of the sea, and empties almost directly into the Baltic at Stockholm.

The Storsjö, (or "Great Lake"), is the largest in Jemtland and lies 983 feet (291.8 mètres) above the level of the sea, and many of the larger bodies of water in Lappland, which are the sources of considerable rivers, or through which they flow on their way to the Gulf of Bothnia, lie at as high an altitude.

The water of the Swedish lakes, as well as that of the rivers, is generally clear and drinkable. Lake Wetter is especially known for its clear, but at the same time turbulent, body of water, as well as for its great depth, (420 feet or 125 mètres.) The rest of the lakes have a depth of from 200 to 300 feet, (60 to 90 mètres), but in all probability, many mountain-lakes in Lappland have a still greater depth.

Of the numerous rivers (or elfs)which flow into the Gulf of Bothnia, the Ångerman elf is the best known, not only for its volume, but for its natural beauty. The Dal elf, which is usually considered as the dividing line between Norrland and the southern part of Sweden, empties further to the south. On the west coast flows the Göta elf, the outlet of Lake Wener, famed for the Trollhätta waterfall, which, though it is interrupted by several rapids, may, nevertheless, be compared with the celebrated cataracts of the Rhine, not only on account of the height of the whole fall (111 feet, 33 mètres), but also on account of its volume of water. But Sweden abounds in such scenery. Almost every river or stream forms a foaming current or roaring cataracts, and there are thousands of them. Even the Trollhätta finds a rival in the Njommelsaska (hare's leap), in Lappland.

One of the peculiarities of these lakes is that they are sometimes interrupted by an almost perpendicular fall the water then spreading out forming a second part of the lake.

The nation possesses in these numerous falls an almost inexhaustible water power, which has not, as yet, been utilized to that extent which it might have been. True, numerous mills and iron works are driven by them, but yet the proportion used, is but a small fraction of the whole. The Trollhätta alone represents a force of 225,000 horse power, which is equal to ten times the steam power of the Swedish merchant navy, or seven times that of the whole Russian marine. This character of the Swedish rivers carries with it, however, the disadvantage of rendering them innavigable, many of the rivers, (the Dal-elf for instance), being barred at their very mouths by a fall, and, as a rule, they are navigable only for a mile or two, except for rafts and small boats, unless they are provided with canals, as the river Göta-elf, of which we will hereafter speak.

GEOLOGY.

Sweden is formed by the two extreme geological formations, the crystalline rocks of the Azoic being, as a general thing, immediately followed by the loose deposits of the Quaternary, while the intermediate formations are but sparingly represented, the Silurian being the only one that has any considerable distribution.

The Azoic Formation extends over the greater part of the country, and is represented by granite, gneiss and other stratified rocks of this formation, which alternate with one another. The gneiss is of both the red and gray varieties, the former being found in the western, the latter in the eastern part. Eurite, Hälle-flinta, which is supposed to form the youngest of the Azoic groups, is of great practical importance, for although it has but a comparatively limited distribution, the most important deposits of iron ores in central Sweden occur in it. They do not form veins, but elliptical beds, which are apparently of the same age as the surrounding rock, which is also true of certain zinc and copper beds. A crystalline limestone, the Swedish marble, occurs in the same rock, and generally in the immediate vicinity of the ore-beds. A similar limestone, along with considerable iron ore deposits, occurs in the gneiss districts, but seems to be confined to that of the younger gneiss.

The granites of Sweden vary in appearance, and belong to different formations, but the greater part of them seem to belong to the Azoic. They occur in large masses, the largest of which lie along the centre of the country, from north to south, so that the granite predominates in the centre and the gneisses along the coast. The coarse-crystalline variety, known as pegmatite or graphic granite, occurs in veins generally in the gneiss, and is quarried, especially in the Stockholm's Skärgård (archipelago,) on account of the pure feldspar which it contains, which is used both abroad and at home, in the manufacture of porcelain-ware.

Among the eruptive rocks, in addition to the granite, occur the porphyries and green-stones (hyperite, diabas, diorite, and trap); the former are quite strongly represented, especially in Dalarne, and are known in foreign countries, as well as in Sweden, on account of the many beautiful polished articles which are made out of them. The greenstones generally occur in small, isolated masses, or as larger or smaller dikes throughout the country, but sometimes as layers (Decken) over the sedimentary strata, of which the mountains of Westergötland form an example. Basalt occurs but sparingly in Skåne.

The Silurian Formation occurs at several places in different parts of the country, as in Skåne, Gottland, (upper Silurian), Öland, along the large lakes, Vener, Vetter, etc., in Westergötland in the so-called Westgötabergen, in Östergötland, in Nerike, and in Jemtland at lake Storsjö, which is the largest of all these occurrences, extending up to Lappland, and includes upwards of 100 geographical square miles, The high mountains to the west of this are formed of metamorphic slates, even to their very peakes, (Åreskutan, Sulitelma), the age of which has not yet been determined with any degree of certainty, but which are doubtless younger than the middle of the Silurian. In Dalarne and Herjedalen are large mountain districts, formed of sandstones and quartzites, which are probably partly of equal age and partly younger than the neighboring Silurian deposits.

The rocks, which undoubtedly belong to the Silurian, occur in about the same order throughout the country, first sandstone resting upon the Azoic, then alum-shale and stinkstone—these two are sometimes considered as belonging to the Cambrian formation—then limestone and slate. These are frequently covered by a layer of greenstone. The sandstone is used as building material and for mill-stones; the alum-shale, either as a source of alum or as fuel in its manufacture or in lime-kilns. The limestone is used as building material, cut into flagging, or burnt into lime. A mixture of ground burnt alum-shale and lime, yields a much-used and durable hydraulic cement.

The rest of the formations down to the quaternary, occur exclusively in Skåne, in the southern part of the Kingdom. There are some deposits of clay and sandstone found in the northwestern part of this province, which are supposed to belong to the end of the *Triassic*, or to the beginning of the *Jurassic* period, and form the only coal bearing district of Sweden. Coal mining is prosecuted at Höganäs, Billesholm, Helsingborg, and at other places. Of late years heavy speculations in these lands have been carried on. The clay is partly fire clay. The *Cretaceous* formation occurs in the southwestern, and in part of the eastern section of Skåne.

The Quarternary Formation of Sweden is partly of glacial and partly of post-glacial origin. The oldest of the former formations is the so-called Krossgrus, or angular gravel, formed as the beds of glaciers during the previous ice period, and which during a succeeding period, when sunk below the level of the sea, more or less completely washed off of the mountains and covered in the valleys by marine deposits. Above the line of these deposits, which is chiefly distinguished by the glacial clay, whose mean height above the present sea level may, in central Sweden, be estimated at about 500 feet (150 mètres), while it rises toward the north and sinks to the south, being in Skåne only from 50 to 100 feet (15 to 30 mètres) above the sea level, come the moraine deposits, which form the surface of the country and almost entirely cover the mountains, but below it, appears the surface of the mountains, surrounded by deposits of diluvial sand and clay, which extend over the greater part of the country. The most peculiar formations of the quarternary are the "åsar" (sand-ridges), occuring principally in the Mälar valley, which are formed of stratified sand and gravel mixed with rounded rocks and boulders. They are generally narrow and high, sometimes running up into a sharp ridge, and their general direction is from north to south. Some of them can be traced for 200 or 300 kilomètres. Part of the city of Stockholm is built upon one of these ridges.

The post-glacical formations consist of clays, which are, however, found only in the neighborhood of the present coast, and of river and fresh water deposits. Of the latter the peat-bogs, alone, are of any practical importance.

The adaptability of a district to agriculture depends upon its lying within or without the boundaries of the diluvial, or the marine deposits, as is seen from the geological relations of the country, which have already been stated, and if within the diluvial, upon the character of the rocks out of which the angular gravel has been formed.

In sections where the marine deposits are wanting, this land has to be used for agricultural purposes, and, though it is difficult to cultivate on account of its stoniness, it affords by no means an unthankful yield, but, on the contrary, if there be an admixture of clayey or calcareous earth, it forms a remarkably productive soil.

The marine clays are, on the other hand easily tillable, on account of the absence of rocks, and are almost entirely devoted to agriculture.

The glacial clays, which lie southward of limestone districts, contain a greater or less per centage of carbonate of lime (20 or 30 per cent. not being uncommon), whereby its productiveness is considerably increased, as is the case with the marls of Uppland.

There is a striking difference in the distribution of the tillable land, in the angular gravel and in the clay districts. In the former the fields lie upon the ledges of the mountains and are seldom large, but are generally small irregular patches, while the principal part of the agriculture of the country is confined to the latter, and the fields are larger and more continual.

The other varieties of soil are devoted mostly to forest culture.

For the Geological Survey of Sweden, see Catalogue, Class 335.

CLIMATE.

The Climate of Sweden and Norway is mild in comparison to their high latitude, a fact which is attributed to the influence of the Gulf-Stream.

There are dense forests, and barley and rye mature in the province of Norrland, while its most southern part lies in the same latitude as the ice fields of Greenland, and its northern in that of barren Iceland. A country extending through as many degrees of latitude must have a great variety of climate. The mean yearly temperature of the northern parts along the coast is + 1° C. = + 34° F. while that of the southern is + 7° to 8° C. = + 44° to 46° F.

The mean yearly temperature of Stockholm is + 5° C. = +41° F. The wells which serve as a measure of the earth's temperature, give about the same figures, the average temperature of a deep well in central Sweden being + 6° C. = + 43°F., while it is not unusual in Lappland to find a deep well covered with ice in midsummer, or a bog, 5 to 6 feet deep, frozen at its bottom; nevertheless, the cereals and potatoes mature in these districts, for although the summer is short, it is very warm and clear. There can scarcely be said to be any night here during the summer, only a twilight, so that vegetation, even in this high latitude, receives the light and heat necessary for its growth and ripening.

The variations in temperature are very great, the thermometer rising in summer to +30° C.= +86° F. and falling in winter to —40° C.= —40° F., at which temperature mercury becomes solid, or a variation of 70° C. = 126° F.

The temperature of the southern parts is also subject to very great changes.

The farmers worst enemy in Sweden is the *frost*, which in a single clear night, perhaps, after a warm summer day, will destroy his brightest prospects, but it is hoped that the increase of tillage, the draining of the bogs and like causes, will at least mitigate its severity, if not altogether prevent it. Such severe frosts are very seldom in the central and southern parts of Sweden.

The lakes and rivers are frozen during the winter season, and navigation is closed on all the canals, the Gulf of Bothnia and the greater part of the Baltic. Göteborg and the harbors on the western coast and in Öresund are more favored, as they are open to navigation the whole year; some of the outharbors of Stockholm are also free from ice the year round, which fact led to the experiment during the winter of 1870 and '71 of keeping up communications with Finland or Russia by means of a steamer built for that purpose. This undertaking was frustrated, however, by the unusual severity of that season, but it is by no means to be considered as abandoned. The object was to keep up a constant transit communication between western Europe and the Russian Empire by way of Sweden.

During the winter season the whole country is generally covered with more or less snow; in Norrland, this is always the case, but not always in the central and southern parts.

The lakes in the south of Sweden are frozen for about 115 days, in the central part for about 150 days, and in the northern for 200 days and upwards; the frozen lakes and snow facilitate the transportation of lumber and the products of mining industry to such and extent, that a winter without snow would by no means be desirable.

The snow frequently drifts bodily, in the open but not in wooded countries; railroad trains have often been detained in Denmark and Skåne by snow-drifts, while they have suffered no inconvenience in the neighborhood of Stockholm.

The annual rainfall in Sweden averages about 522.5 m. m.; there fell however in Göteborg, in the year of 1866, 1188 m. m. The rainfall is generally quite even through the country.

The annual rainfall on the west coast of Sweden

averages, - - - -	715.7	m. m.
in the interior of Götaland, -	545.0	" "
on the southeast coast, - -	429.2	" "
in the Län of Norrbotten, - -	405.6	" "

A Central Meteorological Institute was established in Stockholm in 1873 on the same plan that similar institutions have been established in other countries.

A number of Stations have been established since 1859, where the ordinary meteorological observations have been taken and published under the title of "Meteorological observations in Sweden," (Meteorologiska Iakttagelser i Sverige.) Some of these stations send daily telegraphic reports both to the interior and abroad.

The Central Meteorological Institute publishes a daily "Weather Bulletin" and contributes to the "Bulletin Météorologique du Nord" published by the Scandinavian countries and also contributes observations from four different parts of the country to the simultaneous observations for the northern hemisphere.

Series of various observations have been reserved from the middle and end of the last century. The longest and most complete of these are those from the observatories of Stockholm, Uppsala and Lund.

The registering apparatus of Dr Theorell, has been used at the observatory of Uppsala, since the autumn of 1868; and previous to that time, from 1865 to 1868, the meteorological instruments were observed hourly, day and night, by a volunteer association of students. The observations registered by the registering apparatus is published monthly in the "Bulletin météorologique mensuel de l'observatoire de l'université d'Uppsala."

Hourly observations are published at the expense of private parties. A series of observations for Uppsala, from 1855 to 1862, with three observations daily, has been published separately. Arrangements have also been made by the observatory at Uppsala, that observations shall be taken of the ice on rivers and lakes, of thunder, and of the first appearance of plants and hibernating animals in spring.

POPULATION.

The **Census** of Sweden dates as far back as 1749, when the so-called "Tabellverket" (Statistical Register Office), was instituted, which has since been kept up by the Commissioners of the Statistical Register Office, or the present Statistic Board, of which the Statistic Committee, and the Central Statistic Office, each forms a department. For the last 125 years, therefore, not only the number of marriages, births and deaths can be given, but also the total population; which statements are founded on the returns which the clergy are bound to supply. For the towns of Stockholm and Göteborg, however, it has for the last few years, been considered necessary to make special census by means of official registers in the usual way.*

The total population of Sweden, in the following years, was as follows:

1750	1,763,338
1800	2,347,303
1850	3,482,541
1870	4,168,525
1871	4,204,177
1872	4,250,412
1873	4,297,972
1874	4,341,559

In 1874 the population of Sweden was divided among the different Läns, as follows:

*Compare "Annual Reports of the Central Statistical Office."—Contributions to the Official Statistics of Sweden. Statistics of the population for the years 1851-1874.

Names.	Population of 1874.	1 Kilomètre square.	1 Geographical mile square.
The town of Stockholm,	150,446	40	2,114
The Län of Stockholm,	134,620		
" " " Uppsala,	103,282	20	1,097
" " " Södermanland,	139,216	23	1,222
" " " Östergötland,	262,872	27	1,458
" " " Jönköping,	186,841	18	986
" " " Kronoberg,	163,793	18	981
" " " Kalmar,	238,399	22	1,179
" " " Gottland,	54,499	19	1,043
" " " Blekinge,	130,921	45	2,413
" " " Kristianstad,	228,498	36	1,964
" " " Malmöhus,	330.115	70	3,478
" " " Halland,	130,802	27	1,478
" " " Göteb. & Bohus,	241,936	49	2,623
" " " Elfsborg,	285,217	24	1,296
" " " Skaraborg,	250,257	21	1,657
" " " Vermland,	266,362	18	945
" " " Örebro,	177,084	21	1,127
" " " Westmanland,	121,018	19	1,015
" " " Kopparberg,	184,330	7	359
" " " Gefleborg,	160,487	9	468
" " " Westernorrland,	147,212	6	324
" " " Jemtland,	74,758	1.6	84
" " " Westerbotten,	96,607	1.6	87
" " " Norrbotten,	81,987	0.8	43
Total,	4,341,559	10.6	568

The density of population, which was, in 1750: 4.4 to the square kilomètre, 1800: 6.0, 1850: 9.0, and 1874: 10.6, varies greatly in different Läns, being 70 in Malmöhus Län, and only 0.8 in Norrbotten Län. The greatest density of population is consequently in the southern part of the kingdom, and *vice versa*, as appears from the following table:

Names.	Mainland Square Kil.	Population in 1874.	To 1 Square Kilometre.
Götaland,	86,155	2,504,150	29
Swealand,	75,239	1,276,358	17
Norrland and Lappland,	246,053	561.051	2.3
Tot'l of Sweden	407,447	4,341,559	10.6

If one wishes to make a correct comparison between the densities of population in Sweden and in other countries, one must not forget that Sweden attains a very high latitude, and that more than half of its area is but sparsely inhabited, in comparison with the southern parts of Europe—but by no means so in comparison with its northern position. Skåne, the most southern province in Sweden, sustains a population as large as that of Norrland, (inclusive of Lappland,) though the latter is twenty-three times as large.

Norrland has, however, a bright future in her vast forests, abundant fisheries, fertile valleys and large deposits of ore, which await the hand of industry to develop them.

Railroads have been projected and are now being built, which will soon open up important sections of this country, though their completion may be tardy.

The proportion of males to females, which in 1850, was 100 to 112, has gradually increased so that at present it is 100 to 106,—(1874 : males 2,104,838, females 2,236,721.) There is, however, one district, the Län of Jemtland, where the male sex predominates.

About 13 per ct. of the population of Sweden, live in the towns; the rest (87 per ct.) live in the country, which has of late years contributed much to the growth of the towns.

The actual numbers are in the years	Pop. of Country.	Pop. of Towns.
1850	3,131,463	351,078
1860	3,425,209	434,519
1870	3,628,876	539,649
1874	3,741,369	600,190

Of the 90 towns in the kingdom, the following had in 1874 more than 10,000 inhabitants :

Stockholm,	150,446
Göteborg	63,748
Malmö,	30,676
Norrköping,	26,365
Gefle,	16,787
Karlskrona,	16,643
Jönköping,	12,548
Uppsala,	12,367
Lund,	11,680

The town of Stockholm had in 1850 only 93,070 inhabitants, in 1860: 112,391, and in 1874: 150,446—an increase of about 34 per ct. in 14 years.

During the period from 1861 to 1870, upon an average, 26,645 **marriages** were annually contracted, or 65 to every 10,000 inhabitants, against 76 for the preceeding period, from 1851 to 1860, and 91 for the corresponding period in the last century. The low proportion of marriages during the period from 1861 to 1870, was greatly influenced by the poor harvests of 1861 and 1868; hence, during the succeeding more prosperous years, the proportion has grown more favorable. (In 1871 there were 27,187 ; 1872 : 29,470 ; 1873 : 31,257 marriages.)

The average age for entering into matrimony (second and third marriages included), is, for the men, 30.9 years, and for the women 28.3. The greater number of men enter upon their first marriage in their 27th year, and the women in their 25th. A man very seldom marries before he is of age (i. e. 21 years old), or a woman before she has passed her 16th year. Eighty-five per cent. of the marriages are contracted between unmarried people; 4 per cent. between unmarried men and widows; 9 per cent. between widowers and unmarried women, and 2 per cent. between widowers and widows. Only from 10 to 12 so-called mixed marriages, (between people of different creeds), are annually contracted, and these are the only civil marriages that occur in Sweden. Upon an average 150 marriages are annually dissolved by bills of divorce.

In the year 1870 the population was computed as follows, according to the civil state:

	Males.	Females.	Total.
Unmarried, -	1,263,838	1,288,171	2,552,009
Married, - -	678,926	682,573	1,361,499
Widowers and Widows,	73,022	179,481	252,503
Divorced, - -	867	1,647	2,514
Total,	2,016,653	2,151,872	4,168,525

The period of greatest fecundity is from the 31st to 35th year, and it more rarely occurs that a Swedish woman gives birth to a child before her 16th year than after her 50th.

During the period from 1861 to 1870: 132,442 children were born annually, of which 96,7 per cent. were living, and 3.3 per cent. still-born. Of all the child-bearing women, 1,838 annually were delivered of twins, and 24 of triplets. During the last 20 years six cases of quadruple births have taken place. There are a greater number of males than female births, (1,058 to 1000), which, however, is counter-balanced by a greater mortality of the males, which in the end makes their number smaller.

The proportion of illegitimate births which is of such great importance in forming an opinion of the morality of the people, has, during the last century, unfortunately, been constantly increasing, and is now three times as large as it was a hundred years ago. During the last decennium, about 9.6 per cent. of the births have been illegitimate; 7.6 per cent. in the provinces, and 23.5 per cent. in the towns; Stockholm showing the highest figure, namely 40 per cent., which was still higher during the preceding decennium, but during late years it has decreased to 38 per cent. That the capital is in this respect so conspicuous, is perhaps not so much owing to a greater immorality as to the facilities, which, not only special lying-in-hospitais, but the greater population of the town offer to mothers who wish to conceal their dishonor; and hence, a very considerable number of illegitimate children though born in Stockholm, do in reality belong to other districts of the country. According to the Swedish law, any woman, who is about to be confined, may, if she desires, have the benefit of all possible attendance in a lying-in-hospital, without having even to mention her name.

Foundlings, under which name, probably, many illegitimate children are concealed in foreign countries, *scarcely ever* occur in Sweden. It may further be remarked that a great number of children who are born here previous to wedlock and registered as illegitimate, are legitimized by the consequent marriage of the parents, whereby they are made equal before the law with the legitimate children, under which are included only such as are born of wedded parents. About 10 per ct. of the illegitimate children are born of parents, who have been stated to be betrothed; that is, such as have declared their intention of entering into the marriage relation with one another, although it has not yet been confirmed by the nuptial ceremony. Under these circumstances, and with the knowledge of the increase of illegitimate births everywhere, one might be justified in asserting that Sweden, in this respect, does not appear in a worse light, than other countries.

The Mortality, which during the whole time from 1751 to 1810, remained at about 2.75 per ct., with a decrease during the latter part of last century, has been diminishing, and was for the period from 1851 to 1860 2.16 per ct; from 1861 to 1870 2.02 per ct., (in the provinces 1.93 per ct., in the towns 2.62 per ct.,) and in the year 1872 only 1.63 per ct.—lowest percentage that was ever known; during the last decennium (1861 to 1870,) there have been upon an average 82,233 deaths annually, which number, however, was greatly exceeded in the years 1868 (87,807 deaths,) and 1869 (92,775 deaths,) which fact is accounted for by the poor harvests in the years 1867 and 1868, which brought along with them the scarlitina, measles, nervous-fever and other epidemics. During the good year 1872, there were only 68,802 deaths in the whole kingdom.

Accident with little variation, carries off annually 2,200 victims, of whom rather more than half are by drowning.

The number of Suicides from 1861 to 1870 has annually amounted to 328, (about 261 males to 67 females), i. e., 8.04 in 100,000 inhabitants. In the towns there have been three times as many suicides committed as in the country. The per centage of suicide by different means, are as follows: hanging and strangling, (47.5 per ct.), drowning, (22.1 per ct.,) poisoning, (10.2 per ct.,) stabbing with sharp instruments, (9.3 per ct.,) fire-arms, (8.5 per ct.,) and other ways not known, (2.4 per ct.)

Those persons afflicted with **Mental and Physical Defects** were computed in 1870 as follows:

	Males.	Females.	Total.
Insane or feeble-minded,	4,666	4,443	9,109
Blind, - - -	1,504	1,776	3,280
Deaf and dumb, -	2,370	1,884	4,254
Blind, deaf and dumb,	5	6	11
Total,	8,545	8,109	16,654

With regard to **Epidemics** prevalent in Sweden, and the institutions for the sick, compare Class 346.

In 1870 the population of Sweden was divided, according to their **Religious Creeds,** as follows:

Evangelic-Lutherans, . . .	4,162,087
Baptists, Mormons, Methodists, .	3,809
Reformists, (Calvinists), . .	190
Catholics, Roman, . . .	573
" Russian-Greek, . .	30
Israelites, ...	1,836
Total, ...	4,168,525

The King and the members of the Council of State, as well as every one who holds a clerical office, involving the duty of instructing in religion, or the science of theology, shall profess the Lutheran faith. Persons professing other Christian religions, or the Mosaic doctrine, may be appointed to other offices. The old statute relative to the Diet, which prescribes that only such persons as profess the Christian Protestant Religion shall be elected as representatives at the Diet, was repealed in 1870. According to the Act of June 6th, 1809, the King cannot control or cause to be controlled the conscience of any one, but he shall protect every one in the free exercise of his religion, providing the quiet of the civil community be not disturbed, or any public scandal be caused thereby. Certain measures are provided against the departure from the established church. The so-called law for dissenters (of October 31st, 1873), makes certain provisions for the establishment of special congregations of foreign christian fellow-believers. Monastic orders, either for monks or nuns, or the establishment of convents, are not permitted.

In respect to **Public Education,** it may be asserted, without fear of contradiction, that, with few exceptions, every Swedish major, male and female, (even Finns and Lapplanders), can read print; on the other hand, the art of writing, which is generally known among the younger generation, has, perhaps, not been acquired by all of the older. That such is really the case, will be seen on consulting the investigations that have been made with regard to the knowledge of reading and writing of condemned criminals, and if that be taken as a criterion, the charge of partiality for ones own country can not be made. These investigations for ten years show, with very little or no variation, that of all the criminals the following ratios:

can read and write, . . .	39 per cent.
" read, but not write, . .	58 per cent.
" neither read nor write, .	3 per cent.
Total,	100 per cent.

These three per cent. who can neither read nor write, are probably for the most part minors, so that the remaining 97 per cent., who can read, are adults. [Concerning instruction, see Catalogue, Class 300, etc.]

The Emigration, which in the years 1851 to 1860, included in all 16,900 persons (of whom only a few hundred annually in the years 1858 to 1860), continually increased until 1869, when 39,064 persons left their native soil, but has since that time shown a decreasing tendency, (1870, 20,003; 1871, 17,450; 1872, 15,915; 1873, 13,-

580, and 1874, 7,791.) During the last few years, however, especially in 1874 and 1875, there has been a very considerable counter-stream of returning emigrants. During the period 1861 to 1870, 122,447 persons left the country, of whom, as far as has been ascertained, 88,731 sought their way to North America, whither the usual way is from Göteborg *via* England. In their adopted country the greater number of Swedes are now found in the more northerly states, especially in the upper districts of the Mississippi, (in Illinois, Minnesota, Iowa, etc.) This emigration from Sweden to America is nothing peculiar to our days, for as far back as 250 years ago Swedes sought their fortunes in the new world, where in 1627 they founded "New Sweden," on the Delaware. The first colonists of Pennsylvania were Swedes, (1638.) There is an account of these settlements by Israel Acrelius, who was sent out from Sweden as rector for the Swedish parishes in North America, (1749 to 1756), of which an English translation by William M. Reynolds, was published in Philadelphia 1875 under the title of "A History of New Sweden, or the Settlements on the River Delaware."

The Emigrants of the present times are mostly farmers, factory men, artisans, servants, and common working people, which indicates partly the reasons for their emigration, partly the insight, experience and resources with which the emigrants have gone to meet the future in their adopted country. The increase in the emigration during later years, and the inexperience of the emigrant in general, in looking after his own interests, have called forth the special royal enactments, August 6th, 1864, and February 5th, 1869, relating to the forwarding of emigrants.

Sufficient information about the *immigration* has not been procured, but in all probability it is not very great. During the years 1870 to 1873, upon an average, 80 foreigners were granted the privileges of Swedish citizens; 70 obtained permission to remain in the country, (for the purpose of carrying on some trade), and 75 permission to possess landed property. They are mostly Danes, Poles, and Germans who thus acquire Swedish privileges. The passport-law for foreigners is now abolished.

Sweden is fortunate enough to enclose within its boundaries almost none other than one **Nation,** namely, the Swedish, which speaks one and the same **Language,** which is very like the Norwegian or Danish, and nearly allied to the German. Finnish is spoken among the Swedish Finns, (in the year 1870: 14,932), who live in the most northern parts of the country, principally near the border of Finland, and the Lappish language is spoken by the Lapplanders (6,711), who live in the same neighborhood but towards the Norwegian frontier, but Swedish or Finnish is also known to many of them. There were only 12,000 persons in Sweden, in 1870, who were born abroad, (mostly Danes, Germans, and Norwegians.)

Although **the Lappland race,** which is included in the Swedish population, is small in numbers, it is of special interest, and hence we communicate about this small tribe, which in general is but little known, the following*.

The Lapplanders call themselves Same, (Sabme or Samelads.) They differ greatly from other races, not only in their physical form, but also in certain ancient customs and their former religion. Their language belongs to the Altaic, or Ugorian tongue, in which it is closely allied to the Finnish, and some of the old forms and roots, which in the course of development have been lost in the latter, are found again in the Lappish.

In a physical point of view, the Lapplanders are remarkable for their low stature, slender but sinewy build, and, in consequence of violent bodily exercise and their subsisting on animal food, they generally have a haggard appearance. The color of their skin, hair and eyes are brown, their beards are thin, their cheek-bones protuberant, their chins projecting and their eyes hori-

*According to Baron von Düben: "*Lappland and the Lapplanders*," Stockholm, 1873.

zontal. The shape of the skull is strongly brachycephalous, (*index,* 53.5), and the upper jaw rather projecting.

They frequently have weak eyes, in consequence of the smoke in their dwellings and the reflection of the sun from the sea and snow. With regard to character, they are peaceable, good-natured, thoroughly honest, and, among one another, humorous, but, by the oppression of their neighbors, who are superior in number and strength, they have become suspicious and cunning.

The constant influence of the smoke and the strong contrast from uninterrupted light to darkness, together with their weak eyes, have caused them to form the habit of contracting the eyebrows, which gives them a melancholy appearance—a feature which perhaps also is called forth by the consciousness of the unfavorable circumstances under which they are living.

They are persevering in their work and resolutions and economical, unless subjected to the temptation of drinking, which they can hardly resist. Further, they are kind towards their wives and children, friendly, faithful and benevolent toward one another, yet different degrees of prosperity command more or less respect. They are unusually skillful in making every thing they require for their households, with the exception of cloth and hardware; they are especially very clever in the carving of wood and horn, and the women make very fine embroidered articles of silk and tin wire. They are fond of finery, bright colors, spangles and tinkling ornaments, and value highly articles of silver, and copper utensils. They sew their own clothes, which are made partly of a woolen stuff, (wadmal), partly of dressed or undressed rein-deer skins with the hair on, which latter garment is worn in winter. All the leather clothes, as also the shoes, are sewn with thread which is made out of the sinews of the fore and hind legs or the back of the rein-deer,and the same kind of thread is used in their embroideries of tin, with which they are accustomed to deck their summer garments or the gears of their reindeers.

Their nourishment, namely, meat, milk and cheese, they obtain principally from their herds of reindeer, yet some of them subsist chiefly on fish.

Small game and animals furnishing calaber skins are very much hunted by the Lapplanders, who live in the woodland districts; whereas the so-called Mountain-Lapplanders follow up the chase merely with a view of pursuing and exterminating such beasts of prey as are dangerous for their herds, or for the purpose of obtaining peltry. Although they live principally on animal food, meal (of barley) is seldom wanting, for porridge and unleavened bread; besides they often mix the reindeer's milk with Rumex, Mulgedium, and Archangelica, which they consider a great luxury, they call *Jobmo.* Another luxury is the marrow from the bones of the extremities of the reindeer, which is obtained by crushing them, in the same way as was formerly customary among the people of South Europe, during the pile-work and reindeer period. During late years the use of coffee has very much spread among the Lapplanders, to their pecuniary disadvantage. This is still more the case with Swedish whiskey, which in certain parts, as the Lappland district of Piteå, is immoderately consumed, and thus causing great harm; but, on the contrary, in other parts, especially in the northern Lappish districts of Sweden and Norway, the use of it has in consequence of religious movements, considerably fallen off. Tobacco is used not only for smoking (mostly among the Mountain-Lapplanders), but for snuffing and chewing (principally among the Woodland-Lapplanders.)

The Lapplanders who have kept up their old mode of life, live in tents made of canvass or wadmal, or else in conical "kåtor" (cots,) which are constructed of split timber or thin trunks of small trees, covered with birch-bark, turf or stones; but those who devote themselves to agriculture and cattle-raising, live in frame houses. Most of them own reindeer; the farmers, also, cows and goats, while they have their reindeer taken care of by nomad congeners.

Most of the Lapplanders who possess reindeer are Nomads, and are divided into two classes. The so-called Woodland-Lapplanders have several wooden "kåtor," and move backward and forward during the summer as the pasture is better in one place than in another; in the winter time they wander about the woods more or less extensively towards the coasts, (Bottnen) and every spring they return again to their own districts, in the forests of which they live during the summer.

Every spring the Mountain-Lapplanders wander from the woodlands towards the mountains, where most of them pass the summer, moving about from one pasture ground to another, and pitching their tents in the region of birches or willows. A great number, however, cross the mountain towards the Norwegian coast, (mostly from the district of Torneå, Lappmark to Tromsö Amt), where they spend the summer. In autumn the majority return across or from the mountains into the Swedish woodlands, where they wander about during the winter.

Most of the Nomad-Lapplanders belong to Sweden; the Norwegian Lapplanders are either Mountain-Lapplanders, or are settled along the coasts or rivers of Finnmark as fishermen; the Russian-Finnish are mostly fishermen, and possess but few reindeer, which are principally used for conveying travelers or carrying goods and provisions.

Much having been done in later times, and especially in the years 1840—1850, in Sweden and Norway on the part of the governments to improve the condition of the Lapplanders, their numbers have notably increased. According to the last official returns they numbered in

Norway (1865)	17,178*
Sweden (1870)	6,711
Finland	615
Russia, (1859)	2,207
Total,	26,711

The Swedish, Norwegian and Finnish Lapplanders together possess about 360,000 reindeer, of which the Swedish Lapplanders possess nearly 200,000.

*There are 1,048 individuals of a mixed Lappish-Nowegian race, and 909 of Lappish-Finnish included in this.

ADMINISTRATION OF STATE.

The **Government** is a constitutional monarchy.

The **Fundamental Laws** of the Kingdom are: The constitution (Regeringsformen,) of June 6th, 1809, the regulation of the Diet, (Riksdagsordningen) of June 22d, 1866, the royal succession, (Successionsordningen) of September 26th, 1810; and the law passed July 16th, 1812, relating to the liberty of the press, (Tryckfrihetsförordningen.) The act of the Union, (Föreningsakten) of August 6th, and July 31st, 1815, which, though not belonging to the fundamental laws of Sweden, refers to those of Norway, and determines the constitutional relations in consequence of the union of the two kingdoms under one King.

All state affairs, with the exception of ministerial and military matters, shall be laid before the King in Council of State and there dispatched. Of the ten members of the council of state, seven shall (since 1840), be at the head of so many departments, namely: Justice, Foreign Affairs, War, Navy, Interior, Finance and Ecclesiastics. All the members of the council of state are called Councillors of State, except the chiefs of the Department of Justice and of Foreign Affairs, who are Ministers of State.

The judiciary power of the King is represented by (12—18) Councillors of Justice, who constitute the **Supreme Court**, in which the King has 2 votes, when he participates in its decision.

The cases are arranged by the Lower Court of Revision, which is a sub-division of the Department of Justice. The Chancellor of Justice is in the name of the King the highest accusor; the corresponding official of the Diet is called Justitie-

Ombudsman (Procurator of the Diet, or Attorney-General.)

Each department has an office or bureau of its own, and also each military department has a separate bureau. The head managers of these are called Chiefs of the Expedition, (in the Department of Foreign affairs or the cabinet of foreign correspondence, a so-called Cabinet-Secretary). These seven government offices together with some others nearly connected with them, constitute the Konglig Majestäts Kansli, (H. R. M. Chancery).

Next to the above-mentioned departments, the different branches of administration are managed partly by collegial boards, with a president att he head and councillors as members, and partly by Administrations (Styrelser), with directors-generals as chiefs, who alone decide, and before whom the cases are preferred by the chiefs of the bureau, or by the secretaries.

The members of the Council of State, Presidents or Chiefs of Boards, and similar offices, Colonels of regiments, and the officials in the Foreign Department, holding so-called offices of trust, can be discharged by the King in the Council of State; but other officials and especially such as fill the office of judge, cannot be dismissed without having been previously tried and sentenced, nor transferred to other offices, providing they hold so-called "fullmäkt," (commissions or diplomas) which is usually the case.

The duties of the different departments are as follows:

1.—To the **Department of Justice** or Chancery office, belongs besides questions of Law and charge of prisoners, also, matters relating to the liberty of the press, and the rights of citizens. This department, therefore, includes the High Courts, together with the law-officials and the Prison Committee, together with the prison officials.

2.—The **Department for Foreign Affairs** is with regard to foreign powers common for Sweden and Norway. The chief of this department also manages all the consular business that concerns the united kingdoms in common, but the Kommerse-Kollegium (Board of Trade, under the Civil Department,) directs whatever belongs to Sweden alone, and the Norwegian Department for the Interior, such questions as relate to Norway alone. The Consular laws now in force were enacted April 20th, 1858.

3.—To the **War Department** belongs all the business relating to the regulation and maintenance of the army, the military schools, fortresses, &c. The more minute details of this department belong to the Army Board. For further information see catalogue, Class 345.

4.—The **Navy Department** attends to all matters relating to the navy, the institutions for pilots and coast-lights, nautical surveys, and naval schools. Sub-divisions are the Marine Office, the Pilot Administration, (Lots-Styrelsen) together with all licensed pilots and coast-guards, and the nautical chart office. (Compare Class 345.)

5.—The **Civil Department,** Bureau of the Interior, among other matters, decides upon questions relating to agriculture, mining, commerce, shipping, manufactures and industrial affairs; as also schools connected with these branches,—moreover, roads, railways and canals, together with all the inland and police affairs; in general, all civil business not belonging to another department.

The different branches that belong to this department are: Committee on Statistics, (see upon, page 9.); the Board of Trade whose special duty is to superintend mining, commerce, navigation, manufactures, technical schools, and everything connected with patents; the General Land-surveying Office of the Kingdom, (Rikets General Landmäteri-Kontor) together with all the land-surveying officials and adjusters of weights and measures connected with this office; the Geological Survey of Sweden, (Sveriges Geologiska Undersökning,) the Agricultural Academy, (Landtbruks Akademien) the Agricultural Societies and Schools; the Superintendency of the Towns, the Administration of Public Roads and Canals with its corps of officers; the Administration of the Traffic of the Government Railways, (Kongl. Jernvägs-Trafik-Styrelsen), the Administration of the Construction of Government Railways, (Kongl. Jernvägs-Byggnads-Styrelsen), the Administration of the Construction of Canals and Harbors, (Direktionen för Kanaler och Hamnarbeten,)

The government of the interior is regulated in Stockholm, by a Governor-General, (Öfver-Ståthållare), and in each of the 24 Läns by a Governor, (Landshöfding). The Governors, in the capacity of official authority are called Royal Commanders, (Konglig Majestäts Befallningshafvande). In the absence of the governor, the government of the province is held jointly by one juridic and one cameralistic secretary of the Province, under the title of the Governor's Office (Landshöfdige-Embetet). Subordinate to the government of the province, and acting within more limited districts, are 117 Crown-Bailiffs (Kronofogdar), and 517 Crown-Sergeants, (Kronolänsmän). The government of the towns is exercised by magistrates: Mayor and Aldermen (Borgmästare och Råd).

6.—The **Financial Department** has under its charge the levying of taxes, the control over the production of spirits, and beet sugar, (any other excisable articles do not occur in Sweden), coinage and banking business, customs, posts and telegraphs, crown forests, as also the drawing up of proposals for the Budget, (riksstaten). The government of the small island of St. Barthelemy in the West Indies, the only foreign possession of Sweden, is under this department.

Subordinate offices are: The Board of Domains (Kammar-Kollegium), that takes charge of all the landed property of the state, imposes land-taxes, makes out lists of the various allotments of land in all the different districts, &c.; the Revenue Office, (Stats-Kontoret) that takes charge of the income of the state and defrays its expenses, (part of these are, however, defrayed by the Debt Office of the State, an office under the direct control of the diet); the Mint and the Office where gold and silver are stamped, (Kontroll-Verket); the Exchequer, (Kammar-Rätten), which, among other matters, revises the accounts of the state, (a similar examination is made by the Revisors of the Diet); the Royal Administration of Post, (Kongl. General-Post-Styrelsen); the Royal Administration of Telegraphs, (Kongl. Telegraf-Styrelsen); the Royal Administration of Customs, (Kongl. General-Tull-Styrelsen); the Royal Administration of Forests, (Kongl. Skogs-Styrelsen), together with its Officials; the Board of Public Buildings (Kongl. Öfver-Intendents-Embetet).

7.—Among the duties of the **Ecclesiastical Department,** besides Church and School affairs, is the providing for the sick and poor.

Herein are included matters concerning the Consistories with the Clergy belonging to them, the Universities, the Grammar, and National Schools, most of the Academies and learned Societies, the Archives of the Kingdom, the Royal Library, the National Museum, the Royal Board of Health, (Kongl. Sundhets-Kollegium), togethes with the medical officials; the Society of the Order of the Seraphim, who have the superintendence of the Hospitals, (Lunatic Asylums); Pious Institutions, etc.

ADMINISTRATION OF JUSTICE.

The court of first instance in a town is the **Town-House-Court** (Rådstugu-Rätt), composed of Mayor and Aldermen, (Borgmästare och Råd), and in the country the **District Court,** (Härads-Rätt), where the District Judge, (Häradshöfding) with a Committee (Nämnd), of twelve persons, (Nämndemän), who are elected from among the real-estate owners within the "Härad," or district of jurisdiction, pronounces judgment. The circuit of a district Judge is called "Domsaga," comprising one or more Härad. Of these there are 105. In some of the larger towns there are also police courts, where police matters are attended to.

Courts of appeal are the **High Courts,** (Hof-Rätter). The High Court of Svea is in Stockholm; the High Court of Göta at Jönköping, and the High Court of Skåne and Blekinge, at Kristianstad. The High Court-martial (Krigs-Hofrätten) takes up suits from the Courts-martial, (Krigsrätterna), which are inferior military law courts.

The highest court of appeal is the **Supreme Court,** (Högsta Domstolen), in Stockholm, which passes judgment in the name of the King.

A **Jury** is never impannelled excepting in matters concerning the liberty of the press.

The **Law of the Swedish Kingdom** differs from the laws of other European countries, in that, that it is not based on the Roman (civil) law, but it has sprung up from the wants of the people themselves since the most remote times. The present collection thereof dates from the year 1734; in the course of time, however, it has been altered, and has received many additions, among which the most important is a new penal code (of February 16th, 1864).

The **Forms of Punishment** are: capital punishment, (which is to take place publicly and by decapitation), penal servitude, (for life or from 2 months to 10 years), merely imprisonment, without hard labor, (from 1 month to 2 years), or fines (from 5 to 500, exceptionally 1000 Kr.); in case of no assets the fines are commuted into imprisonment on bread and water (from 3 to 20 days), exceptionally only imprisonment, (from 9 to 60 days.) Special punishment for officials is dismissal or suspension from office for a certain period. Those who are sentenced for more serious offences, are disqualified for office, either for life, or for a limited period, (from 5 to 10 years.)

A special penal law for the military forces was passed on June 11th, 1868, according to which the modes of punishment are like those prescribed in the penal law of the country, with this difference, that capital punishment is sometimes effected by means of shooting, and imprisonment may be changed into being cast into a dungeon. Besides certain disciplinary punishments are prescribed according to a special statute.

Punishments by exile transportation, flagellation, or flogging, do not occur in Sweden.

There has been but one case of capital punishment since 1866. At the end of the year 1872, the prisons contained 774 prisoners for life, 2,809 prisoners undergoing penal servitude for a limited period, (of whom 717 were confined in cells), 101, mere imprisonment, and 93 undergoing punishment by imprisonment on bread and water.* The expenditure for the care of prisoners, in 1872, amounted to $505,500, gold.

According to the official report of the Minister of Justice,† the following persons were condemned by the Court of First Instance, in 1870:

OFFENCES.	SENTENCED TO			
	Death.	Penal Servitude.	Imprisonment.	Fines.
A).—OFFENCES AGAINST THE PENAL STATUTE LAW, OR MARTIAL LAW.				
Religious offences, or Sabbath breaking, - -	......	......	....	86
Transgressions against authorities, - - - - -	......	36	145	775
Forgery, perjury, fraud, etc., - - - - - - -	......	169	65	341
Murder, or manslaughter	1	19		
Chance-medley, accidental manslaughter, or causing or participating in manslaughter, - - -	......	44	8	15
Infanticide, causing abortion, etc., - - - - -	......	63	3	2
Assaults, or battery,	......	135	135	2.051
False accusations, slander, etc, - - - - - -	......	6	46	852
Indecency, - - - -	......	18	7	90
Drunkenness and drinking, - - - - - - -	......	......	14	8,630
Arson, intentionally injuring the owner, etc,,	......	22	21	110
Petit larceny, - - -	......	4	254	661
Theft, and participating in theft, - - - - - -	......	1,581	56	127
Robbery, and attempts at robbery, - - - - -	......	29		
Military transgressions,	.....	30	111	
Other transgressions,	......	7	73	4,892
Total, - - - -	1	2,163	938	18,632
In this sum the following have been counted more than once, - - -	......	219	132	3,189
Number of condemned persons, . - - - -	1	1,944	806	15,443
B.)—OFFENCES RELATING TO THE PRESS. - -	......	......	....	....
C.)—OFFENCES AGAINST THE STATUTES, RELATING TO THE MAINTAINANCE OF ORDER, POLICE REGULATIONS, AND THE LIKE, - - - - - -	......	4	73	12,827
Total number of persons judged, ...	1	1,948	870	28,270

Though upon the whole the offences are decreasing, there are sometimes remarkable variations. In the year 1865 the number of persons sentenced for so-called serious offences amounted to 1,499 (1,252 males and 247 females,) or only 3.6 in 10,000 inhabitants; in 1869, on the other hand, the corresponding numbers were 2,834 persons, or 6.8 in the same number of inhabitants. By special investigations, it is however authenticated that this increase of offences, especially of thefts, was owing to the pecuniary troubles caused by the unfavorable crops in the years 1867 and 1868,* and, likewise, that with the good years that followed, the number of offences again decreased (1870: 1,992 persons, or 4.8 in 10,000 inhabitants; 1872: 1,796, or only 4.2 in 10,000 inhabitants.)

*Annual reports are published by the Royal Prison-Committee under the title: Contributions to the Official Statistics of Sweden, C. Fång-vården, (keeping of the prisoners), 1859-1872.

†Contributions to the Official Statistics of Sweden, Rättsväsendet, (Justice matters), 1857-1872.

REPRESENTATIVE ASSEMBLIES.

The old Swedish National Assembly, which was composed of representatives from four distinct classes (the nobility, the clergy, the townsmen, and the peasants,) called the 4 estates, was abolished by their own consent in 1866, (law of June 22, 1866) so that the Swedish people are now represented by the **Diet,** (Riksdag) which is divided into two chambers, the first and second —which in all questions have the same right and authority. The Diet meets annually (from January 15th until at least May 15th); besides, extraordinary Diets may be convened by the King; the members of the Diet are elected for a certain period; the King is, however, entitled to prescribe new elections before the expiration of that period.

The members of the **First Chamber** are elected for nine years by the provincial representatives (Landsting), without any regard to their place of residence, and by the town deputies (for towns with more than 25,000 inhabitants), one for every 30,000 inhabitants of the Län or town. For eligibility it is required to be 35 years of age, to be possessed of, and to have possessed at least 3 years before the election, ground-property assessed at, at least, 80,000 Kronor, ($22,222 gold,) or a taxable income of 4,000 Kr., ($1,111 gold). The members receive no pay; their number is at present (in 1875) 129.

The Members of the **Second Chamber** are elected for three years, one member for each district of jurisdiction (Domsaga,) 2 members for a district of more than 40,000 inhabitants, and one for every 10,000 inhabitants of the towns, (small towns are united into one constituency). For electoral franchises are required: the right of voting in the community, the possession of ground property worth at least 1,000 Kr. ($278 gold) or the lease hold for 5 years of landed property worth by taxation at least 6,000 Kr. ($1667 gold), or an annual taxable income of 800 Kr. ($222 gold); the elections take place either by electors or direct, whereby each voter has but one vote. For eligibility is required to have electoral franchise and to be 25 years of age. The members of the Second Chamber receive for each Diet, which shall last 4 months, 1,200 Kr. ($333 gold), besides payment of their traveling expenses. Their number at present is 194.

The fundamental difference in the composition of the two chambers, therefore, is: that the First Chamber represents greater wealth and the members are elect for a longer term, 9 years from the date of election; whereas the whole Second Chamber is elected anew every three years; and also that the members of the First Chamber, who may be elected without any regard to their place of residence, receive no pay, which on the contrary is due to those of the Second Chamber, who must be residents of the district they represent.

The Speakers or Presidents (Talmän) and

Vice-Presidents are appointed by the King from among the members of the Chambers.

The members of the Diet who are not in any way restricted, excepting by the fundamental law of the Kingdom, have an unlimited right of moving whatever questions they think proper.

Matters to be debated upon by the Chambers are first arranged by certain **Committees** (Utskott). These are: 1.—The Committee on the Constitution (Konstitutions-Utskottet), for questions relating to the fundamental law, and the examination of the protocols of the councillors of State. 2.—The Budget Committee (Stats-Utskottet) for drawing up the budget. 3.—The Committee on Ways and Means (Bevillnings-Utskottet) for amending the Concession Statutes; under Concessions are included the revenues of the Custom and the Post Office, the duty on stamped paper, spirits, and beet-sugar, and the income tax. 4.—The Bank-Committee (Banko-Utskottet), for the management of the Bank of the Realm, which is an institution of the Diet. 5.—The Law-Committee (Lag-Utskottet), for the law-questions that do not relate to the fundamental laws, as also 6.—So-called Special and Temporary Committees (Särskilda Utskott and Tillfälliga Utskott). A Committee of Secrecy, (Hemligt Utskott), may also be appointed if the King desires it.

Questions, rejected in either of the chambers, are dismissed, excepting such as relate to allowances, which in such a case are decided by renewed voting in common.

The National Debt Office, (Riksgälds-Kontoret) which is under the management of the Diet, has charge of the debts of the kingdom. (The Board that takes charge of the money of the State, or rather of the Government, is the Revenue Office.)

Twelve Revisors, 6 from each Chamber, are annually chosen for the examination of the accounts of the State, which, moreover, are checked by one of the offices of the State (the Royal Exchequer: Kammar-Rätten).

The Diet's accusatory power is excercised by the Procurator (Justitie-Ombudsman.)

For questions relating to canon-law the concurrence of the **Synod** (Kyrkomöte), which meets every fifth year, is required. The members are 30 churchmen, and 30 delegates elected by laymen. The Archbishop is the chairman.

The *capita familiæ* of the nobility, have a **Congress of Nobles** every three years, for the management of their own affairs. The nobility of Sweden no longer possess any prerogatives.

Self-Government, which in Sweden is very ancient, received its present form by the communal statutes of March 21st, 1862, according to which every parish in the country, (2354), likewise every town and a few boroughs, (together 95), form a community, of which such members as pay taxes to the community have to attend to all common matters that refer to the order and economy of said community. Resolutions are decided upon in the country by the **Communal Assembly,**(Kommunalstämma),and in the towns by the **Town-Deputies,** (Stads-fullmägtige), in the smaller towns, likewise in Town-Meeting, (Allmän Rådstuga,); questions relating to the church and national schools are decided upon by a **Vestry-Board,** (Kyrkostämma.)

The Läns also constitute communities, though of a higher order. The self-government in these is executed by the **Government Assembly** (Landsting) which is composed of delegates elected in the towns and districts of jurisdiction, (Härad or Tingslag) of the Län. Towns of more than 25,000 inhabitants are not included in the districts of the Landsting, and are governed by their own town deputies.

MEASURES AND WEIGHTS.

The decimal system for **Measures and Weights,** was introduced into Sweden by a Royal Enactment of January 31st, 1855. The statute of the November 10th, 1865, now in force, prescribes that the length of the second-pendulum measured in Stockholm Observatory at + 15° C. shall be =3.35064 fot; and that the weight of a kubik fot of pure water, at the maximum of density measured in air half saturated with moisture, at + 15° C. and 25.6″ B. (the quicksilver reduced to 0° C.), shall be = 61.522 skålpund.

No other measures or weights shall be used than such as have been adjusted and stamped by proper authorities.

The *unit* for the measure of length is the fot, for superficial measure the quadrat fot, for measure of capacity the kubikfot, for weight the skålpund, the multiples and sub-divisions of which are, for

Measure of Length:

1 ref=10 stång (pole)=100 fot (feet).
1 stång=10 fot.
1 fot=10 tum (inches).
1 tum=10 linier (lines).

Superficial Measure:

1 quadrat ref=100 quadrat stänger.
1 quadrat stång=100 qu. fot (sq. feet).
1 quadrat fot=100 qu. tum (sq. inches).
1 quadrat tum=100 qu. linier (sq. lines).

Measure of Capacity:

1 kubikfot (cubic foot)=10 kannor.
1 kanna=100 kubiktum (cubic inches).
1 kubiktum=1000 kubiklinier (cubic lines).

Weight:

1 centner=100 skålpund (lbs).
1 skålpund=100 ort.
1 ort=100 korn (grains).

Pursuant to the same law, vessels have been measured by the Ny-Läst (= 100 centner), but according to a Royal Enactment of May 15, 1874, such measurement will henceforth be effected after the Moorsom-system in English Register Tons, and it is also ordained (Royal Enactment, October 16, 1874) that one Ny-Läst shall be considered=3.14 tons for sailing vessels, =4.50 tons for steamers, (upon an average one Ny-Läst has hitherto been considered to be =3.27 tons).

Other Legal Measures are:

1 mil=36,000 fot (foot).
1 stig (chaldron of coals)=75.6 kubik fot =12 tunnor.
1 tunna of coals=6.3 kubik-fot.
1 famn (cord) of wood=6 x 8 x 3 fot.

Apothecaries' Weights and Measures are the French gram and mètre.

The Money Weight is also the gram.

The following **old Measures and Weights** are still often used:

1 famn (fathom)=3 alnar (ells).
1 aln=2 fot=24 verktum (inches), (verktum distinguished from decimal tum, now adopted, of which there are only 10 to 1 fot, and 20 to 1 aln).
1 tunnland (the Swedish acre)=5.6 quadrat ref=56,000 quadrat fot.
1 tunna=63 kannor.
1 lispund=20 skålpund of 32 lod.
1 skeppund=20 lispund.

The old and new units, Fot, Kanna and Skålpund, are of equal value.

Concerning the relation between the Swedish and foreign measures and weights, see the table at the beginning of this book.

COINS AND BANKING ESTABLISHMENTS.

Sweden previously based its system of **Coinage** upon silver, but has lately adopted the *gold standard.* The statute of May 30, 1873, relative to the coinage of the Kingdom, prescribes that gold alone shall be the test of value in Sweden, that the unity for the weight of the coin shall be the French gram, and that the unity for reckoning shall be called "*Krona*" (crown) which is divided into 100 "öre;" of gold are coined 10 and 20 Krona-pieces, and a 10 Krona-piece shall weigh 4.4803 gram, and contain 9 parts of pure gold and one part alloy of copper, and consequently 4.032258 gr. of pure gold. For small coins silver and bronzes are used. Of the former are coined 2 and 1 Krona-pieces, (the alloy 2 parts of copper to 8 of silver), 50 and 25 öre-pieces (6 parts silver + 4 copper), and 10 öre-pieces (4 parts silver + 6 copper.) A 1 Krona-piece weighs 7.5 gr. and contains 6 gr. pure silver. Of bronze (95 copper + 4 tin + 1 zinc) are coined 5, 2 and 1 öre-pieces.

Conformable to the decision of a convention held December 18th, 1872, and later decisions, Sweden, Norway, and Denmark have now a common system of gold coinage.

In Sweden no practical difficulty is met with in the introduction of the new system, inasmuch as 1 Krona shall be received in the daily transactions at the same value as 1 Riksdaler Riksmynt (R:dr — the former so-called Riksdaler Riksgälds) which pursuant to the statute of February 3d, 1855, constituted the unity of coinage based on silver, and likewise divided into 100 öre. The coin contained 12 parts of pure silver and 4 of copper, and the small coin was made only of bronze.

A gold coin, called Karolin, (=10 francs) was made a few years ago, but it is no longer continued.

A few old silver coins of the value of ⅔, ⅓, etc., Specie (1 = 4 Kr.), are still circulated, and copper coins in skilling and rundstycke, which belong to the old system of coinage, in which the unit of coinage was Riksdaler Banko (=1½ Kr.) of 48 skillings.

As legal tender is also used *paper money*, the notes of the realm, concerning which the constitution says: "The Diet alone is authorized to issue notes through the Bank of the Realm, which shall be recognized as currency in the Kingdom. These notes shall be paid by the bank on demand, in gold, according to their wording and tenor." Previously to the introduction of the gold standard, this payment was made in silver. The smallest value represented by these notes being 1 Krona, coin of the same or of a higher value is at present very little used in ordinary transactions. The Diet of 1875, has, however, resolved that on a day that shall be fixed by the Directors of the Bank the issue of notes for 1 Kr. shall cease, and the bank-notes shall then be for sums not less than 5 Kr. The other sums represented are 10, 50, 100 and 1000 Kr. Bank of the Realm notes circulate to the amount of from 30 to 40 million Kr.

Besides the Bank of the Realm there are 27 Private Banks that issue notes, of which the stock in circulation amounts to from 60 to 70 million Kr. Their notes, which represent a value of not less than 5 Kr., shall, according to former enactments, be paid on demand in money of the realm, (i. e. silver, latterly gold, or in notes of the bank of the realm), but this obligatory payment is (according to an Enactment of June 12th, 1874), henceforth, whenever new charters are granted or old ones renewed, prescribed to be made only in gold coin.

The **Bank of the Realm**, (Riksbanken), which is managed by the Commissioners of the Diet, (Banko-Fullmägtige) is the principal and oldest bank in Sweden, (having existed since 1668, and being properly a continuation of the one established in 1656 by J. Palmstruch, the first in the world from which notes were issued). Its Head-Office is in Stockholm, and there are 4 branch-offices, (in Göteborg, Malmö, Luleå, and Visby).

Of **Private Banks** there are 2 kinds:

Private Banks that issue notes, to which a charter has been granted for 10 years, and of which all the shareholders, (at least 30 in number), are solidarily, jointly and separately, liable for all the obligations of the banking company. There may also be "sleeping" partners, whose liability is limited by the full value of their shares. The capital stock of a private bank shall amount to at least one million Kr. The ordinance, relating thereto now in force, is of June 12th, 1874. The oldest among these banks, (that of Skåne), was granted a charter for the first time in 1830. At present, their number is 27.

Joint Stock Banking Companies, not issuing notes, (and Joint Stock Loan Companies), of which the first was established in 1863, are based upon the enactment of October 6th, 1848, relating to Joint Stock Companies, and consequently the shareholders of these are liable to the Company only in proportion to the stock they hold. These and similar banks issue no notes. Of these banks there are 8, of which, together with the private banks, monthly reports are published by the Treasury Department.

There are, in addition to these, three similar loan-establishments and also three people's banks, whose operations are founded on the above-mentioned law relating to Joint Stock Companies.

There has also been a third kind of bank, namely, the *Branch-banks,* ("Filialbanker") of which the oldest was established in 1852, but since that time they have gradually been discontinued. The last ceased to exist on June 30th, 1875. These banks issued no notes, but obtained their capital by credentials on the Bank of the Realm. The shareholders were solidarily liable.

Among the banks may also be reckoned several *Banking-houses,* which carry on a complete banking business. To these also belong *Savings Banks* and *People's Banks.* (See below.)

Most of the Private Banks generally have Branch-Offices in various districts of the country, which makes the number of banking establishments in reality much larger.

The above-mentioned banks, and their assets, (aktiva or passiva) June 30th, 1875, are as follows:

A) **Sveriges Riksbank.**—The Bank of the Realm, - - - - - Kr. 94,222,376

B) **Private Banks** (issuing notes):

		Kronor.
Skånes	Enskilda Bank,	41,487,128
Vermlands	"	9,582,802
Kopparberg	"	9.068,704
Östergötlands	"	7,380,574
Smålands	"	14,291,813
Örebro	"	10,607,453
Mälareprovinsernas	"	22,096,392
Göteborgs	"	15,869,716
Stockholms	Enskilda Bank,	27,407,769
Norrköpings	"	10,725,258
Vadstena	"	5,051,831
Hallands	"	3,211,955
Sundsvalls	"	15,898,677
Christianstads	"	13,613,182
Venersborgs	"	6,586,610
Skaraborgs-Läns	"	8,528,112
Gefleborgs	"	7,374,665
Upplands	"	14,653,155
Vesterbottens	"	7,312,904
Christinehamns	"	5,735,710
Borås	"	4,734,445
Södermanlands	"	5,089,341
Kalmar	"	10,482,131
Gottlands	"	3,501,708
Bohus Läns	"	2,234,755
Hernösands	"	7,485,827
Helsinglands	"	8,452,321
	Total, Private Banks, Kr.	298,464,938

C.) **Joint-Stock-Banks,** (Aktiebanker):

	Kronor.
Skandinaviska Kredit—Aktiebolaget	42,529,037
Industri Kredit—Aktiebolaget in Stockholm . . .	5,143,128
Stockholms Intecknings-Garanti-Aktiebolag . . .	18,597,530
Aktiebolaget Stockholms Handels-Bank . . .	12,500,012
" Göteborgs Handels-Kompani . .	14,998,409
" Gefle Bank . .	2,423,834
" Blekinges Bank .	2,559,465
" Göteborgs Köpmans Bank	3,938,221
" Sundsvalls Handels Bank	3,281,070
Total, Joint Stock-Banks, Kr.	105,970,706

Sum Total Kr. 498,658,020

The business of all these Banking-Establishments has increased very much during the last few years, and at June 30th, 1875, was as follows:

Capital and Assets.

	Riksbank. Kr.	27 Private Banks. Kr.	9 Joint-St'k-B'ks. Kr.
Cash	27,361,898	26,342,317	3,200,974
Stock Owners Deposits		39,123,806	
Public Bonds	13,265,402	20,072,982	10,863,129
Bills Discounted	16,392,717	79,287,956	20,964,804
Letters of Credit	10,024,943	58,546,946	16,781,813
Money lent out on interest	25,877,900	57,755,483	39,080,793
Other Claims and valuables	1,299,516	17,335,448	15,079,193
Total	94,222,376	298,464,938	105,970,760

Debts.

Bills circulating,	38,557,023	58,353,855	
Bank Post Bills circulating,	1,899,508	4,608,800	1,659,601
Fuuds deposited,	15,960,989	130,552,599	31,669,532
Funds deposited in Accounts Current,	967,220	19,969,658	12,513,572
Other Debts,	1,075,475	26,595,314	30,184,722
Stock,	25,000,000	49,449,100	22,491,956
Reserves,	10,762,169	8,935,612	7,451,323
Total	94,222,376	298,464,938	105,970,706

The Savings-Banks, the beginning of which may be reckoned from the establishment of a savings-fund for the workmen at Bromö Glass-manufactory, in the Lān of Skaraborg, in the year 1805, although properly the first Savings-Bank was opened in Göteborg as late as 1820, have, especially during the last few years, considerably increased both in number and importance. In the year 1873, they numbered 271, of which 92 were in towns and 179 in the country; during the same year 110,832 new depositors were added to them, while 33,752 retired, so that the whole number of depositors at the end of the year was 563,857.

The business which these 271 Savings Banks transacted in the year 1873, was as follows:

Deposits, ...	Kr. 35,962,766
Withdrawals, ...	„ 21,939,102
Interest, ...	„ 4,450,949
Balance of cash (of the depositors),	„ 106,255,037
Funds belonging to the Savings-Banks themselves, .	„ 5,577,913

The rapid development of the business of the Savings Banks may be seen from the following figures showing the cash on hand belonging to the depositors:

In the year	
1860, ...	Kr. 27,291,937
1865, . . , . . .	„ 35,983,636
1870, ...	„ 57,376,611
1871, ...	„ 71,694,016
1872, ...	„ 87,739,515
1873.	„ 106,255,037

The depositors generally receive 5 per cent. The usual rate of interest in Sweden is from 5 to 6 per cent., but owing to the abundant supply of money it has been down during the last year to 4 and 4½ per cent. The law prohibits lending money at compound interest, or at more than 6 per cent., unless, in the latter case, loans are granted for 6 months, at the most, without mortgage on land.

There are also a few so-called *People's Banks.* Their so-called savings-fund-departments (Sparkasse-afdelningar) are included among the savings-banks. There are also establishments for securing *Capital and Life Annuites* (Kapital och Lifränte-Anstalter).

Loan-Offices for special purposes. *The Bank for advances to Manufacturers,* (Förlagslånefonden), is an establishment, under the control of the Board of Commerce, which grants loans for carrying on or establishing manufacturing business.

The Public Mortgage Bank (Hypoteksbanken), and 10 *Mortgage Companies,* (Hypoteksföreningar), whose business it is to change the floating debts on lands into consolidated debts. These loans are exclusively (since 1861), procured by the Public Mortgage Bank; the common amortization-debt was in 1873: 210,000,000 Kr. ($58,000,000, gold.

There is a *Public Mortgage-Fund for the Swedish towns,* and several *Mortgage-Companies,* which have the same object for the towns as the above mentioned.

The *Iron-Association,* (capital in 1873: 4,968,020 Kr.) and the *Mortgage-Fund for the Owners of Iron-Works* to promote the iron-trade.

A Loan Office, which ought rather to be considered as a charitable institution, is the *Pawn broking Establishment,* of the town of Stockholm, established as early as in 1772 for accommodating the poorer classes with loans upon security of gold, silver, or other movable property. On an average, during the years 1862 to 1871, this establishment granted 147,206 loans, amounting to 1,335,782 Kr., while 121,017 loans were paid in, whereas 24,870 pledges were sold by public auction for want of payment. In recent years, similar establishments have been founded at Göteborg (2), Gefle, Wenersborg, and one more in Stockholm, which, however, have not been able to exterminate private establishments of the same character, where of course the charge of interest is unreasonably high (30 and 40 per cent.)

Insurance Offices are very numerous, partly under the state, and partly private, whose object is, as usual, to grant insurance against fire and sea-risks—on lives, annuities, capital, etc. Besides, there are many foreign Insurance Companies active in the country. As such establishments are not bound to publish their position in any other way than by the review which they must submit to the shareholders, and there is no obligation prescribed in the Swedish law for the insurance of their property against fire, neither the exact number of the different insurance-establishments, nor their operations are known with any certainty. In the year 1870, it was estimated that Swedish property was insured in Swedish companies alone for a value of at least 1,785,000,000 Kr. ($500,000,000, gold).

The Insurance-establishments for Capital and Annuities, which are something between savings-banks and pensionary institutions are 11 in number. In the year 1873 they took charge of upwards of 8,500,000 Kr., but since that time the deposits have very much increased.

The most important among the *Pensionary Establishments* are: The Pensionary Fund of the Army (in 1871 with a capital of 4,451,551 Kr.), the Pensionary Establishment of the Civil Service (5,868,909 Kr. in the year 1873), the Public Fund for Widows and Wards, (4,955,872 Kr. in the year 1871), etc.

Concerning the proper Charitable Institutions see below, Class 346.

FINANCES.

Finances of the State. The constitution of the State prescribes that "The ancient right of the Swedish people of taxing themselves shall be excercised by the Diet alone." The Diet, therefore, on the proposal of the government, determines upon the Budget, or the so-called status of the realm, (Statsreglering) for the following year. The Kingdom having the two offices for the administration of money-affairs, namely, the Revenue-Office (the government's,) and the Debt-Office of the Realm (the Diet's), and many items of the public expenditure and revenue not being included in the Budget, but assigned direct to the Debt-Office of the Realm, (e. g. the expenditure for the Diet, the redemption of the consolidated railway-loans, etc)., the drawing up of the Budget becomes very complicated. To this are, also, to be added several large items, which, in consequence of peculiar circumstances in Sweden, are not at all included in the Budget, such as the maintenance of the so-called "Indelta," (regular) army by "Rotering" and "Rustning" (estimated at 4,000,000 Kr. annually, at least), part of the payment to a number of officials by "Kronoboställen" (land belonging to the Crown, assigned for the maintenance of officials), the keeping in repair of the highways, a burden which falls upon landed property, the pay of the clergy, which is a parochial tax, etc.

On drawing up the Budget the gross-receipts, as well as the expenses are reckoned either as ordinary or extraordinary, and the expenditures are specified under nine so-called "Hufvudtitlar" (nine Headings of the annual expenses of the government(. In case of a deficiency in the calculated income, an order is made out on the Debt-Office of the Realm to be paid either out of funds previously existing, the profits of the Bank of the Realm, or by loans (the latter only for the construction of railways).

The Budget of 1876 is drawn up as follows:

Income (Gross).

ORDINARY RECEIPTS.

Ordinary Rents (Land Tax), .	Kr. 4,505,300
Corn received as tithes, „ .	„ 1,625,900
"Mantal"-money, i. e. Poll Tax,	„ 580,000
Light-dues and Beaconage, .	„ 800,000
Income by the Railways, .	„ 14,600,000
Income by the Telegraphs, .	„ 1,330,000
Income by the Forests, . .	„ 1,000,000
Other sources of ordinary income,	„ 1,475,800
Ordinary Income,	25,917,000

EXTRAORDINARY RECEIPTS.

Customs,	Kr.	20,000,000
Post Office,	„	3,850,000
Stamped Paper,	„	1,750,000
Import on Spirits,	„	13,130,000
Import on Beet-Sugar,	„	60,000
General Concessions,	„	2,800,000
Extraordinary Income	Kr.	41,590,000

Income of the Debt Office of the Realm.

Balances and interest,	Kr.	6,074,609
Share in the profits of the Bank of the Realm,	„	1,250,000
Loan for the construction of Railways,	„	20,000,000
Deficiency to be filled by the surplus of income from other departments,	„	844,404
Income of the Debt office,	„	28,169,013
Total income,	Kr.	95,676,013

Expenses:

ORDINARY EXPENSES.

Head 1.	Royal household,	Kr.	1,266,000
" 2.	Judiciary Department,	„	3,390,000
" 3.	Foreign "	„	609,365
" 4.	Army "	„	11,772,300
" 5.	Navy "	„	4,617,600
" 6.	Civil "	„	13,091,200
" 7.	Financial "	„	11,357,700
" 8.	Ecclesiastical "	„	7,340,900
" 9.	Pensions,	„	1,740,335
	Ordinary Expenses,	Kr.	55,185,400

EXTRAORDINARY EXPENSES.

Head 1,	Kr.	——
" 2,	„	613,882
" 3,	„	——
" 4,	„	6,696,756
" 5,	„	3,154,085
" 6,	„	1,984,782
" 7,	„	570,285
" 8,	„	1,805,910
" 9,	„	503,500
Extraordinary expenses,	Kr.	15,329,200

Exclusive of the Heads, the Railway Buildings of the State,	Kr.	12,000,000

Expenses of the Debt Office of the Realm.

Interest on and amortization of Railway Loans,	Kr.	7,974,954
Advances for the construction of Private Railways,	„	2,000,000
Other expenses,	„	3,186,459
Expenses of Debt Office of Realm,	Kr.	13,161,413
Total expenses,	Kr.	95,676,013

Besides, in case of extraordinary requirements, (during wars, bad crops, and the like), an order is issued at every Diet for a so-called *Great Letter of Credit*, (usually 3 million Kr.), and a *Small Letter of Credit*, (1½ million), to be at the disposal of government.

The chief income of the State accrues from the customs and the tax on spirits.

Since 1864, **duty** is paid only on imported goods. Among these the most important are: Sugar, in 1873, 28 per ct. of the whole customs; woven fabrics, 20 per ct.; coffee, 11 per ct.; tobacco, 10 per ct.; whisky and spirits, 6 per ct.; wine, 3 per ct.; syrup, 2 per ct., etc. The customs depending upon the state of trade must vary accordingly. They amounted in 1870 to 15,782,072 Kr. (in the status of the Realm calculated at 14 millions); 1871: 19,116,601 Kr. (14 millions); 1872: 19,302,770 Kr. (15 millions), 1873: 23,940,226, (16½ millions), and 1874: 29, 442,252, (16½ millions), the highest sum to which the custom duty ever amounted, and to this is to be added 949,590 Kr. in light dues and beaconage. To this income Stockholm contributes about 40 per ct., Göteborg, 30 per ct., Malmö, 10 per ct., etc.

Between Sweden and Norway there is a toll-boundary, but this is now, (by an Enactment of May 29th, 1874), no longer strictly enforced and limited to only a few articles.

With regard to the *tax on whiskey* (brännvin), compare Catalogue, Class 660.

Previous to the year 1855, Sweden owed no **National Debt** to foreign countries, and only a very small one to the Bank of the Realm. For the construction of railways, which began in that year, and which has since gradually increased, several bonded-loans, partly foreign, partly inland, have been raised, and these are paid by amortization. At the beginning of 1875, the whole remaining debt amounted to 37,813,900 Kr. 23,655,150 Prussian Thl. Ct. and 1,649,300 £ *St.* or in all 130,477,920 Kr.(=$36,243,800, gold).

For the payment of these debts several grants have been assigned, and funds formed.

As the National Debt of Sweden has been incurred solely for the construction of Railways, the country is in possession of the full value of its debts, so that whatever besides belongs to the State, is a clear surplus; and therefore the finances of the country are, fortunately, very prosperous. This is also shown by the following review of the Financial Position of the Swedish State at the end of the year 1873:

Active Capital, . . .	Kr.	66,057,926
Railways of the State, . .	,,	123,952,605
Landed property (leased), . .	,,	12,617,249
Forests, ...	,,	29,645,000
Total of Active,	Kr.	232,272,780
National Debts, . .	,,	114,185,926
Amount of Effects in excess of Debts, ...	Kr.	118,086,854

Communal Finances. For the exposition of these, there are no doubt, a number of contributions from different districts, but no complete pictures of the whole. There are a large number of reports at hand from different parts of the country, but they are not sufficient to serve as the basis of a reliable report for the whole Kingdom. It may be stated, however, that the "Landsting" is computed to have a yearly income of half a million Kr., which is devoted to educational institutions, to the maintainance of the poor and other charitable purposes, to public improvements, to agriculture, etc. The sum contributed by the church communities to these purposes is however much larger—that contributed to the public schools alone being over two million Kr. annually.

As another instance may be mentioned, that in the town of Stockholm, all the direct taxes may be calculated at 1 per ct. to the state and 4 per ct. to the community, or together, 5 per ct. of the whole annual income tax.

National Wealth. The assessment taken in 1874 may serve as the measure of the present national wealth:

	Kronor.
Assessment of agricultural landed property, ...	1,778,000,000
Assessment of other ground property	592,000,000
Value of property belonging to the State, Communities, etc., (exempt from taxes), . . .	139,000,000
Estimated income from capital, commerce, industrial pursuits, salaries or pensions, ...	265,000,000

That capital, especially during the last year, has been constantly increasing, has been seen in many different ways, e. g. by a greater activity in business, and the consequence, higher wages of workmen, by large deposits in the banks, by a greater demand for bonds and stocks, by the falling of the rate of interest, etc.

As an illustration, it may here be stated that in in the year 1874 alone, the government granted charters to the following Joint Stock Companies:

	Capital in shares. Minimum. Millions. Kr.	Maximum. Millions. Kr.
10 Railway Joint Stock Companies,	6.2	12.7
135 Joint Stock Companies for Industrial pursuits and Manufactures,	34.9	67.1
24 Joint Stock Companies of Ship-owners,	3.5	11.5
4 Insurance Joint Stock Companies,	3.3	9.0
26 Commercial, Banking and Consumptionary Joint Stock Companies,	1.3	4.6
18 other Joint Stock Companies,	1.0	2.1
217 Total Million Kr.,	50.2	107.0

The corresponding figures were considerably larger for the preceding years.

THE POST AND TELEGRAPH.

The Post is a public establishment which dates from 1636, when regular posts were put in operation all over the country, and in modern times, it has, together with the increased facilities of transport, been greatly developed, but it still travels the greater number of miles on the high-roads; at least such was still the case in 1873: 546,144 Swedish miles to 319,511 by railway, or together 9,252,660 Kilom.; in addition to these there were in, 1873: 173 mail-steamers, mostly belonging to private individuals. The conveying of travelers by stage-coach on the more important high-roads by the arrangement of the postal establishment, is not very extensive (16,908 persons in the year 1873), because the greater number of travellers proper take "skjuts" (extra-posts) at the "skjuts" stations (compare Catalogue, Class 330.)

In the year 1855, a uniform postage of 6 skilling or 12½ öre (in 1858 reduced to 12 öre) for single weight of 4 ort=17 grammes, was introduced all over the country, and at the same time also postage stamps. Later, money-orders, Post-office-advances, and Postal-cards have also been introduced.

Since the beginning of 1873, a new ordinance is in force, according to which the *postage* is 12 öre for a common letter, not exceeding 4 ort, 24 öre for 4 to 25 ort, 36 öre for 25 to 50 ort, while heavier messages are treated as parcels. For local letters, and letters delivered, is charged 3 öre, for postal-cards 10 öre, for despatches under cross-bands "korsband," 6 öre for every 12 ort, for so-called small parcels, not exceeding 1 skålpund in weight, 30 öre, and above 1 and not exceeding 2 lbs, 50 öre. For small cash remittances (not exceeding 50 Kr.) a register fee of 18 öre is charged, and for larger, 50 öre, under the name of Insurance, and 2 öre extra for every 100 Kr. above 1000 Kr. Since the postal treaty at Bern, of October 9th, 1874, has been ratified also on the part of Sweden, the charges for dispatches in general, to and from countries included in the General Postal Union, are: for pre-paid letters, 20 öre per 15 grams; for unpaid letters, 40 öre per 15 grams; for postal cards, 10 öre each; for cross-band dispatches, 6 öre per 50 grams; for registration, 18 öre for each dispatch; and for receipts 12 öre each. For dispatches to and from Norway and Denmark a lower postage is charged, or the same as in Sweden (the single weight is, however, reckoned at 15 grams). Letters from the Government-Bureaus, which formerly were dispatched free of charge, are now (since January 1st, 1874), subject to the same regulations as for private letters; special postage stamps, which are paid for out of the funds of the state, are, however, provided for the bureaus.

Newspapers and periodicals were likewise exempt from postage on account of the stamp duty to which they were subject (even those that were not sent by post); this stamp duty having, however, been abolished since January 1st, 1873, a postage has been imposed instead, which depends upon the size of the periodicals, and how often they are published.

The business of the postal establishment, the chief management of which belongs to the Director of the General Post Office, was in the year 1873, as follows:*

Post-offices, . .	Number,	641
Letters despatched by post (besides Cash remittances),	,,	15,011,874
" foreign, . . .	,,	1,412,689
Cash remittances, . .	,,	1,699,226
" foreign, . . .	,,	145,430
Letters and Parcels of all kinds,	,,	16,711,100
Numbers of Newspapers despatched: inland, .	,,	26,058,840
foreign, .	,,	432,330
Contents of Letters insured,	Kr.	461,028,924
Post-office-orders, . .	,,	2,488,995
Post-office-advances, (Postförskott), . . .	,,	81,318
Income of the Posting Establishment, . . .	,	3,129,000
Expenditure of the Posting-Establishment, . .	,,	2,873,000

In the year 1865 there were only 379 post-offices, 11 million letters and parcels were dispatched, and consequently during the 8 years, 1865 to 1873 the former have increased by 70 per ct. and the latter 50 per ct. Since the beginning of 1874, when the Post-office took the so-called carriage of Government-letters (i. e. the obligation imposed on certain land-holders, in certain cases, to forward official letters in the country), the number of branch post-offices has very much increased, and will probably soon amount to about 2,000, as almost every community will have a post-office of its own.

The **Electric Telegraph,** which was first

*Compare, Contributions to the Official Statistics of Sweden. M.—Postväsendet (Postal Affairs) 1864 to 1873.

established in 1853, has since been extended year by year, so that at the end of the year 1874, there were, at an expenditure by the State of in all, 5,276,990 Kr., 1,058 geographical miles (7,848 Kilom.), of wire with from 1 to 11 wires, or together 2,511 geographical miles (18,633, Kilom.), of wire. In the length of the lines are included 10.7 geographical miles (79 Kilom.) of submarine cables, of which, those leading to Gottland are the longest. Besides, the Swedish State possesses in common with Denmark a submarine cable in the Sound and in common with Prussia, a similar one between Skåne and Rügen, of which the total length is 13.1 geographical miles (98 Kilom.) with conducting wires of in all, 41.9 miles (311 Kilom.) The connection with the Russian empire, besides by a land-line along the Gulf of Bothnia, belonging to the State, is also kept up by means of a submarine cable over the Åland Sea, laid in 1869 by the Great Northern Telegraphic Company in Copenhagen. In 1873 this company also laid sub-marine cables between Sweden and England, and between Sweden and Denmark. Three land-lines of the State lead to Norway.

The total number of the telegraph stations in Sweden, were, in the year 1874:

Stations belonging to the State, . .	132
Private stations, (under the control of the State), ...	19
Railway telegraph stations belonging to the State, ...	138
Railway telegraph stations belonging to Private Companies, ...	184
Signal stations, ...	8
In all, stations, ...	481

Among these, 7 bureaus for the delivery of telegrams in special districts in Stockholm, are not included.

The Director of the Royal Telegraph issues an annual report,* according to which the telegraph of the State has developed rapidly, as the following tabular comparison for 1865 and 1874 shows:

		1865.	1874.
Lines,	Geogr. Miles,	784	1,058
Wire conductors,	"	1,299	2,511
Stations,	Number,	87	159
Telegrams, inland,	"	232,474	772,928
" foreign,	"	95,990	213,469
Income,	Kr.	614,773	1,229,678

Among telegrams dispatched, circulars, meteorological and repeated telegrams are not included.

Of the 159 stations of the State, 75 were managed by females. At all of them Morse's writing apparatus (432 in number) are employed. Besides, in 1874, a Wheatstone's apparatus was put up in Stockholm and at Göteborg.

Of late years post office and telegraph stations have sometimes been united.

The uniform rate all over Sweden is 1 Kr. for 20 words, each not exceeding 7 syllables, with an extra charge of 25 öre for every additional 5 words; 10 öre is further added as carrier's fee. To Norway the single rate is Kr. 2.06; to Denmark, Kr. 1.80, and to other countries it is more depending upon the distance.

The signal telegraph was introduced about the end of last century, and the first telegraphic line for correspondence was carried across the Åland-sea. At the end of 1874, there were for the shipping only 8 stations, namely, 5 in the Skärgård (Archipelago) of Stockholm and 3 in that of Göteborg.

*Contributions to the Official Statistics of Sweden. I. Telegrafväsendet (telegraphic matters) 1861-1874.

MEANS OF TRANSPORT.

Among these are the *high roads*, the *railways*, and the *canals*. See Catalogue, Class 330.

INDUSTRIAL PURSUITS AND COMMERCE.

Domestic Industry has taken a prominent place in Sweden since the earliest times, as is to be expected in a country, where the distances are great, so that the inhabitants, in more than one respect, have had to resort to their own energies; where industrial life, was but little developed; where the long winter evenings have compelled the inhabitants of the country to seek suitable employment within doors; and where, moreover, in certain districts, readiness in art or handiness seems to be innate.

It is, however, the general complaint that domestic industry is on the decline. In consequence, namely, of the more and more reduced prices and the greater perfection and tastefulness of the productions of the manufactories; domestic industry must be diminished in its original form. It were, however, an evil if domestic industry were to cease altogether without being substituted by something else. Independent of the advantage of a small income, or at least of a saved penny, it produces this moral gain, that industry and diligence take up that part of the year, not inconsiderable, when, in consequence of the climate in our country, agriculture, the principal branch of industry, cannot be prosecuted, and which, for want of other occupation, would be devoted to indolence, or perhaps to crime. Domestic industry does not, like manufacturing trades, deprive parents of their children's presence, but makes home a fireside of comfort and prosperity. In those parts where domestic industry is cultivated, there also prevail tidiness and order, even in the houses of the poor. In consideration of that, we ought to try by all means in our power to infuse new life into domestic industry, which, in certain districts at least, has appeared to be rapidly disappearing, and we have thought this possible by imparting to the people taste and readiness in art, as well as a knowledge of the mechanical powers, which now are resorted to in the manufacture of everything on a larger scale, and, therefore, domestic industry now assumes altogether another character than the simple, primitive one of former days.

There are several associations and communities in the country, formed with this object in view, such as the Royal Patriotic Society, founded in 1767, the Agricultural Societies, the Landsting, the Industrial Association in Stockholm, the Society "Handarbetets vänner," (the friends of handiwork) which in particular encourages the child-work, as also other industrial associations, etc. Endeavors have been made to gain this object, partly by publishing suitable tracts, partly by free instruction at schools, or by traveling teachers, partly by premiums or medals, partly by exhibitions, comprehending sometimes the whole Kingdom, sometimes certain Län or parts of the country, and partly by facilitating the sale of the productions of domestic industry. In this latter respect the Agricultural Societies have contributed to the continual exhibition of industrial and hand-made productions arranged in Stockholm under the name of the "Swedish Industrial Magazine." There are also similar places of exhibition, though perhaps smaller, in other parts of the country.

Among all the industrial branches that of *Weaving* is still the most important, even though the peasant does not now, as formerly, in many districts, wear almost exclusively, clothes made by his wife. The chief place for this industrial pursuit is the Län of Elfsborg. We find (see Cat., Class 228) that there are people in these districts who advance money to thousands of women, who occupy themselves with weaving mostly cotton. In Ångermanland they spin and weave fine linens, both plain and figured for tablecloths. In Halland, in Wingåker, (Södermanland), and other places the peasantry make woolen fabrics, etc. It must, however, be born in mind that in these and many other places, weaving constitutes a source of income, and the production is, therefore, calculated for sale, but the industrial art of weaving is practiced in a great many other places, where the manufacture is intended merely for home use.

About these and other female employments, such as *Cushion-lace*, *Hair-work*, *Straw-plaiting*, see Appendix (Women's work).

Among the male employments may be mentioned *Smith's and Joiner's work* of every description, so that in the different parts of the Kingdom are manufactured nails, tacks, horse-shoes, ploughs, scythes, axes, knives, muskets, locks, brass-boxes, pins, etc., and also thrashing machines, vehicles, wooden vessels, staves, weavers reeds, and furniture (e. g. in Våla in Westmanland, and Lindome in the Län of Göteborg, see Cat. Class 217). To this should also be added the manufacture of *clocks, basket* and *straw-work, boot and shoe-making* (for sale) the *dressing of leather, etc.*

Boat-building is a branch of business that is very much followed in certain districts. The boats made in Orust and Tjörn in the Län of Bohus are in great demand, and so are the so-called "snipor" (a kind of boat with both ends pointed) of Westerbotten.

The great development of domestic industry in certain districts, together with the stricter views that formerly prevailed with regard to free trade, called forth, a peculiar kind of commerce, the so-called "gårdfarihandel" (peddling) which, however, in later times, since the former restrictions upon trade have been repealed, and especially owing to the mercantile stores that consequently are allowed to be established in the provinces, has for the most part disappeared. It still happens, however, as a remnant of this peddling business, that Westgothians, or Smålanders travel about the country offering for sale their home-woven cotton or woolen fabrics, or that a Dalecarlian may be met with, far away from his home, for the purpose of selling his substantial clock, or that a Dalecarlian woman ("Dalkulla") may leave her meagre native soil, with her hair-work and horse-hair-work, and wander about, not only her own extensive country, but as far as the neighbouring countries, Norway and Denmark, nay the journey may even be directed to Germany, England, or still farther away.

Mechanical Trades and Manufactures. Ever from the 15th century and until 1846, the mechanical trades in Sweden have been tied by the corporation-laws introduced here after the German pattern, but in the last-mentioned year the *freedom of trade* in Sweden underwent a radical change for the better, which has gained its highest expression in the Royal Enactment of June 18th, 1864, now in force. The first general provision in this enactment, relative to an extended freedom in trading; says, that every Swedish man and woman (with few exceptions) is entitled, both in towns and rural districts, to practice any trading or manufactural pursuit, handicraft or other industrial employment, or to own ships, both for home and foreign trade. To enjoy the right to practice mercantile business, or to sell goods in shops or other warehouses, or with the assistance of any person or persons (other than wife and children living at home) in order to manufacture goods or articles of handicraft for sale, or to engage in any other industrial pursuit, it is requisite to be of good character, and free from all encumbrances, both with respect to person and property, and also to give notification thereof to the proper authorities. From this freedom in trading, are only excepted: bookseller's or printer's business; the distillery or sale of whiskey; the manufacture or sale of gunpowder; dealing in poison or other dangerous materials; the profession of apothecary, or dealing in apothecary's goods; keeping flour-mills or saw-mills; surgeon-barber's business; organ-building; and chimney sweepings, in towns. With reference to all of which special provisions are enacted.

Aliens may own ship property both for home and foreign trade; but his share shall not exceed a third part of the total tonnage of any vessel. Nor shall aliens be the managing owners of any vessel. It shall in each case depend upon special resolution, whether aliens, male or female, who have obtained the King's permission to settle in the country, shall be permitted to practice trade and manufacture, handicraft, or other industrial pursuits.

With regard to the *general relation between masters, engaged in trade, or other industrial pursuits, and their assistants*, it is among other things enacted, that:—

No one shall be engaged as assistant to a dealer, or for work in any manufacture, handicraft, or other industrial pursuit, until after the full age of twelve years. In factories and workshops, no one under the age of eighteen years shall be employed during the night, between the hours of 9 o'clock in the evening and 5 o'clock in the morning; masters in trade and other industrial pursuits, shall, in the treatment and employment of their assistants or workmen, give due consideration to the health and capabilities for labour, and that they, especially those being minors, receive necessary instruction.

By these prescriptions the Swedish law has endeavored to obviate the evils that follow upon the too early application of the energies of children, by which, a strong and healthy race of men will grow up. To what extent the energies of *young men and women* are taxed at factories and manufactural establishments may be concluded by the following figures, which stand for the year 1873:

Workmen over 18 years of age, .	30,537.
Workwomen over 18 years of age, .	11,501.
Total,	42,038.
Workmen under 18 years of age, .	6,239.
Workwomen under 18 years of age, .	3,803.
Total,	10,042.

or together, 36,776 men and 15,304 women. Add to this, 1,254 masters.

The total number of *Manufacturers* and *Handicrafts-people* (male and female,) in the years 1860 and 1873, was as follows:

	1860.	1873.
Owners of Factories (exclusive of companies,)	30,757	2,161
Factory Hands, . .		53,334
Tradesmen, . . .	10,788	17,199
Tradesmen's assistants, .	20,496	25,416
Minors, ...	20,359	28,624

Among the Tradesmen here, are not included such as carry on their trade at home, with the assistance of their wives and children only. If similar minors trades-men be included, as in the public census of 1870, number, considerably higher than those above, according to the statistics of trade and industrial pursuits will be obtained. In the following a more minute account, under the different classes, will be given of the different branches of industry:

The following table will show the total development of *manufactural industry* during the last 43 years:

Year.	Number of Factories.	Value of Production.
1830 . . .	Kr. 1,857.	Kr. 13,175,000
1840 . . .	„ 2,176.	„ 21,200,000
1850 . . .	„ 2,513.	„ 37,092,000
1860 . . .	„ 2,509.	„ 69,109,000
1870 . . .	„ 2,183.	„ 92,281,000
1871 . . .	„ 2,305.	„ 105,236,000
1872 . . .	„ 2,356.	„ 126,312,000
1873 . . .	„ 2,549.	„ 146,869,000

Mines and mining establishments are not included in this table.

All industrial pursuits, and also navigation and trade are under the control of the Royal Board of Commerce, which publishes an annual report.*

This Board also grants *Patents* according to the Royal Ordinance of August 19th, 1856. Patents are granted for a period of not less than three years or not exceeding fifteen in proportion to the nature and importance of the invention, but only on new inventions, relating to, industrial pursuits and art (not on medicines) and also on improvements of older inventions, though not on a mere principle, but on a statement of the manner and method of applying the new invention. The letter-patent in order to be valid shall be published in the official newspaper and the invention shall be brought into practice in the Kingdom within two years.

Otherwise, there are in Sweden, no *privileges* or *mercantile monopolies*, unless among the former may be reckoned the publishing of calendars and the official newspaper, which is reserved for two academies.

Commerce.—The number of people carrying on commerce, was:

	1860.	1873.
Merchants, (men and women)	9,904.	14,605.
Commercial clerks, - -	5,216.	10,389.
Total, - -	15,120.	24,994.
Of these in towns, - -	12,037.	16,632.

* Bidrag till Sveriges officiela Statistik, C.) Bergshandtering (Mining business) 1858-1873; D.) Fabriker och Manufakturer, 1858-1873; E.) Inrikes Handel och Sjöfart (Home trade and Navigation) 1858—1873; F.) Utrikes handel och Sjöfart (Foreign trade and navigation) 1858-1873.

The importance of the different articles, which form the objects of trade with other nations, will be seen by the following list, which shows the value of the Imports and Exports for the year 1873:

	Import. Kr.	Export. Kr.
Live Animals,	508,497.	9,787,169
Animal Food,	17,890,844.	6,937,202
Grain and its products,	18,462,926.	34,020,663
Colonial produce,	45,380,716.	127,319
Fruits and Garden-productions,	3,953,287.	172,516
Spirituous and other Liquors,	7,953,934.	346,290
Raw materials for Spinning,	21,364,281.	311,467
Yarn, Thread, &c.,	10,171,892.	150,118
Manufactures of Spun materials,	39,239,466.	2,060,345
Hair, Feathers, Hides, Leather, Bones, Horn & other substances,	15,425,818.	914,724
Manufactures of Hair, Leather, Bone, Horn, &c.,	750,756.	213,524
Tallow, Oil, Tar, Gum and similar substances,	8,690,156.	1,512,194
Manufactures of Tallow, Oil, &c.,	970,460.	132,274
Wood, (not worked, sawn or cut),	958,053.	96,192,933
Wood, (worked),	971,211.	6,929,228
Colors and Coloring matters,	2,766,556.	179,337
Various other Vegetable matters,	4,903,657.	550,995
Paper, and articles made of Paper,	2,389,397.	2,510,527
Other articles made from Vegetable matter,	143,679.	9,872
Ore, (unroasted),	21,265,601.	991,476
Products from Minerals,	2,026,176.	495,941
Metals, not manufactured or partly manufactured,	8,268,766.	51,905,154
Metallic articles,	11,372,786.	1,860,827
Ships, Carriages, Machinery, Instruments, &c.,	16,048,179.	1,148,471
Money,	8,191,082.	2,099,930
Articles not belonging to any of the above classes,	1,371,549.	343,137
Total.	271,439,725.	221,903,633

The principal *Exports* of Sweden, therefore, are the productions of mines, forests, and agriculture, about which the details will be stated under Classes 111, 620, and 600.

Among the imported articles of greatest commercial importance, are:

Animal food, especially Herrings, Lard and Butter, of which latter article, however, treble the quantity is exported.

Colonial produce, of which was imported in 1873: Sugar and Syrup 81,180,000 lbs., Coffee 26,555,000 lbs., Tea 103,000 lbs., and Tobacco 8,105,000 lbs.

Spirituous and other liquors, mostly Wine, Arrack, and French Brandy (compare Class 660).

Spinning-materials, mostly Cotton and Wool (compare Classes 228 and 235); also yarn and thread; woven goods: Silk-goods to the amount of 2.6 millions Kr.; Wollen, 16.9; Cotton 8.2; and Flaxen and Hempen 2.7 millions Kr.

Hair, Feathers, Hides, Leather, etc., and also Guano, (compare Class 652).

Mineral substances, mostly Coals (compare Class 101) and Salt; Metals, or articles made thereof, mostly unwrought Gold and Silver, and also Iron-rails.

Machinery, etc. (Classes 500-597): mostly Railway-materials.

The details about these and other articles, will be seen under the proper Classes.

In later years the *Foreign Trade* has been continually increasing, and has shown the following variations*:

Years.	Import. Kr.	Export. Kr.	Of this Gold and Silver Coin. Import. Kr.	Of this Gold and Silver Coin. Export. Kr.
1850...	36,354,000	38,625,000	10,000	3,689,000
1860.....	82,469,000	86,496,000	3,030,000	42,000
1861.....	106,570,000	81,084,000	323	930,152
1862.....	98,520,000	86,638,000	1,756,080	119,198
1863.....	96,627,000	92,524,000	518,354	572,200
1864.....	96,549,000	94,003,000	1,274,529	39,435
1865.....	105,863,000	108,086,000	655,977	9,137
1866.....	112,910,000	107,066,000	1,309,951	880,913
1867.....	134,181,000	128,639,000	1,140,837	1,320,000
1868.....	137,740,000	119,524,000	3,327,246	1,360,528
1869.....	136,615,000	125,883,000	4,149,440	2,669,414
1870.....	141,686,000	152,502,000	1,729,114	995,889
1871.....	169,179,000	161,023,000	5,861,734	2,077,027
1872.....	216,366,000	199,815,000	9,714,734	93,360
1873.....	271,440,000	221,904,000	10,833,394	3,077,780

The countries with which Sweden carries on the most extensive trade are: England, total of Import and Export in 1873: 216 millions Kr.; Denmark, 59 millions; Lubeck, 49; Norway, 21; France, 19; Russia, 17; The Netherlands, 15; The United States of North America, 15; Prus-

*If the import in this table exceeds the export, it comes from a different mode of reckoning; for instance, in the value of the imported goods is included the freightage, which is not the case with the exported.

sia, 14; Belgium, 13; Hamburg, 12; Finland, 9; Bremen, 5; Brazil, 4; Spain, 3; States of La Plata, 2; Portugal, 2; Italy, 1.8; The West Indies, 1.3; The East Indies and Australia, 1.3; Algiers, 1 million. If Prussia, Mecklenburg, Lubeck, Hamburg, Bremen and Oldenburg be taken together, the Swedish Trade with Germany (80 millions) will be next to that with England.

The extent of the Swedish *Import* from and *Export* to the following countries, in 1873, is seen by the following table:

	Import. Kr.	Export. Kr.
Norway	13,549,000	7,424,000
Finland	5,554,000	3,614,000
Russia	13,436,000	3,497,000
Denmark	37,240,000	21,874,000
Prussia	6,066,000	8,139,000
Mecklenburg	43,000	548,000
Lubeck	42,963,000	5,611,000
Hamburg	8,593,000	3,230,000
Bremen	4,379,000	408,000
Oldenburg	18,000	313,000
The Netherlands	9,929,000	5,256,000
Belgium	5,905,000	7,363,000
Gt. Britain and Ireland	95,015,000	120,915,000
France	9,367,000	19,189,000
Portugal	1,156,000	1,323,000
Spain	1,694,000	1,565,000
Gibraltar and Malta	....	112,000
Italy	1,187,000	590,000
Austria	38,000	21,000
Turkey	....	....
Egypt	....	525,000
Tripoli, Tunis, & Morocco	....	28,000
Algeria	....	1,028,000
Cape Colony	....	162,000
Other parts of Africa	160,000	104,000
The East Indies and other Oceanic Countries	206,000	31,000
Australia	....	1,107,000
Canada	....	171,000
U. S. of America	7,960,000	6,951,000
The West Indies	1,314,000	31,000
Brazil	3,419,000	674,000
The States of La Plata	2,154,000	100,000
Total	271,440,000	221,904,000

The principal currencies, with which foreign business is done, are £ Sterling, Reichsmark, and Franc.

Owing to the situation of Sweden almost all its foreign commerce is by sea; only from 1 to 2 per cent. of the whole import and export trade is carried on by land, and Sweden contributes for the *sea-transport*, about half the whole number of vessels, or more exactly as follows:

Loaded Ships (Sailing and Steam.)	ARRIVED.		SAILED.	
	No.	Tons.	No.	Tons.
Swedish,	4,367	488,370	7,991	812,480
Norwegian,	630	111,090	2,410	722,030
Foreign,	1,425	403,580	4,512	799,680
Total 1875,	7,422	1,003,040	14,913	2,334,190
" 1870,	5,950	741,070	13,272	2,018,110
" 1865,	4,946	538,360	9,458	1,434,850

The heavy tonnage and the large number of the out-bound (loaded) ships in comparison to that of the incoming, proves that Sweden exports heavy and bulky articles (metal and timber).

In 1873, counted by the tonnage, the proportion of Swedish ships in the import, amounted to 49 per cent., but in the export only to 29 per cent., and in this the Swedish merchant-navy is almost equaled by the Norwegian, which, with its sailing-ships, actively contributes to the export, especially of the Swedish timber from the ports in the Gulf of Bothnia.

In 1873, besides the above stated loaded sailing and steam ships, 11,719 ships in *ballast*, Swedish and foreign, arrived in Swedish ports from foreign countries, and 3,683 such sailed; so that the whole number of the incoming amounted to 19,141, of which 5,052 were steamers, and the number of the outgoing amounted to 18,596, of which 4,775 were steamers.

Sweden also keeps up a very considerable *transport-trade* between foreign countries. In the year 1873 the following number of Swedish vessels arrived from abroad, in ports in the following countries, viz.:

	Ships Loaded.	In Ballast.
In the Mediterranean, Adriatic and Black Seas . .	82	56
In the United States of North America, and Canada .	80	58
In the West Indies . . .	11	4
In Brazil, River Plata, and other countries of South America .	110	29
In the Cape Colony, the East Indies, and other countries of Eastern Asia, and Australia .	22	34
In Norway	226	109
To the Baltic and the German Ocean, as far as the German-Netherland frontier .	1,269	265
In Great Britain and Ireland, and also from the German-Netherland frontier as far as Gibraltar	613	138
Total, 1873,	2,413	693
" 1870,	1,738	580

With regard to the *size of the Swedish Merchant-fleet*, compare Cat., Class 590.

After this general review, we shall proceed to a statistical account of the different branches arranged, class by class, according to the programme for the International Exhibition in Philadelphia.

DEPARTMENT I.—MINING AND METALLURGY.*

MINERALS, ORES, BUILDING STONES, AND MINING PRODUCTS.†

In pursuance of the *Mining Law*, of January 12th, 1855, now in force, any discoverer of Metals and Ores, Pyrites, Graphite, or Coal, unless situated within a distance of 600 feet of a dwelling-house, is entitled to receive from the Inspector of Mines a so-called "Mutsedel" (License) which authorizes the holder to make a trial-experiment, upon which the area (the so-called "Utmål") is determined; generally 600 feet at most, in length and breadth, and for coal 1200 feet, at most, in length and breadth. The owner of the ground is entitled to participate with the holder of the license in the mining to the extent of one half; otherwise he is only compensated for the ground. If the ground belongs to the Crown, the owner's right is transferred, either to the discoverer or to the lease-holder of the estate. In later years when speculations in the Scanian coals have been carried on, on a large scale, it has not been unusual for a single individual or company, to cause as many as a thousand licenses to be issued at one and the same time, in order to secure the right of coal mines in many parishes—an abuse, which in the first instance has called for a limitation to the right of claiming licenses, and which will probably very soon be the cause of a new mining law. If the holder of a license, without due permission, neglect to perform certain minimum amount of work in a mine, he shall forfeit his right to the license.

[CLASS 100.] **Minerals, Ores, etc.** Sweden is very rich in ores, and especially in iron ore, which, however, is not to be found in all the provinces of the country, but is limited to certain districts. Excepting the abundance of iron-ore at Gellivara and some other places high up in Lappland, which, have as yet, however, been very little worked, the largest and thickest beds of ore are to be found within a belt running from east to west, and extending from Uppland and the southern part of Gestrikland through Westmanland and Nerike and the southern part of Dalarne, as far as the eastern part of Vermland. Iron-ore is however to be found to the south of this belt, as in Södermanland and Östergötland; but these mines are not to be compared to the above-mentioned, either in number or extent. In the northern part of Småland, on the other hand, there is a very large deposit of ore, namely, the Taberg, to the south of Lake Vetter. Besides this province is very rich in lake- and bog-ore.

The reason that the production of iron in Sweden, in proportion to that of many other countries, is not considerable, is consequently, not by any means, that there is a scarcity of ore, but

*The contributions on iron ore and iron-manufacture, are mostly by R. AKERMAN, Professor of Metallurgy, Stockholm.

†According to the preliminary prospectus of the classification of the objects that are to be exhibited, they were to be divided into 10 departments, with 10 groups in each, and each group divided into 10 classes, and the numeral of the class should at the same time indicate both the group and the department. For instance, No. 734 was intended to indicate an object as belonging to the 7th department, 73d group, and 734th class. In consequence of this arrangement, no class-number could be lower than 100, and at the same time gaps would necessarily occur in the order of succession, for want of suitable objects everywhere, to carry out the decimal divisions of the departments. On the final drawing up of the programme, the departments were, however, reduced to 7, and the numbering of the groups was done away with, but the rest of the system for classification was maintained; so that the apparent defects here in the order of the numbers of the classes correspond to the official programme.

that there is a difficulty in obtaining the requisite *fuel* for the smelting of it. As stated above, Sweden has no coals, excepting in its southernmost province, Skåne, where, on the other hand, no veins of ore worth working have as yet been found. If to this be added that the Scanian coal-mines, with the exception of a few small seam, have only within the last few years become known to some degree by borings, so that they could not as yet be worked on any large scale, and likewise that the Scanian coal, in consequence of the great distance between Skåne and the Swedish Bergslagerna (the principal mining districts) has at least hitherto been as dear there, as the English coals, which surpass the Scanian both on account of their producing a greater heating effect and a smaller quantity of ashes, it is quite natural that we should be restricted, in smelting the ore, to the fuel, which our forests and peat-bogs can supply, and to foreign coals and coke for the further working of the iron obtained.

The forests in the vicinity of the large mines which have been worked for a long time, have already been exhausted to a very great extent, and it has become necessary to procure the charcoal required for the smelting of the ore, from more distant places; but without railways, it cannot in general, be transported in any large quantities from distant forests; and in the Swedish mining-districts, comparatively few railways have as yet been constructed.

But in proportion as the projected railways are completed (compare Class 332), it will be possible to procure sufficient fuel from remoter forests, which have been to utilize, with the help of the considerable water-power, which Sweden possesses, the abundant ores, on a larger scale. Several large iron works have already been projected, and are about to be built so as to be complete simultaneously with the railways that shall pass by them. We may therefore be justified in saying, that Swedish mining is at present on the threshold of a new stage of development, for just in proportion as the means of communication are improved, the small old iron-works, will no doubt, be abandoned and Companies will be formed for the establishment of larger ones, which may be conducted in a more advantageous manner. The state of commerce during the last two years has, however, been a check on the zeal for the erection of large iron-works, which marked the year 1872 and the beginning of 1873. The prices of iron mines have also been reduced accordingly.

Iron Ores.—The iron-ores of Sweden, properly speaking, consist of *Magnetic iron-ore* (Ferrosoferric Oxide) and *Hematite* (Ferric Oxide) which occur in the primitive formation as beds or bed-like veins in gneiss, eurite ("Hälleflinta"), micaschist, and primitive lime. Besides these, there are also *Lake-* and *Bog-ores*, which, however, are only found in the province of Småland. The former, in order to be distinguished from the latter, are often called *Rock-ores*, and sometimes, as at Grängesberg, Dalkarlsberg, and other mines, they consist of beds of magnetic iron-ore and Hematite, lying side by side. Sometimes these ores may also be found mixed together in the same bed, which, for instance, is the case with the Gräsberg-ore and the magnetic iron-ore of Stora Bispberg; but this is not generally the case, so that one and the same mine yields almost exclusively one kind of ore.

Most of the Rock-ores contain more or less *Quartz*, and this is especially the case with the Hematite; but besides, they are generally, at least the magnetic iron-ores, mixed with other minerals, as augite, horn-blende, chlorite, epidote, garnet, and calc-spar. Lime must, however, be added to most of them, although in general not more than from 10 to 25 per cent. is required to form a bisilicated slag. Not a few iron-ores are already mixed with the above-mentioned minerals in such proportions that they do not require any fluxes, and to these belong, among others, the Dannemora ores. Finally, some iron-ores are rich in *Limestone*, and, in the blast furnace, are mixed with the ores containing quartz, and hence called "blandstenar" (mixing stones). These ores containing lime, are, with few exceptions, magnetic, and often very rich in manganese, as for instance, the Långviks-ore, which contains about 8 per cent. protoxide of manganese, and the ore from Granrot and other mines in Klackberg in Norberg contains nearly 7 per cent. protoxide of manganese.

The *Iron* contained in the Swedish ores varies from 30 to 70 per cent., but the average is from 45 to 55 per cent. Iron-ores occurring in limestone, even when they do not contain more than 20 per cent. of iron, are, sometimes used for mixing with richer quartz ores

The magnetic iron ore of Svartberg, which is used at the Schisshytta, in the Län of Kopparberg for the making of Spiegel-Eisen, is the richest in *Manganese* among the iron-ores that have hitherto been worked in Sweden. This ore contains from 15 to 20 per cent. protoxide of manganese, the cause of which seems to be that the lower layers consist principally of Knebelite. Further, among the iron-ores rich in manganese, the magnetic ore of the Penning-mine in the Län of Gefleborg, which contains from 12 to 14 per cent. protoxide of manganese, deserves to be mentioned.

Most of the Swedish rock-ores contain very little *Phosphorus*, and among those containing the least, may be mentioned Dannemora in the Län of Uppsala with about 0.003 per cent., Persberg in Vermland with 0.004 to 0.005 per cent., and Stora Bispberg in the Län of Kopparberg with less than 0.01 per cent. of phosphorus. In general the phosphorus varies from 0.01 to 0.05 per cent.; but in Sweden there are also rock-ores which contain as much as some tenths of one per cent. of phosphorus. Among others this is the case with *a few* rich iron-ores in the parish of Grangärde and the neighborhood and some of the Gellivara ores. In some rock-ores there has been found as much as 1 per cent. of phosphorus; but such ores have not yet been worked. The phosphorus contained in rock-ores seems in most cases to be due to an admixture of apatite.

The Lake- and Bog-ores often contain a great deal of phosporus, and hence they are generally used only for the production of cast iron.

Some iron-ores contain *Titanium*, and among them the magnetic iron-ore occurring at Taberg, in the Län of Jönköping, deserves special notice, because it is different in many respects from other ores which are common in Sweden. It is interstratified with dark serpentine and in this manner forms a whole mountain, which, however, does not contain more than 30 per cent. of iron. It contains about 6.3 per cent. titanic acid and some *Vanadium*, which metal was first discovered in the iron obtained from this ore.

Most of the rock-ores are mixed with a little iron-pyrites, and sometimes also with other metallic sulphides, but the sulphur is in most cases, almost entirely removed, by carefully roasting. For that purpose, gas-roasting furnaces are almost exclusively used, and the best among them, are those of WESTMAN, (described in WEDDING's revised edition of PERCY's Metallurgy, Vol. II, Part 2, page 485) to which the old gas-roasting furnaces are gradually giving place.

In the year 1873: 19,458,339 centners (827,126,800 Kilogr.) *rock-ore* was raised in Sweden, viz:

Län.	Swedish Centners.
Stockholm	929,333
Uppsala	1,108,980
Södermanland	393,317
Östergötland	224,526
Jönköping	263,574
Kronoberg	460
Kalmar	80,800
Kristianstad	7,200
Vermland	3,001,895
Örebro	5,951,207
Westmanland	2,235,554

Län.	Swedish Centners.
Kopparberg	4,758,986
Gefleborg	472,611
Wester Norrland	17,070
Jemtland	226
Norrbotten	12,600
Total, 1873:	19,458,339
" 1872:	16,938,345
" 1871:	15,215,590
" 1870:	14,508,278
" 1860:	9,290,973

The mines which yielded more than 200,000 centners in the year 1873, were: Utö, (in the Län of Stockholm); Dannemora, (in the Län of Uppsala); Taberg, (in the Län of Jönköping); Philipstads-Bergslag, (in Vermland), of which the Persberg, Yngshytte, Nordmark, and Taberg mines are the principal; the Strossa, Strip, Högborn, Pershytte, Dalkarlsberg, and Striberg mines, (in the Län of Örebro); the Risberg, Morberg and Klackberg mines (in the Län of Vestmanland); the Vinkärn, Bispberg, Rällingsberg, East and West Ormberg, Grängesberg, Gräsberg, and the Släd and Log mines, (in the Län of Kopparberg); and the Nyäng mines, (in the Län of Gefleborg).

Among these the Persberg and Yngshytte mines yielded 1,411,440 centners iron-ore, the Striberg, 1,039,606 centners, Dannemora 777,144 centners, etc.

Of *Lake-* and *Bog-ore* was raised in the year 1873 in:

	Swedish Centners.
the Län of Jönköping,	23,804
„ Kronoberg,	90,502
„ Kalmar,	11,641
„ Skaraborg,	200
Total 1873,	126,147
„ 1872,	292,224
„ 1871,	370,784
„ 1870,	323,436
„ 1860,	522,643

The total quantity of iron-ore raised in 1873, accordingly amounts to 19,584,556 centners,(832,-489,100 Kilogr.) of which 561,264 centners were exported almost exclusively to Finland.

In the raising of the ore there were employed 5,693 permanent workmen, 980 temporary, 382 women and children, together 7,055 persons.

In most of the mines the ore, as well as the water, was raised by means of water power; but at some of them the available water power is either insufficient or too far distant, and hence steam-engines have had to be applied in several cases, so that, in the year 1873, at all the mines in Sweden, 72 of these were used, most of which, however, were only of 15 horse-power.

Other Ores. Among the various kinds of ore which Sweden possesses the *copper-ores*, next to iron, take the precedence. Among these the most important and common are copper-pyrites (yellow copper ore), rarely variegated copper and copper-glance. They are extracted in large quantities at Falun, (or Stora Kopparberget), Åtvidaberg (in Östergötland); Nya Kopparberget, (in Westmanland), Virum, (in Småland), Gustafsberg, (or Huså on Åreskutan in Jemtland), and other places. The copper-ores are mostly smelted in the country, (about which see below, Class 112), but small quantities of the raw copper-ore are also exported (to England); this export has, however, declined of late years, (from 30,000 to 40,000 centners annually before 1871 to 1,567 centners in 1873).

Native Silver and gray copper, (the so-called Fahlerz), have, it is true, been found in this country as mineralogical rarites, but our principal silver-ore is the *argentiferous galena*, as for instance at Sala, Guldsmedshyttan, Falun, East and West Silverberg, and other places. The silver contained in the ore seldom amounts to 1 per cent. These silver-mines are therefore also lead-mines (compare Catalogue, Class 113).

Of all the metallic sulphides, *iron pyrites* is the most common, and is therefore to be met with almost everywhere, here and there impregnating the rocks, or as large stratiform masses which are worth working; as at Dylta, Falun, Väddön and other places. At Ädelfors, Falun and East Silverberg, it has been found to contain a little *Gold*. Iron pyrites is chiefly used for the production of sulphuric acid, green vitriol, and red ochre, (most at Falun and Dylta).

Magnetic pyrites containing *Nickle* is extracted

in some parts of the country, (for which see Catalogue, Class 113).

The only zinc-ore that Sweden possesses, is *Zinc Blende*, which is met with in several places, and in great thickness at Åmmeberg (on the border between Nerike and Östergötland), which mine belongs to the Belgian company, (La Vieille Montagne). The raising of ore has been continuously increasing, so that from 30,000 centners which was raised in 1860, it has since 1865 averaged about 600,000 to 700,000 centners. All the ore is exported, no metallic zinc being manufactured in the country.

Cobalt Ore (Cobaltite) occurs at Tunaberg, Håkansbo, Vena, and some other places, but it is now extracted only at the first-mentioned place, where it is purified by stamping and washing, before it is sent into the market. The production however, seldom exceeds 1000 pounds per annum.

Manganese-ore which is met with at Undenäs, (in Westergötland) Spexeryd (in Småland), Leksand (in Dalarne) and some other places, was raised in 1873 only at the mines of Spexeryd and Hohult (in the Län of Jönköping) when 7,190 centners were produced. The largest production of manganese-ore in the country was in the year 1870: 16,488 centners.

[CLASS 101.] **Coal** has been found in the north-western part of the Län of Malmöhus in Skåne, the southernmost province of Sweden, and recently also in the neighborhood of Engelholm in the Län of Kristianstad, which also belongs to Skåne. It occurs in a formation, the age of which has not as yet been determined with any degree of certainty, but which is generally considered to belong to the Triassic and Jurassic periods. It has been mined in Malmöhus with interruptions, however, since the middle of the 18th century, but only in small quantities.

Most of the coal has been mined at Höganäs, which as was formerly supposed is situated in the vicinity of the northern border of the formation, where the mining began in 1797. Two coal-seams have been worked at Höganäs, of which the upper one, that lies at a depth of from 10 to 200 feet (3 m. to 60 m.; the bed dips from 3° to 5°) and has a thickness of from 0.5 to 1.5 feet (0.15 m. to 0.44 m.) has now been abandoned; the other which lies from 50 to 80 feet (15 m. to 24 m.) deeper, has a thickness of 4.8 feet 1.42 m., but of which not more than 0.6 foot (0.18 m.) is of prime quality, 1.1 feet (0.32 m.) of second, and 0.4 foot (0.12 m.) of third quality, while the rest consists of a carboniferous dark-colored schist. Under this coal-seam, is a bed of *fire-clay* 5 feet (1.5 m.) thick, which is partly raised together with the coal. According to analyses made by E. ERDMANN, in the laboratory of the Geological Survey, samples of the various sorts of Coal have contained:

	Gas.	Carbon.	Ashes.
1st Quality Coal	32.9	64.1	3.0 per ct.
2d "	25.0	54.7	20.3 "
3d "	17.4	39.3	43.3 "

At Höganäs, during the year 1873, was raised:

1st Quality Coal	516,192	Swedish Kubik Fot.
2d "	893,629	" " "
3d "	437,863	" " "
Total,	1,847,684	

About 200 workmen were employed.

Besides in the same year were raised

At Vallåkra . . .	397,284	Kubik Fot.
" Boserup . . .	58,000	" "
" Helsingborg . .	22,320	" "
" Kropp . . .	48,398	" "
" Eslöf . . .	32,800	" "

Or together in the whole Kingdom 2,406,486 Kubik-Fot.

The extent of the coal-formation is, however, not yet ascertained with any certainty, but a number of borings are now being made, and two of them seem to have given highly satisfactory results.

Some of the coals in Skåne can be turned into coke, but in general it does not seem to be the case.

Of coal and coke were imported:

In 1860 . . .	11,791,612	Kubik-Fot.
" 1865 . . .	17,050,586	"
" 1870 . . .	21,146,438	"
" 1871 . . .	22,487,299	"
" 1872 . . .	26,906,103	"
" 1873 . . .	27,248,071	"
" 1874 . . .	29,340,000	"

For **Peat**, see Class 600.

[CLASSES 102 — 106]. **Building-stone, Marble, Cement, Feldspar, Graphite, etc.** *Granite* (and gneiss) is very often used in Sweden as a building material. There are inexhaustible supplies of it, of which especially the gray and fine-grained varieties are employed, although the coarse-grained or red are also used. The foot-wall of most of the larger buildings is of cut granite, and a great many of the bridges; or in recent times, when the arches are made of iron, the pillars and harbour-quays are built of this kind of stone. Cut stones are now likewise used for paving instead of the boulders of granite, gneiss, etc. (generally as large as a child's head), supplied by nature, which were formerly used, and still are, in the small towns. For the erection of solid buildings the Swedish granite is very much in demand, and is therefore exported to Russia, Germany, Denmark, England and France.

Besides being used as a building-material, granite is, in many parts of the country, also used for other purposes, as, for monuments, table-tops, columns, etc. Among the great number of stone-cutting establishments, where such and similar works are made, the following may be mentioned: Malm-ön in the Län of Bohus, Bollö in Blekinge, Hufvudsta near Stockholm, etc. Besides, granite is cut at several of the penitentiaries and houses of correction: as an example, it may be mentioned, that the streets in Stockholm are now being paved, with stones that are cut at Långholm, a penal establishment within the boundaries of Stockholm. Considerable quantities of such pavingstones are also exported.

The specific gravity of the different varieties of granite varies from 2.56 to 2.67. A kubik fot consequently weighs 157 to 164 lbs. (1 Cubic Mètre=2,550 to 2,660 Kilo.) and absorbs, after having been in water for about 90 hours, from 0.03 to 0.07 lbs. (1 Cubic Mètre: 0.5 to 1.1. Kilo).

The *Porphyry*, of Elfdal in Dalarne, is well known both in Sweden and abroad on account of the beautiful polished articles that are made of it. The most common variety has a dark brown groundmass, which contains reddish feldspar-crystals; but other kinds of stone resembling porphyry have also been used for the same purpose, especially varieties of hyperite and granite. The most celebrated work in porphyry (or porphyry-granite) from Elfdal, is the colossal urn at the Royal Summer-Palace at Rosendal, in the Djurgården (Deerpark), at Stockholm, which is 15 fot (4.5 m.) in diameter, 9 fot (2.7 m.) in height, and is reputed to weigh 155 centner, (6,590 Kilo.); next to this is the sarcophagus in Riddarholm Church, for the mortal remains of King Carl XIV Johan (Charles John XIV), which is made after the pattern of the sarcophagus of Agrippa in the Vatican, and weighs 400 centners. This, and other works, which are made out of perhaps the hardest of all known rocks, admit of an extraordinarily fine polish, are very costly, and were executed by common country people. They have now almost entirely ceased to work these rocks.

A very celebrated *Marble-quarry* is at Kolmården, a mountain range between Södermanland and Östergötland. Another similar quarry has been opened at Claestorp in Södermanland. There are also beds in Singön in Rosiagen, which have been considered worth working. Besides these places, there are many others where marble might be quarried, though the lime-stone is generally used only for burning into lime. This marble is primitive lime-stone (crystalline lime-stone) containing a great deal of serpentine, which imparts a greenish color and flamy appearance to the marble. Part of the marble for the New Opera-house in Paris has been sent from Kolmården.

The purer the Swedish marble is the greater is its specific gravity, and the less apt it is to absorb moisture. 1 Kubik-fot weighs 161 to 175 lbs., (1 Cub. Mètre=2610 to 2840 Kilo.) and, after having been immersed in water for about 90 hours, absorbs 0.01 to 0.26 lbs. (1 Cub. m.=0.16 to 4.2 Kilo).

The silurian limestone is more easily worked, and therefore more extensively employed. It is quarried and used for flooring, stairs, exterior covering of walls, etc., but also for finer works, such as brooches, pendants and the like. The cutting of this marble is done in Gottland, Öland, and also in Östergötland, Westergötland and Nerike. The gray stone is chiefly quarried, but sometimes also the red. It can easily be split into slabs and takes a good polish. Large quantities of this stone are likewise burnt into lime, and then alum-schist is frequently used as a burning material.

Sandstone is quarried as a building-material in various places in Sweden, but not to the same extent as in other countries, the cause of which may, among other things, be found in the abundance of granite. Sandstone is however extensively quarried for *Grindstones* and *Mill-stones*, for instance, in Dalarne, Westergötland, Hör, (in Skåne) etc. The mill-stones from the parish of Lugnås in Westergötland are the most celebrated in the country; they are like other stones on the mainland, generally rich in quartz, and hard; on the other hand those from the island of Öland, which are rich in lime, are softer, and mostly used for finer flour. In certain districts, mica-slate is also quarried for mill-stones.

Several varieties of *Clay-* or *Mica-slate* belonging to the primitive formation, are used for *Roofing-slate*. The best known slate-quarry is that in the parish of Fröderyd in Småland, the slate of which, on account of its reddish brown color, has been called copper-slate. There are also quarries in Dalsland (Hällan and Källsviken), Glafva in Vermland, etc. Slate is not generally used in Sweden for roofing, for which purpose sheet-iron, or tiles, and shingles are preferred.

A kind of mica-slate, rich in *Magnesia*, is sought for *hearth-stones* in blast-furnaces. Species of stone still richer in talc, among them the so-called potstone, are in various places worked into household-utensils, such as pots, mortars, etc.

Cement has for a long time been prepared near Wenersborg. For that purpose burnt and ground alum-slate from Hunneberg in the neighborhood, and burnt lime from Kinnekulle, are used. The sluices of the Trollhätta Canal are made with this cement. Of late years a Cement-manufactory has been established at Lomma, not far from Malmö, which is carried on, on a large scale; Alum-slate is, however, not to be an ingredient, but purified clay from the neighborhood. Cement is now also made at other places in Sweden.

Fire-clay is found in large quantities as inter-strata in the Scanian coal-formation and forms a very considerable incidental product of the mining.

Feldspar adapted to the manufacture of porcelainware, is to be found in several places in the country, generally in veins of pegmatite; but it has been made an object of quarrying in the archipelago of Stockholm only. At Ytterby, not far from Waxholm, is a well known feldspar-quarry of that kind, where a number of rare minerals have been found, in which the earth called Yttrium was discovered (together with Erbium and Terbium).

Graphite is obtained in several places in the country, mostly at Fagersta and Norberg in Westmanland. The annual quantity of production amounts to from 1,000 to 1,500 centners.

[Class 107]. **Mineral Waters** are abundant in Sweden, but all the springs are chalybeate and consequently have an inky taste, and leave a deposit of iron-ochre in their discharging channels. The water is as cold as in other cold springs (+6° to 7° C.= +43 to +45° F.) and it is used both for drinking and for baths. Many wells also contain a kind of mud which in consequence of its abundance in silicious infusoria, when applied outwardly, has a beneficial influence in increasing the cutaneous activity. Such mud is also found at many of our numerous watering-places, on our surrounding coasts, which are very much frequented. Among the more frequented mineral-springs, we will mention only: Ramlösa (in Skåne), Ronneby (in Blekinge), Porla (in Nerike), Loka and Sätra (in Westmanland), Medevi (in Östergötland), etc. The Torpa well (on the river Göta) is known as containing a large quantity of iodine. Among all the known watering places in Sweden, as well as abroad, Ronneby is said to contain the largest quantity of iron and alum. As a proof of what the Swedish acidulæ contain, the following analyses of the Ronneby water (made by Dr. N. P. HAMBERG) is given:—

1,000 grams of water contain:	The new Well.	The old Well.
Bi-sulphate of Potash	0.042	0.022
" Soda	0.235	.....
Neutral Sulphate of Soda	.....	0.155
" Ammonia	1.110	0.072
" Lime	0.470	0.240
" Magnesia	0.181	0.032
" Alumina	1.504	0.388
" Proto-oxide of Iron	2.496	0.383
" Manganese	0.144	0.028
" Cobalt	0.007	0.001
" Nickle	0.007	0.002
Chloride of Magnesium	0.095	0.089
Iodide of Magnesium	0.007	traces
Bromide of Magnesium	traces	traces
Silicium	0.096	0.099
Rosin	0.020	0.003
Humic (Krenic & Apokrenic) acid	0.017	0.016
Total fixed constituents,	5.431	1.530

The water in the Old well is used for drinking, and that in the New one for bathing.

METALLURGICAL PRODUCTS.

[Class 110.] **Precious Metals** are scarce in Sweden. *Gold* is found in very small quantity in auriferous-pyrites in a few localities (compare Class 100), but at present it is extracted only from copper-pyrites at Falun. The production is not great: 1870=23.98 Swedish pounds; 1871=14.28; 1872=15.35; 1873=13.65, consequently during the last few years about 6 Kilograms annually.

Silver, which, as shown above (Class 100), is obtained from argentiferous galena, is produced in no great quantity. During the period, 1860 to 1870, the production amounted to from 2,500 to 3,000 lbs. annually (about 1,000 Kilo.), but it has since declined: 1870—2,801; 1871=2,292; 1872=1,747; 1873=1,660 lbs.

For upwards of a century it has been a law in Sweden that all gold, silver, and tin, that is worked for sale, shall be *stamped*, by which means the purchaser is guarded against a spurious article. Manufactured gold may be of three kinds: ducat-gold (23 carats, 5 grains, (refined gold) (24 carats at 12 grains); pistolet-gold (20 carats, 4 grains); and crown-gold (18 carats, 4 grains). Manufactured silver must not contain less than 13¼ lod, (pure silver = 16 lod). Manufactured tin may be of two degrees of fineness: quadruply stamped (0.97 pure tin), and trebly stamped (0.83); certain small articles of tin, may, however, be doubly stamped. The control-stamping is done by the manufacturer, who puts four stamps on his work: the manufacturer's name (cipher), the coat of arms of the town, the degree of purity, and the year (which is indicated by a letter and a figure; e. g. T 7= 1875). The fifth stamp (3 crowns) denotes that the article is of the purity prescribed by law, and is affixed by the proper authorities.

It is therefore prohibited to import gold and silver articles of an inferior quality to that prescribed for Swedish articles. All such foreign articles must, therefore, first be examined and stamped before they may be offered for sale. In order to prevent that gilt or plated articles may, by means of stamps resembling those which are affixed on genuine gold and silver-ware, have a delusive resemblance to these, it is prescribed that on the former shall be affixed the name of the manufacturer, together with his place of residence and the year when the article was made but no other stamp or mark; this also relates to imported articles.

With regard to metal for coinage, see page **21**.

The trade of *Goldsmith* and *Jeweller* is practised by nearly 300 master-tradesmen, besides their assistants, 500 in number. Among the whole number are 40 women, who either assist, or have work-shops of their own. It may be asserted that many of the manufactured articles, especially those made in the larger work-shops of the capital, are quite equal to such productions in foreign countries, both with regard to composition and workmanship. This applies in the first place to large articles made of silver. Gold, as well as silver, is produced in the country, but not in sufficient quantities to meet the demands of the goldsmiths, and hence these materials, as well as all precious stones required must be imported. It is not unusual, however, to find real pearls in Sweden, and sometimes of great beauty, especially in Lappland and Småland. Several species of stones have been found in the country that could be used as precious stones, but they may be looked upon as minerological rarities.

[Class 111.] **Pig-Iron.** The height of the blast-furnaces varies from 30 to 55 fot, (8.9 m.—16.3 m.), the width inside from 5 to 6.5 fot (1.5 m. —1.9 m.), at the mouth or funnel-head, from 7 to 10.5 fot (2 m.—3.1 m.), at the upper part of the boshes, and from 2.8 to 5.2 fot (0.83 m.— 1.5 m.), between the tweers. The capacity of the shafts of the blast-furnaces varies from 900 to 3,500 kub. fot (23.55 —91.60 cub. mètres). In general two tweers are used, in some places three or four, and as a remnant of olden times, sometimes only one. The diameter of the nozzle in blast-furnaces with two tweers is generally between 16 and 20 lines. The pressure of the blast varies between 8 and 30 lines quicksilver, but it is mostly between 12 and 20 lines. Cold and hot blast up to 500° C. is used but generally its temperature scarcely reaches 200°.

At the working of the blast-furnaces, charcoal is exclusively used, but at some furnaces it is mixed with a little wood, yet never more than six to one. Lastly, at some blast-furnaces, where spiegel-eisen is made, the charcoal is also mixed with some English coke.

The charcoal is produced almost everywhere from red and white fir, and every tunna (6.3 kub. fot) contains about 50 lbs. (21 Kilo.) real carbon. The consumption of charcoal for every centner of pig-iron varies from 1.3 to rather more than two tunnor, but in blast-furnaces, where ore from Taberg (in Småland), is smelted, it may amount to as much as four tunnor. The usual quantity of charcoal is from 1.5 to 1.7 tunnor per centner pig-iron.

The smallest blast furnaces produce from 700 to 1,500 centners (30,000—64,000 Kilo.) pig-iron weekly, in the middle-sized, from 1,500 to 2,000 (64,000—85,000 Kilo.) and the largest from 2,000 to 3,000 centners (85,000—127,500 Kilo.).

Most of the pig-iron is intended for fining by the so-called Lancashire-process, and it is therefore run into cast-iron moulds and reduced to the form of broad and flat pieces. The fracture of such pig-iron generally has an appearance of half white and half gray iron, and the mixing of the ores in the blast-furnaces is generally so contrived that they produce bisilicate slag.

The pig-iron intended for Bessemer, on the other hand, is blown gray but is nevertheless mixed with a greater quantity of lime-stone than the above-mentioned.

For the Walloon-fining, adopted at the Dannemora mines, almost perfectly white pig-iron is required or white impregnated with gray dots, like hail-stones, which is run in the form of long pigs. The mixture of ores used for the production of this iron, is among the most basal that are used in Sweden, and the Dannemora ores sometimes contain so much lime and magnesia, that in some instances quartz has been added to the ores before smelting.

Half-white, common Swedish pig-iron generally contains about 4 per cent. Carbon, ¼ per cent. Silicium, and about 0.02 per cent. Sulphur and Phosphorus. The Silicium contained in the Bessemer pig-iron is generally about 1 per cent.

At some blast-furnaces (Schisshyttan and Finnbo) spiegel-eisen is produced, containing much manganese. Both these blast-furnaces are situated in the Län of Kopparberg and use ore from the above mentioned Svartberg.

Common foundry-pig is manufactured by means of a trisilicate admixture of the ores, but its manufacture is not very considerable, as such iron is even imported from England and Scotland. On the other hand, at some blast-furnaces a kind of *cast-iron* is manufactured, which is distinguished for its great strength; at Finspong, among other places, where the cast-iron is used for cannon, shot, railway-carriage-wheels, etc.; at Ankarsrum, where the cast-iron is chiefly used for shot, railway-switches, and crossings; and at Åker, where it is used for rollers, etc.

Lastly, pig-iron is produced for making *malleable iron*; at Åker, Kilafors, and Karlsdal.

The slag of the blast-furnaces is often used as a building-material, and forthat purpose is formed in cast-iron moulds.

Owing to the difficulty of procuring a sufficient quantity of charcoal and ore, there has not been until of late years more than two blast furnaces in one place, and at most of the works there has not been sufficient material to keep one going the whole year round. Both the ore and fuel must in most cases be transported on sledges to the furnace during the winter, and the blasting therefore generally begins with the beginning of winter and depends upon the same for its duration. But it is only in comparatively few localities, that they have been able to bring together, during one winter, sufficient charcoal and ore for carrying on the blasting until the setting in of the next winter. In most cases they have to stop as early as the beginning or middle of the following summer; and the people who have been employed at the blast-furnaces, are then engaged for the harvest. There are, however, instances where blasting has been continued in one and the same place for six years together, without interruption.

At some of the old iron-works that have had better means of transport, during the last few years, besides the old blast-furnaces, new ones have been built, so that at present, there are several works with two blast-furnaces, and at some the Bessemer-process was determined upon last year, but have not yet been completed. Some companies intend to erect as many as three or four blast-furnaces in one place.

In the year 1873 in 213 blast-furnaces, which together were in blast for 43,135 days and nights, were produced 7,987,646 centners pig-iron in pigs, and 145,487 centners in castings, or together 8,133,133 centners (345,771,000 Kilo.). There were employed at the blast-furnaces, 4,206 workmen.

Wrought Iron and Steel. The usual fining process in Sweden is that which is called the Lancashire-process. This is a fracture-fining which is done in covered hearths (catalan-furnaces), and the iron bloom thus extracted is then welded in special furnaces. The hearths have sometimes only one, but generally two opposite tweers. Each tweer in a hearth with two tweers, is about 40 square lines (4 square centim.). The pressure of the blast is about 27 lines quicksilver, and its temperature between 100° and 200° C. For each bloom, rather more than 2 centners (85 Kilo.) pig-iron is generally taken; this quantity varies however, in different places between 1.6 and 3 centners (68—128 Kilo.) The work is carried on with from four to six hands, who relieve one another by turns, so that always two or three are employed at the same time, night and day, uninterruptedly for six days in the week, during which time from 160 to 300 blooms (6,800—12,750 Kilo.) are produced in each hearth, with a waste in pig-iron of 13 per cent., and a consumption of charcoal to the extent of from 1.2 to 1.7 tunnor, according as it has been stored in the coal-shed.

At the larger iron- works the blooms are welded under T-hammers weighing from 80 to 100 centners (3,400—4,250 Kilo.) which are made altogether of pig-iron, but at the smaller works under tilt-hammers with wooden handles, which weigh only about 20 centners

(850 Kilo.), or sometimes under steam-hammers, weighing from 15 to 30 centners (640—1,275, Kilo.)

In later years, blooming-rollers have been introduced in several places, by means of which the welded bloom is, without a repeated heating, rolled into crude bar-iron, which is used partly for making refined iron, partly for cast-steel; in general, however, the blooms that have been treated under the hammer, are suffered to cool, before they are reheated in special furnaces, for the purpose of being finally drawn out under the hammers, or in the rolling-mills. Fagoting is out of the question, excepting for ends, that have been cut off, and refuse iron which has been cut up. Each bloom is welded by itself, and in the smaller iron-works, the welding is occasionally done in reheating or balling furnaces, but mostly in *gas-welding furnaces.*

In some places the blooms are heated with pure charcoal, but generally the charcoal, which alone is too good for the purpose, is mixed with pit-coal, peat, or wood, or only one of these. The welding-furnaces differ according to the fuel used; the greater number of them, however, are modifications of the old Ekman welding-furnaces, which are described in "Das Eisenhütten-Wesen in Schweden," by P. TUNNER, Freiberg, 1858. Of late years they have, however, been more and more supplanted by the Lundin welding-furnaces which are described in the Jernkontorets Annaler" (the Annals of the Iron-Masters Association) for the year 1866, and in "Berg und Hütten-männisches Jahrbuch der K. K. Berg-Akademie" (the Royal Mining-Academy's Annual Register relating to Mining and Smelting) Vol. XVI. These consist of Siemen regenerative furnaces in combination with condensers for removing the great mass of water in the fuel, which in these furnaces is exclusively air-dried saw-dust, wood or peat.

The production of the welding-furnace varies very considerably according as the bloom is drawn out under the hammer, or by rolling, since in the latter case the whole bloom is at once welded and drawn out, whereas in the former, one end of the bloom is first worked, and then, after a fresh heating, the other. A welding-furnace whose product is worked under the hammer, produces weekly from 600 to 1,300 centners (25,500 to 55,260 Kilo.), while such a furnace in connection with a rolling-mill, will turn out in the same time from 1,200 to 2,000 centners (51,000 to 85,000 Kilo.) The quantity of fuel per centner (42.5 Kilo.) bar-iron in the welding-furnace consumed, is from the same cause considerably smaller when the metal is worked by rollers than by the hammer, and varies at the common welding-furnaces from 3.1 to 6 kubik fot (0.081 to 0.157 cubic mètres) charcoal, or from 0.4 to nearly 1 kubik fot 0.010 to 0.026 cubic mètres of pit-coal. The Lundin welding furnaces, on the other hand, generally consume from 3 to 3.5 kubik fot (0.078 to 0.092 cubic mètres) wood, or from 5 to 7 kubik fot (0.13 to 0.18 cubic metre) "Sticktorf" (peat), or about 11 kubik fot (0.29 cubic mètre) saw-dust per centner of bar-iron. Lastly, the waste is also less when the iron is worked by rolls than by the hammer; in the former instance, it is 9 per cent., but in the latter it is about 12 per cent. of the weight of the bloom.

As a matter of course, *rolling-mills* are not suited for small articles, though of late small iron-works have profited by the advantages they offer, and have ceased drawing out the iron under the hammer, and manufacture instead, only blooms. These are afterwards welded and drawn out in a rolling-mill, which is common to several such refining-works.

Besides the Lancashire fining process the so-called Franche-Comté is used, especially at such small iron-works as are not situated in the neighborhood of any rolling mill. This process as it is carried on here, agrees with the former, except with this difference that here, the welding of the blooms is done at the same time in the same hearth.

In the Dannemora-district, the *Walloon-process,* which has been followed from olden times, is still used.

In the year 1873, with 755 *hearths* working, there was produced in the whole country 4,125, 915 centners (175,382,400 Kilo.) *bar-iron,* which employed 6,061 workmen.

Puddling is practiced at some few iron-works, which manufacture their own iron, namely, Motala, Surahammar, Nyby, Kallinge, Gunnebo, Degerfors, and Avesta. The fuel used in the puddling-furnaces is generally English coal, but at Surahammar and Nyby wood is used.

The *Bessemer-fining-process* has been used in Sweden since it was invented, but as late as 1873 only 368,832 centners (15,678,200 Kilo.) Bessemer-metal was produced, and although this process must be consi dered very suitable for Sweden, inasmuch as on the one hand most of the Swedish iron-ores are particularly adapted for it, and on the other the consumption of fuel for the metal produced by it is only about half so great as for Lancashire-iron, yet the Bessemer-process has only during the last few years received general acknowledgment in Sweden. The principal cause of this is no doubt to be attributed to the fact that this *method* requires very expensive appointments; and it is, therefore, only suited for larger iron-works. Further, the Bessemer process is not exactly suited to the manufacture of bar-iron, but had best be followed by the making of the castings, produced into finished articles, and formerly Sweden scarcely exported any iron excepting in the form of bar-iron and blister-steel. In the last few years, however, several Bessemer-works have been erected, so that at present (1875) 15 are completed, and some are building; but several iron-masters, who, a year or two ago, were intent upon adopting this method, have now given up that plan or at least postponed it, especially as the Bessemer castings during these two years have been very difficult to dispose of, while there has been a very fair demand for hearth-refined bar-iron. If, as in 1875, Swedish bar-iron brings as high a price as Bessemer-steel in the market, it is indeed not very tempting to change the old bar-iron works for expensive Bessemer works. On the contrary, during these years two works have ceased manufacturing Bessemer steel and have gone back to the old method of refining.

In the year 1873, thirteen Bessemer-works were in operation, but at three of them, which have small, upright furnaces with weak blasts, the yield was very inconsiderable. Of the whole production or 368,832 centners (15,678,200 Kilo.) Sandviken manufactured 109,253; Forsbacka, 63,488; Westanfors, 57,678 centners, etc. There are converters at all these works.

At all the Swedish Bessemer-works hitherto erected, the pig-iron is taken directly out of the blast-furnaces without being re-melted, and put into the converters. The charge is from about 50 to 90 centners (2,125—3,825 Kilo.) The furnaces have from 6 to 13 tweer-stones and each one of these has from 6 to 13 apertures with a diameter from 4 to 6 lines (12 m. m.—18 m. m.) The pressure of the blast is generally from 200 to 350 lines quicksilver. At Sandviken and the Bessemer-works, erected of late, the blowing engines have from 450 to 700 horse-power, and the process is generally completed in from 5 to 20 minutes.

At some Bessemer-works, one or two per cent. of spiegel-eisen is added at the end of the process, at others, where ores containing more manganese are worked, none is used, and iron of any required degree of softness can be produced.

From 84 to 88 per cent. of the weight of the pig-iron is generally obtained in the form of castings, the waste amounting to only a few per cent. Water-power is exclusively applied at the Bessemer-works, with the exception of three cases, were steam is partly used. Water-power alone, is used at almost all the other iron works; at some, however, there are auxiliary steam-engines, and at others steam hammers.

Since the year, 1868 cast-steel has been manufactured at Munkfors, by the *Martin process* in a Siemens regenerative furnace with a Lundin condenser. Later, this method has likewise been adopted at Lesjöfors and Motala, and besides at one or two other works on trial.

The furnaces are small, holding only from 20 to 30 centners, (850 to 1,275 Kilo.) The fuel is either dried wood or peat, and the consumption is from 10 to 12 cubic feet per centner steel or iron melted. It is a remarkable fact, that in this manner, soft iron can be regularly manufactured, which is afterwards rolled into nail-rods or wire.

At Wikmanshyttan, *cast-steel* is manufactured by the *Uchati-process*, from granulated pig-iron mixed with powdered rich iron-ores, and some powdered charcoal. The melting is done in plumbago-crucibles in common English air-furnaces, which are heated with coke. The steel produced in this manner is especially adopted to the manufacture of such objects as require, at the same time, great strength and hardness, as stamps, hammers, etc.

At Österby not far from Dannemora, cast-steel works have been erected. The melting takes place in crucibles in Siemen-Lundin furnaces, and with wood for fuel.

The Manufacture of Iron and Steel is not yet large enough to satisfy the wants of the country itself; but a better state of things is hoped for within a few years, as some of the Bessemer works now building, are intended for the manufacture of rails and other railway materials, as well as plates.

Motala, Surahammar, Kloster and Boxholm, are the largest of the rolling-mills, which produce *plates*, though at the two last mentioned, only plates, for roofing, etc., are manufactured. At Surahammar, puddled iron is exclusively used for plates, but at Motala, not only that, but Bessemer steel obtained from other works is used. At Kloster, partly Lancashire iron is used, and partly Bessemer from Långshyttan, which belongs to the same company. At Boxholm, Lancashire-iron.

Rails of common dimensions are at present (1875) manufactured at Smedjebacken, where in 1873, 44,274 centners railway rails were rolled, and at Finspong 24,466.

Wheels of wrought iron, for railway-carriages, are manufactured at Surahammar, and at Atlas in Stockholm. *Tires* ar manufactured at Motala and Sandviken of Bessemer steel.

Axles for railway-carriages, are manufactured at Surahammar, of puddled iron, and axles for machineries, at some mechanical work shops, of iron clippings. The principal manufacture of heavy axles is, however, now confined to Motala, where they may be obtained, as desired, either of Bessemer steel, or puddled iron, further at Fagersta and Sandviken, at which works they are exclusively made of Bessemer steel.

Nails are manufactured at many works, and in different ways, as by hand-hammering, cutting, and other modes of manufacture, by means of machinery. Most of the nails are manufactured in the provinces of Blekinge and Östergötland, where they are chiefly produced by means of cutting the plates.

Gun-barrels and *Saw-blades* are manufactured from Bessemer steel at Fagersta.

Wire is drawn at several works. Among the drawing mills, Lesjöfors and Gunnebo, are the principal. Part of the wire is used at the first mentioned work, for the manufacture of *ropes* and *nails*, and at the latter for nails (compare below Class 280.)

The *Production of the Iron Industry* in 1860, 1870, and 1873.

	1860. Centners.	1870. Centners.	1873. Centners.
Rock ore,	9,290,973	14,508,278	19,458,339
Lake and Bog ore,	522,643	323,437	126,147
Total Iron ore,	9,813,616	14,831,715	19,584,486
Crude Iron in pigs,	4,230,246	6,895,794	87,646
Castings directly produced at the Blast Furnaces.	123,144	169,716	145,487
Total pig iron,	4,353,390	7,065,510	8,133,133
Bar, Hoop, Nail, and Wire Iron	3,219,659	4,559,331	4,125,915
Bessemer Steel	. . . .	156,054	368,832
Other Steel	. . . .	130,486	30,767
Plates	569,933	134,857	186,083
Nails	. . . .	112,562	181,305
Utensils, and sundry Iron Manufactures	. . . .	242,278	523,920

The total number of *workmen* employed in 1873 for this production was as follows:

At the Iron Mines,	7,055
„ Blast Furnaces,	4,206
„ Bar Iron Works,	6,061
„ Factories and Foundries,	6,040
Not Classified,	390
Total,	23,752

Import and Export of Iron ware in 1873.

	Import Centners.	Export Centners.
Iron ore,	31	561,264
Crude Iron in pigs	384,423	1,361,619
Cast-iron-ware,	6,229	10,638
Iron-blooms,	24,374	245,700
Anchors, Chains, etc.,	24,270	819
Bar-Iron,	82,256	2,243,497
Hoop-iron, Nail-rods, etc.,	41,214	483,323
Railway-rails,	1,141,623	4,608
Plates, not coated with tin,	97,678	19,095
Plates, tin-plated,	27,172	153
Nails and small iron-ware,	15,878	81,399
Iron-clippings,	17,530	117,493
Steel,	4,647	97,591
Steel work,	101	....
Iron and Steel-wire,	10,046	12,413
	Kronor.	Kronor.
Utensils, Railway-materials and Machinery,	11,657,508	1,010,180

The export of bar-iron was in 1873 unusually small. During the four preceding years, it exceeded 3 million centners per annum.

Although the year 1873 cannot be taken as a standard for the export of Swedish iron, yet the returns for that year being the latest at hand, it is here considered as such.

The exportation of Swedish Iron-ore and Iron to the different countries, is as follows:

Iron-ore, almost exclusively to Finland.

Pig-iron, to England, (1,052,000 centners), Prussia, (89,000), Belgium, Finland, Norway, etc.

Iron Blooms, almost exclusively to England, (225,000).

Bar Iron, to England (1,234,000), North America, (454,000), Denmark, (110,000), Hamburg, (105,000), France, Prussia, Lubeck, Portugal, etc.

Hoop-iron, Nail-rods, etc., to England, (189,000), Russia, (73,000), North America Prussia, France, etc.

Steel, to England, (35,000), Russia, (31,000), Portugal, etc.

From which is seen, that the principal exportation of our iron, is to England. On the other hand all the railway-rails, which we import, are received from England, (in the year 1873 nearly 1,000,000 centners, while during the preceding year was imported about 300,000 centners). This country also supplies most of the imported utensils, railway-materials, and machineries, (in the year 1873 for upwards of $2,000,000, gold.) After England, such goods are mostly imported from Lubeck ($500,000 gold), and then comes Denmark ($220,000 gold). Our utensils and machineries are very often shipped to Russia and Finland.

The *price of pig-iron*, is a question of great importance to Sweden. It is generally fixed during the Hinders-fair at Örebro, and during the Fastinge-fair at Christinehamn. The great demand for iron, of late years, caused unprecedented high prices, but they have fallen again, as may be seen from the following review, which is for 1 centner pig iron delivered at Nora Railway station, in the Lān of Örebro:

In the year 1869,	Kr. 2.65
„ 1870,	„ 2.37
„ 1871,	„ 2.62
„ 1872,	„ 4.25
„ 1873,	„ 6.50
„ 1874,	„ 3.65
„ 1875,	„ 3.50

[CLASS 112.] **Copper,** next to iron, is the most important among the Swedish metals. The principal copper mines, are those at Falun and Åtvidaberg, which have been worked from olden times.

In general, the old method of first producing the matte is still in use, and afterwards, when it has undergone the process of roasting, it is melted into coarse copper, which is ultimately garbled or refined in a reverberatory furnace; but at Wirum, chloric roasting of the ore has been used for several years, instead, with following lixiviation and precipitation of the copper with iron. A method somewhat similar has also been adopted at Falun, since 1874, so that only a smaller portion of the copper there, is now produced by the old methods of melting.

In the year 1873, 26,152 centners (1,111,700 Kilo.) copper, and 2,539 centners, (103,700 Kilo.) blue vitriol, were produced in the country, for which 2,237 workmen were employed. Of late years the production of copper has been on a decline. It reached its highest in 1869, when 51,774 centners were produced. From 8,000 to 12,000 centners generally remain in the country; the rest is exported. Of the raw copper ore, a small portion is likewise exported (to England), but this exportation has likewise decreased very considerably, (from between 30,000 and 40,000 centners annually, before the years 1871 to 1,567, in the year 1873).

Copper is manufactured partly at copper forges and rolling-mills, at which the manufacture in 1873 was stated to be 5,260 centners, partly by coppersmiths, both in the towns and in country, and on a larger scale in some manufacturing towns. In 1870 there were in the country 1,100 coppersmiths, together with assistants. Among the larger copper objects manufactured, are whisky-stills, and apparatus.

[CLASSES 113-114.] **Lead, Nickel, Sulphur, Alloys, etc.** Among the *Lead-* (and silver-) mines, that at Sala, is still the principal. The production of lead has varied much, from about 10,000 or 12,000 centners per annum, during the years 1860 to 1870, to scarcely one-tenth of that quantity at present. 1870=8,802 centners; 1871=2,095; 1872=1,017; 1873=572 centners. Litharge is not included in this.

Leaden shot are made at Sala, and also at Falun.

Although sulphide of *Zinc*, as stated above (Class 100), is mined in great quantity, no metallic zinc, is manufactured in the country.

The *magnetic iron-pyrites containing Nickel*, which is to be found in the country, is seldom rich enough to be worth extracting. The principal Nickel Works are at Klefva, in the Län of Jönköping, and at Sågmyra, in the Län of Kopparberg. The principal production consists of Nickel-copper, and Nickel-matte. The production of Nickel-copper has, during the last ten years, annually amounted to from 500 to 600 centners, (1873=452 centners), and of Nickel-matte to from 1,000 to 8,000 centners (1873=1,287 centners).

From iron-pyrites, besides Red Ochre and Green Vitriol, is also produced Sulphuric Acid and *Sulphur*. The production of Sulphur during the last ten years, has ranged about 10,000 centners annually, of which, in 1870=11,121; 1871=7,871; 1872=7,668; 1873=8,292 centners.

There are three *Brass Manufactories* in the Kingdom, in which common articles of brass are made, and among them pins. Besides, brass is founded by a number of manufacturers, bell-founders, and braziers.

There are likewise some *German-Silver Manufactories*, where the articles are finished; besides, a number of galvano-plastic manufacturers occupy themselves in plating such articles of German-silver as they import.

MINE ENGINEERING—MODELS, MAPS, AND SECTIONS.

[CLASS 120-121.] The importance of mining in Sweden, has called forth the want of Bureaux for directing the same. The Board of Trade, under the Civil Department of the government, is at the same time, the *Bureau for Mining;* but in addition to this, the State maintains a staff of technically trained persons for inspecting, and rendering assistance at mines and works. The country is, therefore, divided into 6 *Mining Districts*, (the Mining-district of Sala not included, which is under the control of a special Bureau), and in each district there is an Inspector of Mines, who is assisted by a Mining-Engineer. The owners of mines can apply to them for consultation, or for the measuring of mines, etc., but for the rest, they have purely administrative duties to perform, as, for instance, to issue "mutsedlar" (mining licenses: see above Class 100,) to watch that the mines are worked in a proper manner, and without any danger to life, to issue reports about the state of the mining, etc.

Besides these government officials, there are others of the same class, at the larger mines, appointed by the companies.

Instruction in the higher branches of mining is imparted at the *School of Mines*, which is connected with the Polytechnical Institute, in Stockholm, and in the lower branches at some minor establishments, Filipstad, Falun, etc., (compare below, about the technical instruction, Class 302).

Accidents in the mines are very rare, as the wall and hanging rocks are either firm, stratified rocks, or granite.

The greatest depth which the mines have reached, is from 1200 to 1300 feet, (about 400 mèters), reckoned from the mouth, and these depths belong to the Sala, Åtvidaberg, and Falun mines, which have been worked from immemorial times.

Maps of Mines, upwards of 200 years old are preserved, and in these, the method of drawing, is the same as in our days, except, that on the old maps, the shafts, galleries, and chambers, are marked on the sectional leaves, which show the different depths, by means of holes cut out in the paper or parchment, to correspond to the openings, which are now distinguished by a black colour. In later times, these maps have sometimes been represented by a kind of *model*, made in such a way as to substitute panes of glass, or wire-network, for the sectional leaves of the map, on which the holes of the mine, have been marked by attaching slips of paper. By this means, a view of the structure of the mine, may at the first glance, be easily obtained.

Concerning the *Geological Atlas*, see Catalogue, Class 335.

DEPARTMENT II.—MANUFACTURES.

CHEMICAL MANUFACTURES.

The development of technical chemistry, has only, within the last few years, assumed any degree of importance, and even now, the home production can only meet the wants of the country, in a few branches, hence the importation of many chemicals is still very great, but the export of others, on the other hand, f. e., Swedish matches, is very considerable, and seems to be increasing. We cannot here, treat of the development of all the branches of technical chemistry in the country, and but briefly, of the more important.

[CLASS 200.] **Acids, Salts, Fertilizers, etc.** Factories have been established for the preparation of *Sulphuric Acid:* in Stockholm, two large ones, namely, Hjerta's manufactory, and Gäddviken's, the latter in combination with the manufacture of superphosphate, at Göteborg, at the Falun copper mines, and other places. The sulphuric acid manufactory at Falun, has lately been greatly extended, with new or remodelled structures. A new such manufactory, was established at Helsingborg, in 1874. It is, however probable, that within a short time, other manufactories will be established, both in the southern and central parts of the country, especially since sulphuric acid, has come into demand for agricultural purposes, and at the super-phosphate manufactories, that are springing up. As raw material for the manufacture of sulphuric acid, iron pyrites are used, of which there are inexhaustible beds, for instance, at the Falun mine, for a manufacture on ever so large a scale; and as iron pyrites, are likewise found in large quantities, in a number of other places in the country; this manufacture seems to have a very promising future.

At Östra Torp, in Skåne, a small *Soda* manufactory, is already in operation; but at Löfholmen, near Stockholm, a larger manufactory is established, for the preparation of Soda, and *Muriatic Acid*, and also of *Glauber's Salt*, and *Nitrate of Ammonia*. This manufactory uses as raw material, besides common salt, also the waste Sulphate of Soda, which is to be obtained from a *Nitro-glycerine* (and Dynamite) manufactory, and at a *Nitric-acid* manufactory, both situated in the neighborhood.

Potash, is boiled in several of the most richly wooded districts. This trade seems, however, to decline, in the same proportion, as wood and timber, increase in value. It is only in the extreme north of Sweden, that *Saltpetre* is prepared, by lixiviating earth and ashes, that have been moistured with urine, and the like; and since the State, purchases all the saltpetre produced in the country in this manner, for the manufacture of gunpowder, the quantity of this preparation, which is to be considered as a branch of agriculture, and of which, only a few centners are delivered by each purveyor, is exactly known. The whole production, amounts at present, to about 2,000 centners per annum, but like that of potash, it is rapidly falling off.

Of *Common Salt*, Sweden possesses only that which is found in the water of the adjoining seas. The attempts which were made in former times, when firewood, had a small or no value, to obtain salt from sea water by evaparation, will scarcely be repeated, at least, not as a branch of industry. About 2,500,000 Swedish centners of common salt, are annually imported.

Fertilizers. An important chemical industry, namely, the preparation of artificial manure, has been developed during the last few years, since the use of artificial manure has become more common among the Swedish farmers. The kind of manure which has been used the longest, and also, in a certain measure has been most in repute, is *Bone-dust*, raw as well as steamed. Among bone-dust manufactories, may be mentioned A. W. FRIESTEDT's manufactory, in Stockholm; the Stockholm Bone-dust Manufacturing Company, at Zinkensdam, near Stockholm; Gustafsberg Bone-dust Manufactory, in Wermdön; Sörquarn Bone-dust Manufactory, in Westmanland; Ulfsnäs Bone-dust Manufactory, in the Län of Jönköping. Nearly all the animal bones which are collected in the country, and which formerly, were exported to foreign countries, especially England, are now used in these manufactories. Considerable quantities of bone, are imported from South America, which are converted into bone-dust or bone-black.

Besides bone-dust, they have now begun to use *Super-phosphate*, in very considerable quantities. It is true, this is principally imported from England, Germany, and Denmark, but there have also been several superphosphate manufactories established in the country, in which the raw material that is imported from abroad is prepared. Among these manufactories, the following deserve to be mentioned:

The Stockholm Super-phosphate Manufacturing Company, at Gäddviken, in the vicinity of Stockholm, the largest in Sweden, established in 1871, on the plan of the modern English super-phosphate manufactories. The raw materials are partly brought from the Company's own apatite-mines in Norway, partly from France or other countries. The manufactory has a sulphuric acid manufactory of its own. In 1874 Gäddviken, sold about 70 or 80,000 centners of fertilizers. The products are of excellent quantity, and excel most others of the same sort, whether of home or foreign manufactories. A company has recently been established at Helsingborg, for the manufacture of super-phosphates, and other fertilizers. It is intended to work up Mejillones-guano.

The "Fertilitas" Joint-Stock Company, at Göteborg, which begun in the summer, 1871, prepares principally Baker-guano super-phosphate and mixtures thereof with Sulphate of Ammonia. It disposed of about 40,000 centners, including imported articles of Mejillones and Coprolite super-phosphate, as well as sulphate of ammonia, Chili-saltpetre, Potash, Salts, Peru-guano, etc., which sale increases from year to year.

The manufactory of A. F. WEDELIN & Co., at Göteborg, established in 1868, produced, in 1872, 36,000 centners, which will probably soon increase to 60,000 or 70,000 centners. As raw material are used Baker and Mejillones Guano,

Sombrero-Phosphate, Coprolite, Spanish Phosphorite, Navassa-Phosphate, &c., to which will probably be added a considerable quantity of Norwegian *Apatite*. The products which are manufactured are superphosphates, which contain 14-15, 16-17 and 20 per cent. of soluble phosphoric acid.

C. F. WÆRN & Co., have for several years past, manufactured superphosphates, in the neighborhood of Göteborg, using for the most part, coprolite from England, as raw material.

At A. W. FRIESTEDT'S techno-chemical manufactory, in Stockholm, established in 1856, are manufactured, steamed bone-dust for agricultural purposes, so-called fodder-bone-dust, white superphosphate, animal charcoal for refining sugar, bone-black and birch-charcoal, for purifying spirits, besides secondary-products, such as spirits of ammonia, "Knochenspiritus," bone oil, ammonia salts, etc. A peculiar kind of bone-dust and bone-charcoal, for etching iron, is likewise produced, and has been used at the arsenal at Carl-Gustafs-Stad, and Husqvarna, for several years. The annual value of the preparation amounts to about $70,000 gold. The raw materials are partly to be had in the country, and partly imported from South America. The artificial manures are disposed of in the central and southern parts of the country, part, likewise, in Denmark and Norway. The bone charcoal is exported to Germany, and Finland, oil and acids, to France, and Belgium.

In the parish of Boda, in Dalarne, a company, under the name of "The Joint Stock Company of Klittberg," intend to work up into suitable manures, the phosphoric beds of conglomerates, which occur there in large quantities, in the silurian formations.*

The State has granted special sums of money for the survey of the extension, and the utilization of the phosphate-bearing beds, and the government has appointed a committee to investigate the matter. The committee has so far shown that deposits more or less rich in phosphates, occur not only in Dalarne but also in other provinces where the silurian formation appears, as in Skåne, Westergötland, Östergötland, Nerike, Öland, and probably also in Jemtland. Further, at Grängesberg, in Dalarne, veins of apatite have been found, although their extension and quality, have not yet been ascertained, nor is it known, whether they will be of any value for agricultural purposes.

Attention has likewise been directed to the existence of *Vivianite* (phosphate of iron) at Wemdalen, in Herjedalen.

It has also been supposed that the deposits of *Glaukonite* bearing lime-stone, schists in Öland and elsewhere, where the Silurian formation occurs, may be successfully prepared and used for the improvement of the soil.

Poudrette is now used every where in Sweden, as a manure, and there are several manufactories for its preparation. Lime is generally used as an admixture. Poudrette is made in the larger towns, and sold in the surrounding neighborhoods. It may, moreover, be mentioned that now, everywhere in the country, as well as at manufactories and larger establishments, where a number of persons are employed, measures have been taken for a more efficient mode of rescuing the excrement.

Recently, they have commenced to collect and to employ as a fertilizer, the *waste* or ejecta at several manufactories, as at sugar refineries, gas-works, soap-houses, tanneries, slaughter-houses, etc.

It deserves special mention, that in Sweden, during the last few years, they have likewise commenced to prepare *Fish-guano*, which in quality and value, competes with the well-known Norwegian. In the Lān of Bohus, or the western archipelagoes of Sweden, they have commenced to prepare *Fish-bone-dust*, which has attracted much attention, and is now used with success for agricultural purposes. In the large island of Oroust, in the Lān of Bohus, a small manufactory

* The conglomerate is burnt, and crushed into a fine powder. The preparation is as yet, used directly, as a means for fertilizing, and improving the soil. At some future time, it is however probable, that acids will be applied.

is already in operation, and it is hoped that in the neighborhood, a sufficient supply of raw material for the annual manufacture of from 10,000 to 15,000 centners, of fish-bone-dust of the best quality, may be obtained.

In the Lappmark of Norrland, they have at length commenced to collect *Rein-deer antlers*, and made trials to treat them in the same manner as animal bones, by which means, manure has been obtained of excellent quality, and equal to the common bone-dust.

The import of guano, and other manures, not specified, is very much on the increase. In the year 1870, it amounted to 121,700 centners; 1871, 243,200; 1872, 404,900; 1873, 429,500 centners.

[CLASS 201.] **Oils, Soaps, Candles, Illuminating and other gases.** The industry of fats is followed up with great energy. In the year 1873, for instance, there was a large *Oil Factory* in Stockholm, a similar one at Göteborg, and no less than 33 of the same sort, in other places in the country, in which chiefly linseed and rape-seed oil, besides oil cakes, were manufactured. A large portion of the linseed cakes which are pressed in Stockholm, are sent to England and Scotland. The value of the two first-mentioned mills, amounts together, to upwards of $470,000 gold, and in all the other mills to nearly $280,000 gold.

The production at 11 *Soap-factories* is stated to have been 11,695,000 lbs. soft soap, and 1,099,-1,099,000 lbs., besides 327,000 pieces, hard soap.

Two *Stearine-candle Manufactories*, in and near Stockholm, produced 3,270,000 lbs. candles. *Tallow-Candles*, are made in the country for home use, but they are also an object of manufacturing industry, from about 750,000 to 1,000,000 lbs. being produced annually.

The raw materials required for the industry of fats, is not produced in the country in sufficient quantities, and from three to four million pounds of olive, hempseed and other oils, from 40,000 to 60,000 centners tallow (from North America, and Russia), as well as very considerable quantities of linseed, and hempseed, and the like, are annually imported.

Of late years the application of *Mineral oils* as illuminating materials has spread very much, partly as photogen, and partly as benzine, which latter is used under the name of "Gas-oil," partly for lighting the streets, in the more distant parts of the larger towns, where as yet it has not been considered advantageous to lay gas pipes; partly in smaller towns and larger establishments. Such gas-oil is used, perhaps, in still larger quantities in small, so-called savings-lamps in private households. The great importance, to which these oils have attained in recent times, have likewise called forth several attempts to obtain them from the silurian formations in the country; but they are now at a stand-still, since people have ascertained that no proper oil-springs are to be found here. The import of fossil oils, of which the greater part is brought direct from North America, amounted, in the year 1866, to not quite 4,000,000 lbs., but double that quantity were imported during the following year. In 1870, it increased to nearly twelve million pounds, and in the year 1873, it came up to nearly twenty millions. A small part thereof, is rectified at some inland manufactories.

Most of the large towns, are now supplied with *Gas-works*, constructed in the usual way. Thus, for instance, in 1872, the conduit pipes in Stockholm, represented a length of 8.1 Swedish miles (86 Kilom.)*, with a consumption of gas during the year of 124,000,000 cubic feet. English pit-coals, are the usual raw material for distillation. At the Hellefors manufactory, in Södermanland, however, so-called wood gas-works are erected, which are intended to use wood in the production of illuminating gas.

[CLASSES 202-203.] **Colouring Materials, Turpentine, Tar, Aseptine, etc.** There are in the towns and country, a number of *Dye-houses*,

*For the sake of comparison, it may be mentioned that the water-works of the town of Stockholm, at the same time, had a length of conduit pipes of 7.5 Swedish miles (80 Kilom.) The water is brought from the neighborhood of one of the former toll-gates of the town.

besides Dyers, which together, employ from 17,000 to 18,000 persons.

A dye-stuff, which is much used in Sweden, for painting houses, is *Red Ochre*, which, besides *Sulphate of Iron*, [Green Vitriol] and *Sulphuric Acid*, is prepared from iron pyrites from the copper mine at Falun, and other places, and also, on a smaller scale at the Alum-works. Such an article, potash-alumina-alum, is prepared from alum-slate, at several places in the country; this slate is likewise used as a fuel, in some lime-kilns. In the year 1873, 35,000 centners red ochre, and 5,000 barrels of alum, were prepared.

The rapid increase, in the manufacture of *Wood oils*, *Turpentine*, *Perma*, (thin tar,) *Spirit of wood*, *Wood-vinegar*, *Tar*, *etc.*, deserves notice. Stumps and roots are used as raw materials. By distillation in closed retorts, etc., a kind of oil is prepared, which can be used in lamps, like photogen, as an illuminating substance. Among the various processes, the use of overheated steam in the distillation, may be mentioned, as at the Wood-oil manufactory, in the parish of Rättvik, in Dalarne. Further, in Småland, they have succeeded in constructing retorts, and furnaces, on such a plan, that the product by a single continuous process, may be obtained so pure, that it needs no further refining. The inventor of this mode of proceeding, is Mr. BRUNO, the owner of an estate in the country, who has erected manufactories of that kind, in the neighborhood of Jönköping.

In Norrland, especially in Westerbotten, the manufacture of tar is carried on in the old fashion, in so-called tar-dales.

The export of tar, which during the years 1871 to 1873, ranged above 200,000 centners, declined in 1874, to 160,000 centners. The principal customers are the Netherlands, Belgium and England. From Finland, on the other hand, from 30,000 to 50,000 centners are annually exported

Under the common appellation of "chemico-technical manufactories," no less than 50 different manufactories, are comprehended in the official reports, where *chemical preparations*, *colours*, *perfumeries*, *mineral-waters*, *etc.* are made.

Among these, is also included a manufactory in Uppsala, for the preparation of a liquid, (invented by H. GAHN, and patented in several countries), called *Aseptine*, and *Amykos*, the antiseptic qualities of which, are mainly due to its chief ingredient, which is boracic acid, and in the latter, also, oil of cloves. Similar preparations, are likewise made at the technical manufactory at Barnängen, in Stockholm.

[CLASSES 204, 205.] **Explosive Substances, Matches.** The manufacture of *Gunpowder*, which formerly was limited to a small number of establishments, having been freed from legal obstacles, is carried on quite extensively; there are now 9 gunpowder manufactories in the country. Among these, Åker and Torsebro supply the Government with a sufficient quantity of gunpowder; formerly Fliseryd and Hysby-Kloster, also contributed to fill the stores. The raw materials, potash, charcoal, and saltpetre, are manufactured in the country, but not in sufficient quantity, and they must therefore be imported. In general, the annual manufacture at the larger powder-mills, exceeds 1.500 centners of inferior, and superior quality.

Nitro-glycerine and *Dynamite*, are manufactured at Winterviken, close to Stockholm, (the first established manufactory of this kind,) and also at Gyttorp, (a powder-mill in Örebro-län,) and at Persberg (in Wermland). Despite all possible care at the manufacture, accidents have occasionally happened. Portions of the manufactory at Winterviken, have exploded several times.

The whole value of the manufacture in 1873, was stated to amount to upwards of $150,000 gold. At the Löfholm soda manufactory (near Stockholm), they make nitrate of ammonia, which of late years has begun to be used in large quantities for the preparation of so-called *ammonia powder*.

A branch of the chemico-technical industry, which has been more rapidly developing year by year, and became of essential importance for the country, is the *manufacture of matches*, which has assumed exceedingly large proportions, especially in the manufactory established in the town of Jönköping. In the year 1874, this manufactory employed 1562 persons, of whom, however, only 762 were permanently employed within the manufactory itself, and the remainder were employed in their own houses, in the making of boxes. The value of the manufacture in the same year, amounted to $697,200 gold. To this vast development, the manufacture of safety matches without phosphorus, which were invented in 1852, has contributed in a very considerable degree, and their use has become so common, that there is now scarcely a place in the civilized world, where these matches (Jönköpings Tändstickor), are not known, and imitated. Besides, there are now Match Manufactories, not only in a great number of the towns, but also here and there in the country, and more are being established. The value of the manufacture of 30 such factories that were in operation in 1873, amounts to about the same sum, as that of the manufactory at Jönköping alone. Upwards of 3,500 persons in all, are employed in the country, in this manufacture. There are also some manufactories established merely for the making of stems, of aspen wood. The chemicals required for the inflammable mass, such as chlorate of potash, chromate of potash, phosphorus, etc., are still imported from England. The following table of the export of matches, will show the great development of the manufacture, during the last few years.

In 1865	2,229,000 lbs.
„ 1870	5,793,000 „
„ 1871	8,351,000 „
„ 1872	12,116,000 „
„ 1873	14,258,000 „
„ 1874	17,271,000 „

In the last mentioned year, this export represented a value of $1,194,400 gold.

England, takes about half the quantity of our matches; Denmark, Lubeck, and Hamburg, are also important consumers.

About some other important chemico-technical branches of industry, such as *refining of sugar*, *distilling of spirits*, *brewing of beer*, etc., see Catalogue, Class 659, etc.

CERAMICS.

[CLASSES 206-213.] **Pottery, Porcelain, etc.** The manufacture of earthen ware is at present carried on in Sweden, at the two China and Faience factories, Rörstrand (established in 1726), and Gustafsberg (established in 1830), the former close to, and the latter two Swedish miles east of Stockholm; at the recently established Faience factory, at Malmö, at the Earthenware factory, and brick-kiln at Höganäs, and at a great number of factories and workshops, for the making of porcelain stoves, inferior faience, common earthenware, earthen tubes and bricks.

The manufactures of Rörstrand, and Gustafsberg, include almost all sorts of earthenware, from the real feldspar porcelain, to the fine faience. The two manufactories are nearly equal in size; they employ together about 1,200 persons, and the value of their manufactures, amounted in the year 1874, to about $750,000 gold. The greater part of their manufacture is sold in Sweden, but there is also a very considerable export to Norway, Denmark, and Russia, and of certain specialities, as, for instance, Rörstrand "Majolica" and Gustafsberg "Parian," also to other countries. Of the raw materials, the clay is brought from England (Devonshire, Dorsetshire and Cornwall), the firestones from Denmark (Möen), and France (from the vicinity of Dieppe), quartz and feldspar from the Stockholm archipelagoes, fire-clay partly from Höganäs, and partly from England. For fuel English pit-coals are mostly used. These manufactories have adopted all the inventions and improvements, in the ceramic art of late years, and they have also contributed their shares, to most of the larger exhibitions, both in Sweden and abroad, and have been awarded high prizes.

The factories at Höganäs, make tubes, waterpipes, and other articles, partly of a brown-colored very compact mass, which is glazed with salt, and partly of a light-yellow mass, which is glazed with lead, and besides, bricks and other articles of unglazed clay. The raw material, consists partly of fire-clay from the coal mines at Höganäs, and partly of clays from other parts of Skåne. As fuel, coals are used, which are raised on the spot.

The manufacture of *Porcelain-stoves*, in Sweden, where such are almost exclusively used for the heating of dwelling-houses, is very considerable, and in most of the towns, there are one or more stove-manufactories, and also many in the country. The panes or tiles for the stoves, are generally made from ferruginous marly clays, either with or without an addition of fine sand, and either coated with a lead-glaze, which is generally made green or brown, but it is sometimes also without a colour, so that the natural yellow, or yellowish-white colour of the clay shines through, or else with an opaque glaze containing tin and lead, which gives to the surface an appearance of porcelain. Among the marly clays, which are used, that in the neighborhood of Uppsala, is the best. The manufacture of stove-tiles, was greatly improved in the decennary 1840 to 1850, by a Mr. WESTMAN, a stove manufacturer, of Stockholm. He introduced a better mode of work, and he also succeeded in producing a fine, and very durable glaze. At present, porcelain stoves of a very fine appearance and good quality, are manufactured at most of the large factories, especially at ÅKERLIND'S, C. A. PETTERSSON'S, and B. H. LUNDGREN'S, in Stockholm, at A. RINGNÉR'S, at Göteborg, at V. E. RINGNÉR'S, at Malmö, at a stove manufactory at Örebro, and at Uppsala, also at the Rörstrand manufactory, where they are made of white faience with a transparent glaze.

The construction of the Swedish stoves, is now very much in favour, so that there is a demand for the manufacture even from abroad.

Common faience with a transparent glaze is, as stated above, manufactured at Höganäs, and besides, at Helsingborg, Oskarshamn, Gefle, and other places.

Earthen-ware, and also *bricks*, and *earthen-tubes*, are manufactured in many places, and generally sold in the neighborhood of the place of manufacture.

GLASS AND GLASS-WARE.

[CLASSES 214-216.] **Glass and Glass-ware.** Among the present glass manufactories in Sweden, that of *Kosta* is the oldest, being established in 1741, and next to that, the *Limmared*, established in 1848. Since that time, many glass-works have sprung up, so that in the year 1873, there were 31 in operation. Most of the glass-works are situated in Småland, Westergötland, and Vermland; there are a few however, in other parts of the country, even in Norrland. At the larger works, the annual production at present, amounts to, from $55,500 gold to $83,300 gold, and for the year 1873, according to returns from all the glass-works in Sweden, it amounts to $786,000 gold. The number of the workers employed at these works, during the year 1873, was stated in the Official Reports, to be 1,670.

The raw material, quartz, is generally to be had in the neighborhood of the glass-manufactories. Sand of the quality most in use, is generally procured from the shores of Lake Wetter, the best from the north end of the lake, in the vicinity of the town of Askersund; finer sand is imported from France. Of Lime, the native varieties are mostly used, partly from the mining district of Nora, in the north part of the Län of Örebro, (primitive limestone), partly in the form of chalk, &c., (from Skåne). For the common sorts of glass, lime from Gottland can also be used. Alkalies, and other raw materials, are mostly imported.

For fuel, fir-wood is almost everywhere used, in some places also peat. A new modification in the manufacture of glass, worth noticing, is the application of the gas furnaces, in the smelting, which, the more they become known and approach perfection, will probably supplant the blast of the old construction.

That the manufacture of glass has been greatly developed in the country, during the last few years, is most distinctly seen by the Custom-house reports: The import is decreasing, while the export is increasing, excepting, however, in the year 1873, when there was an uncommonly large importation. The import during that year was estimated at $253,600 gold, while the export was estimated at $86,600 gold. The preceding year, 1872, the corresponding values were estimated at $145,800 and $65,300, and in the year 1871, at $115,600 and $65,300 gold.

In Sweden, all the usual glass articles are manufactured, with the exception of mirror-glass, which is generally imported from Belgium, or by way of Lubeck. The greater part of the Swedish glass that is exported goes to Norway and Russia, and only exceptionally, to more distant countries, especially as vessels for transporting beer, aseptine, or the like.

Painting on glass, has begun to be introduced during the last few years, by some of the principal glass-manufactories, both on fancy articles and on window glass, on which latter etchings are also made; coloured glass is likewise produced.

There is a special establishment for *grinding glass*, which is driven by water, and employs 25 workmen.

There are 15 small establishments for the *silvering* and framing of *looking-glasses*, which employ 15 foremen and 350 glaziers (workmen included), who put in the plate, etc.

FURNITURE, AND OBJECTS OF GENERAL USE IN CONSTRUCTION, AND IN DWELLINGS.

[CLASSES 217-227.] Sweden, as will be more fully explained hereafter, is particularly rich in forests. In the erection and fitting up of dwelling houses, the *timber industry* occupies a very important place, and in the following, we will briefly consider it.

For the great variety of other objects, which may be brought under this group, only a few references are here given, namely: for *porcelain* to Class 206, for *glass* and *mirrors* to 214, *plate* to 110, *pewter utensils* to 110, *articles of copper* and *brass* to 112 and 113, *articles of iron* to 111 and 280 and the whole account of the manufacture of machinery (Department V), etc. With regard to the fitting up of the Swedish house, in general, whether of the more humble class or more costly, some information is given in Class 342.

The Working of Timber. The manufactures of *Joiner's Work, etc., for building purposes*, such as doors, windows, floors, etc., and also *Cabinet-maker's work*, are produced partly by tradesmen, partly as a domestic industry, and partly by lately established Mechanical-Joinery-Manufactories. To these may be added workshops, which have been established in prisons, and in some public poor-houses, for the employment of the prisoners, or the inmates.

In 1873, according to the official returns, there were in the towns and boroughs, 700 Joiners, together with 1,350 Journeymen, and in the country 820 Joiners, together with 460 Journeymen, or in all 3,330 men, who were employed in joiner's work, as a trade. If on the other hand, such as practice the joiner's trade on so small a scale that they are not registered in the official returns be included, and also such as are employed at the larger country-estates, the number of the joiners will be considerably greater, than that stated. At the census in 1870, were reckoned in all 9000 people, who were employed with joiner's work.

As a domestic industry, this trade is practised almost all over the country; the chairs, however, which are made in the parish of Östra, in the

Län of Westmanland, have a good reputation, as also the furniture of all kinds, which is produced in the parish of Lindome, in the Län of Göteborg & Bohus. The wood, of which these chairs are made, is birch, and likewise that of the better class of furniture which the peasantry manufacture either for their own use or for sale; but a great deal of white or red fir is also used. For superior furniture made by tradesmen proper, the usual kinds of wood, elm, oak, mahogany, walnut, rosewood, etc., are used. At present walnut is most in favour, and this kind of wood has now, in a great measure, supplanted mahogany, which especially formerly, was very much used. A small portion of the walnut-wood is obtained from Gottland and the most southern parts of Sweden, where walnut-trees grow.

The import of such kinds of wood as do not grow in the country, amounted in 1873, for unmanufactured woods, to $38,000 gold, and for manufactured to $92,000 gold, of which the greater part consisted of mahogany veneering, and the like. Other carpenter's and joiner's work was imported the same year, to the amount of $178,000 gold.

The extensive timber-trade of the country seems to call for the exportation of the forest-productions in a shape of greater perfection than that of deals and boards, or square timber and spars; but it is only lately that measures have been taken in this direction, by the establishment of several so-called *Mechanical Joinery-Manufactories*, of which one has been established at Sandarne, near Söderhamn, and one at Luleå; there are three in Stockholm, one of which in particular, (EKMAN'S manufactory) carries on business on a large scale; in Göteborg, two (BARK & WARBURG, STRÖMMAN & LARSSON), and in Uddevalla one. The manufactures of these, in 1873, amounting to about $560,000 gold, comprise the usual articles of joiner's work, or the making of whole houses, of which there were several specimens at the Vienna International Exhibition. One of the Joinery-establishments in Stockholm, is almost exclusively employed in the cutting of veneers. Besides these Joinery-manufactories, there are some saw-mills, as for instance at Sundsvall, at Skutskär in the north of Uppland, at Trollhättan, etc., where boards are planed.

The largest quantity of manufactured timber has hitherto been exported from Göteborg and for the whole of Sweden, it has during the last few years increased to the value of from $400,000 gold to $556,000 gold, in which, however, are not included paper-pulp, and lucifer-matches, important articles for Sweden, and also productions of her forests. In 1873, the export of these joinery-manufactures, furniture and the like, amounted to $290,000 gold, and of such of a coarser description, as handspikes and the like, to $193,600 gold, or together $483,600 gold, of which $195,000 worth was shipped to England, $126,000 to Prussia, $60,000 to Denmark, $56,000 to Belgium, and so forth.

Among the manufactures of split wood, *Cooper's work* holds a prominent place. These are made partly by 200 coopers, registered, together with their 300 journeymen, and partly (by no means on a small scale) as a domestic industry. A country like Sweden, rich in forests, cannot otherwise than induce its inhabitants to procure an extra income from the forest-productions, and the long winter evenings are particularly adapted for joiner's work, and thus large quantities of furniture, vehicles, agricultural implements, articles of cooper's work, shingles and the like, are made. What is made of cooper's work is almost exclusively used in the country, but on the other hand there is a large export of staves and bottoms, which seems to be continuously increasing. In the year 1873, this export amounted to about 2,300,000 oak-staves, and 21,700,000 beach- and other staves. Of the former Norway received 1,800,000, and Denmark 400,000, and of the latter, England 16,500,000, Denmark 4,200,000.

Shingles from ½ to 1 line in thickness by 1½ fot in length are usually handmade, by splitting strait-grained logs of fir wood, but they are also produced by putting a large plane into the frame of a saw, and having it drawn by a horse or an ox along the block of wood which is placed on a trestle. Split shingles are, however, considered better than planed, because the latter are not cloven quite along the fibres of the wood, nor are they so straight as the former. Shingle-roofs are handsome, light and durable, especially when the shingles are inpregnated with a solution of vitriol, and they are also very much in favour, particularly in Norrland, where they are commonly used for the better class of houses. Another sort which is planed, cut out and thicker (from ½ to ¾ inch) is sometimes used for roofing, especially on churches or similar buildings, but they may also be seen here and there, though rarely, as the covering of the walls of an old church, which gives to the building a scaly appearance.

In connection with the statement relative to the Swedish manufacture of matches, were also mentioned some establishments, which manufacture nothing but stems for matches. To these also belongs the so-called *wooden thread*, which is made for the same purpose in Malmö prison.

Turned articles of all kinds are almost exclusively made by tradesmen. Several bobbin-manufactories have quite recently been established, principally with a view for exportation to England; turning has thus begun to be practised on a more business-like scale. Among these may also be included the manufacture of materials for *match-boxes*, which are made on a large scale.

Carving is practised by the peasantry in certain parts of the country (e. g. on the above-mentioned Våla-Chairs), but in general not so much, as for instance, in the neighboring country, Norway. In Sweden it is mostly done by so-called sculptors.

Cork-Cutting, besides being practised by several tradesmen, is, at present, principally carried on by thirteen manufactories, which, in 1873, produced about 1,000,000 gross, worth above $100,000 gold. In Stockholm, there is one establishment where the cutting is done by means of machinery, which is constructed on the same principle as when it is done by hand, and, consequently, the article is considered quite as good as the hand-made. The cork-bark imported in the year 1873 amounted to 19,300 centners. Of cut cork were imported 46,700 lbs., while the export of the same article amounted to 12,600 lbs.

Basket-Work has of late more and more attracted general attention. The productions of that kind have doubtless, in many parts of the country, even formerly, been the objects of manufactural industry, and also of handicraft-pursuit; but especially during the last decennium it has become more and more a prevailing opinion that such articles are especially adopted for domestic industry, and hence, at the expense of the Landsting and Agricultural Societies, gratuitous instruction in this branch has been available to the people, partly in certain schools and partly by travelling teachers in the provinces. In connection with this instruction, straw-work is also taught, and it is therefore to be supposed that these arts are now well known in the country. Willow plantations, for procuring materials for basket-work, are, however, still wanting.

Gilding of Wood is done, partly by handicraftsmen, by gilders and looking-glass makers, partly at manufactories, one of which, situated in Stockholm, carries on a large business, and produces mostly baguettes.

YARNS AND WOVEN GOODS OF VEGETABLE OR MINERAL MATERIALS.

[CLASSES 228-234.] **Cotton Manufacture.** The variations in this industry are shown in the following table of the quantity of *Cotton imported* into the country during the last fifteen years, viz :

In the year	1860,	19,226,000	lbs
,,	1861,	18,146,000	,,
,,	1862,	3,064,000	,,
,,	1863,	1,710,000	,,

In the year 1864,	. .	4,059,000	lbs
„ 1865,	. .	7,600,000	„
„ 1866,	. .	11,006,000	„
„ 1867,	. .	13,468,000	„
„ 1868,	. .	11,417,000	„
„ 1869,	. .	13,153,000	„
„ 1870,	. .	15,111,000	„
„ 1871,	. .	23,937,000	„
„ 1872,	. .	13,348,000	„
„ 1873,	. .	19,307,000	„
„ 1874,	. .	22,130,000	„

The low figures 13 years ago are owing to the American war.

In the year 1873, 21 *Cotton-Spinneries* with 96,300 spindles were in operation, and employed 4,200 workers. The manufacture amounted to 13,760,000 lbs., in all valued at $3,840,000,' gold, so that this branch of industry is one of the most important in the country. It is, however, to be noticed that in the value of the yarn is also included that of the cotton. This production was 784,000 lbs. lower than that of 1872; but compared with the medium of the 5 preceding years, 12,453,000 lbs., the production of the year 1873, shows an increase of 1,307,000 lbs., or 10 per cent. Nevertheless, considerable quantities of cotton yarn are imported, amounting in 1873, to 334,000 lbs. dyed yarn, and 3,577,000 lbs. undyed yarn; the latter amount is as large again as that of the preceding year. The manufactories are situated (in order according to the value of the production), in the town of Norrköping (3), Läns of Elfsborg (3), and Bohus (5), towns of Malmö, Göteborg (2), Uddevalla and Gefle, Län of Blekinge, in Stockholm, and in the Läns of Södermanland, Halland, and Östergötland. Of these the following spun above one million pounds; Berg and Holmen at Norrköping, the Malmö Spinnery, Rosenlund at Göteborg, and Näs and Rydal in the Län of Elfsborg. Kampenhof, at Uddevalla, and Strömsbro, at Gefle, reached very nearly that amount.

In 19 *Cotton-Mills*, with 2,000 workmen, they manufactured in the year 1873: 69,955,000 feet and 5,000 pieces of cotton goods, valued at $2,585,000 gold, which exceeds the average production of the years 1868–1872 by $982,300 gold, or 38 per ct. The mills are situated in Norrköping, (4 with a production valued at $740,000 gold), the Län of Göteborg & Bohus (3), Borås (2), Alingsås, the country district of the Län of Elfsborg (2), Gefle (2), Malmö, Uddevalla, and Stockholm (2). A large mill weaves annually from seven to eight million fot of cloth, and upwards. The largest are the Norrköping Cotton Manufacturing Company, Lim., and the Alingsås Manufactory.

The import of cotton-goods, in 1873, amounted to 2,555,000 lbs., (i. e. twice as much as in the year 1870)., on the other hand, the export amounted to 346,000 lbs.

In 10 *Hosiery Manufactories*, 800 workers were employed (1873), and Stockings, Shirts, Jackets and Scarfs etc. were manufactured to the value of $230,500 gold.

Besides there are several, though small, *Tape-and-Wadding Manufactories* and the like.

Linen-Cloth Industry. The production at the *Linen Yarn Spinnery* of Almedal (near Göteborg), amounted, in the year 1873, to 585,000 lbs. valued at $175,000 gold.

The largest *Weaving Establishment* of this kind is also the Almedal Manufactory, with an annual production of about $1,000,000 fot textile fabrics, besides 15,000 table cloths, amounting in value to at least $83,500 gold. In two other such manufactories the value of the production amounted only to about $300 gold.

The manufactory at Jonsered, near Göteborg, is the most important *Sail-and-Tent-Cloth* manufactory, to which may be added two other such manufactories so that in 1873 the manufacture amounted to 3,272,000 fot, at a value of $289,000 gold. Of this, however, upwards of 3,000,000 fot are produced at Jonsered.

From 600 to 700 persons are employed at *Rope-Making*, partly in the towns, partly in the country itself.

The import of Hemp, in 1873, (mostly from Russia), amounted to 44,600 centners, of Cordage to 1,773,000 lbs., and of Sail-and-Tent-

Cloth to 1,074,000 lbs. Of the latter a small quantity was also exported. The total value of the import of cloth made of flax and hemp was, in 1873, $760,000 gold, and the export $70,000 gold.

Spinning and Weaving form an important *Domestic employment* in Sweden, though perhaps not now so much as formerly; this is mainly in consequence of the cheapness of machine-made productions. The province of Ångermanland, in Norrland, is especially known for its Flax-culture, and fine Linen cloth. Spinning had commenced there at least as early as 1740 to 1750. As a proof how fine linen yarn can be spun, it may be mentioned that in the year 1758, in the parish of Nätra a skein was spun of such yarn, which was 8,000 fot long (2,375 m.) and weighed 1 lod (0.47 ounces=13.3 grams). The Ångermanland Flax is plucked before it yields ripe seeds, and then steeped in water, etc., after a peculiar treatment it is spun into yarn. For the fine linen that is woven in the above mentioned province, the state pays a premium, (hence the appellation " Premium Linen "), and such linen is classified in eight classes. To the first (the coarsest)class belongs such linen as in a warp 3 fot wide (0.891 m.) has from 2,720 to 2,920 threads; after that 200 threads are added to each class, so that the eighth or finest with an equal width has from 4,120 to 4,320 threads. Such linen is bucked in lye and bleached in the sun; but that can only be done in the spring and summer, when the days are long. Therefore whiter linen is made in Norrland than further south, because during that time of the year the days are longer there. For cotton, the chemical mode of bleaching is more common in this country.

In Helsingland and Gestrikland (provinces also in Norrland), a great deal of linen is likewise woven; but in general it is coarser, than that in Ångermanland. The manufacture of linen in Ångermanland, besides for domestic purposes, which in the year 1865 amounted to 1,300,000 fot, has since declined, and in 1873 it amounted to only 38,500 fot. In Helsingland and Gestrikland, in the last-mentioned year, the length of the linen woven amounted to 2,243,000 fot; in the Län of Halland to 540,000, and in three other Läns together, to 131,100 fot.

In the Län of Elfsborg (especially in the southern part), where formerly considerable quantities of woolen stuffs were manufactured, the Cotton Industry, though carried on as a domestic occupation, has assumed such proportions as to be almost a manufacturing industry. The domestic weaving there is, namely, carried on as follows: Certain capitalists advance the yarn required for the cloth, which is then woven according to certain patterns and returned. In that manner many a capitalist employs from 2,000 to 3,000 female weavers. This domestic weaving is with regards to the different sorts divided among the different places, so that in one district the most commonly seen dress-stuffs are manufactured; in another cottons, handkerchiefs or trouserings, in a third, exclusively curtain materials, in a fourth coarse woolen fabrics mixed with hair, such as horse-cloths, carpets, and the like; in a fifth, ticking, etc., by which the skill of the worker is increased. Of late years Jacquard and fancy weaving have been introduced there.

The Weaving Industry considered as a domestic business in the Län of Elfsborg, was estimated in the year 1873, to have produced the following splendid result:

Cottons, ...	32,940,000 feet.
Linens, ...	2,112,000 "
Woollens, ...	528,000 "
Or together,	35,580,000

The manufactories in the country for the making of **Brass wire** or **Brass-wire textures** are of minor importance. The annual value of the manufacture of the two principal is stated to be from $5,500 to $8,500 gold.

WOVEN AND FELTED GOODS OF WOOL, AND MIXTURES OF WOOL.

[CLASSES 235-241.] **Woolen Industry.** The raw material required in the woolen industry is for the most part imported. The importation amounts to from four to five million pounds yearly. The wools are mostly from Germany, the Cape, Buenos Ayres, Australia, and other places, and are generally bought in the European wool markets and at wool sales; of late, however, some has been imported direct from transatlantic ports.

The manufacture of articles of carded wool has its principal seat at Norrköping, where abundant waterfalls offer a good impellant power. In 1873 thirty-eight *Cloth Manufactories* were in operation, at which, in all, 3,301,000 feet of woolen cloth were manufactured, at a value of $2,-445,000 gold, the greater portion of which was produced by the large factories of Drags & Ströms Joint Stock Companies. Besides the woolen-cloth manufactories at Norrköping, there are several of importance in the towns of Halmstad, (with a production in 1873 valued at $498,000), Stockholm (two of which, one near the town, with a production worth about $280,000 gold), Malmö and Landskrona, so that in the above-mentioned year, there were, in the whole Kingdom, fifty-two cloth manufactories, distributed in seven towns, one borough, and in seven country places, in which 4,900 workmen manufactured as follows: 920 feet fine cloth, 45,550 feet middling fine, and 947,980 feet coarse cloth, and 4,469,740 feet besides 17,120 pieces of various textile fabrics, with a total value of $37,500,000 gold. The manufacture of broad-cloth has been continuously increasing of late years. Thus, in the year 1869, the value of the manufacture was only $2,183, 000 gold.

Among the cloth manufactories, are not included six *manufactories for woolen and mixed fabrics*, to which the so-called stuff-manufactories, or the manufactories for flannel and bunting are reckoned. In 1873, the value of the manufacture at these was $210,500 gold.

Besides, there are a great many (46 in the year 1873,) smaller mills for the spinning of *carded wool*, which are spread all over the country, where the greater part of the wool produced is spun into yarn, chiefly for the country people, which afterwards like the woolen yarn spun on their own distaffs, is manufactured by domestic industry into wadmaal, which is used by the peasentry for wearing apparel.

The woolen fabrics manufactured in Sweden, are chiefly sold in the country itself, and only a small portion is exported to Norway and Denmark. The import of such articles on the other hand is very considerable, and amounted in the year 1873, to 3,935,400 Swedish pounds, valued at $4,671,600 gold, an amount that it never came to before. In the same year, 839,400 pounds dyed, and 315,200 pounds undyed mohair and woolen yarn, valued at $1,194,500 gold, were imported.

SILK, AND SILK FABRICS, AND MIXTURES IN WHICH SILK IS THE PREDOMINATING MATERIAL.

[CLASS 242-249]. **Silk Culture.** As early as in the middle of last century, trials were made in the culture of silkworms in Sweden, and also encouraged by the Diet, and supported by pecuniary grants. These were, however, soon withdrawn, and hence not only all the breeding of silkworms gradually ceased, but very considerable plantations of mulberry-trees were either lost, or intentionally destroyed, and it was a long time before new trials were made. The Swedish Society for the Breeding of Silk-worms, under the protection of the then Crown-Princess JOSEPHINE, was not founded until the year 1830, when some interest was again taken in this branch of culture. Since that time, the Society, whose endeavors are supported by the State, has annually distributed seeds, and plants of the mulberry-tree, gratis as well as eggs of the silk-moth, and have tried to spread the knowledge of, and to create an interest in the culture of the silk-worm, by publishing papers and annual reports, though as yet without any noteworthy result. Of late years trials have been made with the oak-eggermoth, in which the public have taken a little more interest, and the favorable results of trials, made by several private individuals, especially during the last few years, bid very fair. If the population would but look favorably upon the culture of the silk-worm, and support the endeavors of the Society, this branch of industry, for which the climate, at least in the southern part of Sweden, is no hinderance, might be very considerably extended.

Mulberries are now mostly planted in Öland and Gottland. The annual Government grant, for facilitating the culture of silk-worms is 4,000 Kr.

The *Manufacture of Silk,* in Sweden, has been carried on without change for centuries, from the times when the rulers thought it a national gain, to call forth at any price, every kind of industry in their own country.

As early as in 1673, there was a silk-mill with fifty looms, in Stockholm, and in that year special privileges were granted for one of the same sort at Göteborg. After the unfortunate wars of Carl (Charles) XII, the manufacture remained in a very unhealthy state, but it rose again into a certain degree of importance under the zealous protection and premium system, which flourished in 1760. At this epoch the number of the silk-operators is said to have amounted to nearly 2000. This number decreased gradually, but the manufacture has uninterruptedly remained the same under all the changes of custom-laws, etc., of modern times. In the year 1845, there were 18 silk-mills in operation, with 600 workmen, with a production valued at $275,000 gold. The introduction of the system of free trade was looked upon as a death-blow to this branch of industry, but the only consequence was that the smaller factories were fused into the larger ones, and the number of workmen employs remained almost unchanged. At this moment there exist but two silk-mills of any importance (both in Stockholm), of which each employs nearly 300 workmen. The value of the annual manufacture amounts together to about $420,000 gold. The trifling culture of silk-worms in Sweden cannot afford any raw-material for the manufacture. The import in the year 1873 of undyed, raw silk was 37,160 pounds, of dyed, 11,730 pounds, of silks and half-silks, 126,000 pounds, the latter valued at $708,400 gold. The principal aim of the Swedish silk-manufacturers has always been to produce good quality, and the firm adherence to this principle, by which it has justly succeeded in acquiring and maintaining a high repute, besides a continuous demand in Sweden and the neighboring countries, perhaps best explains the existence of an industry which belongs to southern countries, for a century, in so high a latitude.

CLOTHING, JEWELRY, AND ORNAMENTS; TRAVELLING EQUIPMENTS.

[CLASSES 250-257.] The manufacture of articles belonging to the *clothing industry,* such as fringe, textile fabrics of gold and silver, embroideries, lace-work, crochet-work, wearing apparel, hats, shoes, gloves, Berlin wool work, artificial flowers, and the like, is insignificant, although they are all produced in several small manufactories, partly as a handicraft, and partly as a domestic industry.

According to the returns of the Census 1870, the number of *tailors* was 13,765 (journeymen and other assistants included), of *seamstresses,* 4,315, and of *shoemakers,* 14,010.

Gloves are made in a few manufactories, especially in Skåne, and these gloves are in favor not only in Sweden, but also abroad. One sort of them, of undyed leather, the "Klippings gloves," are the so-called gants de suède, which are also manufactured on a large scale in Paris, under the same name.

As a remnant of the old monastic period there still exists at Vadstena, in Östergötland, a marked skill in *lace-making.*

For *jeweler's* work, see Catalogue, Class 110.

Most of the articles which can be classed under the name of *notions,* are also manufactured in the country, but not in sufficient quantity, and therefore, there is generally a very considerable import of them from Germany, France and England. The increased importation of most of these articles during the last few years, notwithstanding the considerably increased production at home, is no doubt in consequence of the greater abundance of money.

With regard to some of the more important branches of this industry, the following may be stated:

The manufacture of *Meerschaum, Ivory, Tortoise-shell, Mother-of-Pearl* and *Whale-bone*, is not an object of factory business, but it is included in certain handicrafts, such as turner's, joiner's, and comb-maker's work. The raw materials are almost exclusively imported.

The manufacture of *Articles in Wax* is chiefly limited to wax-candles, tapers, and flowers. Raw wax is exported from Sweden in tolerably large quantities, and of late years the exportation has been continuously increasing; in 1873 it amounted to 18,100 lbs., besides 500 lbs. of bleached wax.

The manufacture of portmonnaie and other small *Fancy articles of Leather*, is carried on as a proper manufacturing business by a company in Malmö, and also a little by the greater saddlers, but for the rest it might be numbered among handiworks of minor importance.

Fancy articles of Bronze, etc., are manufactured partly in several metal and bronze manufactories, partly by upwards of sixty brass founders, who employ at least 100 workmen.

Canes are made partly in the way of a manufacturing business, partly as a handiwork in certain provinces, but *Whips* are mostly made by saddlers.

Umbrellas and *Parasols* are either altogether manufactured in Sweden, or else from imported half-ready-made materials. Thus, in 1873 15,800 skeletons and covers, estimated at $13,600 gold, were imported, besides 17,700 ready-made umbrellas and parasols of silk or half silk, and 153,400 of other kinds.

Combmaker's work is only carried on as a handicraft, and a large quantity of the raw material (horn) must be imported.

Brushmaker's work is exclusively carried on as a handicraft; very considerable quantities are made in the prisons.

There is one factory which is driven by water of 20 horse-power, where upwards of thirty workmen are employed. Besides, large quantities of toys are manufactured, partly as a trade, by turners, pewterers, tin-workers, etc., in the towns, and partly as handiwork in certain provinces. The import of toys which, in the year 1860 amounted to 14,000 pounds, has since uninterruptedly increased, so that in the year 1873 it amounted to 108,000 pounds. The largest sale of toys is by Christmas Eve, when even special fairs are kept for that purpose. This is also the case, though on a smaller scale, on midsummer-day, which is celebrated in Sweden as a great ecclesiastical festival, but still more taken advantage of for recreations in the open air.

PAPER, BLANK BOOKS, AND STATIONERY.

[CLASS 258-264.] The **Paper Manufacture** has increased very much within the last few years, as is seen from the increased export, in spite of the growing home consumption. New mills have been erected in combination with wood-grinding works, and the country has been fully supplied since 1874.

The year 1864 may be looked upon as a turning point with regard to this manufacture, for while about 400,000 pounds of paper were annually imported (which quantity, however, was doubled in 1872, and in 1873 amounted to upwards of three million pounds, which was also continued in 1874 with a slight diminution), the export, which until then was smaller, has since that date been in the ascendency, and is continually increasing, until 1874, when it amounted to upwards of six million pounds, the largest portion of which was exported by the greatest paper mill in Sweden, Korndal (near Göteborg). Besides, there is a very considerable export of *Rags*, which, however, since the year 1872 has been compensated by a still larger import, in 1873, (32,700 centners imported, to 20,500 centners exported).

Some of the smaller establishments have had to give way to the larger ones, which have increased their manufacture most extraordinarily. Twenty years ago there were counted ninety such manufactories, whose manufactures together were valued at upwards of $500,000 gold; in the year 1873, on the other hand, there were only fifty-four, which, with 2,200 workmen, manufactured in all $190,000 gold worth, and among these fifty and odd manufactories there were many whose productions amounted to only about two thousand dollars. There are 17 or 18 factories run by machinery proper. In 1872, at Korndal, the largest of them, 68,000 centners of paper of various sorts, mostly printing paper, were manufactured, but by being enlarged, about 140,000 centners of printing paper could now be manufactured with five machines. The raw material employed consists of wood-pulp, as high as 85 per cent., either mechanically or chemically prepared, and also of straw. The other paper mills, of which the chief product is also printing paper, have, with a few exceptions, two machines, and with these machines from 16,000 to 20,000 centners of printing paper can be annually produced.

The *sorts of paper* which are manufactured are letter-paper, writing-paper, printing-paper, etc., sheeting-paper, "paste-board in long rolls," and the like (which sorts, on account of the climate, have latterly been very much used for the inner covering of dwellings), are manufactured on a large scale at Munksjö (near Jönköping). Paper for bank-notes and stamps is manufactured at Tumba, a paper-mill belonging to the State, and situated a couple of Swedish miles to the south of Stockholm. The Swedish filtering paper, known all over the world, is only manufactured at Grycksbo (in Dalarne). The possibility of producing this fine preparation, is partly owing to the water, which is so pure that it may almost be called chemically pure, and partly to the climate, because in the preparation of the pulp for this sort of paper it is requisite that it should freeze once.

Wood-pulp Paper. In the year 1846, when the German engineer, H. VÖLTER, began his experiments of using, instead of vegetable fibre from flax and cotton, wood fibre, which he prepared by quite a simple expedient, here was the beginning of a branch of industry which is already of great importance to Sweden, since our country possesses just what is chiefly required for it—abundant supplies of fir-forests and large water-falls. The first factory established on this VÖLTER'S system was at Trollhättan, in 1857, and for ten years was the only one of its kind, until here and there in the country they began to establish others, so that in 1870 there were six; but from this time their erection was very rapid till 1873, when there were twenty-seven wood-pulp factories already completed or nearly so; but since that time none have been erected.

This quick development is the more noteworthy as the erection of many of these establishments has cost several hundred thousand Kr.

The observations and inventions made in this branch of industry have not been unnoticed, and therefore the manufactories are calculated to be worked, partly on the chemical, and partly on the mechanical method. The chemical method is as yet so new, that it is difficult to say what development it will enjoy. It is certainly true that in this way a better and more fibrous pulp is obtained, but in proportion to the ground pulp, it is also dearer, especially since caustic soda, which is needed for the manufacture, has considerably risen in price. The grindstones that have hitherto been employed in the mechanical method, have as yet been generally obtained from Germany, the cause of which cannot be that the material required for it is wanting in our country, but rather at the new-established works they have wished to avoid experiments at first, and hence the stones have been brought from such places, where they have already been practically tried. All the machinery, on the other hand, is now made in the country.

The Swedish *Wood-pulp manufactories* extant at the beginning of 1873, may be divided as follows:

I.—*Mechanical,* such of the new works where 100 horse-power is calculated for each grind-stone:

a.—Eleven Völter's Manufactories with vertical grind-stones, and the supplying of the pieces of wood by a screw-mechanism. Of these, the oldest (Trollhättan) has twenty stones, of which the greater number are small; but besides, there are several large establishments with from five to six grind-stones of from 5 to 5½ feet in diameter.

b.—Two Hartmann's, with small vertical grind-stones, and supplied by weights.

c.—Four Siebrecht's, with large horizontal grind-stones, and supplied by hydraulic pressure.

II.—*Chemical,* generally provided with two boilers:

Ten manufactories constructed on different methods (Sinclair's, Lee's, Fry's, etc). The boiling is generally done with caustic soda, in weight about 25 per cent. of the wood, besides, the so-called half-chemical method is applied, consisting in boiling or steaming blocks of wood, and then grinding them in the usual manner. Some of the more recent paper-manufactories in our country manufacture from such pulp, a kind of paper very good for wrappers and sheathings.

The great expectations that were reasonably attached to the paper-pulp industry have, during the last few years, not been quite realized, the cause of which may, in the first place, be looked for in the economical reaction, which, in many parts of foreign countries, followed upon the enterprising activity that distinguished the period immediately preceding the year 1873, besides, it ought perhaps, not be concealed, that there are still some technical difficulties, for the chemical manufactories to conquer. It has been calculated that all the Swedish manufactories, ought to be able to produce about 480,000 centners of pulp annually, of which 350,000 centners, should be mechanical, and 130,000, chemical, but as yet not more than half of that quantity at most has been produced in any year, which, nevertheless, represents a value of several millions of Kr. Of the paper-pulp, part is used for the paper-manufacture in the country, and part is exported (158,-700 centners in the year 1873; 118,100 centners in 1874), mostly to England.

Wall-paper is manufactured in from fifteen to twenty larger and smaller manufactories, and the quantity manufactured in the year 1873, according to their returns, was upwards of 1,333,000 rolls.

Of *Playing-cards,* were manufactured in 1873, in four manufactories, 145,400 packs. Every pack of cards is supplied with a 75 öre (=$0,21 gold) stamp, and the sale of unstamped cards, is prohibited on pain of forfeiting 75 Kr., (=$20,83 gold). Whoever plays with such cards is liable to a fine of 7.50 Kr. The stamp-duty, with which formerly the great Orphan-Asylum was mainly supported, is now paid directly to the exchequer towards the expenditure for the orphan-asylum, and other charitable institutions. The Swedish cards are considered very good. Custom, among the more fashionable people in Sweden, far more than abroad, requires, even at small card-parties in family circles, that new playing-cards shall be used.

Etui-articles, such as small cases and apothecary's boxes, &c., are manufactured on a large scale, by the Joint Stock Lithographic Company, at Norrköping, as well as elsewhere. They also manufacture coloured and stained paper, etc.

In 1873, more than 800 persons practised the trade of bookbinding.

MILITARY AND NAVAL ARMAMENTS, ORDNANCE, FIRE ARMS, AND APPARATUS OF HUNTING AND FISHING.

[CLASSES 265-269]. **Cannon** are now manufactured only at Finspong (in Östergötland), but formerly they were also manufactured at Åker and Stafsjö (both places situated in Södermanland). Finspong, which belongs to a private party (C. EKMAN) is one among the largest works in the country, where, in addition to arms, farming utensils are extensively manufactured, iron wrought and refinings of all sorts are carried on, on a large scale. Cannon and projectiles are not only delivered to the Swedish Government, but also to several foreign powers.

Sweden has 2 *Manufactories of Arms*, namely, Karl-Gustafs-Stad (Eskilstuna) and Husqvarna (at Jönköping), where fire-arms, for purposes of war, as well as for the chase, are manufactured on a large scale. These manufactories, which have been very much enlarged of late, use rolled gun-barrels of Bessemer-steel from the Fagersta Works; but formerly they used mostly barrels made of skillet-steel from Witten on the Ruhr, in Westphalia. Locks, stocks, and other appurtenances are made at the manufactories, from American patterns. Sabres, sword-blades, foils, and bayonets, are likewise manufactured in the town of Eskilstuna.

Besides at Finspong, all kind of *Projectiles* of iron and steel are manufactured at Åker, Hellefors (in Södermanland) and Ankarsrum (in the Län of Kalmar). The good qualities of the Swedish iron are vindicated also in this kind of manufacture.

Small Shot are made at the Sala and Falun mines.

Cartridges for hand-guns, and similar ammunition for larger weapons, are prepared at Marieberg, (near Stockholm) by a division of the Fortification-Corps. In case of need, it can also be produced at the Carlsborg fortress. The copper-plates required for the cartridges, are delivered by the Skultuna Brass Works, (in Westmanland).

Concerning weapons of all sorts, as well as the ammunition, used by the Swedish Army and Navy, see Catalogue, Class 345.

[CLASSES 270–271]. About **Fishing and Hunting** compare Classes 640 and 637.

MEDICINE, SURGERY, PROTHESIS.

[CLASS 272-279.] The making up and selling of *Medicines* are not allowed in Sweden, excepting in apothecary shops, which may be superintended only by examined and duly appointed persons. At the end of the year 1873 there were in the country 217 apothecary shops, which are subject to strict control with regard to the fulfillment of their duties, especially with regard to poisons. Any person, not connected with an apothecary shop, procuring or possessing arsenic without the permission of a physician or other authority, shall, though no harm be done, be fined 25 Kr. ($7, gold).

A few years ago Professor A. ALMÉN, of Uppsala, invented a method of making up and preserving all sorts of medicines, which has proved to be of great practical importance, especially on journeys. The medicines are poured into dissolved gelatine, which is then baked into thin cakes, divided into small squares, each corresponding to an ordinary dose. The leaves, which are thin as paper, can then be easily preserved, and the medicine can thus be immediately used. They have now begun to prepare such *Gelatine medicines* (Gelatinæ medicatæ) in France, Italy, and elsewhere.

Among the more peculiar kinds of medicaments may be reckoned *Aseptine* and *Amykos*, which were likewise invented at Uppsala, by H. GAHN, which has already been mentioned. (Class 202.)

The *Surgical Instruments* which are manufactured in the country (especially those of STILLE, in Stockholm) have gained great repute for their cutting qualities, even among foreigners.

Concerning *Medical attendance* in general, (see Catalogue, Class 346), and especially with regard to Military medical attendance under Class 345.

HARDWARE, EDGE-TOOLS, CUTLERY.

[CLASSES 280-284]. It might be expected, that articles made of *Iron* and *Steel* would be manufactured in large quantities in an iron-producing country like Sweden. It may, however, be asserted that it is not done on a scale, that the celebrated quality of the iron and steel, would warrant. The manufacture of plates, rails, wheels for railway carriages, axles, nails, wire, &c., has already been mentioned in connection with the iron-trade (Class 111), and the manufacture of machinery, agricultural implements, and the like, will be referred to hereafter (Department V).

Other articles of iron-ware belonging to this group, are manufactured partly in mechanical workshops, partly at certain iron-works, partly by thousands of smiths in the towns, as well as in the country, partly in certain country districts, by the peasantry as a domestic industry, where especially knives, axes, scythes, and horse-shoes, are manufactured, but also other articles as nails, tacks, irons for boot-heels, muskets, scissors, keys, etc.

In Södermanland, situated on the banks of the outlet of Lake Hjelmar, is a town with 7,000 inhabitants, whose exclusive branch of business, is hardware, in almost all its branches. In this town, Eskilstuna, the Sheffield of Sweden, the work is divided among a number of small workshops, and here are manufactured on a large scale all sorts of fine iron and steel articles, such as knives, (HELJESTRAND'S razors and STÅLBERG'S table-knives are in high esteem) forks, scissors, swords, foils, sabres, bayonets, iron articles for building purposes (locks, hinges, stove-doors, etc.), house-utensils (shovels, pokers, etc.), carpenter's tools, files, etc. Here is also one of the gun-factories belonging to the State (Karl Gustafs Stad). Iron articles, such as saw-blades and the like, are likewise manufactured at Thorshälla, a town situated not far from Eskilstuna. Here is also a factory for annealing of iron by which articles of cast-iron (such as keys, bolts, etc.), are reduced to malleable iron.

At all these manufactures, Swedish materials are almost exclusively made use of, and at the same time, steel (Bessemer and also some Uchatisteel) has more and more begun to supplant iron. Thus, steel alone is now used for drills and mallets, also on a large scale for engine-axles, and parts of machinery, for which formerly common iron sufficed and which even now is used in many places abroad.

According to the census of 1870 there were 7,300 blacksmiths and 3,700 workmen, exclusive of those employed in mechanical workshops.

INDIA RUBBER GOODS AND MANUFACTURES.

[CLASS 285]. There is a **Gutta-percha** factory in Stockholm, but the most of these articles that are needed, either for their own use or for other branches of industry, are imported, (mostly from Lubeck). The import for 1873 therefore shows 1,260 pounds in an unmanufactured state, but 30,400 pounds in manufactured articles.

CARRIAGE, VEHICLES, AND ACCESSORIES.

[CLASSES 292-296.] **Coach making** is carried on at some large factories, among which that at Södertelje deserves particular mention, also by at least 300 wrights, with 200 assistants, but perhaps most largely as a domestic employment. The Swedish peasant is a very clever worker in wood, and hence he very often manufactures his own vehicles, agricultural implements and domestic utensils. It may be remarked that in all Norrland, two-wheeled carriages with one horse are almost exclusively used, but elsewhere four-wheeled, drawn by two horses, or, in certain districts, by oxen, which is the most common. More than two-draught cattle are but seldom used, although, on account of the natural state of the roads, being, at least in certain provinces, very rugged, drags are scarcely ever used.

The above-mentioned manufactory, at Södertelje is now only a branch of a still larger factory, called the Atlas, lately established in Stockholm, chiefly intended for the manufacture of *railway-carriages*. This establishment already employs 700 men.

In winter, snow and frost generally produce excellent sledge-roads, which appropriately have been called the railways of Sweden. While the snow covers the whole land, swamps and waters freeze, and across them are formed winter-roads, which are not only shorter, but also more even than the high roads, and are therefore very much used. The *Sledges* (sleighs), on account of their simple, light, and suitable construction, deserve a brief notice. While there is nothing remarkable about the small running sledges, it is different with the larger ones. On these there are, namely, no long runners which cannot follow the rough cuts in the road, but two complete small sleighs are placed, one behind the other, under the rack or else under the body of the carriage. These sleighs are made by the peasant, himself, but the more elegant are made by cartwrights.

DEPARTMENT III.—EDUCATION AND SCIENCE.

EDUCATIONAL SYSTEMS, METHODS, AND LIBRARIES.

[CLASS 300.] **I. School-establishments.** (*National Schools.**) The national education in Sweden, is regulated in accordance with a law, which was passed June 18th, 1842, with several amendments made to meet the growing wants of the people.

According to this law, there shall be in every community, and in every parish in the country if possible, at least one *Stationary National School*, with a teacher that has been approved at a seminary.

Two or more parishes forming one pastorate, may, however, either on account of poverty or sparseness of population, unite to one school district, when the instruction is partly given in *Ambulatory Schools* by one or more approved teachers.

Of these two principal kinds of national schools, *stationary* and *ambulatory*, the former are established chiefly in the towns and villages, and also in the most densely peopled provinces, and the latter in places where the population is small in proportion to the extent of territory, and when the variable state of the ground renders it more difficult to visit the school.

There is still a third kind, *Infants' Schools*, which are both stationery and ambulatory. Their establishment began in 1853, at first, in such places as were distant from the national schools; they were intended for giving the children an opportunity of obtaining instruction in the vicinity

*Contributed by the Bureau of National Education, in the Royal Department for Ecclesiastical Affairs, and Public Instruction.

of their homes at a smaller expense. Since the year 1858, however, such schools have been established both in the towns and rural districts, independent of the distance from the national schools. The national schools are intended for such children as have already made some progress.

In 1858, the establishment of the so-called *Higher National Schools* began, the object of which is, to give to such children of the working classes as are gifted with greater capacities and more ardent desire for learning, an opportunity of acquiring, under the guidance of academically trained teachers, a greater degree of education, and of obtaining useful knowledge, without having to be taken from their usual occupations.

The law provides for the establishment of but one school in each parish, but the parishes may establish others at their own discretion.

At the end of the year 1873, when the number of inhabitants in Sweden, amounted to 4,297,972, there were 3,973 national schools, of which 2,805 were stationary, and 1,168 ambulatory, 4,143 infant schools, and 10* higher national schools, or in all 8,126 schools, or one national school for every 1,082 inhabitants, and one infant school for every 1,037 inhabitants, or one national school for every 529 inhabitants.

There is also a considerable number of private schools, especially in the towns, which are under the general supervision of the Board of Public Education.

II. The Management and Control of the Schools. In every school-district, which consists of one or several parishes with schools in common, there shall be a school board, composed of the minister as chairman, and at least four members of the parishes, who are elected for four years.

It is incumbent upon the School Board to superintend all the national and infant schools, to attend to all their concerns, and to watch that the instruction is conscientiously imparted and diligently made use of; to devise rules for the schools with regard to the method of instruction, discipline, time of instruction, etc., which, however, must be submitted for the approval of the Chapter of the Bishopric; to extend a supervision over the private schools within the district in regard to discipline and instruction, and to give to the Board of the Diocese an annual report of the state of the national schools in the district, both in a pedagogical and an economical point of view.

The Bishop and Chapter (Consistory) in every Diocese are bound, in connection with the supervision of the schools in general, which is intrusted to them, to exercise a careful supervision over the national schools, and to watch the management and development of the same, and every third year to send in to the King an opinion as to the state of national instruction in the Diocese, together with all necessary explanatory statements.

The supreme management of the national instruction is exercised by the King through the department for ecclesiastical affairs and public instruction, in which, since the year 1864, a special department has been established for the examination of such concerns as relate to the national education and the supervision of the national schools. The supervision of the seminaries is exercised by the head of this department, but of the national schools by special inspectors appointed by the head of the department for each diocese.

There are at present 49 Inspectors, each appointed for a term of five years, who supervise the schools in their respective districts according to instructions issued by the department.

It is incumbent on the Inspectors carefully to follow the course of the national instruction, to visit in person the national schools in their districts, to procure information about their condition and wants with a view to their improvement and development, and to lay before the School Board and Consistory proposals for improvement whenever the arrangements are found to be deficient, carefully to look after the

*At present 11.

teaching, and to give the teachers necessary instruction and advice as to the method of teaching, etc.

The Inspector shall give to the Consistory of the diocese to which his district belongs a short annual report of what he has done, also, at the expiration of his term of office, a complete report to the department for ecclesiastical affairs and public instruction, which at the same time must contain a complete review of the schools in the district. These latter reports are printed by order of the department, and distributed among the School Board and Chapter, and then these authorities shall take such measures as are suited to the various local circumstances and called for by the suggestions and proposals in the reports.

The Inspectors receive an annual salary, which is fixed for each period of inspection in proportion to the extent of the district; they also receive an allowance for travelling expenses and board.

III. The School Children. Each community may, with the School Board, determine the age when the schooling shall begin, and the law prescribes that this shall not be put off until after the ninth year of the child. It is, however, seldom postponed so long, excepting in such localities where local circumstances or a hard climate render school attendance more difficult. The schooling of the children generally begins with their seventh year and lasts until the fourteenth.

For children who have attained the age of nine years the instruction is compulsory, so that all who are not instructed in private schools, or at home with the permission of the school board, must attend the public schools. The latter must, however, at the end of every term, submit to an examination before the school board, who then decide whether they shall be free from going to school.

The children, whose parents or foster-parents are not able to keep them in clothes and food during the school period, are assisted for that purpose from the almonry.

When parents obstinately refuse to send their children to school, they may be enjoined, after having been warned, to pay for the keeping of their children by other persons.

At the end of the year 1873,* all the children in the country, between the ages of 9 and 14 numbered 734,165, or 17 per cent of the population, of these there were 371,622 boys, and 562,543 girls. In this year, 607,986, or nearly 83 per cent. of all the children were instructed in the national schools, and these were, according to the statements of the school boards, so divided that 288 were instructed in the higher national schools, 239,517 in stationary national schools, 149,565 in ambulatory national schools, and 218,616 in infant schools. Of children bound to go to school, 9,293 were instructed in the public school-establishments (Gymnasiums or Grammar schools, Polytechnic and Technical schools), 29,405 in private schools, 68,682 at home, in all 107,380. This number amounts to nearly 15 per cent. of the children at the school age.

The children bound to go to school, who received instruction consequently, in all numbered 715,366 or above 97 per cent. of the school children.

Of children, who, on account of natural defects, received no instruction, there were in the whole Kingdom 2,678, and of such that for other reasons received no instruction 16,121. According to the statements of the school boards the last-mentioned number of children had received no instruction in said year. Whether they had been instructed in the previous year is not stated. In general, it may, however be taken for granted that no child, sound in body and mind, goes altogether without schooling during the school-age, but at least acquires practice in reading, and generally also in writing and arithmetic.

As a proof of the increase in the number of

*At the computation of the sums which are entered for the year 1873, in this and the following division it has been necessary to use for the town of Stockholm, the corresponding numbers for the year 1874. The discrepancies which consequently may occur in the sums, must nevertheless be considered very trifling, and they cannot perceptibly effect the percentage-figures.

children in the national schools, during the last few years, it may be mentioned that in the year 1865, when, according to the statements of the school boards, there were 631,056 children at the schoolage, only 481,243 made use of the instruction in the national schools, namely, 190,469 in stationary, 157,021 in ambulatory, 133,591 in infant, and 162 in higher national schools.

The number of children in these schools has consequently in eight years increased by 126,743, or upwards of 26 per cent. The increase in stationary national schools has been 49,048, in infants schools 85,025, and in higher national schools 126, while in the ambulatory schools the number of children has decreased by 7,456.

IV. The Regulation of the Schools. The time of instruction in the national schools generally comprises eight months in the year. It is only in a few schools, and chiefly in the southern parts of the country, that instruction is given during nine or ten months. The division of this time which is to be determined by the school board in every community, varies very much in different parts of the country. In most of the places the year of instruction is also to be divided into 2 terms, in some even into 3 or 4.

In most of the ambulatory schools; the instruction is carried on alternately at 3 different stations, during the year, yet in some only at 2, and in others even at 4 or more.

During the reading season the instruction is, in most instances, given on all week days, in some places, however, only on 5 days, the latter is especially the case in the ambulatory schools, where the sixth day is only used for examining the children in the districts, where the school is not open.

The time of instruction is from five to six hours a day, with intermissions of a few minutes between the hours. In some schools instruction is given in the forenoon only, but generally in both forenoon and afternoon.

The schools in the rural districts, where little children are instructed, are divided into two divisions, but where there are no infant schools, into three, which are instructed by the teacher one after another, while the others are employed in quiet exercises. In the towns, on the other hand, especially in the larger ones, the division of the classes is more complete, so that each class is instructed by a special teacher.

The *subjects of instruction* are religion, the Swedish language, history and geography, natural philosophy, geometry and lineal drawing, counting, writing, gardening, singing, and gymnastics.

Of these subjects, in the infant schools, only the rudiments of religion, reading and writing, mental arithmetic, object-lessons, and singing are taught.

In the higher national schools, the same subjects are taught as in the proper national schools, but with more extended courses of instruction. As new subjects, are added free-hand-drawing, and book-keeping.

Industrial schools for boys exist in many places, especially in the towns, and in most of the girl's schools there are opportunities for learning female industry. In some of the larger towns opportunities are also given to girls for practising common household duties, such as baking, washing, ironing, etc., in special so-called schools for housekeepers, established for that purpose.

Those children who are prevented by poverty from availing themselves of the instruction during the whole time prescribed, or such as have not the capacity of acquiring the knowledge that the course of instruction affords, must on leaving the school at least have gone through the following minimum course prescribed by the school laws: Practice in reading, religious knowledge so far as is needed for sharing in the instruction for confirmation, practice in writing, in counting, the four first rules, and practice in congregational singing, with the exception of those who have no natural capacity for music.

The general rules for instruction are, that the exercises in the school shall be chiefly with a view to the development of the mental faculties of the scholars, and that no task, which has not previously been explained by the teacher, shall be given to the scholars to be worked out by them alone; and likewise that the subjects to be taught must be introduced in a suitable order in the instruction; that the children alternately with the reading exercises, shall early practice writing and counting; that the instruction in Bible history shall precede the catechetical instruction, and that the instruction in the other subjects shall not be put off beyond the time when it can be profitably made use of by the scholars.

The last reports show that nearly all the children in the national schools, besides reading exercises, receive instruction in religion, writing, and counting.

With regard to the other subjects taught, the following number of children were instructed in the year 1873:

246,985 children in history and geography.
231,869 " " natural philosophy.
117,041 " " geometry and lineal drawing.
353,217 " " singing.
254,948 " " gymnastics and
59,860 " " gardening.

In *Religion*, the instruction begins with recitals from the Bible history, and these are rendered more intelligible by illustrations, which have been published for the schools. The doctrine of faith is principally taught from Luther's little catechism, an exposition of which, has been published, and may be used by the teacher. The Bible is read at the daily prayers, and in connection with the religious instruction; the children also learn more important scriptural passages by heart.

At the *Reading exercises*, the method of writing-reading-method is more and more gaining ground, and very considerable progress has been made in the accomplishment of reading correctly and well. In connection with this, orthography is prescribed, and the more advanced have exercises in composition.

In *Counting*, the instruction begins with mental arithmetic, and for illustrating the figures, so-called ciphering frames, or other apparatus answering the same purpose, are used. The four first rules are especially well practised, so that the children become thoroughly acquainted with them, and acquire not only expertness in mechanical arithmetic, but also learn the rudiments of counting and the practical application of the same; then they proceed to compound arithmetic.

In *History and Geography*, a knowledge of Sweden is imparted, partly by a connected review, and partly by a detailed recital of the more important events and places, an abridged history of other countries is used, and historical tablets, wall-maps, globes, and tellurions are very generally made use of in order to give a better illustration to what is taught, and thus to facilitate the conception.

Natural Philosophy has, year by year, become of greater importance, and the success is very much promoted by the application of the illustrative materials, which, in recent times, have been procured for the schools. Mural paintings in natural history, collections of plants and minerals, are used, and in many places also physical apparatus.

Geometry is a subject which is not yet so generally taught. It is, however, practically imparted, and generally includes the properties of plain and solid figures, and the art of measuring and calculating the same. In connection with this there are exercises in lineal drawing; but the instruction in free-hand drawing has, as yet, been introduced in only a few schools.

In *Singing* and *Gymnastics*, the instruction is very general, especially in the former, which is practised in almost all the national schools, and in most of the infant schools. For conducting the singing with more surety, organ-harmoniums are to be had by the schools at moderate prices. In combination with gymnastics, there are also military exercises, such as marches, movements, etc.

Instruction in *Gardening* has, as yet, made no great progress. In 1871 there was, however, land appropriated for plantations at 2,166 national schools, and in proportion as it is better arranged for the instruction, the interest for this important subject will no doubt increase.

In 1864 it was enacted that those scholars

who wish to leave the school shall undergo a *pass-examination.* This prescription has been more generally observed every year, and in 1873, 56,815 of the children leaving, stood such a test.

An important part of the regulations, is the continued imparting of instruction to such children as have ceased attending the schools daily. Whenever this is desired, two evening-hours on some week-day are generally fixed upon, for that purpose, in the towns; but in the country a week-day is set apart. These regulations have, however, been slowly developed. In the year 1873, only 27,520 children availed themselves of this instruction.

In some provinces, schools have been established of late years for young men and girls of the peasantry who have already attained an age far beyond that for attending school. These schools (at present 14) which are called *National High-Schools*, have for their object to increase the knowledge acquired in the national schools, and to impart such generally useful knowledge together with the application of the same, as may be of particular importance on entering upon practical duties. Some of these schools have now been successfully in operation for several years.

V. **The Teachers.** In order to be appointed to a *Higher National school*, it is required to have studied at a university. There are special rules given in the school regulations with regard to the appointment of teachers, which have been sanctioned by the King. It is generally so arranged, that after proof has been given before the chapter, by the candidates for the office, the chapter of the diocese, in which the school is situated, proposes the three most deserving, and then the school board chooses one of these as teacher.

With regard to the proper *national schools*, it is required, in order to be appointed regular teacher, male or female, to have gone through a seminary, and to have attained the age of maturity. The appointment to the office of national school teacher, is made by the community in the parish, on the proposal of the consistory, which chooses three from among the applicants, in the order that they deem them most deserving, on account of moral character, knowledge, and skill in teaching.

For the situation as teacher at the *Infant school*, proof of a good character and christian conduct is required, and likewise that they have the requisite knowledge in the subjects to be taught, as well as skill to teach the same. The teachers at the infant schools are appointed by the householders, in consultation with the minister.

Number of Teachers. In the year 1871, the following number was employed: At the *Higher National Schools* 10 male teachers, at the proper *National Schools*, 3,444 male and 564 female teachers; of these 2,970 male and 200 female, or together 3,170 teachers were regularly employed. At the *Infant Schools* 1,585 male teachers, and 2,212 female teachers. The total number consequently amounted to 5,039 male 2,776 female teachers. Of the male teachers 3,215, and of the female teachers 485 had passed their examinations at a seminary.

Of the teachers, 52 were clergymen, and 1,507 vestry keepers.

Salaries. The teachers at the higher national schools, generally receive a salary of from 1,000 to 1,500 Kr., (=$278 to $417, gold,) besides apartments and fuel.

The annual salary of a regular teacher, male or female, at the proper national schools shall amount to not less than 500 Kr., (=$139, gold,) (before the year 1873, 400), including 8 Tunnor (36 English bushels) of cereals, which is always paid in kind. The salary of teachers whose time of service is extended beyond eight months in the year, is increased by two Tunnor of cereals for each month. Every regular teacher, male or female, at a national school, shall also be supplied by the district with suitable apartments, and necessary fuel, and besides have at his disposal a piece of land for the raising of vegetables. By a royal enactment, it is moreover prescribed that every regular teacher, who has kept his office blamelessly for five years, shall receive a salary of not less than 600 Kr., (=$167, gold.)

Of 3,170 regular teachers who were employed at national schools in the year 1871, 2,455 received the lowest fixed salary; 715 received a higher salary, which, in the larger towns often amounted to from 1,000 to 1,500 Kr.

The assistant teachers employed at the national schools, are generally paid by the committees, according to agreement; this is also usually the case with the teachers at the infant schools, who, when they are appointed by the freeholders in the place, are also paid by them. The salaries are fixed by the latter upon consultation with the Chairman of the School Board.

Pensioning of the Teachers. Pursuant to a special royal enactment in the year 1866, the communities are bound to enter, as shareholders for every regular teacher's office at a higher or proper national school, in a pension-fund specially established for teachers at national schools. Shares in the pension-fund are granted for amounts of not less than 500 and not exceeding 1,000 Kr., and the charge amount paid down, not by the teachers, but by the communities, is four per cent. of the share.

The full pension, amounting to seventy-five per cent. of the share, is paid to a teacher if he has served thirty years and attained sixty years of age, and also if the applicant for the pension is afflicted with an incurable disease at that point of life, when his age and term of service together amount to ninety years. Under certain circumstances a smaller pension may be granted; this is determined in proportion to the whole and paid with a certain percentage.

VI. **Normal Schools.** There are eleven schools for the education of national school teachers—seven for male and four* for lady teachers. The supervision of these schools is exercised partly by the Chapter of the Diocese in which they are situated, partly by the head of the Bureau of Ecclesiastical Affairs and Public Instruction, which is established for the management of the national schools.

These schools, for which a new regulation was issued in the year 1865, are divided into three classes, and the course for each class is to last one year. The instruction, which is imparted during thirty-six weeks of the year, is divided into two terms with thirty-six hours in the week, and is gratuitous.

The subjects taught are: religion, the Swedish language, arithmetic, geometry, history, geography, natural philosophy, pedagogical science, methodics, calligraphy, drawing, music, singing, gymnastics, military exercise, and gardening together with the planting of trees.

The instruction is partly theoretical, partly practical. The two first years are principally devoted to the theoretical, which is finished in the third year. The practical instruction is preparatively commenced in the second year by attending the instruction of the teacher in the practical department, and by assisting him. The classes attend in sections. In the third class the scholars who, during ordinary hours of instruction, are summoned to the class-room, to impart instruction in all the subjects that are to be taught and practised in the national school, shall be carefully directed in practical teaching, partly in the school, partly also with small divisions of school-children.

It is to be observed that the instruction shall be on the principle of object lessons as far as possible; that the courses through which the scholars are taken, shall always be so limited that they can make themselves thoroughly masters of them; that the tasks which are given to the scholars for working out at home, shall first be gone through with and fully explained by the teachers, and that the practical exercises in the school strictly conform to the instruction in the seminary, and that they are so arranged, that the scholars obtain a thorough knowledge of that method of instruction, which is best adapted for each subject to be taught, and for each division in the national school.

The instruction in the above mentioned subjects for teaching, and practising, is imparted by

*Two of the seminaries for female teachers were open for the first time, for the school year 1875-1876.

a Principal (Rector) nominated by the King, assisted by Adjuncts and Practical Teachers who are appointed by the respective chapter.

The salary of the Principal is 3,500 Kr., (=$972, gold,) which is increased to 4,500 Kr., (=$1,250, gold,) after ten years' service; that of the Adjuncts for the first few years 1,500 Kr., which, however, after a certain number of years is successively increased to 3,500 Kr.

The number of scholars at the seminaries, which, since the year 1864 has been almost continuously increasing, amounted, in the spring term of 1874, to 790, of whom 585 were males, and 205 females. For the support of poor scholars an annual grant of 55,000 Kr. (=$15,278, gold,) has been assigned by the state. In the spring term of 1874, 232 scholars (161 males and 71 females) were discharged after having passed the examination.

In order to promote the efficiency of *female teachers for the infant schools*, special departments have been established by the state at the normal schools (seminaries) for their training. Further, the state has established a seminary for the training of male and female teachers at the Finnish infant schools, and one for the Lappland infant schools; these seminaries have been opened during the school-year 1875–1876. Schools for the promotion of the training of teachers for the infant schools have been established in special places by the Landsting, and by private individuals.

VII. Cost of the National Schools. The instruction is in general, gratuitous; but the school districts are entitled to demand a small fee from every child that attends the schools. It very seldom happens, however, that they avail themselves of this right.

On the other hand the costs are defrayed by the communities in the following manner, namely: For the erection of school houses, on the same principles as for the building of churches or by a ground-rent, and for the pay of the teachers and the other expenditure by a poll-tax not exceeding 19 öre (=5⅓ cents, gold) for every taxable person, and, if this be not sufficient, and there be no other resources, by a taxation on the same principles as are adopted for the other parochial taxes.

As a support and for defraying the expenditure of the schools, the communities receive, on certain conditions, contributions out of the public purse. These contributions are principally intended for the payment of the teachers and do not exceed 1,200 Kr., (=$333, gold,) for each higher national school; for each proper national school with an examined male or female teacher receiving the full salary and teaching during eight months of the year, they do not exceed 400 Kr., (=$111, gold,) and for each of the other male and female teachers not above 125 Kr. (=$35, gold,) per annum.

Besides, special assistance is granted to poor communities from the exchequer, and the purchase price of the school materials is moderated by the appropriation of a government grant for the making of such materials, and supplying them to the schools at reduced prices.

The costs of training teachers for and the inspection of the national schools, are defrayed altogether with public money, and for the pensioning of the teachers, the state has contributed, partly by a grant for the formation of a fund, and partly by an annual support.

The greater part of the expenditure for the public instruction is the salaries.

In the year 1871, the expenditure for that purpose, for the regular male and female teachers at the national schools, was as follows:

Proper salaries, . . .	Kr.	2,505,849
Fodder for cows, . . .	"	181,099
Fuel, ...	"	177,010
	"	1,863,958
and for assistant female teachers, as well as for male and female teachers at the infant schools,	"	870,885

or a little over the half of the amount required for the salaries of regular teachers. The salaries consequently amounted in all to 2,734,843 Kr., (=$756,679 gold), of which the communities themselves contributed 1,907,505 Kr., (=$429,-863 gold). To this expenditure must further be

added the expense of keeping the school-property in repair, etc., which in the year 1871, amounted to . . . . . Kr. 493,988
and materials, . . . " 172,435
so that the whole expenditure of the communities for the schools, in 1871, amounted to 2,573,928 Kr.. (=$714,980 gold).

The government grants for the year 1871 were as follows*:

Contributions towards salaries, etc., for teachers at national and infant schools, . . .	Kr. 946,822
Contributions for the normal schools, (seminaries for national school teachers), . . .	„ 146,500
Contributions for the inspection of the national schools, . .	„ 40,000
Contributions for the higher national schools, ...	„ 10,000
Contributions for materials for the instruction, ...	Kr. 10,000
Contributions for the support to poor communities, . .	„ 20,000
Contributions for the pensioning of teachers, ...	„ 30,000
Total, ...	Kr. 1,203,322

Consequently, if to the expenditure of the communities, . Kr. 2,573,928
be added the government grants, „ 1,203,322

the expenditure for the schools in 1871 amounted in all to . Kr. 3,777,250
or for a population of 4,204,177 people, nearly 90 öre (=$0.25, gold,) for each individual.

If this expenditure be compared with that of the year 1868, of which the last statistical report has been published, it will be seen that, during this interval the expenditure for the national schools has increased by 343,820 Kr.

The annual receipts by donations for the promotion of public instruction amounted in the year 1871 in all, to 121,133 Kr., (=$33,593 gold), and the balance of the school-fund to 1,688,808 Kr., (=$469,113 gold).

In 1868, the number of school-houses in the whole of Sweden was 3,976, in 1871 4,413. Consequently 437 new houses had been erected in the interval.

VIII. Schools for the Deaf and Dumb, and Blind. There is one State Asylum for the deaf and dumb, and blind, and 13 smaller institutions for the care and instruction of the deaf and dumb.

The first-mentioned institute, *Manilla*, which is under the protection of the Queen-dowager JOSEPHINE, is arranged into two divisions, one for the deaf and dumb; and one for the blind.

The institute is superintended and managed by a Royal Direction, and the supervision of the school itself is exercised by the managing director of the institute, who, at the same time, is the head teacher. The rest of the teachers in the year of instruction: 1874–1875, consisted of 14 male and 11 female teachers, besides 5 handicraft teachers for instructing in the different trades. The time of instruction for a complete course, is computed at from 6 to 8 years.

At the institute, there were in September, 1875, the following number of pupils:

	Deaf and Dumb.		Blind.		
	Males	Fem'l	Males	Fem'l	Total.
Paying at full price,	28	17	10	10	65
Paying reduced price	8	6	...	3	17
Free Pupils,	53	41	17	15	126
Total,	89	64	27	28	208

The annual fee for pupils who pay in full, is 300 Kr. (=$83, gold.)

Instruction is imparted in the same subjects and exercises that are generally taught in the national school, and to the blind also in music and singing; besides, instruction is also given in

*The corresponding grants for the year 1876, are:—

Contributions for teachers' salaries at national and infant schools,	Kr. 1,863,200
For the seminaries for national school teachers, ...	„ 340,650
For inspection of national schools,	„ 65,000
For the higher national schools,	„ 13,200
For the national high schools,	„ 20,000
For materials for the instruction, etc., at the national schools,	„ 16,500
For public instruction among the Finns inhabiting the most northern districts of the country,	„ 12,000
For support to poor parishes,	„ 20,000
Contributions towards the pensioning of national school teachers,	„ 155,000
Contributions to the fund for widows and wards of national school teachers, ...	„ 56,000
Total, ...	Kr. 2,561,550

various practical trades. The speaking-method has been employed in the instruction of the deaf and dumb with success during the last few years. Such as wish to become teachers for the deaf and dumb, may obtain necessary guidance and instruction at the institution.

At the end of the year 1874, the institute possessed a capital of $83,000, gold (exclusive of real estate and inventories). The greater portion of this fund has been formed by donations. The institute receives an annual contribution of $22,500, gold, out of the public purse.

The Manilla institute is situated in the royal deer-garden, "Djurgården" in Stockholm, where, in the year 1864, a large house containing halls for instruction and dwelling-rooms, was erected for the purpose.

The other institutes, for the deaf and dumb, have been erected at the expense of the landsting, communities, or private individuals; the state, however, grants a support of $28, gold, for every pupil, who is there instructed and looked after, and for that purpose an annual grant of $11,000, gold, has been assigned. The number of children, who were instructed and cared for in these establishments, in the year 1875, was 393.

[CLASS 301.] **Higher Education, Elementary Schools, Gymnasiums, etc.** The *object* of the public secondary schools, supported by the State, is, pursuant to an enactment of January 29th, 1859, to impart, a general education, above the range of the national schools, and an elementary knowledge of the sciences, which are further prosecuted either at a University, or at some superior branch school, for some particular science. These schools are called, in Sweden, "Elementar-Läroverk," and hence we retain the name of *Elementary Schools.**

The *Higher Elementary Schools*, have seven classes, and are either so arranged, that the two highest classes are instructed in all the subjects belonging to the Elementary Schools, or only in such subjects as belong to a practical education. Of the latter there is now only one.

The *Lower Elementary Schools*, are those, where such instruction is given on a smaller scale, as is continued and completed in the higher ones, as far as the limits prescribed for Elementary Schools. With regard to the number of classes, they have either two, three, or five. Of those with two classes, only a few remain, which will soon be discontinued or changed into schools with three classes.

Besides the proper elementary schools, there are nineteen so-called *Pedagogies*, established upon the whole with the same object as the elementary schools. The main difference is, that the subjects taught and the courses of instruction at the pedagogies are not restricted by the plan of instruction at the elementary schools, but are determined upon by the Ephorus, at the proposition of the Principal of the school. They have one or two teachers for the literary subjects, and in nine of them there are teachers of music and of gymnastics.

The whole number of the *Elementary Schools* of the State amounts to seventy-seven, and of the *Pedagogies* to nineteen. Of the former, thirty-one are complete; twenty-one have five classes; twenty-three, three classes; two, two classes. All the schools are established either in the towns or the boroughs, none in the country.

A complete *Course of schooling* comprises a period of nine years. The annual period of instruction includes thirty-six weeks, divided into two terms, the autumn and spring term. The autumn-term, which begins at the end of August and ends about the middle of December, takes up about sixteen weeks; the spring-term continues for about twenty weeks, from the middle of January to the beginning of June. In these

* An alteration in the arrangements of these schools has already been determined upon by the government, and partly carried out. The most important points in the new regulation, are, that the reading of Latin, shall begin in the fourth class, and of Greek, in the sixth, and that the instruction in the five lower classes, shall be in common for all the scholars, only with the exception that those of the scholars in the fourth and fifth classes, who wish to read Latin, shall not be instructed in English and vice versa. A proposition for a new school-law has been made by a Commission appointed for the purpose, but it has not yet been examined by H. R. M.

thirty-six weeks is also included a week's holiday at Easter. The number of hours for instruction, per week, is, for the first class, twenty-seven; for the second to the fifth, inclusive, thirty; and for the remaining, thirty to thirty-two, besides the hours required for singing and gymnastics, as well as in the seventh class (the highest) for the optional, Hebrew and English, and also drawing; in the fifth, sixth and seventh classes, all the classical studies; and instrumental music in all the classes. The hours for the compulsory attendance at the singing and gymnastic exercises are from five to seven, per week. It may be remarked that the Principal of the school, if he deems it advisable, has the right to give the scholars in the highest class three holidays every month, but no more. This is intended for the private studies of the scholars.

The daily instruction, from five and one-half to six and one-half hours, varies in different schools, according to local circumstances. At the greater number of schools it is arranged as follows: From 7 o'clock till 9 o'clock A. M., and from 11 o'clock A. M. till 2 o'clock P. M., and two afternoons from 4 o'clock till 5 o'clock P. M. To these are to be added the hours for practising, which are generally in the afternoon. Every day before the instruction begins, and when it is finished, the scholars assemble for prayers. The time devoted for this purpose, about one-half hour, is not included in the time for the instruction.

In the complete elementary schools, instruction is imparted in seven separate classes, of which, each of the five lower (1 to 5) comprises a course of one year, and the two higher ones (6 and 7) each a course of two years. In the three lowest classes the instruction is common for all. From the autumn-term, 1875, the instruction in the fourth class, and from the autumn-term, 1876, also in the fifth, will likewise be in common on all subjects for all the scholars, with the exception that such as wish to learn Latin, shall not be instructed in English, and vice versa. In the sixth and seventh classes the instruction is divided into two departments, namely, the classical with the classical languages and mathematics, as the chief subjects of study, and the practical with no classics, but the time is devoted to practical subjects, especially mathematics, modern languages and natural philosophy. In most of the schools the instruction is common for all on certain subjects, e. g.: religion, history, natural history, and Swedish; in some of the schools the scholars of the different departments have quite a separate instruction.

The subjects of instruction in the different departments and classes, and also the number of hours per week fixed for each subject, will be seen by the following plan of instruction:

PLAN OF INSTRUCTION.

SUBJECTS TAUGHT.						Classical Course.				Practical Course.			
	Class I.	Class II.	Class III.	Class IV.	Class V.	Class VI. 1.	Class VI. 2.	Class VII. 1.	Class VII. 2.	Class VI. 1.	Class VI. 2.	Class VII. 1.	Class VII. 2.
Religion	3	3	3	2	2	2	2	2	2	2	2	2	2
Swedish Language	5	6	6	4	3	2	2	2	2	3	3	3	3
Latin " "	....	....	....	*8	*8	8	8	7	7	....	....	....	....
Greek " "	....	....	....	....	....	6	6	5	5	....	....	....	....
German " "	6	7	7	4	3	1	1	....	....	2	2	....	....
French " "	....	....	....	....	3	4	4	3	3	5	5	5	5
English " "	....	....	....	†8	†8	....	....	....	....	2	2	3	3
Mathematics	4	5	5	5	5	4	4	4	4	6	6	6	6
Natural Philosophy	2	2	2	2	2	....	....	....	....	....	....	....	....
History and Geography	4	5	5	5	4	3	3	3	3	4	4	4	4
Philosophical Propædeutics	....	....	....	....	....	....	....	....	2	....	....	2	2
Natural History	....	....	....	....	....	2	1	....	....	1	1	....	....
Physics	....	....	....	....	....	....	1	2	2	3	3	2	2
Chemistry	....	....	....	....	....	....	....	....	....	2	2	3	3
Mineralogy	....	....	....	....	....	....	....	....	....	....	.....	3	3
Calligraphy and Drawing	3	2	2	....	....	....	....	....	....	2	2	2	2
	27	30	30	30	30	32	32	30	30	32	32	32	32

*Only for those that do not take English.

†Only for those that do not take Latin; one of these hours may, instead, be used for instruction in drawing.

Hebrew and English are optional subjects for the classical course in which instruction is given to the scholars of the seventh class during extra hours. At the request of the parents or guardians, a scholar taking the classical course may be exempted from Greek, and receive other instruction instead, chiefly in English and drawing. On the practical course there are no optional subjects. Children not belonging to the Swedish Church are exempt from religious instruction if the parents or guardians desire it.

In the first class the instruction is generally given by one teacher; in the second and third, there may be from two to four; in the higher classes, at least in the higher schools, the instruction is divided among the teachers according to the subjects.

Instruction in *Gymnastics and Military exercises*, is given in all the classes daily, for half an hour, and besides in the fifth class, one hour, and in the sixth and seventh, two hours weekly, in the *use of arms*. At the beginning and end of the school year, a more extended training with exercises in shooting at targets, field-marches, etc., is given for eight or ten weeks to the scholars of the sixth and seventh classes. At the request of the Ephorus, the colonel of a regiment shall command a suitable officer, not above the rank of captain, to be the leader of these exercises, unless the ordinary teacher of gymnastics is, or has been, in military service for at least five years. An officer thus commanded receives from the State an allowance for his travelling expenses and board, varying in proportion to his rank. For these special military exercises, and for the construction of shooting-grounds, where such do not previously exist, there has been granted an annual allowance of $3,750, gold. At the beginning of each term, all the scholars undergo a medical inspection, and only such as cannot, without risking their health, participate in the gymnastic exercises, shall be exempted.

The instruction in *Music*, consists in singing, and instrumental music, and is so arranged, that every scholar can practise each subject two hours weekly. Instrumental music is optional. All the scholars in the three lower classes must participate in the singing. In the other classes, those are exempted who have no ear and aptitude for music, or, whose voices are undergoing a change.

Drawing is compulsory for the four lower classes, and for the practical course. The hours devoted for that purpose, are stated in the plan of instruction. For the other classes, it is optional, generally with one hour a week for practising. The students of the "practical course," may, if they desire, participate in the optional drawing.

New scholars are admitted only at the beginning of each term; the majority at the beginning of the school-year; very few in the spring. In order to be admitted at such a school, it is necessary to have attained the age of ten years, or at least to come to that age during the course of the term, and must

(1) Be able to read the Swedish language fluently and well out of a book, both Latin and Swedish characters; and to be able to relate the contents of a simple narrative that has been read aloud.

(2) To write a distinct and even hand.

(3) To be somewhat expert in orthography.

(4) To have acquired a knowledge of the Bible-history from an elementary book of instruction, and to possess an insight into the doctrines of Christianity according to LUTHER'S "Little Catechism."

(5) To be expert in the use of the four elementary branches of arithmetic in whole numbers, and also to have acquired some readiness in mental calculation.

(6) To give an abridged account of the geography of Sweden, Norway and Denmark.

Children not belonging to the Swedish Church shall give such proof of their religious knowledge as the principal of the school may deem sufficient.

There is no maximum age fixed upon for a scholar's admittance into the school; nor is there any limit for the number of scholars, either for the whole school or for the separate classes.

Promotion to a higher class takes place in most of the schools only once a year, namely, at the end of the spring-term, which is also the end of the school-year. After having undergone a separate and approved examination, promotion may also take place at the beginning both of the autumn and spring terms.

When a scholar has passed through the seven classes he undergoes an examination that it may be ascertained whether he has acquired that knowledge, education and maturity which it is intended the elementary school shall impart. This examination is called "afgångsexamen," the final examination before leaving the school (about this, see below). A great many, however, leave while they are still in the lower classes.

At the end of every school-year a public *examination* of all the classes takes place. The Ephorus invites a number of the most respectable gentlemen in the neighborhood to attend as witnesses and leaders. The annual examination is partly an account of the course of instruction gone through during the year, partly an exposition of the scholars' progress in singing and instrumental music, drawing, gymnastics and military exercises. When the examination is finished either the Ephorus or the Inspector states the advancements of the scholars; the testimonials with regard to their knowledge, industry and good conduct are read, and premiums and stipends awarded. The whole has an appearance of solemnity, and in many places it assumes the character of a national festivity.

Previous to this examination the Principal of the school shall publish a report for the last school-year.

At the end of the autumn term, there is also a public examination, held at the lower elementary schools, and the five lower classes of the higher, in the presence of witnesses called by the Ephorus.

At the higher elementary schools there is a *final examination* (afgångsexamen), of the scholars who have completed the whole course. It takes place under the control of Censors nominated by the King, and these Censors are generally teachers at the university. The examination is partly in writing, partly oral; that in writing precedes the oral, and takes place in all the schools at the same time. For classicals, the written examination consists of (1), a Swedish composition; (2), a translation from Swedish into Latin; (3), a translation into French or German; (4), the solution of two geometrical and two algebraic problems. Scholars of the practical course shall give the following written proofs: (1), a Swedish composition; (2), a translation into French, and one into German, or instead of either, a translation into English, according to the choice of the scholar; (3), the solution of two algebraic and two analytic problems, and also one relating to mechanics or physics. The subjects and problems required, and the Swedish texts for the translations, are sent from the Ecclesiastical Department, to the principals of the schools. The oral examination comprises the subjects of instruction in the highest class, with the exception of Swedish. A scholar that has been approved at the examination, is declared to be "mature," and receives a testimonial, showing not only his knowledge of each particular subject, but the degree of general maturity that he is considered to possess. An approved final examination entitles to admittance at the university.

Of the 732 scholars (of whom 688 belonged to the schools of the State), who, in the spring-term of 1874, underwent a final examination, 641 passed in writing, and of these, 600 the oral examination; consequently, out of the whole number 91 were sent back in the writing examination and 41 in the oral (of these respectively 46 and 16 scholars of the schools of the State). Among these are included, in the former case 13, and in the latter 10, who, on account of illness, or some other cause, did not attend the examination.

The Board of School Directors. At every such school, there shall be a Principal, ("Rektor") who, besides his office as teacher, is entrusted with the general supervision of the school. At the higher elementary schools, the Principal is generally appointed by the King, for five or ten years; at the lower, on the other hand, he is nominated by the Chapter, for life.*

On certain questions, especially such as relate to the scholars' testimonials, of admittance to, and removal from, the school, advancement, school-fees, discipline, and order of studies, the Principal shall call together the college of teachers, in order to consult on the subject, and decide accordingly. If, on any subject, the principal be of a different opinion from the majority of the college, it is to be submitted to the decision of the Ephorus.

The Bishop, is the Ephorus, of all the Elementary Schools of the State, established in his bishopric. It is his duty to see that the schools, under his superintendence, answer their purposes, and that the teachers in them strictly fulfill their duties. At an elementary school, in a place within the bishopric where the Ephorus does not reside, he appoints an Inspector, who in his place has the general superintendence of the school. If the episcopal office is vacant, all the rights and duties belonging to the Ephorus, devolve upon the Chapter. Teachers' certificates are given in the school of the capital of the bishopric before the Chapter, who also appoint the teachers. The teachers of gymnastics, music, and drawing in the lower elementary schools are appointed by the Ephorus.

Scholastic matters which do not belong to the decision of the above-mentioned authorities, and also complaints against the resolutions of the Ephorus or Chapter, shall be laid before the King by the Ecclesiastical Department. The whole of the school legislation is vested in the King. In questions relating to concessions to the schools, such as the pay of the teachers, the consent of the Diet is required.

*The Chapters consist of the Bishop, as president, and in most cases of the Dean or Provost of the cathedral, and six lecturers from the Elementary School of the town, belonging to the Chapter, as members.

The Teachers of the higher elementary schools are: the Principal, Lecturers, and Adjuncts; in the lower, the Principal and Colleagues; in both, moreover, practical Masters of Gymnastics, music and drawing.

The Principal of a higher elementary school is bound to instruct for from twelve to eighteen hours weekly; in the lower, the Principal instructs twenty, twenty-four or thirty hours, according as they have two, three, or five classes.

The Lecturers instruct weekly from eighteen to twenty-two hours, especially in the higher classes.

The Adjuncts and Colleagues instruct for from twenty-eight to thirty-two hours.

The teachers in the pedagogies have the same duties in regard to instruction, as the Adjuncts and Colleagues.

Besides the general requirements for a government appointment, in order to become a Colleague or Adjunct at an elementary school, it is necessary to have passed the examination for the degree of Doctor of Philosophy, to have taught as teacher candidate, one year at an elementary school, and to have undergone the necessary proof-examination for the office applied for. The Lecturers shall, moreover, have taken the degree of Ph. D., and the Principal shall have passed through, successfully, a Latin disputation. There are special regulations for the Exercise-masters.

When a teacher's office becomes vacant, it is published in the official newspaper by the Chapter, and the subjects belonging to the same are then also made known. When the time of application has expired, the Chapter fixes a day for the examination of the candidates. The Chapter awards testimonials on the specimens produced, and guided by that testimonial, as well as the other testimonials, with regard to the literary merits, experience, zeal and skill of the applicant, appoints the most deserving.

The number of teachers in the schools varies in proportion to the size of the school and the number of scholars.

The following table will give a review of the number of teachers at the different sorts of

ELEMENTARY SCHOOLS.

	Complete.	With Five Classes.	With Three Classes.	With Two Classes.	Total.
Principals	31	21	23	2	77
Lecturers	182	.....	.....	.....	182
Adjuncts & Colleagues	317	113	47	2	479
Teachers of drawing	31	21	23	.....	75
Teachers of Music	31	21	23	2	77
Teachers of gymnastics	31	21	23	2	77
Total	623	197	139	8	967

Of the Pedagogies, those with two classes have a Principal and a Colleague, and also teachers of gymnastics, and of music, but those with one class, have only one teacher, who is generally styled Principal.

Besides the regular teachers, from 60 to 70 extra teachers, have been engaged at the schools for many years. These are appointed by the Ephorus, for one term at a time, at such schools as have not a sufficient number of regular teachers for efficiently carrying out their curriculum.

With the exception of the practical teachers, at the lower elementary schools and pedagogies, and also the teachers of the pedagogies of one class, all the regular teachers have different salaries, according to their time of service. After a service of a certain number of years, if bearing witness of zeal and capacity, a teacher is promoted to a higher salary. The promotion is decided upon by the King, on the proposal of the Chapter which it concerns. Salaries of the teachers are given in the following table:

TEACHERS.	RATES OF SALARY.				
	1.	2.	3.	4.	5.
	Kr.	Kr.	Kr.	Kr.	Kr.
Principals at (a)	4,500	(1) 5,000	.....	....	....
" " (b)	3,500	(1) 4,000	....	....	....
" " (c)	3,000	(2) 3,500	....	....	....
" " (d and e)	2,500	(2) 3,000	(3) 3,500	....	....
Lecturers	2,500	(4) 3,000	(4) 3,500	(4) 4,000	(4) 4,500
Adjuncts and Colleagues	1,500	(4) 2,000	(4) 2,500	(4) 3,000	(4) 3,500
Teachers at (f)	1,500	....	....	....	....
Teachers Gymnastics at (a)	1,000	(4) 1,250	....	....	....
" " " (b)	600	....	....	....	....
Teachers of Gymnastics at (c, d and e)	300	....	....	....	....
Teachers of drawing at (a)	750	(4) 1,000	(4) 1,250	....	....
" " " (b)	450	....	....	....	....
" " " (c)	300	....	....	....	....
Teachers of Music at (a)	750	(4) 1,000	(4) 1,250	....	....
" " " (e)	450	....	....	....	....
" " " (d)	300	....	....	....	....
" " (e & f)	200	....	....	....	....

(a). Higher Elementary Schools.

(b). Lower Elementary Schools, of five classes.

(c). Lower Elementary Schools, of three classes.

(d). Lower Elementary Schools, of two classes.

(e). Pedagogies, of two classes.

(f). Pedagogies, of one class.

(1). After 10 years' service in that capacity at a similar school.

(2). After 15 years' service as regular teacher.

(3). After 20 years' service as regular teacher.

(4). After 5 years' service at the previous rate of salary.

The whole of the allowance of the State in the Budget for 1875, for the Elementary Schools, amounts to $632,500 gold, and for the Pedagogies, to $20,490 gold.

Besides the regular salaries of the Principals, granted by the State, and the personal increase of pay to which they are entitled, they receive from the communities of the towns where the schools are established, houses to live in, or its equivalent in money. At some of the schools the communities have also assigned houses for some of the other teachers.

Most of the teachers receive their salaries in cash. In a few places, the State has appropriated prebends, from which the teachers receive the income.

The extra teachers receive an annual salary of from $278 to $347 gold.

The minimum age (10 years) and knowledge for admission, have already been given. The course extends over a space of nine years. The average age for graduating from these schools should, therefore, be 19, but it is rather higher.

As above stated, there is no limit fixed for the *number* of scholars, neither for the schools themselves, nor for the separate classes. The number will be seen in the following table:

		ELEMENTARY SCHOOLS.				
		Complete	V Cl'ss	III Cl'ss	II Cl'ss	Tot'l
Class I.	Regular Course	1,014	568	357	22	1,961
Class II.	Regular Course	1,337	693	298	29	2,303
Class III.	Regular Course	1,367	561	271	....	2,199
Class IV.	Classical "	828	237	....	....	1,065
	Practical "	394	191	....	....	585
Class V.	Classical "	733	157	....	....	890
	Practical "	226	118	....	....	344
Class VI.	1st Division.					
	Classical Course	683	....	....	....	683
	Practical "	165	....	....	....	165
	2d Division.					
	Classical Course	530	....	....	....	530
	Practical "	69	....	....	....	69
Class VII.	1st Division					
	Classical Course	473	....	....	....	473
	Practical "	58	....	....	....	58
	2d Division.					
	Classical Course	452	....	....	....	452
	Practical "	44	....	....	....	44
Total.	Common "	3,718	1,768	926	51	6,463
	Classical "	3,699	394	....	....	4,093
	Practical "	956	309	....	....	1,265
In all...........................		8,373	2.471	926	51	11821

The number of scholars in the pedagogies was : In nine, of two classes, 144 in the first class, and 96 in the second (the higher); and in ten of one class, 184, or together 424.

There are no boarding-schools. The scholars live either with their parents or board in private houses. Consequently their superintendence out of the school is chiefly committed to the parents or the parties with whom they live.

School-fees. Every scholar, when admitted to a school, shall pay an entrance fee of 6 Kr., (=$1,67 gold). Those who are poor, or come from another school, are exempted.

For every term, the scholars have to pay :

(1) To the furniture fund 4.50 Kr., (=$1,25 gold).

(2) To the Building-fund, which is intended either for repairing or re-building the school-house, 5 Kr., (=$1,39 gold).

(At the suggestion of the teacher-collegium, the Ephorus may exempt poor scholars either from one or both of these payments.)

(3) A fee to the porter for light and fuel, which is fixed every term, according to the requirements. At most of the schools it now amounts to two or three kronor, (=$0,56 to $0,83 gold).

At every higher school there is a *library*, which is open not only to the teachers and scholars of the school, but to the residents of the town and neighborhood. At the proposition of the Board, the Ephorus appoints the librarian, who is generally one of the teachers, and who receives separate pay for this office. Several of these libraries, especially those belonging to schools established in the towns where the Bishops reside, contain very valuable collections of books, illustrated works and manuscripts. The library at Linköping contains about 40,000 volumes, besides 1,500 manuscripts, 500 parchment documents, 1,000 foreign and 12,000 Swedish academical disputations, and also a great number of political and judicial pamphlets, etc. The library at Skara contains upwards of 20,000; at Wexjö, 17,000; at Göteborg, 13,000; at Westerås, 12,000 volumes, etc.

At several of the higher schools there are very considerable *collections* pertaining to natural history, especially zoological ; collections of instruments and apparatus for the demonstration of physics and chemistry, etc.

Funds. Every *Bishopric* shall, for the use of the Elementary schools possess :

(1) A *Building-fund*, the principal income of which consists in the proceeds of one year's revenue of ecclesiastical offices beyond the school, of which the incumbents have either resigned or been dismissed, or have died without leaving a widow or children entitled to a pension, "nådår," (year of grace). The fund is used either for the erection of new school buildings, or for repairing the old ones within the diocese.

(2) A *Premium*-and *Poor-fund*, the income of which is annually divided among the schools of the diocese, to be used for premiums, and to assist the poor scholars.

(3) An *Emeritus-fund*, which is intended for salaries or assistance to teachers who have resigned on account of decrepitude or infirmity.

Every *School-establishment* shall have:

(1) A *Furniture-fund* for the procuring of school materials.

(2) A *Premium-* and *Poor-fund*, the proceeds of which are divided among the scholars partly

as rewards for diligence and progress, partly for assisting the poor and sick.

(3) A *Library-fund* for the purchase and binding of books.

(4) Moreover, each school shall have a so-called *Fund of its own*, principally intended for light and fuel, and for the wages of the porters. Its income consists of the entrance fees and the contributions which are every term imposed on the scholars, in proportion as it may be required.

Stipend-funds presented by private parties as an encouragement for moral and industrious poor scholars, with aptitude and taste for studies, exist at most of the school-establishments.

The school-law prescribes that every *School-house* shall be constructed in keeping with the requirements. The school-rooms shall be sufficient in number and spaciousness, light, cheerful, lofty, provided with fire-places, and generally arranged with strict regard to the health of the scholars and necessary conveniences for instruction.

Several of the schools are built and kept in repair by the towns. When otherwise, the expense falls upon the building-funds, which exist in common for each diocese, and separately for each school. The latter, which have existed only a few years, are as yet very insignificant, and the building-funds of the dioceses have often been insufficient for the wants. In such cases, the Diet has granted allowances to very considerable amounts. Of late the "landsting" have also contributed to the building of school-houses. The towns shall, however, even if they are not bound to build and repair the school-houses, always provide, free of expense, healthy and well situated sites for them, which must be sufficiently extensive, not only for gymnastic establishments, but for the scholars' plays and exercises in the open air.

To give an approximate idea of the cost of a school-house at one of the higher elementary establishments, a statement of the amounts that have been paid lately for the building of some of them is given herewith.

The cost of the school-house at Uppsala, exclusive of the purchase money for the site, amounted to $83,300 gold, of which $57,780 gold for the building and a place for gymnastics; $7,000 gold for warming and ventilating apparatus; $3,900 gold for gas and water-pipes and for a lightning conductor, about $7,000 gold for the furniture; $1,950 gold for an organ and organ-loft; $1,880 gold for the levelling, planting and enclosure of the ground; $1,870 gold for a dwelling for the fire-lighter, and the rest for gymnastic arrangements, fees to the architect, etc. The building contains twenty-six school-rooms, one large hall for prayers and festive occasions, one large room for drawing-lessons, a library, together with a reading-room, one room for music lessons, laboratory, a room for collections pertaining to natural history, store-rooms, and dwelling for the porter. A separate house has been built for the Principal to live in, which cost $3,500 gold. The total expense of the building amounts to about 320,000 Kr. (=$88,900 gold.)

The school building at Norrköping cost	Kr.	293,000
" " " " Gefle "	"	283,000
" " " " Linköping "	"	245,000
" " " " Göteborg "	"	273,000
" " " " Jönköping "	"	222,000
" " " " Karlstad "	"	191,000
" " " " Westervik "	"	151,000

There are but few *Private Elementary-schools*. They are found mostly in the larger towns. Four of them correspond to complete elementary schools, one corresponds to complete practical course, the rest are more or less complete. The complete schools, are privileged to hold pass-examinations with their scholars in the same manner as the public elementary schools.

All the above-mentioned schools are for *boys*. For the instruction of *girls*, there is, besides, the national schools and seminaries established in connection therewith, and schools for special purposes (industrial arts, drawing, music, gymnastics), at which latter, instruction is given to both sexes. There is only one school supported by the State, namely, the "Seminarium," in Stockholm (equivalent to American Normal School) for the training female teachers, together with the "Normal-skolan" (normal school) for girls, belonging to it.

For the support of this school the State has granted $7,000 gold, annually.

At present, there are, in most of the towns, private elementary, or boarding-schools (so-called pensions), for girls. One of these, the Wallin school in Stockholm, has been privileged by the government to hold pass-examinations, according to the ordinance now in force for the higher public elementary schools, and at the same time a dimissory right to the university. The expenses of these private school-establishments are principally defrayed by the payments of the scholars. Only a few are partly supported by the State.

B. **The Universities.** Sweden has two universities: *Uppsala*, the oldest in the North, inaugurated September 21st, 1477, and *Lund*, inaugurated January 28th, 1668.

A Chancellor has the chief management, but the immediate management is effected under the superintendence of a Vice-Chancellor, by the Rector, and the Academical Consistory. Vice-Chancellors are: in Uppsala, the Archbishop; and in Lund, the Bishop. The rectorship alternates yearly among the professors in ordinary. In each university are four faculties: the faculty of theology, of medicine, of law, and of philosophy, of which each form a scientific academical board. The presidents of the faculties, who are called Deans, alternate yearly. Each faculty confers three degrees and dignities of scholarship, namely: the degree of candidate, of licentiate, and of doctor, with the exception, however, that doctors of theology are nominated by the King (without any examination). The dignity of licentiate in philosophy has but lately been added.

The students are divided into provincial unions or so-called nations, which correspond to the bishoprics or provinces of the country. Each provincial union, (thirteen in Uppsala and eight in Lund) is under the superintendence of an inspector (professor), and of one or several curators (younger academical teachers or older students). In the national unions the students are divided into seniores, juniores, and, in Uppsala, recentiores, or, in Lund, novitii. Independent of this, the students frequently belong to one or several voluntary scientific societies (linguistic, philosophic, geologic, etc.) formed by themselves. Among these may also be included the highly valued students' choirs.*

The academical year is divided into two semesters, the autumn semester from the 1st of September until the 15th of December, and the spring semester, from the 15th of January until the 1st of June. As all general instruction in Sweden is given at the expense of the State; so the university education is combined with no other expense for the students, than what is necessary for their stay at the university. The academical instruction is at the same time optional, so that a student attends whatever lectures he chooses. In order to be matriculated at the university, it is required to have gone through a complete pass-examination at one of the higher so-called elementary schools of the country, in the presence of special censors, appointed for the purpose (generally academical teachers). Some private school-establishments, have likewise obtained a similar dimissory privilege. Formerly, this so-called student's examination, was passed at the universities. Recently, ladies have likewise been permitted to pass the student's examination, and as students, to prepare for other examinations. In the spring term, 1875, there were three ladies matriculated as students at the University of Uppsala, where, in 1875, one took the degree of candidate of philosophy.

During the last twelve or thirteen years, the number of students has increased by upwards of 50 per cent. The number of *teachers* and *students*, in the spring term of 1875 was as follows:

UPPSALA.	FACULTY.				
	Theol.	Law.	Med.	Phil.	Total.
Professors	4	5	7	18	34
Adjuncts	3	2	5	17	27
Docents	3	2	2	36	43
Total	10	9	14	71	104
Students	332	142	151	855	1480

*At a prize-festival in Paris among several foreign singing associations, in 1867, the Uppsala Students' Choir took the highest prize.

LUND.	Theol	Law.	Med.	Phil.	Total.
Professors	4	4	5	16	29
Adjuncts	2	2	3	16	23
Docents	1	.....	1	15	17
Total	7	6	9	47	69
Students	112	54	44	313	523

Besides, among the number of teachers at each university, are also reckoned training-masters, namely, in music, drawing, gymnastics, and fencing, and at Uppsala, likewise in horsemanship. Among the officials, are included: librarians, vice-librarians, notaries, clerks, cashiers, treasurers, and amanuenses.

The professors and adjuncts of the theological faculty, draw their principal income from prebends. For the rest, the salary of a professor is 4,500 Kr., which, however, by an extra grant has been increased for the year 1875 to 5,400, and for 1876, to 6,000 Kr., (=$1,667 gold) and that of an adjunct from 2,000 to 2,5000 Kr., which, by an extra grant has been increased for the years 1874, 1875, and 1876, to from 2,400 to 3,000 Kr. The docents receive no salaries, but they have an income partly by stipends, and partly by private lessons which they may give.

There are for the students, and in certain cases also for the younger academical teachers, very considerable funds, which have been raised principally by donations which are managed partly by the Universities, partly by other authorities, and by the students themselves, (by their national unions). These funds are intended for scientific travels, and for the expense of living at the university. The requirements for the obtaining of these, vary very much, generally depending upon the directions of the testators; for instance, relationship to the testator, place of birth, pecuniary position, skill in certain subjects, etc. These funds in Uppsala number about 550, and in Lund about 200 and generally amount to from 100 to 200 Kr. annually; but for docents they may amount to 1,000 Kr., (=$278 gold) and for travelling to several thousand Kronor.

The universities themselves are very wealthy, especially Uppsala, which received among other things from King GUSTAF II. ADOLF upwards of 300 farms, and consequently receives annually about 200,000 Kr. (=$55,500 gold). The government grants for Uppsala are annually, according to the budget for 1876, about 290,000 Kr.; for Lund, according to the budget for 1876, the annual government grant amounts to about 150,000 Kr., or together 440,000 Kr., (= 111,000 gold), to which the salaries are to be added by the State for tithes, etc., that have been withdrawn, amounting to nearly 195,000 Kr., consequently in all, an expenditure by the State of 635,000 Kr. (=$176,000 gold.) At the end of the year 1872 the Uppsala Universiy took charge of 1,758,286 Kr., and Lund of 1,116,523 Kr., landed property not included.

[CLASS 302.] **Professional Schools.—Technical Schools.** Among the *lower* of these are: The Industrial School in Stockholm, five technical and Sunday schools, besides several smaller ones of the same sort, four technical elementary schools, and two lower mining schools, all of which have sprung up within the last twenty years, excepting the Industrial School, which was established in 1846.

The object of the *Industrial School in Stockholm* is to give instruction in such subjects as are necessary for the practising of such trades as require a higher degree of knowledge, and thus to promote the developement and improvement of Swedish industry and trade. The foundation must be theoretical, but the direction practical. The subjects of instruction are: Mathematics, technical and ornamental drawing, calligraphy, stump, lineal and free-hand drawing, engineering, common architecture, engraving, modelling, painting, the Swedish, French, English and German languages, natural philosophy, lithography, knowledge of goods, and book-keeping. The term of instruction lasts from the first of October to the first of May. The scholars are especially such as have already entered upon one of the industrial trades. Of that class 2,523 applied during the year of instruction 1874-1875, of whom 1,735 were males, and 788 females. The immediate management of the school devolves upon a director. At present the number of the head-masters is fifteen, and that of the assistant-teachers sixty. The annual grants of the State amount to 63,275 Kr. (=$17,576).

There are several schools for the instruction of such young men and women as have already commenced a trade. Among these are the so-called *Technical Sunday, and Evening Schools*, in Malmö, Norrköping, Örebro and Borås, in connection with the technical elementary schools of these towns, as well as the technical Sunday and afternoon school at Eskilstuna, which latter, besides the industrial school in Stockholm, is the only one of this kind which is supported by the State. The number of scholars in these schools has of late years amounted to upwards of 1,000 yearly. But besides these schools, there are a great many others with a similar object, which have been established and are supported by the communities, and by the assistance of private donations. To these belong in the first place, the school of the Industrial Society, at Göteborg, in which between 400 and 500 scholars are instructed.

In the *Technical Elementary Schools*, (in Malmö, Örebro, Borås and Norrköping) such as devote themselves to the industrial trades, receive a general theoretical and practical education, as complete as possible. The subjects of instruction are: Mathematics, lineal and free-hand-drawing, modelling, mechanics and mechanical technology, engine work, natural philosophy, chemistry, botany and zoology, languages, book-keeping and commercial science, and also in some of the schools history, geography, mineralogy, geology, singing, etc.

The course of instruction lasts three years. In the year 1873-1874 the number of scholars, who are divided into three divisions, excepting in Malmö, where there are only two, was in all 292. In Borås there is, in connection with the elementary school, a weaving school, which, in the year 1873 1874, was attended by sixteen scholars. The number of teachers in each school is from six to nine, of whom one is at the same time the director. The Government grants for all the technical elementary schools amount to 62,000 Kr., (=$17,200, gold), besides 3,800 Kr. (=$1,-050, gold), for the weaving school at Borås; and in addition to this, the communities provide localities free of expense.

The *Elementary Schools of Mining* at Filipstad and Falun are, properly speaking, private establishments, which are supported either by the Society of Miners or by the Iron-Masters Association (Jern Kontoret).

Higher Technical Schools are: The Polytechnical Institute at Stockholm, and the Chalmer Polytechnical School at Göteborg, the former of which was established, under the name of the Mechanical School, in 1798, and the latter in 1829, although the donation, by Mr. W. CHALMER, Councillor in the Court of Chancery, to which the school in reality owes its origin, was made as early as in 1811.

The object of the Royal *Polytechnical Institute* is to impart the requisite scientific education to such young men as wish to devote themselves to a technical branch of business. Besides, if requested by public authorities, it shall give an opinion on technical subjects and assist private individuals engaged in industrial business with advice and explanations. The subjects of instruction are: pure mathematics, geodesy and topography, theoretical and practical mechanics, descriptive geometry and practical physics, elementary chemistry, chemical and mechanical technology, mineralogy and geognosy, common architecture, the art of constructing roads and canals, and drawing, to which subjects were added, in 1869, mining, metallurgy and smelting when the practical *Mining School* which had existed at Falun since the year 1822 was incorporated into the institute.

The course lasts three years and it is divided into three classes. In the year 1875, the number of the regular scholars was 218, and that of the extra 52. The teachers consist of seven Professors, three Adjuncts, and seven other Teachers. The nearer supervision of the school is exercised by a superintendent under the title of chief director.

The annual government grant is 76,500 Kr. (=$21,250, gold).

The *Chalmer Polytechnical School*, at Göteborg, has the same object as the polytechnical institute, and also the same subjects of instruction, excepting those three belonging to the mining school. The course of instruction lasts three years. The teachers are: one Professor, who is at the same time the Principal, three Lecturers, and six other Teachers. The number of the instructed, partly scholars, partly auditors, for the year 1871-1872 was 149, of whom 35 were from Norway. The annual grant is 32,000 Kr. (=$8,890, gold). The school possesses a very considerable endowment.

All the school establishments for mining and industrial pursuits are entered in the budget estimates for the year 1876, with a Government grant of 291,500 Kr. (=$80,970, gold).

Agricultural Schools. Instruction in theoretical and practical agriculture is given in two higher *Agricultural Institutes* (Ultuna, not far from Uppsala, and Alnarp, near Lund,) and in twenty-seven *Lower Agricultural Schools.* The Ultuna Institute was opened in 1848, and the Alnarp in 1868. The oldest agricultural school was established in 1835, by EDWARD NONNEN, and now there is at least one in every Län (excepting in the Län of Uppsala, where, however, one of the institutes is situated). The agricultural institutes impart a higher scientific instruction to the so-called pupils, whereas the agricultural schools have in view the practical development of able agricultural workmen, but even to these, theoretical knowledge is given. At each of the two institutes there are four free scholarships and at each of the twenty-seven schools twelve free apprenticeships, which include board and lodging. Lower instruction, as in the schools, is likewise imparted at the institutes, in which there are in all fifty-two free places. In 1870 the number of scholars was sixty-three, and of apprentices sixty-one, at the institutes, and three hundred and sixty-seven at the schools.

These schools have contributed much to the development and improvement of agriculture, and they are looked upon with great favor by the public.

For instruction in the *Management of the Dairy*, there are two dairy-schools established, with allowances from the State, at Ultuna, and and at Berqvara, in the Län of Kronoberg, and, besides, instruction is imparted, at well-managed, private dairy establishments, to the dairy pupils that have been admitted by the Administrative Committee of the Royal Agricultural Academy. Instruction is also given in the *keeping of cattle*, the *culture of wool*, subordinate *branches of agriculture, etc.*, by persons who are paid by the State. There are also such persons for the *breeding of fish*, (for which, see Class 640).

In the budget for 1876 is entered a grant of 172,400 Kr. (=$47,800 gold), for the schools for agriculture and industrial pursuits, connected with farming.

Instruction in Foresting. With a view to the spreading, in Sweden, of a general knowledge of everything, relating to the cultivation and management of forests, as well as imparting the necessary insight in huntsmanship, and bringing up a staff of foresters and huntsmen, a special *Forest Institute* was established in Stockholm in 1828. This establishment has now a Director who likewise lectures on the principal branches belonging to the science of forests, one lecturer on the other branches of the science of forests and on mathematics, one on natural philosophy and hunting, and three teachers on secondary subjects. The course lasts two years. In the year 1875 there were twelve scholars at the institute.

For the training of able woodwards, there are in various places in the country, six lower schools —forest schools. Each of these is superintended by a teacher, who is aided in the practical exercises by a forester. The subjects of instruction are much the same as at the Forest Institute, though rather on a smaller scale. The course lasts one year. In 1873 there were at these, sixty-one scholars, and besides twelve at a special forest school supported by the State.

At all these schools the instruction is gratuitous.

For the *Military Schools*, see Class 345, and with regard to the *Nautical Schools*, Class 590.

Instruction in Medicine and Surgery. The *Royal Carolian Medico-Surgical Institute* at Stockholm, the origin of which may be traced as far back as the year 1667, shares with the medical faculties of the universities in perfecting the physicians, manages the principal part of the practical instruction, both in medicine and surgery, at the hospitals of the capital, and is also like the above-mentioned faculties, entitled to arrange about the practico-medical or medical licentiate's examination. The institute is placed under the superintendence of the Chancellor of the University at Uppsala, and the statutes of the university in so far as they can apply to the institute, are to be observed. The number of teachers are at present: eight Professors, five Extra Professors, five Adjuncts and four Docents. Besides the usual duties of instructing and examining the Professors of the institute, have also, (each in his speciality) when requested by the Medical Collegium, to answer questions and to pass opinions on scientific subjects. The number of scholars averages 100. The government grant for the year 1876 amounts to 79,850 Kr., (=$22,180, gold), to which is to be added 12,-280 Kr. (=$3,400, gold), as an extra grant on account of hard times. Their own fund amounts to 92,500 Kr. (=$25,690, gold).

The *Pharmaceutic Institute*, (in Stockholm) the object of which is to impart that knowledge which is necessary for properly practicing pharmacy. The number of students is from sixty to seventy.

Schools for Midwives in Stockholm, (established 1760), at Lund and Göteborg. The course lasts one year. The number of those that pass their examination is annually about 100.

The *Veterinary Institute in Stockholm*, (established 1821) and the *Veterinary School at Skara*, (established 1774) have for their object the training of veterinary surgeons and farriers; but in the latter establishment on a somewhat smaller scale, than in the former. The teachers at the Institute are; four Professors, one of whom is at the same time the Principal; one Lecturer, one Adjunct, and also Assistant Teachers, and one Instructing-Smith; at the veterinary School: two Lecturers, of whom one is the Principal, one Adjunct and one Instructing-Smith. The number of scholars is from fifty to sixty.

Among the medical branch-schools, may also in a certain measure be included the *Royal Central Gymnastic Institute* in Stockholm, established in 1813 by Professor P. H. LING, which has for its object the development of gymnastics in all its theoretical bearings. Also, to train teachers and doctors, partly to give practical instruction and exercise in all parts of gymnastics, as well as to treat such patients as it may be supposed, will be benefitted by gymnastics. The instruction and exercises, are divided into three divisions, the pedagogical, the military and the medical, with one head teacher, and one teacher for each division; besides, there are two female teachers and also extra male and female teachers. Among the head teachers, two are called Professors and one Director. The scholars are partly Officers in the army or navy, partly civilians. The course lasts two years, excepting for legitimate physicians. The number of scholars in 1871, were thirty-seven males and seven females: the institute was further made use of by 1,483 persons, mostly school children.

Instruction in the Fine Arts. The *Royal Academy of the Liberal Arts*, the object of which is to conduct the public instruction in the art of painting, sculpture and architecture, as well as in the other plastic arts. For that purpose there are appointed at the academy: seven Professors, four Vice-Professors, and eleven Teachers. The number of scholars in 1872 was: In the Schools

for Modelling and Antique work, . .	75
In the Architectural School, . . .	20
In the Preparatory School of Design, .	160

Or together 255, of whom twenty-three were females (in the schools for modelling and antique work).

The *Conservatory* connected with the Royal Academy of Music has two divisions, each with two classes. The higher division corresponds to a high school for music. Besides an inspector, the teachers in 1875 were five Professors, twelve Teachers and three Assistant Teachers. The number of scholars was 153, (81 males and 72 females) of whom seven were from abroad.

[CLASS 303.] *Institutions for the Instruction of the Blind, Deaf and Dumb.* See Class 300.

[CLASS 304–305.] **Libraries, etc.** The largest library in Sweden, is that of the University at *Uppsala*, with about 180,000 volumes, 8,000 manuscripts, etc.; the library of the University at *Lund*, contains upwards of 100,000 volumes; the Royal (National) library in *Stockholm* upwards of 150,000 volumes, besides 7,500 manuscripts, exclusive of duplicates and pamphlets; the library of the Academy of Sciences 40,000 volumes upon National History, that of the Carolian Medico-Surgical Institute, 20,000; of the Technological Institute, 15,000; of the Central Statistical Bureau 15,000 volumes. All the higer school establishments, and the provincial unions at the universities have libraries, among which some of those of the schools are very considerable. (Compare the Class 301.) Among a number of other collections of books partly public, partly private, the extensive collections at several of the large estates, where there are also some valuable collections of manuscripts, must not be forgotten.

The *State Paper Office*, (Riks-Arkiv in Stockholm) established in 1609, takes charge of all old records of the Kingdom, among which parchment documents from the period between the eleventh and fifteenth centuries, the registry-book of the Kingdom, (Riks-Registratur) (from the year 1523) as well as all modern State records which are delivered there.

[CLASS 306.] **Printing.** "By the liberty of the press is understood"—according to the Swedish law—"the privilege of publishing works, which is due to every Swede without his being beforehand interfered with, on the part of public authorities; and, further, that the publisher cannot afterwards be made responsible for the contents, excepting before a tribunal, and in no case punished, unless they be distinctly contrary to the law which is established for the preservation of public peace, without withholding public enlightenment."

The law of July 16th, 1812 (the fourth of the fundamental laws of the Kingdom) says, regarding the liberty of the press "that no censure shall precede the publication of any work; that no permission is required for the publication of works; that for the publication of newspapers and periodicals, it is only necessary to send notice to the Minister of State and Justice, and the application for permission is never refused unless the applicant has been condemned for an ignominious crime, or declared unworthy to appear as spokesman for another person before a Court of Justice, nor is permission required for the establishment of a printing office, it being sufficient to give notice thereof to the authorities; a printing office shall, however, be established either in a town or within a distance of one-half Swede mile (three English miles) from one; on every publication shall appear the name of the printer, the name of the place where printed, as well as the year."

The oldest book printed in Sweden ("Vita sive legenda cum miraculis Catharinæ") was printed in the year 1474, and another ("Dyalogus creaturarum moralizatus") in the year 1483, both in Stockholm, and by itinerant printers. Stockholm has in all probability, been in possession of a stationary *printing-office* since the year 1491. At that time letters of indulgence were printed, and also the first book published in 1495 in the Swedish language ("Aff dyäfvolsens frästilse." i. e. On the temptation of the devil.) This printing-office was, however, no longer standing after the year 1498. King Gustaf I, caused another to be established in Stockholm, in 1525, which became the organ of the reformation and the royal authority. The places in which the other oldest printing offices were established are: Wadstena Convent (1495), Uppsala (1510), Söderköping

(1523, removed to Malmö 1528,) Westerås (1621,) Strengnäs (1622,) Kalmar (1626, removed to Linköping 1636,) Nyköping (1645, removed to Göteborg 1650,) Lund (1663,) Visingsborg (on the island Visingsö in Lake Vetter) obtained printing-office in 1666, which was removed to Jönköping in 1688, and in 1707 the first printing office was established in Skara.

In the year 1740 there were in Sweden eighteen printing-offices, of which eight were in Stockholm; in 1840 there were seventy-four, of which nineteen were in Stockholm; in October, 1875, 151 printing-offices divided among seventy-six towns. Of these there are in Stockholm twenty-nine, at Göteborg ten, at Malmö eight, at Uppsala four, in four other towns three, in twenty two, and in forty-eight one printing-office. In these printing-offices are employed as *compositors* 666 journeymen, 472 apprentices and 146 women; as *pressmen*, 156 journeymen, 248 apprentices and 79 women, and as *other assistants* 234 men and 91 women, or in all 1,776 men and 316 women.

Eighty-nine of the printing-offices (of which twenty-three in Stockholm) have machine-presses, amounting in all to 194 (of which 102 in Stockholm.) Of these, nineteen have been manufactured in Sweden, eighty-seven in Denmark, sixty-four in Germany, fourteen in France, (most of them double presses for printing newspapers) and ten in England. In all, 210 hand-presses are used in the printing-offices, (of these, forty-eight in Stockholm) of which 145 were manufactured in Sweden, thirty-eight in Denmark, nineteen in Germany, seven in England, and one in France. Nine printing establishments have eleven "Universals," or "Excelsiors," twenty-three printing establishments (of which twelve in Stockholm) have thirty-three glazing apparatus, and seventeen printing establishments (of which eight in Stockholm) have twenty-four calander presses.

As motive power, thirty-one printing establishments (of which twenty two are in Stockholm) use thirty-four steam engines, two printing establishments caloric engines, two gas engines, one water-turbine and one water-wheel.

Among the productions that have issued from the printing-offices, the *newspapers* and *periodicals* here, as in other places, are especially conspicuous, and of which, in 1871 as many as 216 were published; of these, fifty-two in Stockholm. It is calculated that in the year 1872 the Swedish Post-office carried 8,300,000 copies of Swedish and 400,000 copies of foreign newspapers. Since that time newspaper reading has very much increased in the country. The official newspaper, "Post-och Inrikes-Tidringar" has this year (1876) had its 232d anniversary, and is consequently one of the oldest in the world.

The first *Type-foundry* was established in Sweden in 1737. At present there are two in Stockholm, one on a large scale (P. A. NORSTEDT & SONS) which employs nine foundry-engines, and one at Lund with seven engines.

Stereotyping, which was introduced in 1843, is carried on in connection with the foundry of types, but likewise by other printers. Apparatus for paper-stereotype instead of the common impressions on gypsum, have also been introduced. When greater accuracy is required, as for wood-engravings, etc., electrotyping is also used.

Machine-presses were comparatively early introduced in Sweden, namely, in 1829, (the same year as at Leipzic.) As early as in 1823 Mr. G. SCHEUTZ, of Stockholm, applied for a patent for a printing-press invented by him, "on which the pressure should be produced by means of a roller instead of the common pressing-screw." A press invented by GÖTREK, the book-seller, in the year 1829, and patented the following year, differed from those already known, in so far as an iron cylinder covered with felt was rolled to and fro over the form, instead of sliding the form under the cylinder, which idea is now used for proof-presses. This kind of machine was used in the years 1830--1833 for the printing of newspapers, but it was afterwards superseded. A Swedish mechanician by the name of HOLM, invented in

1840 a printing-press for which he got a patent in Sweden and in England, which is still used in several places, especially in England, and is known under the name of "Scandinavian press." About twenty years ago a mechanician named SAHLBERG, in Stockholm, began to manufacture machine-presses, partly after ZIGL'S model, partly after models of his own. These presses have been much used, not only in Sweden, but in Finland and Russia. Most of the steam-presses now used in Sweden are from EICKHOFF, in Copenhagen; but others of the same sort from KÖNIG & BAUER at Würtzburg, from MARINONI in Paris, etc. are also used.

Iron Hand-presses after the Stanhope-model were at first manufactured at Eskilstuna, by MUNKTELL, and by the above-mentioned SAHLBERG, by the latter on a large scale for Sweden as well as for Finland and Russia, besides several of the more modern presses are used in the country.

A *Numbering-machine* to be used in a common Stanhope press was constructed by BROLING for the printing of the notes for the Bank of the Realm, on the same principle as the self-acting numbering machines of the present time.

About thirty years ago a *Colour-manufactory* was established in Sweden for the printing-offices. At present there is only one of that sort in existence at Söderköping, established in 1870, which supplies very good inks for common printing.

INSTITUTIONS AND ORGANIZATIONS.

[CLASSES 310—311.] Among the establishments for a higher education, besides those mentioned in the previous section, the following **Academies** (all in Stockholm) and **Learned Societies** should be included.

The *Swedish Academy*, established in 1786, which, while developing and giving to the Swedish language definite form, has for its object the spreading and extolling of the glory and memory of the great men who have governed their native country and served and saved the same, as well as to sing to their praise; and thus, at the same time, to extend the glory of the Swedish name and the Swedish language. The number of the members shall always be *eighteen*.

The *Royal Academy of Sciences*, established in 1739, which has for its object the promotion of (physical) sciences. The number of the members are one hundred Swedes and seventy-five foreigners. Under their supervision is the national cabinet of Natural History (*Riks-Museum*, which is divided into six sections, with a superintendent for each, namely, for vertebrated and lower non-vertebrated animals, as well as entomological, paleontological, botanical and mineralogical sections. Besides, there are natural philosophers and other officiates for the observatory of the academy, (the Stockholm Observatory.)

The *Royal Academy of Belles Lettres, History and Antiquities*, founded in 1753 with fourteen honorary members, twenty active and sixteen foreign members, under the supervision of the academy are the National Museum of History and the Royal Academy of Medals, which are managed by a separate Board of Directors, but are kept in the building of the *National Museum* which is intended chiefly for the collections of paintings and sculptures.

The Royal Agricultural Academy, founded in 1811, with 1 Director, 24 honorary, 136 active and 75 foreign members. The academy possesses a so-called field for experiments (near Stockholm). The managing committee of the academy are commissioned, among other things, to have a supervision, next after the chief of the Royal Interior Department, over the agricultural schools in the country, as well as the stock-farms and dairies, belonging to the crown, together with the agricultural engineers, and farmers of the State.

The *Royal Academy of Liberal Arts*, founded in 1735 and intended for the careful direction and promotion of the development and progress of painting, sculpture, architecture and the other plastic arts in Sweden, has one President, ten honorary native members and forty native, as well as an unlimited number of foreign members, female artists and Agrès. A school is connected with the academy. (Compare class 302).

The *Royal Academy of Music*, founded in 1771 with 100 native members, twenty-five females at the most, and an unlimited number of foreign members. About the school of the academy and the conservatory, see class 302.

The Royal Military Academy, founded in 1796 with a view to the promotion of military science. The native members are divided into two classes; in the first are mostly generals, admirals and persons of the same rank, (at present about fifty,) and in the second 120 at the most. The number of foreign members is indefinite.

Besides the above-mentioned Stockholm *Observatory*, there are similar institutions at the two universities at Uppsala and Lund.

Among the learned societies may be mentioned:

The *Royal Society for the publishing of Manuscripts relating to the History of Scandinavia* (founded in 1817 in Stockholm); the *Royal Society of Sciences, at Uppsala* (the oldest scientific society in Sweden, founded in 1710); the *Royal Physiographic Society at Lund* (1778); the *Royal Society of Sciences and Belles Lettres at Göteborg* (1778); and the *Royal Naval Society at Karlskrona* (1771.)

Among these may also be mentioned the *Swedish Society for Ancient Documents*, the *Society of Swedish Physicians*, the *Society of Apothecaries*, the *Society of Gardeners*, the *Society for Native Culture of Silk-worms*, the *Pedagogical Society*, the *Society of Printers*, the *Society of Artists*, the *Society for Northern Arts*, the *Anthropological Society*, the *Mineralogical Society;* the above-mentioned (class 301) *professional unions at the universities*, etc., and, besides several museums, as that at Göteborg, Uddevalla, etc.

[CLASS 312.] **Museums.**—The largest of these is the *National Museum* in Stockholm, which, when the collections in the old so-called Royal Museum had increased so much, that a new locality had to be prepared, was built during the years 1845–1863 for a sum of $623,900 gold, and was ready for the reception of the collections in 1863. These consist partly of collections of works of art in statuary, painting and other objects, (vases, porcelain, ivory articles, mosaics, enamels, etc.,) partly of the historical museum and the cabinet of medals. The collections of art, both of ancient and modern masters, have been greatly increased in recent times by purchases and donations, principally from the members of the Royal Family and the late Lord Steward, Baron VON WAHRENDORFF, and thus the museum now possesses close upon 1,200 oil paintings, 70,000 engravings and sketches, 650 works of sculpture of marble and bronze, besides antique vases, stucco-works, Egyptian antiquities, etc.

The foundation of the Swedish Historical Museum, or the Museum of Antiquities was laid in the latter half of the seventeenth century. At that time, when Sweden had become one of the great powers in Europe, people of all classes applied themselves zealously to the study of antiquities; but in general they were falsely directed, and the result was, that the museum at last embraced principally curiosities. It is only in this century that they have commenced more diligently to collect curiosities found in Sweden, and not until the decennium 1830 to 1840 did they do so systematically, it is only since that time that they have made it their study to bring into the museum, not isolated objects, but rather whole series and rich groups. The collections of the museum are increased yearly by new discoveries, the number of which is continuously growing.

The *antiquities of the heathen times* in Sweden belong to three great periods of culture: the *Stone*, *Bronze*, and *Iron-Age*. The collections of antiquities belonging to the stone-age may be compared with the very largest in Europe.

Among the antiquities of the iron age, those which bear witness to the intercourse between Sweden and other European countries, during the heathenism of Sweden, which extends as far as the middle of the eleventh century, may especially be mentioned. First of all, we here find coins, ornaments, vessels, artistic objects of gold, silver, bronze, and glass, which are, unquestionably, of Roman origin, and belong to the three first centuries of Swedish heathenism. There are also strong proofs that the Constantinian empire, exerted a great influence upon remote Swedish, far upwards of a century, beginning before the close of the fourth.

In the fifth, and the beginning of the sixth century, commercial intercourse was carried on with the Byzantine Empire, which brought a number western and eastern Roman coins into the country, but which scarcely exercised any influence on the culture in the north. During the ninth and tenth centuries, the Swedes carried on a lively intercourse with the East.

Arabian silver, especially coins—about 30,000 have been found in Swedish soil—was brought to Sweden in large quantities. About the year 1000, the lively intercourse with the East ceased, and instead, a close union with Germany and England was formed. While Carolingian coins have only twice been found in Sweden; very large quantities of coins, from the times of the Saxon Emperors, and the last Anglo-Saxon Kings from EDGAR on have been discovered. No museum in Europe—the Russian perhaps excepted—can exhibit such a collection of non-classical objects of silver ornaments, as the national collection in Stockholm.

Two halls in the historical museum of the state, are appropriated for objects from the *Middle Ages*.

Even the first Swedish regents of modern times (after 1523), tried with greal zeal to exalt industry, to which, the circumstance, that Sweden was a refuge for protestants, exiled from other countries, contributed in no small degree. We can, therefore, follow Swedish industrial art from the beginning of *Modern Times*, until the present period, and two halls in the museum are appropriated for specimens thereof.

In the course of time more and more intimate connections were formed with foreign countries; the thirty years' war especially introduced into the country a great many costly ornamented articles. It is well known how rich were Queen CHRISTINA's lists, nevertheless, only a very small share has remained with the Swedish State; the greater portion she either gave away or took with her when she left Sweden.

A large collection of products of industrial art was made by the late King CARL XV and demised by will to the Swedish State.

During the last few years the foundation of two collections which have been laid, both in the capital at present, are private property, but later they will in all probability be delivered over to the State. The museum for Swedish national costumes and national ornaments (or Dr. A. HAZELIUS'S *Scandinavian Ethnographic Museum*) and the Swedish *Trades-union's Museum of Arts and Industry*, founded in 1872.

The two *Universities* of Sweden, and almost all the higher, as well as some of the lower, middle and *classical schools* have collections of antiquities. In some of them are also found objects of modern industrial art.

In the town of Göteborg a museum was opened in 1861, which has rapidly increased, and contains besides natural objects, also antiquities and modern industrial products. There is a similar one, though smaller, at *Uddevalla*.

In *Skokloster* castle, in Uppland, now in the possession of the Count BRAHE family, but formerly belonging to the Field-marshal Count, C. G. WRANGEL, a great number of objects of industrial art are preserved, of which a considerable part was collected by the Field-marshal during his campaigns.

Besides, there are several private individuals who possess large and small collections. The largest of them belongs to CHR. HAMMER, jeweller, in Stockholm.

The *National Cabinet of Natural History* (Riksmuseum) has been mentioned above.

[CLASS 313.] **Music and the Drama.** For *Dramatic Art* there are in Stockholm two national institutions, the so-called Royal theatres (the Great Theatre and the Dramatic Theatre). The Great Theatre was inaugurated as early as in 1782. These theatres receive annually from H. R. M., the King, $16,670 gold, and an equal sum from the public purse. There are several other theatres in Stockholm with stationary companies of performers; but in other towns of the Kingdom, theatrical representations are usually given for a longer or shorter period by travelling companies.

SCIENTIFIC AND PHILOSOPHICAL INSTRUMENTS AND METHODS.

[CLASSES 320–326]. The manufacture of **Mathematical Physical** and **Chemical Instruments,** is generally limited to practical wants and materials for instruction. Larger and more valuable instruments are occasionally imported.

Among the most noteworthy scientific instruments, not only invented, but constructed in Sweden, in recent times, may be reckoned the *Meteorographs* or *Register Apparatus*, which were constructed for meteorological observations, by the lately deceased Dr. A. G. THEORELL of Uppsala.

The registration is effected by attaching to each of the meteorological instruments, a metallic conductor, in such a manner that, on one side, it can be moved along the way which the index of the instrument describes, and, on the other, that it is so connected with the mechanism of the register itself, that the position of the metallic conductors, is accurately indicated, by the recording parts in this mechanism. It is then sufficient to move these parts, so that the conductor approaches the index of the instrument, and to take advantage of the contact for stopping a galvanic current, by the help of which, the movement is checked, so that the recording parts, may indicate the position of the index of the instrument.

This method is applicable for every phenomenon, the course of which can be indicated, by means oi a metallic index, which, by the way, is the case with most of the meteorological phenomena, that, at present, claim the attention of scientific men, such as the temperature, degree of moisture, and pressure of the air, and also its velocity and direction, and the quantity of rain and snow. In this registering apparatus, one of which has been used at the Uppsala observatory, since the year 1868, the recording is effected by means of steel points, which are pressed into paper by electro-magnets.

As the reading off, however, causes a daily recurring mechanical work, the observations are in the later constructions given in printed numeral tables. The parts which here are in connection with the metallic conductors are consequently a system of brass wheels with numeral types engraved on the edge. Further, the moving power, which, in the first meteorographs, consisted in gearings driven by weights, is here an electro-magnet, which is an advantage in so far, that the instrument is kept going of itself as long as the strength of the current is above a certain minimum, and the paper slip that receives the pressure lasts. During this time which may be easily extended to three months, providing the paper roll is carefully wound, and that the number of the observations are four per hour, the instrument ought to be self-regulatory, for the force that is at disposal is also sufficient for the winding of the clock that is necessary for determining the time of the observations.

In an example exhibited in the Vienna Observatory, galvanic conductors are employed, the consequence of which has been that the thermometers can be placed in the garden of the Observatory and the wind instruments (anemometers) on the roof of the tower, which is five stories high, while the register apparatus is placed on the ground floor in the tower.

Meteorologists agree that the meteorological phenomena in the Arctic regions are of great interest for science. It is seen how exceedingly difficult it is to obtain meteorological observations even in these parts of this severe climate, which are comparatively easily accessible, from what is already known of the history of the Swedish Polar expedition of 1872-1873. But a meteorograph of the construction in question would, as above stated, keep going of itself a whole year, providing the observations were limited to one every hour; and granting that several difficulties would oppose the realization of such a result, yet Dr. THEORELL was of opinion that these difficulties would be of such a nature that their removal would be only a question of money, and that the amount required would by no means be as great as that required for the annual wintering in, for instance, Spitzbergen or Beeren Island.

Of scientific instruments of practical value, it may suffice to mention the well-known *calculating machines* which have been constructed by the Engineers A. and E. SCHEUTZ (father and son), and by Dr. M. WIBERG. These instruments print of themselves the results which they calculate. The machine of Dr. WIBERG has lately calculated and printed complete logarithmical tables.

The same Dr. WIBERG, has also constructed a *letter-bag for the emptying of letter-boxes*, which is so contrived, that the lock of the one constitutes the key of the other, by which means, the letters are emptied out of the box, into the bag, without being in the reach of the person who does it. This invention which is used in Sweden, is besides sold both to Prussia and Austria.

For the purpose of measuring geometrical figures, J. P. LJUNGSTRÖM, the Engineer, has constructed a so-called *circular planimeter*, consisting in its most simple form of a circular plate of of glass, through the centre of which passes a vertical steel wheel, that ought to be placed at right angles to a radius which is etched in the pane and marked with a point. When in use, the plate of glass is brought along a rectilineal support (a ruler) so that said point accurately follows the border line of the figure once round. The reading is taken from the wheel which then is turned by friction towards the paper. The instrument measures figures of a width, equal to that of the whole ruler. If very large figures are to be measured (e. g. an ordinary map at once) the instrument is changed, first by a so-called "couple" into a kind of polar planimeter. The "couple" consists of a metal ring, which goes round the pane of glass, together with two legs, one of which is attached to the ring, and the other to the plate. The former moves about a fixed point, while a point marked on the other leg, is moved along the border-line of the figure. The reading off is in this case also done from the steel wheel.

A *distance telescope* (theodolite), with a self-registering scale of distances, has lately been invented, by the same Mr. LJUNGSTRÖM. The difference between this instrument and others of this class, is principally, that the instrument itself, effects all the calculations which otherwise are necessary in consequence of the inclined angles, and also that the distances sought, are immediately marked on the plane-table. The line of sight upon a levelling-staff having been taken by the telescope which is fixed on a ruler that lies on the plane-table, and can swing round on a fixed needle to a piece as large as the part read off on the levelling-staff, is marked on a movable scale on the instrument, upon which a knob being touched, the point of a needle marks the distance on the paper. The calculating operations are effected by the inclined movement of the telescope, which, by means of a curved line, places the scale at such angles to the vertical plane of the line of sight that the sine for these angles constitute the square cosine for the inclined angle of the telescope, and this sine is then projected towards the movable needle.

Among this group may also be reckoned the *air-telegraphs*, invented by Count P. A. SPARRE, (known in France under the name of Sonnerie télégraphique, système Sparre.) The principle is, that a compression of air produced by the pressure on a squeezing together of an India-rubber ball at the one end of a long tube (generally a leaden tube) is immediately transmitted to the other, and there signalizes. This mode of telegraphing is much used in hotels, manufactories, vessels, etc.

Concerning the *Electrical* and *Optical Telegraphing* in Sweden, see page 28; concerning *meteorological establishments*, page 8; *weights* and *measures*, page 20.

Watch and *Clock-making* is carried on partly in large workshops, for instance, in Stockholm, partly as a handicraft both in town and country. About 1000 persons, including upwards of 400 in the rural districts, are occupied in this industrial pursuit, among whom there are some women. Although in some of these shops, new watches are manufactured, such are mostly imported from Germany, Switzerland, and France, partly in the shape of ready-made pocket-watches, large time-pieces and table-clocks, partly, as parts of them without mountings. Steeple-clocks, for railway stations, and other large clocks, are manufactured in the country, chiefly in Stockholm. The skill of the country people in certain provinces is also shown in the manufacture of watches; the house clocks of Dalarne (Mora), for instance, are well known in the country, though not so much for a tasteful exterior as for an accurate motion. It seems, however, that the so-called Schwarzwald (or Dutch) clocks, are supplanting them.

The above-mentioned Dr. THEORELL, has constructed chronometers, the moving power of which, is electricity that draws a spring, which produces the actual impulse; and these time-pieces, therefore, differ from others, in so far that the accuracy of the motion, is altogether independent, of the strength of the current.

[CLASS 327.] Instrumental music being practised in pretty nearly every educated family in the country, it follows as a natural consequence, that the manufacture of the requisite instruments has attained a tolerably high degree of perfection. Swedish *Piano-fortes*, and also wind-instruments have, during the last few years, obtained a prominent place, even at the exhibitions, not only on account of their acoustical qualities, but also on account of their comparatively low price. Most Swedish makers of musical instruments are employed in the manufacture of piano-fortes, and though they perhaps produce from 500 to 600 annually, they do not by far supply the wants of the country, for from 200 to 300 are besides imported annually.

Organs are manufactured chiefly for churches, and in recent times, several valuable ones have been made and generally approved of.

The instrumental music of the country is usually limited to the performances on the *violin*, and in some provinces on the *clarionet*, to which, of late years, the German cabinet *harpsichord* has been added. The violin is especially a favorite instrument, and violin-playing is so generally practised, that in some parishes a violin will be found in almost every peasant's cottage, and probably not least so in Norrland. The manufacture of such instruments is therefore carried on in several places in the country, and though the number of the instruments made is not known, it cannot be small, granting that we know, that from 400 to 500, nay, as many as 1,000 are annually imported.

An ancient instrument, resembling the violin and peculiar to the Northern peasantry, is the

Swedish lyre (*nyckelharpan*), now, however, seldom heard, and almost only in the neighborhood of Uppsala. The tune is played with a bow, on one or two sinew or silk chords, on which the different tones are produced, by means of a key-board, that runs along the finger-board. Several metal strings, which are not touched, strengthen by their consonance the sound.

A peculiar kind of sound-instrument is the *herdsman's horn*, made of wood or birch bark, sometimes of tin-plate, which is used by the herdsmen in the mountainous parts of Dalarne and Norrland, for the purpose of calling the cattle or giving signals. This instrument, which is straight, from five to six feet in length, and without any openings on the sides, has a strong piercing tone, which, if produced by an experienced blower, affords a very agreeable modulation to the ear.

ENGINEERING, CHARTS AND GRAPHIC REPRESENTATIONS.

[CLASSES 330–332.] **Architecture and Civil-Engineering.** For the construction of public buildings and the keeping of them in repair, there are in Sweden three principal bureaus, namely, the Royal Board of Public Buildings, the Board of Roads and Water-works, and the Board for the building of State Railways. The first mentioned under the Royal Department of Finances, ande th two latter under the Royal Department of the Interior.

The Royal Board of Public Buildings (Öfver-Intendents-Embetet) has to draw up plans and make out estimates of buildings projected for the crown, to aid public authorities and communities with advice and explanations, and also, to examine the drawings of public buildings that are to be erected, and, if necessary, to draw new plans; to have the supervision over the houses and buildings belonging to the crown, and also to carry out similar architectural work.

The Royal Board for Roads and Water-works, attends to technical and administrative concerns relating to the construction and improvement of canals, sluices, roads and other means of communication by land and water, harbor-structures, and dredgings, cleansing of waters, and works for promoting great agricultural undertakings by means of draining boggy places and lakes. This board shall also control such works as are carried out by companies, public authorities, or private individuals, and with public money.

With regard to the management of public roads, and canals, and the supervision over buildings, belonging to them, the country is divided into five districts, each under its own chief, with his adjuncts.

These officials, as well as the chief of the board, belong to the corps for the construction of Public Roads and Water-works, and are put on a military footing, and consequently subject to be commanded, in time of war, to serve in the army as engineers. These, (excepting such Civil Engineers, as have passed their examinations, either at the Royal Polytechnical Institute, or at the Chalmer Technological School), constitute the proper corps for civil engineering in Sweden, and hence the officers belonging to the same, when not directly employed in the service of the State, are engaged as assistants in the construction of private railways, at private harbor-work, at water-works for supplying towns with water, etc. Some are even engaged in foreign service. The Corps is composed of one Colonel, one Lieutenant-Colonel, seven Majors, and, for the present, twenty-eight Captains, and thirty-two Lieutenants.

The Royal Board for the Building of State Railways, (Styrelsen öfver Statens Jernvägs-Byggnader), have, since the year 1863, the chief management of the constructions of the trunk-lines of the State-railways, which, when completed, are trafficked, and kept in repair, by the management of the Royal Board for the traffic, on the State-railways.

Buildings. Sweden is rich in building materials; there are abundant supplies of granite and gneiss everywhere for foundations; sandstone in several provinces; lime in every district, and also clay and sand, for the making of bricks; an almost unlimited supply of timber, besides iron, nails, slate, etc. The manner of using these materials may, in genaral, be said to be the same here as abroad; it is, however, natural that, in a woodland country, like Sweden, frame houses are more common than in such places where timber must be brought from other quarters at high prices.

The most common building material for private houses is timber in the rural districts (excepting in Skåne) and in the smaller towns. (Compare Class 342.) For public buildings, such as are erected by the State, bricks are generally used. Among such may be mentioned school-houses, hospitals, prisons, and railway-stations. Since the year 1843, when the first cell-prison was erected, nearly forty have been built, and most of them are noteworthy for their beauty. The railway station-houses, all of which have been erected within the last twenty years, are generally distinguished by great beauty and, in some cases, by great size (the Central Railway Station in Stockholm is 250 feet long). Some of the smaller station-houses as well as the watch-houses, some of which are frame structures, have been copied as models in the erection of private dwelling-houses and farm buildings. Such houses differ perceptibly from the old ones by their far projecting roofs, carved sash-frames and wooden wainscotings, etc.

The development of industrial life in the country has naturally engendered the want of suitable houses for the purpose. As an instance of what modern times, in that respect, has produced, may be mentioned the Karlsvik Manufactory for woollen fabrics, situated in the northwestern part of Stockholm. It was established in 1857, entirely after English pattern, and constructed of iron, stone and glass. The largest workshop, perhaps the largest hall in Sweden, consists of a single colossal room, with a floor-surface of 40,000 square feet, in which there is room for 147 looms. It is covered with a glass roof that rests on 121 hollow iron pillars, which at the same time answer the purpose of escape-pipes for rain and snow-water. In the well-known match manufactory at Jönköping, one of the massive houses contains a work-room that has a surface of 19,400 square feet. The largest building for industrial purposes in this day is doubtless Atlas machinery establishment in Stockholm.

The extent of the country and its development call too urgently for the construction of communications that it should not be heeded. The grants and loans of the State for this purpose have been both large and numerous, but without dwelling upon the efforts put forth by the State, which, in comparison to its means, have been unprecedented, as in the building of the Göta and Trollhätta canals, etc., we may mention that from 1855–71 the government built railroads to the amount of $29,450,000 gold, from 1840–72 it encouraged private enterprises in building railroads, turnpikes, canals, bridges and harbor improvements by grants and loans to the amount of $13,800,000 gold, and from 1872–76 it loaned for the construction of private railroads $2,780,000 gold. The efforts and sacrifices of the communities and individuals in this direction is scarcely to be computed.

We will now consider this important subject in its separate branches.

High Roads. The construction of public roads is a duty that falls upon the communities, assisted by the State: but the keeping of the roads in repair is a duty that falls upon the land-holder alone. The length of the public roads was in 1870, 5,332,035 Swedish miles, (56,995 Kilometres) of which 185,366 Swedish miles were "kungsvägar," (king's roads), namely, roads between towns and other places of importance for traffic. The length of the smaller roads leading to villages and private residences, of which each land-holder has to keep that portion which runs through his property in repair, is not ascertained.

We stated above (page 7) that there are so-called boulder-stone ridges. These contain in certain strata fine sand and gravel; the latter is very much sought and used for the construction of roads and the keeping of them in repair, and also for the terracing of railways. The "Krossgrus"-beds, also contains gravel, though not of such good quality as that in the boulder-stone ridges, and is therefore used almost only where the latter is wanting. In places where level sand-ridges run across an open tract, which is often the case, the high-roads also run along the top of them, or along one side, and consequently be high above the surrounding inhabited country.

It has become very common to have the roads macadamized, especially in Skåne.

In all the towns, and also on all the large high-roads, at distances of from one to two Swedish miles, there are "*skjutsstationer*" ("Gästgifvargårdar"—poststations, in the year 1870: 1524) where the traveller can obtain board and lodgings, as well as carriage and horses. The charge for each horse per Swedish mile, varies according to circumstances; in the towns 1 or 1.60 Kr., and in the country, 0.80 or 1.60 Kr., most frequently 1.60 Kr., to which is added 6 öre for carriage hire. The returns, as to the number of horses procured for "skjuts"—i. e., for forwarding travellers—are not exact; it may, however, be presumed that in the years 1856–1860, they amounted to nearly five millions, in 1861–1865 to a little above three millions, and in 1866–1870, to two millions. The decrease is owing to an extended communication by rail and water, and to the stage-coaches recently constructed for the post-office, by which travellers are also forwarded. Turnpike-toll is not charged, and bridge-toll only exceptionally; but ferriage is paid when the communication is across waters, by means of ferries.

Railways. The oldest railway for locomotives, in Sweden, is the railway which was intended to connect the lakes Mälar and Vener, or the so-called Köping-Hult Railway, which, however, in consequence of the dishonesty of foreign contractors and directors, has not been completed; only a part of it was opened for traffic on March 5th, 1856.

According to a resolution of the Diet of November 18th, 1854, the railways of the State, the so-called trunk-lines, are to be constructed and completed under the direct care, and at the expense of the State, and work commenced the following year, so that part of it could be opened for traffic in 1856; since that time new lines have been opened every year. Until the end of the year 1862, the chief management of the construction of the railways, as well as of the traffic on them, was in the hands of a single individual (Baron N. ERICSON), but afterwards it was divided between the present Royal Board, for building of State Railways, and the Royal Board for the traffic on the State Railways.*

The Trunk-lines, which together form a complete net-work, comprise the following parts:

The West trunk line, Stockholm—Göteborg, (length=42.6 Swedish miles.)

The South trunk-line: Falköping–Malmö (35.6.)

The North-west trunk-line: Laxå–Norwegian frontier (19.5.)

The East trunk-line: Katrineholm–Nässjö (20.1.)

The North trunk-line: Stockholm—northward (completed only as far as the Storvik station on the Gefle-Dala railway=20.4.)

To these are to be added:

The Junction line through Stockholm (0.3 Swedish miles.)

Branch line to the town of Södertelje (0.1.)

---

*The latter publishes annual reports: "Bidrag till Sveriges Officiela Statistik L. Statens jernvägstafik." (The traffic on the State railways): 1862–1873. These reports also contain reviews of the private railways.

Branch line between Hallsberg and Örebro (2.3.)

Branch line from Kil to Fryksta (0.3.)

The trunk lines thus far completed (September 1875) comprise a length of 141.2 Swedish miles (1,509 Kilom. or 938 English miles.)

By the northwest trunk-lines a connection has been established with Kristiania and the Norwegian railways, and a similar connection with Norway will also be gained by the northern trunk-line. This line runs northward through Norrland, then turns and passes through Jemtland to connect with a line which is now being constructed from Trondhiem, in Norway, by which lines, in connection with the Sundsvall—Torpshammar-line, a railway-communication is obtained right across the Scandinavian peninsula, from Sundsvall as far as Trondhiem. A third line of communication with Norway will be obtained by the Dalsland railway which is to be constructed, and put in connection with a Norwegian railway on one side, and with Swedish railways on the other.

Until the 1st of October, 1874, 148,050,000 Kr. (=$41,125,000 gold) had been paid for the construction of Swedish State-railways, of which 131,535,000 Kr. (=$36,537,500 gold) had been borrowed.

The average expense per mile constructed was in 1873: 959,385 Kr. (=127,598 francs per Kilom.*)

The State railways are so-called broad-gauged, or of the normal gauge (4.83 Swedish feet, or 1.435 mètres), with from 21.5 to 22.5 Swedish pounds' weight of rail per foot. There are three classes of carriages, and the prices in the mixed trains are, per Swedish mile, 0.75 Kr. for the first class, 0.55 for the second class, and 0.35 for the third class. In the express trains, in which, as a rule, there are no third class carriages, the prices are: first class, 0.90, and second class, 0.65 Kr.

For the construction of private railways the State has given considerable support as grants and loans, so that at the end of 1871 it had appropriated 14,000,000 Kr. (=$3,889,000 gold). Besides, the Diet, during the years 1872–1876, placed at the disposal of the government 10,000,000 Kr. (=$2,777,500 gold) for annual loans of 2,000,000 Kr. ($555,500 gold). The Diet of 1874 added to this 2,000,000 Kr. The private railways may be divided into two kinds, namely, such as are in connection with the State railways, and such as are not, but which are constructed for a certain traffic. The former (branch-railways) are generally of the same gauge as the State railways, the greater number of the latter, on the other hand, are narrow-gauged, but the rapid development of railway building in late years promises that soon all railways will be either directly or indirectly placed in connection with the main-line system.

Of late years, and especially since the end of 1871, *railway building* in Sweden has taken a great leap, mostly through the enterprise of private individuals, who have been supported by the State. This work has, in proportion to the resources of the State, assumed exceedingly large proportions. At the end of the year 1872 no less than twenty-two private railways, with a total length of 175 Swedish miles, were building. Of these some were already opened for part of the way, and most of them, it was supposed, would be ready within a few years, when the length of the Swedish railways would be at once doubled.

The following table shows how much of the private railways was complete in September, 1875. The lines are arranged in order from the South to the North, and the provinces in which they are situated at the same time specified.

*For the *technical details* of the construction of the State railways the reader is referred to the techno-economical description with illustrations, published by the Royal Board for the building of State railways.

PRIVATE RAILWAYS READY IN SEPTEMBER, 1875.

	Gauge* Sw. ft.	Length Sw. miles.
Malmö-Ystad (in Skåne). . .	4.83	5.9
Lund-Trelleborg (in Skåne) .	4.83	4.0
Ystad-Eslöf (in Skåne) . . .	4.83	7.1
Landskrona-Helsingborg-Eslöf (in Skåne).	4.83	5.6
Helsingborg-Hessleholm (in Skåne).	4.83	7.7
Kristianstad - Hessleholm (in Skåne).	4.83	2.8
Sölvesborg - Kristianstad (in Skåne).	3.59	2.9
Karlshamn-Vislanda (in Blekinge and Småland)	3.59	7.3
Karlskrona-Vexiö (in Blekinge and Småland)	4.83	10.6
Kalmar-Emmaboda (Småland).	4.83	5.3
Vexiö-Alvesta (Småland) . . .	4.83	1.7
Nässjö-Oskarshamn (Småland).	4.83	13.9
Ulricehamn-Vartofta (Westergötland)	3.00	3.5
Borås-Herrljunga (Westergötland)	4.10	3.9
Uddevalla--Wenersborg--Herrljunga (Bohuslän and Westergötland)	4.10	8.7
Lidköping-Skara-Stenstorp (in Westergötland)	3.00	4.7
Hjo-Stenstorp (Westergötland).	3.00	4.4
Mariestad-Moholm (Westergötland)	3.00	1.7
Åmmeberg (Nerike)	4.83	1.2
Halsberg-Motala-Mjölby (Nerike and Östergötland) . . .	4.83	9.0
Vadstena-Fogelsta (in Östergötland)	3.00	0.9
Pålsboda-Finspång (Nerike and Östergötland)	3.00	5.4
Åtvidaberg-Bersbo (Östergötland)	4.00	1.0
Östra-Wermland (Wermland).	4.83	6.4
Nora-Karlskoga (Nerike). . .	4.83	6.8
Vikern-Möckeln (Nerike). . .	2.70	5.1
Köping-Hult (or Köping-Örebro) (Nerike)	4.83	6.6
Nora-Ervalla (Nerike)	4.83	1.5
The Swedish Central Railway (or Frövi-Ludvika) (in Nerike-Westmanland)	4.83	9.2
Storå-Guldsmedshyttan (Westmanland)	4.83	0.5
Wessman-Barken (Westmanland)	4.00	1.7
Köping-Uttersberg (Westmanland)	3.59	3.4
Norberg (Westmanland) . . .	4.00	1.6
Krylbo-Norberg(Westmanland)	4.83	2.0
Skebo-Hollsta (Uppland). . .	3.00	1.1
Uppsala-Gefle (Uppland and Gestrikland).	4.83	12.2
Gefle-Dala—or Gefle-Falun (in Gestrikland and Dalarne). .	4.83	8.6
Marma-Sandarne(Helsingland)	4.83	1.0
Söderhamn (Helsingland). . .	4.10	1.4
Hudiksvall (Helsingland). . .	4.10	1.7
Sundsvall-Torpshammar (Medelpad)	3.59	5.6

*4.83 Swedish feet=1,435 metre; 4.10 feet=1,217 metre; 4.00 feet=1,188 metre; 3.59 feet=1,066 metre; 3.00 feet=0.890 metre; 2.70 feet=0.801 metre.

Together, these completed railways take up a length of 195.7 Swedish miles (=2091 Kilom. or 1299 English miles).

These long chains of railways, belonging to the State, as well as the private ones, are constantly increasing by continued building. A new state line, Karlsborg-Sköfde, of 4.1 Swedish miles, is being constructed, and the Northern trunk-line is about to be increased with 52 miles. Of the more noteworthy private lines, on which they are now diligently working, we will only mention that of Bergslagerna (Falun—Kil—Göteborg) of 49.1 Swedish miles; Halmstad—Nässjö of 16.0; Oxelösund—Flen—Westmanland 14.4; Stockholm—Westerås—Bergslagerna 18.4, etc. About 200 miles are consequently now being constructed.

A review of *all the Swedish railways*, September, 1875, is as follows:

COMPLETED.	Length. Swed. miles.	Kilometres
State Railways,	141.2	1,509
41 Private Railways,	195.6	2,091
Total Completed,	336.8	3,600
ABOUT TO BE COMPLETED.		
State Railways,	56.1	600
About 30 Private Railways,	200.0	2000
Total about to be completed,	256.0	2,600

In 1872, or scarcely four years ago, it was calculated that the total length of the railways which was then 1,893 Kilom., would, within a few years be doubled, and such a result has almost already been attained, inasmuch as we now possess more than 3,600 Kilom. (=2,237 English miles) of railway completed. This sum will average 830 Kilom. for every million inhabitants, which is probably a higher figure than can be shown by any other country. If the 2,600 Kilom (1,700 English miles) which are now being constructed be added, the whole sum, 6,200 Kilom., equally divided, will show the large figure of

1,430 Kilom. railway for every million of inhabitants in the country.

From the official railway statistics, the following figures are given for the year 1873:

	State Railways.	Private Railways.
Railways, number . . .	1	71
Length, Kilom.	1,381	710
Cost of construction per Kilom . . . . . . Kr.	89,757	54,417
Locomotives . . number.	138	86
Carriages	3,889	2,434
Travellers conveyed . .	2,557,543	1,475,694
Goods, Swedish centners.	28,239,527	45,873,728
RECEIPTS.	Kr.	Kr.
For passenger traffic . .	4,910,819	1,253,328
For freight traffic	6,637,286	4,277,714
For sundries.	161,483	127,347
Total.	11,709,588	5,658,389
Expenditure.	6,186,167	2,838,542

Only the most important of the private railways on which traffic was carried on in 1873 are included in the above review. The receipts of the State railways for the year 1874 amounted to 14,061,576 Kr. (=$3,350,450 gold).

Canals.* The construction of canals can be traced as far back as the beginning of the fifteenth century. It may, however, be taken for granted that in reality no canal provided with sluices was completed before the years 1596–1606, when a canal supplied with (probably three) wooden sluices, was constructed around the water-falls of the town of *Torshälla* for the purpose of placing the town of *Eskilstuna*, in communication with Lake Mälar. Of late years this canal has been re-dug, and the sluices rebuilt under the direction of Major A. GRAFSTRÖM, so that they now have a depth of 8½ Swedish feet, 24 feet in width at gates, and 140 feet in length. The lift is nearly 20 feet.

This stream, the so-called Eskilstuna River, forms the outlet of lake Hjelmar into lake Mälar, and presents a second fall of 5 feet at Eskilstuna, near lake Hjelmar, two-thirds Swedish miles or four and a half English miles, above the first, which is also passed by means of a canal.

The most noteworthy *canals* in Sweden are, the *Trollhätta* and *Göta canals* which together, with large intermediate lakes, form direct communication, from the Baltic to the Kattegat, 39 Swedish miles (417.9, or 25.9 English miles), in length.

The largest lake in Sweden, Wener, discharges its water mostly through the river Götaelf, into the Kattegat. This river, about seven Swedish miles, (46 English miles) long, is navigable, but is interrupted by several large water-falls. These are nearest to Lake Wener, the falls at Rånum, 19′ in height, the falls at Trollhätta, famous for their natural beauty, with a total height of 111′; and the smaller falls, at Stallbacka, Åkerström and Lilla Edet.

At the last mentioned place, the building of a sluice, was commenced almost simultaneously with the above mentioned canal at Thorshälla, and completed in 1607, but it has since been rebuilt several times. At that period, the digging of a canal past the falls at Rånum was also undertaken, and zealously patronized, by CARL IX. in honor of whom it still bears the name of *Carlsgraf.*

The bold idea of passing round the largest of the falls at Trollhätta, seems to have emanated from EMANUEL SWEDENBORG, the renowned seer and man of science, who drew to it the attention of CARL XII. and gained this high-minded king's approval. POLHEM was commissioned to draw up a plan for carrying out this grand undertaking, which was also completed during the lifetime of the king, but at his death the work ceased. It was not until the years 1793—1800, under the direction of E. NORDWALL that those works, which now have the name of *Trollhätta Canal* were quite completed, after plans previously drawn up by DANIEL THUNBERG. Although this canal with it sluices, still exists and is used, yet at the side of it another canal was construcled by Baron NILS ERICSON, during the years 1837—1844, which, with its 11 sluices of cut granite

*The following account of canals and harbors has been contributed by Mr. A. M. LINDGREN, captain in the corps for the construction of public roads and water-works.

presents one of the finest specimens of that kind of structure any where to be seen. The sluices are 120 feet in length, 10 feet in depth, and 24.5 feet wide between the gate posts.

The whole number of sluices that occur between Lake Wener and the Kattegat are 16, and the total difference of water from Lake Wener to the sea, 148.5 feet.

The *Göta Canal* connects Lake Wener with the Baltic, and the intermediate lakes, Wiken (the highest point of the canal, whose surface lies 308.2′ above the level of the sea), Wettern, Boren, Roxen and Asplången. Although diggings for this canal were commenced as early as in the 16th century, yet no work in earnest was undertaken until the beginning of this century, when the work was completed under the direction of Count BALTZAR BOGISLAUS VON PLATEN, during the years of 1810—1832, at a cost of 15½ million Kr., (=$4,300,000 gold). The plans which were followed during the work, though with great deviations, were worked out by the engineers DANIEL THUNBERG and THOMAS TELFORD.

The niveau of Lake Wener lies 160′ below that of Wiken. To get over this difference of level, 19 sluices were required. From Lake Wiken, on the other hand, the vessels are let down to the level of the Baltic, by means of 35 sluices. The artificial part of the canal is 8 Swed. miles, 7,100′, (54 Eng. m.), and the total length from Lake Wetter to the sea, is 17¾ Swed. miles, (118 Eng. m.)

The depth of the canal is 10′, the width of the bottom 36′ to 40′, the depth of the sluices 10′, the width between the gate-posts 24.5′, and the length between sill-miter locks 120′. There are 27 culverts, 34 bridges across the canal, and upwards of 20 places for loading and discharging.

Among the oldest of the canals in Sweden, is the *Hjelmare Canal*, which, with a total length of 1¼ Swedish miles, (8 Eng. m.), connects Lake Hjelmar and the river Arboga, which again flows into Lake Mälar. This canal was first constructed in the years 1629 to 1639, but it has since been re-constructed several times; the last time by the engineer J. EDSTRÖM, during the years 1821 to 1830. It has 9 locks, and one pair of dam-gates. The draught of water is 7′, and the sluices are 24 feet in the least width, and 120′ in length. The canal's total difference of level is 77′.

Among the canals of an older date may also be included the *Strömsholm Canal*, which connects Lake Borken and Lake Mälar, the latter situated 336,4′ lower than the former. By this canal, which was first constructed by J. ULFSTRÖM, during the years 1787 to 1795, a communication was opened with the mining districts in the interior, for a distance of nearly 9½ Swed. miles (63 Eng. m.) in length. It was re-constructed during the years 1842 to 1860, by J. KLEEN, and is supplied with 1 regulating sluice, 5 half-sluices, 25 locks which are 5 feet deep and 18 in width of gate, and from 70′ to 80′ in length, the greatest sinking of any of the sluices is 20′.

The *Kinda Canal* is to be considered as a branch of the Göta canal; it runs from Lake Roxen directly south, and has been brought into existence, by the canalization of the river Stång, by which stream, the lakes Rengen, Jernlunden and Åsunden discharge into Roxen. By this canalization, which was carried out by A. GRAFSTRÖM, during the years 1865–75, a connected water-passage of seven and a half Swedish miles (fifty English miles) in length, has been opened into the interior of the country. The difference between the water-level of Rengen and that of Roxen, is 176.4′, and fifteen lift-locks have been built for raising or lowering the vessels that height; the greatest fall at any of the locks is 16½′. The depth of the canal is 5′, and the least width of lock is 16½′; the length of the locks is 98′. The lowest of them, at Linköping, has the same dimensions as the locks of the Göta canal, and besides form the inlet to a spacious harbor-basin. The cost of the canal was 1,493,000 Kr. (=$360,-000 gold.

The *Dalsland Canal*, was constructed during the years 1864–68, by Baron N. ERICSON, at a cost of 1,365,000 Kr. It connects the large and elongated lakes, Stora Lee and Lelången, &c., and the Lake Silen not only with one another, but with Lake Wener, so that by this work a connected navigable passage, of 23¾ Swedish miles (158 English miles) across the frontier of the Kingdom, and into Norway, has been opened. The total lift of the canal is 200′. The number of sluices is 25, or 28, if the branch canals to Silen, and at Snäcke to Ånimmen be included; their depth is 5.5′, the width of gate 14′, and the length 100′.

The *Södertelje Canal* joins Lake Mälar with the Baltic at the town of Södertelje. The total length of the canal is 17,068′ (3 English miles), of which 6,475 are dug through a gravel ridge, which, in some places, is as much as 100′ high. There is but one sluice, with 10.8′ of water at the lowest level of the Baltic, and 12′ at the lowest of lake Mälar. Its least width is 29′ and the length is 140′. The canal was completed during the years 1806-1819.

The *Sluice of Söderström* in Stockholm, likewise joins Lake Mälar with the Baltic. This sluice is 12′ deep below the lowest water-surface of the Baltic, and 13′ deep below that of Lake Mälar; it is 32′ broad and 152′ long.

Besides, there are canals in connection with sluices, at *Forshaga* (the river Klar-elf), *Karlstad* (the same river), *Seffle* (the mouth of the river Byelf) which canals are connected with Lake Wener; *Filipstad-Sjöändan Canal* (between the lakes Daglösen, Aspen, and Lungen) in Vermland; *Hörken Canal* between two lakes named Hörken, and the canal at *Knopfors*, both in Nerike; *Åker Canal* in Uppland; *Tamm's* or *Dellen Canal*, between the lakes Dellen in Helsingland, and the *Medelpad Canal* between the lakes Stöde and Refsund as far as Pilgrimstad in Jemtland.

To these are to be added ten canals dug *without* sluices, so that the whole number of canals in Sweden is 28.

With regard to the construction of the sluices, it is worth remarking that it, in most cases, corresponds with that of the sluices of the Trollhätta, and the Göta canal, the sluices being built of blocks of granite, sandstone, or limestone, and cemented together, either with Portland cement or other sorts of cement from Berg, Fålhagen, and other places in Sweden.

Hollow quoins, gate chambers, and sills are generally made of well cut granite, and the sluice-chambers and bottoms of rough-cast square stones as they have been blasted. At some places, as for instance at the sluices of Tannefors, in the Kinda Canal, there are to be seen not only lift-walls, but clap sills, cut out in the rock itself.

It has generally been preferred to construct the sluices on a basement of rock; very few rest on an artificial foundation, which, in that case, usually consists of piles or beams. The whole of the sluice in Stockholm has been built in a caisson, the bottom of which, now constituting the support of the sluice, rests partly on piles, partly on a firm natural foundation.

At present there are only two sluices in Sweden that have been built of *timber*, namely, the sluice at Eskilstuna, and the upper sluices of the Snäcke canal, between the lakes Ånimmen and Ärren.

At the construction of the sluices of the Dalsland canal, they tried for the sake of economy to build the side-walls without the use of mortar or cement, but which have been tightened by means of clay-walls carefully constructed behind them. This is also the only elevated-canal (kanalbro) in Sweden. At Hofverud it has been carried across the falls, by means of a bridge made of iron-plates, which rests on basements of granite masonry, and has a span of 110′.

The larger among the old sluices, and especially the more recent ones, are conspicuous not only for a careful and durable mode of construction, but for pleasing and tasteful forms, the sluice-chambers generally presenting curved lines in both the horizontal and in the transverse sections.

The traffic on the canals in 1873; was as follows:

CANALS.	Sailing Vessels and Boats.	Steam Vessels.	Traffic-Receipts.
	No.	No.	Kr.
Trollhatta,	4,867	2,290	327,224
Göta,	2,873	1,617	212,694
Kinda,	973	1,007	28,563
Södertelje,	1,926	1,789	34,695
The Stockholm Sluice,	9,374	1,730	45,261
Strömsholm,	3,572	912	142,176
Eskilstuna, (2 canals),	288	999	15,326
Hjelmare,	398	134	15,115
Dalsland,	2,298	1,261	43,220
Seffle,	715	131	15,802
Forshaga,	926	....	23,869
Filipstad Bergslag's	2,553	1,165	24,582
P. A. Tamm's,	8,421	2,461	6,989
Norrsback,	3,526	1,829	4,685
13 other canals,	6,347	5,564	13,555
In all 28 Canals,	49,057	22,889	953,356

Harbours. Our country, as is known, is by nature supplied with many large and small harbours, of which some have not required any improvements at all, to make them answer their purposes, whereas on others, large amounts of capital have been spent for their improvement and supplying them with such structures as are required for the convenience of an extended commerce; comparatively speaking, however, the object has been attained without spending such large sums as they have done abroad. The imperceptible tides on our coasts, give to our harbours quite a different character from such as are situated on coasts where they are greater. The proper harbour basins, therefore, need not be shut off from the outer roadsteads by means of entrance sluices, which is necessary, for instance, on the coasts of England and Holland, so that the harbours are *always* open to vessels going or coming

The same character that belongs to our harbours along the coast-line, also belongs to our numerous harbours in the interior, along the shores of the large lakes Wener, Wetter, Malar, etc. There are only two harbours in the country that have basins that are shut off by sluices, namely, the Linköping harbour at Nyquarn, and the harbour at Karlstad.

With regard to their object, the greater number of them are commercial harbours. Separate harbours for the wants of the Navy, with various establishments belonging to them, have been arranged at Karlskrona and at Skeppsholmen in Stockholm.

During the years 1840—1872 supports to the amount of 4,203,122 Kr. (=$1,167,534 gold) were given out of the public purse, as grants and loans for the building or improving 48 separate harbours, which have been constructed by private communities, which have also contributed large sums of money.

The principal outer commercial harbours in the country are Hernösand, Gefle, Stockholm, Norrköping, Westervik, Kalmar, Karlskrona, Simbrishamn, Ystad, Malmö, Helsingborg, Varberg, Göteborg, Uddevalla, and besides almost every coast town has a harbour of its own, more or less conveniently arranged. In Gottland, besides at Visby, there are harbours at Sandhamn Slitö, and other places; in Öland there are the harbours of Borgholm, Mörbylånga, Färjestaden, etc.

Along the shores of Lake Wener there are the harbours of Wenersborg, Åmål, Mariestad, Lidköping, Karlstad, Kristinehamn, etc.; at Lake Wetter, Askersund, Motala, Vadstena, Grenna, Jönköping, Hjo, etc., and besides a harbour is to be constructed at Karlsborg. Along the shores of Lake Mälar, besides at Stockholm, there are harbours at Vesterås, Köping, Arboga, and Strengnäs.

The piers of the harbours are generally constructed of blocks of granite and gneis (exceptionally of limestone), which rest on a lower bed, the skeleton of which generally consists of timbered wooden cases, which are filled and surrounded with stones. The waters of our coasts being generally free from the sea-worm which elsewhere is so destructive to timber, it has been possible to apply this mode of building without incurring any inconvenience. In places, where the bottom has not been to depend upon, beddings of fascines have been used.

There are *Wharfs* for ship building at most of the harbours in the kingdom, and besides at numerous places along the coasts, where the inhabitants frequently carry on ship-building as a branch industry, together with agriculture.

Dry-Docks, with mechanical workshops belonging to them, for the repairing of vessels have been constructed at Göteborg, Malmö, Karlskrona, (6 in number), Norrköping, and Stockholm (2). Besides, there are 3 at Göta Canal, namely, at Söderköping, Motala, and Sjötorp, and also one at the Hjelmare Canal. A new dock (300 feet in length) has been decided upon to be built at Djurgården, near Stockholm, for the use of the R. Navy.

Most of our docks have been blasted in the rock, and they are supplied with gate-posts and entrance walls of square blocks of granite. The Malmö dock, which has been built in a place very unsuitable for such a structure, was constructed altogether in a timbered caisson. Col. C. J. BEIJER carried out the difficult work.

The oldest of all the dry-docks in the country was constructed in Karlskrona, by POLHEM, and the other five docks that are there, have been built since 1755 by DANIEL THUNBERG.

The docks at Karlskrona have the following dimensions, namely the old repairing dock, 250 feet in length, the gate opening 52 feet, and 17 feet in depth; the five new docks from 220 to 290 feet in length, from 51½ to 52 feet in width and 20 feet in depth.

The Malmö dock is 200′ in length 34′ in width at the entaance and 12.5′ deep.

The Stockholm dock, is 250′ long, 50′ broad and 14′ deep. All the depths are reckoned below the lowest water surface.

Excepting the Malmö and Oskarshamn docks, which are shut by means of floating-gates, the rest are supplied with double entrance-gates.

Slips for the convenience of navigation, have latterly been arranged in various parts of the country, as for instance, at Göteborg, Kalmar, Stockholm, etc.

[CLASS 333.] **Military Engineering.** See Cl. 345.

[CLASS 334.] **Naval Engineering.** Of canals, harbours, docks, etc., an account has been given above. Concerning coast-lights, pilot-establishments and life-boats, see class 590 in which a general rewiew of the Swedish Merchant fleet occurs. About the R. Navy, information will be given under Class 345.

CLASS 235.] **Maps.** The making of various charts and maps, geometrical, geographical, &c., was originally entrusted to the "Landtmätare" (landsurveyors), but their office has since been limited to the measuring and mapping of landed property, corresponding very nearly to what is known in other countries under the name of the Bureau of Cadastre. BURÆUS, the first director, was commissioned as early as 1628. One of the most common duties of the surveyor, is the legal sub-division of the land (*laga skifte*,) especially of that belonging to larger villages, where it has been divided into small lots, owing to the growth of the village; but, it has afterwards been found to be more advantageous, to unite these into larger or even into a single lot. After these lots have been measured and adjusted, they are portioned to the inhabitants; and it sometimes happens that some of them have to leave the village, and erect their houses on the lots assigned them. In this manner a village of five, ten or fifteen households is sometimes almost entirely dissipated. A pleasant village of twenty or more households is an exception. The law authorizes any petty land-holder to call in the assistance of the surveyor for a new adjustment of the land, and perhaps the disjoining of a whole village. This important law dates from 1827.

The extensive sub-division of land in Dalarne, has given rise to a special kind of "legal division," the *storskifte*, or great division. Another duty of the land measurer, is the *afvittring* or limitation of land, the principal object of which is to separate private property, especially forests, from that of the crown, and to divide latter into settlements. This work is now nearly completed in all the provinces, except Lappland.

Of the maps designed by the land-measurer, as well as of the description of the lands, three copies are generally made out, of which one is kept by the land holder, one (the original) is deposited in the land-measuring office of each province, and the third in the general land-measuring office in Stockholm. As stated above, these maps correspond in certain respects to the cadastreal maps abroad, or Doomsday-book in England. They are not published, and their scale is usually 1-4000, though the scales 1-2000 and 11-000 are also authorized.

The corps of land-surveyors, at the head of which is a director-general, is at present composed of about 600 persons, distributed among the different Läns, or provinces. It is to them a landed proprietor has to apply, if he wants any land on his estate measured, but he has to defray all the consequent expenses. Thus, about 700,000 Kr. (about $200,000) are annually expended by the Swedish land-holders, independent of the expense of procuring hands to assist. The annual grant of the State, for the whole land-surveying staff, amounts to nearly 300,000 Kr., ($83,300 gold) so that the total expense amounts to at least one million Kr. per annum. It must, however, be admitted that these sums have been well employed. Few measures have advanced Swedish agriculture more than these "laga skiften," which have caused a general improvement of the land. It is at the same time to be remembered that the greater part of the Swedish land belongs to the peasantry, and that their tillages are comparatively small, considering the extent of the arable land they possess.

The economical surveying of Sweden. For the geographical survey of the Swedish country parishes, which formerly appertained to the Central Land-measuring Office, a special office called *Rikets Ekonomiska Kartverk* (the office of the economic survey of Sweden), was instituted in 1859, with the object of obtaining an accurate knowledge of the area of the country, and of its natural divisions, from an economical point of view.

This office is divided into two departments, namely, the general, for the country in general, and one specially for Norrbotten, which, comprehending the most northern part of the country, requires, on account of its vast extension and imperfect cultivation, a separate management.

The maps of the former department are on the scale of 1:20,000. They are formed by means of connecting geodetical maps, according to the fixed position of triangular. It is, however, to be remarked, that the whole of the triangulation is done by commissioned officers of the topographical corps.

The maps of Norrbotten, which have also topographical object, are made partly on a scale of 1:20,000 and partly on one of 1:50,000, the latter being especially used for Lappland. This is the first time that the proper topographical maps of this remote region have been made.

The districts where cartographic surveys have hitherto been made, are the middle of Sweden, (the part measured between 1860 and 1871: 235 Swedish square miles=78,255 Eng. square miles), and part of the province of Norrbotten (820 Swedish square miles=27,350 Eng. sq. miles) Lithographic maps have been published of the Läns of Uppsala and Örebro, of some parts of the Läns of Kopparberg and Stockholm (the country district), of part of Östergötland (on the scale of 1:50,000), and of several districts of Norrbotten, (on a scale of 1:100,000). From these cartographic leaves 36 district maps of the middle of the country, and 5 of Norrbotten districts have been published. Although the surveys for these maps are continued at the expense of the state, the publication of them will depend upon the communities and private individuals, who will have to defray the expenses. The grant in the budget for 1876 is 87,000 Kr., (=$24,270 gold) of which 30,000 Kr. is for Norrbotten. The persons employed for the work consist of 19 cartographers and 18 assistant-designers, of whom 8 are females, and besides, 2 staff-officers commanded.

The office of the Economical Cartography of Sweden had one time a director of its own, and at another it was superintended by the Director of the Central Land-Measuring Office, while the Cartographic Department for the Län of Norrbotten has been under the supervision of the Governor of that province. Since the year 1873 both the offices have been under the management ot the Staff General of the topographic division.

Topographical Maps. As early as the beginning of the 17th Century, as stated above, cartography was inaugurated in Sweden, at the expense of the state, by the agency of the Land-measuring Office, which was established at that period, and instructed to draw up not only geographical maps of the main land and waters of Sweden, but also the so-called geometrical maps of more limited districts, in order to secure the right of posession, and for the settling of disputes among neighbors, with the ownership of land. The office performed the first part of its duty, by publishing maps of the whole country, as well as several of its districts, but within a short time the geometrical maps, absorbed the whole attention of the office, which ceased the publication of geographical maps, in 1789.

The work of the Land-measuring Office, in the latter direction, was continued by a private individual, Baron S. G. HERMELIN, (ob. 1820), of maps, engraved on copper, not only of all the provinces of Sweden, but of Finland. This atlas, together with all the plates, has been bought by the state, and several of the maps are still published, from time to time, under the direction of the topographical division of the Staff-General.

A complete atlas for the whole kingdom, was, however, not completed until the year 1805, when the "*Fältmätnings Corps*" (Military Corps of Topographic Engineers), was organized. This corps, which, in 1838, received the name of "*Topografiska Corpsen*," (the Topograghic Corps), was commissioned to prepare a complete topographic map of the country. Since the beginning of the year 1874, this corps has been joined to the Staff General.

The *method of projection* is that called the increasing conical; it gives to the space, providing it is not too large, an absolutely correct shape, an advantage obtained by allowing the scale to *increase*, not only towards the north, but the south, proceeding from the middle parallel. The meridians are indicated by straight lines, and the parallels by concentric circles. The cone, by the development of which the surface of the maps is obtained, cuts the terrestrial spheroid along two parallels, 56° 57′ 31.5″ and 64° 22′ 56.5″, by which the error of projection is equal to zero (0). The greatest error of projection amounts to 0.0021; it occurs at the frontier, latituded to the north and south, 65° 50′ 20.4″ and 55° 21′ 19.4″, and also at the latitude which is equal to half the number of the degress of the conical angle, or 60° 44′ 29.6″. The meridian which passes at 5 degrees to the west of the observatory of Stockholm, and which, likewise, coincides correctly enough with the middle meridian of the Scandinavian peninsula is adopted as the principal meridian.

A triangulation of the first order, surrounds the coasts of the south and middle of Sweden; it is connected with other triangular claims, executed with the same care along the meridians, as well as the parallels. By triangulation of the second and third order, between and within the chains of the principal triangulation, a number of points sufficient for the atlas, have been obtained in the southern parts, but not yet in the northern. But, inasmuch as the southern and central parts of Sweden, will soon be completely triangulated, the geodesical operations in the north may be protected with greater vigor. The officials of the Hydrographic office, have already commenced their surveys by a triangulation, extending from that of the Russian-Scandinavian measurement of degrees, in the vicinity of Haparanda, along the western coast of the Gulf of Bothnia. This work will be continued by the united efforts of the officials of the Hydrographic Office and the Topographical Division of the Staff-General.

The Stockholm observatory is the initial point of the whole Swedish primary system. Besides, the observatory of the University of Lund, has been connected with the primary system, by a special triangulation, under the supervision of the Academy of Science, in Stockholm. Further, for the sake of control, the polar altitude has been ascertained at different times, at several trigonometrical points; the position of the net is fixed by azimuthal determinations of one of the sides of the triangle, extending from the Stockholm Observatory, and of several other points of the system. Of the *bases*, determining the length of the sides, only six may be considered as being equal to the demands of the present times, with regard to exactness. Of these lines, one was measured in 1840, by the former topographic corps, by means of a BESSEL'S Apparatus, three in 1863, by the Academy of Science, for the European measurement of the meridian, with an apparatus of STRUVE (slightly modified), and two during the years 1870–73, by the topographic corps, with the above-mentioned apparatus, borrowed from the Academy of Science. Besides, there are three bases of an older date, measured on the ice by means of an older apparatus.

During the last two decennaries, a beginning has been made for a complete *hypsometrical* measuring. This measurement is effected partly by the topographic division of the Staff General, and partly by the Commissioners of the Geological Surveys. The work of these two bodies is done on the same plan, and in connection with each other. The measuring is effected by means of levelling the standard, being the average height of water in the Kattegat and the Baltic, such as it has been found to be during a long series of years, by hydrographic observations made from the light-houses. Level-lines have been brought across the country, from sea to sea, in several places. The general direction of these lines is from east to west, and they are intersected by other lines, running north and south. From these principal and controlling lines proceed detailed levellings, by means of which the number of points necessary for the map are determined. Besides, in later years trigonometrical levelling has been combined with the triangulated surveying.

The *scales* of the different maps are: for the general map 1:1,000,000; for the maps of the provinces 1:200,000; for the special maps 1:100,000; for the original maps (sketch on the field) 1:50,000. For special maps of certain positions and localities, is used a scale of 1:20,000, or 1:10,000, and even larger, according to the object of the map.

The special map (or 1:100,000) is divided into rectangular leaves of two Swedish feet (594 m. m.), by 1½ (445 m. m.) The leaves, of which the sides are either parallel or perpendicular to the principal meridian, are numbered in Roman figures to the west and east of this meridian; with Arabic figures from the north to the south, from the perpendicular of the meridian at 72° Lat. N. The maps to the east of the principal meridian are marked with the letter Ö (Öster=east), and those to the west with the letter W (Wester=west); thus, Stockholm, for instance, is situated on the map V. Ö. 32 (five east, No. 32), each map receives its name from a town, or some other locality of importance, situated on the same.

As stated above, copies of all the geometrical maps are kept at the general land-measuring office in Stockholm, and the originals are preserved in special archives in the respective provinces. These maps, on account of their number and the large scale on which they are drawn up afford a medium of facilitating the military cartography of the country, which it would have been wrong to neglect. And accordingly, since the year 1812, a system of cartographic sketching, or groundwork (*stom-kartor*), has been introduced, to which all the geometrical maps, which have not been considered unfit for use on account of their age, or for other reasons, have been transferred, on the scale adopted for the military maps. In districts of which there have been no suitable maps, measurements of certain lengths have been made and incorporated into the ground-work by the aid of the trigonometrical points. Surveys in the field have then been made on copies of this ground-work.

Such has been, and still is, to a certain degree the mode of proceeding for the composition of maps. Henceforth it will be different, since the economical surveying of Sweden has been placed (in 1853), under the management of the topographic division of the Staff-General. This staff, making use of their determination of places, and with the same mode of projection, is drawing a general map of the middle and southern portion of Sweden, on the scale of 1:20,000. In those districts, where the operations of the Office of the Economical Surveying, precede the military surveys on the scale of 1:50,000, the maps of the Economic Surveying, will be reduced to that scale, and the topographic surveys effected on a copy of these reductions.

The surveys for the military atlas, were at first made on the scale of 1:100,000, on which the whole of the coast-district, and a great part of the middle of Sweden, or the whole district of the large lakes Vener, Vetter, Hjelmar, and Mālar, or together a territory of 1,500 Swed. sq. miles, (66,000 Eng. sq. miles). This work showed the difficulty of producing a sufficiently exact and complete map of a country, with a surface so intersected as that of Sweden, unless the surveys were made on a larger scale. In 1844 the scale of 1:50,000 was adopted, which has been in use since that time, and on which, in the south of Sweden, and area of about 25,000 Eng. sq. miles has been surveyed. The topographical surveys, executed by divisions of 10 to 12 officers, under the command of a staff-officer, are performed with all the exactness that the adopted scale will admit. The slopes are determined by means of a small leveling instrument, and transferred to the map after the shading scale. The above stated measurement of heights have not yet advanced sufficiently far, to precede and serve as a direction for the topographic operations. Wherever these measurement have taken place, the heights are inscribed on the original maps, to the number of from 20 to 25 points per square mile, and afterwards their absolute altitude. The maps are then reduced to the scale of 1:1000,900 to serve for the engraver. Simultaneously with the survey, a topographic, military, and statistic description of the district delineated is prepared.

Previous to the year 1857, the *map* on the scale of 1:100,000 was kept secret. At first there were only hand-made copies of it; but in 1826 it was ordered to be engraved, and the engraving to be executed by the officers of the corps, who on their official oath were responsible for the secret keeping of the map, both before and after its completion. The engraving was done on copper, and, with the exception of the names, by etching. In 1857, when the King, at the request of the commander of the topographic corps, permitted the publishing of the above-mentioned maps, 20 maps were found to be too old for publishing, and 11 were not published until corrected after a previous survey. The engraving of the more recent maps, have been executed with the burin by artists, of whom some have been permanently attached to the corps, and others have done piecework. Since 1857, 36 leaves have been engraved in this manner.*

Since 1832, it has been incumbent upon the topographic corps, in proportion to the progress of the military atlas, and by making use of the materials of the same, to publish maps of the Swedish Lāns, on the scale of 1:200,000, accompanied with statistical descriptions. Of this atlas, 15 maps, including 10 Lāns, have been engraved on copper with the burin. In 1872, the king ordered that this special publication should be postponed until further notice. Since the year 1865, the general map on the scale of 1.100,000 has been in hand. It is to be published in 3 leaves, of which one is already completed, and one is being engraved.

Further, the topographic division is occupied

*In future, the staff-general intends, as soon as practicable, to substitute for the copper-engraving the heliographic method invented by MARIOT, which has been purchased by the Swedish state.

in drawing up military maps on a larger scale, for the purpose of exhibiting strategetic points of importance. These are kept secret.

An annual grant of $28,000 gold, reckoned from the beginning of the year 1875, has been assigned in the budget, for the topographic work of the staff-general, exclusive of salaries of staff-officers, who are employed in topography, The income from the same purpose.

In later years, *private individuals*, have likewise been very active in tartographic work.

Major A. HAHR, by applying the surveys of the topographic corps, or, where such had not yet been made, by using the best material at his disposal, has published a general map of the middle, and southern parts of Sweden, on the scale of 1:500,000, and a similar one for the north of Sweden, on the scale of 1:100,000. The former, engraved on copper, has been published in 8 leaves, and the second, lithographed, in 2 leaves. HAHR has, likewise, published and caused to be lithographed for the use of schools, a physical and political map in 8 leaves, of the middle and south of Sweden. The late King, CARL XV, contributed very considerably, out of his own private funds, towards this atlas. The maps and the plates have now been handed over to the topographic corps, and the latter serve for new impressions in proportion as the old ones run out.

Lieutenant TH. A. VON MENTZER has published, for the use of schools, very good maps, not only of Sweden and the neighbouring countries, but of other parts of Europe, and the different quarters of the world. The same author has also published maps of the expeditions of the Vikings, and of the maritime and commercial routes of the ancient inhabitants of the North, as well as an atlas for universal history, and other maps for the ease of young students.

Several private cartographers, have with the pecuniary assistance from the State, published maps of the Northern parts of Sweden. Thus there are: by L. E. ÅHRMAN a map in two leaves of the province of Gestrikland on the scale of 1:100,000; by P. WIDMARK a map, in one leaf, of Helsingland, on the scale of 1:200,000; by FRESE, a map of the diocese Karlstad (Vermland) on the scale of 1:200,000; by M. R. STIERNSTRÖM, a map in four leaves of the Län of Westernorland on the scale of 1:150,000; by S. J. WESTRELL a map in one leaf of the Län of Jemtland, on the scale of 1:500,000; by ALBIN and by T. F. NORDBECK, another map of the same Län in fifteen leaves on the scale of 1:200,000; by C. A. PETTERSSON, a map in one leaf, of the Län of Norrbotten on the scale of 1:1,000,000.

E. G. LJUNGGREN has published a map of the towns of Sweden and their territories.

A copy of the nine Southernmost leaves of the map of Sweden, by the staff general on the scale of 1:100,000, has been published in Copenhagen. on the scale of 1:200,000, by I. H. MANSA.

Nautical Charts. The *Sjökarteverk* (Hydrographic Office) is in a military and technical point of view, under the management of the minister of naval affairs, and its duties are principally the following:

(1). The *hydrographic surveying*, (on convenient scales,) of the coasts of the country, and the larger navigable lakes; the sounding of lakes the sounding of shoals and sand banks and the general exploration of the nature of the navigable waters, surrounding the country, in proportion, as it may be deemed necessary for navigation or the defence of the coasts; preparatory operations for nautical cartography, such as triangulation, magnetic observations, etc., so far as they may not be necessary for the office, and when they have not been previously executed with sufficient accuracy.

(2). *Publication of Charts, etc.*, the construction of original charts, and the reproduction of these charts by engraving, or any other suitable means, for the purpose of keeping them at the disposal of navigators; the preparation and publication of descriptions of channels, coasts and other necessary matters concerning navigation.

The persons employed in the Hydrographic Office, consist of one chief, and a requisite number of officers, and other assistants. This number are at present 4 naval officers and one designer. Besides, for the annual hydrographic surveys, other officers of the Royal Navy, are commanded according as there may be occasion; in general from 7 to 9 officers are engaged for all the hydrographic expeditions.

Besides, 3 engravers, 1 guillocheur, and two plate printers, are at present employed at the office. All these persons work by the piece. The government grant for the office amounts to $16,-500 gold per annum. The fixed pay of the chief and the other officers is defrayed separately by the budget for the naval department; but smaller salaries for special work done for the office are charged to the office. The annual income by the sale of charts amounts to $4,500 gold.

Previous to the year 1860, the hydrographic surveys were principally made by means of sailing vessels and rowing boats; but since that year steamers have been used, and now when practicable, are always used. Unfortunately, the narnow channels in various "skärgårdar" (archipelagoes) make the use of rowing-boats indispensable. It is natural that the use of steam has considerably accelerated the hydrographic work, and it has also gained very much in accuracy especially in moderately windy weather, when the application of steam would allow the continuation of a work, that must have been interrupted much sooner, if rowing-boats had been used. The variety in the nature of the Swedish coasts and archipelagoes, has, however, made it necessary to use vessels greatly differing in size and power, to adapt means of working to the requirements of the localities. During later years, the vessels employed have consisted of a steam gun boat of 60 horse power for soundings in the sea, and of vessels belonging to the hydrographic Office, viz: 2 steam schooners of 30 and 15 horse power, 5 steam tugs of 8 horse power, 1 open steam sloop of 5 horse power, and, besides, 2 schooners and 1 yacht have been used as lodging vessels. During the year 1862—1871 the office was principally occupied with soundings along the coasts of the country, surveys of the "skärgård" (archipelago) of Stockholm with its vast labyrinth of isles, reefs and channels, and the triangulation of the northern coasts (the gulf of Bothnia), where no triangulation as yet had been made, and to which place the hydrographic surveys will be transferred in a few years.

As an instance of the rapidity with which hydrographic surveys may be performed when steam is used, we may mention that the "skärgård" of Stockholm, the most extensive, the most dense and the most difficult to survey, in this immense chain of islands, which skirt the greater part of the Swedish coasts, this skärgård including the space at sea which separates the isles, and which has been surveyed, encloses an area or 180 geogr. sq. miles (9,910 kilom. c.) The hydrographic surveys were continued for 10 summers, averaging 5 months each, and the total number of hands employed, were 67 commissioned officers, say 6.7 per annum, and 592 non-commissioned officers, engine-men and sailors, averaging 59.2 men per annum. Consequently, the area annually measured and sounded with all possible accuracy was 18 geogr. sq. miles (991 kilom. c.) or about 2.7 sq. miles (14.8 kilom. c.) per officer during 5 months work annually.

The hydrographic charts of the coasts, archipelagoes, and lakes of the interior of the country are generally on the scale of 1:20,000 is used. The soundings near the coasts, and also within sight of land, are delineated on the scale of 1:50,-000, and those in the sea generally on the scale of 1:100,000. The method of projection, is the intersecting conical, or that used by the topographers of the Staff-General for terrestrial maps.

The office publishes, for the use of navigators, in general, charts of channels, on scales varying between 1:300,000 and 1:350,000, including all the seas washing the coasts of Sweden; coast-charts, on the scales of from 1:200,000 to 1:250,000; and special charts, on the scales of from 1:50,000 to 1:100,000. The atlas published, is designed after the progressive, or Mercator's projection,—with the exception of special maps, which are constructed after the intersecting conical method, as for the hydrographic surveys. The whole atlas, which is engraved on copper, undergoes an annual re-examination. The collection of charts published by the office, includes only the Baltic with its gulfs, the Kattegat, and the Skager-Rack, as far as Lindesnäs, in Norway; at present it consists of 1 chart of routes, (carte de cours), 7 channel-charts, 19 coast-charts, and 15 special charts, together 42 charts.

Besides, the Office publishers, under the title: "Den Svenske Lotsen," (the Swedish Pilot), a description of the navigation in the waters washing the coast of Sweden and the neighboring countries, of which work new and revised editions appear as often as called for. Lastly, it annually publishes two numbers of "Underrättelser för Sjöfarande" (Information for Navigators), containing the most important notices, official or non-official, received by the office, about discovered shoals, the construction or modification of lights, and other nautical marks, etc., on all the coasts in the world.

Geological Survey of Sweden. The question about establishing Geological Surveys in this country at the expense of the State, was moved, first in 1855, by a petition made by the Agricultural Society of the Län of Uppsala, for a grant from the State, for a geological survey of that Län, the Society offering to pay half of the expenses, and afterwards, by the expressed wish of the Seventh Swedish Agricultural Congress, that accurate geological surveys, should be made, as soon as possible, all over the country, at the expense of the state.

On receiving favorable reports, both from the Agricultural Academy, and the Academy of Sciences, the Government proposed to the Diet to assign for these surveys a grant of 60,000 Kr. (=$16,666 gold) for the three years from 1858 to 1860, which was agreed to.

The instructions given by the Government, on the 27th of April, 1858, for the establishment of geological surveys, prescribe, that they should be made on a common plan, and principally with the object of examining the geognostic relations of the country, with a three-fold view to scientific, agricultural, and industrial investigations, and to publish the result by means of maps and detailed descriptions,

The surveys were commenced in the year 1858, and were at first conducted in the Län of Uppsala, and the neighboring parts of the Läns of Stockholm and Westmanland, in order first to construct a map of the basin of Lake Mälar.

The result of the work during the first two years, based on the map of the Staff-General, on the scale of 1:50,000, having been laid before the Diet, in 1859, the latter declared, that it would be of special importance, to have the geological maps, published on a scale sufficiently large, for the sake of reproducing completely, and with requisite clearness, all contained in these maps, that could serve for a guide for agricultural or other industrial purposes.

The geological survey of a country like Sweden, must necessarily be combined with great difficulties, on account of the uniform nature of the rocky surface and the want of great intersections. A petrographic map alone, on a large scale, would be fatiguing, but this inconvenience has been avoided by also reproducing the strata and their extention. Owing to this procedure, which is also beginning to be adopted abroad, the map, while it gives a true representation of the country, is of direct interest to the agriculturalist, which is not the case with an ordinary geological map.

The scale of 1:50,000, which was exclusively used in the beginning, is now used only in such parts of the country, as make this large scale necessary, either on account of the variety of their formations, or on account of their geological importance in an economical point of view. In more uniform regions, and in the more thinly populated districts, as for instance, Småland, the scale of 1:100,000 has been found sufficient for the survey, and that of 1:200,000 for the maps published. They also indicate the moveable strata, and the rocks visible on the surface, without indicating the ground, but they are also accompanied by maps exclusively petrological with indication of the ground.

As a base and form for the geological maps, the original map of the staff-officers on the scale of 1:50,000 has been generally used, and also, the economical maps published in the same scale, and lastly the maps of the staff-officers on the scale of 1:100,000.

The extent of ground surveyed on the scale of 1:50,000 at the end of the year 1874, amounts approximatively to 366 Swedish square miles (41,800 kilom. c.), and that surveyed on the scale of 1:100,000, to 70 Swedish square miles (8,000 kilom. c.).

At the end of the year 1874, were published 57 lithographic maps, on the scale of 1:50,000, together with the relative descriptions; 5 maps are about to be made, and 22 have been partially surveyed. Two maps on the scale of 1:200,000, together with their descriptions, have already been published, and two are being engraved.

The geological surveys are accompanied by levellings, by means of ordinary instruments. The distance surveyed during these levellings in the years 1862-1874 represents a length of 1,128 Swedish miles (12,000 kilom.).

Simultaneously with the surveys for the geological maps of the country, on the above mentioned scales, materials have been collected during several years, for a general geological map of the country. Special explorations have been made for this purpose, and in particular in the more distant, and therefore, less known districts of the country, such as Dalarne, Herjedal, Jemtland and Lappland. Several monographs and scientific memoirs have been published, which are based on more detailed geological and paleontological surveys. These kinds of publications are constantly increasing. Besides the purely scientific and cartographic work, another duty connected with the geological survey, is to provide for the wants of practical geology. For that purpose, special surveys are conducted in those districts of the country that contain coal and ore, (an extensive exploration will begin this year, 1875, in Lappland, which is especially rich in ore) and also operations in connection with technical economy and agricultural geology.

Another object of the geological survey is to furnish materials for national archæology; simultaneously with the geological explorations, the sepulchral fields of the pre-historic periods and other stationary monuments are carefully noted and reproduced on the maps, by means of special signs.

In the above manner, the commission of the Swedish geological survey is endeavoring to fulfil their duty to produce a geological atlas of the country, (to constitute a scientific institution) to serve technical industry, mining and agriculture, by means of practical geological investigations, based on scientific principles. The grants voted by the Diet for the geological survey have gradually increased, and in the budget for 1876, they represented a sum of 70,300 Kr., (= $19,528 gold).

The functionaries of the geological survey, permanently employed are 12 in number, the director included. In summer this number is more or less increased, by the employment of extra assistant geologists, who execute principally the more mechanical part of the work. The winter months are devoted to the construction of maps, to the preparation of descriptions and monographs, to chemical analyses, and to microscopic studies, etc., all of which is done is done in a locality belonging to the State, containing work-rooms, a chemical laboratory and museum; this museum which contains, besides some small rooms, one large room with galleries, 120 feet (36 metres in length) and occupying two stories, is distinguished for its practical and elegant arrangements.

Above (page 5), we have given a general review of the *Geology of Sweden*.

PHYSICAL, SOCIAL, AND MORAL CONDITION OF MAN.

[CLASS 340-341.] We have already given a partial account of the physical development and condition of the Swedish population, a further account is given in the following, under the head of dwellings and mode of living; the same is in part applicable to their ailments.

Further, see class 650.

DWELLINGS.

The Peasant's Home.*—If we turn our attention upon Skåne, the richest and most southern province of Sweden, we find in the northern part a style of architecture corresponding with that of the more northern provinces; the dwellings are large, well-built, and generally two stories high; while in the southern, where the purely Scanian style finds expression, the architecture is peculiar and almost unique, its counterpart being found nowhere in Sweden, except in the neighboring province of Halland, which, especially in the southern part, presents a great resemblance to Skåne.

In the Scanian plain, the peasants' farm-houses are united, so that their out-walls form a sort of court-yard. In the beginning this was, in all probability, not only done in imitation of the old castles, but also as a defensive measure; but now, as the peasant no longer has to provide himself against a siege, these buildings offer other advantages; the supervision of the owner is rendered easier, the cattle are kept from straying off, and the peasant, not being entirely out of doors, is protected from the winds while he prosecutes his winter's employment. But the protection from the weather is quite another, if one enters a peasant's dwelling of proper construction, and the traveller, be his habits of life never so refined, will find here an air of comfortableness, for draughts through the floor are impossible, even though a violent snow-storm rage over the open country.

The walls and floors of the houses are made of clay. The skeleton is made of a hewn framework with lining walls, and the intervening space is filled with moistened clay and long straw; the roof is made of spars from twelve to sixteen feet in length. They have begun to burn the clay into bricks, which gives the houses a pleasanter appearance. Some of the newer dwellings are entirely made of brick or granite. The older houses are painted white.

The dwelling consists of a lobby with the sitting-room on one side, and the summer-room (bärstuga) on the other. Of the lobby itself may be remarked that it contains a stairway leading to the garret and a pantry. The sitting-room is the more important one, and has a depth equal to the whole width of the house. The entrance-door was near the inner wall, so that on entering one faced the wall next the court-yard, which was provided with three windows; on looking out of one of these windows, the first thing that met one's gaze was the *goose-bench*, where the geese were set in the spring; then the *table-bench*, which extended along the yard-wall to a closet; in the corner, in front of this bench, and from which it derived its name, stood a solidly made table with a top of dark polished slate; between the cupboard and the kitchen door stood another bench used for the same purpose as the table-bench. These benches were wrought with great care, and formed a sort of chest which was filled with straw; the smaller one, and sometimes the larger one also, was covered with "smordatyg," a kind of matting wrought with flowers, fruits, and other figures, in brilliant colors. The closet in the corner was frequently made of carved oak, and had an upper and lower department; these were divided into smaller compartments by means of columns, and provided with shelves. Here the peasant kept his various documents and

* From a treatise by Dr. R. BERGSTRÖM, Librarian.

money. On the shelves stood the family library, a brandy-bottle with glasses, a tobacco pipe, and coffee-cups, in order to be in readiness in case of the arrival of strangers or visitors. On the other side of the kitchen-door stood a birchen chair, bottomed with straw, generally the only one in the house, and near the chair stood the kakelugn.

The name *kakelugn*, porcelain stove, is misapplied, in that, that this stove was an iron one, heated from the kitchen, though the greater part of it stood in the dining-room. The fuel was turf, and consequently the cheering flame of the northern fireplace was wanting. The sides of the stove were ornamented with figures—St. George and the Dragon, Adam and Eve under the Tree of Knowledge, Sampson tearing open the Jaws of the Lion, The Last Supper, etc., in bas-relief. The stove rested on a foundation of bricks, or upon high wrought-iron feet, and was very thick and solid. The old and popular forms have but lately begun to be replaced by others.

Immediately on the other side of the stove stood the "fireside-bench," on which the peasant rests during the day, in the winter, but which otherwise served as a sleeping-place for the children. A small sofa stood against the far wall under the window, and there came the double bed, the end of which, which was turned toward the room, was converted into a cupboard in which the dishes for the entertainment of visitors were kept, and the side next to the room was also provided with a pair of doors so that it resembled a second closet. On the bedstead, a good distance from the floor, lay several beds, the lower one of straw. From above was suspended a rope covered with some kind of cloth, and provided with a handle in order to facilitate the raising up as the sleeper sunk deep into the soft beds. The bedsteads were painted with brilliant colors, as were the rest of the furniture. At the foot of the bed, and between it and the pantry-door, stood the wall clock. On the opposite side hung a small fringed towel, and thus, with another step, we have completed the round of the sitting-room.

The Bärstuga, or summer room, had no fireplace; here the mother, daughters and servant-maids kept their clothes in chests which were painted blue, with huge tulips, from the pencil of the country artist, and provided with black mountings; besides the clothes-chests there was, generally, in this room a long table, together with a place of honor for a visitor, and between the table and wall a bench, besides a shut-up double-bedstead, a few chairs, and the loom, which, as well as sundry other articles, used to be taken into the summer room when not needed for a short time.

In one of the other rows were the lodgings for strangers, where travellers used to be accommodated with night quarters, the man-servant's room (the maid-servants were in the sitting-room, where they also slept at night), and the reserve room, which the old people occupied when the eldest son married, after having stipulated for certain necessaries, *e. g.*, corn, milk, turf, etc. The other rows contained stables, barn-floors, store-rooms for the turf and implements, etc. All the windows looked into the yard, in which stood the corn-ricks, if there was room for them, and there was generally a well. There were two gates to the yard, one facing the road leading to the village, and the other the "tomt," or the piece of ground nearest the yard.

In the dwellings of the cottagers there was neither larder nor summer room, but the sitting-room was fitted up as in the houses of the wealthy.

The kitchen was also the brew-house: besides the hearth it had a "kölna" (drying-oven), and a baking-oven, the vault of which, to save space, was built outside of the main building, and covered with a thatched roof of its own.

In the outline and coloring of all the ornaments there was something of "instinctive certainty." Whatever might have been remarked against them, there was a kind of *style* in them which had sprung up on native ground, and been developed without any foreign influence; it is true the models might have been found partly in the gentlemen's houses one or two centuries earlier, but the people had used them freely. Besides the ornaments on the stove, and the carved and painted furniture, the embellishments consisted in "pictures" from the Holy Scriptures, pasted on the white-washed walls, and historical pieces by a country artist. Birthday congratulations, with painted wreaths which encircled verses and names neatly written in court-hand, and tablets in memory of departed relatives (both kinds under glass and framed), were also seen on the walls, as well as a few flower-pots in the windows.

In the rest of the arrangements there was the same harmony and self-agreement. The unity is now disturbed—we have therefore used the perfect form—and it is perceived that a transition period is at hand. Thus, for instance, the old stone-floor sprinkled with sand is beginning to be exchanged for a floor of smoothly planed boards, but which is not kept much cleaner than the former was. The olden turned wooden dishes and platters, and the round or square boards on which meat or pork was cut, have begun to be mixed with crockery-ware, and even forks are seen among the formerly all-prevailing pocket-knives, of which every one had his own. Newspapers and periodicals also begin to peep forth: formerly nothing of the kind was seen but the Bible and psalm-book, and a few other religious books and songs and legends, "printed this year"; also the indispensable almanac which used to have its place on a beam in the ceiling, right over the peasant's seat, at the upper end of the large table.

How different from this Scanian home is the peasant's house north of the river Dalelf! We will suppose that we are in *Ångermanland*, and are approaching what seems to us a large village. If we ask our driver or guide about the number of peasants, or cottagers, who live here, we shall be astonished at the fewness that the answer indicates, supposing we compare it with the chaos of houses before us. On approaching a little nearer, a number of larger or smaller houses that can scarcely be comprehended at a glance are seen thrown promiscuously together without and particular order or symmetry, and enclosed with fences which form tolerably rectilinear figures. All the houses are built of logs laid on the top of one another, and hewn on the sides, which are turned outwards and inwards, and the crevices stopped with moss. In case the owner has accustomed himself to a little more comfort, or if the "dry-wood" nearest the village has already been cut off, so that the fuel must be brought from a distance, the houses are sometimes caulked on the inside with tow (stry) instead of moss, by which means the warmth is better retained. If the owner has a taste for neatness, and can afford it, the houses are also lined with boards, and painted with red ochre, which latter looks very well in contrast with the white window-frames. Some of the well-to-do peasants paint their buildings altogether white.

The roof is either of birch-bark, boards, or shingles.

The main building is generally a two-story house; but the upper floor is often not fitted up, and remains so, even so far that a proper flooring is wanted. Before the entrance, which is in the middle of the house, on the side towards the yard, there is always a landing, which is often at some distance from the ground, so that a few steps leading to it are needed. The landing is sometimes covered with a roof, ornamented with carved ledges and supported by pillars, or side walls of pierced work. In the lobby are two doors. One opens into a large room, inside of which are one or more smaller rooms—chambers—frequently furnished in the town fashion with sofas, bedsteads with magnificent down beds, sheets and worked quilts, ratan-chairs, chests of drawers, pier-glasses, curtains, etc. The rooms are warmed by means of hearths, or brick stoves, and the walls are covered with glazed paper, or with newspapers, which are pasted on and colored with lime-water. The family never occupy these rooms, excepting when strangers arrive; they generally occupy the spacious kitchen, and the other of the two doors in the lobby opens into it. Here is a prodigious fire-place, with its hearth of brick or iron, and the indispensable coffee-pot always in readiness; and on the hearth blazes from morning till night the wood fire.

Wooden laths are hung parallel to the ceiling, and next to the fire-place, on which timber is placed to dry; and there the never-failing rifle-gun, together with the powder-horn and the eathern bullet-pouch, has also its place. Along the walls stand large, unwieldy tables, often provided with leaves; further, an enormous cupboard, consisting of a closet, surmounted with shelves reaching to the ceiling, and completely filled with bright cooking utensils, pewter plates and crockery; then a massive chest, gaudily painted, and provided with the initials of the father of the family, the last letter being always an **s** (*i. e.*, son).*

The old wooden vessels are gradually giving place to earthenware. "Träkoxarna" are circular, oval, or irregular vessels of knotted birch, of various sizes, generally varnished and painted with fancy flowers, as are also the spoons and ladles of birch. The silver is brought out only when visitors are entertained. The peasantry of no other country possesses so much silver spoons, goblets, etc., as the Swedish. The cooking utensils, of tinned iron and copper, are always kept bright.

Here we also find those peculiar and substantial bedsteads which reach to the ceiling and consist of two or three horizontal partitions, with room for two persons in each, and on the front side are frequently provided with doors, so that from the outside it may be taken for a closet. The end of the bedstead is actually a closet, generally fitted as follows: undermost a long drawer, answering the purpose of trundle-bed, and above doors to a compartment with shelves; uppermost, above an opening about breast-high, are again doors for shelves and drawers. In this special bedstead-closet the peasant keeps his valuables, money, and documents relating to his farm. Sometimes this closet is ornamented with pictures taken off bon-bons and pasted on, keepsakes from the fair and an odd silver watch or two. Undermost in the bedsteads is straw; sometimes, when it is to be quite genteel, straw and down beds over that, often reindeer hides; further, though not always, a coarse sheet, and uppermost, as a quilt, very suitable for the climate, the sheep-skin, in the long fleece and cleanliness of which the Norrlander takes a certain pride. The walls are generally covered with simple paper, but sometimes they remain bare. The upper story, when fitted up, consists of spare rooms for visitors, similar to the large room and chambers below.

The family, however, generally occupies this house only in the winter. Toward summer they remove to the smaller house (the brew-house), which consists of a kitchen, fitted up in the same manner as in the main building, but somewhat smaller, and a room with a fire-place; and sometimes, but not always, with a separate entrance; this room is otherwise occupied by some pensioner ("födorådstagare"), unless there is another house at his disposal.

Separate houses are built for the stables, cow-house, threshing-floor, granary, dairy, barns, smithy, and such others as belong to a well-regulated peasant's farm, and these are sometimes duplicates, and thus arises that chaos of houses which must astonish every traveller. Even as many as twenty houses may be seen in a single peasant's farm-yard. This extravagance, which has grown a custom, can only be accounted for by the abundance of timber, which induces the peasant, when it is necessary to in-

* The Swedish peasantry generally have no family name, but only a Christian name, to which they add that of the father in the genitive, together with "son" or "dotter" ("son" or "daughter"): *e. g.*, Karl Johansson is "Karl Johan's son" (Charles John's son); his son would be called Karlsson; Karin (Catherine) Johansdotter is "Karin Johan's daughter," and so on.

crease his store-room, to build still another stable or barn, rather than add to the old one.* The forest must, however, suffer in the end from such extravagance, and the fact that the forests are rapidly becoming remoter from the larger villages must be traced to this building and the wasteful consumption of fuel. At a large peasant's farm a man-servant has constant employment during the winter in sledging and chopping fire-wood.

Peasants who are not so well off, as well as settlers and cottagers generally, have their dwelling-house fitted up as the brew-house of the more wealthy, though the walls are frequently unpainted, and the inside without papering. The dust-heap, which has been placed immediately at the side of the landing to the lobby for convenience sake, is often very unpleasant. The bleak northwest wind often blows right through the house, and sometimes even a "necessary" is wanted.

There are collections of huts on many of the forest-pastures, which are distant from the farm to which they belong. These huts are fitted up as kitchens, dairy, and cow-houses.

Large peasants' houses, however, do not, by any means, belong exclusively to Norrland and modern Skåne. As far back as 1817, a writer says, in his description of *Östergötland*, that in the country districts of this province are generally found "lighter and more comfortable dwellings than in many other provinces of the kingdom. Even in districts without forests, two-story houses of white or red fir timber are no longer rare." Further, the same writer says: "Almost everywhere the roof of the main building is lined with boards, and thatched, or covered with birch bark and turf, and the cow-house is only thatched. Among the more wealthy peasantry it is now, however, customary to roof dwelling-houses, as well as out-houses, with tiles. The painting of the houses with red ochre, which is the fashion in some places, gives to the villages a pleasant aspect." This quotation brings us to the consideration of the peasant-architecture of Central Sweden, which is at present representative for the whole country.

Traces of that equalization which is the boasted characteristic of the present are found everywhere, and here this "levelling" seems to be working out a decidedly good work for the country. A better taste in the erection of buildings and regulation of their manors has already been instilled into the peasant; and fortunately improved peasant architectural models had already begun to be followed at that period when the law of 1827, regarding the subdivision and redistribution of land, began to be executed.

The railways, however, appear to have contributed more than anything else to the wakening of the peasant's sense of the beautiful, and that not only by their buildings, which have been constructed with praiseworthy regard for their architecture, but also by the opportunities for travelling which they afford. On journeys which, previous to the railways, could scarcely have been thought of, even on pleasure excursions, etc., the peasant will now see a great deal, and during the long hours in the trains animating conversations are entered into with persons of the more educated classes, who take pleasure in communicating with the cheerful and humorous peasant.

The progress in agriculture, and the departments immediately connected with it, must be acknowledged as astonishing, especially for the short time which is still in the memory of the majority. It cannot, forsooth, be concealed that the still-existing, though perhaps vanishing type of the Swedish peasant's yard, is, on a whole, an index of the agriculture of the country. The cow-house and other houses, belonging to the economy of the farm, are small and miserable, while the dwelling-houses are comparatively large and magnificent. The main building is the chief point that first attracts the eye, like the

* The custom of using compounds of the word "hus" (house), *e. g.*, "redskapshus" (room for implements), "svinhus" (pig sty), etc., where no longer separate *houses* for different purposes exist, but only divisions in the same house, implies that this multiplicity in the mode of building has been general in the country.

churches in the small provincial towns. The old type, as we have said, is about to become extinct, and that very soon. In many places it is already quite so, as for instance, in the western woodlands of Nerike and their vicinity, which we will now consider.

This development calls for that state which must come, sooner or later, when the line of demarcation, which separates the peasant from the gentleman, begins to be more indistinct, or altogether expunged; and as our object here is to depict only the more typical portions, we restrict ourselves to what we would call *the middle class of the peasantry.* It is his home—the middle-sized farm—with which we will occupy ourselves.

Any *hip-roofed houses* (ryggås-stugor), with windows on the roof, are scarcely seen any longer, nor any of those antiquated houses with galleries round the sides (such as were represented at the late Paris Exhibition by a copy of the celebrated historical Ornäs Cottage), probably originating from the middle ages, and which are probably imitations of the castles of that period. At present the peasant's house is built of rough-hewn timber, with protruding corner-joints, and two stories high, the one below containing a lobby, sitting-room, and kitchen. The upper story is also divided into three apartments, corresponding to those below. The entrance to the dwelling—which is always, excepting in rare cases, situated in a village—is at the corner of one of the long sides.

The houses are built parallel to the public road, if one passes, or to some stream in the neighborhood, or in case the country is undulating, parallel to some ridge or valley, and sometimes they are built north and south, according to the compass, and generally with the front exposure to the south.

On entering the lobby, one sees, in case the stair-case to the upper-story is to the right, a door on the left. leading to the sitting-room, the common working and sleeping-room of the family, generally from 14 to 16 feet long, and occupying half of the ground-floor of the house. To the right of the door opening into the sitting-room is the large, open fire-place, mostly built of stone; further to the right, beyond the fire-place, there is still another door, which opens into the kitchen. The low chamber—the tall peasant can often touch the ceiling with his hand—is rather poorly lighted with only two, sometimes three, windows, with small panes, one of which is in the front, another in the end, and the third, if it exists, is in the back of the house. The walls are plastered and whitewashed. The unpainted ceiling, of planed boards, rests on strong beams; both the ceiling and timbers have grown brown with age and smoke. The floor is made of planed boards. In the kitchen, to which there is another entrance, besides the one already mentioned, at the back of the house, or in the lobby, there is only exceptionally more than one small window. The kitchen fire-place is open on two sides; from one of the two sides where it is backed (by a wall) a prodigious baking oven opens to the hearth, in the inner corner of which is the real fire-place. The flue right over the fire-place is shut with a damper, and above this is the chimney, with which all the fire-places of the house are connected, by means of pipes.

The bed-room, situated above the sitting-room, which, as a rule, is not fitted up, and without a fire-place, is used as a clothes-closet—often as a storeroom for certain eatables, such as eggs, dried meat, etc., and in the summer as a milk and general store-room, and therefore the spinning-wheel, the loom, etc., are put there when they are not needed.

The chamber, or the spare room, reserved for guests, namely, for more esteemed guests (others must be contented with the sitting-room), is, on the other hand, generally fitted up with more style than the sitting-room.

The outer roof, with an under layer of narrow rounded pieces of wood, has a double covering consisting of, first, birch bark, and then a layer of turf, a material protecting as well as durable.

The houses are frequently lined with boards and painted with red ochre.

If a stranger enters such a house, with its low roof projecting scarcely three-fourths of a foot, with the sitting-room browned by time and smoke, it does not strike him with its harmonious proportions, nor yet does its cleanliness nor air of "well-to-do" render it very inviting to him.

But on a winter night, however, when all are collected round the fireside, it assumes quite a different character. The men then enjoy a repose which the uninterrupted work during the other seasons but sparingly affords them; and the women who, when they have done their tasks in the cow-house, have no longer any employment out of doors, are now busy indoors, and the spinning-wheel hums cheerily. The traveller who, nearly frozen by the north wind, and fatigued by the length of the road, is passing outside in the dark, casts longing glances towards the fireside, which sends its rays through the window, unobstructed by any envious curtain, and feels why the word *home* is the substance of so much that is dear and valuable.

This mode of building and fitting up of houses, though it is still predominant, is not the only one, and is rapidly passing away.

One-story houses are also seen, especially on smaller peasants' farms, but the fitting up of the rooms is then similar to that of the ground-floor of the former two-story house, sometimes, however, with this difference—that here are two "sitting-rooms" (stugor) of the same size, one on each side of the kitchen, which is in the centre of the house. In other respects, we may say that the number of rooms is the only thing in which the whole of this group of dwelling-houses—large, middle-sized and small—differ from one another.

These classes of buildings, of which we have spoken, are disappearing very rapidly, so that in some parts, especially in those of which we have mentioned, they are already quite scarce, and in their stead houses of an altogether different style, and with a considerable degree of elegance, are being built. The turf roof—which was not ugly on the smaller huts, painted with red ochre, but abominable on the larger houses—is giving place to the light shingle roof, with a projection of from 2½ to 3 feet, which appears to a good advantage, even after having been weathered.

The influence of new models can be seen in the general character of the buildings, *i. e.*, in the symmetrically-built doors and windows, etc. The logs no longer protrude at the corners, and the greater care which is bestowed on every detail has removed that appearance of decay which was attendant upon the former mode of building. In many cases the landing to the lobby is covered by a light roof which forms a sort of verandah, and contributes much to the appearance of the dwelling.

The size of the dwelling still depends upon the abundance of timber and the wealth of the owner. The taste varies a little in different places—essentially influenced, as it appears, by the neighborhood of a railway or some building serving as a model—but two-story houses are only exceptionally built. The fitting up otherwise remains unaltered in its leading features: sitting-room (stuga), which still has its former signification, lobby and kitchen; and, as before, according to circumstances, one or more rooms. But these are now lighter, more cheerful and suitable; each window has six large panes of glass, three in height; the rooms are higher, 8½ to 9 feet, or still more, as also the well-finished panelled doors. Double windows, which retain the warmth much better than a single one, formerly adopted only by the gentry, are no longer a luxury, while painted walls and ceilings, in the better rooms even papered, hide the formerly visible layers of timbers, and that rather as a rule than an exception.

The tendency to build large houses, which has also been noticed by travellers, does not seem to abate, and wherever buildings are erected they are designed on a much larger scale than the mode of life and position of the inmates would warrant. This kind of extravagance does not testify in favor of the Swedish peasant's frugality, nor for his unpretendingness. There may perhaps be vanity in this extended mode of building, but it exhibits at the same time a noble feature in the character of the people—a disposition for sociability and hospitality, which distinguishes the Swede in every station. It would be vain to try to argue away this national characteristic, to make it a virtue of necessity, in a country where the distances are great, the means of communication undeveloped, and houses of entertainment for travellers are few and bad, depending upon the necessity of reciprocal services, for it still exists undiminished, even when these feasible causes—over the greater part of the country—have long since ceased.

The beneficial influence of modern times is also perceptible in other buildings belonging to the farm. The small houses, which are comprehended under the common appellation of out-houses, and which are scattered about at random, have given way to new, elegant and well-arranged ones. The close and dark cow-house, where the cattle in winter pined in darkness and vitiated air; the stable with its sloping stall or stalls, its roof scarcely proportioned to the height of the horse, and its door of still smaller dimensions; the barns into which the fodder must be put through narrow openings in the walls, and the damp timber-roofed cellar, which must be rebuilt every fifth or tenth year, no longer exist. The cattle are now placed in high and well-lighted and ventilated houses, and in suitable stalls, no longer close to the walls, but at a short distance from them, so as to afford space for a passage, through which the fodder is carried to welladapted racks or mangers. Formerly it was thrown on the floor, where it was wasted or made unsavory by being trod on. In the gable end there is usually an opening through which the excrements are thrown out. A gutter runs through the middle of the stable for conducting the liquid excrements to the dung-heap. The principal entrance is on one of the long sides. On the side opposite the opening to the dung-hill is the "feeder," a partition along the whole width of the house, where the fodder needed for the day is kept. On proceeding further in the same direction, one comes to the barn or threshing-floors and granary, between which the barn is situated. Sometimes there are also under the same roof a house for implements, stable and a wood-house, but generally the latter forms a house or two of itself. To the barns and threshing-floors are large doors or gates, which admit the corn being *carted* in; and wherever the situation makes it practicable it is so arranged that the fodder can be taken in the same manner into the spacious hay-loft, which occupies the whole top part of the building.

In the central part of Sweden the *building material* is still wood, mostly red fir, to which the climate imparts a firmness and strength that this wood does not attain in more southerly climates; exceptionally white fir is used, which is softer than the red. Other materials are also exceptionally used, but only for the cow-house, which here and there is built of stone. Sand and lime, which of late have been used, have proved to be both a good and cheap building material; and the still-increasing price of forest productions, for which there is a great demand, have made it a general wish that "moulded houses" might become more general. Vaulted cellars of granite, built underneath some of the houses, for the purpose of saving a separate roof, are an innovation which has rapidly been adopted.

With regard to the **furniture**, it is much the same in the sitting-room, whether among people in different circumstances, or in different districts. It is here in no way conspicuous, neither in number nor appearance; it consists of a shut-up bedstead, with three or more sofa-beds, a folding-table, a press, and a cupboard, or a chest of drawers, a few chairs, and a ponderous house-clock. The whole is simple, serviceable, and not uncomfortable; being suited to the mode of life of the inmates, as well as to their wants. The father and mother's common resting-place is a *shut-up bedstead;* but not after the model of that which is seen among the other classes, which is made longer when pulled out, but in such a way as to increase the width when the peasant's bedstead is drawn out. Some more ornamenting, a few simple borders, and very primitive carvings, nevertheless, distinguish this piece of furniture from the sofa-beds, the sleeping-places of the children and servants. The back of the bedstead, which is turned towards the wall, is higher than any of the other sides, like the back of one of our common sofas, having the shape of a horizontal brace. The side-pieces, which are on a level with the lowest points of the back-piece, are nearly one foot higher than the upper edge of the front side. A thick quilt covers the bed, which, when one has risen, is immediately shut up. Over the bedstead, on a nail, by its strap, hangs the father's gun; below that, on a simple cushion —a squirrel's fur, or something like—hangs his watch. The sofa-beds have a straight back-piece, and sides in the shape of squares or something similar; stuffing and ornaments are dispensed with. For the night the lid-seat is raised, and the outer side is pulled out, as on the large bedstead. In the shut-up sofa is room for more than one person. Sometimes, instead of shut-up sofas, such made of frame-work are seen, on which the back and side-pieces—of the same height—are made of thin pieces of wood, resembling a railing; these rail-sofas have feet, and do not rest on the side-pieces, which on the former reach down to the floor. They are also, or at least are intended to appear, more elegant. In *one* respect the sleeping-places of the peasantry correspond: they are, namely, very short; shorter (six feet exactly) than they ought to be, and from one to one and a half feet shorter than those belonging to the other classes.

The *table*—generally there is but one in the room—is about four and a half feet by two, and rests on solid legs, which for further security are kept together by as many cross-pieces of wood of equal strength. On each side there is a leaf, hung on hinges; these leaves can be turned up, and to support them there are two legs, fastened with wooden cross-pieces, which turn on vertically placed axes. On week-days, however, this table is seldom used, but instead a peculiarly constructed piece of furniture, which at first sight looks like a three-legged chair, with a support for the back; on a closer inspection the seat is found to be double, with hinges on the front side, and when it is opened out forms a table, the fourth leg of which is the support for the back. It is true this table is small, but large enough for the humble meals. The unstuffed chairs, sometimes with backs of thin pieces of wood, often, however, with merely a cross-piece for a back, do not in any way deviate from the simplicity of the whole.

The *press* is generally divided into two parts, separated by an open room, which sometimes—as an old-fashioned bureau—is covered with a sloping lid. Otherwise the shape and fittings vary. In the press are kept sundry articles, which the thrifty housewife would not like to see scattered about, such as sewing things, and so forth. A simple border at the top is the usual ornament, and the doors are paneled. The lower part of the press is frequently used as a cupboard—now in the shape of a chest of drawers, as a rule breast high, now in the shape of a room, with shelves and two doors, and above them a couple of shelves abreast.

The *bedstead* is generally in the corner obliquely opposite the door of the sitting-room; the space between the bedstead and the kitchen door is usually filled up by a sofa-bed, while the opposite wall is taken up by two of the same sort, between which, if the space admits, a table sometimes is placed. The folding-table takes up the space before the gable-window; on the right and left are a couple of chairs, and on each side of these the press and the cupboard. One often sees hanging in a corner a small press, about three feet high, of which two sides are attached to the corner of the room; and three face the room, the middle one of which being the largest is also a door. In this *corner-press* will frequently be found an oblong bottle, holding about ¾ kannor, on one side of which is etched a royal cipher, surmounted with a crown, or else a ship, and also some cornet-shaped glasses. In the bottle is the never-failing "bränvin" (whiskey).

At the side of the bedstead, on the gable-wall, is generally seen the ponderous house-clock, with its large dial-plate, nearly a foot in diameter. It is a *Dalecarlian clock*, and a fine specimen of domestic industry in Sweden, though perhaps the case, about seven feet in height, and resembling an urn, drawn out at both ends, does not prove a particularly tasty form; the practical wants have here been yielded to: a sufficient height for the weights, and a broad centre for the oscillation of the pendulum. This kind of clock, made of brass and iron, or of wood and iron, generally runs exceedingly well, and its self-taught manufacturer has even understood to make it strike the quarters, and to show the day of the month, etc.

To the household articles may further be added a small *library*, the principal contents of which are the Bible and psalm-book—several copies—various books of sermons and devotional works by Luther, Arndt, and other fathers of our church. Besides these are seen the law-book, some juridical manual, the ordinances relating to the community, as also minor works on economy; further ballads and tales, stitched together, copies of the cheap editions of "Frithiof's Saga," and "Fänrik Stål's Sägner," and historical works. Scarcely ever is a novel seen. This little library, the worn volumes of which bear witness to its having been diligently used, has its place sometimes on a shelf on the cupboard, and sometimes in a special little press with glass doors, and sometimes on a shelf which is nailed high up on the wall. A few flower-pots are seldom missing in the windows—balsamines, geraniums, fuchsias, aloes, roses. Also a few pictures on the walls.

Finally to the fittings belong some iron hooks in the ceiling, supporting long poles, on which have been placed some coarse cakes of unbolted rye-meal for drying. Round the fire-place, likewise, near the ceiling, is fixed a pole, which is bent after the outline of the hearth; on this the family at bedtime hang their stockings, etc., to dry.

Such is the comfortable and suitable fitting-up, and such are the household articles in a peasant's cottage of the middle class, but which are rapidly disappearing. The time which has elapsed since this change began, and the present, may be divided into two periods. During the first were seen, here and there, household articles foisted in, for the presence of which no apparent reasons could be assigned, and which did not harmonize with the rest: they were the wreck of past prosperity, which, by the public sale at some baronial hall, had found their way to the peasant's cottage. At length collectors of "curiosities and antiquities" discovered what precious remnants from the time of LOUIS XIV and other periods had been stored away in the peasant's humble home, and from that time these relics began to be bought up by collectors, amateurs, and private persons; but it is not uncommon even now to find in the peasant's cottage a faceted mirror, a commode of the rococo period, or a precious cabinet from the 17th century; but the peasant will not part with them as cheaply as formerly, but often greatly over-values them.

In the second period begins that imitation which is expressed by the exchange of certain pieces of furniture, especially the press and the cupboard, for others, *e. g.*, commodes, chiffonniers, etc., which were poor imitations of ugly models. A change has also simultaneously taken place in their taste for colors, so that the former prevailing dark brown is exchanged for a lighter one—yellow, light or reddish brown; the flowers and bouquets, on a light blue ground, which they were so fond of seeing on the doors of presses, cupboards, and clocks, are quite out of fashion. Most fortunately, culturing art—if we may use that expression—has, perhaps in the eleventh hour, begun to turn her attention towards the naive art, which, unknown, or despised and ridiculed, sprang up among our peasants. There are many suggestions to carry out, tendencies to follow up, and precepts to be heeded, as everything acquires an incalculable value by being entirely native.

The period of transition that we spoke of was

an expression of the prosperity and the steady advance of culture among the majority. A third period is near at hand. Almost everywhere, in the articles that are now added to the household, may be recognized the hand of the experienced artisan —often found to be that of a mechanic who has returned home, after having been trained at the polytechnic school—less parade and greater regard to form are noticeable.

The sitting-room, however—if we may once more enter it—maintains its quality of being the work-room of a thriving agricultural family: this stamp remains despite the complaints of a pretended luxury; despite the fact that white curtains soften, and blinds shut out the light; that a looking-glass hangs on the wall; that the illumination from the wood-fire is in a great measure displaced by the cheaper lamp; and that the paint on the furniture is covered with a coat of varnish, or exchanged for a polish. It may appear that the peasant, returning home from the field or the wood, soiled by his work, or drenched by the rain, would not move about in his nail-shod shoes, and so forth, with the same comfort among these articles, which seem to call for greater care than the former, and yet it is not so: the peasant has adopted different manners from those of his forefathers.

We have confined ourselves to the room which constitutes the home of the family; but we will also say something about the rest. The serviceable furniture in the *kitchen* consists of an unpainted but white-scrubbed table—or a couple of them—and a shelf for kitchen utensils and other vessels. One is astonished at the number of copper vessels—pots and pans, milk-bowls, water-cans, etc.—and some of these holding as much as a tun! which, besides pewter articles, are often seen in the old peasants' houses. They are remnants from the time when there were no savings or other banks to which one might commit the management of one's savings, but was obliged either to hoard them, or to lend them in the neighborhood, or to invest them in articles of more lasting value—which at the same time were convenient for a dower to a future son-in-law. Hence originated the above-mentioned profusion in silver, large tankards, drinking-cups, etc., at the quantity of which one is astonished at great feasts, but without which, neither festivals, baptisms of children, nor funerals can be celebrated. With regard to the kitchen it may further be noted that the earthen vessels, dishes, and plates, formerly in use, have now begun to be supplanted by the stronger china-ware.

The *chamber* is of less interest. It was here the modernization seems to have been first introduced, while the sitting-room (stugan) remained longer closed to it. The paltry finery, which formerly at times made this room amusing to look at, has given way to greater solidity: thus, for instance, the paper cut out to represent curtain-holders is no longer seen, nor the chandelier made of a hoop, wound round with colored paper, and hanging by strings from the ceiling. Still are seen on the walls, most frequently in a frame with glass, those quaint congratulations: paper with wreaths of flowers, or artistically cut, in the centre of which is the congratulation neatly written in black letter, in metrical form, to the young daughter or son of the house on some *name-day* of theirs. Here are also found a great many of those little nick-nacks with which woman loves to adorn her home: worked table-cloths, and white, knitted quilts, now and then bought ones, but as often made by the daughters of the house. A photographic album is now seldom wanting, filled with the photographs of the family, their relatives, and friends.

Time has also wrought changes in the furnishing of the rest of the house, but space will not allow us to dwell upon them. "Luxury" has not created poverty, at least among this class, whose corn-fields were never better drained and manured, whose cow-houses were never so well filled with fat cattle, and whose implements are of the most approved patterns.

The Citizen's House. — From the simplest country cottage to the most magnificent houses in towns, or manors in the country, there are so many gradations that no line of demarcation can be drawn. The better houses of the peasant are equal, or even superior to the more humble ones of the citizen, and in completeness the latter surpass such houses as are called palaces. Consequently no particular style can be specified for the citizen's dwelling-house. The claims of a person building a house are, under the best circumstances, that it shall be substantial, comfortable, and outwardly neat.

As for the situation of the house, there is, in the towns, not much choice; an inhabitant may build on his own ground-plot, but according to the particular building regulations of the town. In this respect there is greater freedom in the country, where, in general, people are allowed to build their private houses as they choose. In case the owner himself chooses the site for his house, he neither seeks the greatest eminence nor the hidden valley, but rather a small hill covered with foliage, and sloping towards a lake or some other water.

The materials are either bricks or wood. Wooden houses are principally seen in the north of Sweden, both in the towns and country; brick houses in the south of Sweden and in the northern towns.

A substantial kind of wooden house is built on a foundation of granite, and mostly of squared timber carefully put together. The crevices between these timbers are driven with iron wedges and then caulked with oakum, so that the walls are as tight as the sides of a ship. There are, however, houses built of timber which is dressed on only two sides; the inner and outer, on the other hand, are round, and dressed off when the house is finished. The crevices thus caused are larger than when square timber is used, and are filled with moss, oakum and plaster. When the house is built the outer walls are colored with red ochre or a solution of vitriol, and when it has dried for a few years, it is weather-boarded, and at the same time ornamented with borders, pilasters, etc. It is afterwards painted—in the country generally white, but sometimes yellow; in the towns grayish white, green or red, which makes the reflection of the light from the house milder to the eye. In the towns wooden houses are not seldom plastered, particularly the older ones, either with mortar alone, which is caused to stick by means of wooden pegs fixed in the wall, or with mortar on tiles with which the walls have been covered.

The more substantial houses are built of brick and mortar on a foundation of granite or sandstone. When the house has dried for a year or two, the outside is plastered and smoothed, and frequently painted white. Bricks and mortar being easily worked, these houses are generally richer in ornaments than the wooden ones. The roof is covered with shingles—mostly the wooden houses in the country—tiles, slates, or sheet-iron. The floor is double; the space between is filled up with sawdust or, for want of this, with dry clay. The walls are commonly lined inside with pasteboard. The window-openings—from twenty to thirty square feet—generally have six panes of glass. The height of the houses are generally, for wooden houses two stories, for those of brick three, and in the larger towns four, the ground floor and entresol included. In the towns where building lots are expensive, and the want of outhouses not particularly great, there are generally cellars of brickwork under the houses for the preservation of food and the keeping of wood. In the country they have detached cellars of masonry underground—ice-cellars overground. The other outhouses are generally placed like detached wings to the main house. These wings likewise contain dwelling-rooms for the servants. A Swedish house of brick or wood, when carefully built, affords even in the severest winter a very comfortable residence. In Norrland, on a cold winter day, the thermometer will sometimes show — 40° Celsius (= — 40° F.), while inside the wooden house there is fresh air at + 18° to + 20° C. (64° to 68° F.)

For towns, boroughs, and other places with a dense population, there is a *Building Regulation* of May 8th, 1874, in force, which, among other things, prescribes that at the building of new towns, or the regulating of old ones, the streets are to be made at least 60 feet broad (exceptionally at least 40). The dwelling-houses must not be built higher than 5 stories, ground-floor included; and no house, as far as the eaves, may exceed in height the width of the street, increased by 5 feet. All houses must be roofed with some non-combustible material; at corner houses the corner must be cut off, and the height may be modified by the width of the crossing streets. Pure white must not be used for painting the outside, but some other color not injurious to the eye. In dwelling-houses the floor is to be laid at least 1 foot above the ground, and the height of the rooms must not be under 9 feet (in garrets, exceptionally, 8 feet). In churches, school-houses, theatres, and similar buildings, all the doors shall open outwards.

With regard *to the inner fittings*, it is to be remarked that the floors are exclusively of wood, except in brick houses, where the floors of the lobbies, as well as the steps, are of cut limestone (marble). The floors of the dwelling-houses are partly laid of planed white or red fir, mostly unpainted, or in squares or similar forms painted, partly marquetry with wood in one or more colors. The ceilings are either of plaster of Paris and white, with some decorations either in plaster or colors, or of wood painted white, or covered with whitewashed canvas or pasteboard. Ceilings hung with tapestry, or variegated, are not in vogue. The walls are papered, or sometimes, especially in saloons, painted either on the brick wall itself, on panelling or canvas. Walls hung with gobelin tapestry or gilt leather, and ceilings with richly-cut sandstone ornaments, are now seldom seen, except in the most elegant houses. The rooms are warmed (p. 57) by the excellent Swedish stoves, which are heated with wood; iron hearths are used in the kitchens. The stove in the saloon is often ornamented with one or more fixed mirrors, which latter also usually belong to the fixtures of the house. For the winter double windows are put in, which very considerably conduce to the warmth of the room, prevent draught, and the outer window from being covered with frost. One window in each room has a so-called wicket-window (lättruta) for ventilation, which is also obtained by ventilators in the stoves. In most of the stoves in the dining-rooms there is a small cupboard or niche with brass doors, in which, during the cold season, plates are put to be kept warm. The size of a common sitting-room is from 200 to 300 square feet by 10 to 12 feet in height.

In the country, and generally in the small provincial towns, the owner himself occupies the whole of his house without letting; but in the larger towns one house most generally holds several families, one on each floor. In Sweden the desire to have many rooms is very great, and in the country, naturally, this luxury can be more easily attained. Besides the rooms which are used by the family more or less, there are also spare rooms, so-called guests' rooms, one or more, which are kept in order the whole year round to accommodate their friends. In the towns, on the other hand, no separate spare rooms are used.

The proportion between a person's income and his want of dwelling-rooms is partly stated in the ordinance, now in force, relating to taxes, which prescribes that a house rent of from 300 to 500 Kr. shall be considered equivalent to an income of at least 3 times that amount; a rent of from 500 to 1,000 Kr., 4 times that amount; from 1,000 to 1,500 Kr., 5 times; and a rent above 1,500 Kr., at least six times that amount.

The rule is that an ordinary family in a tolerably good position is supposed to need: an antechamber, a room for the master, dining-room, saloon, bedroom, nursery, kitchen and pantry, besides wardrobes, larder, etc. The annual rent of such a floor, in a good situation, is at present, in Stockholm, from 1,200 to 2,000 Kr. ($330 to $550 gold). In the larger houses of the more populated towns there is a porter or door-keeper, and the floors are supplied with gas and water; nor are closets wanting.

At the census in Stockholm, in 1868, it was ascertained that there were 6,239 dwelling-houses, namely: 4,011 of brick, 1,806 of wood, 410 of brick and wood, and 12 of other building materials. Of these houses, 2,034 were of 1 story, 1,972 of 2 stories, 1,041 of 3; 956 of 4; 228 of 5, and 8 of 6 stories. Together they contained 83,050 dwelling-rooms and 22,505 kitchens, of which only 543 dwelling-rooms and 241 kitchens were situated under ground. Divided among the population of the town, this number will average 1.29 person to each room. In Göteborg, for the same year, the proportion was 1.65.

The stair-cases of the brick houses are of stone (seldom of iron); the garrets have brick floors, and are besides partitioned off by iron doors from the inhabited part of the house. Between the houses are fire-proof walls (*i. e.*, the walls next to the neighbor's premises have no windows or other apertures). Wooden houses are not allowed to be built any more in Stockholm. Those which still occur are in the outskirts of the town; they are small and old, and are disappearing rapidly.

The Swede is fond of fine *furniture*. It is also asserted, if he has any more money than he particularly needs, he either gives an entertainment or buys a new set of furniture; and it appears, in this respect, as if the tendency were on the increase. The furniture is generally of fir, but veneered with walnut or mahogany, or else made of solid oak or more valuable wood, which is especially the case with table tops, chairs, etc. Nice furniture of a cheaper wood is also used. Iron for furniture in dwelling-rooms is used only exceptionally for bedsteads. Most of the furniture is manufactured within the country.

Houses for the Working Classes.— Since three-fourths of the inhabitants of the country, according to the census, subsist from agriculture and its allied branch pursuits, it follows as a natural consequence that most of the manual laborers are found among the agricultural classes. The laborer among them, in the capacity of male or female servant, always boards with his master, and is also lodged, or else he is a so-called "statkarl," *i. e.*, a person who, besides a cash salary, receives an annual allowance in kind for his subsistence ("stat"), which includes lodging. A third kind of laborer in the employ of the landholder is the "torpare" (cottar), who in reality is a kind of lease-holder of land and houses, and who pays the rent by so many days' labor. The Swedish agricultural laborer, therefore, as a rule, need not have any trouble in procuring a dwelling. This also applies to such as are employed at mines, iron-works, saw-mills, or other manufacturing establishments in the country. The owners of the works provide, at least their permanent work-people, with lodgings, and the extra laborer ought not to have any difficulty in finding shelter with the peasantry, who generally have room to spare.

It is quite different, however, with the laborer in the towns, where, as a rule, the employer does not provide lodgings, but every one must take care of himself. With the development of manufacturing industry in the towns, and the constantly increasing stream of unencumbered workmen, the question about houses for working people has, especially of late years, become a matter of greater importance; and still more so, since in Sweden, as in many places abroad, the populations of the towns have begun to increase at such a rate that as yet it has been impossible to erect a corresponding number of houses, which has had an injurious effect both on poor and rich. Individual enterprise, the larger industrial establishments, workmen's unions, or institutions, have therefore in many places tried to remedy this evil, and consequently we find so-called houses for the working classes in our larger towns, such as Stockholm, Göteborg, Norrköping, Jönköping, Malmö, etc.

For want of materials for a complete account in this respect, the following may be stated only with regard to *Göteborg*, from which it may be seen how they have tried to solve this difficult problem. To this we ought also to add the observation, that Göteborg may be supposed to be the place where they have been best able to find means for the solution of the question.

At Göteborg there are two classes of houses for the working people, such as are only intended for letting, and such as may, on stipulated terms, become the property of the tenant.

1st. *Houses designed only for letting:*

The Old Houses for the Working Classes in Göteborg. These were established in 1846 with an irreversible loan of 75,000 Kr., given by private individuals on obligations at 4 per cent. interest, and guaranteed by the town. At present there are several houses—some small and some large—that have been built out of this capital. Together they contain 16 dwelling-places, each consisting of 1 room and a kitchen, pantry, and wood-cellar, and 24 dwelling-places, each consisting of a so-called "spis-rum", or a room with a kitchen-grate. The rent is 10 Kr. a month for the former, and 7 Kr. a month for the latter. The assets of the houses at the end of the year 1874 were 88,000 Kr., consisting in the value of the houses erected; and the liabilities 75,000 Kr., in the irreversible loan.

Robert Dickson's Establishment. This was founded partly in 1857 by a donation of 150,000 Kr., partly in 1858 by a testamentary disposition of 180,000 Kr. by the late Mr. ROBERT DICKSON, merchant. The stipulations attached to it by the donor were that, with a view to the moral and economical improvement of the working classes, healthy and comfortable dwelling-houses should be built and the tenements let at a moderate rent, in preference, to members of the proper working classes. For the promotion of order and cleanliness within the dwellings the tenants were also subject to certain obligations, among which may be mentioned, not to receive any persons as inmates of the house, excepting those belonging to the family. It was further stipulated that out of the net proceeds 90 per cent. should be employed for the further erecting of dwelling-houses for the working classes, and the remaining 10 per cent. should be put aside for a fund, which, on the proposal of the directors, and the approval of the municipal board of the town and the governor of the province, might be used for such generally useful establishments as would be supposed could conduce to the comfort and improvement of the workingman. The supervision and management, not only of this establishment, but the old dwelling-houses for the working classes in the town, is entrusted to a board of directors appointed by the Local Government Board, and their accounts and management are examined by auditors appointed by the same authority.

Since the year 1858, 26 houses in all have been built out of the capital given, in four different places; of these the first six are built of timber, all the rest of brick. These houses contain 180 separate dwelling-places, of which 44 consist each of 2 rooms and a kitchen, 132 of 1 room and a kitchen, and besides 4 single rooms without kitchens. And for the convenience of the tenants, a house containing a laundry, bake-oven, and an ironing-room, has been erected on each of the four building sites. Each dwelling has also a pantry and wood-cellar of its own. The amount of rent, which since the beginning of the establishment has remained the same, and in proportion to current prices has been very low, has, however, this year (1875) been raised, and is at present: for 2 rooms and a kitchen 15 to 15½ Kr., for 1 room and a kitchen 8½ to 12 Kr., and for a single room 4 Kr. by the month. The capital has since 1858 increased from 330,000 Kr. to 553,300 Kr., and consists in houses to value of 414,500, building fund saved for the further erection of houses 113,800, and the 10 per cent. fund 25,000 Kr. The managers have this year bought a large building site, with the intention of erecting 14 houses, each to consist of 8 dwelling-places, and the work is already commenced. It may be anticipated that this establishment, at some future time not very distant, will develop into greater importance.

The Joint Stock Company in Göteborg for the erection of dwelling-houses. This Joint Stock Company, which was sanctioned during the latter part of the year 1874, and established in order to counteract, though it might be but temporarily, the seriously increasing want of dwelling-houses, caused by the great influx of laboring people, had already at the beginning of this year (1875) completed two large frame houses, each containing 20 dwelling-places, consisting of a room with a kitchen-grate walled in; and during the summer 12 others were built, each containing 6 such rooms as stated above. The rent is 7.50 Kr. a month for each dwelling. According to the rules of the company no profit is aimed at, and a larger dividend than 5 per cent. on the capital paid in is not allowed. The capital is at present 100,000 Kr. ($27,800 gold).

2d. *Houses for the Working Classes intended, on stipulated terms, to become the property of the tenant.*

The Göteborg Savings Bank's Dwelling-houses for the Working Classes. Since the year 1869 the principals of the savings bank of the town of Göteborg have put aside a part of the annual profit with the intention of erecting healthy and suitable houses for the working classes, which might, on stipulated terms, become the property of the tenants. The sum which, until this year, has been assigned for that purpose amounts to nearly 30,000 Kr., and for the promotion of the undertaking the savings bank has further granted loans to the amount of 56,000 Kr. on security in the houses erected. Hitherto 8 houses have been built, each containing 2 dwelling-places, of which one has 2 rooms and a kitchen, and one 1 room and a kitchen; and 10 houses, each containing 2 dwelling-places of 2 rooms and a kitchen each, and one single room. The first 8 houses erected have been sold for a deposit of 300 Kr. and a monthly rent of 22 Kr.; the time for the payment in full being 18½ years, at the expiration of which they become the property of the tenants. For the houses that have been last erected, and for which offers are to be lodged just about this time (summer, 1875), the deposit is calculated at 400 Kr., and the monthly rent at 52 Kr. The time for the payment in this case will be 20 years.

The Göteborg Joint Stock Company for the erection of Dwelling-houses for the Working Classes. This company, which was established in 1873, and has a paid-up capital of 319,000 Kr., has already erected 18 houses, and 14 houses are being built. Each house contains 2 dwellings, consisting of 2 rooms and a kitchen each, and 1 room with a kitchen-grate walled in. A small garden-plot is attached to each house. The terms on which these houses may become the property of the tenant are, that he on the signing of the contract pays 400 Kr., and afterwards 52 Kr. per month in advance. Further, he is bound to keep the property in repair, to have it kept clean, but he is exempt from taxes on the same. He shall also reside on the premises, but he may let to respectable people whatever is not needed for his own use; the rent, however, in this case must not exceed 7.50 Kr. per month for a room, 6 Kr. for a kitchen, or 10 Kr. for the room with the kitchen-grate. No public house or tavern business is allowed to be carried on on the premises. Whoever complies with these conditions for 20 years becomes the owner of half of the house, which part has a value of 8,000 Kr.

These, as well as the houses erected by the Göteborg Savings Bank, are of brick and tile-roofed.

Besides these houses, the *Göteborg Workmen's Association* have formed a company for the erection of houses for the working classes, but the company has not yet commenced its operations.

[CLASS 343.] **Commercial Systems and Appliances** are described under the section Commerce (page 29); Coins and Banking Establishments (page 21); Post and Telegraph (page 27); Means of Transport (page 100), etc.

[CLASS 344.] **Money, Mints and Coining.** See above page 21.

[CLASS 345 A.] **Government and Law.** We have given a general account in the introductory part, under the section Administration of the State (p. 15); Administration of Justice (p. 17); Representative Assemblies (p. 19); Patents (p.

32); Post and Telegraph (p. 27), etc. Separately, some information is also given about the prison arrangements (p. 18).

It consequently remains to give a somewhat detailed account of the *forces, military and naval, for the defence of the country.*

THE ARMY.*

[*Class* 345 *B.*]

A.—ORGANIZATION AND ADMINISTRATION OF THE ARMY.

THE Army organization of Sweden is based on the Cadre System. The Regular Army (Stammen), or peace-establishment, is obtained by Enlistment, "Rustning" ("Array," or the furnishing of men and horses for the Cavalry), and "Rotering" (furnishing of men for the Infantry). The Reserve, which, after previous training, is called in only in case of war, is made up by Universal Conscription ("Värnepligt"). The troops levied by the "Rotering," and "Rustning," are comprised under the general name of the "Indelta" Army.

CADRE TROOPS.

I. *Enlisted Troops.* Enlistment for military service is only allowed within the country, and all disputes in connection therewith are decided by the civil authorities.

The enlisted man must be free from physical infirmities and faults, and have a height of at least 5 feet 5.8 inch, Swedish (1.66 Mètres). He shall not be less than 17, nor more than 30 years of age. The term of service is generally 6 years. After having served his time, the soldier is entitled to a discharge, unless his term expire during the periodical regimental drill, in which case he is bound to remain in the service until the end of the manœuvres. In exceptional cases, however, his Colonel (or Regimental Commander) has the right to discharge him earlier, except in time of war, when no enlisted soldier can be discharged for any other cause than sickness. A soldier may also receive his discharge before the end of his term of service, in consequence of disability for military service, and for the commission of dishonoring crimes. Every enlisted soldier, belonging to a garrison regiment, obtains the right to a pension after serving 20 years in full, and attaining the age of 40.

These forces are garrisoned the whole year, and do duty in the larger towns and fortresses, with the exception, however, of one regiment, of which the officers and men are only called in yearly for short drills, and are absent on furlough in the intervals.

Of enlisted garrisoned troops, the effective numbers are:

Infantry	1,552 men.
Cavalry	980 "
Artillery	4,075 "
Engineers	600 "†
Total	7,207 men.

Of enlisted troops, not in garrison, there are:

Infantry	476 men.‡

II. "*Indelta*" *Troops. a.* "*Rotering*" (Infantry). For nearly two hundred years the different provinces have each undertaken, on condition of exemption from the former levies, to furnish a certain number of soldiers. For a more

* Contributed by the Staff-General.—The following gives an account of the Army as actually existing. It should, however, be observed, that several propositions for the reorganization of the Army have been submitted to the Diet by the Government, but, as yet, none has been adopted.

† A new Battalion of Sappers of 360.

‡ A regiment is now under formation, but only one company is yet raised.

equal apportionment of the duty thus undertaken, the Provinces have been *divided* ("indelta") into so-called "rotar" (soldiers' cantons or districts). Each canton ("rote") consists of two whole farms ("gårdar"); sometimes, however, the half is counted as a whole. In the course of time it became necessary, owing to improved cultivation, to make some slight modifications. The new (295) cantons that have thus arisen have partly been employed in improving the old districts.

One of the farms in the district is called the "Stam-Rote" (Head Canton), and on it the soldier's cottage is generally situated. Its owner, in the capacity of Canton-Master ("Rote-mästare"), is responsible for the duties, in common, of the canton. The canton is bound always to keep a soldier, and to find his pay and house. In time of war the cantons are exempted from the duty of recruiting.

The recruits are inspected for approval at musters, held twice a year, before the Governor of the Province, and the Commander or Colonel of the Regiment. Here the agreements entered into, between the canton-owner or keeper ("Rote-hållare") and the proposed recruit, are confirmed. The recruit must be over 17, and under 25 years of age, and his height must not be less than 5 feet 5.8 inches, Swedish (1.66 mètres). When the recruit has been received as a soldier, he can neither be dismissed as unfit, nor discharged without the consent of his canton-owner, unless through age, sickliness, or bad conduct, he be found incapable or unworthy for further military service. The right to a pension is attained at the age of 50, and after having served 30 years. Men serving in Rifle Corps are an exception, they being entitled to the pension at the age of 45, and after 25 years of service.

The soldier's emoluments are fixed for each man, by a contract entered into by him and the Canton-Master. They generally consist in the *Bounty* ("hand-money", värfningspengar), which varies between 10 and 100 Kr.; further, a *yearly pay* of 2 to 15 Kr., and, finally, the "*Hemkall*" (or "torp," farm laborers' homestead), which must consist of a small cottage, with requisite outhouses, some land, etc. On an average, the private soldier's income from his canton can be estimated at 150 Kr.

During his attendance at the yearly regimental drill, or when ordered out on other military service, the soldier is maintained at the expense of the State.

Originally the canton had to furnish the soldier's clothing, but at present it is, until further, absolved from this duty.

The total number of Infantry cantons is 20,376, of which, however, 2,074 are appointed to pay the regimental bands and non-commissioned officers. Of the remaining 18,302 effective cantons, 180 furnish troopers, for whom horses are supplied by cantons, specially set apart for that purpose.

b. "*Rustning*" (Cavalry).—By the term of "rustning" is meant the duty attached to the ownership of certain lands, to engage, support, and equip a trooper, together with a charger fully efficient for military service, on condition of certain mitigation in the rent on such lands. Where the rent was considered too low, an additional sum towards the "rustning" was appropriated from the rent of some other farm. This rent has received the name of "Augmentation Rent" (augments-ränta).

For this duty of "Rustning," which was introduced at the same time with the "Rotering," and shared on the same grounds, contracts called "Rustnings-bref" (or "Letters of Array") were made between the State and every separate Arrayer ("Rust-hållare").

By virtue of such contract the Arrayer is released from payment of nearly the whole "ground-rent," *i. e.*, the legal tax on his land (and, in most cases, he receives a separate augmentation rent), and is exempted from Rotering. On the other hand the Arrayer is bound, in time of peace, to furnish an efficient man, and to defray all expenses, and medical attendance, to supply and maintain his outfit, equipage, and accoutrements, to furnish and maintain an approved charger, with saddle and saddlery complete, and finally, to take charge of and keep the kit and equipment of the trooper and horse, and to disburse all charges for his baggage and appointments. The average annual cost of the Cavalry "Array" may be estimated at 350 Kr. for each "Arrayer." The array and augmentation rents together amount to sums varying between 240 Kr. and 420 Kr.

The Arrayer is bound, within a period of six weeks, in time of peace, to fill any vacancy occurring in his canton. The recruit shall not be less than 17 or more than 25 years old, and his height must be at least 5 feet 5.8 inches, Swedish (1.66 mètres), with the exception, however, of young men under the age of 21, who can be approved of if measuring the 5 feet 5 inches (1.63 mètres).* Otherwise, respecting enlistment, discharge, and pensioning, the same regulations are in force for the Cavalry (rusthåll) as for the Infantry (rotehåll) previously described.

The supplying of vacancies of cavalry horses (called "remounting", remontering) is also the duty of the Arrayer, and the new horses (called "remounts") are examined at so-called Remounting-Inspections, held twice yearly, by the Governor of the Province and the Colonel or Corps-Commander.

In consequence of an increased want of infantry, a part of the cavalry regiments have been transformed into infantry, but they still retain their original nature of cavalry regiments. Instead of the abatement in costs for Cavalry Array, arising through this alteration, the arrayer of these "dismounted" regiments contributes a "charge for horse vacancies." Instead of this charge some of them furnish a horse for the artillery exercises.

At present there are 6,505 Cavalry Cantons, of which, however, 724 are appropriated to the payment of musicians and under officers. The effective force is, accordingly, 5,781 men, of whom 2,661 serve as Infantry, and 3,120 as Cavalry.

RESERVE FORCES.

I. *Extra Infantry Array* (Extra Rotering). At the time when the old Infantry Array was introduced, some parts of the land were exempted from this duty. The inequality of taxation that resulted from this arrangement gave rise to the subsequent introduction of a law by which this so-called "privileged land" was subjected to "extra array." The "extra cantons" (extra rotar) thus formed are, however, exempted from all duty of recruiting in time of peace. But—in contradistinction to the rule applying to the other "arrays" in the regular "Indelta" army—they are obliged, during war, to furnish men, and to supply them, also, with clothing.

In order, nevertheless, to have a supply of horses in readiness at the breaking out of war, agreements have been made with the extra canton owners to supply a horse, instead of an untrained recruit.

At present the number of extra cantons amounts to 2,671.

II. *Universal Conscription Troops.* The duty of every citizen, to defend his country, has been known and admitted in Sweden, from time immemorial. This obligation has been put into practice, with more or less severity, at different periods, and thus there have been times when here, as elsewhere, the duty has existed only as an idea, while at other times it has been one of the fundamental principles of the Constitution.

At present, every Swede is "värnepligtig", *h. e.* liable to personal military service; or, in other words, to enter the *Universal Conscription* (Bevāring). Neither exemption by payment nor substitution is allowed. The conscript's military service commences in the year following that in which he completes his 20th year, and finishes in the year in which he attains 25 years of age.

The following persons are, however, legally exempted from conscription, viz.: Those who are

* The maximum height allowed for a recruit is nowhere stipulated, either in the enlisted or Indelta Army.

incapacitated or totally unfit for military service, owing to physical deformities or defects, sickness, and constitutional unsoundness or debility; those who are engaged in military service, or in the pilot and lighthouse services; postillions and mail-carriers; armorers, artisans and mechanics employed in the workshops of the Artillery and Navy; artisans and workmen at small arms factories, powder and sulphur works; and, finally, such persons in the service of the State as the King deems proper to release from this duty.

The Conscription Force is divided into five classes, according to age. In time of war, or else whenever required in defence of the Kingdom, the King can levy one or more classes for military service, either from the whole country or from particular provinces. In time of peace, on the contrary, only the two youngest classes can be called out every year for 15 days' drill. Further, masters, mates, engineers, and other persons and seamen employed in the Merchant Navy, are exempted from drill and military service in time of peace. They are, however, in time of war bound to serve in the Royal Navy up to their 35th year.

While in active service the conscripts are under martial law, but else under civil law.

The country is divided into separate Conscription Districts for the Army and Navy; but the Island of Gottland, however, having an exceptional Law of Conscription, is not included therein. The conscripts are distributed among the enlisted and Indelta regiments or corps in their respective districts.

Every youth, on attaining the age of conscription, shall appear personally at the Muster of Conscripts, which is held in the month of April, every year, within each separate district. The musters are held by the Governor of the Province, in the presence of the Colonel commanding the Infantry Regiment quartered within the district, and is assisted by a Commissary of Musters and a Surgeon. At the muster the men are approved and enrolled, or else rejected. In the latter case they have to present themselves again at the muster of the ensuing year. The conscripts, on the other hand, who are rejected or exempted on legal grounds, receive a so-called Free-Letter (or Certificate of Exemption, "Fri-Sedel"), signed by the Governor.

In districts where, besides Infantry, Artillery or Cavalry is stationed, a small contingent is also selected for distribution among the latter services. In this case the conscript's choice is taken in consideration. At present the Conscript Troops are divided into Military and Naval Troops, but of late years the whole force has received its training in the Army. The strength of the first class is about 20,000 men, and of all the classes about 80,000 men.

Of special Conscription Corps, with a permanent cadre of officers, but no permanent force of rank and file (stamtrupp), there is one regiment* and two battalions.

TERRITORIAL TROOPS.

I. *Defence of the Island of Gottland.* Owing to its considerable distance from the main land, the Island of Gottland is particularly exposed to the attack of an enemy. Under such circumstances, and as it may often become difficult to send reinforcements from the main land, the inhabitants of the island have engaged to supply a separate National Militia (National Beväring), in which every man of the population, capable of bearing arms, is obliged to serve. The age of conscription commences with the 18th and ends with the 50th year. But the conscripts remain in a reserve from their 50th to their 60th year, to assist in the construction of field-works, etc. This National Militia cannot be ordered beyond the boundaries of the island, and stands under martial law only while in active service.

At the annual musters, every man capable of bearing arms, and not unfit for service owing to age or sickness, is enrolled. Householders, tenant farmers, etc., form a separate corps that is not ordered out on active service except in cases of most pressing necessity.

* This regiment is being disbanded.

The National Militia is only organized as Infantry and Artillery. The Infantry consists of 4 battalions of 7 or 8 companies each; the Artillery consists of 3 Foot Batteries. The rank and file of the Infantry is made up of conscripts between 18 and 45 years of age, and men in the Reserve, of from 45 to 50 years old; the rank and file of the Artillery is composed of a cadre of 75 enlisted privates, and 200 conscripts between 21 and 30 years of age, who are selected from among the infantry-men by the commanding officers of each battery.

The officers of the National Militia, as in the rest of the army, are appointed by the King, while the non-commissioned officers are elected by the rank and file, so that one Corporal is nominated by every 25 men, and one Under-officer by every 50 men.

The men are drilled 6 days every year. Ammunition and arms are provided at the expense of the State, and the men themselves keep and account for these articles. They are exercised in their own clothes, and receive compensation for wear and tear. The troops also supply their own rations, for which the State pays every private 37 öre daily.

The total strength of the National Militia in 1872 was 6,335 men (exclusive of the Reserve), which is 11.7 of the population.

II. *The Volunteer Rifle Corps* ("Skarpskytteföreningar"). The Army Organization of Sweden, based on a small standing army and an undeveloped militia institution, has not been able to satisfy the demand of the patriot for a strong and efficient defence. The Corps of Rifle Volunteers have become the visible evidence of this feeling of insecurity, and their object is to constitute, even in time of peace, an organized voluntary defence to co-operate with the forces established by law.

The Regulations, contained in the Royal Order of March 8th, 1861, respecting the Corps of Rifle Volunteers, provide as follows, viz:

Every Corps of Rifle Volunteers is entitled to decide and order its own internal organization, but such corps is bound to undertake the obligations that are necessary, in order that the King, as Commander-in-Chief of the Military Forces of the Kingdom, may be able—not only in time of peace, but also on the breaking out of war—to issue orders for the effectual employment of all the available forces for the defence of the Kingdom. Every Volunteer Corps shall therefore be allotted to a certain District, Assize, or Parish, irrespective of the different craft, profession, or social position of the members, and they shall be subordinate to the Commanding Officer ("Öfverbefälhafvare"), appointed by the King, from among three persons nominated. Should a war arise between Sweden and a foreign power, or the peace of the Realm be so seriously threatened by external enemies that it should become expedient or necessary to place the army in the field, every Volunteer corps shall further be liable—upon receiving orders to that effect from the Government officer or authority who shall be appointed thereto—to perform the military service or duties to which the corps be ordered, within the district wherein the corps has elected to serve.

If, finally, a Volunteer Corps be called out for active service, its members shall be subject to Martial Law.

The total force of Rifle Volunteers on the 31st of December, 1874, was 13,778 men.

THE COMMAND OF THE ARMY.

The grades in the command are *Commissioned* and *Non-commissioned Officers* and *Corporals.*

The *Commissioned Officers* are divided in three classes: *General, Regimental,* or *Field,* and *Company Officers.*

The first class comprises 5 ranks: *Field Marshal* (a rank that is only conferred during war), *General, Lieutenant General, Major General* and *Adjutant General* (not conferred since 1842).

The second class has three grades: *Colonel, Lieutenant Colonel* and *Major.*

The third class consists of *Captains, Lieutenants* and *Sub-Lieutenants* (Cornets and Ensigns).

The *Non-commissioned*, or *Under-Officers*, are: Sergeant Majors ("Bombardier" Sergeants, or "Styckjunkare" in the Artillery, "Conductors" in the Royal Engineers), Color and Company Sergeants ("Under Conductors") and Sergeants ("Furir" or "Forager" Sergeants only in the Infantry).

The *Corporals* are classed as: "Distinction" Corporals (1st "Constables" in the Artillery), Corporals and Vice-Corporals (2d "Constables" in the Artillery.

Every grade is distinguished by its separate marks, worn on the uniform. In some of the ranks there are, under different denominations, several classes of salaries, which, however, except in the grade of Major, entail no alteration in the right of command.

The King alone appoints and promotes officers to the commissioned grades. To obtain a first commission it is necessary to have gone through a course of study at the Military College. There is a regulation by which it is provided that persons may be promoted to the grade of commissioned officer without passing any examination, if they have been in actual service for six years as non-commissioned officer, and at least two years of that time as Sergeant-Major; but this regulation is very rarely applied. In the lower grades, after the first commission, promotions generally take place according to seniority, but Artillery and Engineer officers are required to have passed an examination at the Military High-School (Staff-College, "Krigshögskola") before promotion to the rank of Lieutenant. Officers of higher grades are promoted only for merit.

Non-commissioned Officers are appointed and promoted by the Colonel (or Corps Commander), as also Corporals of all grades, on the nomination of the Captain commanding the company.

The salary of the officers and non-commissioned officers in the enlisted regiments is paid quarterly, in cash. But the manner of paying the "Indelta" forces, on the contrary, is based on the "Indelta" system, *i. e.*, the salaries are paid from the rents of certain lands, or farms, the revenues of which are appropriated to the maintenance of the Army, or consist in the actual proceeds of such farm-lands.

Both officers and non-commissioned officers are bound to support, clothe and equip themselves out of their salaries, and in the "Indelta" Army to reside permanently in the district in which their respective regiments are raised ("regementets ständ"). The non-commissioned officers, however, receive an additional allowance for clothing, and a part of their accoutrements is supplied at the expense of the State.

Likewise those officers who are required to be mounted are bound to purchase and keep one or more service chargers out of their salary; only captains and subalterns in the Artillery, and officers of the "Pontoneer Battalion" and "Field Signal Company" are mounted at the cost of the State.

Corporals have the same income as private soldiers, but receive an additional allowance in cash.

For the pensioning of officers and non-commissioned officers there is a common Army Pension Fund, formed partly by a State grant, and partly by certain stipulated deductions from the salaries of all officers.

In general cases, in order to receive a pension, the applicant shall have been in the service 30 years, and reached the age of 50. Non-commissioned officers of the enlisted garrison regiments are, however, entitled to a pension after 25 years of service, and at the age of 45. Any person so seriously injured in war, or in the service, as to make his retirement compulsory, receives a pension corresponding to his rank, and besides, if the casualty occur in war, he may receive an increased pension. Officers and non-commissioned officers, who have served a certain number of years over the age entitling to a pension, and who further undertake to hold themselves in readiness for active service, within the country, in case of war, receive a supplementary pension out of the Government Funds. There are also private funds for the pensioning of officers and non-commissioned officers. For the army there is, further, a common Fund for Widows and Wards, from which pensions are paid to widows, and to children during their minority, of the officers and non-commissioned officers who have been members of this fund; * there is also, in nearly every regiment, one or more similar funds for the rank and file.

Corporals are entitled to a pension at the same age, and on the same conditions as privates. However, men who have served as corporals during the last three years of their term of enlistment, receive a pension one grade higher than they would have been entitled to as privates. Vice-Corporals do not enjoy any advantages above the privates with respect to pensioning.

It should be remarked, regarding the relation of officers to civil society, that except during active service every military man is subject to the same laws and regulations as other citizens; accordingly, except during war, any person serving in the Army can be elected member of the Diet. In the Oath of Allegiance he further promises both to defend the Royal Power, and to conform to the Constitution of the Realm. Military officers and officials, in common with all persons in the pay of the State, are, however, prohibited from carrying on retail business, or any trade.

Reserve Officers.—Beside the officers in the cadres there is a number of reserve officers, unattached to any regiment or corps, and a definite number of pensioned "disposable" officers. The former may be ordered on duty both in time of peace and war, while the latter are only bound to serve within the country in case of war, up to the age of 60 or 65. The age depends upon the rank held by such an officer.†

* In this connection it may be observed that every officer is entitled to marry without the permission of his superior officer, and is only bound to send in a notification of the fact.

† There are also "half-pay" officers and non-commissioned officers for the Reserve Batteries of the Artillery.

The officers of the "Corps for Road and Water-Works" (Väg och Vattenbyggnads Corpsen), who, under ordinary circumstances, are employed as engineers at public works and buildings, can also be ordered on duty as Engineer officers in the army during war.

In order to have a sufficient number of candidates for the non-commissioned grades ready for service in case of war, agreements to that effect are made with Conscripts suitable for promotion. These so-called "Conscripts-Elect" (Bevärings Eliter) enjoy certain advantages for the extended service to which they become liable. They can afterwards be promoted to "Conscript-Corporals" and "Under-Officers." The number of these is not great.

Colonels of regiments are also entitled to receive and nominate so-called "Volunteers." This name is given to young men who receive neither bounty nor pay, and during peace are not bound to any stipulated term of duty, but enter the service with the object of promotion to the non-commissioned grades, or of being admitted to the Military College.

Administration and Command of the Army.

The *King* has the supreme command of the military and naval forces of the realm.

Next to the King the Minister of War is Commander-in-Chief of the army, in which capacity it is his duty to decide with full and supreme authority on all matters relating to the discipline of the army.

The *Minister of War* is the chief department of the army, and to it belongs the management and decision of all questions concerning the organization of the army. It is divided into two sections: the "*Chancery Office*" (Kansli-Expedition), and the "*Executive Office*" (Commando-Expedition). To the former section belongs the preliminary treatment of all affairs that, according to the Constitution, require to be submitted to the King in Council of State, and to the latter all other military matters.

The highest administrative department of the

army, called the "*Army Administration,*" is subordinate to the Ministering of War, and is divided into four sections, or departments, viz.:

1. The *Artillery Department*, at the head of which is the "*Master-General of Ordnance*" (General commanding all the Artillery forces, General-Fälttygmästare), manages and decides on all matters relating to the material of the artillery, arms, and ammunition of the army, etc.

2. The *Fortification Department*, at the head of which is the *General, commanding the Royal Engineers* (Fortifikationen), manages and decides on all matters relating to the building and repairs of fortresses, billeting and quartering of troops in the Capital, etc.

3. The *Commissary Department* (Intendents-Departementet), at the head of which is the *Commissary General-in-Chief* (General Intendent), manages and decides on all matters relating to the recruiting, remounting, equipment, and supplies of the army, etc.

4. The *Civil Department*, at the head of which is the *Paymaster-General* (General-Krigskommissarie), manages and decides on all matters relating to the pay and "Indelta" establishment of the army, etc.

For military purposes the kingdom is divided into five *Military Districts*. All the forces cantoned in such district are under the orders of a general officer, Commandant of the District (General Befälhafvare), with the exception of the Regiments of the Guard, that form a separate brigade, commanded by the General (Chef) of the "Brigade of Life-Guards," and the National Militia of Gottland, that is under the orders of a separate military commandant (Militär-befälhafvare). Besides the engineer troops are also under the immediate command of the Fortification General (Chefen for Fortifikationen), the artillery under the command of the Master-General of Ordnance, and the cavalry (excepting a cavalry corps in the Province of Jemtland, standing under the immediate orders of the District Commandant) under the command of the Inspector-General of Cavalry.

The *Staffs* of the army—besides the Aid-de-Camps attached to the King and Royal Princes—are: the General, the Artillery and the Engineer (or Fortification) Staffs.

In the year 1873 a reorganization of the Swedish *General Staff* was effected. Its *personnel* is now composed of: 1 Chief (Commander), 14 Head-Adjutants, and 24 Staff-Adjutants. To the former class belong 1 Colonel, 3 Lieutenant-Colonels, and 10 Majors; to the latter 16 Captains and 8 Lieutenants. The Head-quarters of the General Staff has 4 Divisions or Sections: viz.: for Communications (Roads, etc.), Military Statistics, Military History, and Topography, employing in all 22 officers. Officers detached on special duty are: 1 Assisting the Minister of War, 1 Assisting the Chief of the General Staff, 5 in the Executive Office of the War Ministerium (Kommando-Expedition), 5 as Commanders of the Staffs of Military Districts, 1 assisting the Inspector-General of Cavalry, 1 for the Brigade of Life-Guards, 1 assisting the Military Commandant of Gottland, and 1 at the Commissary Department of the Army Administration.

Candidates ("aspiranter") for the General Staff must go through a course of study in the General Staff Department of the Military Academy (Staff College), assist three consecutive years at the drill, exercise, and manœuvres of the branch of service to which they belong, and be employed in the staff duties of their regiment. They must subsequently serve 2½ years in the General Staff, of which two summers and one winter in its Topographical Department. Further, they must go through the yearly exercises in the branches of the service to which they do not belong, and finally be sufficiently skilled in riding.

The *Artillery Staff* consists of a certain number of officers detached for the duty, serving under a separate staff commander, as the staff of the "Master-General of Ordnance."

The *Fortification Staff* comprises all the engineer officers of the army, and furnishes the engineer and pontooneer regiments with officers.

Strength of the Army and Organization of its different Services.

The *Infantry* of the army consists of

2 Regiments of Life Guards,
2 " " Life Grenadiers,
1 " " Marines.*
17 " " Infantry,
1 " " Rifles (Fältjägare).
1 Battalion " Grenadiers,
1 Corps " "
3 " " Rifles.

In times of peace each infantry regiment is divided into 2 battalions, and each battalion into 4 companies. A corps corresponds to 1 battalion.

There are, altogether, 48 battalions of infantry.

There are, in addition, cadres of officers for 2 conscription battalions.

The *Staff of an Infantry Regiment* consists of

1 Colonel, commanding the Regiment,
3 Majors, commanding Battalions,
1 Captain, or Subaltern, Regimental Quartermaster,
2 Lieutenants or Ensigns, Adjutants,
1 Regimental Chaplain,
3 Surgeons,
1 Regimental "Auditor"† ("Auditör"),
1 " Paymaster ("Skrifvare"),
2 "Muster Writers" ("Mönster Skrifvare"),
2 Battalion Adjutants;
1 Regimental Commissary,
1 " Sergeant-Major ("Fältväbel"),
1 " Drum-Major,
10 " Musicians,
2 Armorers ("Gevärshandtverkare").

The staff of a corps, or single battalion, is somewhat smaller.

A *Company* comprises

1 Captain, commanding the Company,
2 Lieutenants,
1 Ensign,
1 Company Sergeant-Major,
1 Color Sergeant,
2 "Forager" Sergeants ("Fourirer"),
12 Corporals and Vice-Corporals,
5 Musicians (Drummers, etc.), and about
120 Rank and file.

As a rule there are, besides, 4 captains and 4 sergeants divided between the 2 battalions of the regiment.

From each company 4 men are selected for duty as sappers ("infantry pioneers") and instructed, under separate officers, in the construction of field-works and bridges, etc.; also 8 "sharp-shooters" (riflemen), who practice to attain great skill as marksmen; and 1 nurse-soldier, who is trained at some hospital.

In the time of war the regiment is formed into 3 battalions, of 800 men each, by calling in the reserve.

The *Cavalry* consists of

1 Regiment of Horse Guards,	4	Squadrons,
1 " " Hussars,	10	"
1 " " "	6	"
1 " " "	5	"
1 Corps " "	5	"
1 Regiment of Dragoons,	10	"
1 Corps " "	5	"
1 " " Mounted Rifles,	2	"
Total,	47	"

The *Staff of a Cavalry Regiment* consists of

1 Colonel, commanding the Regiment,
2 Majors,
1 Captain, or Subaltern, Regimental Quartermaster,
2 Regimental Adjutants,
1 " Riding-Master ("Stallmästare"),
1 " Chaplain,
1 " "Auditor,"
2 to 3 Surgeons,
1 Paymaster,
1 Regimental Veterinary Surgeon,
2 "Muster Writers,"
1 Armorer (Pistol Smith), and
1 Saddler.

The Staff of a Cavalry Corps is somewhat smaller.

* It is being disbanded.
† Consulting advocate at courts-martial, etc.

To a *Squadron* belong
1 Captain, commanding the Squadron,
1 Lieutenant,
1 Cornet,
1 Troop Sergeant-Major,
3 Sergeants,
6 Corporals and Vice-Corporals,
3 Musicians (Trumpeters, etc.), and
83 to 93 Men.

There are, in addition, in some regiments and corps, from 3 to 6 officers and 3 to 6 under officers for the different squadrons.

On the war footing the strength of the squadrons is increased to 100 men.

The *Artillery* will consist of 30 batteries, forming 3 regiments of equal strength; besides, there are also 6 garrison companies, a reserve of 9 batteries, and a Pyrotechnical Corps ("Fyrverkarecorps"). The artillery is composed of rifle muzzle-loading cannon of 9.65 Cm., 7.69 Cm., and 6.68 Centimètres calibre. Of the above thirty batteries, twelve are 9.65 Cm. "riding"* (åkande), ten 7.69 Cm. "riding," six 7.69 Cm. horse,—and two 6.68 Cm. foot-batteries.

Beside the artillery above mentioned, there are, as previously stated, 3 batteries in Gottland, of which one is a 9.65 Cm., and two are 6.68 Cm. foot-batteries.

A regiment of artillery is formed of 5 divisions, and a battery is divided into 3 sections or detachments, each having 2 guns.

The *Staff of an Artillery Regiment* consists of
1 Colonel, commanding the Regiment,
2 Lieutenant-Colonels,
4 Majors,
6 Captains,
3 Lieutenants,
6 Sub-Lieutenants,
1 Regimental Riding-Master,
1 First Chaplain,
1 Regimental Surgeon,
3 Battalion (Assistant) Surgeons,
1 Paymaster,
1 Battalion (Second) Chaplain,
1 "Auditor,"
1 Veterinary Surgeon,
3 "Bombardier" Sergeants (Sergeant-Majors),
6 Sergeants,
2 "Staff" Trumpeters.

A *Battery* will consist of

	9.65 Cm. "Riding."	7.69 Cm. "Riding."	7.69 Cm. Horse.	6.68 Cm. Foot.
Captain commanding the battery	1	1	1	1
Captain commanding the park	1	1	1	1
Lieutenants commanding detachments	2	2	2	2
Sub-Lieutenant commanding detachment	1	1	1	1
Sergeant-Major, (Battery Adjutant)	1	1	1	1
Sergeant-Major (Park Under-Officer)	1	1	1	1
Sergeants, (Cannon Commanders)	3	3	3	3
Battery Trumpeter	1	1	1	1
"First Constables" (Corporals)	5	4	4	4
"Second Constables"	7	7	7	7
"Detachment Trumpeters"	3	3	3	3
Privates	88	88	103	61
Battery Artificers	2	2	2	2
Horses	20	20	26	10

A *Fortress or Garrison Company* (Battery) will consist of
1 Captain, commanding the Company,
1 Lieutenant,
1 Sub-Lieutenant,
1 Sergeant-Major,
2 Sergeants,
5 Corporals ("Constables"),
1 Trumpeter, and
50 Privates.

The *Pyrotechnic Corps* consists of 2 officers, detached from the artillery regiments, 1 foreman, and 25 men.

On the war footing the Conscripts are called in and the number of horses to each battery increased, partly by "extra array" and partly by purchase.

* So called from some of the gunners riding on the carriages. Such batteries are intermediate between a horse and foot-battery.

A *Battery on the war footing* will have

	9.65 Cm. "Riding."	7.69 Cm. "Riding."	7.69 Cm. Horse.	6.68 Cm. Foot.
Officers	5	5	5	5
Non-commissioned officers	6	6	6	6
Privates (of cadre)	104	94	109	64
" (of reserve)	64	49	43	68
Horses	160	134	161	88
Guns	6	6	6	6
Wagons, carts and carriages	4	12	12	12

Besides, for each battery there is to be 1 Accountant, 1 Veterinary Surgeon, and 1 Farrier.

The *Engineer Troops* consist of 1 battalion of "pontoniers" and one "field signal company," and besides, a battalion of sappers is being organized. The "pontonier battalion" comprises a staff and 3 companies of pontoniers.

The *Staff of the Pontonier Battalion* consists of

1 Major, commanding the Battalion,
1 Captain ("Tyg-kapten," in charge of material),
1 Lieutenant, Adjutant,
1 Battalion Surgeon,
1 Veterinary Surgeon, and
1 Under Conductor (Sergeant).

A *Pontonier Company* comprises

1 Captain, commanding the Company,
2 Lieutenants,
1 Sub-Lieutenant,
4 Non-commissioned Officers,
2 Musicians,
12 Corporals and Vice-Corporals,
18 Artificers and Armorers, etc., and
88 Privates.

The *Material* of the Battalion consists of 3 ponton trains, with each of which can be constructed a standard or "normal" bridge, 176 feet in length, for all arms.

To the "*Field Signal Company*" belong

1 Captain, commanding the Company,
2 Lieutenants,
1 Sub-Lieutenant,
4 Non-commissioned Officers,
24 Corporals and Vice-Corporals,
2 Musicians, and
94 Privates.

The *Material* of the Field Signal Company consists of 3 divisions, each having the fixtures requisite for 2 stations and 36,000 Swedish feet (10.7 Kilom.) of telegraph wire. In the intervals between the periodical drills and manœuvres, the pontonier battalion has 20 and the field signal company 10 horses. For drill and campaign service the necessary extra horses are provided in the same manner as in the artillery.

The *Battalion of Sappers* is to have the same strength and organization as the pontonier battalion.

Exclusive of these engineer troops there are, as mentioned above, in every infantry regiment 2 non-commissioned officers and 32 privates selected for sappers (called "infantry pioneers"), who are trained in field-works, during a term of 4 years, by officers detached for the purpose from the same regiment. Before undertaking the direction of these exercises the officers themselves must go through a preliminary course of practical study and instruction, together with the officers of the Royal Engineers.

Of the above-mentioned 32 men and officers, one-half is relieved and replaced by new men and officers every two years. The relieved detachment returns to the ranks, thus forming within the regiment a permanent trained reserve of sappers, comprising both officers and privates, the number of which may be estimated at not less than 6 officers, 6 non-commissioned officers, and 100 men, as soon as the present system has been fully developed. These sappers always remain in the ranks of the regiment, but when necessary they can be detached, partly to smaller works requiring skilled labor, and partly to act as foremen at more extensive works, where the full strength of the regiment is required. Their material consists of 2 wagons, each drawn by 3 horses, and in most respects of similar construction with the common train-wagons of the army, but each carrying a small iron ponton, inside of which are packed a variety of engineering tools (shovels, pickaxes, etc.), for about 150 men, and outside some bridge-building materials of the lightest description, calculated for the use of smaller detachments, and as a help in the construction of temporary bridges.

[See TABLE, page 146.]

(B) CLOTHING AND EQUIPMENT.

I. *Uniform.* (a) *Enlisted Troops.* Under the particular supervision of the colonel of the regiment and the superintendence of the Army Administrative Department (Armé-Förvaltningen), and *Administrative Commissariat Board*—organized at the head station or depot of every regiment, and consisting of a field-officer as chairman and two other officers and a regimental intendant as members—manages and directs the procurement and maintenance of the uniform of the rank and file, also when on detached service. To that effect the Board receives from the Army Administrative Department a yearly "clothing grant," the amount of which is based on estimates, made at the end of each year, of the current prices, partly of clothing materials and wages, and partly of ready-made articles, regard being had, in all cases, to the time that the different articles of clothing and equipment are appointed to be used.

The Board is entitled to make agreements with all privates, who are found desirous of such arrangement, by which the men themselves undertake to furnish and keep in repair such articles of their kit, as are most exposed to wear and tear, compensation being made for the same, according to certain regulations.

The allotted clothing grants are accounted for, annually, by the Board, and the Crown credited for all or any surplus arising therefrom.

(b) *The "Indelta" Cavalry and Infantry raised by "Cavalry Array"* ("Rusthålls Infanteriet"). For all these regiments and corps* the respective "Cavalry Arrayers" provide, maintain, and keep the articles of clothing. They are in general allowed—when they find it to be expedient and compatible with their interests—to make personal arrangements; but in this case tenders for the deliveries are to be called for *publicly.* The articles provided cannot be received and approved unless they have been inspected and found to agree with the regulated samples and models, both as to cut, make, quality and other particulars.

(c) *The "Indelta Infantry Array."* In every regiment and corps raised by Infantry Array in the Indelta Army the supply, maintenance and care of the private soldiers' clothing† is directed by a Commissariat Board, consisting of the colonel of the regiment or corps commander as chairman and three officers as members. In time of peace the Board receives from the Army Administrative Department, for the defrayment of the expenses, a yearly money-grant, the amount of which is calculated from the current prices of the materials of the uniform and the cost of labor, and also casual payments, as for instance, compensations for wear and tear of uniforms during service, for the accidental loss of articles, etc., etc.

The men are always provided with one new and one perfectly serviceable uniform. The first, called the "parade suit," (Lifmundering‡) is deposited and kept at each respective "Canton," under the care and responsibility of the "Canton Master"; and the "drill uniform" (exercis-mundering, undress or fatigue uniform), is in the soldiers' own keeping.

* With the exception, however, of a corps of Mounted Riflemen, for which there is a Commissariat Board, which manages the supply, repairs, and keeping not only of all clothing but also all regulation articles belonging to the uniform, together with accoutrements, kit and saddlery, for certain yearly money grants, assigned and payable to the Board by the Army Administrative Department.

† Except the "Capote," or great-coat, an article supplied and kept in repair direct by the Crown.

‡ The terms "parade" and "undress" uniform do not refer to uniforms of separate cut and model, the only difference between parade and undress, with the privates of the "Indelta Army," consisting in the head-dress worn.

ABSTRACT OF THE STRENGTH OF THE SWEDISH ARMY IN 1875.

	Staff.						Companies, Batteries, Squadrons.								Artillery Artificers, &c., & Pyrotechnic Corps.						Horses. †		
	Generals.	Other Commissioned Officers.	Non-commissioned Officers.	Civil Officers.	Personel of Bands.	Total.	Officers.	Non-commissioned Officers.	Veterinary Surgeons of Squadrons.	Bands, Trumpeters and Drummers.	Corporals.	Artificers, etc.	Privates and Volunteers.	Total.	Non-commissioned Officers.	Civil Officers.	Artificers, &c., & Bombardiers	Total.	Grand Total.	Cannon.	Ordinary.	Extra (Hired).	Total.
General Officers	9	..	..	..	..	9	..	..	..	..	..	..	....	....	..	..	..	..	9	..	....	..	....
General Staff	..	38	..	..	..	38	..	..	..	..	..	..	....	....	..	..	..	..	38	..	....	..	....
Artillery	..	66	27	30	6	129	195	177	..	147	498	60	3,327	4,404	7	31	102	140	4,673	234	616	475	1,091
Engineer Staff and troops	..	31	15	12	..	58	20	20	..	10	72	90	438	650	..	..	..	..	708	..	30	..	30
Cavalry	..	43	1	75	1	120	172	198	47	143	310	..	3,970	4,840	..	..	..	..	4,960	..	4,490	..	4,490
Infantry*	..	178	73	256	256	763	966	802	..	928	2,304	..	20,622	25,622	..	..	..	..	26,385	..	....	..	....
Total	9	356	116	373	263	1,117	1,353	1,197	47	1,228	3,184	150	28,357	35,516	7	31	102	140	36,773	234	5,136	475	5,611

ADDITIONAL.

In the *Gottlands National Beväring (Militia)—Conscripts:*

Non-commissioned Officers	199
Musicians, &c.	76
Corporals and Vice-Corporals / Privates (Infantry and Artillery, &c.)	7,777 ‡
Total	8,052

In *other Regiments and Corps of the Army (Conscripts):*

Non-commissioned Officers	3
Corporals and Vice-Corporals	8
"Conscripts Elect" (unpromoted)	21
Privates (Infantry, Cavalry and Artillery)	85,400
Total	85,432 §

* Not including the Marine Regiment and "Life Regiment" of Conscripts (Lif Bevärings Reg.) but including the permanent cadre of officers of the Gottland National Militia.

† Besides the chargers that are to be provided and kept at their own expense by General Officers, Officers of the General Staff and Cavalry, Artillery Field Officers, and mounted Infantry Officers.

‡ According to the Returns of the 1st October, 1873.

§ According to the Returns of the 1st October, 1873, there is the "Naval Conscription" (Sjöbeväringen), making about 20,000 men, who are drilled in the army, and the Voluntary (Scharp-Schooters), 13,778 men, on December 31st, 1874.

The private soldier generally provides his own shirts, stockings, shoes and boots, for which he receives a regulated compensation in cash for each day these articles are worn while on duty; but, however, in the event that his term of duty in any year should not amount to full 30 days, he is nevertheless allowed the compensation for wear and tear for the whole of that term.

When new articles are made for parade wear the corresponding articles, previously worn at parade, are reserved for use at drill and in undress, and the uniform and articles worn in undress by the private till that time, in case they no longer are of service as uniform, become the private property of the soldier.

On marching, at the commencement of a campaign, the rank and file is dressed in the parade uniform.

Any surplus arising in the Commissariat Funds cannot be used for any purposes that are not connected with the clothing of the regiment; but such surplus money remains under the administration of the Board, which gives an account of it to the Army Administrative Department.

(a) *Rank and File of the "Universal Conscription."* For the supply of clothing for the conscripts there is, also, at each cadre regiment and corps, a Conscription Commissariat (or Clothing-Board, Bevärings-Beklädnads Direktion*), consisting of a major as chairman and two officers as members. This Board, upon which devolves the same duties as on the Commissariat Board of the cadre troop, has at its disposal a certain annual money-grant, calculated from the length of the ordinary term of drill; as well as a compensation for wear and tear for every day that the uniform is used over and above that term. The conscripts, as well as the regular privates, arc supplied with one new parade and one thoroughly serviceable "drill uniform," which are kept in storehouses situated on the drill and camping grounds.

* Three conscription corps, in which the cadres consist only of officers, have no Commissariat Board, but the clothing and all other articles for the troops are provided and managed directly by the Crown.

All cloth needed for the Army, as also all woollen stuffs for lining, are provided by the Army Administrative Department, and on requisition issued to regiments and corps from the stores of the Crown, the value of the deliveries being deducted from the sums granted yearly for clothing. The cloth is manufactured from pure, unadulterated wool, and shall have been shrunk before receipt in the Government Stores.

Other materials and articles required for the uniform are purchased by the respective Boards, generally from contractors at public auction (entreprenad auktion).

The chairmen and members of the above-mentioned Boards do not, as such, receive any separate salary.

II. *Accoutrements and Kit.* (a) *Enlisted Army.* The articles of accoutrement (belts, etc., "remtyg") and kit, and the saddlery of the cavalry, in these regiments, are furnished and maintained by the Administrative Boards (Förvaltnings Direktioner), in the same manner as has been cited above, regarding the clothing.

(b) *The Indelta Cavalry and Infantry raised by Rusthall.* All accoutrements, saddlery, and harness for the Cavalry of this class, as well as the articles of accoutrement for the Infantry of the "Cavalry Array" (Rusthåll), are furnished and maintained by the "Cavalry Arrayers," but the other articles of the kit and equipment of both Cavalry and Infantry are supplied by the Crown. The repair of the latter articles is superintended directly by the Army Administrative Department, with the aid of reports, drawn up and remitted from the regiment to the Department.

(c) *The Indelta Infantry.* The supplying and keeping of the articles of accoutrement is managed direct by the Army Administrative Department, at the expense of the Crown, from yearly reports sent in to the Department. The personal articles of accoutrement are in charge of the private, but all other articles of kit and equipment (utredning) are kept and preserved by the "Canton Masters."

(d) *Rank and File of the Universal Conscrip-*

tion. The Crown also supplies the Conscripts with the articles in question. All matters relating to new supplies or repairs of these articles are submitted to the decision of the Army Administrative Department, which issues the new articles, if found necessary, and the requisite means for effecting repairs. The articles are stored in warehouses situated on the camping grounds.

III. *Baggage and Camp Equipage* (Tross). All baggage-wagons and carriages, and all articles required for the field-equipment of the rank and file, both of the enlisted and indelta troops, and the conscription forces, are provided at the cost of the Crown, and issued from the Army Administrative Department. Of the baggage-wagons and camp-equipage allotted to regiments and corps, a part is kept in the store-houses of garrisoned towns, and at the encampments; and a part in baggage-sheds situated within the respective company-districts, or cantons, of the "Indelta" Army.

(C) ARMS OF THE SWEDISH ARMY.

Since 1867 the Swedish Infantry is armed with breech-loading rifles of the Remington system. These guns, as well as the carbines of the same system, with which a part of the Cavalry is armed, are made at either of the two Small-Arms Factories of Karl Gustaf's Stad (Eskilstuna), or Husqvarna. The first of these factories belongs to the Swedish State, and the second belongs to a private company.

The calibre of the rifle is 12.17 millimètres, its weight 4.7 kilogrammes, its length, together with the bayonet, 1.85 metres, and its cost, when manufactured at Karl Gustaf's Stad, 25 kronor, and when delivered from Husgvarna, about 35 kronor. The carbine weighs 3 kilogrammes, and it costs about 27 kronor when manufactured at Karl Gustaf's Stad.

The cartridges have copper cases, are constructed for rim-ignition, and weigh 35 grammes, of which the projectile weighs 24, and the charge 4.25 grammes.

Every Infantry private carries altogether 80 cartridges in his pouch and knapsack, and, besides, the battalion ammunition-wagons carry 40, and the other ammunition-wagons 50 rounds each.

The initial velocity of the projectile of the rifle is 400, and of the carbine 340 mètres.

For the rifle, the radius of the circle surrounding the best half of the hits, at the following ranges, is: 100, 200, 300, 400, 500, 600 mètres, 12, 24, 35, 48, 60, 73 centimètres.

The Swedish Cavalry is armed with sabres, and revolvers of Francotte's system. A part of the Cavalry (about one-fifth of the force) has, in addition, carbines, and another lances.

The Artillerymen are armed with sabres, and, besides, all non-commissioned officers and corporals, and a part of the privates, with revolvers.

Ordnance, Carriages, and Wagons of the Field-Artillery. Since 1864 the *Field-Artillery* has been armed with rifled muzzle-loading cannon, of cast-iron, cast and finished at either of the Gun-Factories of Finspong, in Östergötland, or Åker, in Södermanland.

The guns used are of three calibres, viz.: 9.6, 7.7, and 6.7 centimètres; of the smallest bore, however, there are but few; their respective weights are: 640, 380, and 250 kilogrammes, and their cost, 400, 300, and 265 kronor.

The projectiles are: shells (explosive grenades), shrapnel shells, fire-grenades, or incendiary shells, and case-shot. The first class of shells have percussion caps of about the same construction as the Russian; while the shrapnel shells have time fuses, in all essential respects similar to the Austrian. The fire-grenades are filled altogether with an inflammable compound, burning with a very hot and large flame, and fired by slow match. The case shot are enclosed in canisters of zinc-plate, and filled with langrel of forged iron.

The shells weigh respectively 7.8, 3.9, and 2.3 kilogrammes; the shrapnel shells are of the same weight; but the case-shot and fire-grenades are a little lighter.

The charges used in horizontal firing (firing-charges), the cases of which are made of silk-waste, weigh 1.3, 0.8, and 0.5 kilogrammes, and give the shells an initial velocity of 380 mètres; the charges for firing with elevation (throwing-charges), as in the Italian Artillery, are transported in packets made up to the weight of the "firing-charge"; the smallest throwing-charge weighs one-fifth of the "firing-charge."

The probable deviations, in firing with shells of the first description, are, at the following

ranges:	750,	1,500,	2,000 mètres.
Longitudinally,	6.2	12.7	16.3 "
"	11.6	18.2	19.8 "
"	15.0	19.0	23.0 "
Transversely,	0.3	0.7	1.2 "
"	0.5	1.3	2.2 "
"	0.4	1.1	1.9 "

With regard to the rifling of the field-pieces, a modified La Hitte system has been followed, which is exactly similar to the Norwegian system, described in "Revue de Technologie Militaire," Tome V.

The *Carriages and Wagons* of the batteries that are equipped with guns of 9.6 or 7.7 centimètres calibre (batteries belonging to the Field-Army proper) are mostly of models adopted in 1831, and consist of gun-carriages, ammunition-wagons, spare gun-carriages, forge-wagons, and store or baggage-wagons.

All of these carriages and wagons, with the exception of the store-wagons, which are exactly like the baggage-wagons of the Army, have similar wheels, and generally similar fore-carriages; besides, wagons and carriages belonging to the same kinds of batteries, excepting the ammunition-wagons, also have similar hind under-frames. The gun-limber and carriage are connected by means of a pintail placed in a movable shaft or lever; the back part of the gun-carriage tail rests on a pivot-rail, in most essentials like that of the Austrian gun-carriages.

The gun-limber, when empty, weighs 580 kilogrammes, and, without their equipments, the weight of the gun-carriages is respectively: for the heavy gun 600, and for the light gun 430 kilogrammes.

The light gun-carriages, as also all ammunition-wagons, are drawn by six, and the heavy gun-carriages by eight horses. The draught-burden, per horse, with carriages completely equipped, and men mounted in their places, is about 300 kilogrammes for the gun-carriages, and about 420 kilogrammes for the ammunition-wagons, but the burden per horse, with field-forges and store-wagons, amounts to at least 470 kilogrammes.*

The number of shots, per piece, carried in the gun-carriages is 27 for the heavy, and 34 for the light gun; in the battery ammunition-wagons there are respectively 112 and 120 shots per piece; the spare ammunition carried with the Parks of Army Divisions consists of respectively 43 and 59 rounds per gun.

The percentage of different kinds of shot in the total supply of projectiles is, for the heavy gun: shells 50, shrapnel shells 33, "fire-grenades" 6, and case-shot, 11 per cent.; and for the light gun: shells 45, shrapnel shells 42, "fire-grenades" 2, and case-shot 11 per cent.

The *other Artillery Material*—constituting the Ordnance of Coast Fortresses—consists of: various old smooth-bore pieces, cannons and mortars, some rifled pieces of heavy ordnance, and a small number of armor-breaking (siege-) guns. The rifled battering-pieces, rifled on the same system as the guns of the Field-Artillery, have a calibre of 12.18, 16.72, and 20.23 centimètres; the guns of the first two calibres are of cast-iron, weighing respectively 1,700 and 4,200 kilogrammes, and cost about 850 and 1,650 kronor; the 20.23 centimètres guns are made of Bessemer steel, strengthened with a layer of rings of the same metal, and weigh 7,600 kilogrammes.

The carriages of these pieces are of cast-iron.

As armor-breaking guns are used: partly rifled pieces of 24 centimètres calibre, in all essential

* Trials are now being made with a gun-carriage and limber, and an ammunition-wagon, with under frame-work of sheet-iron, but in other particulars nearly the same as those in use at present. A new field-forge, exactly like the store-wagon, with respect to the carriage-body and frame, has been recently adopted.

respects resembling those of the French Navy, and, partly, smooth-bore pieces of 28.6 centimètres calibre; the last named (weight 1,400 Kilogrammes, price 7,500 kronor), fire a chill-moulded solid ball, weighing about 85 kilogrammes, and having an initial velocity of about 490 mètres.

The carriage of the 24 centimètres gun is of wrought-iron; the recoil is checked by hydraulic pressure, and the gun runs back of itself to the parapet.

A gun of 27 centimètres calibre (French Navy system), and a muzzle-loading mortar of cast-iron are yet under trial.

(D) FORTRESSES AND ENGINEER MATERIAL.

(a) *Fortresses.* The fortresses of Sweden are: Karlsborg, Waxholm-Fredriksborg, Kungsholm, Drottningskär, and Karlsten.

Karlsborg is the chief depot or store-fortress of the country, and therefore occupies an important position in the Swedish system of defence. This fortress is situated on a cape in Lake Wettern, west side, at the point where the Göta Canal enters that lake, and consequently it occupies a central position with reference to the middle and south of Sweden, and has, also, good lines of communication, both by sea and land, to nearly all parts of the Kingdom. The fortifications facing the lake consist of connected earthen walls (*breastworks*) having a profile of more than the usual thickness, and outside of these ramparts there is a detached wall of masonry. On the land side the fortifications consist of several works situated in front of each other. The inmost line of defence consists of a casemate serving as barracks for the garrison, and extends across the whole fortress toward the lake, so that it intersects the large earthen walls previously described.

The works of *Waxholm-Fredriksborg* are designed for the defence of the principal entrances to Stockholm. The Fortress of Waxholm is built on a rock, situated in the sound separating the islands Waxön and Rindön, and consists almost exclusively of casemates. The Fortress of Fredriksborg is located on the island Rindön, and defends the sound between the latter and island Wermdön. This fort has been constructed during the last six years, and consists principally of armor-clad batteries, armed with 24 centimètres and 27 centimètres guns. The minor inlets are filled up and defended by detached works.

Kungsholm-Drottningskär. These forts defend the chief channels leading to Karlskrona. Fort Kungsholm lies on a rocky islet, east of the principal inlet to the port, and the citadel of Drottningskär, west of the same inlet. These forts, consisting hitherto of works and lines of batteries, built of masonry, are being reconstructed, and the principal lines of defence will consist of armor-clad batteries. The minor inlets are blocked up and defended by detached works.

The fortress of *Karlsten* lies on a rocky island on the west coast of Sweden, 4 Swedish miles from Göteborg and 1 Swedish mile from the main land. This fortress, which has now lost its military importance, was designed to defend the entrance to the harbor of Marstrand, and to serve as the head station of the Swedish gunboat squadron (skärgårdsflottan) on the west coast of Sweden.

(b) *Military Bridge-building Material.* At present 3 new ponton trains are being manufactured, and there are 3 of somewhat older date. All are constructed according to the system of Birago, but more or less altered.

Each of the three older trains consists of: 15 ponton carriages drawn by 6 horses each, 1 field forge wagon, 1 wagon for material, 1 ambulance wagon, and 2 store wagons, for which 11 saddle horses and 115 draught horses are required. Forage wagons are procured according to demand.

The first two trains have wooden pontons, but the third iron. The wagons of the latter train are furnished with springs, but not the others.

The ponton wagons carry 15 ponton halves, together with four trestles and other materials for a so-called normal or standard bridge 176 feet in length, resting on pontons and end abutments; but by using all the trestles and some additional rafters and planking there are supports and other requisites for a bridge 264 feet long, of the full normal breadth and bearing capacity. The material of a ponton train suffices for bridges respectively 7½ feet broad and 242 feet long, or 5 feet broad and 330 feet long, or 3½ feet broad and 418 feet long. The ponton train can also be employed in all other works in which such materials are used.

These pontons have proven entirely satisfactory on all occasions when they have been tried, both as to strength and solidity, and are easily manageable in the water; but the transportation on land is effected with some difficulty, partly on account of the wagon's weight, but more especially on account of the unwieldy system of horsing with six draught animals.

The three new bridge trains will each comprise 28 wagons, drawn by 3 horses each; and all are perfectly alike as to make, but differently loaded, viz.: 24 as ponton and 4 as baggage wagons, and for which will be required altogether 8 saddle, 84 draught, and 8 spare horses, or a total of 100 horses. The bridge wagons carry 16 ponton halves and 8 trestles, with other materials for a bridge 10 feet in breadth (calculated for the greatest possible bearing capacity), either on pontons alone or trestles alone, and 180 feet in length; or with both pontons and trestles, 240 feet long; for the passage of troops in regular marching order 338 feet long; and for infantry marching in columns and formed in two files 480 feet long; in all these cases without the use of any temporary and additional materials. In the store wagons are carried 4 days' rations for 100 men and 1 day's forage for 100 horses. All of these wagons are so constructed as to allow of the cooking of the rations while on the march.

The ponton train can be separated into 4 sections, each comprising the materials required for a bridge of one-fourth of the above-mentioned length, with victuals for one-fourth of the troops and horses.

All pontons are made of sheet-iron; the top beams and lower cross beams or ties of the trestles are somewhat lighter than in the old bridge trains, but are furnished with more iron mountings.

All the wagons, without any alterations, can be packed as pontoon, trestle or baggage wagons. They are made almost exclusively of steel, will turn round completely without cranking, and have a self-acting brake for the fore wheels, worked by the wagon's own pressure on declivities. The three draught horses are harnessed abreast, the driver has his place on the wagon, so that none of these horses are ridden. When crowded, the width of the three horses is the same as the breadth of the ponton, and the width between the outer tracks is the same as that of the wheel tracks.

(c) A *Field Park of Engineers*—which accompanies an army corps, for use in such field works as are performed under the direction of sappers, but with working parties taken from the Infantry—consists of 18 wagons harnessed with three horses each, viz.: 1 staff wagon, 10 tool and implement wagons, 2 ponton wagons, 2 wagons for sapping and mining materials, 1 field forge, and 2 baggage wagons. Each of the tool wagons carry supplies for 200 men. The bridge wagons resemble very nearly those of the Infantry pioneers, and are strictly intended for use in the construction of temporary bridges.

(d) *Material of the Infantry Pioneers.*—The plan adopted in its construction is: that this material should be capable of conveyance in any infantry baggage-wagon, and accordingly the pioneer-wagons are of the same build and dimensions as the ordinary baggage-wagons of the army, the only difference being that they are of iron for the sake of greater lightness, and that, instead of the ladders and baggage-chest carried on baggage-wagons, the pioneer-wagons have a small sheet-iron ponton. The build of the wagon has made it necessary to construct this ponton in two halves, the front part 4½ and the hind part 8 feet long. All tools are carried in the ponton halves, for which purpose there are in the front part two low chests, one over the other, which contain all small tools and nails, and also serves as a seat for the driver; in the hind part are packed all large tools and implements, together with cordage and oars, etc.* On top of the hinder ponton half lie six ladder-platforms (bridge plank), of which three are locked fast as a covering for the tools, and besides 1 trestle-top, 1 spare pole, 2 hand-spikes, etc., etc.

The "ladder-platforms" are 10 feet long, 1 1/3 feet broad, and constructed so that they can be rapidly coupled together, two and two, with iron hooks, thus forming a bridge flooring 20 feet in length and capable of carrying 10 to 12 men.

For each wagon are required 1 driver and 3 horses, and for packing and unpacking, a detachment of 8 men. Every infantry regiment has 2 wagons of this description, each containing the necessary articles. The tools carried with a regiment may, therefore, under ordinary circumstances, be calculated to suffice for a working party of 300 men.

The bridge-building materials furnish 6 double bridge platforms or plankings 20 feet in length, 2 whole or three half pontons (on the two front halves being coupled together as one), and 2 trestles, the legs of which consist of carriage-shafts or hand-spikes.

A whole ponton, used as a boat, will carry 12 men. Two whole pontons, floored with "ladder-platforms," form a convenient ferry for 25 men, or for a baggage-wagon, or for 1 horse. Four pontons, with 12 double ladder-platforms, constitute a ferry 20 feet long and 16 feet broad, which will carry 4 horses, or 50 men. Land bridges are constructed from the trestles, with a flooring of ladder-platforms. Two whole pontons and the ladder-platforms belonging to them will give a bridge 60 feet in length for infantry in two files, or for light vehicles carefully drawn by men. Three half pontons, 2 trestles, and the accompanying ladder-platforms, laid in a single line, will form a bridge 120 feet long for one file of men.

The wagon and ponton, fully packed, can be launched backwards into the water, and floats; there being also convenient room in the wagon for the 8 men in attendance, and the horses swim alongside. In this manner all can be rowed across a lake, assuming the weather to be calm.

(e) *Field Telegraph Material.*—The manufacture of material for the Field Telegraph Service was commenced in this country in 1868. The apparatus is transported in wagons drawn by 2 horses, and resembles in all essentials the Swedish baggage-wagons.

A detachment comprises 2 station-wagons, each containing the apparatus and material requisite for erecting 2 stations; 2 pole-wagons, carrying 150 poles and 20 lengthening rods each; 2 wagons for materials, each with 30,000 feet of galvanized iron wire, spun in 4 coils; and 6,000 feet insulated cable, together with the necessary insulators and tools.

Besides, every detachment has 2 forage and store-wagons, designed exclusively for provisions, forage, and baggage.

As a rule a whole detachment is used in establishing a line, and to insure greater rapidity the work is carried on simultaneously at two different points of the same line; each detachment may be subdivided into two equal and independent sections.

The stations are generally established in tents, or in houses, if at hand. The wire is paid out at once from the wagons, when feasible; if not, the roll of wire is carried by 2 men, wearing supporting slings, or belts adapted for this purpose. The holes for the poles are made with iron crowbars. The wire is rolled up directly on the wagon, either by means of one of the wagon wheels, which through a simple mechanism makes the wire roller revolve, or else by a windlass. When carried by hand the wire is wound

*It should be specially observed that, in order to insure the smallest possible weight and at the same time the greatest strength requisite, most of the tools and implements are made of Bessemer steel.

off from the roller by means of a common winch.

For optical signaling flags are used by day and lanterns by night. The latter are useful, also, as carriage-lanterns, but have movable blinds for the purpose of emitting the light a longer or shorter time.

(E) SANITARY DEPARTMENT.

In *time of peace* the sanitary care both of the army and navy is superintended and directed by the Chief Medical College, or Board of Health ("Sundhets Kollegium"), one of its 4 members being appointed referent, who brings all questions relating to the Army Medical Service before the college. All surgical instruments and articles for the dressing of wounds, etc., to be used in the army, are procured and kept in efficient order through the Army Medical Office ("Fältläkare Kontoret"), which is under the superintendence of the above-mentioned board, and serves also as a dépôt for articles of this description. The Army Medical Staff consists of 2 Physicians and Surgeons-in-Chief of the Army, 5 Chief or Field Surgeons, 38 Regimental Surgeons, 68 Battalion Surgeons, 5 Garrison and Fortress Surgeons, and 47 Assistant Surgeons—total 165. The Naval Medical Staff consists of 1 Physician and Surgeon-in-Chief, 2 Regimental Surgeons, 4 Battalion Surgeons, and 17 Assistant Surgeons—total 24.

In case of war a Surgeon-General (or Medical Director-General) is appointed. This officer stands under the immediate orders of the Commander-in-Chief, and superintends the Sanitary Service of the army.

The *Personnel* further consists of

(A) *Surgeons* (Physicians).

(a) *With the troops.*

3 Surgeons to each battalion of infantry and corresponding force of cavalry.

1 Brigade Surgeon and 2 Battalion Surgeons to each brigade.

1 Divisional Surgeon and 2 Battalion Surgeons to each division ("Fördelning").

4 Surgeons with the artillery reserve.

The Surgeon-General and 3 Surgeons at headquarters.

All medical officers of the army are mounted, with the exception of Assistant Surgeons, who travel with the ambulance wagons.

At least 1 Surgeon from each battalion, and a requisite number of ambulance soldiers, are detached for service with the ambulances (Field Hospitals); the whole of this medical force being under the supervision of the Brigade Surgeons.

(b) *At Hospitals.*

1 Chief or "Field" Surgeon for every 300 or 400 men, or more.

1 "Hospital Surgeon" for 100 men.

1 Under or Assistant Surgeon for 50 men.

(B) *Apothecaries* (Army Chemists). 1 with each movable ambulance or stationary hospital.

(C) *Ambulance Soldiers and Hospital Attendants.*

(a) *Ambulance Soldiers* (or "Instrument Carriers," Kartusch-bärare). These men have attended a course of study and been trained to dress wounds and attend the sick in accordance with prescribed regulations. Three men from each battalion accompany the surgeons.

(B) *Litter Carriers* ("Förbinderi Soldater"). Sixteen men detached from each battalion; 8 men and 1 corporal from each battery; besides an additional troop under the name of "Reserve Ambulance Detachment," consisting of 7 men and 1 corporal from each battalion of infantry, and 4 men from each squadron and battery.

(c) *Hospital Warders* (or Assistants), principally for service at hospitals: 2 per cent. of the total force of the army or army corps.

The Hospital and Ambulance *Material* in use is

(A) *With the Forces.*

(a) *For each Battalion.* 1 instrument case (Medicinal Kartusch), containing the most indispensable instruments, articles for dressing wounds, and restoratives.

One battalion hospital store wagon, with an instrument and medicine-chest, bandage-pouches, with rollers, etc., for dressing wounds, sufficient for 100 wounded, litters and all the necessary articles for 25 beds.

One battalion ambulance wagon for removing the wounded or sick.

(b) *For each Brigade.* One reserve hospital store wagon, fitted up with instruments, etc., in the same manner as the battalion hospital store wagon, only that it contains a larger supply of medicines, bandages, and appliances for the dressing of wounds.

One reserve ambulance wagon (similar to the one mentioned above).

Five baggage wagons, each carrying provisional hospital material for 40 beds.

(c) *For each Division.* The same number of wagons as for the brigade.

(d) *For the Artillery Reserve.* Instrument cases and wagons, according to the strength of the force.

(e) *For the Head-Quarters.* One spare hospital store wagon and 2 ambulance wagons.

(B) *At the Ambulance* (place of dressing wounds, etc.) are stationed the battalion and brigade hospital store wagons, ambulance wagons, baggage wagons, and other vehicles temporarily procured.

(C) *Field Hospitals* (or Portable Ambulance Hospital) provided for about 100 invalids.

The hospital articles required are supplied from the brigade baggage-wagons, from special store or baggage-wagons, and from stores in the neighborhood.

(D) *Fixed or Stationary Hospitals.* The hospital articles and material are drawn from the chief stores of the army as requi[illegible]

By an Accessory Treaty of December 13th, 1864, Sweden joined the Geneva Convention.

All surgical instruments required for the army are made by Mr. ALB. STILLE, surgical instrument maker, Stockholm.

(F) INSTITUTIONS FOR MILITARY EDUCATION, INSTRUCTION, AND TRAINING.

I. **Enlisted Troops.**—The Wermland Rifle Corps, which is not garrisoned, has similar camps of exercise, and drills the same number of days, as the "Indelta" Infantry, and the training and instruction of the non-commissioned officers and privates of this corps is consequently treated of under the heading "Indelta Troops."

In all other regiments, *that are garrisoned*, the enlisted recruits are drilled with their respective regiments, during the term required for their approbation in all parts of their military duties. The duration of the recruits' drill ("Recruit School") is accordingly indefinite, and varies from 3 to 5 months.

The yearly "drilling time," as it is called—when all persons on furlough or leave of absence are bound to attend for training in company (battery, squadron), battalion (divisional), and brigade drill and exercise—lasts three months, commencing the 1st of April or the 1st of May.

At all garrison regiments schools are established, where the private soldiers are during the winter instructed in reading, writing, and arithmetic.

II. **"Indelta" Troops.**—These regiments, as well as the Wermland Rifle Corps, have short periods of drill and exercise, at times appointed by general orders. The duration of the exercises depends on the amount of the appropriations made for this purpose by the Diet. At present the troops are trained in the following manner:

Infantry. The recruits are trained during two consecutive years at so-called Recruit Meetings (or Drills, "Rekryt-Möten"), which are appointed to last 40 days each year, and the first year the recruits are besides trained separately during the 20 days of the Regimental Meeting (or Camp of Exercise), the whole term of training for recruits thus amounting to 104 days. The "approved" private soldiers and riflemen ("approberade", *i. e.*, passed from the class of recruits) are drilled 20 days at the regimental camps, and further, during the months of August and September every year they have also to attend the company rifle practice, to practice firing at target. Those who are to be trained as "sharp-shooters" (or marksmen, 8 men from every company) have, in addition to this, 8 days' target practice every year with their regiment.

Cavalry. The recruits are trained during 2 consecutive years at "drill squadrons" (when new chargers are also mustered). If the number of recruits should not be sufficiently large to allow of the efficient carrying on of the exercises, the colonels are empowered to fill up the squadrons from the "approved" men. The duration of the training is fixed at 90 days a year, and the "approved" (or trained) troopers are drilled for 26 days at "regimental camps of exercise," held yearly.

Here would appear to be the appropriate place for a review of the yearly *manœuvres*, at which all the troops are collected, as also for an account of the training given to *pioneers*, *ambulance attendants*, *armorers*, and *farriers* (serving in the ranks of their respective regiments).

During the last days of the regimental camps the troops of the military districts are assembled, under the superintendence of their respective district commandants, for training in "*Field Service*" (tactics, outpost, and picket duties, etc.) On these occasions the forces are always divided into 2 bodies, which represent antagonistic armies. Hereafter yearly autumn manœuvres are to be held. To the last-mentioned manœuvres regiments are ordered, independently of the division, into military districts, so that the force then assembled amounts to about one-fifth to one-fourth of the total strength of the standing army.

The *Pioneers* (or Sappers), of which the regulated number is 4 per company, both in the enlisted and "Indelta" infantry, are selected from among the young privates who have passed the recruits' school and have attended the yearly "regimental camp of exercise" once at least. They serve as pioneers during 4 years, and then return to the ranks. All the pioneers are assembled for general exercises during the "officers'" and "regimental exercises," and are then trained by officers specially detached for this duty, so that they are afterwards capable of constructing small field fortifications and performing ordinary engineers' work, and are competent to act as foremen at the construction of larger works of this kind.

Ambulance Soldiers serve as assistants to the Army Medical Staff and as attendants on the sick, for which purpose they previously go through a special course of study at some stationary military hospital. Their regulated number is 1 private per company, or squadron, and 3 per battery.

Armorers (private soldiers). By the "Regulations" a certain number of these men are to belong to every regiment and corps of infantry. The soldiers who are to be trained for this purpose go through a course of training in the repairing workshops of the artillery; the course embracing the instruction requisite to enable them subsequently, not only to execute the necessary repairs, but also to assist in the inspection and care of small arms.

Farriers. In every regiment and corps of cavalry there are to be 3 farriers in each squadron. The troopers who are to serve in this capacity go through a course of training at the veterinary schools of the kingdom.

III. **Reserve Forces.** Of the Reserves the "*Beväring*" (conscripts) alone is drilled in time of peace, and of its 5 classes only the 1st and 2d are exercised during 15 days each year. In their second year of military service the conscripts are drilled together with the regular soldiers in the ranks of the cadres, during a part of the "camps of exercise."

IV. **Territorial Troops.** 1. *Defence of the Island of Gottland.* The company or battalion exercise of the "National Conscription" (or Militia, "Beväring") is held 6 days annually with the Infantry and "Landstorm" (Reserve-Conscription), company- and battalion-exercise being performed alternately every other year.

"Battery camps" (Möten) for the Artillery are also held 6 days annually.

The "Cadre Battery" of the Artillery, on the other hand, receives a longer training, altogether corresponding with what has above been stated of the exercises of enlisted troops in garrison.

2. *Volunteer Rifle Corps.* These corps have the right to fix the duration and frequency of their own musters for drill; but every corps, in order to become entitled to a state subsidy granted for this purpose, must go through certain target practice and drill, the extent and order of which is regulated by the War Ministerium.

V. Officers of the Army.

1. OFFICERS ON FULL PAY IN ACTIVE SERVICE.

A. *Non-Commissioned Officers.*

(a) *Infantry.* There are two schools for the training of aspirants to the non-commissioned grades, viz.: The non-commissioned officers' preparatory school and the non-commissioned officers' school.

The *Non-Commissioned Officers' Preparatory School.* To this school—where the instruction is given at the same time as in the "Recruit School," separately for each regiment, and in which the term of study for the "Indelta" Infantry and Wermland Rifle Corps is appointed to last 42 days every years—10 soldiers or volunteers (privates) with requisite officers are ordered from each battalion; but in the enlisted Infantry the number of pupils detached to the schools, and the time of training, vary according to the requirements of the service. The object of this school is, that pupils shall receive the preliminary instruction requisite, in order that they may afterwards be fitted advantageously to go through the "Non-Commissioned Officers' School." The course of instruction embraces: 1. Reading from print and handwriting, and accounting for the matter read. 2. Writing, partly from copies, and partly, for the more advanced pupils, after dictation, the latter including also instruction in orthography and punctuation. 3. Arithmetic—the four operations in simple numbers, decimal fractions and compound calculation. 4. Soldiers' instruction (in the duties of the service). 5. Corporals' instruction. 6. Instruction in the use and care of small-arms. 7. Drill, in close and open order. 8. Field and outpost duties, etc. 9. Gymnastics. 10. Bayonet exercise. 11. Swimming (where opportunities offer).

The *Non-Commissioned Officers' School.* This school, established for the use of the whole "Indelta" Army and the Wermland Rifle Corps, is open yearly during 120 days, from May to September. It is located at the Fortress of Karlsborg, where the officers and pupils are lodged in barracks during the term. 1 non-commissioned officer, and 10 corporals, "volunteer" soldiers, or privates from each battalion, are ordered to the school, besides the requisite number of officers and teachers. In the enlisted infantry the number of pupils and the time of training vary according to the requirements of the service. With respect to the instruction the Non-Commissioned Officers' School is divided into 3 classes. The 1st Class, Corporals' School; the 2d Class, Non-Commissioned Officers' School; and the 3d Class, a school for those pupils who have been found to have the necessary attainments for following the course of study in this higher class. Instruction is given in the following subjects and exercises, viz.: Reading, writing, arithmetic, practical geometry, corporals' instruction (in the various duties of the service), and regulations, articles and statutes of war; musketry tactics, field fortification, military surveying, elementary surgery (art of dressing wounds), field, outpost, and skirmishing service, etc., drill, target-practice, gymnastics, fencing and swimming.

(b) *Cavalry.* There are also "Non-Commissioned Officers' Preparatory Schools" and "Non-Commissioned Officers' Schools" for the cavalry. Each regiment has a school of the former class, which is held for the same length of time as the "Drill-Squadron" in the "Indelta" Cavalry, *i. e.*, during 90 days, and the number of pupils appointed to the school is 12 men per

"Battalion" (5 squadrons). In the Enlisted Cavalry the term of training and number appointed may be increased, if profitable. The instruction comprises: Reading, writing, orthography, written reports, requisitions, and accounts; arithmetic ("quatuor species" in simple and compound numbers, and decimal fractions), Troopers' and Corporals' Instruction, Mappery, Horsemanship, Farriery, Art of dressing wounds, Service Regulations, Articles of War, Knowledge of Signals, Pronouncing of the words of command, Duties of Squad and Flankering leaders, Field and Picket duties (covering troops, etc.), Target-practice, Gymnastics, Fencing, Riding, Practice in shoeing and currying horses, and Swimming.

The Non-Commissioned Officers' School of the "Indelta" Cavalry is held during 90 days (1st July–28th September), every year, at Stockholm. Besides the requisite number of officers, there are appointed to the school 1 non-commissioned officer from every "Battalion" or Corps of the "Indelta" Cavalry, and 1 man, either Corporal, Vice-Corporal, "Volunteer," or private from every "Indelta" Squadron. Regarding the division into classes, and the subjects of instruction, the same, or similar rules and plans as are in force in the corresponding Infantry School, are followed.

The non-commissioned grades in the Infantry and Cavalry are: Corporals, comprising Vice-Corporal, Corporal, and "Distinction"-Corporal (highest rank of Corporal), and Under-Officers, consisting of "Forager" Sergeants (Furirer, lowest rank of Infantry Under-Officers), Sergeants, and Sergeant-Majors. For promotion to the grade of Vice-Corporal, private soldiers, who have been "approved" in drill, are only required to have passed an examination in the "Corporals' Instruction," while, in order to be promoted to Corporal, they are required to have passed the 1st Class of the Non-Commissioned Officers' School, to have received the certificate of "approved" for their studies there, and to have passed an examination in "Service Regulations" at the regiment. Those who have satisfactorily passed the 2d Class, and taken the foregoing examination at the regiment, are competent to be appointed Non-Commissioned Officers.

(c) *Artillery.* In each of the 3 Artillery Regiments the theoretical instruction is placed in the hands of the Regimental Department of Instruction, where 1 Captain, 1 Lieutenant, and 2 Non-Commissioned Officers act as teachers. The term lasts from the 1st of October till the end of April, and the School consists of two Divisions, viz.: the *Lower*, for the training of non-commissioned officers, and the *Upper*, in which officers are prepared for entering the Military Academy (or Staff College). [For the instruction in the Upper Division, see below.]

The Lower Division consists of 3 classes. The course of studies comprises, in the 1st Class: reading, writing, arithmetic, and gunnery ("Artillery"); in the *2d Class:* writing, arithmetic, planimetry, and stereometry, gunnery, and instruction in the army organization and land defences of Sweden; in the *3d Class:* arithmetic, geometry, mechanics, gunnery, fortification, and linear drawing.

The theoretical instruction is followed by practical exercises carried on during the course of the summer, and attended by the pupils who have studied at the school during the preceding winter.

At the conclusion of the theoretical instruction, the pupils are examined. After passing an "approved" examination in the studies of the 1st Class, the artilleryman becomes competent for promotion to "2d Constable" (Corporal), if he be also approved in the practical duties of the service, and in regulations. Pupils who have duly passed the required examinations in service regulations and articles of war, have gone through the Non-Commissioned Officers' School in an approved manner, and passed satisfactory examinations in the courses of study of the 2d and 3d Classes, are entitled to further promotion, an examination from the 2d Class being required for promotion to "1st Constable" (Corporal) and Sergeant, and from the 3d Class for promotion to Sergeant-Major (Styckjunkare).

There are separate schools for riding, fencing, and gymnastics at each regiment.

The practical "Non-Commissioned Officers' School" of the Artillery is held separately in each regiment, during 6 to 8 weeks every year, 3 or 4 pupils from each Battery being appointed to the school, due attendance at which is one of the requirements for promotion to the grade of Corporal.

(d) *Engineers.* (Fortifikationen.) The Non-Commissioned Officers' School, at which instruction is given from the 1st of October to the end of April, is divided into 5 classes, viz.: a preparatory class for the private soldiers in general; the 1st Class, in the studies of which pupils are required to pass an "approved" examination for promotion to Vice-Corporal; the 2d Class, for promotion to Corporal; the 3d Class to Sergeant; and the 4th to Sergeant-Major.

The instruction does not comprise regulations and other instructions in the duties of the service, as a separate examination in these subjects must be passed by the men before they are allowed to enter on the duties of their respective grades.

Practical exercises in geometry, field-surveying, leveling, and fortification, take place under the direction of officers detached for the purpose, and are attended by the pupils of the school separately and by the whole force of the corps together. (For the last-named general exercises, "the Engineers' Field Exercises at Karlsborg," see below.)

The course of instruction comprises: In the *Preparatory Class:* Reading, writing, and arithmetic.

In the *1st Class:* Reading, writing, arithmetic, geometry, field-exercises, and fortification.

In the *2d Class:* Reading and writing, arithmetic, geometry, field-exercise, and fortification.

In the *3d Class:* Orthography and writing (written reports and requisitions, etc.), arithmetic, planimetry, stereometry, field-exercise, musketry, gunnery, fortification, field-surveying, leveling, architecture, and drawing.

In the *4th Class:* Swedish composition (theme-writing), arithmetic (embracing both common arithmetic and algebra), planimetry, stereometry, trigonometry, mechanics, field-exercise, musketry, gunnery, fortification, topography, architecture, intrenchment and architectural drawing, and mapping, together with practice in coloring (maps, etc.) and tracing.

(B) *Commissioned Officers.*

In order to become eligible, in time of peace, for an officer's commission, in any regiment or corps of the Army, it is, among other requirements, necessary to have passed through a course of study at the Military College (Krigsskolan). [His Majesty, the King, can, nevertheless, give a commission to any non-commissioned officer without his having passed the Military College, provided that he has served in a distinguished manner as non-commissioned officer for six years, two of which at least must have been in the highest non-commissioned grade; but such promotions are now of very rare occurrence.] The Military College, which is located in the Palace of Karlberg, in the immediate vicinity of Stockholm, is common to candidates for officers' commissions in all branches of the military service. Since 1873 the college is a purely military place of education; where only such are received as have passed a complete dismissory examination from some elementary school,* and who, besides, during two "camps of exercise," viz., the "Recruit Camp" (or drill-meeting) and the "Regimental Camp," have had opportunity to test their efficiency for the service, and have been so tested by the officers of the regiment in the ranks of which the candidates are desirous of entering as commissioned officers. The principal features of the regulations of the Military College are:

In order to obtain admittance, as pupil in the Military College, the applicant shall have gone through the full course of study at a complete Elementary School, besides having proved themselves fitted for the military profession at one "Recruit Camp," and one "Regimental Camp,"

* Compare class 301.

where they must have shown themselves fully qualified in the drill and other exercises in which they have taken part.

The pupils have to remain at the Military College two summers—when they are trained in practical exercises—and one autumn and one spring term, when they are chiefly occupied with theoretical studies.

The practical exercises in the summer comprise: drill (manual and company, etc.), field exercise, rifle and target practice, gunnery exercises (firing at horizontal and elevated ranges), field-fortification and bridge-building, practical geometrical exercises, field-surveying and practical topography, and swimming; and during the terms: drill, fencing, sword and bayonet exercise, gymnastics and riding.

The theoretical course embraces: articles and statutes of war, drill, exercise and service regulations, tactics and strategy, musketry, gunnery, military engineering (fortification and bridge-building), topography, and the drawing up of reports and other service-despatches; besides artillery (ordnance and small arms), fortification, military bridge-drawings, and mappery.

After having completed the course of study at the Military College, and passed the officers' examination, the cadet (or aspirant) is eligible for appointment as officer to any branch of the Army.

The Military College is calculated for the reception of one hundred students annually.

The present State grant for the Military College amounts to 79,888 kronor.

2. OFFICERS OF THE RESERVE.

In addition to "officers remaining in the Army" (unattached), and "disposable officers," there are, also, half-pay officers in the Artillery (from the beginning of the year 1873, for the mobilisation of the Reserve Batteries), and officers of the Public Roads and Water Works Corps (Väg-och Vatten-byggnads Corpsen).

The *Half-pay Officers* of the Artillery, having received the same training and education as the full-pay officers of corresponding ranks, an account of their training may here be omitted. Their liability to service is confined to the ordinary yearly drilling time (see above).

All the present officers of the *Public Roads and Water Works' Corps* have followed the complete courses of study at the Superior Military Academy for Officers of the Army, of which further mention will be made below. But, having been debarred from this academy since 1870, those who hereafter wish to obtain commissions in the Corps are now trained as *Civil* Engineers, at a Polytechnic College, which, under the name of the "Polytechnical Institute," is established in the Capital. The course at this college is three years, and the instruction comprises: mathematics, mechanics, physics, chemistry, mechanical and chemical technology, descriptive geometry, geology and mineralogy, topography, architecture (common and hydraulic), and the construction of roads, etc.

For the purpose of practically training the officers and non-commissioned officers, a series of drills and exercises, known under the name of Officers' Meetings (*Befälsmöten*) for each regiment, are held yearly in the spring, before the commencement of the other regimental exercises or "camps." With the "Indelta" Infantry and Wermland Rifle Corps these exercises are carried on during 10 days, and besides all the officers and non-commissioned officers of the respective regiments, 20 corporals, "volunteers," or private soldiers from each company, are ordered to join. In the "Indelta" Cavalry these officers' meetings last 20 days, and are attended by all officers and non-commissioned officers, and 12 men, corporals, "volunteers," and troopers, per squadron. In the artillery all officers and non-commissioned officers are exercised separately for 20 days before the commencement of the other general drill. In the other garrison regiments the officers' drill is appointed to last during the time considered necessary by the colonels of the regiments.

In order that the officers of regiments may receive a more thorough training, both practical and theoretical, in certain branches of the science of war, there are the following exercises and establishments, viz.:

District Manœuvres. It is intended that these manœuvres shall be held 14 days annually, districtwise, with the requisite number of field officers, captains, or regimental quartermasters, appointed from the regiments and army corps, in accordance with the "Regulations;" but the execution of these exercises depends upon the sufficiency of the amount voted for the purpose by the Diet. The commanding officer (a colonel or lieutenant-colonel) for each district is appointed by the King, and assisted by an officer of the general staff. The regimental officers attending the exercises command in turn, the field officers being appointed by the king, and the others by the respective commanding officers (colonels or lieutenant-colonels of their regiments).

School of Musketry. In order to spread a more intimate knowledge of small arms throughout the army, officers from all infantry regiments and corps are ordered to attend at the School of Musketry, which meets two years out of every three at the Royal Palace of Rosersberg (4 Swedish miles from Stockholm). The number of pupils is so proportioned that during the course of 3 consecutive years 1 officer from each battalion shall have received instruction. Besides the pupils and a requisite number of armorers and attendants (as batmen, etc.), the personnel consists of 1 officer in command and an adjutant, and 3 teachers, of whom 1 instructs in the ballistic, 1 in the technical, and 1 in the practical part of the studies. The course is completed in 2 months, and both the commanding officer, the teachers, and the pupils receive a special allowance during the time they are attached to the school.

Gymnastic Central Institute. This establishment is situated in Stockholm, and its object is to train instructors in fencing and gymnastics for the elementary schools, orthopedic gymnasts (for curative gymnastics), and officer instructors in gymnastics for the regiments. Fourteen officers from all the regiments and army corps, and 2 from the navy, are ordered yearly to go through the course, besides many officers volunteer to attend the instruction. The staff of instructors receives emoluments or fixed salaries, and consists of 1 Director (also Chief Instructor for the Military Department), 2 Professors or Chief Instructors (1 for the Pedagogic and 1 for the Medical Department), 3 Instructors, and an indefinite number of assistants. The pupils ordered to the school receive a day allowance during their stay. The course is completed in 2 years. The term lasts from the 1st of September to the 15th of April, and the instruction is both theoretical and practical. The annual State grant amounts to 29,400 Kr., and the total income of the institute to about 40,000 Kr.

Inspection of Small Arms. Each year one or two officers of the infantry are required to qualify themselves for the inspection of small arms, and are ordered to attend a course of practical instruction of 8 months' duration, at the Karl Gustaf's Stad Small Arms Factory, at Eskilstuna, which is the property of the State, and is under the supervision of the Artillery Department. During their term of attendance the officers receive the daily allowance usual for detached service.

The "Pioneer Officers" receive their technical training during the exercises of the engineers at Karlsborg. Every other year 1 officer from each infantry regiment, and every fourth year 1 officer from each corps is detached, in order to take part in these exercises, which are carried on during 30 days annually. These officers receive an extra allowance during the time of attendance. In order to accustom the infantry regiments more thoroughly to the conducting and execution of engineering work ("field works"), it is regulated that both the officers and non-commissioned officers of pioneers, as well as the men themselves, shall not serve in the capacity of pioneers for more than 4 years, and that at the expiration of this time they are to be replaced by others.

Riding School. As a requisite for promotion to lieutenant in the cavalry, cornets (sub-lieutenants) must previously go through a 2 years' course in the Riding School at the Palace of Strömsholm (situated between Westerrs and Köping). Artillery and engineer officers must also attend the school. The instruction, which is given from the 15th of September till the 15th of March, comprises riding (3 to 5 horses daily, 1 "Manège" horse, 1 or 2 horses for breaking in, and 1 so-called "field charger"), practical "knowledge of horses," fencing, gymnastics, target practice with the revolver on foot and on horseback, and besides equitation (theoretical), farriery, and the veterinary art. The breeding and training establishment, also situated at Strömsholm, furnishes a supply of riding horses, and every officer is entitled to bring 1 service charger to the school. The officers of the school are 1 Commanding Officer ("Chef," who is also Director of the Breeding Establishment), 1 Head Riding Master, 2 Instructors in Riding, 1 Instructor in Fencing and Gymnastics, and 1 Teacher of the Veterinary Art and Farriery.

From the 16th of March to the 1st of May the Riding School is also open to infantry officers About 10 infantry officers yearly avail themselves of this permission, in order to qualify themselves for the posts of regimental adjutants.

The *Military Academy* (or Staff College), which must be attended by officers as a requisite for appointment to the General Staff, and for promotion to the rank of lieutenant in the Artillery and Royal Engineers.

For admittance to the academy as a student the requirements are: that the applicant shall have done duty as officer at least one year, and that he shall have passed a preliminary examination. This examination is held at the 3 artillery regiments,* where, in the upper division (see above) of the respective regimental departments of instruction, the officers are prepared for this examination. The instruction imparted for this purpose is partly intended to serve as a repetition of the subjects studied for the officers' examination, but more especially to confirm and extend their knowledge of mathematics. During the term of instruction, which is carried on for 2 winters, from the 1st of October till the 1st of April (though the course may be completed in 1 winter), an opportunity is offered the infantry officers attending the academy to perfect themselves in riding at the riding schools of the artillery regiments. Officers who have passed the preliminary examination, held in the month of April every other year, are entitled to present themselves at the Military Academy on the 15th of July, and report themselves for matriculation as pupils.

The buildings of the Military Academy contain apartments for the commandant ("chef") and adjutant, tutors ("repetitörer") and students, and are situated at Marieberg, near Stockholm. The personnel consists of: 1 commandant, 1 adjutant (and librarian), 1 accountant, 1 physician, 11 professors, 2 assistant teachers, and 4 "tutors." The number of pupils in each course varies between 30 and 50. The course of study is of 3 years' duration; the academic year lasts from the 15th of July to the 1st of May, and during the remaining part of the year the students rejoin their respective regiments to attend the regimental drills and exercises.

The instruction embraces the following subjects: Mathematics, mechanics, descriptive geometry, physics, chemistry, gunnery, fortification, tactics and strategy, military history, architecture, mathematical geography, topography, military geography, and the French language. Instruction is also given in artillery and fortification drawing. The practical exercises, carried on as part of the course, are in gunnery, construction of bridges and fortifications, and surveying (topography). The pupils also visit the artillery workshops, ordnance foundries, powder works, and small-arms factories, etc.

* The officers of the Royal Engineers receive their instruction at that corps' own school, at Stockholm, where they also pass the preliminary examination in question.

The foregoing subjects are not all obligatory for the whole body of students, neither are they studied by all of them to the same extent, as the courses of instruction are divided into three separate branches or sections, viz.: for artillery officers (one superior and one inferior course), for engineer officers, and for officers of other arms, regard being had in the latter section to the qualifications required for future appointment to the general staff.

A yearly state grant of 42,366 Kr. is paid to the Military Academy.

We finally proceed to mention the exercises, recurring yearly, that may be considered as practical schools for the application of a superior military education. They are:

The *Exercises* (or "voyages") *of the General Staff*, which last a fortnight, and are attended by all officers and aspirants to the General Staff, who are in active service and who can be spared from other duties during that time. The exercises are carried on, alternately, in different parts of the country, the sites chosen being the most important, strategically considered.

The *Common Artillery School of Gunnery*. The exercises are held at Tånga Hed, situated on the railway line that connects Stockholm with Göteborg, and 6 Swedish miles from the last-mentioned city. The school is assembled for 16 days in the month of July, a certain number of artillery officers (ranging between 20 and 36), who have prepared at the Military Academy, being ordered to attend, yearly. During this time a series of gunnery exercises are carried on, alternating with lectures.

The *Field-Exercises of the Royal Engineers*, at Karlsborg. In addition to officers who have prosecuted their studies at the Military Academy, all officers and non-commissioned officers of engineers, who can be spared from other duties, are ordered to attend these exercises, and all the private engineers who are designed for promotion to corporal join in the exercises; and further, as previously stated, during 30 days, those officers of the Infantry who are to be trained as Pioneer officers. The school is assembled at the Fortress of Karlsborg, and the term of training is appointed to last 35 days.

THE NAVY.*

[*Class* 345 *C.*]

A.—THE ORGANIZATION OF THE NAVY.

THE Swedish Navy is designed for the defense of the Swedish coast. It has been divided into squadrons several times, lastly in 1866, when the Navy was reorganized. In 1873 the Coast Artillery and the Navy were united, and form at present one department under the name of the Royal Navy.

The King is Commander-in-Chief of the Army and Navy.

Next to him, the Minister of Marine is the commander of the naval forces.

The *Navy Department* (Sjöförsvars-Departementet) consists of two divisions—one bureau of chancery (Kansli-expedition), who attends to all matters that are to be determined by the King in Council of State, according to the fundamental law; one commander-in-chief's bureau (Kommando-expedition), who attends to all matters relating to commands.

Under the Navy Department are:

* Contributed by the Commander-in-Chief's Bureau of the Navy Department.

The Head of the Navy (Chefen for Flottans Militär personal), who has a staff for his assistance, and in a military point of view the nearest command of the military officers, and who is responsible for their efficiency of service.

The Bureau for Naval Affairs (Förvaltningen of Sjöärendena), which is the Navy's highest administrative authority. The president must have the rank of flag-officer. The board is assisted by a bureau of chancery and a treasury.

The Pilot Department (Lots-Styrelsen). See below, class 590.

The Hydrographic Office (Sjökarteverket). See above, class 335.

The Naval Academy (Sjökrigsskolan). See below.

The Superintendent's Office of the Marine Engineers (Öfver-Direktörs Embetet vid Marin Ingeniör Staten), which is the technical authority for the construction of ships, machinery, houses and waterworks for the Navy. The staff is composed of 1 superintendent (managing director), 2 directors, 7 engineers and extra engineers, 2 architects, and 2 draughtsmen.

The Military and Technical Bureau, whose duty is to assist the minister of marine in military technical questions. The bureau is divided into three departments — military, dock-yards, and constructions.

The Naval Stations at Karlskrona and Stockholm. Each station is divided into a military depot and dock-yard.

The military depot is under the superintendence of a military chief. The military chief at Karlskrona is at the same time chief commandant there. For the assistance of the military chief there is a military and a civil bureau, and a board of directors for managing the clothing department.

Under the military chiefs of the stations are: The military corps, the medical staff, the clerical staff, and everything connected with clothing, provisioning and the care of the sick. The medical staff under the military chief at Karlskrona is composed of 6 physicians and 5 medical stipendiaries, the clerical staff of 3 clergymen and 3 teachers, the civil staff of 7 officials. The medical staff under the military chief in Stockholm is composed of 3 physicians and 10 medical stipendiaries, the clerical staff of 3 clergymen, the civil staff of 4 officials.

The Dock-Yard is under the supervision of an intendant-in-chief (warfs-chef), who is responsible for its administration. For the assistance of the intendant, he has a bureau of chancery, an audit-office, and an adjutant. The administration of the dock-yard is divided into four departments, namely: the engineer, artillery, equipment, and submarine warfare department, each under a chief of its own.

Under the intendant-in-chief are: the dock-yard staff, the stores and materials of the dock-yard, houses and buildings at the station. The civil staffs under the chiefs of the dock-yard are composed of 23 officials in Karlskrona, and 14 officials in Stockholm.

The working force at the dock-yards, the "båtsmän" excluded, consists partly of a permanent staff, partly of temporary workmen. The permanent corps of engineers consists of 26 persons in Karlskrona, and of 20 in Stockholm. At the Karlskrona dock-yard, the corps of workmen, in the beginning of 1875, was composed of 61 non-commissioned officers and foremen, and 665 shipwrights, and at Stockholm of 43 non-commissioned officers and 143 carpenters and mechanics.

(B) THE MILITARY STAFF.

In the same manner as the army is composed of national militia (indelta), enlisted (värfvade), and conscription troops, so is the Navy composed of "båtsmän" (sailors, paid and kept, like the "indelta" in the army, by the landowners),* boys, a corps of seamen and naval conscripts (sjöbeväring). The commanders are composed of a corps of non-commissioned officers, and a corps of commissioned officers.

* This duty of the landowners is called "Båtsmanshåll."

The Båtsmanshåll, for which farms are expressly reserved, in districts situated near the sea-coast, is founded on the same principles as the rest of the "indelningsverk" (appointments of lands and rents for the "indelta" of the army and navy). The "båtsman" is raised, kept, clothed, equipped, on the same principles as the privates of the "indelta" army.

There are 31 companies of "båtsmän," and the full number of the force is 6,571, of which there are at present 1846 vacancies. The annual expenditure of the "Rote" (the farmers who are bound to furnish the sailor) for one man averages 113 Kr. When the men are on duty they are clothed, kept, and paid by the government. The annual cost for the clothing of a "båtsmän," calculated for the time he is on duty, is 85 Kr. 11 öre, and the food about 55 öre per day.

The Corps of Apprentices. The number of the corps, which is regulated according to the requirements for the recruiting of the corps of seamen, is 280, and this number is divided into two companies, which are stationed at Karlskrona. The age for admittance into the corps is from 14 to 16. To be rated as ordinary seamen, it is required to have attained the age of 18 in combination with proportionally developed bodily strength, and practical skill.

The Corps of Seamen is recruited from the apprentices, who are entered at the age of maturity and must serve in the corps for 6 years. The corps consists of 600 men, who are divided into 6 companies, 4 at Karlskrona, and 2 in Stockholm. They are also divided into five classes, with regard to the pay on shore, which ranges from 127 Kr. 75 öre to 401 Kr. 50 öre per annum. The men who are continuously on duty are clothed by the State, and receive their rations in natura, and an extra daily pay when commanded to go to sea. The annual cost for the clothing of a sailor is 108 Kr.

The Conscripts. All the sea-faring persons registered as master-mariners, mates, engineers, sailors, and stokers, between 20 and 25 years of age, being exempt from all military drill in time of peace, are bound to serve during war. The number amounts to about 1,000 master-mariners, mates, and engineers, and 6,000 sailors.

The conscripts drawn in the coast districts are called naval conscripts (sjöbeväring) and allotted to the navy, but in time of peace they are drilled in the army. These young men, bound to serve in time of war, are divided into five classes according to age, and amount in round numbers to 26,000.

The Corps of Non-Commissioned Officers. This corps is exclusively recruited from the corps of seamen. In 1866, when the Navy was divided into coast-artillery and the navy, some of the supernumerary non-commissioned officers were transferred to the Reserve List. The number of those who still are on this list is 30.

According to the organization in 1873, the corps of non-commissioned officers of the Navy is composed of

20 Chief Non-commissioned Officers (called "Flag Under-Officers").
75 Non-commissioned Officers of the 2d Class.
95 Non-commissioned Officers of the 3d Class.

190 Total.

The non-commissioned officers are divided into the following classes, intended for duty on board, namely: 65 belonging to the quartermaster's staff, 65 to the gunnery, 40 to the boatswains, and 20 to the ship-stewards.

The Corps of Commissioned Officers. In order to get a commission in the Navy, it is required to have passed through the Naval Academy. Officers of the grade of Captain or higher, may be transferred from the active to the Reserve List, to which, at present, 73 officers belong.

The active corps consists of:

2 Flag-Officers (Admirals).
6 Commodores.
20 Captain-Commodores (Post-Captains).
43 Captains (Lieutenant-Commanders).
43 Lieutenants.
26 Sub-Lieutenants.

140 Total.

(C) THE TRAINING OF THE CORPS.

The Seamen. Those belonging to the seamen's corps, as well as those belonging to the "båtsmanshåll," are divided into three classes, namely: seamen of the 1st (leading-seamen), 2d (able seamen), and 3d class (ordinary seamen), besides the class of recruits. The seamen of the 1st class consist of such as are intended when on board, and sometimes also on shore, to do duty as non-commissioned officers (petty officer-corporals) as well as such as are intended for foremen.

The men belonging to the 3 seamen's classes are divided into 3 sub-classes in proportion to their term of service and good conduct, and when on board they receive pay which varies accordingly.

First and second class seamen are divided among the following six branches, by which the selection of suitable men for the cadres for manning the vessels is greatly facilitated, namely: Torpedo corps, gunners, sailors, stewards, stokers, and mechanics.

The men are drilled at training-schools, one at each of the naval stations. All "båtsmän" recruited begin their course before the 15th of September, and all boys rated as mature, who do not possess the knowledge required for an approved recruit, shall begin the recruits' course on the 1st of October.

The instruction comprises separate courses for the recruits' class, and the 3d, 2d, and 1st of the seamen's classes.

The exercises are continued throughout the whole year, during winter on shore, and for about four months during the summer on board the training-ships of the school.

Such of the "båtsmän" as are considered unsuitable for sea-service are engaged as dockyard-båtsmän, and are employed as workmen at the dock-yard. In each company of båtsmän two-thirds are intended for sea-service, and one-third for dockyard-service. In the same proportion as recruits are advanced to a seaman's class the corresponding number are removed to be dockyard-båtsmän.

The Non-commissioned Officers. There is a preparatory school at each of the naval stations, intended for future non-commissioned officers of all staffs, and a school for non-commissioned officers, divided into the quartermasters', gunners', boatswains', and stewards' classes.

In order to be admitted into the non-commissioned officers' school it is necessary to be a first-class seaman, and to have gone through the preparatory school. The course of instruction lasts from October until April.

The Commissioned Officers. A military college, which has for its principal object the training of naval officers, was established in Stockholm in 1748, and afterwards removed to Karlskrona. It was then again established in Stockholm, and it continued to be in common for the training of officers both for the army and navy until 1867, when a special *Naval College* was established in the Capital for the training of officers for the Royal Navy. The school is under the supervision of the head of the Royal Naval Department, and is divided into two divisions—a preparatory division, with four classes, and an upper division with two classes. The course is calculated to last six years. The number of pupils and cadets is about 46. They have yearly practical exercises. The annual number of naval cadets passing the lieutenants' examination is from 5 to 6. For promotion in the navy no further proof of knowledge is required. The annual government grant for the school is 24,720 Kr.

(D) THE BUDGET.

The whole grant for the Naval Department for the year 1876 amounts to 7,771,685 Kr. 40 öre. Of this 127,837 Kr. 60 öre is for the Headquarters, or the Administrative Department of the Royal Navy, and sundry expenses, 2,136,692 Kr. 98 öre for the men and officers, 4,020,894 Kr. 82 öre for the material, 550,000 for naval expeditions, and 936,260 for the pilot-corporation, coast-lights, and life-boat establishment, and also for the hydrographic bureau, and the navigation schools.

(E) THE FLEET OF WAR.

The first steam-boats intended for war-steamers were the paddle-steamers, "Oden" and "Gylfe," which were built in 1835, and a few years later, in 1841, the Swedish fleet was increased by a larger armed steamer, the paddle-corvette, "Thor," with an engine of 200 nominal horse-power, which was built in the mechanical workshop at Motala. Our first man-of-war screw-steamer, with the machinery below the water-line, is the corvette, "Gefle," which was built in 1847, and supplied with a machinery of 300 nominal horse-power. This steamer was also built at Motala, where also our first armor-plated man-of-war, the monitor, "John Ericsson," of 1500 tons burden, and fitted with a screw and machinery of 150 nominal horse-power, was built in 1865. The vessels belonging to the Swedish Navy are enumerated in the following table:

	Armor.					Number of Guns.					
						Rifled.					
	The hulk.	Fire-front of the turret.	Speed in knots.	Nominal horse-power.	Crew.	Cm. 27	Cm. 24	Cm. 16	Cm. 12.18	Smooth bore.	Total.
ARMOR-PLATED VESSELS.	Decim. inches.										
3 Monitors	4.00	8.80	6–7	450	240	..	4	..	..	2	6
1 Monitor	4.17	15.08	7–8	160	80	..	2	..	..	..	2
3 Small Turret-boats	2.14	5–9	4–6	53	96	..	2	..	..	1	3
7 Small Turret-boats	2.14	14.12	7–9	350	315	..	7	..	..	..	7
14				1,013	731		15			3	18
STEAMERS WITHOUT ARMOR.											
1 Line-of-battle (screw) ship	....	....	7	350	735	..	..	..	..	66	66
1 Frigate	....	....	11	400	316	..	..	8	..	8	16
3 Corvettes (one building)	....	....	10–12	1,100	565	..	..	7	12	3	22
2 Gun-boats (one building)	....	....	12–13	350	142	2	..	..	..	..	2
10 Gun-boats	....	....	8–9	600	390	..	..	..	10	..	10
2 Despatch or Commander-in-chief's ships	....	....	10	230	141	..	..	..	..	5	5
1 Transport	....	....	10	140	48	..	..	..	..	..	..
20				3,170	2,337	2		15	22	82	121
SAILING VESSELS.											
1 Frigate	....	....	....	....	340	..	..	..	..	36	36
4 Corvettes	....	....	....	....	998	..	..	..	..	86	86
4 Brigs	....	....	....	....	249	..	..	..	.	10	10
1 Schooner	....	....	....	....	38	..	..	..	..	8	8
10					1,625					140	140
ROWING VESSELS.											
34 Gun-sloops	....	....	....	....	....	..	..	..	..	..	60
48 Gun-yawls	....	....	....	....	....	..	..	..	..	..	48
5 Mortar-boats	....	....	....	....	....	..	..	..	..	..	5
87											113

The Swedish Navy consequently possesses 14 armor-plated vessels of in all 1,013 nominal horse-power, and 18 guns, of which 15 are rifled and armor-penetrating. The rest of the steam fleet consists of 20 vessels of in all 3,170 horse-power, and 121 guns, of which 39 are rifled, and 2 of these armor-penetrating of 27 cm. calibre. The sailing and rowing vessels, the former 10 and the latter 87 in number, are in all mounted with 253 smooth-bore guns.

Great attention has during the last few years been paid to submarine warfare. For the movable defence, Harvey's towing-torpedo was purchased in 1871, and Whitehead's self-acting fish-torpedo in 1875.

The cost of the whole steam fleet amounts to nearly 15 million Kr., of which 1,800,000 Kr. for the line-of-battle ship the "Stockholm," 1,255,000 Kr. for the steam-frigate "Vanadis," 1,100,000 Kr. for the steam-corvette "Balder," 1,150,000 Kr. for the steam-corvette "Saga," 370,000 Kr. for each of the gunboats "Blenda" and "Disa," 1,120,000 Kr. for the monitor "Loke," and 950,000 Kr. for each of the other monitors, the "John Ericsson," the "Thordön," and the "Tirfing." The cost of the small turret-boats varies from 137,000 Kr. to 329,000 Kr.; together they cost 2,572,000 Kr. The cost of the ordnance is not included in these sums.

The Artillery employed for the Navy is:

27 cm. rifled breech-loading guns, of cast-iron, with 2 layers of steel hoops, chiefly after the French system, of about 20 calibres in length, and provided with 5 parabolic grooves. They weigh, together with the mechanism, 24,043 kilo., and cost about 38,000 Kr. The weight of the solid shot is 216 kilo., of the hollow shot 144; the greatest charge of gunpowder is from 38 to 40 kilo.

24 cm. rifled breech-loading guns, of cast-iron, with steel hoops, after the French marine system. Their weight is 14,766 kilo., and the cost, according to present rates, 22,000 Kr. Their solid shot weigh 144 kilo. The initial velocity has been proved during the last experiments to be 415 mètres.

16 cm. rifled breech-loading guns, of cast-iron, with steel hoops, likewise after the model of the French marine. Their weight is 5,312 kilo., and the cost 6,400 Kr.; their solid shot weighs 48.45 kilo.

12.18 cm. rifled muzzle-loading guns, of cast-iron, with steel hoops, Swedish model, and made at Finspong. Their weight is 1,870 kilo., and the cost 2,200 Kr.; their shells weigh 15.72 kilo.

6.7 cm. rifled muzzle-loading guns, of cast-iron, like the field guns of the land artillery. They weigh 250 kilo., cost 270 Kr., and are designed for use in effecting a landing. Their projectile weighs 2.25 kilo.

Mitrailleuses of the Palmcrantz-Wiborg model. This mitrailleuse is composed of ten gun-barrels of the model adopted for the Army and Navy. The price is 3,000 Kr.

38.1 cm. smooth-bored muzzle-loading guns, of cast-iron, American model. A gun of this kind weighs 18,860 kilo., and costs 15,000 Kr. The solid shot weighs 205 kilo.

26.7 cm. smooth-bored muzzle-loading guns, of cast-iron. They weigh 12,700 kilo., and cost 7,500 Kr.; the solid shot weighs 68 kilo.

Of older models:

22.6 cm. smooth-bored guns for hollow shot.
20.2 cm. " " " "
20.2 cm. " " solid shot.
17.75 cm. " " " "
16.7 cm. " " " "
15.53 cm. " " " "
12.17 cm. " " " "
9.62 cm. " " " "
32.66 cm. mortar.

The projectiles of the largest of the above-mentioned guns are of cast-iron, case-hardened. As a means of igniting the charges in shells time and percussion fuses are used.

The latest *Small-arms* adopted for the Navy are:

Breech-loading rifles of the Remington system, provided with sword bayonets. These weapons are of the same construction as those of the Army, and require the same ammunition, so that all the statements relative to the latter weapons also apply to the former, with the exception of the cost price, which is as much higher as the sword bayonet is dearer than the ordinary bayonet, or 7 Kr. Such a weapon, together with a sword bayonet, costs, according to the present prices, 41 Kr.

Revolvers of a similar model as those of the Cavalry, and also revolvers on the Lefaucheux system.

The other small-arms are of older models, and the following:

Breech-loading rifles with a calibre of 14.84 millimètres.

Muzzle-loading rifles with a calibre of 15.44 millimètres.

Smooth-bore muzzle-loading muskets.

Smooth-bore pistols, as well as pistols fixed on the gunwale, with a calibre of 40.97 millim., for which not only a solid ball is used, but also small shot.

Cutlasses.

Boarding-axes, and

Pikes.

BENEVOLENCE.

[*Class* 346.]

CHARITY, which bids us care for the poor and needy, has formed an element in the Statute Laws of the Kingdom from time immemorial, even long before the clergy were enjoined in 1686, to care for the needy in their respective parishes, but these Poor Laws and their amendments exacted almost too much from the parishes and admitted of frequent abuse; in order to avoid this a new Poor Law, with certain restrictions, was enacted, June 9th, 1871, which is now in force.

This law provides that only children, and such as in consequence of age, sickness, or natural defect, are unable to work, and have no means of their own for their support, shall have an unconditional right to charitable assistance from the community to which they belong, whereas in other cases it will depend upon the approval of the Charity Commission. A person who is able to work shall support himself and those of his children who are under age; a husband his wife; and children their parents. For the support of servants, operators, and such workmen, together with their wives and children, the employer is responsible during the validity of the agreement between them. Any one who, by indolence or indifference, brings upon his non-aged child, or his wife, such distress that charity must be applied for, or if he suffers his children to go begging, or begs himself, he may be punished with hard labor. All that ask for alms, either by words or gestures, of any one but the proper authorities, are considered as beggars.

In order to be able to fulfil their duties with regard to the maintenance of the poor, nearly every parish has at least one poor-house, in which principally aged persons are taken care of. In 1870 there were 2,500 such poor-houses in the country. Children, on the other hand, are frequently sent out to board with families. During the above-named year 85,150 persons, old and young, were wholly supported at the expense of the Charity Commission, and 119,230 persons were temporarily relieved. At this rate it may be calculated that 3.6 per cent. (3.3 per cent. in the country, but 5.5 per cent. in the towns) of the population of the Kingdom were receiving relief, but in reality this number is too small, as the children belonging to the families have in many cases not been counted separately. The total expenditure, which for 1865 was stated to be 3,856,862 Kr., and for 1870, 6,022,345 Kr., is put down much too low, as many items (such as dwellings, fuel, food, etc.) have often not been included. It is easily understood, under such circumstances, that the maintenance of the poor is looked upon as one of the heaviest duties of the community.

Besides this public Charity Institution, there are a great many establishments which have charity for their object, such as the institutes for the deaf and dumb, and the blind (compare above under Class 300 A), orphan-asylums, day-nurseries, lying-in-hospitals, homes for the incurable. In the Great Orphan Asylum in Stockholm, there are always about 150 infants who are nursed within the establishment, and from 3,000 to 4,000 children are boarded at its expense, mostly in the country.

Provision for the sick is another means by which distress is relieved, and which is becoming more general year by year. It has been stated above (page 214) that an apothecary's business cannot be carried on by others than properly qualified persons; this also applies to the practice of medicine. Quackery is, therefore, strictly prohibited. The supervision of the medical treatment of the sick and the sanitary arrangements belongs to the Board of Health; but for the insane-asylums (mad-houses) there is a separate commission, the Corporation of the Order of the Seraphim. Besides medical practitioners, who are always legally authorized, there is a town-physician appointed in every town, and in some of the rural districts there are so-called physicians of the provinces, and specially appointed doctors for the hospitals and insane-asylums. That there are medical staffs attached to the Army and Navy has been stated above. In the year 1873, there were in Sweden 61 hospitals, including those for syphilitic diseases, with, in all, 3436 sick-beds, besides 24 other establishments for the sick (children's homes and the like not included), with 1,154 sick-beds, 9 insane-asylums with 1,154 sick-beds, 217 apothecary's shops, 558 appointed or practising physicians, 2,043 midwives, 186 veterinary surgeons. The number of vaccinations during the same year amounted to 83 per cent. of the births during the preceding year. The average expense for the attendance of each patient in the hospitals was 1.12 Kr. per diem.*

During the ten years, 1861–1871, 129,181 persons (15.71 per cent. of all the deaths) were the victims of *epidemic diseases*, which occurred in very different degrees of severity: The years 1861 and 1867 were very lenient, but 1862, 1866, and 1869, were so much the worse. The epidemics which carried away the above-mentioned victims were the following: Scarlatina (28,836), typhus, measles (morbilli), diphtheria, hooping-cough (pertussis), croup (laryngitis membranacea), small-pox (variolæ), cholera (5,322), diarrhœa, dysentery (dysenteria), brain-fever (meningitis cerebro-spinalis), puerperal fever (febris puerperalis), ague (febris intermittens), raphania, mumps (parotitis), and scurvy (scorbutus) (113). The worst cholera years were: 1834 (12,637 deaths), 1850 (1,811), 1853 (8,511), 1854 (1,152), 1855 (2,302), 1857 (3,771), and 1866 (4,706). During the other years cholera occurred either not at all or only in a few cases.

Of people afflicted with leprosy (lepra) (which is a very common malady in Norway) there are in Sweden but a small number, from 70 to 80 persons, mostly in the province of Helsingland.

[CLASS 347.] In addition to the provisions for the sick in the Army, made by the government, private individuals have interested themselves in the sanitary cause and formed, Dec. 3, 1864, the "SWEDISH CENTRAL ASSOCIATION FOR THE VOLUNTARY TREATMENT OF THE SICK AND WOUNDED IN WAR," under the presidency of H. R. H. the Duke of Östergötland (now H. R. M. King Oscar II). The association commenced its existence not only with the coöperation of public authorities in this country, but also of the International Committee at Geneva and kindred foreign associations.

According to the rules adopted May 24, 1865, but a little altered in 1871, the objects of the association are:

In time of Peace. (*a*) To spread a knowledge of the necessity of improved methods of treating the sick and wounded during war, of the insufficiency of the means at the disposal of the Army Administrative Department and of the improvements made in other countries by the publishing and distributing of tracts. (*b*) To encourage the formation of branch associations. (*c*) To solicit contributions of money, means of conveyance, and other necessary articles from the public. (*d*) To procure and train volunteers for the nursing of the sick and wounded. (*e*) To enter into combination with similar associations in other countries, and especially that of Geneva.

In time of War. (*a*) To place at the disposal of the Army Administrative Department materials and trained volunteers for the care of the sick and wounded. (*c*) To assist as far as they can in the arrangement of the conveyances and hospitals.

* Two Medical Reports of the diseases treated and the regimen prescribed are annually published, and they belong to the general series (Bidrag till Sveriges officiela statistik), namely: K) I of the Board of Health (Sundhets Kollegium) for the years 1861–1874, and K) II of the Board of the mad-houses for the years 1861–1874.

The association will likewise procure suitable employment for soldiers who, either by wounds or sickness, have become less able to work; and to succor soldiers' families, or widows and orphans.

One of the main objects of the association has been the procuring and training of nurses. With this latter object in view, Miss E. RAPPE, a lady zealous in all philanthropic undertakings, was sent to London, in 1866, to go through a course of instruction at the "Miss Nightingale Institution." Whereupon, after having completed the course and returned to Sweden, she was appointed as superintendent of the new Academical Hospital at Upsala, where all the nurses employed by the association since that time (1866) have been trained. The nurses employed by the association at present number 66, the majority of whom have been trained at the Academic Hospital.

At the International Exhibition in Paris, in 1867, where the association was awarded a prize for articles exhibited for the treatment of the sick, and, likewise, at the exhibition in Vienna, in 1873, the association had delegated members who were commissioned to take cognizance of and to procure such objects as are within the sphere of the association. A member of the association was likewise present at the diplomatic conference at Geneva, October, 1868, and the conference in Berlin, April, 1869.

Under the auspices of the association, Professor ESMARCK'S "The first dressing on the battle-field," and his lecture on "The strife of philanthropy against the horrors of war," have been translated into the Swedish language, and a number of copies sold, others distributed for the use of the Army, and to several hospitals.

In consequence of letters received, not only from the International Committee at Geneva, but the Central Committees at Berlin and Paris, requesting contributions for relieving the distress caused by the Franco-Prussian war, 1870–1871, the association determined, at a meeting on August 26th, 1870, to remit to the "Agence Internationale," established at Basel by the International Committee at Geneva, a sum of 20,000 francs, amounting to nearly half the capital then possessed by the association, together with 27 cases containing sundry hospital articles, valued at upwards of 20,000 francs, contributed by the public at the solicitation of the association, were sent from Stockholm to the Basel agency, and from the towns of Göteborg and Malmö similar articles of about the same value, as well as money collected to the amount of 176,775 francs, to be employed where most needed during the vicissitudes of war, without any regard to the nationality of the sufferers.

At the suggestion of the association and the Royal Board of Health, H. R. Majesty ordered, on the 21st of October, 1870, that 4 physicians, 2 of whom were chosen by said board and 2 by the association, should go to the French-German seat of war. Though none of the physicians thus sent (all of whom were members of the association) were assigned duties by either of the belligerent armies, they had opportunities, not only at the headquarters of the German army at Versailles but also at several hospitals in France and Germany, to make many important observations concerning the treatment of the sick and wounded, which they reported to the association.

The association's collection of models and materials for the sick has gradually increased by generous gifts from the members of the royal family, as well as from private individuals. Large quantities of linen have been collected, which has been partly presented, partly collected by the association's ladies' committee, who have made bandages of the linen that has been received.

Pursuant to a proposal made by H. R. M., the present King, to establish an ambulatory hospital brigade, a sloop of war and a gun yawl have been fitted up as hospitals and transports, by the association, and these vessels were employed in the neighborhood of Stockholm during the military exercises in 1872.

In case of a war breaking out, in which Sweden-Norway may have to participate, the association enters the service in the Army under the command of the Administrative Department, and subject to certain regulations, which provide that the volunteers shall in no case act on their own responsibility, but shall be subject to the official staff.

Collaterally with the Association a corps of ambulatory hospital volunteers has been formed in the capital who have offered to assist the Association in case of need. At present this corps consists of 24 members, who, according to the rules adopted for the corps, have either passed a requisite examination, or shall do so within two years from the time of their joining the corps.

Lastly, we may add that a military medical association has been formed among the physicians of the Army and Navy, the Central Committee of whom will publish a periodical. The "Association for the treatment of the Sick" have embraced the opportunity of availing themselves of this periodical as a medium for the spreading of such notices as concern the duties and interests of the volunteers for the treatment of the sick and wounded in war.

With regard to others, besides the above-mentioned *Co-operative Associations*, we may mention that there are several in the country, such as the Military Club, the Physicians' Association, the Apothecaries' Society, the Industrial Union, etc. (compare Class 311). The order of the Freemasons, which may be included in the number, support a large orphan asylum in Stockholm.

[CLASS 348.] Respecting the division of the inhabitants of the kingdom according to *Creed*, see page 302.

[CLASS 349.] *Art and Industrial Exhibitions* take place continually at our museums, also on a larger scale at certain intervals, when generally the neighboring countries, Norway, Denmark, and Finland, are invited to participate. Such was the nature of the Industrial Exhibition which was held in Stockholm in 1866, and likewise the meetings of naturalists and lawyers, which in recent times have been held in the Scandinavian countries. Among these may also be included the meetings of students which have been alternately held at the northern university towns. In 1873 an International Archæological Congress was held in Stockholm, and the same year the Permanent Statistical Commission also met at Stockholm.

Agricultural Fairs are held annually in almost every province by the Agricultural Societies. The General Agricultural Meetings, which are held at intervals of a few years, sometimes in one place, sometimes in another, attract visitors not only from different parts of the kingdom but also from abroad.

DEPARTMENT IV.—ART.

SCULPTURE AND PAINTING.*

[CLASSES 400–413.] A glance at the Swedish art of a century ago takes us back to the reign of GUSTAF III., through whose efforts Sweden advanced to a foremost position in literature and art, especially in literature and dramatic art, but some of the important names in fine-art also belong to this period.

In order to judge correctly of the direction taken by Swedish fine-art in the latter half of the 18th century it is desirable to study the history of the building of the palace in Stockholm, by *Nicodemus Tessin, Jr.*, and its artistical ornamenting, an occurrence of special importance in the history of Swedish fine arts.

It is here to be considered, however easily it may be accounted for, that Tessin, at the building of the palace, made no use whatever of the Swedish school founded by *Ehrenstrahl*, inasmuch as its tendency was too strongly German, whereas Tessin favored the French taste in decoration. It was Tessin and his family who were chiefly instrumental in introducing this style

* Contributed by Professor E. BERGH

into Sweden, and the building of the palace afforded the best opportunity.

The French artists called into the country by Tessin exercised, however, no particularly great influence on the native artists, as the deranged condition of the country's finances, after the unfortunate wars of CARL XII., caused an interruption in the building of the royal castle. So much the greater, on the other hand, was the influence of those Frenchmen who were called into the country by *Carl Gustaf Tessin*, who after the death of his father superintended the building of the palace, with *Carl Hårleman* as assistant architect.

In 1728, when the State had so far recovered from the prostration caused by the unfortunate wars of CARL XII. that the Diet could grant the sums necessary for the completion of the palace, C. G. Tessin procured the services of a number of foreign artists, among whom may be mentioned: *G. T. Taraval*, the painter; *Lelièvre*, *Belletti*, *Bouchardon*, *l'Archevesque*, *Masreliez*, sculptors, and *Sergel*, embroiderer in gold.

These foreigners and some Swedes, as *Johan Pasch* and *Olof Arenius*, formed the circle of artists of which Tessin was the soul and centre. Through his influence a school of design was established, which was directed by Taraval, and in 1735 incorporated as the *Royal Academy of Design*. Thus, an institution was called into existence on which the votaries of art in Sweden could rely, and where new beginners could receive instruction. This school did not fail to produce its effects.

Among the scholars of the Academy we find the Crown Prince GUSTAF (afterwards GUSTAF III.) and his brother, and the instruction received while in this school doubtless contributed largely to the development of the monarch's taste for art and artistic occupations.

Among the prominent scholars of the Academy may be mentioned *Carl Gustaf Pilo*, who, however, soon (1740) settled in Copenhagen, where he became eminent, and was appointed Professor and Director of the Academy founded by Frederick V., but after having remained there for thirty years he returned to Sweden, and was appointed Director of the Academy at Stockholm; *Lorenz Pasch*, *Peter Krafft*, and *G. Lundberg* (Crayonist), who were the principal portrait painters of the Gustavian period.

The greatest among the scholars of the modern school were, however, *Louis Masreliez* and *Tobias Sergel* (sons of the above-mentioned artists of the same names); *J. Säfvenbom*, the oldest landscape-painter in Sweden, likewise, probably received his first instruction in this school.

A little later (1766) a school for engraving on copper was added to the Academy, under the direction of *Peter Floding*, which artist, under the guidance of *Jacob Gillberg*, had acquired great skill in chalcography.

Notwithstanding the opportunities which the building of the palace afforded to the more advanced, and the instruction which the Academy offered to beginners, the emigration of the Swedish artists, who sought their fortunes in foreign countries, still continued. It has been stated above that Pilo went to Copenhagen, and so did *Mandelberg*, who likewise was appointed professor there. *Alexander Roslin* (born 1718) left Sweden in 1745, and repaired to Paris, where he remained the rest of his lifetime, and became one of the most celebrated portrait-painters of his age. In the year 1774 he visited Sweden, after having previously in 1771, in Paris, painted the likenesses of GUSTAF III. and his brothers, CARL and FREDRIK, which painting is still one of the ornaments of the National Museum in Stockholm. He died in Paris, in 1793, without having been exposed to the dangers of the revolution.

The celebrated miniature painter, *Peter Adolph Hall*—"le Van Dyck de la Miniature"—likewise sought and found his fortune in Paris, but was driven to Belgium by the storms of the revolution, where he died, at Liège, in 1794. *E. Cogell*, who was appointed professor at Lyon; *N. Lafrensen*, the distinguished water-color painter, who returned from Paris to Stockholm, in 1791, where he painted a superior portrait of GUSTAF III. *Elias Martin* visited England, where he was highly esteemed as a historical painter, but was recalled by GUSTAF III. in 1791; in later years he painted mostly landscapes, which were greatly appreciated by his contemporaries. *Adolph Ulrich Wertmüller* (born 1749) received a small stipend in 1772, and went to Paris, where he acquired great fame, and while there he painted a picture, "Queen Marie Antoinette with her Children," which is considered the best portrait of this unfortunate queen (it is now in the National Museum in Stockholm). Wertmüller returned to Sweden in 1797, but soon after went to America, where he died in 1812.

Sergel had in 1761 been awarded the great medal of the Academy, and in 1767 he received a stipend for travelling abroad. Two years later he was followed by Masreliez, so that Sweden, at the ascension of the throne by GUSTAF III., was almost destitute of prominent native artistic talent of art. Those who still remained in the country, deserving to be mentioned, were: *Hoffmann*, who, after a prolonged sojourn in Paris and Rome, returned in 1771 (his chief work is probably the altar-picture in Clara Church, Stockholm), and *Pilo*, who returned a year later, but resided in his native place, Östergötland, until GUSTAF III., while on a visit at Nyköping, met him, and was so favorably impressed with his works that he engaged him to paint a picture of his coronation; Pilo at the same time was appointed Director of the Academy. The death of GUSTAF III. prevented the completion of this picture, which is in the Museum at Stockholm in its unfinished condition.

Peter Hillerström, who, as a youth, was employed under Taraval at the building of the palace, and was educated as a tapestry-weaver, for which purpose he was sent to Paris, but after having had an opportunity of studying with Boucher he gave up weaving altogether, turned painter, and represented common-place scenes of his age. A dry conception and a feeble coloring often impaired the value of his numerous works.

It was natural that GUSTAF III., with his intense love for the beautiful, though his knowledge was rather superficial in the fine arts, should not be satisfied with the service rendered the fine arts by the above-named artists; he therefore determined to recall the principal Swedish artists who were abroad. In this he did not succeed with Roslin, who, as stated above, only paid a short visit to his native country; on the other hand, Sergel obeyed the king's summons in 1777, and took the place of his former teacher, l'Archevesque, who was obliged to resign on account of his health, and to return to his native town, Montpelier, where he died in 1778.

Sergel had already acquired great fame abroad, especially by his "Faun," and his statues, "Diomedes" and "Othryades"; but his being called home was no doubt a misfortune with regard to his development as an artist, for in all probability if he had been able to finish his studies among the classical scenes and associations of Rome, he would have been an artist, perhaps superior, but certainly equal to Canova, the plastic, who gave tone to the statuary of his time. In Rome, by the order of the Countess Dubarry, he modelled his incomparably beautiful group, "Amor and Psyche," which were executed in marble for GUSTAF III., and which is now one of the most beautiful ornaments in the Swedish National Museum. As a melancholy proof of the activity to which the favor of GUSTAF III. forced him, may be seen a few steps from the above-mentioned group, the most repugnant abuse of antique work, an imitation of the well-known antique statue, "Venus Callipygos," represented with the features of a court-beauty (the Countess Höpken). Among the best works of Sergel may further be mentioned: "Venus stepping into the bath" (executed for Count Cederhjelm of Säby), "Axel Oxenstjerna and the Muse of History," a number of church monuments, as that over Cartesius (in Adolf-Fredrick's Church, in Stockholm), and innumerable portrait-statues, busts, and medallions. The most important of these works, one of Sergel's master-pieces, is the statue of Gustavus III. on the quay in Stockholm, which was ordered by the burghers of Stockholm in 1790. In this statue the old Roman spirit seems to have awakened anew in Sergel; GUSTAF is represented at the moment he steps on shore presenting the olive-branch to his country as a sign of peace. Sergel died in 1814.

Four years later, in 1781, *Masreliez*, the painter, returned. He had studied principally at Bologna, where he was so highly appreciated that he was made a member of the academy of the city. Next to Sergel, he was the most prominent artist in the time of GUSTAF III. Inasmuch as Masreliez's natural talent was not at all suited for easel pieces, and monumental works were but seldom offered, this master left but few works of importance. Among them may be mentioned the altar-piece in the Maria Church, in Stockholm, painted in oil before his departure. This painting is, however, of far less importance than the fresco paintings in the Haga pavilion, which represent scenes from Greek mythology, with arabesques, which plainly show that he had diligently studied decorative painting, and that he may be looked upon as Sweden's classic artist, though he could not always lay aside the rococo style that characterized the times. He exercised his principal influence as teacher at the Academy, where he was appointed Professor in 1784, and Director in 1806. He died in 1810.

The love of GUSTAF III. for the scenic, one of the most prominent traits in his character, caused him to see the greatest talent of all the artists at his court, in the French architect, *Louis Desprèz*, whose acquaintance he had formed in Rome. Desprèz was an excellent draftsman, and was looked upon by the king as the perfect artist, a suitable person to be appointed, not only royal decorative painter, but also to execute one of the few historical paintings of the Gustavian period, "The Battle of Hogland" (in the Royal Palace at Rosenberg), a painting of no great merit. Després had but little opportunity of practising his own art, architecture, further than drawing plans, the most important of which was a plan for a large palace at Haga, the foundation of which was laid in 1786, but which was never finished on account of the king's death.

Peter Hörberg, born in Småland in 1746, the son of a soldier, Åke Hörberg, is perhaps the most peculiar phenomenon in the art of the Gustavian period. He was endowed with a most extraordinary discrimination in colors and a lively imagination, and would doubtless have arisen to a prominent position in the history of art had he had even a moderate art education, and not had to contend against such serious financial embarrassments; but as it is he can only be looked upon as a curiosity. He was a member of the Royal Academy, and died in 1816.

In architecture, after the time of Hårleman, if Desprèz, whose activity was mostly confined to the sphere of projects, be excepted, the first place was held by Superintendent *Adelcrantz*, whose most important works are Adolph Frederich Church and the Opera House in Stockholm; and later by *Erik Palmstedt*, who rebuilt "The Torstenson House," after the model of the Opera House for the Princess Sophia Albertina, and who gave, in the Stockholm Exchange, though in the details it is not very tasteful, a well-proportioned specimen of the Gustavian architecture. "Norrbro" (the Northern Bridge) was constructed by him after designs by Adelcrantz.

In *chalcography*, which during the time of liberty was very well represented in Sweden, *Fredrik Akrell* and *Jacob Gillberg* were prominent, both trained in Floding's school; the latter, in particular, has produced very good works. The art of coining medals was worthily represented during this period by *Gustavus Ljungberger*.

The School of Design, established by Tessin, which in 1735 was styled Drawing Academy, and received a support from the State, was reorganized in 1768, and at the proposal of Mr.

Adelcrantz, the Superintendent, was changed from a school of design into a school of arts, under the name of "Academy of Painting and Statuary." Its members were *Rehn*, *John Pasch*, *l'Archevesque*, *Lundberg*, and *Fehrmann* as the founders, and *Säfoenbom*, *Lorenz Pasch*, *Floding*, *Gillberg*, and *Ljungberger* as "fellows." L'Archevesque was the first Director of the new Academy. The existence of the new school was, however, perilled, inasmuch as the ruling political party, called "the caps," entertained the plan of refusing it any support; but the Revolution of GUSTAF III. intervened and saved the Academy. In the years 1773 and 1777 the support was increased, and consequently the instruction was considerably extended. The position of the Academy was further guaranteed by the patriotism of the Director, *Gerhard Meyer*, who in his will bequeathed the Academy his house, which is still standing. The collections of antiquities, etc., necessary for the instruction could now be arranged, and the exhibitions set down in the regulations of the Academy set on foot. These exhibitions showed a noticeable progress in the activity of the Academy as an establishment for instruction, although dilettanteism was rather largely represented.

Notwithstanding these seemingly favorable circumstances, it cannot be said that the Academy produced in the following period any prominent artist. The unfortunate political circumstances were perhaps in a great measure the cause. There were no doubt able teachers, such as Sergel, Masreliez, and *Von Breda*. The latter had returned from England, where he studied under Reynolds, and his fame having reached his native country before him, he was immediately appointed professor. The principal representatives of Swedish art at this period were: *Peter Krafft, Jr.* (born 1777), who studied at David's, in Paris, and was a very skilful portrait painter, in which branch he produced some good works. Most of them, however, carry along with them the stamp of business, and betray no other effort than that of gain. He died in 1863. *Gustaf Erik Hasselgren* succeeded Hillerström to the professorship in 1817. His most important work was the altar-piece in the Jacob Church, in Stockholm, which, however, was removed to make room for a painting by his more successful rival, *Fredrik Westin* (born 1782), who was placed by his contemporaries on a level with the most prominent painters. The present times cannot coincide in that opinion, for the style and manner in which he represented scenes from the Greek mythology, or allegories, is feeble and expressionless. He appeared at once as a portrait-painter and a painter of church-pieces. In the latter direction the altar-pieces of Jacob and Kungsholm churches are his chief works.

Erik Gustaf Göthe, the sculptor (born 1779), perfected himself under the guidance of Sergel. In 1803 he went to Italy, where he remained for 7 years. In the course of this time he produced, among other things, his "Recumbent Bacchanalian." On his return to his native country he continued his activity, and the most prominent among his works are the monuments of Axel Fersen and Magnus Stenbock, his "Hebe," "Venus," "Amor," etc. He was commissioned by CARL XIV. to model the statue of CARL XIII., which was erected in the present "CARL XIII'. Square," in Stockholm. It certainly cannot be said of his more fortunate competitor, *J. N. Byström* (born 1783), that he was an artist of greater merit; but he had gained the favor of CARL XIV., which was also visible by a number of orders, as "Juno with the Hercules Child"—his greatest work (now in the National Museum, in Stockholm)—"Bachus," "Hera," "Hymen," statues of CARL X., XI., XII., etc. This predilection of the king for Byström exercised an influence on most of the Mœcene of the time, and the numerous orders which the artist consequently received placed him in a very comfortable financial position, but also contributed to the production of works seemingly hurried over, as if made merely for sale, and hence but few of his works are found satisfactory on a nearer inspecti

With the exception of Byström, who mostly resided in Italy, the rest of the above-mentioned artists were directors of the Academy, which after 1812 was called "*Academy of the Liberal Arts.*" Notwithstanding it had at that time six regular and three extra professors, besides several other teachers, the instruction does not seem to have been carried on with any particularly great zeal, which may be inferred from the establishment of a society called "Society for the Study of the Arts," in opposition to the Academy (1814). Its object was, partly to complete the insufficient academical course, partly to make episodes from the northern "saga" and history subjects of artistic treatment, in opposition to Greek and Roman history, which the Academy, imitating the French, always brought forwards as subjects of study. The proper founders of this society were *Johan Gustaf Sandberg* (born 1782), *Bengt Erland Fogelberg* (born 1786), and *Johan von Breda*. They were joined by *Karl Johan Fahlcrantz*, the landscape painter, and *Alexander Lauræus*, the genre painter. This society shared the interest which the so-called "Gothic Alliance" manifested for ancient northern subjects, and at their request P. H. LING, the poet, and founder of Swedish gymnastics, held a series of lectures on the application of northern mythology in the fine arts. It is also, no doubt, to be attributed to the influence of Ling that Fogelberg began to give plastic form to the "Asa" gods.

A contention arose between this society and the Academy, which, in 1818, took the outward form of a Northern Exhibition, arranged under the auspices of the "Gothic Alliance," and independent of the Academy, where Fogelberg appeared with his northern mythological images, Sandberg with "the Valkyrias," and Fahlcrantz with northern landscapes. This difference was, however, adjusted by some of the members of the Academy joining the "Alliance;" Fogelberg receiving from the State a stipend for travelling abroad, and Sandberg, in 1821, being received as a member of the Academy.

Fahlcrantz (born 1774) was perhaps the most gifted among these contemporary artists, but yet a child of his age, inasmuch as he put aside any earnest study from nature, and mostly derived his inspirations from engravings after Claude Lorrain, which is plainly reflected in his Swedish landscapes. He died in 1861.

Architecture, in this period of "still-life," shared the same stagnation as the other branches of art. The works of *Tempelman*, *Sillén*, *Gjörvell*, *Sundwall*, and others, which are represented by the "Keyser House," in Stockholm (built by Sundwall), and the "Carolina rediviva," at Uppsala, with their paucity in taste, show no trace of the great traditions of Tessin.

In 1815, *C. D. Forssell*, engraver on copper (born in Skåne, 1777), was recalled from Paris by CARL XIV. He had become well known in Holland and France. His most important work after his return home is the portrait of CARL XIV., after Gérard. He was almost the only engraver on copper of this period, which is not to be wondered at, inasmuch as this art, which, during the period of liberty, was very much in favor, was afterwards put in the background by lithography, to which Forssell's pupils, *Cardon*, *Carl Johan Billmark*, and others, went over.

In *Miniature Painting*, *Lorenz Sparrgren* (deceased 1831) was an uncommonly talented artist who surpassed his contemporaries, *Andersson*, *Gillberg*, and others by far. This art is also its last representative since the time of Sparrman was *Way* (died 1873).

The *Art of Coining Medals*, which has been on the decline since the death of Ljungberger, was practised by *Grandel*, *Frumerie*, *Salmson* and *Lundgren* (father and son). In our days *Ludvig Ruben* has executed several copper plates of uncommon finish and merit. The principal ones are "Judith with the Head of Holofernes," after Allori, the artist's own portrait, and "Madonna della sedia," by Raphael, which, almost completed, remains unfinished in consequence of his death in 1875.

The movement in a national direction which "The Society for the Study of the Arts" called forth, exercised in the immediate future no lasting influence on Swedish art, and with the exception of the northern mythological images of Fogelberg, there is scarcely a trace left. The contention between the different opinions, however, awakened criticism, and the reciprocal and perfect satisfaction with everything and anything ceased. The artists felt the necessity of keeping pace with the development of art abroad. Therefore about the year 1820 another period of emigration commenced, which, however, was of quite a different character from that during the period of liberty, inasmuch as its principal object was the pursuit of knowledge in the foreign schools of art, but not to seek reputation and fortune. In 1818 Lauræus repaired to Paris; two years later Fogelberg, Salmson the medal coiner, and *Axel Nyström* the architect arrived there. In 1822 these artists went to Italy, where they met with Byström and *Hjalmar Mörner*, who had left Sweden in 1816. Lauræus died in Rome, 1823. But a short time previously *Olof Johan Södermark* had joined the circle of northern artists on the banks of the Tiber. For the next 25 years the Swedish artists who went abroad for study gathered around this nucleus, and remained for a longer or shorter time in the eternal city. Among them may be mentioned *A. C. Wetterling*, *C. G. Plagemann*, *R. W. Ekman*, *C. A. Dahlström*, *C. S. Bennet*, *G. W. Palm*, *J. M. Stäck*, *E. Lundgren* *U. Troili*, *P. Södermark*, *Jr.*, the architects *F. W. Scholander* and *A. Törnquist*, and later the painters *N. J. Blommér* and *L. A. Lindholm*, together with the sculptors *C. G. Qvarnström* and *J. P. Molin.*

During this period a new life was infused into the art of this northern circle, and the best works of that period were produced in Rome. Among these are Byström's "Juno with the Hercules Child at her Breast;" Fogelberg's northern mythological images "Odin," "Thor," and "Balder," and his monumental statues of Gustavus Adolphus (for Göteborg), BIRGER JARL and CARL XIV. (for Stockholm), and many pictures of national life and Italian scenes.

Rome was the centre of congregation for Swedish artists till about the year 1850, when, owing to the realistic tendency of modern art, it changed to Paris, though a few artists had already taken up their residence there as early as 1830, among whom were *Carl Fredrik Kiörboe* and *Peter Wickenberg;* the latter of whom had already, in 1840, earned the reputation of being a most skilful genre and landscape painter, and especially of winter scenes. He died while still young, in 1846.

Johan Wilhelm Carl Wahlbom went to Paris in 1838, where he remained for some time; later he studied in Germany and Holland, and then returned to Sweden, but went south again on account of his health. He chose Rome for his residence, and while there painted some of his best pieces. A complete apoplectic lameness forced him, however, to seek medical assistance in England, where he soon after (1858) died.

Johan Christian Berger perfected himself as marine painter in Paris and England, but especially in the latter country. He seems to have made Turner's rather fantastic style and manner of painting his pattern. He died (1871) in Sweden, where he had resided a long time.

It was natural that these artists, who had resided in foreign countries, should give a new life to artistic study in their own country. The branch of art which reaped the first fruits thereof was the Academy of *Architecture*, under the direction of *Nyström*, who educated several clever scholars, among whom were: *Törnquist*, *Åbom*, and *Scholander*, the latter of whom was made director after Nyström, and further developed it. The instruction was also improved in the other schools, though the older artists already mentioned continued to direct them for some time.

The realistic tendency became more and more prevalent, and soon infected the German schools. In Sweden it found adherents, under whose influence *Johan Boklund* went to Munich in 1846, and was followed by *Johan Fredrik Höckert.* The latter went to Paris in 1850, where his paintings repeatedly met with great applause, and after having in an uncommonly short time acquired the technical routine of the French school, he was, at the International Exhibition, in 1855, awarded a medal of the first class for his picture, "A Sermon in a Lappish Chapel." He returned to Sweden, where he died in 1866. In 1855 Boklund also went to Paris, where he, with several other Swedish artists, studied at Couture's.

Düsseldorf was likewise a school where most of the artists, who went abroad during the decennium from 1850–60, sought to perfect themselves. The main cause of this was the acquaintance with the works of Tideman and Gude at the Academy's Exhibition in Stockholm, in 1850. These works with their northern character, technical finish, and realistic conception, made a great impression on the young students at the Academy. It cannot be denied that Swedish art acquired a northern and national character, which was wanting up to that time.

In the beginning of the decennary, 1850–1860, *Quarnström* returned to his native country, where he has remained with few interruptions, and executed many monumental works; as, Tegner's Statue at Lund, Berzelius's in Stockholm, Engelbrekt's at Örebro, etc.; he also exerted a powerful influence on the instruction in drawing at the Academy, and was its director from 1854 until 1867. A little later Molin returned from Italy to Stockholm, where he also executed several monumental works, as: The Statue of King OSCAR I. (in Göteborg), the group "Bältespännarne" (the belt-tiers, gladiators), the Statue of CARL XII. (in Stockholm), and the monumental fountain, which was not raised in Stockholm until after the death of the artist, in 1873.

In 1856 Boklund returned to Stockholm, where he was appointed Professor at the Academy in the same year, and was commissioned to found a school for figure-painting. After the death of Quarnström he became Director of the Academy. In 1861 there was added to the Academy a landscape-school, founded by Professor *E. Bergh.* The Academy is now open to both sexes.

The *Stockholm Art Union*, which now has opened a suitable and permanent show-room for the works of the artists, has essentially contributed to the vigorous life which has been manifested in Swedish art in the course of the last few years.

ENGRAVING AND LITHOGRAPHY.

[CLASS 420–421.] ENGRAVING ON COPPER, especially in earlier times, was very much practised. Our first work of copper-plates is a rare book of heraldry, printed in 1650. At present copperplate is used almost exclusively for cartographic purposes. The topographical maps of Sweden and also the marine charts are printed from copper-plates. For the topographical maps trials have been made with a heliographic method invented at Vienna, which has been purchased and applied by the Swedish State.

[CLASS 422.] Wood engraving is very ancient, and was used as early as 1483 in the printing of a book of that date as a reproductive art. Xylography has of late become of great importance through the ateliers, established for illustrated newspapers and periodicals, also for obtaining copper-plates.

[CLASSES 423–424.] LITHOGRAPHY. Of the various modes of multiplying drawings in Sweden, as elsewhere, the different branches of Lithography are mostly employed. This art was introduced into the country about 1818, but in the beginning it was not much used for artistic purposes, for which copper-plates in mezzotinto was still in favor; but after 1825, the great progress of lithography in other countries was also acknowledged in Sweden, and K. *v. Scheele* having, in Munich, under the personal guidance of *Senefelder*, acquired a thorough knowledge of technics, and some very prominent artists in copper engraving having devoted themselves to lithography, there arose, in proportion to our circumstances, a really splendid practice in lithographing. Though it be granted that, in Sweden, many of the circumstances which, in other countries, call forth and maintain lithography, it may be asserted that the different branches of this mode of reproduction have, in general, kept even pace with the progress made in other countries.

This may, however, not be so much the case with regard to the proper *artistic lithography*, on the very natural ground that in a thinly peopled country like Sweden, there be but a very limited sale of more expensive works.

Of *the manner of engraving* on stone we may be justified in saying that it has attained a comparatively great degree of perfection. Various illustrations in scientific works, principally in those published by the Academy of Sciences, and also several cartographic works, are productions of this kind that deserve especial notice. Two of the official atlases of Sweden are published by means of lithography; one of them, our chief *chromographic* work, has hitherto been engraved and printed in the lithographic establishment of the staff—a private establishment with a kind of an official stamp about it; the other was formerly engraved chiefly by females employed at the cartographic establishment, and printed in a private printing office, but this is now also done at the lithographic establishment of the staff.

The *Lithographic Fly-press* was early introduced in Sweden, and is now very common.

Pursuant to a government resolution, and with the support of the State (in the shape of rent-free premises) "the lithographic establishment of the staff" was founded in 1873, with a view to the promotion of the application of modern expedients in reproductory art, principally in cartography. This establishment is, moreover, provided with a photographic and galvano-plastic workshop, and has of late been very much and successfully employed in photo-lithography and helio-engraving.

There are some very extensive lithographic establishments in Stockholm, the central printing office, the lithographic establishment of the staff, *A. L. Norman*, *A. Schumburg*, besides many smaller ones. This branch of industry is carried on on a very large scale, almost exclusively for industrial and mercantile purposes, in Norrköping, by the Joint Stock Lithographic Company (*Lithographiska Aktiebolaget*), which, in connection with this business, is also employed in the manufacture of paper boxes, envelopes, etc. There are also lithographic printing offices in Jönköping, Örebro, Göteborg, Malmö, Gefle, etc.

PHOTOGRAPHY.

[CLASS 430–432.] *Photography* has not as yet been much resorted to in Sweden for reproductions on a larger scale, with the exception of the above-named Lithographic Establishment of the Staff, which of late years has extensively employed photo-lithography and other modes of reproduction where the help of photography is required. Photography is largely used for the taking of portraits. In Stockholm alone, there are as many as 50 photographic workshops, and as the other towns are proportionally as well supplied, it is evident that the photographic art is much practised in Sweden. It may also be asserted that the productions of the cleverest of them are quite as good as any of the kind abroad.

INDUSTRIAL AND ARCHITECTURAL DESIGNS, MODELS AND DECORATIONS.

[CLASS 440–443.] Engraving and tracing rose-engine patterns, as well as pattern-drawing in general, and decorative painting, are practised in the country for usual purposes; but they cannot exactly be said to take a very prominent place, with the exception perhaps of the scene-painting for the royal theatres in Stockholm. Instruction in these subjects is given both at the Academy of the Liberal Arts and at the Technical Schools.

DECORATION OF POTTERY, CERAMIC AND GLASSWARE; MOSAIC AND INLAID WORK.

[CLASS 450–453.] MOSAIC and similar works are not, properly speaking, objects of industrial activity in Sweden; it is, however, not uncommon to meet with articles of fine workmanship, as for instance table-tops made of differently colored

Swedish marbles that have been joined together. Such articles, made of porphyry, are also sometimes seen.

Of greater importance are the numerous wooden articles which are manufactured in our joinery establishments. Inlaid floors, generally of oak, are made in many places not only for home use but also for exportation.

[CLASS 454.] MISCELLANEOUS OBJECTS OF ART are often met with, especially in our older churches, and it may therefore be in place to point out what has been preserved of *the ecclesiastic art* of the middle ages.

Most of the objects which were used for Catholic worship were no doubt destroyed during the Reformation and by the simultaneous reduction, and since that time war and fires have devastated many of the churches. There are, however, still many and valuable remnants, partly in the churches, and partly in public collections. The most important of these collections are those in the National Museum at Stockholm, the Museum at Lund, Enånger Church in Helsingland, etc.

Among the church ornaments *the painted glass windows* ought especially to be mentioned, which have been preserved in no small number, especially in the island of Gottland, which, owing to its commerce, was very rich during the middle ages, and where ecclesiastical art, during that period, was more highly developed in many directions than on the main land.

Sweden still possesses many *church-bells*, which are highly valuable on account of their age, and on some of them there are inscriptions in runic characters. Four bear the several following dates — 1228, 1238, 1345, and 1493. Another bell, with an inscription only in Latin characters, was founded in 1293.

Altar-ornaments from the middle ages still exist in great numbers. There are two valuable ornaments of that sort, from the earlier periods of the middle ages (antemensale, cross, etc.), of oak, coated with chased and partly gilt copper, of which one from Broddetorp church in Vestergöthland (Westergötland), is now in the National Museum, and the other is in Lyngsjö church in Skåne; and also an antependium (altar-cloth) of green velvet embroidered with gold-thread, from Biskopskulla church in Uppland, now in the National Museum.

The greater number of the Swedish churches, even the smaller parish churches in the country, seem to have been provided with *altar-shrines*, with carved, painted and gilt images, during the latter centuries of the middle ages. Of those which are still preserved in the National Museum, four were made during the years 1468, 1475, 1514, and 1526. The most valuable altar-shrine in Sweden is probably one, with magnificent paintings, belonging to the cathedral at Strengnäs, which was made at Brussels about the end of the 15th century.

The principal of the numerous isolated *saintly figures* that have been preserved till our times is the representation of the struggle between St. Göran, or George (rather larger than life), and the dragon, which valuable work of art was presented by the Regent STEN STURE, *Sr.*, to St. Nicholas' church in Stockholm, in the year 1489, and it is now in the National Museum.

A great number of *crosses, chalices, patens, censers, lavatories, holy-water pots*, and other *vessels belonging to the church* are still extant. Several wooden crosses, with enamelled copper plates, from the 12th century, are in particular deserving of notice. There are also to be found cèboria and monstrances, most of them of gilt copper, as well as sacrament-houses of wood with rich gothic ornaments.

Among *reliquaries* we may especially mention some reliquaries of wood coated with embossed and gilt copper, the shrine in Wadstena church, in which the bones of the holy BRIGITTA are now preserved, a costly reliquary of a large cylindric rock-crystal, from the Westerås cathedral, now in the National Museum, two silver reliquaries in the form of arms for the bones of the holy Eskil and the holy Brigitta, etc.

In the National Museum there is preserved an iron wreath with a runic inscription, belonging to a *chandelier* from Väte church in Gottland. Besides, there are in the museum, partly in the churches, other chandeliers, candle-sticks, candle-staves, etc.

Baptismal-fonts, chiefly from the 12th and 13th centuries, have been preserved in great numbers. Most of them are round, but some are square. Many of them are beautifully ornamented in relievo, and runic inscriptions on them are not rare.

Tombstones, from the different periods of the middle ages, also occur in great numbers, and on the oldest of them there are often runic inscriptions. There is a tombstone in the National Museum, from the middle of the 12th century, in the form of a church with its choir, with rich and tasteful foliated ornaments, which was brought from Botkyrka in Södermanland. There are inscriptions on it both in runic and Latin characters. A monumental plate of copper, with figures engraved on it and an inscription, lies in Vester-Åker church in Uppland. A piece of superb embroidery on green satin, which formerly lay in Skokloster church in Uppland, over the grave of the "holy" Holmgeir Folkunge, who was beheaded in the year 1248, is preserved in the National Museum.

A great quantity of *priest's vestments*, from the middle ages, made of costly materials and ornamented with rich embroideries in silk and gold, are preserved in the National Museum, in Uppsala cathedral, and in many other places. In 1818 they found in the river Motala, Östergötland, a large, round, magnificent buckle of gold, set with a number of precious stones, which had no doubt been worn by some high ecclesiastic. The most costly among the mitres that have been preserved from the middle ages is one that belonged to the bishops of Linköping, and which is now preserved in the National Museum. It is richly set with precious stones and real pearls, and ornamented with enamelled plates of silver (émail cloisonné) from the 12th century.

DEPARTMENT V.--MACHINERY.

MACHINES, TOOLS, APPARATUS AND MOTORS.

[CLASS 500–589.] The manufacture of machinery in Sweden, which, in proportion to the population, is carried on, on a very large scale, takes place partly in mechanical workshops established for the purpose, partly in similar establishments, but in connection with the manufacture of iron. In the report on the iron trade (class 111), therefore, it was not possible to avoid touching upon this kind of manufacture also, though, properly, it must be considered as belonging to this class (500) as well as to the industry of the metals in general (class 280). This occasionally close connection between the iron works and the mechanical workshops makes it difficult to say how great the number of the latter properly is, since it greatly depends upon how one reckons.

According to the official trade reports, there were in Sweden, at the end 1874, 98 so-called *mechanical workshops*. But knowing, as we do, that the numerous iron works, which manufacture machines, and especially agricultural implements, on a far larger scale than many of the proper mechanical workshops, are not included in this number, the figures are in reality much higher than those given. On the other hand, it cannot be denied that, among the workshops, there are many, in Stockholm, whose operations are quite inferior as compared with the larger mechanical workshops. Thus, in 1874, we reckoned in all 49 so-called workshops in Stockholm; but, inasmuch as 3 of these (Bergsund, Bolinder's, and the Great Dock Yard) stated their united productions to amount in value to nearly 4½ million Kr., the value of the manufacture of the remaining 46 did not amount to more than 1⅓ millions in all.

The declared value of the manufacture of all the workshops in the kingdom is much less than that which the manufacture of machinery and implements in the country has reached. This applies also to the stated number of mechanical workmen employed. However, waiving these circumstances, and only considering the returns, we shall perceive how rapid and vast has been the development during the last few years, as appears from the following review of the workshops, viz.:

Year.	Number of Works.	Number of Workmen.	Declared Value. Kr.
1860	71	2,900	4,702,000
1865	97	4,900	7,926,000
1870	92	5,100	9,286,000
1871	95	6,100	10,827,000
1872	94	7,600	15,677,000
1873	87	8,800	19,522,000
1874	98	10,200	24,383,000

Thus, while the number of the workshops has remained much the same during the last ten years, that of the workmen has doubled, and the manufacture is now three times as large as ten years ago. From 1870 to 1873 the value of the manufacture was doubled.

Despite this vast development, the demand for machine-made manufactures has increased even more rapidly, especially for railway materials, which is largely due to the rapid development of the railway system. The united endeavors of the many workshops have, therefore, not been able to prevent an annual importation of very considerable quantities of implements and machinery, principally from England, whereas there has been a very considerable exportation of agricultural implements. The value of this import and export is stated in Kr., as follows:

Year.	Import.	Export.
1860	2,208,000	38,000
1865	2,870,000	65,000
1870	2,990,000	847,000
1871	3,754,000	398,000
1872	6,306,000	834,000
1873	11,658,000	1,010,000
1874	17,000,000	1,651,000

Add to this the import and export of steam-engines and boilers:

Year.	Import. Kr.	Export. Kr.
1870	91,000	2,000
1871	38,000	32,000
1872	586,000	119,000
1873	1,079,000	80,000

Judging from several circumstances, the home-consumption of the production of the mechanical workshops must have been continuously on the increase. The number of ships built, either entirely of iron or with double hulls of timber and the frame of iron, is continually increasing. At the numerous waterworks they are far from being so generally satisfied with wooden wheels as formerly, whereas iron turbines are now required instead. The mechanism in mill works and the like must now be of iron; the peasant's threshing machine, formerly so simple, now requires a cast-iron wheel. The agricultural implements are being made more and more exclusively of steel and iron, etc. All these facts together will explain how it is possible that, in spite of the numerous workshops, and the really vast production of some of them, the export has not been larger, and that the import, on the other hand, is so considerable.

The mechanical workshops are scattered throughout Sweden. They are to be found in all the towns, at least in the tolerably large ones along the coast, with the exception of those situated in the most northern part of the Gulf of Bothnia, and also in several parts of the interior. Among the latter there is the *Motala* mechanical workshop, which is the largest in Sweden.

This establishment, founded in 1822, takes its course from the junction of the Göta Canal with Lake Vetter, has been continuously extended, and, being situated in the interior, branch establishments have been established, especially for the building of larger vessels, one on the coast of the Baltic (in 1841) and another on that of the German Ocean (in 1859), namely, the Motala Dockyards at Norrköping, and Lindholmen, near Göteborg. The number of workmen at all the workshops, including a rolling-mill attached to the principal establishment for the purpose of manufacturing iron, is from 2,000 to 2,500; and, as early as 1871, the declared value of the machinery and vessels turned out by the workshops at Motala and from the dockyards at Norrköping, amounted to 1,350,000 Kr., and of those at Lindholmen to 950,000 Kr., so that, if the value of the production of the rolling-mill, estimated at 1,300,000 Kr., be added, the value of the total annual production will amount to the considerable sum of upwards of 3½ millions. For the year 1872 the declared value was 5½ millions, and it has since remained at about 6 million Kr. per annum.

And this production will be increased hereafter by that of the large, new iron works, Bångbro, which has quite recently become the property of the Motala company, and where manufacturing has just commenced. Bångbro is situated 16 Swedish miles north of Motala, and is connected with it by rail. But this is not all. The Motala also possesses an old and well-known mechanical workshop at Nyköping (near the Baltic), where, however, no work has been carried on for several years; but it is understood that operations are to commence again, which will be greatly facilitated when a railway to Nyköping, which is now ready, is opened for traffic.

The impellent power for the mechanical workshops is either water or steam (in the towns generally the latter). The Motala mechanical workshop and rolling-mill are driven by 7 water-wheels and 11 turbines, of in all 1,035 H. P., of which 1 turbine is of 250 H. P.; also a steam-engine.

Among other large mechanical workshops deserving to be mentioned are *Bergsund*, the *Great Dockyard*, *Bolinder's workshops*, and the *Atlas*, all four in Stockholm; that at *Oskarshamn*, at *Trollhättan*, *Keiller's*, at Göteborg; *Kockum's*, at Malmö; that at Eskilstuna (*Munktell's*), *Arboga*, *Köping*, *Gefle*, *Landskrona*, and *Hellefors* (in Södermanland), etc. The declared value of the annual production at the most of these is from 1 to 1½ million Kr. Among the numerous iron works employed in the manufacture of machinery and implements, we may here mention *Öfverum*, *Finspong*, *Näfveqvarn*, *Ankarsrum*, *Åker*, *Lesjöfors*, *Forsvik*, etc. Of these works, Finspong is especially worth notice, not so much for its manufacture of machinery but for its extensive manufacture of cannon and military ammunition, and as a very large estate, etc.

This industry has advanced so far, that at the different workshops they are beginning to devote their attention exclusively to special branches. Thus for instance, *marine engines and ships* are produced chiefly at Motala and its branch establishments (the monitors for the Navy and from 30 to 40 large and small vessels annually), and also in Stockholm, at Bergsund, and the Great Dockyard, at Oskarshamn, and at Göteborg, etc.

Land-machinery, likewise at these places, and also at Trollhättan (locomotives and portable engines), at Bolinder's, in Stockholm (saw mills), at Eskilstuna (portable engines), at Malmö (locomobiles and railway carriages), etc.

Railway material—Locomotives at Trollhättan and Motala, carriages at the Atlas and its branch establishment at Södertelje, as well as at the workshops at Göteborg, at Kockum's (Malmö), at Landskrona, etc. (For the manufacture of rails, carriage-wheels and axles compare above, class 111).

Agricultural implements at Öfverum, Göteborg, Näfveqvarn, Åker, Ankarsrum, Malmö, Forsvik, etc.

Most of the Swedish *steamers* are constructed at the Swedish workshops, and the number of these steamers having been continuously increasing. That mostly Swedish iron and steel are used for all these and similar works has been stated above, and also that steel is taking the place of iron. With regard to ingenuity and efficiency as well as elegance in construction, we may be allowed to assert that Sweden can, without fear, compete with any other nation, being able to produce such well-known names, as for instance, *Samuel Owen*, *John Ericsson*, *Carlsund*, etc.

What distinguishes the Swedish steamers is their construction, which, owing to the excellence of the materials, can combine lightness with strength. Therefore, when a ship happens, for instance, to run aground, some of the plates may be bent, but they do not break, and the rest of the ship remains uninjured, so that when the damaged plates are replaced by new ones, she is as good as new again.

WATER TRANSPORTATION AND APPLIANCES.

[CLASSES 590–593.] THE MERCHANT FLEET. Among the men who have distinguished themselves in *ship-building* in Sweden, Admiral *Fredrik Henrik of Chapman* (born September 16th, 1721, died August 19th, 1808), takes the first place. He raised ship-building to a theoretical science. Most of the ships of the present time are founded on data stated in his writings, though of course with such modifications as have been called for by the introduction of steam-engines and iron and steel coatings.

In the numerous dock-yards (see above, class 330) which are to be found along the Swedish coast, a great number of merchant ships are annually built, for which the forests of the country furnish the wood. The northern dock-yards on the shore of the Gulf of Bothnia use fir-wood for ship-building. When these forests do not reach as far as the shore, the timber is carried there along the numerous rivers which intersect these northern provinces of Sweden.

With regard to the oak-forests the circumstances are not so favorable. In the provinces, in which they occur, namely, in those situated to the south of the river Dal, the supply of oak is, however, sufficient to satisfy the wants for the building of merchant-ships. Large blocks of oak required for ships of war have, on the other hand, had to be imported from Northern Germany for many years.

At the numerous mechanical workshops (A 500) in the country where they are employed in ship-building, among which the Motala with its branch establishments at Göteborg and Norrköping takes the lead, Swedish iron is exclusively used as a building material. At these mechanical work-shops several ships of war have been built; among the most important of these are the monitors, for the Swedish and the Norwegian navies.

The Swedish merchant navy, from as far back as we have any reliable returns, has been continuously increasing, not only with regard to the number of ships, but also to the tonnage. The various sea-ports in the country have, however, not profited to an equal extent by this development; on the contrary, some have shown a marked retrogradation. In this respect the capital is especially conspicuous. At the beginning of this century it possessed 234 sailing-vessels of a burthen of 37,830 tons, but in 1870 it had only 150 vessels of 15,795 tons burthen, of which nearly 100 were steamers, and most of them had engines of only from 5 to 15 H. P. It is different with the second town in the Kingdom, or Göteborg, which in 1800 possessed 168 sailing ships of 20,660 tons burden, which number decreased in 1835 to 70 vessels of 11,582 tons burden, but it has since gradually increased to 174 vessels of 50,050 tons burden, so that at present Göteborg is the richest in ships of all the Swedish seaports. Second in rank is Gefle, which at the beginning of the century possessed 54 vessels of 7,832 tons burden, but in 1870 it had acquired 72 vessels of 27,600 tons burden. The other principal seaports are the Norrland towns Sundsvall and Hernösand, and in 1870 Stockholm was reckoned next in importance. Since that time, however, the state of things has changed a little, so that the order of precedency, estimated by the tonnage, was, in 1873, Göteborg, Gefle, Stockholm, Helsingborg, Sundsvall, Hernösand, etc.

At the end of 1873 the Swedish merchant fleet was composed of the following ships:

	Sailing Vessels.		Steamers.			Total.	
	Number.	Tons.	Number.	Tons.	Horse power	Number.	Tons.
Ves. bel. to towns	1,223	227,370	407	47,780	17,381	1,630	275,150
Ves. bel. to coun. districts.	2,112	155,350	158	3,810	2,386	2,270	159,160
Total..	3,335	382,720	565	51,590	19,767	3,900	434,310

The smallest of the vessels here included measure 10 tons. Concerning the mode of measuring Swedish vessels, see above, page 57.

The *crews* of all these 3,900 vessels, including the commanders, amount to 24,750.

In the same year (1816) that they made the first experiments with *steamers* in Paris, or three years later than when the first steamer plied the Thames, similar experiments were also made in Sweden on Lake Mälar with a small boat only 32 feet (9.5m.) in length. The proper history of steam voyages in Sweden, however, commences with the voyage of the Amphitrite from Stockholm to Vesterås, in the summer of 1818. The commercial interest of Sweden admonished the nation not to allow the new means of communication to go unemployed. The progress in this department has indeed been both great and rapid, especially since the Göta canal (September, 1832) was completed and opened to traffic. That part of the steamboat navy which belongs to private parties was as follows, during

1830	10			
1840	50	of	1,954	H. P.
1850	67	"	2,939	"
1860	203	"	9,332	"
1870	388	"	11,626	"
1873	565	"	19,767	"

As appears from this review the increase in mechanical power has not corresponded to the increase in number of steamboats during the last decennary. This is accounted for by the great number of small steamers of less than 10 H. P. by which the total number has been increased. In 1860 one could only count 26 of that sort, but 10 years later there were 112 of in all 577 H. P., and consequently averaging but very little above 5 H. P. In 1873 the corresponding number was stated to be 136 of 917 H. P., which increases the average power to 6.8 H. P. This great number of small boats, to which we may further add 27 of about 10 H. P., is something quite peculiar to Sweden, or, perhaps more correctly, to Stockholm, in the watery dominion of which town most of them ply about in all directions, thus affording cheap and convenient means of communication. The numerous steamers which keep up the passenger traffic along the coasts of the country, as well as communication with foreign countries, are generally of about 100 H. P., and are all distinguished by their symmetry and elegant fittings. They are constructed of Swedish iron in Swedish mechanical work-shops, and have occasionally had opportunities of giving astonishing proofs of their excellent material and good construction.

Concerning the trade that is carried on by the Swedish private sailing and steam vessels, see above, page 80.

Navigation Schools. [For the training of commanders for the Merchant Fleet.] Navigation-schools have been established [for training] in nine towns: Stockholm, Göteborg, Malmö, Karlshamn, Kalmar, Vestervik, Visby, Gefle, and Hernösand, which are under the Navy Department. The school is divided into three classes. In the first (the lowest) class, which has for its object the training of second mates, instruction is given in arithmetic, geometry, and navigation; in the second class, which is designed for first mates, or second-class sea-captains, the subjects of instruction are the same, though on a more extensive scale, and besides, trigonometry, astronomy, and marine law; in the third class, which is for first-class sea-captains, besides the subjects mentioned above, instruction is also given in navigation, astronomy, physical mechanics, and in the rudiments of ship building. The term of instruction lasts from October until April, when there is an examination. In the spring of 1875 the following number were examined: 274 second mates, 64 first mates, or second captains, 107 sea-captains, of whom 22 of the first and 3 of the captains' classes had not gone through any navigation-school.

For the training of qualified *Engineers* for passenger-boats, and *Engine-drivers* on the State and private railways, instruction is given in six of the navigation-schools in the construction and handling of steam-engines. In the above-mentioned year 87 passed the so-called machinist-examination, and 184 passed the examination required for being entitled to command a steamer.

In the navigation-school at Göteborg there is also a division for *ship-building*, which has for its object the training of ship-wrights and foremen for the dockyards. The course lasts two years.

The Government grant for the navigation-schools is 75,800 Kr.

In Stockholm there is an establishment for the training of able *seamen*. It was founded by *Abraham Rydberg*, whose name it bears, and at the beginning of 1875 it had a capital of 252,566 Kr. In 1873 the number of scholars at the practical school for sailors was 70, of whom 7 had remained from the preceding year.

Pilot and Light-house Establishments. The chief management of these, as well as of the Life-boat Establishment, which is connected with the same, belongs to the Directors of the Royal Pilot Administration, under the Royal Navy Department. The *Board* is composed of 1 Pilot-Director and Chief, 8 civil officials, 5 fire-engineers, 3 district-chiefs, and 15 division-chiefs (3 pilot-captains and 12 pilot-lieutenants). The *body of pilots* proper on January 1st, 1875, was composed of 58 master-pilots, 576 government-pilots, 111 extra pilots, and 111 pilot-apprentices, or in all 856 pilots. The crew on board the two steamers belonging to the pilot establishment consists of 20 persons. The *body of fire-guards* comprises 176 persons for the coast-lights, and 61 for the light-ships, or in all, 237 persons.

The whole pilot and light-house establishment, for which consequently 1125 persons are needed, is maintained by the light and beacon dues, which are now paid only by ships, in proportion to their burthen, that arrive from, or clear for foreign ports, and that not more than once a month, or for more than five months in the year, though they may make several voyages abroad. The surplus remaining after the above-mentioned expenses have been paid is used for defraying the costs of new lights and for the improvement of old ones. According to the budget estimates last established the expenditure for the pilot and light-house establishments amounts to 800,460 Kr., of which 332,345 Kr. is required for the lights, and 12,000 Kr. for the life-boat establishment. In this expenditure the pilot-dues received by the pilots and divided among themselves are not taken into account. In 1874 they amounted to 672,965 Kr. for 55,697 pilotings effected.

The accounts about *light-houses* are but scanty until 1652, when the supervision over the lights was entrusted to a government-board, although no accessible records give us any detailed information as to the light-houses then extant. The Landsort light-house, outside Stockholm, is the oldest coast-light in Sweden about which we have any reliable information. Fires were lighted there at least in 1669; but the light-houses at Kullen, Nidingen, and at Falsterbo were, however, constructed at a much earlier period, but yet during the time when Skåne and Halland were Danish possessions. "The fire-pan" on Kullen was erected in 1560.

In the oldest light-houses either pit-coals or oil-lamps, the latter being placed in front of mirrors, were used for producing the illumination. To burn a candle or oil-lamp in a lantern without any means to increase the effect seems also to have been a mode of illuminating. The coals were burned either in a basket or an iron pot, which was placed either on the roof of the light-house or in some other elevated position, sometimes in a basket (fire-pan) appended to one end of a balancing-pole. Such a "fire-see-saw" or "fire-beacon" was used at Falsterbo until 1796.

At the Örskär light-house, to the north of Stockholm, mirrors were used from the time of its construction in 1687. After the erection of the present massive light-house (supplied with winding stairs) instead of the former wooden one there were introduced in 1740 five concave, polished steel mirrors, each 2 feet 2 inches in diameter, supplied with six lamps, and this light was during its time considered the best in the Baltic, "nor was its equal to be found in many places." In 1768 it was enacted that four revolving mirrors should be used. Each mirror, independent of the rest, was set in motion about a vertical axle, by means of poles from the axle of the mechanism, and was consequently a revolving light, though probably not because it should be distinguished from any other for which it might have been mistaken—which at present is the object of our revolving lights—but that it might, by the application of a smaller number of movable mirrors, give a light, though it were with interruptions, in every direction over the sea. At the Korsö light-house, not far from Stockholm, there were at first two lanterns, put out on stages made for the purpose, one on each side of the tower. Later two mirrors were employed, which revolved about a horizontal axle by means of clock-work in order to illumine that part of the horizon that was needed.

Later, improvements were made in the pit-coal fires by enclosing the fire in a lantern with glass windows, by placing under the hearth a tube, intended for the reception of the ashes, that extended through the whole tower, or part of it, and by the coals being hoisted up with a winch.

At present there are no coal fires used in the Swedish light-houses. They are all supplied either with improved *mirror apparatus* or with *Fresnel lens apparatus*. The first light-house erected with lens apparatus was the southern one at Vinga, near Göteborg, which was lighted in 1841. In 1843 the light at Falsterbo was changed into a lens light. Not only in these, but also in the lens lights that have since been erected, where, for the purpose of utilizing that portion of light passing upwards and downwards, silvered mirrors were used, these have been exchanged for catadioptric lenses, so that all the lens lights now consist of a dioptric middle part, a catadioptric crown above, and a ring below the middle part, *i. e.*, the light from the lamp in the focus of the apparatus is made to pass out horizontally by refraction in the lens of the middle part, and both by refraction and reflection in the crown above and the ring below.

The mirrors now employed in light-houses always have silvered reflecting surfaces. In form they are either parabolically concave mirrors, or else so-called sideral lights, composed of two mirror surfaces, the one above and the other below the flame.

The considerably increased number of light-houses in recent times, by which the distances between them have been diminished, have made it necessary, in addition to the old modes of preventing mistakes—namely, by means of employing one stationary or two stationary, or by means of strong intermitting lights—to use colored lights, generally red, or by varying the intensity, *i. e.*, stationary lights varied by strong flashes, partly with varying red and white lights, and other variations.

In two new lens lights, with white and red flashes, the change of color is from white to red without any interruption of the light, which makes the characteristic of the light more apparent than when the different blazes are divided by dark intervals.

In recent times *light-houses* of iron, partly open towers, partly of iron plates, have been more generally used in Sweden than elsewhere. Those that were formerly built were either of stone or wood.

Besides the so-called coast lights, which, together with the light-ships, are kept up by the State, there are also several smaller ones, so-called ledfyrar (lead-fires) and harbor lights, which are generally kept up by communities or private individuals.

Provided it be not otherwise prescribed the fires are *lighted* at sunset and kept burning until sunrise during the whole year, when the navigation in the vicinity of the light is not stopped by ice. *The light-ships* are annually sent to sea when there is no longer any danger of ice, and are again removed when the ice becomes dangerous. In places where bells or gong-gongs are used for giving *signals of warning* in foggy weather, it is done at short intervals, and always with several strokes or flourishes immediately after one another. At some light-houses signals from vessels are replied to by gunshots. At the Vinga light-house (in the Kattegat) they have put up a fog-horn of American construction, which every minute, in foggy weather, sounds a strong and shrill trumpet-peal continuing for about 5 seconds, and, under favorable circumstances, it may be heard at a distance of from 1 to 1½ geographical miles.

In various places along the coast, and in Gottland, the population carrying on fishing are entitled, whenever required, to light so-called fisher-fires in order to guide fishing-boats out at sea. There must always be two close to each other, and not strong enough to be mistaken for the strong light of the present light-houses. In the lakes, and in several canals in the interior of the country, coast lights are kept up either by private communities or companies (in Lake Vener there are no less than 38 such). All those which are not under the control of the State are not included in the following review of the Swedish light-houses in 1874:

	Coast Lights. Number.	Light-ships. Number.
Gulf of Bothnia	20	4
The Baltic	38	4
The Sound	5	2
The Kattegat	17	..
Lake Vener	1	..
Lake Vetter	1	..
Total	82	10

Of these lights 16 belong to private parties, the rest (76) belong to the State. At the beginning of this century the number of lights was only 12, for 9 of which coal fires were used, and for the remaining 3 oil lamps with mirrors.

The Paternoster Light-house, on the west coast outside Marstrand, and the Häradskär, on the east coast between the towns of Norrköping and Vestervik, are lens lights of the first rank arranged on open iron turrets. The Paternoster Light-house was completed in 1868. The total cost, including lantern, amounted to 123,249 Kr.; that of the lantern, together with the illuminating apparatus, 49,886 Kr. The iron turret, which stands on a cliff, is 108 feet high. A light-ship costs nearly 100,000 Kr.

The Life-preserving Service, which is under the Royal Pilot Administration, is managed by an Inspector, who is bound to visit and to inspect all the stations twice a year, as well as to make experimental trials and to see that the staff and materials are kept in proper order.

The first safety stations were established in 1855, namely, at "Mälarhusen" and "Brantevik," on the south coast of Sweden. The number was afterwards gradually increased until 1866, when 12 stations had been established. The number has not since been increased. There are:

3 complete stations (supplied not only with life-boats, but also with rocket apparatus),

6 boat stations, and

3 rocket stations (1 rocket station was established in 1875).

The safety crew consists of, at each complete station and boat station, 1 superintendent, 1 steersman, and 10 boatmen; at each rocket station, 1 superintendent and 4 assistants.

The annual salary is, for each superintendent from 70 to 84 or 96 Kr., for the steersmen 30 Kr., the boatmen 24 Kr., and the assistants 18 Kr. For each life-preserving expedition each superintendent and steersman receives 6 Kr., each boatman 5.50, and each assistant 3.50. For experimental trials each superintendent receives 2.25 and each of the rest 1.50 Kr.

The annual expenditure for the support of the life-preserving service generally amounts to about 12,000 Kr. annually. The original cost of the various stations amounted in all to 49,950 Kr. The annual expenses, including fees and 2 experimental trials, generally amount to,

For each complete station, 660 Kr.
" boat station, 600 "
" rocket station, 270 "

All the life-boats are of wood and clincher-built, partly after English models and partly after Danish. They are 28.2′ (8.37m.) long, 7.5′ (2.23m.) broad, and with a complete crew and the bottom valves shut, their draught is 10′′ (0.25m.) With the valves open they draw as much again. The life-boat last procured, which was built in the Royal Dock-yard at Karlskrona, after English model, surpasses the rest for its good qualities.

When the crews have had opportunities of thoroughly testing these boats, they seem to place full confidence in them, and do not hesitate to go to sea in them in any weather. Nor has as yet an accident happened at any of the numerous expeditions that have been undertaken to save human life, though some have taken place under most unfavorable circumstances.

A life-boat will hold 24 people, and on life-saving expeditions during heavy storms, the sea running high and the valves being open, it has carried as many as 23 persons, and brought them safely ashore.

In order to convey a life-boat from one part of the coast to another there is a special transportation car that is drawn by 6 or 8 horses or oxen.

At the rocket stations "Dennet's" apparatus is used. The distance of throwing attained by this is generally from 900 to 1,000′ (270–300m.)

From October 5th, 1856, when the life-saving apparatus was first introduced in earnest, until November 15th, 1872, 611 persons were saved, partly by means of the life-boats, partly by means of the rocket apparatus, and partly in coast-boats with crews from the life-boats.

Despite all precautions to prevent accidents at sea, such a thing is of course impossible, especially along so extensive and rocky a coast as that of Sweden. The following *shipwrecks* and accidents have occurred off the Swedish coasts:

	Sailing vessels.	Steamers.	Total.	Of them totally lost.
In 1866	104		104	48
1867	155		155	70
1868	118	8	126	48
1869	121	6	127	58
1870	90	15	105	22
1871	174	24	198	74
1872	193	17	210	114
1873	136	30	166	39
1874	142	34	176	49

The many accidents in 1872 were especially caused by the storms on the 11th, 12th, and 13th November.

DEPARTMENT VI.—AGRICULTURE.

ARBORICULTURE AND FOREST PRODUCTS.

[CLASSES 600–606.] Sweden is very rich in forests, and supplies not only nearly all the timber for home consumption, but also very considerable quantities for foreign markets. Foresting is becoming of very great importance to Sweden, especially as the lumber trade is assuming such gigantic proportions.

Although a very considerable part of the country—namely, Lappland, where most of the forests have not been divided between the crown and the inhabitants—has not as yet been fully surveyed, the Swedish *forests* are estimated to extend over an area of 1,537.8 Swedish square miles (=67,836 English square miles, or 175,690 sq. Kilom.), which amounts to 42.8 per cent. of the mainland of the kingdom. In this forest territory mountain ranges (fjäll), mountains, and bogs are not included. About ⅔ds of all the forests of the kingdom are situated north of the river Dal, and very few in the most southern parts of the country.

If we include those forests that will in all probability be allotted to the crown parks as already belonging to it, especially those in Lappland, amounting to about 4,000,000 tunnland (nearly 2,000,000 hectares or 5,000,000 acres), the area of the public forests may be estimated as follows:

	Swedish Tunnland.
Crown parks	5,555,000
Woods belonging to the royal estates..	30,000
" " " landed property set apart for the maintenance of officials	1,012,000
Woods belonging to charitable institutions	66,000
Court District (Härads) Commons....	220,000
Parish Commons	8,000
Mining "	50,000
Oak-tree Plantations	1,000
Quicksand Fields	5,000
Total	6,947,000

This territory (=3,429,000 hectares or 8,474,000 acres) includes nearly 20 per cent. of all the forests of the country, and the remaining 80 per cent., or 28,640,000 tunnland (=14,138,000 hectares, or 34,937,000 acres) consequently fall to the share of *private* owners.

During the latter years about 200,000 Kr. have annually been assigned for the purchase of ground for the laying out of new crown parks.

About 3,000 tunnland of the government forests, where the timber has been cut off, are annually replanted.

The forests consist principally of red and white pine, intermixed with birch, alder, and asp trees, to which are added, in the districts to the south of the river Dalelf, oak, and in the most southern provinces beech forests.

Besides the above-stated proper forests, there are also, belonging not only to private estates, but also to landed property appropriated for officials, to royal estates, and farms belonging to institutions, considerable pasture grounds, mostly overgrown with birch, asp, alder, and oak; occasionally with ash, elm, maple, linden, and fir trees. These grounds may most nearly be compared to the middle forests of Germany. In a few places, in the middle and southern parts of the country, are some inconsiderable mulberry plantations.

The *management* of the woods belonging to private individuals is as yet altogether free, with the exception of the island of Gottland, where (pursuant to the Royal Enactment of September 10th, 1869) the useless destruction of forests is prohibited, and Norrbotten, the most northern län of the kingdom, where (pursuant to a Royal Enactment of September 29th, 1874) small timber (7 inches in diameter at a distance of 16 feet from the base) must not be exported or cut in a saw-mill, excepting for domestic use. Public opinion, however, seems more and more to call for legal restrictions even with regard to the management of these forests.

The public forests are under the superintendence of a Forest Board (Skogsstyrelse),* which belongs to the Financial Department, and the management is entrusted to forest officials, of whom there are 7 Forest Inspectors, 80 Rangers (Overseers of Hunting Districts), and 300 Crown Huntsmen and Foresters, besides extra officials. The revenue from the public forests amounted in 1874 to 1,174,000 Kr., while the corresponding expenses amounted to 377,000 Kr.

The *Consumption of the Forests.* That Sweden depends almost exclusively upon its forests for fuel, etc., for the greater part of its extensive mining operations, has already been stated (p. 37). The burning of charcoal on a large scale is carried on in most of the provinces in the kingdom, but most extensively in the proper mining districts, *i. e.*, the central part of the country. It is further obvious that Sweden, in consequence of its northern situation, requires a very considerable quantity of fuel for domestic purposes, and the abundance of forest has by no

* This Board now publishes annual reports, principally on the Public Forests, under the title, "Bidrag till Sveriges Officiela Statistik" (Contributions to the Official Statistics of Sweden). Q. Skogsväsendet (Woods and Forests), 1870–1872.

means contributed to economy. It cannot, however, be denied that the peasantry have begun to entertain more reasonable views in this respect. There is also great extravagance in the size and number of the buildings in the country, with the exception of the towns, the province of Skåne (where only the frame-work is of wood), and large estates. To this, besides the fuel required for industrial establishments, may be added timber for carpenter's work, ship-building, and the like, the custom of enclosing with a peculiar kind of wooden fence the so-called "Gärdesgårdar" (constructed by means of a double row of fir props, in pairs, each pair being held together by rings of twisted fir or willow twigs, between which are placed sufficiently long, slender pieces of split timber in a slanting position); not only the private properties themselves, but the various subdivisions of the land belonging to them, etc. To this consumption is to be added all that is required for the vast exportation, and the total amount of timber felled in the Swedish forests yearly may be estimated as follows:

	Cubic feet.
Timber for fuel.................	890,000,000
" " carpenter's work......	110,000,000
" " exportation...........	150,000,000
Total..........	1,150,000,000

Or upwards of 30,000,000 cubic mètres.

The exportation of timber increased from 1865 to 1872, since which time it has slowly decreased. The export of boards and planks alone from 1865 to 1874 is here cited:

	Cubic feet.
In 1865.........................	58,173,000
1870.........................	77,378,000
1871.........................	80,798,000
1872.........................	90,762,000
1873.........................	88,376,000
1874.........................	81,640,000

The whole export of forest productions in 1873 was as follows:

		Cubic feet.
Timber and spars of large dimensions, pieces..................	552,800	11,111,000
Timber and spars of smaller dimensions, pieces..................	1,608,500	9,126,300
Timber for building purposes, masts and spars of smaller dimensions, pieces..........................	578,400	6,227,600
Sleepers, pieces....................	688,400	384,400
Pit props, pieces....................	15,261,400	13,143,600
Boards and planks, dozen..........	4,396,707	88,376,400
Deal ends..........................	....	3,248,400
Lath-wood..........................	....	503,700
Borders and ribs, pieces...........	623,200	....
Wood for fuel,......................	....	1,578,500
Wood for hoops, pieces...........	44,500	....
Wood for oars, "	28,800	....
Staves of beech, "	21,695,500	....
Staves of oak, "	2,313,200	....
Wood, dressed, Kr..................	172,200	....
Wood, undressed, Kr...............	1,755,300	....
Tar, Ctr..........................	206,500	....
Pitch, Ctr.........................	3,200	....
Rosin, pounds.....................	29,000	....
Lamp-black, pounds...............	439,400	....
Bark..............................	....	152,000

The total of this export, so far as it is stated in cubic measure, amounts to 134,000,000 cubic feet, and if to that be added the other articles of export, besides taking into consideration the loppings, one might be justified in estimating the quantity cut down for exportation at upwards of 150,000,000 cubic feet (4,000,000 cubic mètres).

The value of the timber exported in 1873 has been estimated in the official returns at 100,000,000 Kr.

The Swedish timber, like the Swedish bar-iron, which finds its way to ports in all parts of the world, is in demand everywhere, especially *boards* and *planks*, of which, as an instance, in 1873 upwards of 1,000,000 cubic feet were shipped direct from Sweden as far as Australia; 500,000 to the Brazils, etc. More than the half of the timber exported goes to England, where, in 1873, of boards and planks were sold 47.5 million cubic feet; and next to England, France 18.4 million cubic feet, and Belgium 4.5 millions. Considerable quantities are also exported to Prussia, Denmark, Lubeck, Spain, etc.

Of *square-cut timber* (beams and spars), reckoned by the number of pieces, England took the most, 631,000 pieces; Denmark, 523,000; further Prussia, 466,000; France, Lubeck, Belgium, the Netherlands, etc., smaller quantities.

Timber for building purposes, masts, spars, of smaller dimensions, were almost exclusively shipped to the Netherlands (339,000 pieces), and to England (223,000).

Special attention should be given to the unfortunately extensive export of *pit props*, which are almost exclusively shipped to England (15,163,000 pieces). Almost the whole of the small remainder (76,000 pieces) goes to France. Hitherto these pit props have been shipped only from the west coast of Sweden, especially from Göteborg; but they are now shipped on a small scale also from the Baltic, principally from the coast of Småland; the pit props shipped from that quarter have, however, been twice as large as those from Göteborg.

The largest timber is exported from ports on the Gulf of Bothnia, especially from its southern part, between the rivers Dalelf and Ångermanelf, where the towns of Gefle, Söderhamn, Hudiksvall, Sundsvall, and Hernösand are situated. A great number of *saw-mills* have been built in this district at the numerous waterfalls, and as steam-mills. In 1870, in one län, Westernorrland, there were no less than 31 steam saw-mills, and this number has since greatly increased. Besides steam saw-mills, there are numerous others, especially such as are driven by water, where timber is sawn for sale and for domestic use. Moreover, the numerous rivers, small and large, afford an easy mode of transporting timber and logs from the interior to the coasts by means of rafts, a method which is very much used; and whenever there are any hindrances in the streams capital is not spared to remove them.

Concerning the *manufacture of timber*, see CLASS 217.

PEAT.*

[CLASS 607.] The great extent of the peat-bogs in Sweden, comprising about a twelfth part of the area of central Sweden and averaging about 6 feet in depth, seems to imply that the peat manufacture ought to be old in this country; but, nevertheless, it is not so, owing principally to the facility of obtaining large supplies of cheap fuel from the forests. In such parts of Skåne and Bohuslän as are destitute of wood, peat has, it is true, been the chief fuel for many years, but it is only during the last twenty years that the peat-bogs have been more extensively developed; however, there remains much to be done before it can be said that the application of peat has become general. Of late years there are many who have given the public information concerning the peat-bogs, and the preparation of the peat, which is necessary for its most advantageous use. Foremost among the writers on this subject is L. B. FALKMAN, Director General for the Land Survey, who, in his meritorious work, "Om de Svenska Bräntorf-mossarne," Stockholm, 1870, has given a very instructing account of the standpoint of the peat industry in general at that time, and the most advantageous modes of preparation.

The increased value of all forest productions during the last five years, and the continuously-increasing demand for fuel, have still more directed people's attention to the working of the peat-bogs, and have given an impetus to the endeavors to utilize them in the best manner possible, to which the Jernkontoret, as well as several agricultural societies, has contributed a great deal.

The preparation of peat for fuel, not being subject to any taxation whatever, and there being no detailed returns of the production, it is difficult to state even approximately the quantity prepared. By the aid of private information we may, however, be able to throw some light on the progress of one of the principal branches, that of machine-made peat. During 1865, about 50 machines, of Swedish make, for the preparation of peat, were in use. By the beginning of 1876, about 350 machines more, of various dimensions, had been manufactured in the country, besides some scores imported; and hence, during ten years, this part of the production had in all probability increased eightfold. If we take 5,000 Tunnor per machine as the average, the machine-made peat alone would amount, to correspond in

* Contributed by A. WERNER CRONQUIST, Engineer.

value as a fuel, to 50,000 cubic fathoms of fir-wood. Whether cut or trod peat increased in the same proportion we cannot determine.

The methods of working adopted in Sweden at present are:

The preparation of peat by cutting, which is done with a common spade, and the peat has the form of a brick. Cutting with a spade with an upright wing (the Bavarian method), as well as dividing the cutting between two laborers (the Dutch method).

The preparation of peat by treading, as is generally done in Hanover and Westphalia, is very common. The kneading (treading) is, however, no longer done by men or horses, but by various sorts of kneading machines (pug-mills), of which we will merely mention a large one for steam-power, consisting of a horizontal cylinder 1½ feet in diameter and 12 feet in length, where the peat is worked by knives fixed on axes, which rotate with a velocity of about 100 revolutions in a minute, and a smaller kneading machine for hand-power, consisting simply of a quickly-rotating grooved roller, which presses the peat against a firm plate or background.

Inasmuch as the peat-bogs which contain good peat generally abound in roots, stumps of trees, or stones, the peat cannot be cut to advantage, but it must be shaped by means of a machine, which works the peat at the same time. Among the great number of machines which are used in this country for peat, of any particular form, we may mention

The machine for cylindrical peat (tube-peat machines), constructed by S. H. SAMUELSSON, which consists of a kind of peat-press, chiefly made of wood, with an elevator, which connects the top part or mouth of the press with that part of the bog from which the peat substance is to be raised. The machine is either single or double. In order to keep the former in motion, are needed a horseman and five other attendants; for a double machine steam-power is required and double the number of workmen. The peat is dug up and thrown into the elevator, which raises and discharges it into the mouth of the press, which thus is continuously supplied with the crude peat. The latter, without being moistened, is a little bruised by the press, upon which it is sufficiently compressed, and at last it comes out in the form of a cylinder, on a table standing at the foot of the press. Each such cylinder is from 5 to 7 inches in diameter, with one, two, or three tubes about 1 inch in diameter, which run through the whole length of the cylinder, which simply needs air-drying before use. It is said that, with the assistance of practical workmen, one can produce by the single machine from 2,000 to 2,500 pieces of cylindric peat per day, equivalent to from 45 to 55 Swedish tunnor; and by the double machine from 5,000 to 7,000 pieces, equivalent to from 110 to 150 tunnor. The price of preparing the peat is stated at 12, 15, 20 or 25 öre per tunna (6.3 cubic feet) 100–150 Swedish pounds.

In 1872 this machine was reconstructed by Mr. ROOS, of Norrköping, who manufactures strong, substantial, and well-finished machines for making cylindric peat, which have been very extensively used, so that at present there are about 150 of them in the hands of the public.

Eichorn's ingenious idea to manufacture so-called "kultorf" (peat balls) has been, by the endeavors of Messrs. VON HORN and THUNBERG, most highly developed. Two large "kultorf" (peat ball) manufactories have been established, one at Wårgårda, the other at Wång. Since stationary manufactories of that sort are very expensive, and the carriage of the raw material increases the cost of manufacture, Messrs. THUNBERG and ANREP, while maintaining the principle on which EICHORN'S machine for preparing peat is founded, have brought into the market machines for shaping peat, which, in a constructive point of view, may probably be among the best that has been produced in any country.

There are many other machines, among which Schlickeysen's, Garret's, and Leo's are the most important.

POMOLOGY. [CLASS 610-611.] See Department VII.

AGRICULTURAL PRODUCTS.

[CLASS 620-624.] RURAL ECONOMY. It is estimated that in Sweden 3 million people, or ¾ of the whole population, derive their subsistence from farming and its branch occupations. This occupation has in all times been highly esteemed, and the Swedish peasant has always been a free and an independent man. Such a thing as a farm laborer tied to his native soil never existed in Sweden.

Swedish legislation acknowledges no other limits for *the division of the land taxed* than that the tenant shall be "besuten," *i. e.*, that a household of at least 3 able-bodied persons can subsist on the piece of ground allotted. Smaller tenements ("lägenheter") may also be separated from the farms, either for ever or for a certain period, by means of which "torps" (cotters' tenements) spring up. At present the land is divided as follows:

Owners of not exceeding 4 Swedish Tunnland (5 acres) cultivated land..	65,000
Owners of from 4 to 40 Swedish Tunnland (from 5 to 50 acres) cultivated land..........................	165,000
Owners of from 40 to 200 Swedish Tunnland (from 50 to 250 acres) cultivated land....................	26,000
Owners of above 200 Swedish Tunnland (250 acres) cultivated land.....	2,650
Total number of landowners..	258,650

The total of the allotments of land amount to about 300,000, to which are to be added 185,000 cotters' places and other tenement lands.

In a cameralistic point of view the Swedish land comprises 67,770 "Mantal" or "Hemman," which in olden times generally corresponded to so many farms, each conducted by one peasant's family; but in the course of time, especially through the advances made in agriculture, they have altogether lost this signification, and only constitute so many units for the taxation.

The whole of *the mainland* (exclusive of paddocks and pastures, barren rocks and the like) embraces:

	Swedish Tunnland.	Acres.
Gardens and the like...	56,000	68,000
Fields and other cultivated tracts of ground	5,359,000	6,538,000
Natural meadows......	4,004,000	4,885,000
Woodland	35,587,000	43,411,000

The cultivated land does not represent more than 6.6 per cent. of the whole area; but this low figure is accounted for by the existence of the extensive waste lands in the north of Sweden; add to this 4.8 per cent. for the natural meadows and the result will be 11.4 per cent.; but Skåne, the southernmost province of the country, represents 52.5 per cent. of the area of the province.

In such a country as Sweden *the climate* cannot but vary very much. The climate of southern Sweden surpasses in mildness that of northern Germany. Thus, for instance, in Skåne, rape, but not beets, are cultivated as oil-plants; and the sugar-beet yields excellent crops. In the northern parts of the country, which are mostly covered with woods, pastures, lakes, and bogs, and where the mountains attain a very considerable height, the climate raises great obstacles to agriculture, so that in these parts of the country, besides the felling of timber, the breeding of cattle must be the chief aim of the farmer.

The great variations of the country *in a geological point of view* have been touched upon above (page 7). In the woody and mountainous districts gravel of crushed stones (Krossgrus), with a small portion of clay and sand, is chiefly found, while in the open country the soil consists partly of argillaceous morain matter, mixed with a considerable portion of lime in the lower strata, partly of stratified clay and stratified marl, and partly, and most commonly, of field-clay (post-glacial clay). The open country of Sweden has generally a fertile soil, which, if well cultivated, is not at all inferior in production to that of any other country. The upper soil frequently rests on strata of marl, and *marl*, where it exists, is generally used in the southern and central provinces of Sweden as a fertilizer. *Limestone* occurs in many places in the country, and is likewise used for the improvement of the cultivated land.

The aspect of agriculture on the larger estates is quite in keeping with the times. The fields are drained and supplied with marl; the fallow-ground is limited, and partly sown. The cultivation of bulbous plants is gradually increasing, as well as a more rapid succession of crops from the same land. Large quantities of artificial manures, bone dust, superphosphate guano, alkaline salts, sulphate of ammonia, and Chili saltpetre are now generally used at many of the larger farms, and not seldom also at the smaller, by which the production of corn and roots, and other feeding herbs has of late considerably increased. The houses and implements—the latter mostly of iron—are excellent, and fine herds of different breeds are met with in various parts of the country. In the southern parts of the country the black cattle are generally tethered during the summer and stable-feeding is being more generally introduced. Higher up in the country it is more common to make use of the pastures.

*The oldest *husbandry* in Sweden consisted in "*Svedjelandsbruk*," *i. e.*, the forest was felled and the stumps were burnt, upon which the ground was sown with rye. This mode of tillage is now only used in a few places in Vermland and some other forest districts. Upon that followed "*hackebruk*," when the soil was worked with a mattock, and the stones picked and piled up into large or small heaps. The ground thus broken up was then annually sown as long as it would yield a moderate crop of grain, but when that was no longer the case, it was again left to its natural state. Thus the land first cleared has since been overgrown with forest, and everywhere in the woods heaps of stones from the "hackebruk" period are met with, and also traces of ditches.

In many places in the northern provinces the land is still tilled in "*ensäde*," *i. e.*, it is annually sown in the spring with corn, potatoes, or flax, and when that no longer pays it is discontinued, and the land becomes "svaljord" (lay-land). It will gradually be overgrown with grass, and it is then used partly as pasture-ground and partly as meadow-ground. Having been covered with grass for a series of years until another upper soil (humus) has been formed, the fertility returns and the land is again cut and for some time used for sowing, upon which it is again left to be overgrown with grass. This kind of husbandry, the most primitive of all, is no more practised excepting in the most northern provinces (Norrland), where, as in the other parts of the country, farming is now generally carried on on the system of twifallowing and trifallowing, and in various places by differently arranged rotations of crops and *koppelbruk*.*

Twifallowing is most common in Upland, Vestmanland, and Södermanland, or in the provinces that surround Lake Mälar. *Trifallowing* mostly occurs in Östergötland and Westergötland, in Nerike, in Öland and Gottland, as well as in the Län of Gefleborg, Westernorrland, and some parts of Kopparberg.

Fourfallowing is more uncommon, and occurs in Falbygden and some other parts of Vestergötland and Dalsland, and also in Småland, Blekinge, and Roslagen, as well as in the districts of Nedan Siljan, and Ofvan Siljan of the Län of Kopparberg, where trifallowing, nevertheless, is also practised.

Rotations of cropping are common in Scania, not only at the larger estates but also among the peasants, and in the other southern and central provinces at all almost all the larger estates and farms, and in the latter provinces likewise at many of the smaller farms. "*Koppel*"-*farming* is most common in Vermland and Dalecarlia, but, like rotations of cropping, it is practised here and there in the country at the larger estates,

* The following (as far as page **221**) is partly from contributions by Professor *J. Arrhenius.*

* Dividing the land into parcels and allowing part of it to lie fallow.

where the limited extent of the natural pasture and meadow-grounds makes the cultivation of grass a necessity.

Rotation of cropping occurs in many modifications from 4 to 12 fields. The oldest "koppel"-farming in Dalarne was of 10 years, and now "koppel"-farming occurs in many places of from 6 to 16 years rotation, the latter often with a double sowing of grass, or a sowing of grass and clover both after manured winter-crops, and summer crops, when manured and hoed roots had been the preceding crop. At present the same principles are followed in "koppel"-farming as in rotation of cropping, viz., corn and feeding-herbs follow after one another, so that cerealia and foliferous plants alternate; and, therefore, "koppel"-farming arranged in that manner is *rotation of cropping with fields of clover and grass for several years.* The last-mentioned modes of "koppel"-farming are, with regard to the agronomy of the country, the most suitable, and—by the grass fields that last for several years and a larger cultivation of bulbous plants—they admit of profitable dairy-farming and cow-keeping, which have found such favor with the public that there is a very considerable export not only of cattle but of dairy products.

The cereal grasses which are most cultivated in the country are: wheat, rye, barley, oats, buckwheat, peas, vetch, broad-beans, and lentil. Of *plants for spinning*, flax and hemp are cultivated; and of *plants for expressing oils*, autumn and spring rape.

Wheat, which no doubt ripens in all parts of the country, is, properly speaking, not cultivated in Norrland, where *barley* is the chief species of corn. The latter is likewise of great importance in Skåne. *Rye* is mostly grown in the provinces about Lake Mälar, and especially in Östergötland, as well as in Skåne. The best crops of *oats* are obtained in Skåne, Westergötland, and Vermland; but in Norrland the culture of oats is very limited. *Buckwheat* mostly belongs to Skåne; *pease* and *vetch* are cultivated in all parts of the country, excepting in the extreme north; *broad-beans* and *lentils* mostly in the southern parts of the country. The principal *district for flax* is the Län of Westernorrland (Ångermanland); *rape* belongs almost exclusively to Skåne.

Of *roots* grown on the farms are, potatoes, turnips, cabbage-turnips or Swedish turnips (Rutabaga), carrots, and beets; of the latter, both the ordinary as well as the sugar-beet, which latter has of late begun to be cultivated with great success for the sugar-mills established in Skåne.

Potatoes, which were introduced into Sweden for the first time in 1723, did not begin to be generally spread until 40 years later, at least not among the peasantry. At present potatoes are not wanting even high up in Lappland.

For sowing on *grassland* intended to last for several years, they use red clover (Trifolium pratense), Alsike clover (Trif. hybridum), white clover (Trif. repens), timothy grass (Phleum pratense), and various other grasses, and in low marshy places also fox-tail (Alopecurus pratensis).

The Alsike clover, which is a native of central Sweden, deriving its name from the parish of Alsike, between Stockholm and Uppsala, is the most hardy of all the species of clover, and in the northern provinces it is exclusively cultivated instead of the red clover, which does not thrive there. Large quantities of seeds from the Alsike clover are exported, when it is known under the name of *Swedish clover*.

The cultivated land was cropped in 1873 as follows:

	Swedish Tunnland.	Acres.
Winter-corn	831,000	1,014,000
Summer-corn	1,767,000	2,156,000
Pulse	110,000	134,000
Potatoes	300,000	366,000
Other roots & bulbous plants	23,000	28,000
Flax and Hemp	30,000	37,000
Grass	1,484,000	1,810,000
Other species of plants	7,000	8,000
Fallow	807,000	985,000
Total	5,359,000	6,538,000

On these fields the following species of corn were *sown* the same year, viz.:

KIND.	Quantity Sown.	
	Swedish Tunnor.	English Bushels.
Wheat, Winter	86,400	391,900
" Spring	7,900	35,800
Rye, Winter	570,900	2,589,600
" Spring	8,300	37,600
Barley	472,500	2,143,300
Oats	1,491,000	6,763,200
Mixed Corn	168,900	766,100
Pease	63,300	287,100
Beans	11,700	53,100
Vetch	32,800	148,800
Buckwheat	600	2,700
Potatoes	1,485,000	6,736,000
Flax (and Hemp)	21,000	95,300
Rape	100	500
Turnips, White Beets, Grass-seed		

If we now take for granted that in ordinary years the yields are of winter-corn from 8 to 9 times the quantity sown; of spring-corn from 5 to 6; and of potatoes from 7 to 8, it will be easy to calculate what an *average harvest* in Sweden yields. In reality a somewhat similar method is used after the completion of the harvest in order to be able immediately to determine the approximative quantity of the most important species of corn gathered, and this calculation gave the following result for the years 1874 and 1875:

Harvest.	1874.		1875.	
	Swedish Tunnor.	English Bushels.	Swedish Tunnor.	English Bushels.
Wheat	735,400	3,335,800	717,000	3,252,300
Rye	4,253,900	19,295,700	4,368,000	19,813,200
Barley	2,665,200	12,089,300	3,461,100	15,699,500
Oats	6,649,800	30,163,500	10,487,100	47,569,500
Mixed Corn	924,200	4,192,200	1,241,900	5,633,300
Pease, Beans, Vetch	425,100	1,928,300	718,500	3,259,100
Potatoes	11,697,400	53,059,400	11,867,900	53,832,800

The harvest of 1874 was not considered to come up to an average one.

For 1873, on the other hand, when the harvest was above the average, the Agricultural Societies reported* the estimates of harvest as low. It ought to be remarked that these figures have been proven to be rather too low, especially with regard to potatoes.

Harvest, 1873.	Swedish Tunnor.	English Bushels.
Wheat	673,800	3,056,400
Rye	3,873,000	17,567,900
Barley	3,088,200	14,008,100
Oats	8,727,100	39,568,000
Mixed Corn	1,091,100	4,949,200
Pease, Beans, and Vetch	605,300	2,745,600
Rape	6,600	29,900
Potatoes	9,630,500	43,684,000
Other Roots and Bulbous Plants	1,053,200	4,777,300
Linseed	48,200	218,600
	Swed. cent.	Kilogram.
Flax and Hemp	95,900	4,075,000

Tobacco is also grown, especially in the neighborhood of Stockholm, and several other towns where there is plenty of manure. The produce of the tobacco plantations round about Stockholm was stated to be, for the year 1870, nearly 5,000 Ctr. (213,000 Kilo.), and of those about Kristiania 3,000 Centners (128,000 Kilo.), but the extent of the produce of the whole land is not ascertained. (Compare Class 661.)

Of the harvest in 1873, 358,500 Tunnor of corn and 1,530,100 Tunnor of Potatoes, were used for the distillation of spirits. For the feeding of domestic animals, about 2,500,000 Tunnor are probably annually required.

If this be deducted, and, further, the amount of the corn sown as seed, as well as the import and export, be taken into consideration, the *home consumption of corn* per individual may be calculated at:

Wheat	0.18 Tunnor	= 0.8	Bushels.
Rye	1.02 "	= 4.6	"
Barley	0.53 "	= 2.4	"
Oats	0.35 "	= 1.6	"
Mixed Corn	0.19 "	= 0.9	"
Pease	0.11 "	= 0.5	"
Potatoes	1.53 "	= 6.9	"

In all probability the consumption of potatoes is, however, rather above 1½ tunna per individual; it is probably about 2 tunnas (= 9 bushels).

* Contributions to the Official Statistics of Sweden. (N) Agriculture and the Breeding of Cattle. Reports of the Agricultural Societies, 1865–1873.

Rye is the chief grain used by the Swedes for bread. Barley is used for bread in Norrland, oats in Dalecarlia, Vermland, Dalsland, Bohuslän, and partly in Småland, but rye is used in all the other provinces, and also to a certain extent in the above-mentioned provinces. The Swedish bread is generally baked into hard, thin cakes, the oaten and barley bread even as thin as paper. Similar hard bread (Knäckebröd), peculiar to the North, is, nevertheless, crisp, and it may be kept a long time, almost as long as one likes. The art of baking this kind of bread does not even extend to the southern parts of Sweden.

Sweden produces more grain and cattle than she consumes, and hence there is annually a very considerable *Export*, especially to England. The export of grain comprises principally oats and barley, whereas no small quantities of rye and rye-meal are imported from Russia and Finland, and wheaten flour from Denmark. The export of oats has been continuously increasing during the last ten years, the poor years, 1867 and 1868, excepted. In the beginning of the decennary it comprised annually about 6 million Swedish cubic feet (4.3 mill. bushels), and in 1870 it had increased to 20 million cubic feet (14.4 mill. bushels), but since 1871 it has been rather less.

The import and *export* of grain were as follows:

Cub. Ft.	1870.		1874.	
	Import.	Export.	Import.	Export.
Wheat......	247,800	484,400	84,000	228,000
Rye.........	1,065,200	539,700	6,370,000	18,400
Barley, Malt	120,500	2,552,700	710,000	1,562,000
Oats........	....	20,161,900	....	17,226,000
Centners.				
Flour, Wh'n	248,800	25,500	525,000	52,000
Meal, Rye..	547,900	14,500	1,180,000	36,000

That the figures representing the import for 1874 are higher, and those representing the export lower than the corresponding figures for 1870, is owing to a somewhat more unfavorable harvest in the former case.

Potatoes, properly speaking, are not an article for either importation or exportation. To prevent the importation of the destructive Colorado-beetle, it was resolved on July 16th, 1875, that potatoes, before they are allowed to be imported into the Kingdom from North America, shall be minutely examined and cleaned, whereas peelings, earth, and vessels that have been used for keeping them shall be burnt; it is, however, permitted that the packing need only be washed.

LAND ANIMALS.

[CLASS 630-636.] DOMESTIC ANIMALS. The number of these in 1873 were as follow:

	Number.
Horses over 3 years...............	400,900
Horses under 3 years..............	55,000
Oxen............................	288,800
Bulls...........................	46,400
Cows............................	1,340,600
Neat-cattle under 2 years..........	505,600
Sheep...........................	1,695,400
Goats...........................	121,800
Pigs............................	421,800

and in Lappland, nearly 200,000 reindeer.

According to this there are to every 1,000 people 106 horses, 508 neat-cattle, 423 small cattle, and 98 pigs. Owing to the development of dairy farming of late years, in quality as well as in quantity, this ratio has become greater. Thus, only 5 years ago, or in 1869, it was respectively no more than 101, 451, 399 and 82.

As *draught-cattle* on the farm, horses and oxen are employed, the latter, however, mostly in Södermanland, Småland, and in some parts of Westergöttland. In Norrland the ox is so little used as a beast of draught that it may almost be said that he is scarcely seen there.

There is a large export trade in dairy products, as well as in corn, mostly to England via Göteborg. A great deal of butter is, however, sent across the sound to Denmark, possibly for re-exportation. In its place we receive large quantities of butter from Finland. Pork, which of late years has begun to be imported on a large scale, is mostly from North America.

The imports and exports for 1870 and 1874 were as follows:

Import and Export.	1870.		1874.	
	Import.	Export.	Import.	Export.
Live Stock.				
Horses, Number...............	1,370	810	1,700	2,450
Horned Cattle, "	520	13,510	1,040	22,900
Sheep, "	370	8,930	130	21,600
Pigs, "	930	16,830	2,200	11,000
Products of Breeding:				
Meat, Centners.............	12,110	2,050	16,500	2,100
Pork, "	31,440	2,780	226,200	8,600
Cheese, "	7,930	4,000	16,400	3,670
Butter, "	47,400	54,680	37,300	68,900
Tallow, "	34,600	......	54,300	......
Hides and Skins, "	77,950	11,520	66,000	20,000
Wool, Pounds..............	4,253,000	43,180	3,910,000	84,600

Concerning *the treatment* of cattle and *improved breeding*, see class 680.

[CLASS 637.] WILD ANIMALS. The game law of October 21st, 1864, now in force, protects during certain seasons the following species of animals, namely: the elk, roe-buck, deer, wild reindeer, beaver, hare, capercailzie (*Tetrao urogallus*), black grouse (*Tetrao tetrix*), hazel grouse (*Tetrao bonasia*), moor hen (*Gallinula chloropus*), woodcock (*Scolopax rusticola*), ptarmigan (*Lagopus alpina*), willow grouse (*Lagopus subalpina*), red grouse (*Lagopus scoticus*), partridge (*Perdix cinerea*), swan, wild duck, eider duck, double snipe (*Scolopax major*), and the common snipe (*Scolopax gallinago*). The elk, properly speaking, belongs to the large forests of central Sweden and the south of Norrland, whereas the roe-buck, deer, partridge, and red grouse (the latter introduced from Scotland) inhabit the south of Sweden. The wild reindeer is still occasionally found in Lappland; but whether the beaver is still to be found there can scarcely be decided. The ptarmigan and hazel grouse occur almost exclusively in the mountainous districts of Norrland. The rest of the above-mentioned species of game are spread quite equally over the country. What the yearly profit of the chase is would be impossible to decide. Large quantities of capercailzie, black grouse and ptarmigans are brought from Norrland to Stockholm, especially during the winter season.

Among injurious *animals of prey*, specified in the game law, are lynxes, bears, wolverenes (gluttons), wolves, foxes, martens, otters, seals, eagles, eagle-owls, hawks, and falcons. Whoever kills a specimen of any of the four first-named animals of prey, whether grown or young, receives from the government a reward of, namely: for a bear, 50 Kr.; for a wolf or lynx, 25 Kr., and for a wolverene, 10 Kr. It is therefore known exactly how many of these have been killed. Of later years they seem to have diminished very considerably, and in several districts they are apparently altogether exterminated. Thus, for instance, in all southern Sweden, not a single wolf (as far as we can learn) has been shot since 1867. During the cold winter of 1874–75 some wolves were, however, seen in the southern parts of the country. Upon the whole it seems as if the larger beasts of prey were almost altogether confined to the desolate forests of Norrland and Lappland.*

Upon an average there were killed annually:

	1856–1860.	1861–1865.	1866–1870.
Bears	124	106	99
Wolves.........	174	111	47
Lynxes	175	136	107
Wolverenes......	122	110	139

Formerly, premiums were also paid out of the public purse for the shooting of foxes and birds of prey, but such premiums have not been paid since 1869, and therefore there are no data

* In the face of these facts, how ridiculous are the tales that foreigners, who are but little acquainted with Sweden, still occasionally spread, namely, that even in the streets of Stockholm people cannot walk with perfect safety, on account of wild animals. But such reports require only to be hinted at without any further proofs.

as to the exact number killed, which, of course, is no longer carried on with the same zeal as before. The greatest number of foxes killed was in 1867, when, as far as has been ascertained, 18,023 were despatched; in 1868 no less than 27,762 birds of prey were shot.

During the years preceding 1869 the government paid annually, for animals of prey killed, upwards of 110,000 Kr., but at present not one-tenth of that sum is paid. The destruction caused to the domestic animals by the animals of prey may be estimated at from 70,000 to 80,000 Kr. per annum.

[CLASS 638.] *Insects.* The raising of bees is a very ancient industry in the North, since even the mythological "sagas" tell us how the gods drank their mead in Valhalla, and likewise how the ancient champions, after the combats of the day, emptied their drinking-horns of mead. Mead is a kind of ale brewed from honey, and mixed with a small quantity of sweet gale (*Myrica gale*). Other times brought other customs, and the raising of bees, apparently, began to be neglected, but it has now again begun to attract attention. Although there are no complete statistical accounts, yet this branch of industry is not so inconsiderable, since in 1872, for instance, no less than 3,200 bee-hives were reckoned in one-fourth of the whole number of parishes in the Län of Göteborg & Bohus; 5,000 in the northern part of the Län of Elfsborg; 1,300 in half the number of parishes in the Län of Uppsala, etc. The last-mentioned Län is situated at the northern extremity of the proper region for the Swedish apiary, for farther to the north, or in all Norrland, it is very rare to find a beehive. The long winters there are very unfavorable for the raising of bees. Of late years about 20,000 pounds of beeswax have annually been exported, and about 6,000 to 7,000 are imported.

The silkworm has been noticed above, class 242.

MARINE ANIMALS, FISH CULTURE, AND APPARATUS.*

[CLASSES 640–648.] *Fisheries.* Sweden, as stated above, with an extension of upwards of 14 degrees of latitude from north to south, has a sea-coast equal to about two-thirds of its total boundary-line, and which in many places is indented with large bays, and girted with many archipelagoes (skärgårdar). Besides, the country is intersected by numerous streams and lakes, so that a twelfth part of the area of Sweden consists of water. The waters on the coasts differ considerably from one another, as well as from the waters of the lakes, which also differ from one another, which also causes differences in the fish fauna, which is very rich in species.

Fishing is the fourth branch of industry in point of importance in Sweden.

The most important fisheries carried on in Sweden are the following:

1. *Fisheries in the lakes and archipelagoes of the kingdom.*
2. *Salmon fisheries in the rivers and archipelagoes.*
3. *Herring-fisheries in the Baltic, and on the coasts.*
4. *Fisheries on the Banks, in the Kattegat, and the German Ocean.*

1. *The fisheries in the lakes and also on the Baltic coasts* are, in the south of Sweden, carried on principally for the Perch (*Perca fluviatilis* L.), the Pike-perch (*Lucioperca sandra* CUV.), the Pike (*Esox lucius* L.), the Bream (*Abramis brama* L.), and other fishes of the carp tribe, as well as for the Burbot (*Lota vulgaris* CUV.), the Eel (*Muræna anguilla* L.). In the lakes in the north of Sweden are caught especially some species of the genus *Coregonus*, and also the above-mentioned species. The fisheries in the lakes and on the shores are carried on as a chief

* Contributed by Dr. HJ. WIDEGREN, Intendant of Fisheries.

branch of industry by a population of fishermen residing on the shores; as an extra branch by farm-people, cottagers, handicraftsmen and soldiers, who either possess fishing-licenses, or have procured such by agreement.

As statistical returns of the fishing-industry here have been collected only for a few years, it is not yet fully known either how many persons are annually employed in the fisheries in the lakes and on the shores, or the value of the tackle that is used, nor yet the value of the fish taken at these fisheries. It appears, however, from what has been ascertained in certain provinces that this branch of industry is of the greatest economical importance. To make this clearer it is sufficient to mention that in one of the smaller provinces of the country, Nerike, 500 persons share in the fisheries in the lakes, and the tackle they use amounts in value to $9,500 gold.

In the other provinces, with the exception of Skåne and Blekinge, the lake-fisheries are carried on as a branch industry by a far greater number of persons. The salmon-fishery in Lake Wetter may be estimated to amount to about $30,000 gold annually. On the coast of the Län of Kalmar the coast-fishery is carried on by 200 persons, who are exclusively supported by it, and by 700 persons, who, though not exclusively, yet chiefly subsist therefrom. These people possess fishing-tackle worth $31,000 gold.

The products of the lake and shore fisheries are mostly disposed of in a fresh state in the neighborhood of the fisheries. As there are no taxes on the products of this industry nor limit to the catching, it is impossible to state the yearly income of the communities from this source; the best criterion that State has been able to obtain whereby to judge are the number of persons engaged and the value of their tackle.

2. *Salmon fisheries.* These fisheries are carried on in the Norrland rivers from the end of May until the beginning of September; in the rivers in the west of Sweden (Wiska, Ätra, Nissa, Laga, Qvistrum) from the beginning of April until the middle of July, and along the coasts of Skåne and Blekinge in the winter months, when the ice does not prevent. The richest salmon streams are the Torneå, Luleå, Umeå, Ångerman, and Ljusne rivers in Norrland, and further, the above-mentioned rivers on the west coast, the salmon of which is held in higher esteem than that on the east coast, and which is quite as good as the Scotch. The largest salmon fisheries in Sweden are those at Elfkarleby in Uppland and at Mörrum in Blekinge; the annual income from the former is on an average $11,000 gold, and from the latter about $8,300 gold.

The salmon is now-a-days mostly disposed of in a fresh state, in the country and also abroad, in which latter case it is packed in ice and shipped, via Stockholm or Göteborg, by merchant-houses to England and Germany, especially to Berlin. The greater part of the salmon that is taken on the south coast of Sweden in winter is sent to Germany or Denmark for smoking. According to the last returns as to the revenue from the salmon-fisheries 27 salmon-streams of the kingdom gave an annual income of $170,000 gold. The salmon-fisheries along the coasts of Skåne and Blekinge are computed to bring in on an average $33,300 gold yearly.

3. *The herring fishery in the Baltic and along the coasts.* This fishery, perhaps the most important of all, is carried on from Cape Kullen in the Sound as far as the inmost part of the Gulf of Bothnia, and mostly in open boats, with a crew of two or three men. The fishermen use partly stationary and partly drag-nets.

On the southern coast of the country the herring-fishery is carried on by a population who live together in large fishing villages, and obtain their subsistence entirely from the fishery. Along the coasts of the inner Baltic, from Kalmar to the Län of Norrbotten, as well as of the island of Gottland, the herring-fishery is carried on by people who live in the interior and only visit the archipelagoes during the fishing period, and by fishermen who reside on the various islands.

The Baltic Herring, or *Strömming*, a smaller variety of *Clupea harengus* L., is sold either fresh, or bloated, in the towns along the coast, or else pickled, in barrels. This pickled article is mostly sold in the country, but of late years it has also been exported to the German ports. As pickled herring is the daily food of the Swedish peasant a sufficient quantity cannot be procured in the country, and large quantities are imported from Norway (in 1872, 1,603,300 cubic feet, in 1873, 1,134,100, and in 1874, 1,147,000).

Along the coast line from Kalmar to Malön, in the vicinity of Haparanda, the herring-fishery is carried on with 3,275 boats, and according to the latest returns it may be calculated that about 66,500 barrels strömming are annually pickled. In the Blekinge archipelago, according to the returns, 47,732 barrels were pickled in 1868, and in the Län of Malmöhus and Kristianstad, where the herring-fishery is carried on with 686 boats, 13,600 barrels of herrings were pickled in the same year. The greater part of the catch in these two last-mentioned Läns is, however, sold fresh to the inhabitants of the fertile plains of these provinces.

In the island of Gottland the herring-fishery is carried on by 1,911 people, with 606 boats, and in 1869 the catch was estimated at 30,070 barrels.

Upon an average it may be calculated that on the east coast of Sweden 150,000 barrels of Baltic herrings are annually pickled, which article at the prices of last year represents a value in money of 3,000,000 Kr.

Besides the Strömming-fishery, which is carried on in the Baltic, Herrings (*Clupea harengus*) and Sprats (*Clupea sprattus*) are also caught during the autumn and winter months in the Kattegat on the coast of the province of Bohuslän. The sprats caught are partly sold fresh and partly pickled, or salted as anchovy and so-called "dainty herrings free from skin and bones." Of these very considerable quantities have been exported during the last few years. The catch of herrings in 1871 was valued at 88,847 Kr.

4. *The Bank fisheries in the Kattegat and the German Ocean* is carried on near the coasts with small but decked vessels, and on the banks in the Kattegat and off the west coast of Norway with larger vessels, so-called bank-skates, which have a burden of from 20 to 60 Lasts (65 to 200 tons), and a crew of 12 or 14 men. As tackle for the bank-fishery the so-called "Storbackor" is used. It is a line, with a hook, that is laid out on the banks to a depth of 100 fathoms. As a bait, is used either muscles or bits of fish. With this tackle are caught the Cods and Haddocks (*Gadus morrhua* L., *G. virens* L., *G. æglefinus* L.), the Ling (*Molva vulgaris* NILSS.), the Thornback (*Raja clavata* L.), and the Halibut (*Hippoglossus vulgaris* CUV.). Of the fish caught, part is sold fresh, but the greater part is prepared into "stockfish," or salted, either by Norwegian merchants or fish-curers in the Län of Bohus, and from the liver "cod-liver oil" is prepared and the roe is salted in order afterwards to be sold for bait to the sardine fisheries in France. In 1874 there were in the Län of Bohus 112 Bank-fishing vessels, with a manning of 1181 men. According to calculation, the catch in the course of the year represented a value of $400,000 gold. In the same year 839 centners stockfish were exported from Göteborg to England.

Mackerel-fishery is also carried on along the coast of the Län of Bohus, by 1465 men with 381 boats. The revenue of this fishery amounted, in 1874, to $67,400 gold.

The *Lobster-fishery*, in the Län of Bohus, was, in 1874, computed at $40,000 gold, and the *Oyster-fishery* at $3,000.

For the *Superintendency and Improvement of the Fisheries*, the following officials are appointed:

An Intendant of the fisheries in the fresh waters and on the east coast of Sweden, with two Assistants and one Instructor in fish-breeding. Besides these government fishery officials, there are in certain provinces and waters so-called fishery-*overseers* appointed, whose chief duty is to see that the enactments relating to the fisheries are observed. Of these overseers some are paid by grants from the State, others partly by

"Landsting" and Agricultural Societies, partly by the owners of the fishing-waters.

The next direction and superintendency over the sea-fishery on the west coast of the Kingdom is entrusted to an *overseer*, who stands under the control of the Governor of the Län of Göteborg & Bohus.

Pursuant to the Royal Letter of February 12th, 1864, and the Royal Enactment of November 7th, 1867, the *Fishery-Intendant* has the following duties to perform, chiefly with the help of his assistants:

(*a*) To make surveys of the fisheries in the different parts of the country.

(*b*) To make proposals for suitable protective laws for different districts and water systems, and to lend a helping hand to the administrative officials in matters relating to the legislation and management of the fisheries.

(*c*) To collect materials and prepare reports for the fishery statistics.

(*d*) To have the superintendency of the Normal State Establishment for the breeding of fish, and other establishments of the kind.

(*e*) To direct the appointed fishery overseers.

ANIMAL AND VEGETABLE PRODUCTS.

(Used as food or as materials.)

[CLASSES 650–656.] The greater number of substances belonging to the ANIMAL KINGDOM, such as *meat*, *butter*, *cheese*, *tallow*, etc., have been referred to above (Class 630). Eggs are also an important article of export; upwards of 3 million being exported yearly, chiefly to Norway and Denmark.

About *Honey* and *Wax*, see class 638.

Hides and *Skins* are objects of considerable importance, both industrial and commercial.

In 1873 there were 693 *leather manufactories* in Sweden, of which 200 were in the towns and boroughs, and the rest in the rural districts, employing 2,000 workmen. Besides, there were 260 tanners with 510 assistants, who were carrying on tanning as a trade. The manufacture, which is steadily increasing, amounted, in 1873, to 3,627,000 pounds of sole-leather and leather dressed in train oil, for which 600,000 hides and skins of an aggregate value of 7,850,000 Kr. were consumed. In 1872 a manufactory was established in Stockholm for the dressing of kid-leather (so-called handskskinn), which is considered quite equal to the best foreign (at Worms). The country does not produce a sufficient quantity of raw material for the currying, and hence a considerable quantity, especially of South American and East Indian hides, is imported. The importation in 1873 amounted to 121,800 centners hides and skins, of which 24,900 centners were dressed. There is also an export from the country.

In the manufacture of *saddlery* are employed 1450 handicraftsmen, together with their workmen.

[CLASS 657.] FLOUR AND MEAL. Although Sweden exports corn on a large scale, nevertheless corn, flour, and meal are imported in very considerable quantities, especially rye-meal, which is chiefly imported from St. Petersburg, and wheaten flour, which is principally brought from Denmark and also from Stettin. The annual import of ground-corn averaged, during the last five years, as follows:

Grits...............	Centners	5,000
Flour, Wheaten.....	"	265,000
Meal, Rye.........	"	540,000
" other kinds...	"	10,000

For principal grains exported and per capita consumption, see class 620.

How much grain is ground or malted in Sweden cannot be stated in figures, as there is no duty on grinding or malting. With a knowledge of the grain production of the country, and by deducting the difference between the export and import, as well as what is needed for seed, it may be estimated that from 10 to 12 million Swedish tuns (from 45 to 55 million bushels) grain are annually ground. The numerous waterfalls in all parts of the country afford abundant opportunities for the erection of grit-mills; but besides, in the middle and south of Sweden, especially in Öland, a number of wind-mills are used. In the towns, particularly in the large ones, several steam-mills have been erected. The so-called "fire-mill" in Stockholm has existed since 1804; this structure, which has recently been rebuilt, after a Bohemian model, attracts attention by the grand scale on which it has been erected, and carries on its manufacture. The mill has, namely, 23 pair of stones, besides peeling-mills, and the like, and grinds weekly 1,000 Swedish tuns. Uddley mills, in the neighborhood of Stockholm, which are driven by water-power, are now (1875) being reconstructed for 24 pair of stones.

For finer grinding French stones are used in Sweden; but besides, the country possesses good mill-stones in Öland, Lugnås (in Westergötland), Hör (in Skåne), Dalarne, etc.

[CLASS 658.] STARCH. The manufacture of starch and dextrine has of late years been considerably developed. The production of starch, chiefly from potatoes, was, especially formerly, carried on as a domestic occupation and in connection with farming. Of late years, on the other hand, several suitably constructed small manufactories have sprung up for this branch of industry, in Småland, Westergötland, and several other provinces.

[CLASS 659.] SUGAR AND SYRUPS.* Sugar-refining has been carried on in Sweden for a long time, and at present five-sixths of the sugar used in the country is refined in Swedish refineries. From 1860–1870 the yearly importation of raw sugar ranged from 35 to 40 million pounds, in 1873 it was 45,840,000 lbs., and in 1874 42,700,000, of refined sugars from 6 to 8 million lbs.; in 1871 and 1872 this amount was doubled, and in 1873 it was 24,800,000 lbs.; but in 1874 it declined to 22,150,000 lbs.

The importation of syrup, which amounted in 1860 to 1,000,000 lbs., has continually increased, and amounted, in 1874, to 13,600,000 lbs.

The sugar-refineries, of which there were 24 30 years ago, have decreased in number but increased in production. In 1873 there were but 12 in the Kingdom, with 1820 employees; in Stockholm 5, Göteborg 2, Landskrona, Norrköping, Vadstena, Halmstad, and Malmö, one each. The largest of these are *Tanto* in Stockholm, *Rosendal* and *H. Carneggie & Co.*, in Göteborg; each of these refine from 8 to 10 million lbs. sugar and syrup yearly. In 1873 their aggregate production was 43,023,000 lbs. sugar, valued at $4,824,600 gold; and 7,842,000 lbs. syrup valued at $288,000 gold. This is one of the most important branches of industry in the country, reckoned according to the value of the production.

Among the above-mentioned sugar-refineries are included 5 beet-sugar manufactories, which, in 1873, manufactured 5,922,000 lbs. of sugar and 2,927,000 lbs. of syrup.

After a few preparatory experiments on a small scale in Göteborg, for several years, the first large *beet-sugar manufactory* of this kind was established at Landskrona in the beginning of the decennary 1850–1860. In the years 1852–1854 trials were made with the cultivation of the sugar-beet, in almost all the southern and central provinces of Sweden, and numerous experiments were made by the Royal Agricultural Academy during these years, as to the quantity of sugar contained in the beets raised in the country. These, in general, gave very satisfactory results; but the manufactory at Landskrona remained the only one of its kind for many years, inasmuch as there were many difficulties to conquer before it was possible to cultivate the beet on a sufficiently large scale to justify the establishment of a manufactory and supply it with the necessary raw material. Not until the Säbyholm estate had

* From contributions by Prof. C. E. BERGSTRAND.

been purchased and devoted to cultivation of the beet by the Landskrona Co., was it possible for the new establishment to produce beet-sugar with profit.

The manufacture of beet-sugar was still exempt from duty; but the uncertainty as to how long this would be the case may have been the cause that very little attention was paid to the subject, until the Diet, in 1869, decreed that the manufacture should be exempt from duty until July 1st, 1873, but then subject to a successive taxation for 12 years, after which time there will be a fixed tax which shall be a certain percentage of the import duty on sugar. The duty is paid by the weight of the beets, 100 pounds of which being estimated to yield 6¼ pounds of raw sugar.

Shortly after this rate of taxation had been introduced, 5 new beet-sugar manufactories were established in the country on a very large scale, namely, at Inedal, close to Stockholm (built in 1869), at Halmstad (1870), at Arlöf, in the neighborhood of Malmö (1870), at Wadstena (1871), and at Ljung estate (1872); the two last-mentioned are in Östergötland. At the Ljung and Landskrona manufactories, the press-method has been adopted, and at the rest the diffusion method.

At the Arlöf manufactory about 2,000 centners of beets are worked up daily, or about 300,000 centners yearly, of which the company grows only about 12,000 or 15,000 centners; but they obtain a supply from the neighboring estates, so that the manufactory has not as yet been short of raw material. The beets have generally been of a good quality, and contained from 12 to 13 per cent. sugar, and upwards.

Since all these manufactories, which work up very large quantities of beets (during the manufacturing year, January 9th, 1873, to January 9th, 1874, 731,355 centners, according to the basis of taxation adopted, equivalent to 4,570,969 lbs. of sugar), commenced their operations, only the Scanian manufactories at Landskrona and Arlöf have continued their work on the same scale as before (with the exception of the Inedal manufactory, which converted in all 411,755 centners beets = 2,573,469 lbs. sugar, with a duty of 41,175 Kr., during the year, January 3d, 1874, to January 3d, 1875). In Skåne there are more sugar-beets raised than the sugar factories can use, so large quantities are exported to Denmark, and used for the manufacture of *beet-coffee* at the chiccory manufactory at Kalmar.

That they have been obliged to almost discontinue the manufacture of beet-sugar in Central Sweden is owing to the want of raw material. We may rest assured, however, that the experience gained in Skåne will soon spread throughout the country, and that the people will see the advantage in the cultivation of beets, not only for the promotion of industry, but for agriculture in general, and thus the manufacture of beet-sugar will soon revive and become a profitable branch of industry.

The beets mature in Central Sweden, though it was feared by many that they would not, but in all cases where they have not, it has not been the fault of the climate, but due to late sowing and the want of proper attention.

Of late they have commenced, in some places, to produce the so-called *lime-sugar*, as a suitable raw material for the sugar manufacture, as the great distances to the factories make it impracticable to transport the beet itself. This is rapidly becoming a domestic and agricultural branch of industry. The beet-roots are grated, heated, and pressed out, and the juice cleared by means of milk of lime, and evaporated to a consistency of from 30 to 32 degrees Baumé, or boiled down to about 1.26 specific gravity. When the juice has cooled new-slaked lime is added, and then the lime-sugar is immediately formed as a granular mass. Trials have been made in the chemical experimental establishment in the Royal Agricultural Academy, in Stockholm, as early as 1870, since which time lime sugar has been produced according to the directions received, in Blekinge, and at Årås, in Westergötland, though only by way of experiment and on a small scale.

The culture of potatoes, which is carried on

very generally, for the manufacture of spirits, evidently delays the introduction of beet raising. Soil and manual labor are called into requisition for this purpose, and the farmer thinks he profits as much as if he cultivated beets, or perhaps more.

[CLASS 660.] **Corn Brandy.** In Sweden the distillation of spirits has been, with the exception of short interruptions, exclusively a branch of agricultural industry since the earliest times. In general every landed proprietor had the privilege of distilling, and was at liberty to carry it on on any scale he chose. This afforded the proprietor a very convenient mode of converting his agricultural products into an easily transportable article, while at the same time the waste was applicable for the improvement of the farm. Inasmuch as the duty on the distillation, which the State imposed in proportion to the size of the implements, was very moderate, it followed as a natural consequence that the distillation was universally carried on. The proprietors generally found it profitable to distil spirits even from their own products, so that for about 40 years corn brandy was produced in upwards of 170,000 different places in the country.

It was natural that such a system would be injurious in many respects. The implements were of the most simple construction, and were used in such a manner that the raw materials employed gave comparatively poor returns, so that the production was no more than sufficient for the home consumption.

The establishment of larger distilleries on an improved plan gradually took the place of the small ones that were scattered over the country; but still, as late as 25 years ago, corn brandy was manufactured in 700 distilleries worked with steam, and in 37,000 smaller ones. However, another inconvenience now arose. The larger apparatus and improved technical methods which supplanted the small and imperfect stills caused a fall in the price of corn brandy to such a degree that quite a panic arose with regard to the moral and economical existence of the nation.

With this danger before their eyes, the government and the representatives tried, in 1854, by vigorous measures to eradicate the evil. Two laws were passed, one relative to the distillation, and the other to the retailing of corn brandy, and with these two laws, the former of which was not fully put into effect until 1860, the Swedish distillation of corn brandy entered upon a new stage, and at the same time an essential diminution in the above-mentioned abuse of intoxicating liquors was brought about.

The object of the new distillation law, which has gradually been reached without any change in the fundamental principle, was the limitation of the manufacture to a smaller number of stills, the placing of these under public inspection, and the raising of the price of the manufactured article. The law provides that in every distillery at least 200 kannor (523 litres) of the normal strength (50 per cent. alcohol, at a temperature of + 15° C.) shall be manufactured daily, on which an excise duty of 80 öre per kanna of the normal strength is imposed; that at every distillery, as long as the manufacture is continued, an official, who is paid by the State, shall be appointed, whose duty it is to measure the manufactured spirits, and, in order to guard against fraud, carefully to superintend the distillation. All these officials, or so-called comptrollers, are subordinate to the chief comptrollers, who are appointed for the districts. Periodical reports of the distillation, etc., are sent from the chief comptrollers, as well as from the comptrollers, to a special office, under the head of which the whole staff of comptrollers are placed.

The enforcement of this law met with great resistance on the part of the smaller landholders, who feared that it would turn the distillation of spirits into a complete manufacturing industry, and thus be isolated from agriculture. In regard to these agricultural interests, certain stipulations have been made with a view to the prevention of too great a concentration of the manufacture. It is therefore generally not permitted for more than seven months in the year (January to April and October to December), and at no distillery is it allowed to exceed 1,200 kannor per day.

How great the annual *production of corn brandy* was in the country before the application of the above-mentioned law cannot be determined with any degree of certainty. The returns fluctuate between 30 and 50 million kannor (78 to 130 million litres). Considering the large number of distilleries, the latter figure is, however, the more likely of the two. Since 1860, on the other hand, the returns are to be depended on, and show that during the period 1864 to 1873, when the number of distilleries varied between 400 and 600, the annual production of corn whiskey averaged 14,800,000 kannor (38,740,000 litres). In 1873 the production amounted to 18,064,544 kannor, for which an excise duty of 14,038,620 Kr. was paid to the State, while the cost of controlling and receiving amounted for the year to 387,207 Kr., or 2.76 per cent. of the excise duty.

The raw materials which are principally used for the distillation of spirits are potatoes and grain, besides small quantities of various other kinds, such as beets, beet molasses, reindeer moss, etc. Of the two first-mentioned materials there were used during the 10 years, 1864 to 1873, on an average 1,523,000 cubic feet grain of various sorts and 8,877,000 cubic feet of potatoes annually.

Reindeer moss, which has begun to be employed of late years, is deserving of particular notice. Professor STENBERG, in Stockholm, having deemed this species of moss particularly suitable for the object in question, made some experiments on a large scale in 1868, the result of which was that in the following years quantities of reindeer moss were employed at several distilleries. The yield has, however, proved very variable, inasmuch as it depends partly upon the quality of the moss itself, and partly upon the process. Upon an average every centner of reindeer moss has yielded about 6 kannor of whiskey of the normal strength; yet with careful management as much as 9 kannor have been obtained. Upon an average about 300,000 kannor of moss whiskey are manufactured annually, and there is no doubt that in years when potatoes fail this raw material, of which Sweden possesses inexhaustible supplies, will be employed on a far larger scale.

The annual *import of distilled spirits*, which chiefly consist of arrack, rum, and French brandy, averaged in the above-mentioned period (1864–1873) about 1,000,000 cans (nearly 2½ million litres) of the normal strength, whereas no export worth mentioning took place.

The *retailing of spirits* is subject to a special duty which is computed to amount to 25 or 40 öre for every kanna of spirits sold. The licenses for this sort of trade are granted by the community, who also receive the revenue of the taxes, which are so divided that one-fifth falls to the Landsting, one-fifth to the Agricultural Society, and three-fifths to the community. The revenue which was thus divided in 1873 amounted to 1,997,345 Kr.

A branch of industry of considerable importance and peculiar to Sweden is the manufacture of the so-called Swedish **Punch**, a liquor prepared from arrack or rum, water and sugar, which is exported, and has found its way to countries even beyond Europe.

Wine is manufactured from certain kinds of fruit, such as currants, gooseberries, cherries, and likewise, on a small scale, from foreign raisins and inferior wines. The annual production from five such manufactories is stated to be 300,000 kannor.

Ale and Porter. The brewing of beer, as a domestic branch of industry, has been generally practised in the country from the most remote times. On the other hand, the development of the same to a more extensive industry stands in a near connection with the diminished consumption of corn whiskey, which the new legislation with regard to the same has caused. Since that time the consumption of beer has increased, and a great number of breweries, not only for Bavarian and Scotch beer, but for various other sorts, have been established. Of late years Swedish beer has become rather an important article of export. The manufacture of ale, as well as of porter, being, however, entirely exempt from duty, whether direct or as an excise upon malt, materials are wanting for the calculation of its real extent. The manufacture of porter at one brewery in Göteborg was stated to be 1,100,000 kannor in 1873.

Although the *Hop culture* in the country is very ancient, neither a sufficient quantity nor a suitable quality for the superior sorts of beer is produced, and consequently from 5,000 to 6,000 centners of Bavarian hops are annually imported.

Vinegar. The vinegar manufactured in Sweden is generally prepared from diluted corn whiskey. At the distillation of wood some wood vinegar is also obtained as a by-product, though not in any quantity worth mentioning.

[CLASS 661–662.] BREAD. See CLASS 620.

[CLASS 663.] **Manufacture of Tobacco.** There are no detailed returns of the tobacco manufactories before 1780, when their number was 72, with 677 workmen and a production of 236,600 pounds smoking tobacco, 997,000 pounds chewing tobacco, and 137,800 pounds snuff, or together 1,371,400 pounds tobacco and snuff. Until 1830 there was only a slight change in the number of factories, as well as in that of the workmen, since the former amounted to 77 and the latter to 695. On the other hand, during these 50 years, the production, which then amounted to 891,500 pounds smoking tobacco, 771,300 pounds chewing tobacco, 1,286,200 pounds snuff, and 7,200 pounds cigars, or together 2,956,200 pounds, had more than doubled. In that year (1830) the manufacture of cigars commenced in Sweden.

In 1873 the manufacture of tobacco was carried on in 102 manufactories, where 3,575 workmen were employed, and during the 43 years since 1830 the production had very considerably increased, so that the same amounted to 1,269,200 pounds smoking tobacco, 1,250,300 pounds cigars, 2,049,200 pounds various sorts of tobacco, and 6,634,900 pounds of snuff, or in all 11,203,600 pounds, amounting in value to 8,902,000 Kr. Among the above-mentioned manufactories there are only a few that carry on their business on an extensive scale.

The import of tobacco in the form of leaves and stalks, which in recent times has remained steady at about 6,000,000 or 8,000,000 pounds, rose in 1874 to 10,350,600 pounds. To this is to be added an annual import of from 50,000 to 60,000 pounds of cigars and about 30,000 pounds of rolled tobacco. Of cigars a few thousand pounds are generally exported.

TEXTILE SUBSTANCES OF VEGETABLE OR ANIMAL ORIGIN.

[CLASS 665–669.] For WEAVING see CLASS 228–249.

MACHINES, IMPLEMENTS AND PROCESSES OF MANUFACTURE.

[CLASS 670–675.] In proportion to the great development of agriculture in Sweden of late years, the want of improved *agricultural implements* and machines has become more and more urgent, and it is now not uncommon to find at moderately large farms implements which formerly were found only on the very large estates. Expensive threshing and reaping machines, portable engines and the like are coming more in use throughout the country.

This continuous and greatly-increasing demand has not been able to be met by the home production at Öfverum, Näfveqvarn, Göteborg, Malmö, Trollhättan, Eskilstuna, Ankarsrum, Åker, Forsvik, etc., though on an extensive scale, and has induced a very considerable importation of agricultural implements. Thus thousands of American reaping machines are probably now imported.

The Swedish *agricultural implements* have been honorably noticed at the international exhibitions. Being made of excellent iron or steel, they combine a suitable construction with lightness and strength, and a cheapness that can scarcely be competed with. The demand for Swedish implements for exportation (especially for Russia) has therefore considerably increased of late years, and the reason why this exportation is not still larger than it actually is may be found in the fact that the Swedish workshops are too much taxed by native wants to be able to supply the demands of foreign markets. There are several factories for the making of agricultural implements being established, while those already existing are being extended.

AGRICULTURAL ENGINEERING AND ADMINISTRATION.

[CLASS 680-683.] The chief direction of agriculture belongs to the Royal Civil Department and the *Royal Agricultural Academy* (Landtbruks-Akademien) in Stockholm, which was founded in 1811, and is also a central establishment for the improvement of agriculture, and provided with a station or chemical experiments. The special care of the improvement of agriculture in the various provinces devolves upon *the agricultural societies*, which publish annual reports.*

For the draining of the upper soil and the irrigation of the meadows, as well as for assisting in agricultural improvements, etc., 12 *agricultural engineers* are appointed, who are paid out of the public purse, and when requested by the farmers in the country they shall assist in these and other matters. We are in a great measure indebted to these engineers for the breaking up of so much land and drawing off of water, the drainings, fertilizing with marl, and other agricultural improvements, which annually take place. Thus, in 1873, at least 55,000 tunnland were drained in the country.

With regard to the *manures* used in Swedish husbandry, see class 200.

For *the improvement of the breed of cattle* in the country, breeding cattle have been purchased from time to time, and cattle of the short-horned, Ayrshire, Pembrokeshire, Voigtland, and Algauer breed have been placed at different stations. Besides, the Dutch black cattle have always been valued, and were introduced in the country long ago, especially in the southern and central parts. In recent times, several *Joint Stock Dairy Companies* have been formed, and dairy-economy has in general made great progress since the method of cooling with iced water, which was invented by Mr. J. G. SWARTZ, of Hofgården, in Östergötland, has been more generally adopted.

Two travelling instructors are paid by the government to give advice and explanation about the rearing, raising, feeding, and other particulars with regard to *the management of horned cattle*, as well as to the improvement of them by the choice of suitable animals for breeding. These persons also give instruction about the treatment of the milk in the making of cheese and butter, and also designs for suitable houses for the stock farm and dairy.

For the improvement of the *Wool and Sheep farm* a special official, paid by the government, is appointed, who annually inspects the sheep farms belonging to the State, and assists private sheep-masters with advice and information about the rearing of sheep and other things connected with the same.

There are 3 *studs* in the country, Strömsholm, Flyinge, and Ottenby, of which the first-mentioned was established as early as 1694. The total number of horses in 1874 was 334; of these 124 were stallions. Besides, in the cavalry regiments there are stallions belonging to the squadrons and companies. The annual grant for the purchase of animals for breeding is 50,000 Kr., and for prizes on horses there are very considerable funds. Since 1868 there have been annual horse races at Stockholm, Göteborg, and Helsingborg.

The Working People employed on the Farm, besides the grown children of the peasantry, are generally servants of either sex. The former are partly cotters (torpare) with a piece of land, for the rent of which they render a cer-

* Contributions to the official statistics of Sweden. (N) Jordbruk och Boskapsskötsel (Agriculture and the Breeding of Cattle). Reports by the agricultural societies for the years 1865–1873, together with an abstract made out by the Central Statistical Bureau.

tain amount of labor; and partly servants hired by the year. The last-mentioned receive a salary in cash, and either board at their master's or have a household of their own, founded on an annual allowance in kind ("stat").

The salary of a man-servant, legally employed, who boards with his master, varies very much in different parts of the country, but it may be estimated at from 100 to 200 Kr., and for a maid-servant at from 50 to 100 Kr. The daily wages during the summer months for a farm laborer is from 1 to 2 Kr., and for a female from 50 öre to 1 Kr. The allowances in kind ("stat") and salary for a servant hired by the year, who has his own household ("statkarl"), vary considerably in different parts of the country, but in the middle of Sweden they may be estimated as follows:

Wheat, 2 cubic feet.
Rye, 27 "
Barley, 12 "
Pease, 2 "
Potatoes, 12 " together with a piece of land calculated for the planting of 6 cubic feet of potatoes.
Herrings, 80 pounds.
Salt, 40 pounds.
Hops, 2 "
Wool, 2 " or food for a sheep.
Milk, new, daily, ½ can.
" skimmed, daily, ½ can.
Additional allowance (safvelpenningar), 20 Kr.
Earnest-money (städsel), 5 Kr.
Wages, 50 Kr.

The whole, together with the cash amount, estimated at 350 Kr. Besides, such a "statkarl," who in general is married, has free lodgings, fuel and medical attendance; moreover he is exempt from all taxes, both to the state and the community, these being paid by the master. For a head servant, and also for one that superintends the cattle, both the wages and the allowance in kind are much greater than for a common farm laborer. We may therefore in general estimate the value of the allowance in kind ("stat") and the wages for a man at from 300 to 500 Kr., and for a female servant at from 200 to 300 Kr.

TILLAGE AND GENERAL MANAGEMENT.

[CLASS 690–692.] The different modes of cultivating the soil have been noticed above, class 620.

DEPARTMENT VII.---HORTICULTURE.*

[CLASS 700–737.] In all probability gardening began during the middle ages, and was then called into life by the monks, who introduced various kitchen and medicinal plants into the country, which since that time have grown wild in abundance. It was not until the latter half of the 16th and beginning of the 17th century that the large baronial country seats sprang up, and the people, after a nearer contact with foreign countries, had become acquainted with their customs and shared their riches, that foreign plants were introduced into our country on a larger scale; but it was not until the latter half of the 18th century that gardens were laid out and a horticultural literature arose.

But it is only in this century that horticulture has tried to keep even pace with agriculture, which had been rapidly developed, and if we take into consideration the sacrifices which private individuals have made in this respect, as well as the readiness and liberality with which the state has repeatedly encouraged and supported it, we cannot be surprised by the success with which it has met, and though this branch of industry is not the source of great income, it contributes in no small degree to the national prosperity, and serves to embellish and refine the outward life. Further to the north, gardening has likewise made rapid progress, and has surpassed the expectations of even the most sanguine.

* Contributed by Professor N. J. ANDERSSON.

The public horticultural institutions are the following:

(1) The *Royal Agricultural Academy*, which has a section for gardening, and, on its property, "the field for experiments," possesses a large space, where a considerable number of fruit trees, park trees, and ornamental shrubs are raised, and trials are made to acclimate and utilize these, as well as our kitchen herbs and decorative plants.

(2) Of *Botanical gardens* we have two, namely, one at Uppsala, in lat. 59° 51½′, which takes up a large area with extensive grounds and spacious hot-houses, which contain ancient classical specimens from the time of LINNÆUS, and many new plants from distant countries; and one at Lund, in lat. 55° 42′, which was laid out a few years ago, and is supplied with houses and auxiliaries to meet the demands of the present times, so that it may be truly said of this garden that for academical instruction, it is the most suitable in existence, and at the same time an ornament to the town and province where it is situated.

(3) Under the supervision of the Agricultural Academy are the two *Agricultural Institutes* of the kingdom, the one at Ultuna, near Uppsala, and the other at Alnarp, near Lund, in Skåne; and also 27 agricultural schools, of which there is at least one in each province. In their gardens a great number of scholars (in 1871 no less than 529) are annually instructed in gardening.

The special gardening establishments are: The *Bergius Establishment for Instruction in Gardening*, placed under the inspection of the Royal Academy of Sciences, was established as early as 1784, by the eminent naturalist, P. J. BERGIUS, principally for agricultural plant-training and gardening, and since 1832 the *School of the Swedish Horticultural Society* (Svenska Trädgårdsföreningens läroanstalt), where at present between 20 and 30 scholars go through a two years' course in horticulture. Besides, a great number of men are trained at the Agricultural Academy's Field for Experiments (in arboriculture), and also at the Royal Country-seat, Haga (in forcing fruits and floriculture).

Further, special societies for the promotion of gardening are the following: *The Horticultural Society at Göteborg*, which has laid out an exceedingly fine park and beautiful garden, in which there are several hot-houses that shelter a large collection of exotic ornamental plants, and others remarkable on account of their organization. Since 1848 a society of friends of gardening has flourished in Stockholm under the name of *The Gardeners' Society* (Gartner Sällskapet). There are also such societies in Uppsala, Örebro, Karlstad, Linköping, and Westerås.

It may also be mentioned that at Haparanda and Piteå a *Town-park* has been laid out at the expense of the inhabitants, which contains several foreign trees and shrubs; and that at Östersund, Umeå, and Hernösand town-gardeners were engaged not long ago; and also that at Gefle, Uppsala, Linköping, Skara, Karlstad and Visby, such an official has been placed at the head of a garden belonging to the Län, from which a number of trees, shrubs and flowers are spread throughout the country.

Now, if to this be added, that especially fruit trees, from the Agricultural Academy's Field for Experiments, and also from the Swedish Horticultural Society, are sold in the country, as well as by several richly-supplied *market-gardeners*, chiefly at Stockholm, Göteborg, Norrköping, and Helsingborg, a few Royal country-seats, and large private estates; and that a very considerable number are imported from Scotland, England, Holland and Northern Germany, *i. e.*, Berlin, Lubeck, Travemunde, and Hamburg (mostly trees and ornamental plants), Erfurt, Quedlingburg, and other places (mostly seeds), it will be seen that horticulture is an important branch of industry in Sweden.

Also most of the *Royal country-seats* have extensive *parks* and good gardens, beautiful flower parterres, and superior hot-houses, as at Haga (among the best in the country), Ulriksdal, and Drottningholm in the vicinity of Stockholm, at Tullgarn in Södermanland, and Beckaskog in Skåne, where many young people are instructed both theoretically and practically in gardening, and who afterwards exercise a beneficial influence upon the gardening of the country. At the numerous *large estates* that are to be found in Uppland, Södermanland, Nerike, Östergötland Skåne, Halland, and the vicinity of Göteborg, the grounds are magnificently laid out, often in the English provincial style, and supplied with ornamental flower parterres, and frequently with costly hot-houses (at one of these estates there are no less than 18 hot-houses), in which plants from southern climates are raised, and which with regard to form, taste and luxuriancy are not far behind those of foreign countries.

Likewise at the *Seminaries for the Training of Teachers for the National Schools* of the country from about 700 to 800 scholars are instructed in horticulture; and at the stationary *National Schools*, the number of which at present is 2,540, instruction in gardening is enjoined, and the community is bound to assign requisite land for plantations, where the scholars can raise trees, which they afterwards transplant into their future dwelling places, in which manner a knowledge of this branch is diffused among the peasantry, and whose best fruits will be reaped among the lowest class of society.

And lastly, students are often enabled, by *grants from the state*, to travel abroad in order to make themselves acquainted with the mode of laying out gardens there, and by that means acquire experience or increase their knowledge.

It is not possible to state how great a part of the *superficial area* of Sweden is *occupied by gardening* at present. According to the last official statistical returns, 56,000 Swedish tunnland (68,000 acres) were taken up by the culture of trees, hops and vegetables.

It is obvious that the state of culture in a country like Sweden, which extends far towards the north, must vary very much, and present an interesting picture of the gradations it undergoes in proportion to the latitude, which is also distinctly marked in the variations of the native flora of the different provinces.

In this respect Sweden is generally divided into the following 3 regions:

(1) The *Region of the Red and White Beech*, or Southern Sweden. This extends, though the above-mentioned species of trees are cultivated as high as 60° north latitude, from the most southern part of the country, from 55° 20′ to 57° 5′ on the east coast, but on the west coast as far as 59°. Wheat and buckwheat thrive here. Walnuts, chestnuts, peaches, apricots and grapes ripen in the open air; the greater number of the fruit trees, ornamental shrubs and plants, which thrive in Denmark, and to a certain degree in the north of England and Northern Germany, grow very well here. Among these, though some need the greatest care, may be mentioned: *Aucuba japonica, Bignonia radicans, Broussonetia papyrifera, Clethra paniculata* and *tomentosa, Catalpa syringæflora, Ephedra, Hibiscus syriacus, Paliurus aculeatus, Pawlownia imperialis, Platanus occidentalis, Prunus lauro-cerasus* and *lusitannica. Robinia pseudo-acacia* grows to an almost gigantic height; several species of oak, even such as belong to the south of Europe, attain a considerable height; *Castanea vesca* becomes upwards of 150 years old, the box between 2 and 3 hundred and 8′′ in diameter; many needle trees, as *Thuja plicata* and *occidentalis, Salisburia, Taxus hibernica* and *Cupressus Lawsonii*, thrive exceedingly well; *Taxus baccata* has a stem of 3′′ in diameter; *Liriodendron* becomes almost 30′ high and produces an abundance of flowers, and in one place there is a specimen of *Magnolia acuminata* which is 40′ high and has a stem of more than 1′ in diameter.

Göteborg, situated on the west coast, has a milder climate, owing to its uniformity, than the east of Sweden in the same latitude.

The following ligneous plants: Alnus cordifolia, Aralia spinosa, Amygdalus communis, Berberis Darwinii, Carya alba, amara und virginiana, Clematis lanuginosa, Evonymus japonica and radicans, Fothergilla alnifolia, Wistaria sinensis, Hydrangea hortensis, Ilex acquifolium, Pterocarya caucasica (becomes very large), Rhododendron ponticum, Spiraea prunifolia, Skimmia japonica, Quercus ægilops, Cephalotoxus, Chamaecyparis sphaeroidea, Pinus Douglasii, grandis, Menziesii, khutsow, retinospora, ericoides, leptoclada and pisifera, Thuja gigantea, and Lobbii and Sequoja gigantea, do well here. The native species which characterize this region are: Sorbus aria, Acer campestre, Cornus sanguinea, Evonymus europæa, Ligustrum vulgare, Lonicera periclymenum, Coronilla emerus, together with Helianthemum fumana and œlandicum in the Baltic islands, the Genista, and also some of the more southern forms of the families Rosa and Rubus.

(2) The *Region of the Oak* extends as far as the river Dal, 60° N. L., though this tree is cultivated as far as Sundsvall (62° 20′) on the east coast. Rye, barley and oats are the chief species of corn, tobacco is cultivated with success, and though the culture of kitchen vegetables, both in the open air and in hot-beds, give excellent yields, and several species of fruit come to perfection during the course of the year, and during very favorable summers even walnuts, grapes (especially the American species), and wall-apricots.

Of the trees that thrive in the latitude of Stockholm a few are given below:

Acer negundo.
Aesculus machrostachya.
Ailanthus glandulosa.
Azalea pontica.
Berberis buxifolia.
Caragana chamlagu.
Castanea vesca (8–10′ high, bush-shaped).
Chamæcyparis nutkaensis.
Clematis patens.
Clethra alnifolia.
Cotoneaster microphylla.
Cotoneaster Simonsii.
Cratægus pyracantha.
Liriodendron tulipifera (a bush only 6′ high).
Lonicera sempervirens.
Mespilus germanica (bears fruit annually).
Pinus canadensis.
" cephalonica.
" cilicica.
" Nordmanniana.
" orientalis.
Prunus triloba.
Rhamnus canadensis.
Rhododendron catawbiense.
Rhododendron dahuricum.
(Ribes sanguineum).
Cupressus Lawsoniana.
Cydonia japonica.
Erica herbacea.
Fraxinus lentiscifolia.
Hypericum hircinum.
Lespedezia bicolor.
Ligustrum ovalifolium.
Spiræa ariæfolia.
" bella.
" cantonensis.
" Thunbergii.
Weigelia amabilis.
" rosea.

Of the native plants which characterize these districts, Fraxinus excelsior, Acer platanoides, Ulmus montana, Tilia europæa, Alnus glutinosa, Rhamnus frangula, and Viburnum opulus extend as far as Ångermanland; Sorbus scandica, the most peculiar tree of the north, as far as Jemtland, whereas Sorbus fennica, Taxus baccata, Prunus spinosa, Crataegus oxyacantha and monogyna, Cotoneaster vulgaris, Lonicera cœrulea, Berberis vulgaris, and Rhamnus catharticus are scarcely to be found beyond this region.

(3) The *Region of the Gray Alders, Needle-trees and Birches* includes Norrland as far as the boundary of the Swedish highlands in Lappland. Barley is the chief kind of corn, although it has been found that rye, and, not seldom, wheat, will grow. Flax and hops have been cultivated in a very high latitude; red and black currants, with several other kinds of berries, are indigenous, but gooseberries are more sensitive, and any proper cultivation of fruit trees cannot be carried on to advantage, though in Östersund and Skellefteå apples occasionally, and gooseberries with still greater certainty, ripen.

The time of vegetation is very short in the north, scarcely more than two, at most three months. For many perennial plants the summers are sufficiently long and the abundance of snow forms an excellent protection against the severity of the winters; therefore several bulbous and foliferous plants thrive exceedingly well as far northward as the mountain ranges, and most of the kitchen vegetables, excepting beans, thrive, though not so well, farther south, yet well enough to become very savory, and to form peculiar varieties.

As high up as Piteå the following ligneous

plants are stated to thrive without a winter cover, viz.:

Amelanchier Botryapium.
Amygdalus nana.
Caragana altagana.
" arborescens.
Cornus alba.
" sanguinea.
" sibirica.
Crataegus coccinea.
" glandulosa.
" sanguinea.
Cytisus elongatus.
Eleagnus macrophylla.
Evonymus europæa.
Ligustrum vulgare.
Lonicera alpigena.
" coerulea.
" pyrenaica.
" tatarica.
" Caprifolium.
" Periclymenum.
Lycium barbarum.
Mahonia aquifolium.
Philadelphus, species plurimac.
Pinus austriaca.
" balsamea.
Pinus Cembra.
" mhugus.
Populus balsamifera.
" laurifolia.
" candicans.
Pyrus baccata and prunifolia (with ripe fruit).
Ribes multiflorum.
Rubus odoratus.
Salices, species multæ.
Spiræa, species plurimæ.
Sambucus racemosa.
Symphoria racemosa.
Syringa chinensis.
" josikæa.
" vulgaris.
Thuja occidentalis.
Viburnum acerifolium.

Besides, of Swedish species:

Corylus avellana.
Cotoneaster vulgaris.
Sorbus aria.
" scandica.
Viburnum opulus, var.

Besides our pines and the birches, which form connected, and as it were primitive forests, this region is marked by the following ligneous plants, although they extend further south: Alnus incana, Prunus Padus, Sorbus Aucuparia and Populus tremula, among which are seen in large quantities, Myrica Gale, and above all numerous species of Salices, and as small shrubs Empetrum and several Ericaceæ; besides, near the coast there are Myricaria germanica and Hippophaë rhamnoides.

From this brief survey it appears that the vegetation of Sweden is a mixture of northern and southern species, or more properly of an arctic and a southeastern, Asiatic character; for on a minute comparison with that of adjacent countries it is seen that our high northern flora is identical with the circumpolar, and that they are to be found again in the districts east of the Baltic and north of the Gulf of Finland, and that the least agreement is with West Europe. At the end of the glacial period the Swedish flora had quite an arctic stamp, and extended farther towards the south than at present; after that, species from central Asia were introduced and spread through central and northern Europe.

1. Fruit Trees.

That fruit trees were cultivated in Sweden as early as the 11th or 12th century seems certain, for as early as the year 1300 the law provides punishment for whoever steals fruit out of another person's garden. But what progress this culture made in the course of years; which were the original species; what new species appeared, and how these came to perfection in our regions, or which were considered as more peculiar, we have very incomplete or no information.

The following varieties of the apple are more generally and successfully cultivated:

Astrachan, red and white, delicious and transparent, native.
"Edel-Borsdorfer", especially in the southern parts, bearing abundantly.
"Zwiebel-Borsdorfer."
Red Cardinal.
Red Colville.
Charlamowsky.
Prince's apple.
Gravenstein.
Irish peach apple.
Emperor Alexander.
Danzig Kantapple.
Scarlet red Parmaene.
Ribston pippin.
Winter postof ("Grågylling").
Lorraine Rambour.
Reinette de Canada.
Yellow Richard.
Princesse noble.
Bohemian rose apple.
Thorn pippin.
Pigeon rouge.
Pigeon blanche.

To these may be added the following, which have more of a native origin, and are more characteristic for our country:

Hampus.	Kafvelås apple.
Josephine.	Stenkyrke "
Orange apple.	Stäringe "
Rosenhäger.	Hörningsholm apple.
Glass apple.	Åkerö "
Kanicker.	Börringe "
Melon apple.	Ringstad "
Wine "	Fröåker "
Lemon "	Kesäter "
Lord's "	Mälsåker "
Maiden's apple.	Stenberg "
Säfstaholm apple.	

In general, the apple trees in Sweden bear fruit in abundance, which in succulence and flavor is excelled in few other places. However, it frequently happens that unfavorable weather, or still oftener the larvæ of the butterfly (however not in such a manner as in Germany), cause such injuries and devastation that the apples are either not developed, or ripen too late.

Of *Pears* the following species are considered the most suitable:

Green Magdalen.	Cattilac ("Pundpäron").
Round "Mundnetz" pear.	Winter-Nelis.
English summer butter pear.	Fulvous butter pear.
Gansell's bergamots.	Louise bonne d'Aorange.
Good greys ("Gråpäron").	Windsor pear.
Capiaumont.	Espereus bergamotte.
Napoleon's butter pear.	Diel's butter pears (Beurré Diel).
Saint Germain.	Winter Dechants pear.
Duchesse d'Angoulême.	Flemish beauty.
Dutch fig-pear.	Bonchretien.
	Doyenné.

As peculiar varieties, may be mentioned different species of Bonchretien, Fullerö-Hofsta, Larsmäss (early and common), Wennström Grenna, Sörmland, and Stenberg pears.

The climate is less favorable for pears than for apples. Even when cultivated as wall-fruits in the southern parts of the country, the foreign varieties bear no comparison with those abroad, and the winter pears, especially, often fail.

Cherries of all sorts thrive well as far north as Stockholm. Both the acid and sweet varieties sometimes grow wild. Of the different species of *Graffion* (Bigareau) the yellowish red Dönissen's, and Napoleon's yellow, and also the large black ones are generally cultivated; of the *Heart Cherries*, Fromm's Black, Knight's Early Elton, Lucien, Early May, and Winkler's White; of *Sweet Cherries*, the Common May Cherry and the Red Muscatelle; of *Acid Cherries*, the Common Small, the Large Glass Cherry of Montmorency, and the Large Glass Cherry, and of the *Morello*, the common Brown Cherry, the Brown Brussels, the Ostheim, and the Prince's Cherry.

Of *Plums*, in the middle of Sweden, the best sorts are:

Green Gage.	Real early damask plum.
Red egg-plum.	King's plum of Tours.
Apricot plum.	Red Emperor's plum.
Jefferson.	Lawrence's Favourite.
Washington,	And more rare:
Early English damask plum.	Hackman's plum.
	Theresia, etc.

When the weather, in autumn, is unfavorable, the last-mentioned sorts do not bear well; otherwise plums ripen even in the middle of Norrland, but not farther north.

It has been stated above that in the south of Sweden *Apricots*, *Peaches*, *Nectarines*, *Walnuts* and *Chestnuts* are cultivated in the open air, and ripen. The three first-mentioned are also trained in the middle of Sweden, in hot-houses; nay, the early orange apricot ripens on an espalier even about Stockholm. Among peaches, the double Montagne and Admirable are mostly cultivated. The walnut tree grows in Skåne, Gottland, and Kinekulle, where it attains a very considerable height; and at Stockholm it has occasionally borne ripe fruit. Castanea vesca, on the other hand, which in Skåne attains great height, is at

Lake Mälar frequently nothing but a stunted shrub.

2. **Small Fruits** or Bacciferous Shrubs.

It has been mentioned above that Sweden is very rich in productive and savory berries, which are eaten in their natural state, either with or without milk, or else preserved, and that in such large quantities that they, especially the red bilberry, form an article of export to distant southern countries. Such are the Red Whortleberry (Vaccinum vitis idæa), the Raspberry, the Blackberry (Vaccinum myrtillus), the Strawberry (Fragaria vesca), the Cloudberry (Rubus chamemorus)—which, however, is more plentiful in the north—which occur all over Sweden in the mountainous districts as far as the region of the birch; the Bramble, which belongs mostly to the coast line of the southern parts, and the arctic raspberry "åkerbär" (Rubus arcticus), which represents the high north. In the mountains black and red Currants grow wild, and at last we have the Alpine Currant (Ribes alpinum), the Swedish Cornel (Cornus suecica), the Cranberry (Oxycoccus palustris), the Crowberry (Empetrum nigrum), and others, which, however, are seldom eaten.

1. The *Gooseberry* (Ribes grossularia). The early Swedish green, rough-fruited small gooseberry thrives well as far north as North-bothnia; the red preserve gooseberry is considered the best, of which the following sorts are cultivated: Alicant, Bloodhound, Red Warrington, Rifleman, London, etc.; of the *green*, Dutch Wing and Green Ocean; of the *yellow*, Bird Lime, Cottage Girl, Smiling Beauty, and Early Sulphur; of the *white*, White Champagne, White Manchester, and White Smith.

2. The *Currant* (Ribes), R. rubrum, *red* currant: Red Dutch, Caucasian, Ruby Castle, and Versaille; *white*, White Dutch, generally cultivated, as is also Gaundin fruit blanc, Transparent white, and Imperial à fruit blanc; *black* (R. nigrum), Neapolitan (Black Naples), the best.

3. The *Raspberry* (Rubus idæus), the double-bearing (excepting Belle de Fontenay) and the yellow raspberry (excepting Yellow Antwerp, which is very much cultivated) are less suited for our climate, and of the red the following are the more generally cultivated: Fastollf, Hornet, Paragon, Red Chili, and Victoria.

4. The *Bramble* (R. fruticosus) is unfortunately very little cultivated, and most of the new American varieties will not thrive and ripen in our climate.

5. The *Strawberry* (Fragaria) is cultivated in many varieties as far as southern Norrland, though scarcely on a scale worth mentioning. Of the monthly strawberry, the Gloire de St. Genis-Laval is considered the longest bearing; and of the pineapple strawberry, Doctor Hogg, Louis Marie, Lucas, Mammouth (thrives as far north as Haparanda), Empress Eugenie, Princesse Royal, Sir Harry, White Pineapple, etc.

6. The *Grape* (Vitis), as above mentioned, is trained on espaliers in many places, in Skåne as well as in Gottland, and generally yields a luxuriant ripe fruit. The sorts which are mostly used are Frankenthal, Chasselas blanc and Fontainebleau, Large Syrian and Early Leipzig, and sometimes Precoce de Malingre. Grapes very seldom ripen near Stockholm, and then generally only of the American Vitis labrusca. In hothouses, on the other hand, this fruit is cultivated on a large scale almost everywhere in the south and middle parts of Sweden, and whoever has seen grapes from Öfverås at Göteborg, from Haga at Stockholm, or from Salsta in Uppland (not to mention the princely estates in Skåne and Östergötland), can testify that they are fully comparable to those of the rest of Europe.

7. The *Pineapple* (Ananassa) is cultivated at several large estates, and yields good ripe fruit. The sort which is mostly raised is Old Queen.

3. **Kitchen Vegetables.**

While the ligneous plants, which we cultivate on account of their fruit, are in a greater degree subject to climatic circumstances, the nutritious plants which our gardens yield in large quantities are, with few exceptions, much alike all over the country; and while many of them decrease in size the farther to the north they are cultivated, others gain in flavor, so that few of them are carried there from the southern provinces. Although it is only lately that this kind of culture has been successfully carried northward as far as the Polar circle, yet even in this short time some peculiar varieties have been developed, from the seeds of which plants have been reared in the south with great advantage, and which are hardier and whose fruit ripen sooner.

(A) *Tubers or Esculent Roots.*

1. The *Potato* grows as far north as the Lappland Highlands. Of all the cultivated ground in Sweden 5.6 per cent. was taken up by potatoes in 1873. The average crop is 12,000,000 Swedish tunnor (= 55,000,000 English bushels). Of these, together with other esculent roots, 1½ or 2 million tunnor are used for the distillation of brandy, 2½ million tunnas for domestic animals, and 1½ million tunnas for seed, but the rest for food; by which it is seen that the potato forms a component part of the nourishment of our people.

The potato, of which there are several hundred varieties in the country, has been cultivated in Sweden for over 150 years, during which time several varieties have been produced which are well adapted to the climate, such as the potato of Svartsjölandet, Öland, etc. For cultivation in the open air the American rose potato is considered the best, and for hot-house culture the ash-leaved kidney, or else the long six-weeks' potato, and others.

The potato disease, which has infested our country for nearly three years, but seemed to have disappeared for a few years, appeared again in 1872. (For the Colorado Beetle compare CLASS 620.)

2. The *Turnip* (Brassica Rapa), of which at least 20 to 30 different sorts are cultivated, namely, of the *white* two round and 3 oval (tankards); of the *yellow* three round, green-topped, and four red-topped, and the oval. For culinary purposes the May turnip and others are cultivated as far north as the Highlands, and generally require 2 months for their development.

3. The *Swedish Turnip* or Rutabaga (Brassica Napobrassica) is cultivated as far north as the potato, and requires at Stockholm nearly 4 months to ripen. It yields from 400 to 600 tunnas per tunnland, and occurs in 3 principal varieties: the reddish yellow, the white, and the large grayish-red; the green-topped yellow is considered the best. The turnip-rooted cabbage, or *Kohl-Rabi*, is very little used as a nutritious plant. It occurs in two varieties, the green and violet, and endures a northern climate; yields ripened seeds.

4. The *Radish* (Raphanus sativus) appears in several varieties, which ripen in from 40 to 60 days, of which the black round and long are the best; it is raised as far north as Norrbothen. Among the varieties of the *Little Radish*, the early round red ones, the white and yellow monthly radishes, the oblong high-red, the red with white root ends, and the long red glass radishes, are the best.

5. The *Horse-radish* (Armoracia). The largest quantities and best quality is raised about the town of Enköping, in Uppland.

6. The *Carrot* (Daucus Carota) occurs in many varieties. The long red Altringham is the best, and is cultivated in the gardens. It grows farther north than other varieties. After that the best are the Horn and Brunswick. For hot-beds and early cultivation in the open air, the Danwick and the Early Dutch Carrot. The White Carrot is more seldom cultivated.

7. The *Parsnip* (Pastinaca) thrives, but not very well in Norrland. The round turnip-shaped ones (panais de Metz) are the earliest. They require for their development 80 days.

8. The *Beet* (Beta vulgaris) occurs in two sorts: The *Red* Salad Beet, which is cultivated in numerous varieties as far north as Norrland. The common dark-red, Dutch, and Bassano beet are the best; they ripen in 90 days. Of the Beta vulgaris the small white is cultivated in large

quantities for the manufacture of sugar, and the large round or oblong yellow and red for feeding cattle. The beet does not thrive in the north of Sweden, but about Stockholm it yields sugar in such quantities that it has been considered profitable to establish a sugar-mill. In Skåne and the other southern provinces it is still more productive. Of the *Great White Beet*, Beta Cicla Mangold, or poirée grosse blanche, the large leaves, or midribs and stalks, are often eaten as salad and spinach.

9. The *Hamburgh Parsley* (Apium Petroselinum dissectum), of which the Skirret parsley is the earliest, but will scarcely endure the winters. The Bardowik, on the other hand, is more hardy, but it must be covered with earth in winter.

10–20. The *Skirret* (Sium Sisarum), *Salsafy* (Tragopogon porrifolius), *Scorzonera* (Scorzonera hispanica), *Chicory* (Cichorium intybus), *Jerusalem Artichoke* (Helianthus tuberosus), *Chervil* (Chaerophyllum bulbosum L.), and *Celery* (Apium graveolens) are also cultivated in northern Sweden, whereas *Wood Sorrel* (Oxalis esculenta and lasiandra), *Lamb's Lettuce* (Campanula rapunculus), "*Ardacha*" (Lathyrus tuberosus), and *Cyperus* (Cyperus esculentus), *Arach* (Aracacha esculenta), the "Erdkastanie" earth-chestnut (Bunium bulbocastanum), and the *Groundnut* (Glycine apios) occur only in the southern parts of the country, and even there only occasionally.

21. The *Onion* (Allium). The sorts which commonly occur in Sweden are: 1. The *Red* (A. Cepa), of which the Dutch flat dark-red is the best; then the sulphur-yellow, the onion for frying, called the Madeira or Portugal Onion; and lastly, for pickling, the White Dutch, White Nocera, and the Potato Onion. 2. The *Shallot* (A. oscalonicum), of which the large Danish is the best. 3. The *Leek* (A. porrum), of which the summer sort is probably the best, but does not endure the winter unless protected. Of the Winter Leek, which occurs in several varieties, the pearl onion, which on cutting the stalk forms small onions, is cultivated the most. 4. The *Garlic* (A. satinum) is not used in the preparation of food. 5. The *Winter Onion*, or "Lauch" (A. fistulosom). 6. The *Chive* (A. schoenoprasum). 7. The *Rocambole* (A. scorodoprasum) and the *Bear's Garlic* (A. ursinum) grow wild; the former as far north as the shores of the Arctic Ocean, the two latter only in the middle and southern parts of Sweden. In Norbotten the Chive, the Red Onion, the Leek and Shallot are grown as far north as the Highlands.

22. *Asparagus* (Asparagus officinalis) grows wild in several parts of Sweden, and 3 or 4 sorts (of which the most noteworthy are the Giant, Erfurt, Darmstadt, Grayson's Giant, and the Sutton's true Giant Asparagus) are cultivated for food, but scarcely beyond the middle of Sweden, whereas as ornamental plants as far as Torneå.

(B) *Folious Plants.*

23. The *Cabbage* (Brassica oleracea) thrives in northern Norrland.

(a) The *White Cabbage* is mostly propagated from Swedish seed that produces the so-called Swedish flat-headed cabbage, which in numerous varieties appears in the different districts of the country, and is cultivated as far north as Norrland, although there, in the northern parts, it often fails, and hence it is mostly imported from the south, where it ripens in 3 months, although it is not gathered until the cold sets in.

The *Red Cabbage*, or *Red Hearting Cabbage*, is a variety which, however, is less common, and the *Pointed*, or *Sugar-Loaf Cabbage*, of many kinds, which are cultivated on account of their earliness.

(b) The *Savoy*, or *Crisped Cabbage*, of which the Waterloo, the Yellow Curled Blumenthal, and the Chou Marcelin have proved the best, but are very little cultivated.

(c) *Rosettes*, or *Brussels Sprouts*, are so very hardy that they endure the open air and are gathered even in winter.

(d) The *Winter Cabbage*, *Borecole*, *Greens*, or *Green Kail*, and *Red Cabbage* (B. sabellica), vary very much with regard to the color of the leaves.

This sort, of which the low green or red curled is considered best, is on account of its hardiness of great importance in the high North. Special sorts are the Plumage or Feather Cabbage and the Palmtree Cabbage, which are mostly cultivated as ornamental plants; the Giant, or Cow Cabbage, which is used for feeding. All these are less hardy than the former.

(e) *Cauliflower*, of which the Early Erfurt Dwarf is the earliest and best. The Amager, and the early and late English Cauliflower, which are cultivated as far north as Torneå, and with us produce very good seed, are also commonly used. A peculiar variety of this is the *Broccoli*, which, however, is seldom cultivated. Less common are the "Schnittkohl" (very hardy) and *China Cabbage*.

24. *Salad* is obtained from the following plants:

(a) Genus *Lactuca*, namely: (1) The *Leaf Salad*, which is made use of in autumn and winter; *Cabbage Salad* (of which the *yellow Stoneheaded* (Steinkopf) is planted early, and the *large yellow Asiatic* later), and the "Bindsalat" (blanched summer salad of L. sativa, which seeds well and is cultivated high up towards the North). (2) The *Perennial Salad* of L. perennis is very early; and (3) The *Asparagus Salad* of L. augustana.

(b) Genus *Cichorium*, namely: *Endive* of C. endivia, among the numerous forms of which the Large Escurial, the Large Curled leaves, the Light Green, and the Moss Endive are considered the best. The bleached leaves of the C. intybus are also sometimes used.

(c) Genus *Fedia* affords spring salad, Lamb's Lettuce (F. olitoria); little used.

(d) Genus *Taraxacum* produces Lion's-tooth salad (T. officinale); but little used.

For the same purpose the following are likewise cultivated:

Spinach (of Spinacea), partly *Prickly-seeded*, partly *Smooth-seeded*, of which the Gaudry Spinach is the best variety, and is cultivated in the mountain districts of Lappland. Other sorts are: *New Zealand Spinach* (of Tetragonia), which, however, is seldom used; *Phytolacca esculenta*, *Basella*, *Claytonia*, *Hablitzia*, *Chenopodium*, *Quinoa*, etc. Further, the following, the leaves of which are sometimes used in salad, grow wild: *Chenopodium bonus Henricus* (Wild Spinach), *Water-Cress* (Nasturtium officinale), and *Winter-Cress* (Barbarea vulgaris Br.)

Rhubarb. Several species of the genus Rheum, which all, especially the so-called Queen Victoria and Prince Albert, are successfully cultivated even as far north as the mountain districts of Lappland.

Orach (Atriplex hortensis L.), of which those with yellow leaves are mostly used as culinary plants, and those with red as ornamental plants. They thrive as far north as Norrland.

Dock (Rumex Patientia L.), and likewise the *Common Sorrel* (Rumex acetosa), grow most luxuriantly in the Highlands of Lappland, where there is also Mountain Sorrel (Oxyria).

Parsley (Apium petroselinum) thrives as far northward as the Highlands. The common curled-leaved is the best. Myatt's garnishing and Mitchell's Matchless are the most ornamental.

(C) *Leguminous Plants*.

25. *The Pea* (Pisum sativum). Of the pea there are two principal varieties: The common Field Pea, which is cultivated on a large scale (thus in 1873, for instance, 63,300 Swed. tunnas were planted in the whole kingdom, and 370,000 tunnas reaped), and the Garden Pea. The latter alone requires our attention here. In the middle of Sweden the following sorts are considered the best:

Of the *Sugar Pea*: the Large Sabre and the Early Humble Dutch.

Of the *Early*: Daniel O'Rourke (ripens in Norrbotten in less than 3 months), Early Wonder, Dickson's Favorite, Harrison's Glory, Auvergne, Fairbaird's Surprise, and Laxton's Prolific.

Of the *Later Green*: Scymetar and Caper.

Of the *Later White*: Waterloo, Victoria, Thurston's Peliance; and

Of the *Wrinkled Marrow:* Champion of England, British Queen, Knights, White and Green Mammoth, etc., are cultivated as far as the Lappland Mountains, especially a middle-sized sort with succulent and savory small pods, which is also, under the name of "the Norbotten Sugar Pea," successfully planted farther south, where it has proved very hardy, early, and productive.

26. The *Lentil* (Ervum Lens), the *Chick Pea* (Cicer aristinum), and the *Winged Pea* (Tetragonolobus), are more seldom cultivated, the last-mentioned occasionally as ornamental plants.

27. The *Kidney Bean* (Phaseolus). (a) The *Common Kidney Bean*, or Runner (Ph. vulgaris L.) Among the most common in this country are the Common Black (from Swedish seed) the Large Kidney Bean, the Algerin Large Black, and the Roman Wax-Bean, a variety of which is the *Early Dutch*, or *Very Earliest Dwarf*. (b) The *Scarlet Runner* (Ph. multiflorus Lam.); and (c) The *Dwarf* (Ph. nanus L.), of which the Common Brown is the best known; then the Early Yellow, Flageolet, Eagle and Negro. In general, beans do not thrive well in Norrland.

28. The broad bean (Vicia faba L.) is likewise represented by many varieties, and also the Windsor and Mazagan. They are cultivated as far as the mountain districts of Lappland, and produce good crops.

(D) *Vegetables from various Plants.*

29. The *Cucumber Tribe* forms three species:

(a) The *Cucumber* (Cucumis sativus). In general most of the green sorts are suited for cultivation in the open air, and especially the Westerås Cucumber (which has received its name from the town of Westerås, in Westmanland, where its culture is very old and carried on on a very large scale for pickling), the Russian and Early Grape, and also the Common Early Green and White Snake, and the Early White Dutch. In hot-beds all the sorts can be cultivated; the most common are White Snake, White and Green Non Plus Ultra, Man of Kent, Cuthill's Black Spine, White West Indian, White Astracan, Arnstadt Green and White Giant Snake, etc. In hot-beds the early sorts give a good result even in Norrland.

(b) The *Melon* (Cucumis melo L.) is with us, at least in the middle of Sweden, seldom cultivated excepting in hot-beds, and for that purpose any sort can be used. The *Watermelon* (Cucurbita citrullus L.) frequently occurs.

(c) The *Gourd* (Cucurbita pepo L.) is mostly reared on account of its multifariously varying and often wonderful form; as food (even for cattle) occurs: the Succada (Vegetable Marrow) and Custard Squash, and other varieties, which often attain an enormous size and a weight of 20 kilogrammes. They produce crops as far north as the middle of Norrland.

30. The *Artichoke* (Cynara scolymus L.), of which the Large Violet, or Red English, and Large Brittany are considered the best, and are successfully cultivated as far north as the middle of Sweden, and bear flowers which in size and flavor often excel the foreign ones. The Spanish Cardu (Cynara cardunculus) does not endure our winter, but it is nevertheless grown, and its blanched leaf-stalks are used.

31. *Mustard* (Sinapis). Two sorts are grown: the Common Mustard (S. alba) and Black Mustard (S. nigra), but mostly only at small farms. *Spanish Pepper* (Capsicum annum L.) generally occurs only as an ornamental plant, whereas of late the cultivation and use of the *Tomato* (Lycopersicum esculentum Mill.) has increased.

(E) *Aromatic Plants.*

32. The following plants, chiefly used for the seasoning of food, are cultivated in most parts of Sweden, and those marked with a (*) likewise in the north: *Sweet Marjoram** (Origanum majorana L.) and *Winter Marjoram* (O. majoranoides), *Thyme** (Thymus vulgaris), (Cerifolium sativum), *Spanish Chervil* (Myrrhis odorata Sc.), *Anise* (Pimpinella anisum L.), *Sweet Basil* (Ocymum basilicum L.), *Dill* (Anethum graveolens L.), *Tarragon* (Artemisia dracunculus), *Fennel* (Anethum fœniculum L.), *Hyssop** (Hyssopus officina-

lis), *Coriander* (Coriandrum sativum L.), *Cress* (Lepidium sativum L.), *Indian Cress** (Tropæolum majus L.), *Caraway* (Carum carvi), *Summer Savory** (Satureja hortensis L. and S. montana L.), *Lavender** (Lavandula Spica), *Balm* (Melissa officinalis L.), *Spearmint* (Mentha viridis), *Burnet* (Poterium sanguisorba L.), *Sage* (Salvia officinalis L.), *Rue* (Ruta graveoleus L.)

(F) *Technical Plants.*

33. *Hops* (Humulus lupulus). The hop has probably been cultivated in Sweden from the earliest times, for it is mentioned in the laws in the beginning of the fourteenth century; at present it occurs wild in abundance even in Norrland. Owing to the extensive manufacture of beer the cultivation of the hop has of late years increased very much, especially the foreign varieties, and it is successfully cultivated even in Norrland at from 6 to 8 Swedish miles from the coast.

34. *Hemp* (Cannabis sativa) is cultivated in Norrland as far as the common rye boundary, though nowhere in large quantities. C. gigantea is used as ornamental plants.

35. *Flax* (Linum usitatissimum) is likewise a plant that seems to have been cultivated in the earliest ages. In Norrland, the provinces Ångermanland and Helsingland are especially known by their linen industry, which is dependent upon the cultivation of flax; and likewise certain parts of Småland and Westergötland. The land devoted to the raising of plants for spinning amounted in 1873 to about 30,000 tunnlands, which produced a return of 4,000,000 kilogrammes spinning material.

36. *Rape* occurs with us in 2 species: the *Cole Rape* (Brassica napus oleifera) and *Turnip Rape* (Brassica rapa oleifera, rapeseed). The culture of the former is most considerable in Skåne and in Gottland; the latter thrives as far north as the basin of Lake Mälar.

37. *Tobacco.* Of this plant, *Nicotiana tabacum*, and the variety Amerfort, *Nicotiana macrophylla*, and var. Gaundie, and, most commonly, *Nicotiana rustica*, are cultivated, generally in the neighborhood of towns, where manure and hands for gathering the leaves are easily obtained; however, this culture scarcely reaches beyond the middle of Sweden. At Åhus, in the Län of Kristianstad, where the culture of tobacco is said to be the oldest (since the middle of the eighteenth century), the production in ordinary years amounts to 170,000 kilogrammes, and in the neighborhood of Stockholm it is somewhat larger.

WOMAN'S WORK.

(By the Hon. Mrs. Rosalie Olivecrona.)

During the last twenty or thirty years an earnest movement, aiming to extend woman's sphere of action and knowledge, has been manifested throughout all civilized countries Nor has this movement been unknown in Sweden, but has steadily progressed. The best evidences thereof are, on the one hand, the many educational institutions, which during the last twenty years have been established for, or made accessible to the female sex, in order to give it the advantage of a more thorough and systematic Education. On the other hand, we perceive an increased willingness, not only on the part of private persons but also on that of state authorities, to admit women to trades and offices.

With regard to what has been done in order to promote female education, a list of the schools and educational establishments which are open to women, will, undoubtedly, give the best illustration.

(1.) *The Royal Seminary in Stockholm for the training of female teachers in the high branches of education*, established 1861. The number of teachers is 18, of pupils 65. Two hundred and eighty-eight pupils have gone through the Seminary, of which two hundred and three have received diplomas as teachers. The course embraces three years, and the instruction is free. The branches taught are :

(*a*) *Obligatory:* Religion, History of the Church, Swedish language, comprehending Northern mythology and Icelandic, French, German and English languages, History, Geography, Natural Philosophy, Hygiene, Mathematics, Pedagogy, Singing, Drawing, Gymnastics.

(*b*) *Optional:* Botany, Zoology, Chemistry, Physics, Physiology, Geometry, Algebra and French, German and English conversational excercises.

Last year stipends were distributed to 13 pupils.

(2.) *The Royal Normal School for Girls*, being at the same time a school of practice for the pupils of the Seminary, established 1864. The number of teachers is 23, scholars for the school year (1874–1875), 271. Branches of instructions: Religion, Swedish, French, German and English languages, History, Geography, Natural Philosophy, Arithmetic, Geometry, Object-Lessons, Writing, Singing, Drawing, Gymnastics, Needle-work.

(3.) *Higher Schools for Girls*, based on the same principles and with mostly the same subjects of instruction as the Normal School, there are further:

(*a*) In Stockholm, five private schools, the oldest established 1831, the youngest dating from 1870, with an aggregate number of 117 teachers and upwards of 800 pupils. To one of these has been added since 1870, three upper classes, with the purpose of preparing the scholars for entering the University. Additional studies for these classes are: Latin, Algebra, Physics, Chemistry, Philosophical Propedeutics. Six young ladies have already passed this examination with great credit, two of them were also examined in Greek. By a letter patent of October 16th, 1874, this school has obtained dimissory right to the University, for five years.

(*b*) In Uppsala three, the oldest established 1849, the youngest 1870, with an aggregate number of 81 teachers and 366 scholars.

(*c*) In Göteborg four, with 65 teachers and 531 scholars.

(*d*) In all provincial towns of any importance, except a few among the most northern. The oldest date from 1847, but the greater number from 1860–70. Many of these schools have been established by lady teachers, who have received their education at the Royal Seminary.

In none of these schools is the instruction gratuitous. At the Diet of 1873, the Government asked for a grant in order to establish higher schools for girls in four provincial towns. This was to be the first step towards procuring to the female sex, the advantage of almost gratuitous instruction which has long been enjoyed by the male sex. The Diet rejected the royal proposition, but granted a yearly allowance of 30,000 Kr., to the support of already existing female schools. In 1875 eleven schools received appropriations out of this sum.

(4.) *Classes for the Higher Education of Women*, established 1865 by Miss JENNY ROSSANDER. The lessons are given by way of lectures, and comprise the following subjects: Swedish and French languages, Swedish Literature, Swedish and Universal History, Esthetics, Archæology, Geography, Natural Philosophy, Geometry, Arithmetic, Algebra, which are all optional. The number of teachers is at present three male and five female, with 43 scholars, besides 45 who are entered as auditors.

(5.) *The Royal Academy of Music or Conservatory*, where female pupils have been admitted since 1854. The number of teachers is 20, of whom 3 are females. Subjects of instructions are.

Harmony, Composition, History and Esthetics of Music, Singing, playing of Organ, Piano, Violin, Violoncello, Double-bass and Wind-instruments, Italian language and Declamation. The instruction is free.

The greatest number of female pupils during one year was 157; last term (the autumn 1875) they numbered 72. Examination as organist, comprehending Harmony, Singing, playing of Organ and Piano, has been passed by 66 females. Examination as Director of Music, comprehending Harmony, Counterpoint, History and Esthetics of Music, Instrumentation, Singing, playing of Piano, Violin and Violoncello has been passed by one lady, who also received the highest testimonial as Organist.

(6.) *The Royal Academy of Fine Arts* was opened to lady pupils in 1864, though with some restriction as to the studies, which for ladies comprehend:

Drawing, Painting, Anatomy and Perspective. The instruction is free.

The number of female pupils is limited to 25 and consequently there are always many competitors for the vacant places.

(7.) *The Industrial School* in Stockholm. Instruction in the branches mentioned below has been imparted to females since 1854, viz: Drawing, Painting, Modelling in clay, wax and parian, Lithography, Xylography, Chalcography, Perspective, Calligraphy, Book-keeping, Lacquering, Arithmetic, Geometry, Swedish, French, German and English languages. The instruction is almost gratuitous, except for languages.* The number of Students in 1875, was seven hundred and eighty-eight female pupils, among whom one hundred and sixty were engaged in technical pursuits. The same year there were 47 female competitors for prizes, ten of whom succeeded.

(8.) *The Telegraphic School*, established 1873 in Stockholm, by the telegraphic board of administration with a view to give females instruction in subjects required for competency as telegraph operators. For admission to the school a preliminary examination must be passed. It comprises: Arithmetic, History, Geography, Swedish, French, German and English languages. The course of instruction is free, and embraces three months. The branches taught are: Physics, Telegraphy, Art of Telegraphing, Calligraphy, Regulations. The present number of teachers is six, of pupils fifty-nine.

(9.) *The Royal Central Gymnastic Institute*, where ladies are trained as teachers of gymnastics. Subjects of instruction are: (*a*) *Theoretical:* Anatomy, Physiology, Hygiene, Pathology, Gymnastics. (*b*) *Practical:* Exercises in pedagogical and medical gymnastics and their application. Since 1820 female teachers of gymnastics have been engaged at the Institute. In 1875 five female pupils passed their examination. The instruction is free.

(10.) *Lying-in Hospital for instruction in Midwifery*. Such are to be found in Stockholm,

*The school-fee is limited to 50 öre per month, with an addition of 50 öre a week (3 hours) for each language.

Göteborg and Lund, where gratuitous instruction is imparted in this branch of medical science, together with cupping, bleeding, vaccination, and the nursing and rearing of infants. The course is annual with some additional time for those, who wish to be allowed the use of obstetrical instruments, which is generally the case. This privilege was granted to the Swedish midwife as early as 1829, though not without a strong opposition. Experience has, however, shown that this was a proper course, and a Finland physician attributes the small percentage of deaths among the Swedish child-bearing women to this circumstance. We give the following as an illustration of this assertion. In 1860 two hundred and five deliveries with instruments, were performed by midwives—189 with obtuse, 16 with sharp instruments. Of the mothers 200 recovered, of the children 149. In 1869 there were 362, of which 341 with obtuse, 21 with sharp instruments. Of the mothers 347 recovered, of the children 270 were born alive. The course of instruction for midwives has already been established upwards of 200 years in Stockholm. 1760 several reforms and improvements were made in the institution and the instruction made more systematic. The number of pupils at present is 52, of whom 12 receive board and lodging free of expense. In Lund this course of instruction dates from the beginning of the century, and the number of pupils is 15. In Göteborg the institution was not established till 1856, the number of pupils varies from 30 to 40.

In the end of 1875 the number of midwives all over the country was 2,043, of whom 156 practised Stockholm.

(11.) *Seminaries for the training of female teachers for the Primary Schools.* One in Stockholm established 1866, with 12 teachers of whom 6 are female, and 110 pupils, and one in Skara, with 88 pupils, established 1856, and reorganized 1866. Two new ones were established 1875, one in Kalmar, and one in Falun. The instruction is free, and comprises: Religion, Swedish language, Arithmetic, Geometry, History, Geography, Natural Philosophy, Pedagogy, Calligraphy, Singing, Linear Drawing, Gymnastics, Gardening, Swimming.

To these Institutions belong also since 1867 the *Seminaries for the training of teachers for Infant Schools*, and schools of practise.

(12.) *Primary Schools*, scattered all over the country. In 1874 they numbered: Stationary Schools 2,674, Ambulatory Schools 1,149, and Infant Schools 4,298, with an aggregate number of upwards of 2,800 female teachers, and 358,000 female pupils, of whom 4,058 belonged to the community of Stockholm. The subjects taught are: Religion, Swedish language, Arithmetic, History, Geography, Physiology, Object-lessons, Calligraphy, Singing, Gymnastics and Needlework.

(13.) *High Schools for Peasant girls.* The first one of this kind was established 1870, but is already closed. Five others have since been established on the same principles and impart instruction in Religion, Swedish language, History, Geography, Arithmetic, Geometry, Physiology, Natural Philosophy, Calligraphy, Book-keeping, Drawing and Needle-work. These schools are to be considered as a continuation of the Primary school, and their aim is to develop the intellect of the young country women. The experiment is as yet too new and too little tested to admits of a judgment concerning it usefulness.

(14.) *Industrial and Sewing Schools* for poor children are to be found in many towns and even in the country. The children are gratuitously instructed in spinning, weaving, sewing, marking and knitting, in some schools also in crochet and straw work.

(15.) *Schools for the training of Maid Servants.* Such are to be found:

(*a*) In Stockholm, three, viz: 1. *The Murbeck Institution*, established as early as 1747, but not till 1770 fitted for its present object. Three hundred and four girls have been brought up and sent out as servants, places having been provided for them. Forty-four girls are at present accommodated there. The branches taught are the same as in the Primary School, with addition of baking, washing, ironing, spinning, weaving and knitting. 2. *The Malmquist Institution*, which may be said to date from 1852, when Mr. and Mrs. MALMQUIST, actuated by christian charity, took care of eight destitute children. This small beginning has gradually developed into a well-organized institution, still under the supervision of this worthy couple. Altogether 397 girls have received shelter, board and instruction at this institution, among whom, 14 have got situations as teachers, and 146 as servants. Instruction is given in the same branches as in the above mentioned school. In both these institutions children are received at an early age. 3. *The Practical Housekeeping School*, opened 1870, numbers 18 scholars. Twenty-two girls have gone through the course of instruction, which embraces three years, and got situations as servants. Conditions of admittance are: to have attained the age of fifteen, and gone through the Primary School, as the instruction only comprises the practical knowledge necessary for servants.

(*b*) In Göteborg, a *Practical Housekeeping School* established 1865 on the same principles as the last mentioned. The number of scholars is 25. One hundred and three girls have gone through the school, of whom 60 have got situations as servants. To this school belong a laundry and a bakery, by means of which no inconsiderable revenue is obtained. It contributes also to its self-support by receiving school boys as day boarders. A "crèche" where babies are received for the day, giving the maidens opportunity to get experience and insight in the nursing of infants. Similar schools, either established or organizing, are also to be found in many other provincial towns.

(*c*) *Children's Homes*, which also have for their object the training of girls for domestic servants. Among these the one established in Stockholm, 1860, by the Princess Eugenie deserves to be particularly mentioned. In 1868 it was removed to the Isle of Gottland, and is situated in the immediate neighborhood of Fridhem, the summer residence of the princess. The children are received at an early age and get the same instruction as in the Primary Schools, with the addition of needle work and domestic employments.

(16.) *Dairy Schools*, of which there are two public ones, one at the Agricultural Institute of Ultuna and one at Bergquara. At each of them six female pupils are taught in all that belongs to the management of dairies and cattle, and pay for their instruction, board and lodging, by work. Each school receives an annual allowance from the State of 3,000 Kr. Private dairy schools are provided by agricultural societies in two different counties, without support from the government. Besides at thirteen well-managed dairy farms in different parts of the kingdom, instruction in butter and cheese making is given to female pupils engaged by the special committee of the Royal Agricultural Society. Their instruction, which includes a two-years' course, is paid by a yearly allowance from the State, in all of 2,000 Kronor. These pupils are also taught writing, orthography and arithmetic. It is not uncommon in Sweden to have women take the whole care of the dairy cattle on a farm as well as to do the indoor work of the dairy.

(17.) *Sunday and Evening Schools* where poor children, for a couple of hours in the afternoon receive instruction by young ladies, are also to be found all over the country. The branches taught, on Sundays, religion and singing; on week days, writing, reading, spelling, arithmetic, natural philosophy.

(18.) *Mending Schools*, where poor girls are taught by young ladies to mend their clothes neatly and properly.

The Swedish women themselves have been unsparing in their efforts to procure for their sex the means of obtaining useful knowledge and they have in more than one way contributed to earn for it the educational advantage above mentioned. The "*Tidning för Hemmet*," (Home Review) started 1859 by two ladies and still edited by one of them, has always been a warm and energetic advocate for woman's cause. The object of this review has ever been to hold up to woman a high moral and intellectual standard, and to effect through her, many a social improvement. A *Reading Room for Ladies* and a *Circulating Library* were established in Stockholm, 1867, by the editors of the review, with a view not only to diffuse a taste for good reading, but also to put it within the reach of persons with limited means. This review is not the only representative for woman in our periodical literature, but she has also in several other instances made herself known both as editor and contributor. Besides this the Swedish women have taken a prominent part in working the field of literature, and we have a comparatively great number of talented authoresses, among whom none are more worthy of being remembered and honored than Mrs. Lenngren, (born 1754, died 1817) whose poetry is unsurpassed in humor and elegant versification; and Fredrika Bremer, (born 1801, died 1866) known and beloved all over the civilized world. Many translations are also made by women.

Music is cultivated with predilection as is shown in the first place by many far-famed Swedish singers, as for instance, Jenny Lind, Louise Michaëli, (born 1830, died 1875) and Christina Nilsson, and in the second by the prominent place this accomplishment holds in the general education. We have also some female composers and in the department of woman's work at the International Exhibition of Vienna, 1873, there were compositions for the orchestra, violin and piano, evincing natural talent and a good musical education.

The first Swedish lady, who in this century distinguished herself as a painter, was Sophie Adlersparre, (born 1808, died 1862). Many difficulties, against which she had to struggle, have gradually been removed, and the Swedish female artist occupies to-day a respected position. Several female painters, such as Amalia Lindegren, Agnes Börjesson, Josefine Holmlund, Sophia Ribbing, Adelaide Leuhusen are known and respected even beyond their native country.

Sculpture, the noblest and most difficult of the fine arts, is also cultivated by some lady-amateurs, among whom, a member of our royal family, the Princess Eugenie, holds an eminent place.

Mrs. Lea Ahlborn has been engaged since 1853 as medal stamp cutter and engraver at the Royal Mint, in Stockholm and enjoys in this vocation a high reputation.

At the Royal Academy of Science females are often employed to draw and paint Swedish plants for scientific purposes.

Wood carving is executed by female workers with skill and taste. The most eminent among them was Sophia Isberg, (born 1819, died 1875) the daughter of a poor tailor, who early evinced artistical talent in this branch of art. Her workmanship was distinguished for a great variety of ideas, often historical, and for an elaborate execution. She had received prizes at exhibitions in Stockholm, Göteborg, Paris, London and Vienna. Some of our best photographic ateliers are conducted by ladies, and many ladies find employment in this pursuit. Xylography, lithography and engraving are also successfully pursued by females.

At the Archives of Swedish Maps eight females have since 1860 been engaged as assistant designers, besides whom several others obtain temporary employment.

In the *Copying Office* opened 1864, through the exertions of the editors of the Home Review, many ladies find remunerative employment by copying and translating. Even at some of the State Departments females are employed in copying.

The legislative power has not only co-operated with the advocates of the woman's question in increasing for her the opportunities of obtaining instruction, as shown above, but has also been willing to assist her efforts to find new means for self-support—efforts so much the more necessary, as machinery has deprived her of many means of support formerly available to her.

Thus, the rights mentioned below have successively been granted to the Swedish women by the enactment of different laws, viz: 1853 and 1859 to get employment as teachers in the primary schools; 1861, to act as organist and to practise as surgeon and dentist after having produced proofs of competency; 1863, to hold with some restrictions, inferior post and telegraph offices; 1870, admission to the universities after having passed the student's examination, and to the medical profession after having produced requisite proofs of competency.*

The practical results of these grants may be seen by the following statements:

More than 3,000 female teachers are engaged in the public schools and among them several teach drawing and music in boys' schools. Female teachers are also engaged at private schools for boys, especially in the lower classes. Even at schools for the deaf and dumb, the blind and idiots many females are employed as teachers.

As organists, are engaged 2 females.

At telegraph offices: (*a*) regulary employed, 103; (*b*) temporarily employed, 6; (*c*) supernumeraries, 161, =270.

At post offices, 164.

There are two lady dentists, and 3 surgeons in the Kingdom.

In 1867, a course of instruction with a view to train nurses for the sick was opened at the University Hospital, in Uppsala; it is superintended by a lady who was trained for her profession at the Nightingale Institution for the training of Nurses in London. Thirty-eight nurses have received instruction, † and afterwards obtained situations at other hospitals. Two ladies have also gone through the same course of instruction in order to prepare themselves for the office of matron at hospitals.

In the hospital belonging to the *Deaconesses' Institution* ‡ in Stockholm, which accommodates 40 patients, all the attendance is performed by deaconesses with assistance of one physician. Most of the medicine there used is also prepared by them. Deaconesses are much sought for as nurses in families.

During the period of 1871-1875 nine young ladies have passed the student's examination. Of these, however, only two have for any length of time continued their studies at the University of Uppsala. One of them has taken the degree of candidate for the degree of Ph. D., at the Philosophical Faculty and thus gained the right to aspire to the office of assistant teacher at the higher public schools for boys. The other is successfully pursuing her studies as candidate for the degree of M. D., at the Faculty of Medicine.

Even in other respects the State has been willing to satisfy the just and reasonable claims of woman, as may be shown by the following laws: 1845—equality of inheritance for son and daughter was established, and the wife received equal right with the husband to their common property; 1846—woman was granted the right to practise industrial professions or carry on retail business

* Three stipends have already been founded for female students: one of 1,229 Kr. belonging to the University of Uppsala, may be aspired to by female students in general, another of 6,000 Kr. exclusively for female students of medicine, pursuing their studies at the Carolinian Institute, in Stockholm, and a third one of 1,000 Kr., for female students of medicine at the University of Lund.

† This instruction has been provided by the *Society for the aid of the sick and wounded in war*, and the nurses are at the disposal of the Society in case of need. The total number of nurses, trained at different hospitals for the service of the Society, amounts to sixty-six.

‡ This institution, modelled on that of KAISERWERTH, was founded 1851, with very limited resources, its chief object being to train nurses for the sick. Gradually the sphere of its activity was extended by the addition of several other works of charity, such as: a school for poor children, (1852), a home for destitute children (1853), a reformatory for woman, *the Magdalen Home*, (1857), a reformatory school (1862), a school for the training of maid servants (1875). Since 1864 the institution has gained possession of an extensive property in the immediate vicinity of Stockholm, where buildings have been erected to serve its different purposes. In 1872 a chapel was also built upon the premises. The institution numbers at present 110 members, of whom are 64 deaconesses, 28 sisters of probation and 18 novices. Of these 55 serve in the establishment and the rest are engaged at other hospitals, poorhouses, schools, children's homes, orphan asylums, reformatories, etc.

in town or country; 1858—to claim, if she wished, the right of being of age when 25 years old, which restriction was removed in 1863, when she was unconditionally declared of age at 25. In 1864 her rights to trade and industrial pursuits, were enlarged, and in 1872 was adjudicated to a woman of age, full right of disposing of herself in marriage—father's, brother's or kinsman's consent having hertofore been necessary. 1874—a Married Woman's bill was passed by which she was entitled (1) to manage that part of her private property, set aside for her personal use in the marriage contract; (2) to dispose of her own earnings.

Through the exertions of several ladies a Society was established in 1873, the object of which is to secure to married women the right of administering their own property. This society has subscribed a sum of 3,000 Kr. to be awarded as prizes for the best essays on a projected law, which adjudges to married women full right of administering and disposing of her own property, inherited or earned, that it may not be lost by the mismanagement of the husband or seized to pay his debts.

The efforts to find new means of self-support for woman have also met with a favorable co-operation from the public at large. Thus many females have lucrative employment as clerks in private banks, savings banks, life insurance companies, joint stock companies, commercial offices, etc., also, at the railroad offices and stations many women are employed as clerks. There are even instances of ladies being superintendents of branch departments of private banks, and, in one town, the municipal treasurer is a lady.

The admittance of the sex to commercial and industrial pursuits has proved a source of lucrative employment. Thus in 1873, the number of women engaged in trade amounted to 4,381, of whom 2,764 managed their own business, and of women occupied in industrial pursuits to 17,171, of whom 640 were themselves owners of factories and workshops.

Even in the mechanics woman is not wholly without representatives. Some very ingenious machines have been invented by a lady, an apparatus for tuning organs and harmoniums, favourably spoken of by competent judges; and an improved construction of Grover & Baker's sewing machine. Several females work as watchmakers, some independently, others as assistants. Two sisters are successfully carrying on the goldsmith business; female shoemakers, lacemakers, glovers, book-binders, japanners, mother-of-pearl-workers, rope makers, glaziers, hatters, comb makers, painters, turners, upholsterers, bakers, confectioners work on their own account. In many other trades, as for instance tailor's, furrier's, goldwire-drawer's, gold beater's, tinner's, brewer's, potter's, women perform part of the work. Most of the weavers employed in the manufactories are women. In many printing offices women are employed, and there are some exclusively managed by females. In 1874 the number of women engaged in this trade was 282. At the china manufactories, Gustafsberg and Rörstrand, a great deal of the work is performed by women, particularly modeling and enamel-painting. As industrial pursuits, exclusively belonging to the sex, may be mentioned: plain sewing, making of dresses, stays, bandages, artificial flowers and lace, knitting, crochet, netting, embroidery, millinery and hairdressing. Women from Dalarne, one of the northern provinces, make clever gardeners.

Among the efforts made by women to be of service to their own sex, may also be mentioned: *The Governesses Mutual Annuity Fund*, founded by a lady in 1855, in order to secure a small annual income to aged female teachers. Owing to some defects in the organization this institution was about to collapse after scarcely five years existence. It is now reorganized on sounder principles, and the plan for the paying out of the annuities is based on the same system as the one adopted by *The Mutual Annuity Investment Society*. At the age of 55 the share-holders receive an annuity of 9 per cent. on the paid investments, which have increased by the interest being added to the capital, and by the gains derived from the investments of contributors, who have died before the said age. The capital of this Fund amounts to at present 155,358 Kr. The number of share-holders is 218, of whom 99 receive annuities to an amount of 7,236 Kr. The total paid out in annuities since 1860 is 56,-649 Kr. The institution is entirely under female management, the board consisting of nine ladies.

For such productions of female workmanship, which do not generally belong to the industrial market, a sale-room called the *Beehive* was opened in Stockholm 1870, and has proved successful. Similar establishments have also sprung up in several provincial towns. In order to procure employment for poor women, there are not only in the capital, but in every town of any importance. *Ladies Societies* by the means of which such work as spinning, weaving, knitting and sewing is distributed to those who cannot otherwise find employment.

Many benevolent societies and charitable institutions for the relief of suffering humanity, have also been established by ladies. Among them may be mentioned: *Society for the relief of the poor*, founded and presided over by the Queen; *Societies for the Promotion of womanly industry* under the patronage of the Queen Mother; *Lotten Wennberg's* fund for the Destitute*, founded by the late Queen LOUISA; *Friends of Poor Children* under the patronage of Princess EUGENIE. The first idea of the *Patriotic Association* originated with the late Queen LOUISA, who thereby wished to induce the working classes to provide against old age and times of need by making small investments in Insurance Companies. Among charitable institutions may be mentioned: *The Crown Princess Louisa's hospital for sick children*, accommodating about 60 patients;† *The Home for released female prisoners*, founded 1860 by the present Queen with a view of assisting women punished for crime, to reform and redeem their character. One hundred and twenty-four persons of that class have left the institution after having got suitable employment. The *Asylum for Pauvres Honteuses*, established 1862 by the Countess VON SCHWERIN, and endowed by FREDRIKA BREMER, gives a quiet and comfortable home to 48 elderly ladies, most of whom have seen better days.

The corner stone of a building for the same purpose in commemoration of King OSCAR I was laid in 1873, by the Queen Mother, who also defrayed the expenses, on the 50th anniversary of her arrival in Sweden. The building is to be opened during the winter of 1876, and has accommodations for 50 inmates.

The Silent School (for the deaf and dumb) in Stockholm, dating from 1861, and the *Asylum for Idiots*, (the first of its kind in Sweden,) in Sköfde, established 1866, are both founded by women of small means and modest position, but warm hearts, and are at present institutions of considerable importance. There are a great many other associations and institutions in the varied field of philanthrophy, which owe their origin to female charity and energy, but the above mentioned may be considered the most noteworthy.

The domestic industry of the country-women consists chiefly in spinning and weaving for the use of the family. In several provinces, as for instance Ångermanland in the north of Sweden, where the soil is favorable to the cultivation of flax, this industry has however a considerable extent, and the linen there manufactured by hand forms an important article of commerce within the country. Though this fabric as to evenness and colour may be excelled by foreign manufactures, it is considered to wear better. In Wing-

* Miss LOTTEN WENNBERG, (born 1815, died 1864) was during many years a most active and indefatigable friend of the poor in the capital.

† The first fund for this hospital was obtained through a legacy from a medical man. The sum being insufficient to carry out the plan, the executors of the will addressed themselves to the Crown-Princess LOUISA and the ladies of the capital with the happy result that the design of the benevolent testator soon could be realized.

åker, in the middle of Sweden, yarn and textile fabrics of undyed wool are produced for the home-market in no small quantities, and women from that neighbourhood travel about offering their wares for sale. In another of the middle provinces, Westergöland, white and coloured cottons as well as stuffs of cotton and wool are manufactured by hand in the homes of the country-people and this industry is carried out to a great extent. Contractors, generally wealthy peasants, furnish the working materials, pay small wages for the making, and these goods are carried all over the kingdom by pedlars. They meet even in Norway with a ready sale.

Knitting forms also a part of the domestic industry, and the peasant-women knit not only stockings for the use of the family, but even warm and strong jackets for the seafaring men. In some provinces curiously worked and highly ornamented worsted mittens are also made by the women.

Another branch of female industry is lace-making, but it is limited to certain parts of the country. It flourishes mostly in Wadstena (Östergötland) and its vicinity, and derives its origin from old times, when it constituted one of the chief occupations of the sisters of the far famed nunnery of Wadstena, founded by ST. BRIGITTA in the XIVth century. By want of good patterns and proper encouragement this industry had, however, gradually degenerated, till the late Queen LOUISA, the consort of CARL XV, tried to elevate it by distributing new patterns and better thread among the lace-makers.

That her efforts as well as those of others to the same purpose have not been unsuccessful, is shown by the fine specimens of elaborate workmanship which are obtained from Wadstena. Unfortunately, however, this industrial pursuit is still carried on rather unsystematically, so that extensive orders can seldom be executed.

Even in Dalarne, in the north, and in Skåne and Blekinge, in the south of Sweden, lace-making, though of another kind, belongs to the domestic industry, but the lace is only manufactured for the use of the inhabitants themselves, as it is required for their national costumes, which have remained unchanged for centuries. In those few provinces, where national costumes are still worn there is more variety in the domestic industry, and the women are more skilled and display more taste in their workmanship. It is very interesting to observe their carefully executed embroideries of quite a peculiar kind, the tasteful, richly coloured textures, which are used for their costumes and which are manufactured with very imperfect implements. What adds to the interest is, that most of the patterns used for lace, embroidery and textile industry have been handed down from generation to generation for centuries back. Many Dalecarlian women are also skilled in making ornaments of hair, such as chains, bracelets, brooches, &c., which they peddle on foot, not only in Sweden but even in the neighboring countries.

In these parts of Sweden, where the national costumes are still in use, female industry and taste is not only displayed in articles of dress, but even in curiously woven and embroidered carpets, cushions, curtains, etc. On festive occasions the walls of the cottage may be seen decorated with a kind of ancient gobelin tapestry, sometimes representing scenes from the bible, carefully preserved as precious heirlooms of the family.

Even the farthest part of the inhabited north, Lappland, exhibits proofs of female industry. The women make not only all the garments used, which partly consist of a coarse worsted material, partly of the skin of the reindeer, but also the shoes. Moreover, they ornament their costumes with curiously woven, gaudy colored belts and a richly embroidered bib, called "åtså leppa," on which they pride themselves. For embroidering, a kind of wire made of zinc is used, but their common sewing thread is made of the sinews of the reindeer, carefully twisted together.

As the directors of the International Exhibition in Vienna, 1873, wished to see the female industry of the respective countries represented, a committee of Swedish ladies undertook to arrange a section for Woman's Work in the Swedish department at the exhibition. The programme of this committee was to collect specimens of all the different kinds of exhibitable work, performed by Swedish women of all classes of society. In order to form a more correct judgment about the articles sent for that purpose, a preliminary exhibition was held in Stockholm in the spring of the year. Many hitherto little known or observed productions of female domestic industry, especially what regards the peasantry, attracted considerable notice. This gave rise to an association, *Friends of Female Domestic Industry* (Handarbetets vänner) which was organized in the spring of 1874 with a view to promote and develop female industry on the basis of native art. This association, which has met with much sympathy, is endeavoring to save from oblivion ancient patterns and modes of workmanship, and to introduce new ones based upon native art, for which purpose designs from Swedish ornaments and objects of art from mediaval and ancient times have been collected and applied to articles used for the comfort and ornament of home. It encourages also lace-making and textile industry by hand, by means of which are manufactured a kind of carpet rivalling in beauty the renowned Turkish carpets, but differing from them by their peculiar designs derived from ancient objects of native art. It gives employment to a considerable number of women, and has received and executed orders not only for the home-market, but even from Russia, England, Germany and Austria. Among its patronesses are also the present Queen and Queen-mother, and it has received a grant of 1,000 Kr. from the Government. This association has already arranged two exhibitions of female work, with working divisions where lace-making, weaving, &c., have been executed. At the last one, which took place in the spring of 1875, children between 5 and 14 years of age were also invited to take part in a competition for prizes, embracing the following kind of work : plain sewing, knitting, lace-making, weaving, mending; and for boys, wood-carving, chip and basket-work. About 80 children were entered as competitors, and prizes were awarded to 42 of them.

Associations for promoting Domestic Industry. (Hushållningssällskap) exist all over the kingdom and have been very successful in carrying out their object, viz: to promote domestic industry among the country people, male as well as female. They employ many female teachers, who give instruction not only to the children in the primary schools in the country, but also to peasant-women, and this instruction embraces chiefly different kinds of weaving, basket and straw work. Encouraging results of such efforts may be noticed at the annual exhibitions of these associations. The making of straw hats for their own use has long existed as a domestic industry among the country people, but been in a rather backward state till, through the efforts above mentioned, an improved method has been introduced and the taste for this useful pursuit more developed. During the last 15 years one teacher has given instruction in this branch of industry to more than 1,000 pupils varying in age from eight to seventy-three years. In one year orders for 4,000 straw hats were received from Norway by one of the Swedish border-provinces.

COMPARATIVE TABLE OF MEASURES, WEIGHTS AND COINS.

Sweden.	France.	England and North America.
1 fot,	0.296906 mètre,	0.97412 foot.
1 aln,	0.593812 mètre,	0.64941 yard.
1 mil,	10.6886 kilomètres,	6.64171 stat. miles.
1 quadrat ref,	0.088154 hectare,	1.21784 acre.
1 tunnland,	0.49366 hectare,	0.2199 acre.
1 quadrat mil,	114.247 kilomètres carrés,	44.1124 sq. miles.
1 kanna,	2.6173 litres,	0.57606 imp. gallon.
1 kubik fot,	0.02617 mètre cube,	0.92435 cub. foot.
1 tunna,	1.6489 hectolitre,	4.5365 bushels.
1 skålpund (℔),	425.0758 grammes,	0.93713 pound av du pois.
1 centner,	42.50758 kilogrammes,	0.8367 hundred weight.
1 ton,	1 tonneau,	1 ton.
1 krona,	1.39 franc (1 fr.=0.72 kr.)	£0.055 (£1=18.16 kr.) $0.268 gold ($1=3.73 kr.)

SWEDISH CATALOGUE

II.

EXHIBITS.

INTERNATIONAL EXHIBITION, 1876,

PHILADELPHIA.

SWEDISH CATALOGUE

II.

EXHIBITS.

INTERNATIONAL EXHIBITION, 1876.

PHILADELPHIA.

Press of HALLOWELL & COMPANY,
121 South Third Street,
PHILADELPHIA.

CONTENTS.

R. SWEDISH COMMISSION TO THE INTERNATIONAL EXHIBITION.

PRESIDENT,

BERGSTRÖM, P. A.,—*Late Minister of Interior; Governor,*	Stockholm.

VICE PRESIDENT,

TROILIUS, C. O.,—*Director-General of Government Railways,*	Stockholm.

MEMBERS:

DARDEL, F. L., DE,—*Director-General, Board of Public Buildings,*	Stockholm.
DICKSON, CH.,—*M. D.,*	Göteborg.
FOCK, A. H. E., *Baron,—Chief of Board of Controls,*	Stockholm.
SCHOLANDER, F. W.,—*Professor, Academy of Fine Arts,*	Stockholm.
LUNDSTRÖM, C. F.,—*Manufacturer,*	Stockholm.
ELFVING, N. H.,—*U. S. Consul,*	Stockholm.
STENBERG, S., *Professor, Carolinian Medico-Chirurgical Institute,*	Stockholm.
ÅKERMAN, A. R.,—*Professor, School of Mines,*	Stockholm.
BOLINDER, J.,—*Manufacturer,*	Stockholm.
LENNING, J.—*Manufacturer,*	Norrköping.
LUNDSTRÖM, C. L.,—*Manufacturer,*	Göteborg.
BREITHOLTZ, CL. G.,—*Colonel of Artillery,*	Stockholm.
PEYRON, K.,—*Captain in the Navy, Chamberlain,*	Stockholm.
WIDMARK, E.,—*Chief of Board of Public Education,*	Stockholm.
WIDEGREN, H.,—*Superintendent of Fisheries,*	Stockholm.
SIDENBLADH, P. E.,—*Secretary of the Central Bureau of Statistics,*	Stockholm.

SECRETARY,

NORRMAN, C. G. V.,—*Captain of Fortification,*	Stockholm.

RESIDENT COMMISSIONERS IN PHILADELPHIA.

JUHLIN-DANNFELT, C.,—*Commissioner-General,*	Stockholm.
BILDT, CHARLES, *Chamberlain,—Assistant-Commissioner,*	Philadelphia
WESTERGAARD, L.,—*Consul,—Assistant-Commissioner,*	Philadelphia

BERGMAN, G. W.,—*Captain of Artillery,—Special Commissioner, Army Department,* Stockholm.

BRUSEWITZ, E.,—*Engineer,—Special Commissioner, Metallurgical Department,* Stockholm.

HERMELIN, O. *Baron,—Special Commissioner, Fine-Art Department,* Stockholm.

JACOBI, A. E.,—*Engineer,—Special Commissioner, Machinery Dep't,* Stockholm.

MEIJERBERG, C. J.,—*Professor, —Special Commissioner, Educational Department,* Stockholm.

ASSISTANTS.

LINDAHL, J., *Dr. Ph.,—Secretary,* Lund.

HEADDEN, WM. P., *Dr. Ph., Assistant Secretary,* Philadelphia

ISÆUS, M.,—*Architect,* Stockholm.

POSSE, FR.,—*Count,—Superintendent of the Machinery Department,* Stockholm.

SWEDISH MEMBERS OF THE INTERNATIONAL JURY.

Group I, ÅKERMAN, A. R.,—*Professor, School of Mines,* Stockholm.

" II, NORDENSKIÖLD, A. E.,—*Professor, Academy of Science,* Stockholm.

" IX, ARNBERG, CARL, Stockholm.

" XXI, ÅNGSTRÖM, C. A.,—*Professor, Polytechnical Institute,* Stockholm.

" XXVII, DARDEL, F. L., DE,—*President, Academy of Fine Arts, Director-General, Board of Public Buildings,* Stockholm.

" XXVIII, TORELL, O. M., *Professor, Chief of the Geological Survey of Sweden,* Stockholm.

SECRETARY TO THE JUDGES.

HOFFSTEDT, W.,—*Engineer,* Stockholm.

ERRATA AND ADDENDA

Page 1, line 7, read 90 per cent. instead of 9.

" 3, No. **10**, read Cl. 335 instead of 320.

" 4, No. **15**, read Cl. 505 instead of 565.

" 5, No. **19**, read **C. A. Kullgren's Enka,** (*Widow*), and add to "Prev. Aws.:" Vienna, 1873, Medal of Progress.

" 6, No. **23**, read **Stenkolswerks** instead of **Stenkolworks**, and *Höganäs* instead of *Höganas*.

" 6, No. **29**, read Vemdalen instead of Vendalen.

" 16, No. **16**, read Åker instead of Aker.

" 42, *CLASS 250*, add:

Fyrwald, C. J. M. Stockholm.
Military Trimmings.

Morell, S. O. & Co. Stockholm.
Military Equipment.

" 45, No. **171**, read **Malmö** instead of **Mamlö**.

" 47, No. **179**, read Cl. 262 instead of 252.

" 48, No. **187**, read Husquarna instead of Musquarna.

" 50. No. **190**, add to articles exhibited: **Breech-loading Apparatus for eleven and ten inch Guns.**

Page 51, add:

CLASS 278.

Kongl. Krigsministeriets Fältläkare-Kontor. *Royal War Office, Sanitary Department.* Stockholm.
Hospital Carriage.

" 53, No. **219**, read Cl. 224 instead of 210.

" 53, No. **229**, read **Uddeholms** instead of **Udderholms**.

" 79, line 36, read *CLASS 515* instead of 514.

" 82, *CLASS 570*, read **430. Björkman.**

" 82, " read **431. Kristinehamns.**

" 83, *CLASS 573*, add:

Surahammars Bruks Aktiebolag.
Railway Wheels and Axles. (See Cl. III.)

" 83, add:

CLASS 577.

Fagersta Bruk. (See Cl. III.)
Tramway Rails, Street-car Wheels and Axles.

" 86, No. **457**, add to articles exhibited: **Cereals.**

" 86, *CLASS 621*, read **460. Hofmeister** instead of **640.**

" 86, No. **461**, read **Berggren** instead of **Beggren.**

INDEX.

COMPARATIVE TABLE OF WEIGHTS, MEASURES AND COINS.

SWEDISH.	AMERICAN.
1 Fot	=0.97412 foot.
1 Mil	=6.64171 statute miles.
1 Kubikfot	=0.92435 cubic foot.
1 Skålpund	=0.93713 pound avordupois.

1 Krona=100 öre=0.268 dollars gold.

(Compare PART I.)

DEPARTMENT I.

MINING AND METALLURGY.

A.—MINERALS, ORES, BUILDING STONES, AND MINING PRODUCTS.*

CLASS 100.

	Import Duty in United States.	Sweden.
COPPER-ORE, each lb. of fine copper, contained therein, .	9 per cent. of 3 cts. per lb.	free.
IRON-ORE, ...	20 per cent.	free.
NICKEL- and ZINC-ORES, ...	10 per cent.	free.
LEAD-ORE, ...	1½ cts. per lb.	free.
LIMESTONE, ...	20 per cent.	free.

1. Adelswärd, Th. *Baron.* Åtvidaberg.

Copper-ores, with accompanying minerals' from the mines of Bersbo and Grönhög.

(**Metallurgical Products** obtained by the refining processes.—See Cl. 112).

Previous awards: Paris 1855, London 1862, Stockholm 1866, Paris 1867, Copenhagen 1872, Moscow 1872.

The working of these copper mines, which had sunk into neglect, was revived in 1755, but the mines were not put in full operation until 1762, when a company was formed. In 1783, the shares of this company had already been bought up by Baron ADELSWÄRD, and the mines, with the adjoining estates, were turned into entailed estate.

The number of employees in the mines and in works, 1874, were:

	Mining.	Smelting works.	Total.
Men, . . .	148	106	254
Old men, . .	13	27	40
Young men over 17,	113	23	136
Boys under 17, .	...	45	45
Woman and children, ore-assorting,			280
" " dross-picking,			89
Total employees, ...			844

The power required for the mining is supplied by two stationary steam-engines of 15 H. P. each, and 2 steam-engines of 10 and 12 H. P. respectively.

For the smelting-works the necessary power is supplied by water-engines of about 50 H. P.

The production during 1874 was 375 tons of refined copper. The raw material used was 9,469 tons of ore, which was melted with dross from former meltings as an alloy.

The refuse consisted of zincic oxide partly in form of powder, partly deposited on the walls of the furnaces, and was sent to Germany as a zinc-ore.

The largest part of the products were exported to Germany via Lubeck and Stettin.

There are established for the benefit of the operatives, savings-funds, pension-fund, schools, parish-library, and bath-houses. There is a co-operative society, of which the workmen are members. They are also furnished with free medical attendance and free medicines in case of sickness.

2. Aktiebolaget Bofors-Gullspång. *Bofors-Gullspång Co. Limited;* by P. Lagerhjelm. Bofors.

Iron-ores. (See Cl. 111).

3. Berg, Axel. Wårby, Stockholm.

Iron-ores.

4. Berg, Gottfried. T. Wårby, Stockholm.

Nickle-ores from Nätra in Westernorrland and Langtjernberg in Dalarne.

Zinc- and **Lead-ores,** from Nasafjäll.

5. Fagersta Bruk. *Fagersta Iron and Steel Works;* by Chr. Aspelin. Westanfors.

Iron-ores and Limestone. (See Cl. 111).

* A pamphlet containing analyses of Swedish ores is being published by the Swedish Iron-Masters Association, and can be procured at the office of the Swedish Commission.

6. **Collective Exhibits of Jern-Kontoret.*** *The Swedish Iron-Masters Association.* Stockholm.

General Map of the principal Mining Districts in Sweden; **Collection of Minerals,** illustrating the said map; **Maps of several Mines**; **Drawings of Blast-furnaces,** old and new, and of the **Gas-welding furnaces,** mostly used in Sweden.

Iron-Works, partaking in the **Collective Exhibition** of **Jern-Kontoret:**

1. **Avesta-Garpenbergs Aktiebolag.** *Avesta-Garpenberg Co. Lim.* Avesta.

Iron-ores from the mines of Uddevalla in Norberg, Långvik, Knapergrufvan, Gröndal, Rullshytte, Spetal, Kärrgrufvan. (See Cl. 111).

2. **Björneborgs Bruksegare.** *Proprietors of the Björneborg Iron- and Steel-Works;* by O. Nordenfelt. Björneborg.

Iron-ores from Persberg, Sanna, and Hofsta. (See Cl. 111).

3. **Degerfors Aktiebolag.** *Degerfors Co. Lim.;* by Jos. Larson. Degerfors.

Iron-ores from the mines of Persberg, Vikers Striberg, and Dalkarlsberg. (See Cl. 111).

4. **Ekman, Carl.** Finspong.

Iron-ores from the mines of Färola, Nartorp and Stenebo. (See Cl. 111).

5. **Hermansson, C. T.,** *Count.* Ferna, Bernshammar.

Iron-ores from the mines of Marnäs, Hilläng, Drag, Byberg, Gräsberg, Hällsjö, Nyberg, Spetal, and Kolningsberg. (See Cl. 111.)

6. **Hofors' och Hammarby Bruksegare.** *Proprietors of the Hofors & Hammarby Iron-Works;* by H. Petré. Gefle.

Iron-ores from the mines of Malmberg, Gröndal, Penninggrufvan, Nya Kärrgrufvan, Storberg, and Nyäng. (See Cl. 111).

7. **Larsbo-Norns Aktiebolog.** *Larsbo-Norn Co. Lim.;* by H. P. W. Gahn. Kåfalla.

Iron-ores. (See Cl. 111).

8. **Laxå Bruks Aktiebolag.** *Laxå Iron-Works Co. Lim.* Laxå.

Iron-ore. (See Cl. 111).

9. **Lesjöfors Aktiebolag.** *Lesjöfors Iron and Steel Co. Lim.;* by G. Ekman. Långbanshyttan.

Iron-ores from the mines of Persberg, and Långban, among which are samples of crystallized **Magnetic Iron-ore** and **Specular Iron-ore, Hausmannite** and **Limestone.** (See Cl. 111.)

10. **Lindberg, Lars.** Kohlsva.

Iron-ores. (See Cl. 111).

11. **Löfvenskiöld, Salomon.** Nissafors, Jönköping.

Iron-ores. (See Cl. 111).

12. **Ramnäs Bruks Aktiebolag.** *Ramnäs Iron Works Co. Lim.;* by Fabian Tersmeden. Ramnäs.

Iron-ores, from the mines of Norberg, and Meling. (See Cl. 111).

13. **Rettig, C. A.** Kilafors, Gefle.

Iron-ores. (See Cl. 111).

14. **Schisshytte-Molnebo Bruk.** *Schisshytte-Molnebo Iron Works.* Morgongåfva.

Iron-ores, Knebelite, Zinc-ores, and **Galena.** (See Cl. 111).

15. **Stockenström, A. von.** Åker, Mariefred.

Iron-ore. (See Cl. 111).

16. **Stora Kopparbergs Bergslag.** Stockholm.

---

*The *Jernkontoret* is an association, composed of the iron-masters of Sweden, nearly all of whom are members. The object of the Association, is the promotion of the Swedish Iron Industry, which it effects by advancing money to its members, to assist them in extending their works; and by making appropriations for experimentation, and the investigation of new processes and improvements.

The Association meets every third year, in Stockholm, to discuss business matters of common interest, as well as Technical questions. During the interval between the regular meetings of the Association, the management of its business is entrusted to five ordinary, and five extra administrators, who are elected at the regular meetings.

The Association was founded in 1745; its capital accreed from the annual contributions of the iron works is $1,380,-000, gold; its income for 1875 was $67,000, gold, and expenses, $48,000.

Iron-ore from the mines of Wintjern, Skinnaräng, Gräsberg, Tuna-Hästberg. (See Cl. 111.)

17. **Sundström, J. O.** Charlottenberg.

Iron-ore. (See Cl. 111).

18. **The New Gellivara Co. Lim.**; by J. A. Wikström. Luleå.

Iron-ores from different mines of the Gellivara Mountain in Westerbotten. (See Cl. 111.)

19. **Österby & Strömbacka Bruksegare.** *Proprietors of the Österby & Strömbacka Iron Works;* by Baron G. Tamm. Österby, Dannemora.

Iron-ore from the mines of Dannemora. (See Cl. 111).

7. **Larsson, P. M.** Löa, Rällså.

Iron-ore from various mines. (See Cl. 111).

8. **Sandvikens Jernverks Aktiebolag.** *Sandviken Iron Works Co., Lim.* Gefle.

Iron-ores. (See Cl. 111).

9. **Schough, Robert.** Luleå.

Iron-ores from the mines of Luossavara and Killinge, in Norbotten.

Copper-ore from the mine of Huornats, in Norbotten.

10. **Sveriges Geologiska Undersökning.** *The Geological Survey of Sweden.*

Geological Collections. (See Cl 320).

11. **Uddeholms Aktiebolag.** *Uddeholm Co. Lim.:* by E. G. Danielsson. Råda.

Iron-ores from the mines of Taberg, Nordmarken, Finn-mossen, Persberg, and Långban. (See Cl. 111).

CLASS 101.

	Import-Duty in United States.	Sweden.
COAL—Anthracite, ...	free.	free.
" —Bituminous, ...	75 cts. per ton.	free.

12. **Höganäs Stenkols Verks Aktiebolag.** *The Höganäs Coal Mining Co., Lim.* Höganäs.

Samples of Coal.

Profile of the Coal Stratum, natural size.

(**Saltglazed Clay-pipes,** for water-pipes, etc.—See Cl. 206).

(**Fire-bricks. Samples of Fire-clay,** crude, prepared.—See Cl. 207).

(**Flooring** and **Flagging.**—See Cl. 208).

(**Saltglazed Pottery,** for household use.—See Cl. 210).

Prev. Aw.: Malmö, 1857 (silver medal); Agricultural Fair of Skåne, 1861 (silver medal); 11th General Swedish Agricultural Fair (gold medal); Malmö, 1865 (silver medal); Stockholm, 1866 (silver medal); Paris, 1867 (large gold medal and bronze medal); Göteborg, 1871 (silver medal); Copenhagen, 1872 (silver medal).

Agencies have been established in Stockholm, Göteborg, Gefle, Norrköping, Kristianstad, Kristinehamn, Malmö, Ystad, and Copenhagen.

The business of the company embraces mining, and manufacture.

The coal-mining was commenced in 1796 f the manufacture in 1827.

The company employs 750 persons, of which are:

Officers, 10.
Full-grown workmen, 653 } Wages $0.28 to
Boys, 92 } $0.83, gold, per day.
Women, 5, wages $0.18 to $0.20, gold, per day.

The power required is supplied by eleven steam-engines, with 350 H. P.

The production during 1874, consisted of:

Fire-bricks, . .	pieces,	2,227,542
Fire-clays, prepared, .	cub. feet,	92,461
Pottery, . . .	pieces,	144,059
Fire-clay, . . .	cub. feet,	222,669
Coals, ...	" "	1,650,544

The discount at wholesale is from 5 to 10 per cent.

The value of the production amounted—

In 1864, to . . .	gold,	$135,000
In 1869, to	"	131,500
In 1874, to	"	198,000

The government taxes on this last amount were $728, community taxes $4,278 gold.

The raw materials mined in 1874 were:

Coal, ...	cub. feet,	1,169,000
Clay, ...	" "	465,000

The coal-ash mixed with one-seventh part of slacked lime, partly in form of bricks, partly as mortar, is used as material for erecting factories and workmen's-buildings.

312,000 fire-proof stones, and 10,000 cubic feet of clay are annually exported to Denmark, and smaller quantities to Russia and Germany,

The following funds have been established for the benefit of the workmen:

Burial, sick, and widow-funds, amounting to . . .	gold,	$7,500
Savings-bank, deposited by workmen, ...	"	7,750
The Friese-fund for workmen's widows, whose husbands have been injured in the mines,	"	650

For the children of the workmen are established:

Two Common Schools.

Three Primary Schools.

One Industrial School for girls.

Besides these are established: reading-rooms; a library, which is annually increased; water-works at several places in the manufacturing districts, with filtering reservoirs, thus procuring good drinking water; hospital and physician. For the enjoyment and recreation of the workmen a large park is laid out, in which is built a dancing-floor, where a band of twelve persons plays every Sunday afternoon. The company provides a competent teacher for the instruction of this band. All workmen have free dwellings, with garden-plots, and free fuel.

The works constitute a separate parish of 2,433 members, for which the company provides a minister.

15. Samuelson, T. H. Töskefors. Råda.

Turf. (See Cl. 565).

16. Westerlund, A. F. *Engineer*, Nybro. Kalmar.

Turf, from the middle stratum of the Nybro-bog, which can be cut, dried, and used without being mixed with other turf or pressed, which is not the case with the upper and lower strata.

Prev. Aw.: Moscow, 1872 (silver medal, first class); Diplomas for samples of peat at Agricultural Fairs in Sweden.

The factories are situated at Wexiö and Nybro, the former was established in 1874, the latter in 1875. There are employed

At Wexiö, 12 men, 2 women, and 6 children.
At Nybro, 5 " 2 " " 2 "

The peat is ground and pressed at Wexiö by a 10 H. P. steam engine.

The annual production at Nybro amounts to $1,250 gold. The works are about to be increased both in size and number.

CLASS 102.

	Import Duty in United States.	Import Duty in Sweden.
MARBLE, veined, in blocks, . . .	50 cts. per cubic foot, and 20 per cent.	free.
" polished slabs of, not exceeding two inches in thickness, .	25 cts. per superf. foot, and 32 per cent.	free.
" other manufactures of . . .	50 per cent.	free.
OTHER building and monumental stones, . . .	$1.50 per ton.	free.
GRANITE, dressed and polished, . . .	20 per cent.	free.

17. Berg, Gottfr. Wårby, Stockholm.

Works of polished **Porphyry,** from Elfdalen, Dalarne, yellow and light-green **Serpentine,** from Torsåker, Gestrikland.

18. Klintberg, J. W. & Co. Wisby.

Table-slabs of Gottland Marble, rich in fossils and of various colors. **Jewelry of the same material** as broaches, ear-rings, cuff-buttons, studs, shawl-pins, bracelets and paper-weights. **Grindstones of Gottland sandstone** of various sizes. **Collection of fossils** and **samples of Marble.**

Prev. Aw.: Stockholm, 1866, (diploma of honor); Gottland Economical Society, 1869, (silver medal); Moscow, 1872, (silver medal); Vienna, 1873, (two diplomas of merit); Mariestad, 1874, (silver medal); Gottland's Agricultural Society, 1875, (silver medal).

Agents in Stockholm, Göteborg, Lund and Ronneby. Commission to agents 8 or 10 per cent.

The manufactory was established in 1865, and gives employment to twenty-two workmen and eight boys, of whom four are under fifteen years of age; in addition to these, four goldsmiths are employed in setting. The wages are from fifteen to eighty-five cents per day. At present the work is made by hand, but horse-power will soon be applied, which is likely to reduce the prices by 10–20 per cent. The waste is used for glass, soda and lime manufacturing. In 1874 the value of the manufacture amounted to $12,000 gold, and it has for the last five years increased by 50 per cent.; the government taxes are $16.40 gold and the community taxes $56.40 gold. A small quantity is sent to London and Paris; but very little has been sold abroad. Foreign tourists, however, make some small purchases on visiting Wisby.

In Wisby a workman's society with a savings-bank exists, to which some of the workmen belong. The boys attend the schools, and the proximity of the sea furnishes a good opportunity for bathing.

19. Kullgren's C. A., Widow. *Uddevalla.*

Monuments, Columns, Table-tops, Paper-Weights, all made of polished granite.

Prev. Aw.—London, 1851 (bronze medal); Malmö, 1865 (silver medal); Stockholm, 1866 (bronze medal); Wenersborg, 1872 (gold medal); Copenhagen, 1872 (silver medal); Moscow, 1872 (gold medal); Mariestad, 1874 silver medal).

The stone-cutting works were established in 1844, the polishing works in 1871.

In the works are employed 135 men, twelve women, and twenty children under fifteen years of age. Nearly all work paid for by the job at a certain price per piece, and per square foot completed.

The stone-cutting is all done by hand, but in the polishing works a steam-engine of ten H. P. supplies the power required.

The annual production amounts to from 100,000 to 200,000 cwt., and consists mainly of cut granite for the construction of breakwaters, quays, bridges, docks and houses, monuments, columns, pedestals, paving-stones, flaggings, curb-stones, etc. The government taxes on this production are $31.50 gold, and the community taxes $195.25 gold per annum.

The refuse is used for paving-stones, gravel for macadamising, beton-gravel, etc.

The products of the manufacture are mainly exported to Germany, Denmark and England. For the benefit of the operators an obligatory savings-fund, a fund for assistance to the sick and infirm, and a school are established.

20. Nya Marmorbruks Aktiebolaget. *New Marble-works Co. Lim.* Norrköping.

Manufactured articles of Marble.

CLASS 103.

	Import-Duty in United States.	Sweden.
ROMAN CEMENT	20 per cent.	free.

21. Skånska Cement-Aktiebolaget. *Scanian Cement Co. Lim.;* by R. F. Berg. Lomma, Malmö.

Portland Cement in barrels.

(**Bricks** of the company's own manufacture, joined together by cement and loaded for stretching and breaking. See class 206.)

(**Castings** of Cement. See class 208.)

Prev. Aw.—Moscow, 1872 (silver medal); London, 1874 (bronze medal); Malmö, 1875 (silver medal).

Cement-factory and brick-yards at Lomma, six miles north of Malmö. Lime-quarry and lime-kiln at Limhamn, about three miles south of Malmö.

The lime-quarry is very old, was formerly worked by another firm. Brick-yards established by another firm. The cement-factory, established in the fall of 1873 by the present company.

All work done by the job. The number of workmen varies with the different seasons. The maximum is 300 to 400 men; no women employed. Of the employès, ten, at the most, are under fifteen years of age.

The power required is supplied by five steam-engines, aggregating 150 H. P.

The production in 1874 consisted of

Portland Cement, . . .	64,000 cub. feet.
Sundry Brick Manufactures, such as building, roofing-bricks, drain-pipes, etc. .	5,000,000 pieces
Limestone quarried, . . .	610,000 cub. feet.

The value of this production amounted to about $138,900 gold, though it was the first year the cement-manufactory was in operation. The government taxes during the same year were $170 gold, and the community taxes were $439 gold.

The raw materials used in the cement manufacture are clay and wet lime-stone. For fuel, coke, manufactured on the spot from English coal, is used.

The Cement is exported to Norway, Denmark and Russia. The lime-stone to Denmark and Germany.

For the benefit of the workmen a sick-fund and a library have been established, and steps have been taken to encourage the making of deposits in the savings-banks of the neighborhood.

CLASS 104.

	Import-Duty in United States.	Sweden.
FELDSPAR,	20 per cent.	free.
FIRE-CLAY,	$5 per ton.	free.
FIRE-BRICK,	20 per cent.	free.

22. Rörstrands Aktiebolag. *Rörstrand Co. Lim.* Stockholm.

Feldspar. (See class 210.)

23. Höganäs Stenkolworks Bolag. *Höganas Coal-Mining Co.* Höganäs.

Fire-clay ; Fire-brick.

CLASS 105.

	Import-Duty in United States.	Sweden.
GRAPHITE,	free.	free.

24. Berg, Gottfr.. Wårby, Stockholm. **Graphite.**

CLASS 106.

	Import-Duty in United States.	Sweden.
GRINDSTONES, FINISHED,	$2 per ton.	free.
MILLSTONES,	20 per cent.	free.

25. Gottland's Slipstens Bolag. *Gottland Grind-stone Co.* Burgsvik.

Grind-stones.

The company began working in 1873, and 40,000 grind-stones have annually been manufactured, with a value of $16,600 gold. Refuse pieces of the sand-stone are used for grinding marble, etc. Export to Denmark, Finland, Russia and Germany.

26. Karlson, Gust. & Martin. Lugnås.

One Grind-stone for coarser work.

The manufacturing of grind-stones and mill-stones is only carried on as a home-industry. The stones are mostly sold within the country or in the eastern parts of Norway.

27. Berg, Gottfr. Wårby, Stockholm.

Grind-stones, Mill-stones from Wyk, Bohuslän.

CLASS 107.

	Import Duty in United States.	Sweden.
MINERAL WATERS, artificial, in bottles, not containing more than one quart,	3 cts, each bottle & 25 per ct.	free.
PHOSPHATES,	free.	free.

28. Berg, Chr. L. Eriksberg, Stockholm.

Mineral Waters.

29. Berg, Gottfr. Wårby, Stockhom.

Vivianite from Vendalen, Jemtland.

30. Mineralwatten Aktiebolaget. *Mineral Water Co. Lim.* Stockholm.

Mineral Waters.

B.—METALLURGICAL PRODUCTS.

CLASS III.

	Import Duty in United States.	Sweden.
IRON, in bars, ...	35 per cent. of the import price, but not less than 1 ct. per lb. for ordinary sizes, or 1½ cents for extra sizes.	free.
" " pigs, ...	$7 per ton.	free.
" " sheets, ...	$1,25 per bdl.	free.
STEEL, in bars, billets, coils, ingots and sheets, valued at 7 ct., or less per lb., . . .	2½ cts. per lb.	free.
" " above 7, not above 11 cts. per lb., .	3 cts. per lb.	free.
" " above 11 cts. per lb., . . .	3½ ct's per lb.	free.
" In blooms, cast-tires, axles, shafts, and other forgings in the rough, . . .	90 per ct. of 45 per ct.	free.
" In other forms, not otherwise provided for,	90 per ct. of 30 per ct.	free.

31. Aktiebolaget Bofors Gullspång. *The Bofors Gullspång Co., Lim.;* by P. Lagerhjelm. Bofors.

(**Iron-ores.** See Cl. 100).

Pig-iron, Blooms, Bar-iron, Wire-rods and **Iron-plate.**

Prev. Aw. Stockholm, 1866 (honorable mention); Paris, 1867 (honorable mention); Vienna, 1873 (medal of merit).

Agents: Messrs. J. A. KJELLBERG & SÖNER, Göteborg.

The rolling-mill at Bofors was established in 1865. At present mining is carried on in Nora and Karlskoga, mining districts of Örebro Län; refining at Bofors and Björkborn, of the same Län, and also at Gullspång in Westergötland and Wägsjöfors, in Wermland. There are blast furnaces at Qvarnstorp, Lönnhyttan and Granbergsdal.

The works use 500 H. P., and employ 200 workmen.

The production during 1874 was 6,000 tons in bars and rods, and that for 1875 is estimated to 8,500 tons.

An Aid-Society is formed for supporting the sick, and the workmen themselves contribute to its fund according to their wages.

Directors: Messrs. C. O. KJELLBERG, C. F. GEIJÉRSTAM and P. LAGERHJELM, General Manager.

32. Fagersta Bruk. *Fagersta Iron- and Steel-Works;* by Chr. Aspelin. Westanfors.

(**Iron-ores,** raw and roasted. **Lime-stone.** See Cl. 100.)

Pig-iron and **Blast-furnace-slag.** A series of broken nine-inch **Bessemer Steel Ingots** of various temper, with **blooms,** forged from pieces of the same. **Slag** from the converter.

Bessemer Steel, square and round, from ⅝ inch to 5 inches diameter.

Spring-steel from 1½ to 4 inches.

Crank-axles, Shafts and various **forgings for machinery.**

(**Forged Spikes, Nails** and **Nail-rods; Cut Nails** and **Flat-iron** for **Cut Nails,** see Cl. 284.)

(**Saw-blades.**—See Cl. 510.)

(Railway apparatus: **Axles,** among which is one tested by several strokes. **Springs** and **Buffers.** See Cl. 573.)

(**Tram-way rails** and **Angle-steel,** see Cl. 577.)

Plates. Plate-slabs, forged and broken for showing the fracture. **Plate-slabs, rolled** (a **Steam boiler** made from Fagersta-steel, and showing its toughness.

Gunbarrels:

(a.) A series, showing the different stages in the manufacture of Gunbarrels, that are rolled over balls, from punched pieces.

(b.) A Gunbarrel that has been subjected to trials at the gun-factory of Husqvarna.

(c.) Five Gunbarrels, that have been submitted to severe trials at the gun-factory of the Swedish government.

(d.) A series of gunbarrels, showing the different stages in the manufacture of gunbarrels from hammered solid pieces.

Tools for rock-drilling.

Tool-steel. A series of broken ⅛-inch square steel showing, the different fractures on account of different degrees of carbonization.

Steel bars of various temper, welded together and broken to show the fracture.

A series of **Products from the Bessemer converter,** taken out at different periods of the blow, with samples of slag, taken at the same time.

Steel from Fagersta Bessemer works of several degrees of hardness, tested at the testing works of Mr. D. KIRKALDY in London. The whole, forming a very complete series of experiments, made for investigating the strength of the material by tension, elasticity, compression and torsion, etc.

Reports of the results and commentaries, by Mr. KIRKALDY, as well as a *Special Catalogue,* containing chemical analyses of the Fagersta products, and certificates as to the quality, are to be obtained at the office of the Swedish Commission.

The manufacture is carried on at Fagersta, Westanfors and Fliken.

Prev. Aw.: Paris, 1867 (gold medal); Copenhagen, 1872 (silver medal); London, 1873 (medal); Vienna, 1873 (medal of progress).

The Fagersta Iron-works are very old, and the Bessemer process was introduced as early as as 1867, and although the method at that time was not so developed as it is at present, the first "blows" were made with perfect success, on account of the good materials used.

For the iron and steel manufacture are employed about 250 workmen, with wages of from $11 to $34, gold, per month, and 10 boys under 15 years with wages of $4 to $8, gold, per month.

The annual production of Bessemer ingots is about 3,100 tons; all the ingots are manufactured into blooms, slabs, axles, machinery, railway material, springs, tool-steel, plates, sawblades, gunbarrels, spikes, etc.

Besides the pig-iron used for Bessemer, they use about 2,000 tons for making Lancashire iron.

Raw materials used:

10,100	tons of iron-ore.
1,072,000	bushels charcoal.
150,000	cub. ft. of coal.
20,000	" " " coke.

About 300 tons of scraps are obtained annually, that are partly sent to England and partly remelted at the works.

Government taxes, ...	$ 300, gold
Community taxes, ...	$1,300, "

The iron and steel is consumed mostly in Sweden, and the rest sold in Denmark, Norway, Germany, England and in the United States of America.

The works are driven partly by water, of about 750 H. P., and partly by steam engines of 70 H. P.

For the production of pig-iron two blast-furnaces are used, and, for converting the pig-iron into steel, two Bessemer converters, of a capacity of three and one-half tons each.

The steel is made by the direct process, the iron is taken in a ladle from the blast furnace to the converter, and the steel is always blown without addition of spiegeleisen. As the excellent ore used for the Bessemer pig-iron is taken from mines in Norberg, belonging to the works, the mixture of ore is always the same and consequently the quality of the steel is constantly uniform.

The steel used, for a great variety of manufacture, can, by the absolute absence of sulphur, and the extremely small quantity of phosphorus (0.02 per ct.), as well as the high amount of manganese (4 to 5 per ct.), be made of any desirable temper, from the softest (containing 0.10 per ct. of carbon), suitable for plates, wire, etc., to the hardest tool-steel, of 1.00 per cent., and upwards, and the certificates, specified in the special catalogue of the Fagersta exhibition, as well as the account of the very interesting illustrations of the tension, etc., of the material, speaks highly in favor of the production.

33. Gysinge Bruk. *Gysinge Iron-Works.* by G. Benedicks. Gefle.

Pig- and **Bar-Iron.** Brand: 

The manufacture was commenced in 1678. There are seventy men employed in the works.

The power required (200 H. P.) is supplied by water.

The annual production consists of about 1,200 tons bar-iron, with a value of about $160,000, gold. The old Walloon process is used.

The production is exported to England, France and America.

The area of the estate is about 50,000 acres, about 43,600 of which are woodland.

For the benefit of the workmen are established a savings-bank, pension-fund, primary school, common school, industrial school for girls' library, etc.

34. Collective Exhibition of Jern Kontoret. *Swedish Iron-Masters' Association.* Stockholm.

(**Maps, Collection of Minerals, Drawings of Blast-furnaces, etc.** See Cl. 100.)

Iron-works partaking in the **Collective Exhibition** of **Jern Kontoret:**

1. **Ankarsrums Bruk.** *Ankarsrum Iron-Works;* by A. De Maré. Ankarsrum.

One 9.24 inch **cast-iron-shot** with bronze studs.

One **ditto,** broken for showing the fracture.

One 11-inch **chilled cast-iron shot** with copper belts.

One 11-inch **chilled cast-iron shot,** broken to show the fracture.

Chilled cast-iron double-pointed crossing.

Chilled cast-iron single-pointed crossing.

Blooms.

Bar-iron.

Wire-rod.

Swedish wrought-iron for blister steel.

Prev. Aw.: Vienna, 1873, as partaking in the Coll. Exh. of Jern-Kontoret, (Diploma of Honor.)

Prev. Aw.: London, 1862, honorable mention; Stockholm, 1866, first prize; Paris, 1867, bronze medal; Copenhagen, 1872, silver medal; Moscow, 1872, silver medal; Vienna, 1873, medal of progress.

One of the two railway crossings has been used 8½ years in the station of Arvika.

The manufacture of pig-iron commenced 1827, of castings, 1835, and of bar-iron, 1855. In the establishment are employed 625 men and 375 women.

The iron-products are exported to Norway, Denmark, Finland, Russia, England, Germany, France, etc.

2. **Avesta - Garpenbergs Aktiebolag.** *Avesta Garpenberg Co. Lim.* Avesta.

(**Iron-ores** from the mines of Uddevalla in Norberg, Långvik, Knapergrufvan, Gröndal, Rullshytte, Spetal, Kärrgrufvan.—See Cl. 100.)

Pig-iron from Dormsjö blast-furnace.

WS

Blooms of **Steel-iron** from Garpenberg, broken to show the fracture.

AG

Blooms from Avesta, broken to show the fracture.

GD

Steel-iron from Garpenberg.

AG

The pig-iron is made at Avesta, Dormsjö and Fors' blast-furnaces, and the wrought-iron at Avesta, Brattsfors Talbo, Fors and Åsgarn, all these manufactories belonging to the Company.

3. **Björneborgs Bruksegare.** *Proprietors of Björneborg Iron and Steel-Works;* by O. Nordenfelt. Björneborg.

(**Iron-ores** from Persberg, Sanna and Hofsta.—See Class 100).

Pig-iron and **Slag,** from the blast-furnace.

Bessemer-steel ingots.

Steel-bars, showing the fracture.

Prev. Aw.: London, 1862, for Pig-iron, Bar-iron and Steel, of the brand:

London, 1873, at the exhibition in Albert Hall.

Agencies in Göteborg, London and Sheffield.

The manufacture of Bar-iron was commenced 1656, when the works were established; of Pig-iron in 1852, and that of Bessemer-steel in 1874.

In the works, 84 men, and 6 boys under 15 years of age, are employed. The total amount of wages paid them is $47 gold, per day.

The power required for the manufacture of pig-iron, is supplied by steam-engines of 40 H. P., and water-engines of 25 H. P. For the manufacture of Bessemer-steel, water power of 750 H. P., is available. At present, 400 to 500 H. P. only, are employed.

The last years' production consists of over 7,000 tons of pig-iron, and 1,300 tons of Bessemer-steel ingots, the whole having a value of about $204,000 gold.

The raw materials, used for this production were:

Iron-ores, . . 12,238 tons,
Limestone, . . 1,040 "
Charcoal, . . 1,205,000 bushels,

and of the pig-iron produced, 1,720 tons were converted into Bessemer-steel.

The Bessemer-scrap is remelted in a Lancashire hearth, and then drawn into bars.

All the steel is exported to Sheffield.

Government taxes:

on Pig-iron, . . $89.00 gold.
on Bessemer-steel, . 88.00 "

Community taxes:

on Pig-iron, . . $61.00 gold.
on Bessemer-steel, . 58.00 "

Six per cent. of the earnings of the workmen, are deposited in a life annuity insurance-institution.

A common and a primary school are established at the works.

4. **Degerfors Aktiebolag.** *Degerfors Iron-works Company;* by Joseph Larson. Degerfors.

(**Iron-ores.** See Cl. 100.)

Samples of **Pig-iron**:

Blast-furnace slag.

Bar-iron bent so as to show that it is free from cold, and red-shortness.

Boiler-plate, a piece of the same brand, bent cold, and another bent warm.

Wire-rod No. 6 W. G., 700 Swedish feet long, and weighing 78 lbs.

Iron-bars, round and square, of different dimensions:

Angle-iron, 4 by 4 and 3½ by 2½ inches:

Bundles of square and flat **Nail-rods** and **Rivet-iron**:

Samples of broken bars showing the fracture.

Agents: Messrs. A. FRÖDING & Co., Göteborg.

The works were established in 1863, by the Ölsboda Company. The present owners bought the works in 1870, and have constantly extended the same since that time.

Prev. Aw.: Vienna, 1873, as partaking in the collective exhibit of Jernkontoret, Diploma of Honour.

The number of employees are: In the manufacture of iron, 270 men and 40 boys. On buildings, etc., 90 men.

Their wages are: first-class workmen, $275 to $550 gold, per annum; others from $165 to $275 gold; boys from $55 to $100 gold per annum.

At present the power is supplied by water engines of 550 H. P., but through water-works already built, the total available power amounts to at least 1,400 H. P. Besides this, a 4-ton steam-hammer is employed.

In the year of 1874, was made at the works, 4,243 tons of pig-iron, and during the same year were drawn in the rolling mill, from own billets, 3,507 tons, principally wire and nail-rods; from billets made at other forges, 1,434 tons; total, 4,941 tons.

The value of the annual production is about $270,000, gold. The government taxes are about $360, gold, and the community taxes $792 gold.

For the manufacture are constructed one blast-furnace, seven Lancashire-hearths and rolling mills for bar-iron and rods, two puddling-furnaces, steam-hammer, and one train for boiler-plates up to five feet in width.

Most of the bar-ends from the mills are re-rolled, the rest being re-melted with charcoal, and the iron thus produced, is used for special purposes.

Most of the production is exported, principally to America, Germany, England and France.

All the children of the workmen receive instruction at the Company's expense.

The workmen deposit their savings in the savings bank of Kristinehamn, the nearest town. A few of them also have deposits in the Interest and Capital Insurance Association of Stockholm.

A so-called Co-operative Society has been established with a share capital of about $1,400 gold, mainly subscribed for by the workmen themselves. Its main object being to buy the necessities of life at wholesale, and to retail them to members at cost. During last year its sales reached the considerable sum of $29,722 gold.

5. **Carl Ekman.** Finspong.

Materials for **Gun-pig-iron.**

(**Iron-ores** from the mines of Färola, Nartorp and Stenebo, see Cl. 100).

Limestone and calcined ores from the same mines.

Samples of the 1st, 2d and 3d class of **Gun-Pig-Iron** from the blast furnace, and the corresponding **Slag.**

Samples of the 2d, 3d, 4th, 5th, 6th, 7th and 8th class of **Gun-Pig-Iron**, from the re-melting furnace.

Forge Pig-iron, grey, white, and mottled.

Pig-iron for malleable castings, white and grey.

Forged **Blooms** and rough **Bars**, **Iron Rails, Angle Iron**, rolled **Flat-Iron** for cut nails, round, square and flat **Rolled Iron Bars.**

(Two chilled **16 centimeters Shot**, cast from Finspong gun pig-iron, of which one is broken to show the fracture.

One **12 centimeters Shell** and one **16 centimeters Shell.**

Two chilled **24 centimeters Shot**, cast from Finspong gun pig, of which one is broken to show the fracture. See Class 267).

(Chilled **Railway Wagon Wheels**, see Class 573).

Prev. Aws.: First Prizes at the exhibitions of London, Paris, Vienna and Moscow.

The business embraces iron works and machine shops, together with mining, forresting and farming.

Branches: Sten blast-furnace, Latorp forges, Fiskeby estate, and others.

The manufacture was commenced in the seventeenth century.

The employees consist of:

Managers, Engineers, Foreman, and Office-Assistants, . .	39
Regular workmen, . .	650
Variable " . . .	196
Women in the farming, .	20
Boys and girls under 15, . .	30
Total employees ,.	935

The workmen have free lodgings, firewood at a low, fixed price, and wages according to skill.

The 1030 H. P. required, is supplied partly by water, and partly by steam-engines.

The production, during 1874, consisted of:

Pig-iron, . . .	7,917 tons.
Bar- Rod- Hoop- and Shaped-iron, .	4,370 "
Billets, . . .	208 "
Guns and Shots, . .	625 "
Sundry Castings and Machine Parts, (Shafts, Axles, etc.), . .	416 "
Nails and Railway Bolts,	125 "

Planks and Boards 2,000 Standards. and besides Farm Produce.

The value of this production amounted to $555,600 gold, besides the value of the farm produce. The value of the manufactures has doubled within the last 12 years.

The raw materials used in the above production were:

Iron-ores, . .	16,500 tons.
Charcoal, . .	2,538,000 "
Limestone, . .	. 1,650 "
Timbers, . .	60,000 pieces.

The pig-iron, as well as the bar-iron are manufactured with charcoal, the pig-iron for guns and shot is blown with cold blast, and from particular ores, suitable for the purpose.

The products are mostly exported. At Finspong and Latorp are established 2 schools with 3 male teachers, 7 female teachers, and about 270 children. At Sten is established a school with one teacher and about 50 children. The works employ a physician, who resides at Finspong, at which place also a drug-store is maintained at the expense of the proprietor. Workmen with families receive gratuitous treatment in case of sickness. At Finspong is established a hospital with 8 beds, and a "home" for such as have been disabled or have grown infirm, at present 7, and an assistance-fund for sick workmen. The savings-bank of the Län, which has branches in the parishes, is patronized by the workmen.

6. **Hermansson, C. T., von.** *Count.* Ferna.

(**Iron-ores** for the manufacture of Spiegeleisen, from the mines of Marnäs and Hilläng; for the manufacture of rolled bar-iron, from the mines of Drag, Byberg, Gräsberg, Hällsjö, Nyberg, Spetal, and Kolningsberg.—See Cl. 100).

Specimens of **Spiegeleisen** and **Bar-iron.**

Prev. Aw.: Vienna 1873, as partaking in the Collective Exhibition of Jern-Kontoret, Diploma of Honor.

The manufacture was commenced over 200 years ago.

The works are all situated in Westerås Län, at Ferna, Bockhammar, Kedjebo, Trummelsberg, Finnbo, Björnhyttan, Wirsbo, and Bennebo.

The 200 H. P. required for the works is supplied by water, and in case of scarcity, steam-power is employed.

The annual production consists of about 4,000 tons of Bar-iron of the following dimensions:

Square-iron from 5 millim. to 55 millim.

Round-iron from 5 millim. to 55 millim.

Flat-iron from 10 by 2½ millim. to 120 by 25 millim.

The Institutions for the benefit of the workmen are similar to those generally established at such works in Sweden.

7. **Hofors & Hammarby Bruksegare,** *Proprietors of Hofors & Hammarby Ironworks;* by Hj. Petré. Gefle.

(**Iron-ores** from the mines of Malmberg, Gröndal, Penninggrufvan, Nya Kärrgrufvan, Storberg and Nyäng.—See Cl. 100).

Roasted Iron-ore from the same mines.

Pig and **Blast Furnace-slag.**

Blooms.

Iron-bars, forged.

Nailrods, in bundles.

Samples of Iron, bent cold, and others punched red hot, to show that it is free from redshortness.

Prev. Aw.: Vienna, 1873, as partaking in the collective exhib. of Jeru-Kontoret, (Diploma of Honor).

8. **Larsbo-Norns Aktiebolag.** *Larsbo-Norns Company;* by H. P. W. Gahn. Kåfalla.

Iron-ores (See Cl. 100).

Pigi-ron and rolled **Bar-iron.**

Prev. Aw.: Vienna, 1873, as partaking in the collective exhibition of Jern-Kontoret Diploma of Honor.

Agents in Stockholm, Messrs. A. W. FRESTADIUS & Co., and others.

The works embrace: Larsbo-Norns and Wikmanshytte Iron-Works in Dalarne, and Ramnäs Rolling-Mills in Westmanland, besides mines, forests, and farms.

The annual production consists of:

Pig-iron,	6,000 tons.
Rolled Bar-iron,	1,900 "
Forged Bar-iron,	1,400 "
Cast-steel,	100 "

9. **Laxå Bruks Aktiebolag.** *Laxå Iron-Works Co., Lim.* Laxå.

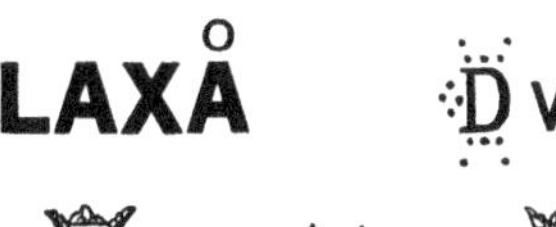

D VC

DB
L

(**Iron-ore.**—See Cl. 100).

Pig-iron, Blooms, and **Bar-iron, broken iron-bars,** showing the fracture, **round iron-bars,** bent into knots and spirals.

Prev. Aw.: Bronze medal, Stockholm 1866; Gold medal, Moscow 1872.

The works, established as early as the 17th century, employ for the manufacture of

pig iron, 30 hands.		
blooms, 50 hands.	}	130 laborers.
wrought iron, 50 hands.		

The water-power .	180 H. P.
The steam-power . .	40 H. P.

During the last years an average of 7,000 tons of iron-ore have been used for producing pig-iron, which, with the addition of 1,700 tons of pig-iron from other furnaces, have been refined into wrought-iron.

10. **Lesjöfors Aktiebolag.** *Lesjöfors Iron and Steel Co. Lim.*; by G. Ekman. Långbanshyttan.

(**Iron-ores** from the mines of Persberg and Långban, among which are crystallized **Magnetite** and **Specular** ore, **Hausmannite** and **Limestone.** See Class 100.)

Pig-Iron and **Blast-Furnace slag.**

Bessemer-Steel Ingots. Brand:

GE

Bessemer-steel Bars of various dimensions. Brand:

EKMAN & CO.,
BESSEMER
CAST STEEL.

(with from 0.75 to 0.80 per ct. of carbon).

One Bar, contaning 0.15 per cent. of carbon.

EKMAN & CO.,
BESSEMER,

One bundle **Wire,** No. 4, W. G.

EKMAN & CO.,
BESSEMER.

containing 0.15 per cent. of carbon. One bundle **Wire,** No. 4. W. G.

EKMAN & CO.

Wire Ropes.

Prev. Aw.: Silver Medals: Stockholm, 1851 and 1856; Paris, 1855 and 1867; Bronze medals: Copenhagen, 1872; Vienna, 1873.

Agents—Messrs. EKMAN & Co., in Göteborg. The company owns Lesjöfors Iron-works with blast-furnace, and Bessemer works, at Långbanshyttan, both in Wermland. The wire manufacture was commenced in 1856, the manufacture of steel by the Siemens-Martins process in 1871, and by the Bessemer process in 1875.

In the different manufactures of the company are employed 190 workmen, of which four are under fifteen years of age. They are mostly paid by the piece, and their wages amount to from eight to twenty-five öre (2½ to 8¼ cents per hour.

In this statement are not included the workmen required for the work in the woods, the lumber business, farming work and mining.

The power required, is at Lesjöfors supplied by motors of 250 H. P., and at Långbanshyttan of 500 H. P.

The manufacture consists of pig and bar-iron and steel made by the Siemens-Martin and Bessemer processes, together with the manufacture of these products into various objects,as wire ropes, nails, etc. The quantity of the production is varying, according to the state of the market, which has especially influenced the produced amount of iron.

The value of the manufacture during 1873 amounted to $200,000 gold, against $97,100 gold in 1868; herein, however, are not included light wire wares and pig-iron.

As an exact book-keeping shows that under present conditions the agriculture in this district, although necessary for other industries, gives only loss, the taxes on real estate and business of the company are charged entirely to the business, and amount to the government to $800 gold per annum, and to the community more than one-half that sum, not counting maintainance of roads, poor-taxes, school-taxes, etc.

The raw materials annually used are about 4,200 tons of iron-ore from Persberg and Långban mines, 550,000 bushels of charcoal, and 4,219 cords of wood.

The Bessemer ingots are taken as hot as possible from the moulds and introduced into a re-heating furnace, where their temperature becomes more uniform, whereupon they are immediately drawn into blooms.

The products are partly consumed in Sweden and partly exported.

For the benefit of the workmen at Lesjöfors are established savings-funds, together with interest insurance-fund, co-operative society,which, from its earnings is allowed to pay two per cent. on the capital paid in, but must use the rest for mutual beneficial purposes; a common school with two graduated male and three female teachers. At Långbanshyttan, a school with one graduated male and two female teachers. Besides, these, are in both places established industrial schools for girls, reading societies with libraries.

It is probable that the manufacture of pig-iron will be about 2,100 tons per annum, from which will be manufactured about 850 tons Bessemer steel, and about 850 tons Lancashire iron and steel of various kinds, together with some Martin steel.

11. **Lindberg Lars.** Kohlsva.

(**Iron ore.**—See Class 100).

Roasted iron-ore, Pig-iron, and **blast furnace-slag, Blooms,** broken to show the fracture; **Rods,** and **Wire.**

Prev. Aw.: Vienna, 1873, as partaking in the collective-exhib. of Jern Kontoret Diploma of Honor.

12. **Löfvenskiöld Salomon.** Nissafors, Jönköping. (See Class 100).

Magnetic iron-ore, Pig-iron, Blast furnace-slag, Billets, Bariron, of different shapes.

Prev. aw. Vienna, 1873, as partaking in the collective exhibiton of Jernkontoret, Diploma of Honor.

The manufacture commenced in 1712. Branch manufactory at Rasjö, in the Län of Jönköping. In the works are employed 3 assistants and 38 workmen, altogether 41 employees, with wages amounting to $4,400 gold, per annum. The necessary power is furnished by water engines of 90 H. P.

The annual production during the last ten years has been about 400 tons bar iron of various dimensions, with a value about $23,600 gold, which sum, during the last few years, has increased about $4,200 gold, owing to the high cost of manufacture. The raw materials were 119,500 bushels of charcoal and 500 tons of pig iron.

The refuse from the manufacture is remelted and sometimes refined.

The annual exports were about 200 tons bar-iron.

13. **Ramnäs Bruks Aktiebolag.** *Ramnäs Iron Works Company Lim.;* by Fabian Tersmeden. Ramnäs.

Iron-Ore from the mines of Norberg and Meling (see Class 100).

Roasted Iron-Ore, from the same mines; **Limestone.**

Pig-iron from the blast-furnaces at Seglingsberg, along with the slag

Blooms, from Ramnäs.

Rolled Iron-Bars.

Prev. aw.: Vienna, 1873, as partaking in the collective exhibition of Jern-Kontoret, Diploma of Honor.

The smelting of the ores is carried on at Seglingsberg and Mattsbo. The Rolling Mills are at Ramnäs, where in 1875, 5,330 tons of iron of different kinds were drawn.

During the same year were produced at Seglingsberg, 2,550 tons of Pig iron, at Mattsbo, 2,100.

14. **Rettig C. A.** Gefle, Kilafors.

(**Iron-ores.**—See Cl. 100).

Pig- and **Bar-Iron.**

Prev. aw.: London, 1851 and 1863; Stockholm, 1866, and Vienna, 1873, as partaking in the collective exhibition of Jern-Kontoret, Diploma of Honor.

The manufacture under the present brands commenced in 1840.

In the works are employed 112 men and 14 boys. The power required is supplied by *water engines* of about 200 H. P., and a steam engine of of 20 H. P.

The annual production is about 1,600 to 2,100 tons of pig and 1,500 tons of bar-iron, for which a tax of $550 gold is paid to the government, and $830 gold to the community.

The raw materials used annually are: 5,000 tons iron ore from the mines of Hammarin and Ramhäll, 1,250 tons from the mines of Bispberg and Norberg. The production is exported to England and America.

For the benefit of old and infirm workmen, a pension fund is established. Four schools for the children of the workmen are maintained by the proprietor.

The brand mostly used by the Kilafors Works, during the last three decades, is

In the manufacture of gray pig-iron a blast, with a temperature of about 392° F., is used, but for white malleable pig-iron, and forging pigs, a blast with a temperature only =158° F. The gray pig iron, which contains about 2 per cent. of manganese has with advantage been used for the Bessemer process, and the white pig iron as material for malleable pig-iron, iron, for blister steel and wire, as well as for steel made by the Siemens-Martins process. The steel- and wire-iron is manufactured by the Lancashire process, and the welding is done in a hearth (not a welding-furnace), invented by the owner of the works.

15. **Schisshytte-Molnebo Bruk,** (*Schisshytte-Molnebo Iron Works*) Morgongåfva.

(**Iron-ores, Knebelite, Zinc-ores, Galena**—see Cl. 100.)

Spiegeleisen of the brand:

W28B

(**Bars of Lead.**—See Cl. 113).

Prev. aw.: London, 1173, medal; Vienna, 1873, bronze medal.

Branch works at Rämen, in Dalarne.

The present firm succeeded ALEX KEILLER & Co., in 1872.

In the works are employed 70 men and 5 boys under 15 years of age.

The power required is supplied by water and steam engines, together 25 H. P.

The production during 1874 consisted of 3,330 tons of the different products, for which the government taxes were $263 gold, and the community taxes $300. For the production of one ton spiegelisen are used:

Iron-ore, . . .	tons	2,03
Limestone, . . .	"	0.18
Coke, . .	bushels	13,80
Charcoal. . . .	"	197

The exports go principally to England and Germany.

16. **Stockenström A. von.** Aker, Mariefred.

(**Iron-ore** and **Lime.**—See Cl. 100.)

White pig iron:

Blast furnace slags.

Prev. aw.: Medals, in London, 1851 and 1862; Paris, 1855 and 1867; Copenhagen, 1872; and Stockholm, 1866. Diploma of Honor, in Vienna, 1873, as partaker in the Coll. Exh. of Jern-Kontoret.

The production of the kind of pig iron exhibited was commenced in 1868.

The power required is supplied by water.

The raw materials used are ores from Skattvång, Bredsjönäs, Utö, and Uddevalla mines.

Limestone from Bredsjönäs and Kalkbro.

The productions are exported to Belgium, France, England, Germany, Russia, Switzerland. There are beneficent institutions, funds, schools, etc., for the workmen.

17. **Stora Kopparbergs Bergslag.** Dalarne. Head-office in Stockholm.

(**Iron-ores** from the mines of Wintjern, Skinnaräng, Gräsberg, Tuna Hästberg.—See Cl. 100).

Roasted Iron-ores, from the same mines.

Pig Iron, made from these ores.

Blast-furnace slag.

Blooms and **Billets,** from different kinds of pig iron, marked:

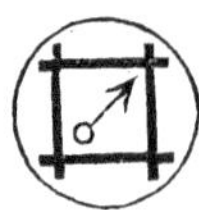

LX

Bar-iron, marked:

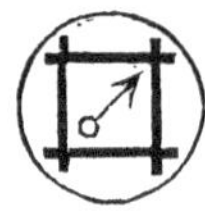

from blooms of the same brand:

Bar-Iron, marked:

from blooms of the brand:

Bar-Iron, marked:

from blooms of the brand:

Bar-Iron, marked:

LX

from blooms of the same brand.

Iron samples with holes, punched in red heat, to show that it is quite free from redshortness.

Prev. Aw.: Bronze-medals in Paris, 1855; London, 1862; Stockholm, 1866; Moscow, 1872. Silver-medal in Copenhagen, 1872; and Diploma of Honor in Vienna, 1873, as partaking in the collective exhibition of Jern-Kontoret.

The iron-works were commenced in 1736.

18. **Sundström, J. O.** Charlottenberg.

(**Iron-ore.**—See Cl. 100).

Pig-iron and **Bar-iron.**

(**Nails.**—See Cl. 284).

Prev. Aw.: Copenhagen, 1872; Vienna, 1873, medal of merit.

The manufacture of bar-iron was commenced in 1863; the manufacture of nails, by the exhibitor's new process, in 1872; and the manufacture of pig-iron in 1873.

In the works, are employed 167 men, with wages of about $1.10, gold, per day, and 17 boys, with wages of about $0.45, gold, per day, or altogether, 184 workmen.

The power required for the operation of the works, is supplied by water-engines of 200 H. P., and steam-engines of 20 H. P.

The production in 1874, consisted of

625 tons of rail-spikes,
1,400 " pine- and oak-spikes,
1,650 " bar-iron,

with a value of $310,000, gold, on which the government taxes were $83, gold, and the community taxes, about $550, gold.

The raw materials used for this production, and for making 4,000 tons of pig-iron, were as follows:

Iron-ore,	6,500 tons.
Charcoal,	1,080,000 bushels.
Coal,	32,000 cub. ft.
Coke,	19,000 "
Turf,	225,000 "
Sawdust	162,000 "

For the manufacture of wrought-iron, Lancashire hearths are used. In the manufacture of bar-iron, welding furnaces for peat and sawdust of LUNDIN'S patent are used, and also a welding furnace for wood and coal of W. WENNSTRÖM'S construction.

In the manufacture of rail-spikes machines of C. ÖSTLUND'S patent are employed; and in the manufacture of pine- and oak-nails, machines of the exhibitor's patent.

The bar-iron is exported to America, France, England, and Norway.

The rail-spikes are sold in Sweden and Norway. The pine- and oak-nails in Sweden, Norway, Finland, and Russia.

In America, the bar-iron is known under the following brands:

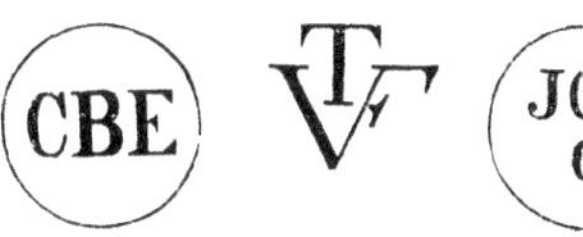

LANCASH
GASWELDED.

For the benefit of the workmen, a savings-bank, a school-house, and a singing-class have been established at the works.

19. **New Gellivara Co. Lim.**; by J. A. Wikström. Luleå.

(**Iron-ores.**—See Cl. 100).

Products therefrom.

(**Nails.**—See Cl. 284).

(**Forest products.**—See Cl. 600).

(**Agricultural products.**—See Cl. 620).

After many years' suspense, the manufacture of pig-iron was taken up again in 1874, and that of bar-iron in 1875.

The whole number of employees was last year 1500 men, with an average fee of $0.55 gold per day. The amount of the production was: 1200 tons pig-iron and castings, 9,200 standards, deals and battens. The whole production is exported to England and France. Taxes paid to the Government amount to about $2,200 gold, and to the community, about $4,500 gold.

20. **Österby & Strömbacka Bruksegare.** *Proprietors of Österby & Strömbacka Iron Works;* by *Baron* G. Tamm. Dannemora.

(**Iron-ores** from the mines of Dannemora.—See Class 100.)

Roasted-ores from the same mines.

Pig-iron from the same ore.

Slag from the blast-furnace.

Cast steel ingots, from Österby. Brand:

DANNEMORA

Bessemer Steel-ingots from Iggesund:

Bessemer Steel-bars.

Crucible Cast Steel-ingots from blister steel.

Iron-bars from Österby.

35. **Larsson P. M.** Löa, Rällså.

(20 specimens of **iron-ore** from 7 different mines; the Stråssa ore being mostly used for making pig iron.—See Cl. 100.)

5 **pigs of cast-iron,** 2 of which are cast in moulds, 2 in open sand.

N6R

The old blast furnace erected at a very remote period was enlarged in 1872.

Water power 30 H. P.

In making the pig-iron, ores from 6 mines are mixed in the following proportions:

Stråssa	ore	50 per ct.
Blanka	"	15 "
Ingelshytte,	"	15 "
Grängsten	"	10 "
Smålberg	"	5 "
Damgrufva	"	5 "
		100 per ct.

36. **Motala Mekaniska Verkstads Aktiebolag.** *Motala Mechanical Co. Lim.;* by E. Unge. Motala.

Iron and **steel** in **bars, plates** and **sheets,** with **products of working.**

37. **Sandvikens Jernwerks Aktiebolag.** *Sandvikens Iron-Works Co. Lim.* Gefle.

(**Iron-ores.**—See Class 100.)

Pig-iron, Blast-furnace slag.

Bessemer steel ingots.

Piston rod for a steam hammer.

Crank for a steamer made from Bessemer steel.

Shaft for a steamer, made from Bessemer steel.

Locomotive Crank made from Bessemer steel.

Railway wagon wheels, made from Bessemer steel.

Tires and **Axles,** made from Bessemer steel.

Steel, in bars of various dimensions, made from Bessemer steel.

Prev. aw.: First prizes at Göteborg, 1860; London, 1862; Stockholm, 1867: and Moscow, 1872.

The director of the works, Mr. FR. GÖRANSSON, was rewarded with the large gold medal of the Swedish Iron-Masters-Association (Jernkontoret), in 1865.

Agencies in Stockholm, Christiania, Copenhagen, St. Petersburg, Moscow, Düsseldorf, Paris, London, and Sheffield.

The manufacture of Bessemer steel was commenced in November 1857, at the Edske blast furnace, and the Högbo iron-works, and was in 1873 concentrated at the iron-works then erected at Sandviken.

In the works are employed 700 men, besides forest workmen and miners.

In the Bessemer steel-blowing, which is carried on with 2 convertors, are employed upwards of 600 H. P., of which about half is steam and half water-power. Steam engines are besides available to increase this power, in case of necessity, with about 150 H. P. In the tire mill and the smaller rolling mills, water or steam-power, about 185 H. P. is employed.

For the Blowing-engines for the blast-furnaces, ventilators, cranes, and other accessory machines, steam and water of about 150 H. P. are employed. For the forging are employed the following steam hammers:

1	steam hammer of	15 tons weight.
1	" " "	5 " "
2	" " "	2½ " "
2	" " "	1 " "
2	" " "	4 cent'rs "

The works can produce per annum:

about 4,200 tons of tires.
" 1,700 " " axles and machine parts.
" 1.000 " " steel in bars for tools, etc.

The value of the manufactures during 1874 amounted to nearly $500,000 gold, and the average value for the last five years has been $430,500 gold. The raw materials used in 1874, consisted of:

Ironore, principally from Bispberg, Norberg, Långvik, and Nyäng mines,	9,750 tons.
Limestone, . .	1,417 tons.
Charcoal, . .	1,300,000 bushels.
and for welding furnaces and steam boilers,	
Coal, . . .	10,000 tons.
Wood, . . .	1100 cords.

By the use of excellent ores, mixed in such proportions, as experience and careful observation have indicated, and melting exclusively with charcoal, a quality comparable with the best cast steel, is obtained, though with a price of production which is slightly higher than by the common Bessemer process.

The largest part of the refuse is remelted in the blast-furnaces.

Over half of the manufacture is exported to Norway, Denmark, Russia, Germany, France, England.

For the benefit of the workmen, are established at the works:

A branch of the Gefle savings-bank.

A sick and burial fund.

A school with 4 classes, managed by 1 male and 3 female teachers; and a library.

An industrial school for girls, with one female teacher.

A society of the Workmen's Musical Society under whose auspices evening schools have been opened and public lectures occasionally given.

From the beginning of the manufacture, the confidence in its products has been constantly increasing, and orders have been received to such a degree as to necessitate yearly extensions of the works.

38. Surahammars Bruks Aktiebolag. *Surahammars Iron Co., Lim.*; by C. Alexanderson. Westerås.

Railway-axle with **two wheels.**

Mould for spoke of a wheel.

Iron puddled with wood as fuel.

Round-rolled puddled steel and iron.

Iron, puddled by gas.

Wheelcentre forged from one piece.

Wheelcentre outturned at the nave.

Crooked **rail-way wheel-axle** notched, and then cut into two pieces.

Tap cut out of a railway axle.

Old railway axle and **wheels** with **tires** of puddled steel.

Special catalogues are to be obtained at the office of the Swedish Commission.

Prev. Aw.: London, 1862, medal; Paris, 1867, bronze and silver medal; Copenhagen, 1872, silver medal; Moscow, 1872, the great gold medal.

The pig is converted into wrought iron by puddling, the only fuel used being either wood or turf. Coal is never used.

The annual production is about:

Plate, ...	1000 tons.
Railway, wagon wheels and axles,	1100 "

and a small quantity of common bars.

The raw material used a year is about

Pig iron, ...	2100 tons.
Blooms, ...	300 "

About 500 tons tires are annually bought for the wheel manufactory.

The government taxes amount to about $150 in gold, community taxes $300 gold.

The value of the annual production is about $240,000 gold and it has increased by $125,000 gold since the year of 1868.

The products are principally exported to Russia and Finland, but partly also to England, France, and Germany.

In the works are employed 167 laborers and 31 boys.

All the children of the workmen receive instruction at the expense of the company or the parish. The company has erected two school houses; one of them is used as a meeting place by the workmen's union.

39. Uddeholms Aktiebolag. *Uddeholm Co. Lim.;* by E. G. Danielsson, Uddeholm, Råda.

(**Iron-ores** from the mines of Taberg, in Wermland, Nordmarken, Finnmossen, Persberg, and Långban.—See Cl. 100).

Roasted Iron-ores, from the same mines, and **Limestone.**

Pig-iron, from these ores; **Slag** from the blast-furnace.

Bessemer Steel-ingots, for plate and hard steel; and **Slag** from the converter.

Siemen-Martin Steel-ingots, for nail and wire-rod.

Lancashire-iron for wire and other manufacture.

Bundles of **Iron-rods** and **Wire-coils.**

Iron-rods, bent, twisted, and knotted.

Siemen-Martin-Steel, flat and square.

Wire-rods from the same material.

Axles from Siemen-Martin-Steel.

Anvils from Bessemer-steel; **Pinch-bars; Sledge-hammers; Rock Drilling Tools; Springs.** All made of Bessemer-steel.

Lancashire-iron bent and twisted, cold; broken **Iron-bars** for showing the fracture.

Prev. Aw.: Medals in London, 1851; New York, 1853; London, 1862; Stockholm, 1866; Paris, 1867; Copenhagen, 1872; Moscow, 1872; Diploma of honor in Vienna, 1873, as partaking in the collective exhibit of Jern-Kontoret.

Agents in Göteborg.

The mining is carried on in the mining districts of Wermland, and the iron and steel manufacture, at the Uddeholm Iron Works, in the same Län.

CLASS 112.

	Import-Duty in United States.	Sweden.
COPPER, in plates, bars, ingots, etc., ...	5 cts. per lb.	free.

40. Adelswärd, Th., *Baron.* Åtvidaberg.

Copper in **ingots,** with specimens illustrating its various **stages of production.**—(See Class 100).

41. Skultuna Aktiebolag. *The Skultuna Co. Lim.;* by O. W. Löwenborg, Westerås.

Copper in various stages of production.

Brazen Hardware. A price-list will be found in the office of the Swedish Commission, in the Main Building.

Prev. Aws.: Bronze Medals in Stockholm, 1866; Copenhagen, 1872.

Agencies in Stockholm, Göteborg, Gefle, and some other Swedish towns.

The works are situated on the estate of Skultuna, and were established in 1611 by the Government, and have afterwards been improved and extended by private owners.

In the works 150 men and 20 boys under 15 years of age are employed. Their wages are paid, in accordance with the ancient custom, partly in stores and partly in cash.

The power required is supplied by water-engines of 227 H. P.

The annual production in 1869 amounted to $91,772 gold; in 1874 to $193,300 gold, for which the Government taxes were $277 gold, and the community taxes, $286 gold.

This production consisted of:

Copper.—Sheet, bolt, ...	2,100 cwt.
tubes, wire, ...	465 "

Brass.—Sheet, wire-cloth,	1,654 cwt.
Chandeliers, journal-boxes, candle-sticks, compass-boxes, bottles, pots, spittoons, kettles, boxes, tubes, etc.,	744 "
boiler tubes,	1,167 "
Guilding Metal.—For cartridges,	1,074 "
Yellow Metal.—For sheathing ship-bottoms, bolts and nails,	1,420 "
Pinchbeck.—Tea and coffee-pots, etc.,	43 "

The raw materials used were .

Copper,	7,200 "
Zinc,	1,780 "
Tin,	40 "

All melting and annealing is done with gas, which is made principally from peat, but also from sawdust, stumps, and sprigs. Before it is used the gas is purified from water and acids by surface condensation.

The refuse from the copper is re-refined, when it cannot without such process be used for making brass. The refuse from the brass is melted, after being carefully assorted with regard to alloy.

The exports are: To Finland, sheet and manufactured copper; to France, brass wire, there used in the manufacture of artificial flowers; to England, copper wire.

For the benefit of the employees, sick and burial funds are established. The school instruction is well provided for; it is conducted by three teachers in three separate schools at the works, besides which there are A B C-schools on the surrounding farms belonging to the estate. But besides all this, the workmen assemble two evenings during the week and attend lectures in natural philosophy, history, geography, etc., and get instruction in writing, arithmetic, and drawing.

CLASS 114.

	Import-Duty in United States.	Import-Duty in Sweden.
BRASS, in bars or pigs,	15 per cent.	free.
" in sheets or manufactured,	35 per cent.	free.

42. Skultuna Aktiebolag. *The Skultuna Co. Lim.;* by O. W. Löwenborg, Westerås.

Brazen Hardware. A price-list will be found in the office of the Swedish Commission Main Building. (See Class 112.)

DEPARTMENT II.

MANUFACTURES.

A.—CHEMICAL MANUFACTURES.

CLASS 200.

	Import-Duty in United States.	Sweden.
CHEMICAL PREPARATIONS, not otherwise provided for.	20 per cent.	5 per cent.
ACIDS, boracic,	free.	free.
" nitric, chemically pure,	10 per cent.	free.
" " not chemically pure,	free.	free.
" sulphuric, fuming,	1 ct. pr. lb.	½ öre pr. lb.
" " others,	free.	½ öre pr. lb.

43. Aseptin-Amykos Aktiebolaget. *Aseptin Amykos Co. Lim.;* by *Dr.* Fr. Söderlund. Uppsala.

Single Aseptin for preserving cooked food, soup:, butter, milk, etc.

Double Aseptin for preserving raw meat.

Aseptin for preserving corpses from decomposition, for anatomical preparations.

Amykos for the **Toilet,** valuable on account of its destroying and keeping off infusoria; it is an excellent mouth wash, and tooth preserver, an excellent cosmetic, and anti-epidemic.

Concentrated Amykos of far more powerful effects than the former; it is a very valued remedy in all parasitic diseases, ulcerating sores, rheumatism, etc., as well for man as beast.

Prev. aw.: Vienna, 1873; Paris, Geogr. Congress, 1875, diploma of merit.

The manufacture of these preparations was commenced in 1870, by the inventor, the late chemist, HENRY GAHN, and the present company was formed in 1871.

The use of the preparations of HENRY GAHN, as well of the aseptin as of the amykos, is based on that circumstance, that, while these substances are perfectly harmless to the human body, they destroy those organisms of the lowest order, infusoria, which not only attack our food ana soon destroy it, but also ourselves as well living, when favorable conditions present themselves, as after death.

Price-list of the Aseptin-Amykos manufacturing Company:

Single- and Double-Aseptin,	$0.28,	gold,	pr pack.
Preparation-Aseptin,	0.42,	"	" jar.
Toilet-Amykos,	0.28,	"	" bot'l.
Concentrated Amykos,	0.56,	"	" 1 litre
" "	0.37,	"	" ½ "
" "	0.23,	"	" ¼ "

Single- and Double Aseptin are also sold in bulk, the former at $0.46, gold, per lb., the latter at $0.43 per lb., all net price, when at least 10 lbs. are ordered at once.

The Amykos is also sold by the *kanna* (=0.58 gallon), the Toilet-Amykos, at $0.55, gold, per *kanna*, and the Concentrated Amykos at $0.83 gold per *kanna*, all net price, when at least 10 *kannor* are ordered at once.

44. Bengtsson, B. Östra Torp, Trelleborg.

Calcinated Glauber's salt.
Calcinated soda.
Hydrochloric acid.

45. Eurenius & Svalander. Stockholm.

Chemicals.

Factory established in 1875.

Raw materials are sulphates from the neighboring nitric acid factories, pyrites, refuse from mineral water factories, witherite, etc.

The pure acids are obtained by double distillation of the raw acids.

There are 3 men employed in the factory who receive from 55 to 70 cts. per day, and in case of sickness free medical attendance.

46. Friestedt, A. W. Stockholm.

A case with flasks, containing samples of various **preparations of bone** and **wood.**

Prev. aw.: London, 1862, bronze medal; Stockholm, 1866, bronze medal; Stockholm 1868, silver medal; Paris, 1867, diploma of merit; Göteborg, 1871, bronze medal; Moscow, 1872, gold medal; Copenhagen, 1872, bronze medal; Vienna, 1873, diploma of merit.

47. Gullbergs Aktiebolag. *Gullberg Co., Lim.;* by Th. Gullberg, Göteborg.

Sulphuric Acid, several kinds, in glass bottles.

Fertilizers in glass jars.

Prev. aw.: Vienna, 1873, medal of progress; Uddevalla, 1874, silver medal.

Agencies in Stockholm, Norrköping, Malmö, Helsingborg, and Kristiania.

The manufacture was commenced in 1868, by Mr. Theodor Gullberg, the present manager of the company.

From 40 to 45 men are employed.

The power required is supplied by three steam engines of together 32 H. P.

The production during 1874 consisted of:

Sulphuric acids, . . .	70,000 cwt.
Superphosphates, . . .	65,000 "

The prices of these manufactures are according to strength and percentage.

The value of the manufactures depends on the raw material used.

The increase in the value of the annual production has been about 12 per cent. during the last years.

The raw materials in 1874, consisted of:

Pyrites, ...	45,000 cwt.
Soda-saltpetre, . . .	1,000 "
Raw material for superphosphates,	30,000 "

The refuse, glaubersalt, is manufactured into soda.

The taxes are about $410 in gold per annum.

The acids are exported to Norway and Finland.

CLASS 201.

	Import-Duty in United States.	Import-Duty in Sweden.
CANDLES, stearine and adamantine,	5 cts. per lb.	5 öre per lb.
" paraffine,	8 cts. "	5 öre "
" spermaceti and wax,	8 cts. "	3 öre "
" all others,	2½ cts. "	3 öre "
SOAPS, of toilet or shaving,	10 cts. pr. lb. and 25 pr. ct.	12 öre "
" soft,	1 ct. per lb. and 30 per ct.	3 öre "
" others,	1 ct. per lb. and 30 pr. ct.	5 öre "
OILS, animal n. o. p. f.,	20 per ct.	2 öre "

48. Liljeholmens Stearin Fabriks Aktiebolag. *Liljeholmen Stearine Manufacturing Co., Lim.* Stockholm.

Stearine-candles, stearine, oleine, and **glycerine.**

Prev. aw.: At all larger exhibitions since 1851.

The manufactory was established about 1838.

In the manufactory are employed 65 men, and 65 women.

The power required is supplied by steam-engines of about 20 H. P.

The production during 1874, consisted of:

Stearine candles, . . .	18,500 cwt.
Oleine, ...	6,200 "
Glycerine, . . .	750 "

with an aggregate value of $420,000, gold.

The increase in the production during the last 20 years has been from 5 to 10 per cent. or more per annum.

The government taxes in 1874, were $222 in gold, and the community taxes $103 in gold.

The raw material consisted principally of oxen-tallow, in 1874, about 28,000 cwt.

The only thing peculiar in the production is the treatment of the wicks.

The refuse consists of 750 cwt. of stearine pitch, principally used in the manufacture of gas.

A small part of the production is exported to Norway.

The workmen are provided with free dwellings, by the owners of the manufactory.

The business of the company is transacted by L. J. HJERTA, Stockholm.

49. Sjöberg, A. P. Malmö.

Grease for car-wheels and engines.

Prev. aw.: Malmö, 1875, bronze medal.

50. Werner, Carl Oscar. Stockholm.

Chronometer Bone-oil.

Free from acids, does not dry nor oxodize, protects from rust, and is free from stearine.

The manufacture was commenced in 1874, after 7 years of experiments and observations.

The production during 1874, was 225 lbs. of chronometer-oil at $42 gold per lb. At wholesale 20 per cent. discount.

The refuse consists of bones, hoofs, etc.

Exports only to St. Petersburg, Russia.

Certificate.

LABORATORY OF THE TECHNOLOGICAL INSTITUTE,
St. Petersburg, Dec. 12th, 1874.

The samples of bone-oil 1 and 2 produced by MR. WERNER, have been analyzed in the Laboratory of the Technological Institute, with the following results:

Bone-oil No. 1, is transparent and colorless has a Sp. Gr, 0.901; solidifies at—5°C.; its fluidity compared with that of water is 0.09; it contains no adulterations, no mineral acids, or other chemical reagents.

This bone-oil is well adapted as a lubricant for even the most delicate mechanism, as it does not become pitchy or oxidize, and effectually protects the apparatus from rust.

Bone-oil No. 2, is transparent of a yellowish color, has a Sp. Gr. 0.909; solidifies at—3.5° C.; is of the same purity as No. 1, and as a lubricant is applicable to all machines, clocks and chronometers excepted, for which purpose No. 1 is expressly manufactured.

Signed,

Professor WILESCHINSKY,
Director of the Technological Laboratory.

CLASS 202.

	Import-Duty in United States.	Import-Duty in Sweden.
INK, Indian,	35 per cent.	free.
" others,	35 per cent.	5 öre pr. lb.
VARNISHES, valued at $1.50, or less, per gallon (8 lbs. to a gallon),	50 cts. pr. gal. and 20 pr. ct.	10 öre "
" valued higher,	50 cts. pr. gal. and 25 pr. ct.	10 öre "

51. Ekman, C. L. Stockholm.

India and **writing-ink,** the former article, intended for artists and draughtsmen, does not decompose on exposure to the air; the latter remains unaltered by the influence of light or chemical reagents, and does not corrode the steel pen.

52. Gullberg's Aktiebolag. Göteborg.

Ink. (See Cl. 200.)

Specimens of dyed materials.

53. Lundgren, P. W. Stockholm.

Copying ink.

54. Strandberg, Fr. A. Jönköping.

Ink, Varnishes.

CLASS 203.

	Import-Duty in United States.	Import-Duty in Sweden.
PERFUMERY, alcoholic,	$3 per gal. and 50 pr. ct.	40 öre pr. lb.
" containing no alcohol,	50 pr. ct.	4 öre "

55. Aseptin Amykos Aktiebolaget. *Aseptin Amykos Co., Lim.;* by Dr. Fr. Söderlund. Uppsala.

Amykos, for the toilet. (See Cl. 200.)

56. Granholm, J. P. Stockholm.

Rectified amykos.

57. Pauli, F. Jönköping and Stockholm.

Perfumery and **toilet soaps.**

Prev. aw.: Göteborg, 1860; London, 1862; Stockholm, 1866; Copenhagen, 1872.

Branch manufactory in Stockholm.

The manufacture was commenced in Jönköping 1841, in Stockholm 1876.

The power required is supplied by a steam-engine of 8 H. P.

In 1864 the production had a value of $13,800 gold, in 1874 this had increased to $56,000 gold.

The government taxes on this later sum were $56 gold, and the community taxes $250 gold

In the manufacture of perfumes and toilet-soaps, are applied the newest processes and machinery used in the most prominent perfume-manufactories of France and England.

The exports go to Finland and Norway.

This manufactory, established in 1841, was the first in Sweden to manufacture perfumery on a large scale. In the preparation of extracts the exhibitor is at present the only one in the country applying the processes and apparatus used at the factories in the south of France—Grasse, Canne, Nice and others.

CLASS 204.

	Import-Duty in United States.	Sweden.
MATCHES, ...	35 pr. ct.	2 öre pr. lb.

58. Uddevalla Tändsticksfabriks Aktiebolag. *Uddevalla Match Manufacturing Co., Lim.* Uddevalla.

Matches.

59. Aktiebolaget Nya Tändsticksfabriken. *New Match Manufacturing Co. Lim.* Stockholm.

Safety-matches.

Prev. aw.: Moscow, 1872, silver medal; Vienna, 1873, diploma of honor.

Agencies in London, Hamburg, Danzic, and Barcelona.

The factory was established 1870, and gives employment to 130 working people, of both sexes, about one-fourth of which being 14 to 20 years of age. The power is supplied by a 15 H. P. steam-engine.

60. Blombacka Aktiebolag. *Blombacka Co. Lim.* Molkom.

Matches.

Company formed 1873, employs 12 men, 10 women, 7 boys and 20 girls. All are paid by piece work. Engine worked by means of a turbine wheel, with a capacity of 20 H. P.

Most of the manufactured products are shipped to England, smaller quantities to Finland, Russia, Germany and China.

61. Bodé, Patrik, for *Gnesta Match Factory.* Stockholm.

Paraffined, safety matches, veneer, for match-boxes and **splinters,** intended for foreign match manufactories, in want of suitable wood.

Agencies in London, Berlin, Kristiana, and Helsingfors.

The manufacture was commenced in 1873.

The employees at the factory consist of manager, foreman, and book-keeper, 15 workmen, 17 women, and 20 children, under 15 years of age. Besides these, women and children of the neighborhood are employed in making match-boxes, at their homes, as is also the case with the prisoners, of two country prisons. All the work at the factory is done by the job, and the average earnings have been, for men $0.85 gold, women $0.28, and children $0.14 gold, per day.

The power required is supplied by a portable steam-engine, of 4 H. P.

The products are exported to Norway, Denmark, Finland, Russia, Germany, and England, to which latter country, nearly the whole production is shipped.

62. Holmberg, Eric. Södertelje.

Safety-matches, in wooden and paper boxes.

Prev. aw.: Moscow, 1872, bronze medal.

Branches in Stockholm and Uppsala for manufacture of boxes.

The manufacture was commenced in 1872.

In the manufacture are employed 13 men, 14 women, 20 boys, 15 girls, and, outside of the factory, 20 to 30 persons in Södertelje, and about 80 prisoners in the prisons of Stockholm and Uppsala.

The yearly production is about nine million boxes of matches, with a value of about $33,300 gold, for which the taxes are about $70 gold per annum.

The raw material for matches and boxes are 30,000 cubic feet of aspenwood, besides chemicals.

Nearly the whole production is exported to Hamburg.

To a savings fund for monthly deposits in savings-bank of Södertelje, the operatives make weekly contributions of 10 per cent of their wages.

63. **Jönköpings Tändsticksfabriks Aktiebolag.** *Jönköping Match Manufacturing Co., Lim.* Jönköping.

Safety-matches.

64. **P. E. Kreuger & Jennings**; by Eric Kreuger. Fredriksdahl, Kalmar.

Safety-matches.

Prev. aw.: Kalmar, 1870, first prize. Has not participated in any other exhibition.

The manufacture was commenced in 1867.

In the manufactory are employed 50 men, with wages from $0.40 to $0.85 gold, per day; 150 women, with wages from $0.20 to $0.40 gold, per day, and 100 boys and girls, with wages from $0.15 to $0.35 gold, per day.

The power required is supplied by a steam-engine of 8 H. P.

Safety-matches in boxes are sold, delivered on board of vessel, in Kalmar, in cases containing 7,200 boxes, at $3.61, gold, per thousand boxes. Safety-matches in capsules, are sold in whole cases of 10.000 capsules, at $2.78, gold, per thousand.

The raw materials used in the manufacture are:

Aspenwood, ...	40,000	cub. ft.
Pine boards, ...	504,000	sq. feet.
Chlorate of Potash, .	250	cwt.
Paraffine, ...	350	"
Glue, ...	450	"
Gum Arabic, ...	200	"
Amorphous Phosphorus, .	20	"
Umbre, ...	20	"
Pulverized manganite, .	30	"
Dextrin (potato), . . .	10	"
Nitrate of Lead, . . .	3	"
Hyposulphite of Soda, . .	3	"
Blue paper, ...	1,000	reams.
arton paper, etc., . . .	600	"

The steam-engine is supplied with fuel, almost exclusively from the refuse of the aspenwood.

The exports, which principally go to South America, India, China, Germany, England, and other countries, are about 2,000 cases, of 50 gross, per annum.

The workmen have established a savings-bank, to which the proprietor of the manufactory has given $70, gold, as a reserve fund.

65. **Körner, Ferd.**, for *Ellbo-Göteborg Match Factory.* Göteborg.

Matches.

Prev. aw.: Paris, 1867, great prize medal; Moscow, 1872, medal, Vienna, 1873, medal of merit.

Tändstickor, (matches)	Price per gross, free London.		
white boxes } in cases à 50	1 s.	6	d.
blue boxes } gross.	1 s.	9½	d.
Favorite Tändstickor, made especially for damp climates, will keep any length of time, in cases à 50 gross,	1 s.	7	d.
Elephant Paraffine Matches (English shape) in cases à 20 gross	2 s.	6	d.
Ellbo Paraffine Matches (Swedish shape) in cases à 50 gross	2 s.	0.	d.
Göteborg Kali Tändstickor (safety matches) in cases à 50 gross	2 s.	2	d.
Universal Safety Matches (English shape) in cases à 25 gross	4 s.	0.	d.

66. **Lindahl, J. F.** Kalmar.

Safety matches.

Prev. aw.: Vienna, 1873, medal of merit.

The manufacture was commenced in 1865.

In the manufactory are employed 25 men, 50 women, 15 boys and 25 girls.

The power required is supplied by a steam engine of 8 H. P.

The price of matches is 13 Kr. ($3.61 gold) per 1,000 small boxes, and 3 Kr. ($0.83 gold) per gross of large boxes.

The raw materials used are, at least 30,000 cubic feet of aspenwood and sundry chemicals.

The steam-boiler is heated with the refuse from the aspenwood.

The whole production is exported to Germany, England and all trans-atlantic countries.

The operatives have established a savings-fund among themselves.

67. Lovers Fabriks Aktiebolag. *Lover Manufacturing Co., Lim.* Waxtorp, Kalmar.

Paraffined safety matches, without phosphorus, in boxes.

Phosphorus matches, in boxes and capsules.

Aspen wood, aspen veneer, as well for boxes as for matches.

Prev. aw.: Kalmar Agricultural Society diploma of merit.

Agencies in Hamburg and London.

The manufacture was commenced in 1874.

In the manufactory are employed 16 men, 12 women, 40 boys, and 80 girls, which number of employees will soon be doubled.

The power required is supplied by water engines.

In the manufacture are annually used: Aspen wood, 10,000 cubic feet; paper, 1,000 reams; and sundry chemicals, 200 cwt.

The largest part of the production is exported to Hamburg and London.

For export the paraffined safety matches are packed in chests containing 50 gross of boxes in 6 zinc cases, each containing 6⅓ gross. In chests containing 50 gross of boxes in one zinc box.

68. Norrköpings Tändsticksfabriks Aktiebolag. *Norrköping Match Manufacturing Co., Lim.* Norrköping.

Impregnated safety matches. Particular attention is called to the impregnated safety matches, which have that advantage over the common ones, that they *do not glow after being blown out*, and that *the composition, after being burned out, does not drop off*, but that the match after combustion gives quite a strong piece of charcoal as a residue.

Prev. aw.: Moscow, 1872, large silver medal; Linköping, 1873, silver medal by the Agricultural Society Östergötland; Vienna, 1873, diploma of merit.

Agencies in Hamburg, Paris, Amsterdam, Antwerp, and St. Petersburg.

The manufacture of common safety matches was commenced in 1870, that of impregnated matches in 1872.

In the manufactory are employed:

35 men,		at $0.46 gold per day.
70 women,		at 0.28 " "
14 boys, 17 girls,	under 15 years of age,	0.19 " "

Women and girls mostly have job work whereby their earnings vary from $0.15 to $0.55 gold per day.

The power required is supplied by a steam-engine of 16 H. P.

The production at present is about 80,000 boxes of matches per day, giving 24,000,000 boxes per annum, valued at $90,000 gold. The net price for the common safety match is 13 Kr. (=$3.61 gold) per 1,000 boxes, and for the impregnated safety matches 14.50 Kr. (=$14.03 gold) per 1,000.

The following tabular statement shows the value of the yearly production since the factory was established:

In 1870 its value was	$ 5,500 gold.
" 1871 " "	23,900 "
" 1872 " "	35,000 "
" 1873 " "	43,000 "
" 1874 " "	32,500 "

The peculiar treatment of the matches by the manufacture is the above mentioned impregnation, by which their quality is generally improved. The refuse from the aspen wood is used for fuel.

The largest part of the manufacture is exported by way of Hamburg to China and South America, part of it also to Germany and Russia.

For the benefit of the workmen a sick-fund is established, to which they pay a part of their weekly earnings, and from which they, in case of sickness or death, receive assistance.

69. Strengnäs Tändsticksfabriks Aktiebolag. *Strengnäs Match Manufacturing Co., Lim.* Strengnäs.

Safety matches, which can be lighted only by rubbing against the tables on the sides of the match box.

Agency in Stockholm.

The manufacture was commenced in 1874.

In the manufactory are employed 12 persons at $0.55 gold per day, 60 persons at $0.35 per day, and 10 persons at $0.28 per day.

The power required is supplied by a steam engine of 10 H. P.

The value of the production during 1874 was $60,000.

The refuse is used as fuel for the steam-boiler.

The workmen have formed a society of 100 members, intended to give help to members in case of sickness, during which they receive $2.00 gold per week, during three months if necessary.

70. Tändsticksfabriks Aktiebolaget Phœnix. *Phœnix Match Manufacturing Co., Lim.;* by A. C. Holm. Malmö.

Phosphorus and **safety matches,** in boxes.

Agencies in London, Hamburg, Vienna, and several other cities in Europe.

The manufactory commenced operation in 1874.

In the manufactory are employed:

42 men, wages by piece-work,	$0.50 to 0.85, gold, per day.
30 women,	0.40 to 0.50, " "
25 boys, 40 girls,	0.25 to 0.35, " "

besides those employed in the manufacture of boxes, which is done at home. The consumption of boxes at present, is about 50,000 per week.

The power required is supplied by a steam-engine of 25 H. P.

At wholesale of the phosphorus and safety matches, 10 per cent. discount is allowed.

The refuse, from the box and splinter making, is employed as fuel for the steam-boiler. The ashes are used partly for the manufacture of poudrette, and partly for fillings.

The phosphorus and safety matches are exported to most European countries, South America, Cape Town, Java, and China.

71. Tändsticksfabriks Aktiebolaget Vulcan. *Vulcan Match Manufacturing Co., Lim.* Göteborg.

Matches.

72. Westerviks Tändsticksfabrik. *Westervik Match Factory;* by Algot Lagerquist. Westervik.

Safety matches.

Prev. aw.: Moscow, 1872, (medal); Vienna, 1873, diploma of merit.

Agencies in Hamburg: DOMNICKS & Co.

In the factory are employed 160 men and women and 121 children. A steam-engine of 12 H. P's capacity.

The average value of the annual production has amounted to $30,000, and nearly the whole of said has been shipped via Hamburg to China and South America.

The government taxes are $28, and the community taxes $37 per annum. A fund for the benefit of the sick is established among the working men.

73. Wisby Tändsticksfabriks Aktiebolag. *Wisby Match Manufacturing Co., Lim.* Wisby.

Safety matches, in boxes.

Prev. aw.: Gottland's Agricultural Society, 1875.

Agents in Amsterdam, Berlin, Cologne, London, Hamburg, Riga, St. Petersburg, Singapore and Stockholm.

The factory has a steam engine of 16 H. P., and employs a foreman, book-keeper, 12 men, 20 women, 40 girls, 36 boys, and 300 hands engaged outside.

The materials used are Aspen and Fir-wood, Chemicals, Zinc, etc., to an annual value of $16,700 gold.

The average production is from 10 to 15 million of boxes per annum.

The machines are of the latest and most improved construction. The refuse is sold for wood pulp.

As taxes to the government is paid 1 per cent. and to the community 4 per cent. of the annual income.

The whole production goes via London, Hamburg and Amsterdam, all over the world.

Commission 3 per cent. Order to be sent to Mr. R. LUDWIG, in Stockholm.

A savings-bank is founded for the benefit of the work people, and a fund for the sick is to be formed.

74. Ystads Tändsticksfabriks Aktiebolag. *Ystad Match Manufacturing Co., Lim.;* by W. & T. Peterson, Ystad.

Safety matches.

Prev. aw.: Vienna, 1873, diploma of merit.

The manufacture was commenced in 1871.

In the manufactory are employed:

1 Foreman, with a salary of	$700	gold pr.	annum.
1 Bookkeeper, " "	275	"	"
1 Engineer, " "	195	"	"
23 Workmen, with wages of	0.70	"	per day.
10 " " "	0.42	"	"
16 " " "	0.21	"	"
36 " " "	0.14 to 0.35		per day.

The power required is supplied by a steam-engine of 10 H. P.

The annual production in value amounts to about $55,600, gold.

The refuse is used as fuel for the boiler.

The entire production is exported to England, Germany, Austria, Denmark, Spain, North and South America.

For the benefit of the workmen, a savings-fund has been established, which fund, at the end of the year, is distributed among them.

B.—CERAMICS, POTTERY, PORCELAIN, ETC.

	Import-Duty in United States.
STATUES of TERRA COTTA in bas-relief,	40 per cent.
EARTHEN and STONE-WARES, to wit: brown earthen and common stone-ware, not ornamented,	25 per cent.
CHINA, PORCELAIN, and PARIAN-WARE, gilded, ornamented, or decorated,	50 per cent.
" " " " plain white,	45 per cent.
ALL OTHER earthen and stone-ware or crockery-ware, n. o. p. f., white, glazed, etched, printed, painted, dipped or cream colored, composed of earthy or mineral substances,	40 per cent.

	Import-Duty in Sweden.
STONE-WARE and FAIENCE, white or one-colored, not painted:	
(*a.*) plates,	per lb. 3 öre.
(*b.*) other articles,	" 5 "
" " " painted or printed:	
(*a.*) plates,	" 6 "
(*b.*) other articles,	" 8 "
PORCELAIN and PARIAN, white or one-colored,	" 10 "
" " " gilded or with painted figures or flowers,	" 20 "
CROCKERY-WARE, n. o. p. f., and TERRA-COTTA,	" 3 "
TILES and BRICKS, all kinds,	free.

CLASS 206.

75. Gustafsbergs Fabriks Intressenter. *Shareholders in Gustafsberg's Manufactory.* Stockholm.

Terra-cotta and **architectural pottery.** (See Cl. 210.)

76. Helsingborgs Jern och Lerkärlsfabriks Aktiebolag. *Helsingborg Iron and Stone-ware Manufacturing Co., Lim.* Helsingborg.

Terra-cotta.

Saltglazed stone jars, measuring from 6 Kannor (600 cubic inches), down to $\frac{1}{16}$ Kanna (6.25 cubic inches.)

CLASS 207.

77. Höganäs Stenkolsverks Bolag. *Höganäs Coal Mining Co.* Höganäs.

Fire-clay goods. (See Cl. 101.)

CLASS 210.

78. Höganäs Stenkolsverks Bolag. *Höganäs Coal Mining Co.* Höganäs.

Tiles for flagging. (See Cl. 101).

79. Gustafsbergs Fabriks Intressenter. *Shareholders in Gustafsberg Manufactory;* by W. Odelberg. Stockholm.

(**Terra-cotta** and **architectural pottery.**—See Cl. 206).

Faience.

(**Biscuit-ware** and **Parian.**—See Cl. 212).

(**Porcelain** and **argentine.**—See Cl. 213).

(**Table china.**—See Cl. 218).

(**Majolica.**—See Cl. 211).

Prev. aw.: Malmö, 1865, silver medal; Stockholm, 1866, silver medal; Paris, 1867, silver medal, with honorable mention; Moscow, 1872, gold medal; Copenhagen, 1872, silver medal; Vienna, 1873, medal of merit.

The factory was established in 1826. The workmen, numbering about 400 in all departments, are paid by the piece, the size and character of the piece determining the price.

A discount of 30 per cent. is allowed at wholesale.

In 1875 the business of the company amounted to nearly $300,000 gold.

The principal export is to Norway, while but small quantities are sent to England, Germany, France and Russia.

For the benefit of the workmen have been established a sick and burial-fund, with a capital of over $1,660 gold, to which the participants make monthly contributions; a poor-fund, to which 15 per cent. of the earnings of the laborers is contributed, and out of which a physician is paid, medicines purchased, two schools supported, and orphan children and such as are unable to work, receive aid; a co operative society is formed by the employees, with a capital stock of $2,800 gold.

A savings bank, reading room, and library with over 500 vols., are also established at the works.

80. Rörstrands Aktiebolag. *Rörstrand Co., Lim.* Stockholm.

(**Feldspar.**—See Cl. 104.)

Faience, plain and decorated.

(**Majolica** and **pallissy.**—See Cl. 211).

(**Biscuit-ware** and **parian.**—See Cl. 212).

(**China,** plain and decorated.—See Cl. 213).

(**Table-sets.**—See Cl. 213),

(**Stoves.**—See Cl. 222).

Prev. aw.: Malmö, 1865, silver medal; Stockholm, 1866, silver medal; Paris, 1867, 2 bronze medals; at this exhibition the articles exhibited by the company were termed by the jury "*superior products*;" Vienna, 1873, medal of progress.

The factory at Rörstrand was established 1726. A branch manufactory was established in in 1874, at Arabia, Helsingfors, Finland.

In the factories are employed: 293 men, 161 women, 56 boys, and 29 girls under 15 years of age; together 539 employees.

The power required for the manufacture is supplied by one steam-engine of 90 H. P., and one of 15 H. P.

The production during 1855, amounted to $88,900 gold; during 1865, to $135,000 gold; and during 1875, to $375,000 gold, for which latter production the government taxes were $310 gold, and community taxes $1,886 gold. At wholesale 10 to 35 per cent. discount is allowed.

In 1874, the production consisted of:

Faiance, plain,	to the value of	$115,830	gold.
" decorated,	" "	159,720	"
China, plain,	" "	14,330	"
" decorated,	" "	13,580	"
Damaged articles,	" "	12,940	"
Plaster of Paris,	" "	4,170	"
Feldspar, . .	weight,	25,000	cwt.

The raw materials for this production are: Gypsum, quartz, feldspar, kaolin and other clays, together about 120,000 cwt.

The refuse consists of broken gypsum forms, used as fertilizers, and broken capsules, from which fire proof bricks are made.

For the benefit of the operatives are established:

1. Two sick and burial-funds, to which the operatives pay a monthly fee, and to which the company besides gives an amount, corresponding to 25 per cent. of the contributions made by its employees.

2°. A primary school for forty children, for which the company provides the room, and pays the teacher.

3°. A Sunday-school for forty boys under 15 years of age, employed in the factory, the teacher being paid by the company. Free medical attendance; circulating library; temperance restaurant; grocery and provision store.

4°. Bath-house.

CLASS 211.

81. Röstrands Aktiebolag. (See Cl. 210). **Majolica** and **palissy-ware.**

CLASS 212.

82. Gustafsbergs Fabriks Intressenter. (See Cl. 210).

Biscuit-ware and **parian.**

83. Rörstrands Aktiebolag. (See Cl. 210).

Biscuit-ware and **parian.**

CLASS 213.

84. Gustafsbergs Fabriks Intressenter.

Porcelain and **argentine.*** (See Cl. 210).

85. Rörstrands Aktiebolag.

China, plain and decorated. (See Cl. 210).

C.—GLASS AND GLASSWARE.

	Import-Duty in United States..
GLASS-WARE, cut, engraved, painted, colored, printed, stained, silvered or gilded,	40 per cent.
" plain, mould or press, n. o. p. f., ...	35 per cent.

	Import-Duty in Sweden.
GLASS-WARE, plain, and druggist's glass jars with printed signatures, . .	per lb. 3öre.
" cut, engraved, etc., ...	" 15 "
" chemical, ...	free.

CLASS 215.

86. Brusewitz, Fred. Limmared.

Glass for different purposes, such as house utensils, **chemical** and **pharmaceutical glassware, preserving** and **packing vessels,** and different kinds of plain, cut or otherwise.

(**Decorated glass.**—See Cl. 216).

A price-list is to be had at the office of the commission.

Prev. aw.: London, 1852; Stockholm, 1866; Paris, 1867; Moscow, 1872; Vienna, 1873, besides at several exhibitions in Sweden.

Branch manufactories at Bollsjo and Strömsforss. The manufacture was commenced at Limmared, in 1748, at Bollsjo, in 1568, at Strömsforss, in 1871.

In these factories are employed 4 men with wages over $550, gold, per annum, 40 men with wages from $275 to $550, gold, per annum, 10

*The *argentine* or *silver-plated china* was invented by MR. EILEV HANSEN, Engineer at the Gustafsberg Factory, who engages to establish works for the manufacturing of argentine in any part of Europe or America.

women and 54 younger workmen with varying wages.

The necessary power is supplied by a steam engine of 15 H. P., and water engines of 35 H. P.

The value of the production in 1864, amounted to $37,500, gold; in 1874, to $80,500, gold, the government taxes on this production were $555, gold, and the community taxes $277, gold.

The raw materials used for this manufacture in 1874, were 6,000 cords of wood, 600,000 lbs. fire-proof clay, 75,000 lbs. quartz, 220,000 lbs. alkalies, 140,000 lbs. lime, 3,000 l s. saltpetre, 100 lbs. smalt, and 1,500 lbs. manganite.

The refuse at Limmared is manufactured into inferior glass, at Bollsjö and Strömforss.

In 1874 small quantities of glassware were exported to Belgium, Norway and Denmark.

For the benefit of the employees, schools, reading rooms and bath-houses have been established.

87. Reymyra Aktiebolag. *Reymyra Co. Lim.* Remyra.

Glass-ware of 1st and 2nd quality.—See Cl. 216).

Prev. aw.: First-class medal in Stockholm, 1851; Malmö, 1665; Copenhagen, 1872; Moscow, 1872; honorable meution in Paris, 1855.

The works were founded in 1810, and the manufacturing commenced in 1812.

At present 124 men, 11 women, 77 boys and 12 girls under 15 years of age, are employed.

The work-people are paid by the piece, and the wages average $33,500, gold, per annum. Grinding and breaking-machines are worked by a stationary steam-engine of 16 H. P., and the preparing of peat for fuel by a portable engine of 8 H. P. The materials used are quartz, alkalier, lime, arsenic, etc., amounting to a weight of 9,000 cwts. per annum.

All the refuse in some way or other is made use of in the manufactory. Furnaces and tools are all of the most improved construction. The articles manufactured, consist chiefly of household utensils, physical and chemical apparatus, etc., partly made of first, partly of second crystal; the former surpassing the latter in transparency, refraction of light and intensity of sound. The value of the manufactured wares for the business years 1874-75 was $116,700, gold, being $65,000, gold, more than that of 1869-70. At wholesale, the prices are reduced by five to twenty per cent. The government taxes amount to $507, gold, and the community taxes to $578, gold.

During the last years the exports to Norway, Denmark and Russia, were valued at $6,000 to 8,000, gold.

The company has a church and school of its own, and keep a drug store in common with the community. There is also a hospital with eight beds, and a savings fund, to which the workmen contribute five per cent. of their wages.

CLASS 216.

88. Brusewitz, Fr. (See Cl. 215).
Decorative glassware.

89. Reymyra Aktiebolag. (See Cl. 215).
Decorative glassware.

D.—FURNITURE AND OBJECTS OF GENERAL USE IN CONSTRUCTION AND DWELLINGS.

CLASS 217.

	Import-Duty in United States.
HOUSE-FURNITURE, WILLOW-WARE and CABINET-WARE, finished,	35 per cent.
" " " not finished,	30 per cent.
	Import-Duty in Sweden.
HOUSE-FURNITURE, of such woods as grow in the country, ...	per lb. 3 öre.
" of such woods as do not grow in the country, massive or veneered with, and GILDED FURNITURE, ...	" " 5 "
(If upholstered, but without cover, no additional duty to this rate; if upholstered and dressed with cover, 20 per cent. additional duty is added.)	
WILLOW-WARE and BASKETS of course material, ...	" " 4 "
" " others, ...	" " 25 "

90. Backman, J. F. Stockholm.

Fire and **burglar-proof safes,** made of Swedish material; the spaces between the walls are filled with alum, sawdust and chalk.

Prev. aw.: London, 1862, medal of honor; Stockholm, 1868, 1st prize; Copenhagen, 1872, diploma; Wien, 1873, medal of progress.

The factory was established in 1854, and gives employment to 30 persons.

91. Clarberg, F. A. Stockholm.

Jewelry case.

92. Glömsta Fabriks Bolag. *Glömsta Manufacturing Co.* Huddinge.

Varnished pine furniture, consisting of **garden table, sofa,** and 4 **chairs,** which can be folded together, and are easily transported; **night table,** which can be taken apart, and **foot stool.** (See engravings at the end of catalogue).

Prev. aw.: One silver cup and several smaller prizes at the exhibitions of the Agricultural Society of the Län of Stockholm; Uppsala, 1874, bronze medal.

The products are at present sold in Stockholm, Norrköping, and Visby.

The manufacture was commenced in 1871, and is now about to be extended.

Women are employed in the varnishing department of the factory. All work is paid for by the piece. At wholesale a discount of 10 per cent. is allowed.

A small portion of the products is exported to Norway, Finland, and Germany.

For the employees, opportunity for reading is given, and during the winter months, lectures are given two evenings during the week.

93. Holm, F. F. W. (*Deaf and Dumb.*) Stockholm.

Set of counters,	price, $10 gold.
Writing desk,	" 14 "
Cigar-case,	" 12 "

all inlaid work.

(**Model** of the Gymnastic Hall at Manilla, with apparatus.—See Cl. 340).

Prev. aw.: London, 1870; Stockholm, 1870; Moscow, 1872; Copenhagen, 1872; Vienna, 1873; Berlin, 1874.

94. Låstbom, Sven. Stockholm.

A corner cabinet of Swedish **birchwood,** veneered on the front part with handsome, waved birch-veneer (not from mazer or root-wood,) and on the sides with the common smooth kind.

Prev. aw.: Paris, 1867, honorable mention.

The manufacture was commenced in 1849.

The wages of journeymen cabinet-makers, at present, are 50 per cent. higher than three years ago, or from $4.17 to $7.00 gold per week.

95. Peterson, C. E. Stockholm.

Table.

96. Rambach, C. Stockholm.

Chair in north style, designed by N. M. MANDELGREN, and made of oak from the Swedish line-of-battle-ship "*Äpplet,*" sunk the 5th of June, 1676, and partly risen 1870.

97. Rusch, P. O. Göteborg.

Japanned furniture, cigar cases.

98. Sandberg, A. & Cook. Stockholm.

Walnut writing chair, in renaissance style.

Prev. aw.: Stockholm, 1866, silver **medal**; Paris, 1867, diploma of merit; Copenhagen, 1872, diploma of honor.

99. Wahlström, S. F. Stockholm.

Products of **basket-makers'** industry.

Prev. aw.: Copenhagen, 1872, medal second class; Vienna, 1873, medal of merit.

The factory, established in 1864, employs 8 able workmen, who receive, as wages, 33⅓ per cent. of the wholesale price of the fabrics. During last year 30,000 lbs. of willows (various species of *Salix* were used.

100. Österberg, C. G. Jäder, Eskilstuna.

School furniture.

CLASS 218.

	Import-Duty in United States.
ARTICLES OF GOLD, SILVER, OR GERMAN-SILVER, ...	40 per cent.
" OF OTHER METALS, gilt and plated, or not, ...	35 "

	Import-Duty in Sweden.
ARTICLES OF GOLD,	per art. 5 öre.
" OF SILVER,	" 3 "
" OF OTHER METALS, gilt, silver, or nickel-plated,	per lb. 30 "
" OF ALLOYS, not gilt or plated,	" 15 "
" OF COPPER, polished,	" 30 "
" OF " not polished,	" 15 "
" OF TIN, painted or japanned,	" 30 "
" OF LEAD OR ZINC, painted or japanned,	" 15 "
" OF TIN, not painted or japanned,	" 15 "
" OF LEAD OR ZINC, not painted or japanned,	" 3 "

101. Brusewitz, Fr. (See Cl. 215).
Table glass.

102. Guldsmeds Aktiebolag. *Goldsmiths' Co., Lim.;* by Alf. Ambrosius. Stockholm.

One **silver drinking cup,** in northern style, richly chiseled and adorned with medallions of CARL XIV JOHAN, OSCAR I, CARL XV and OSCAR II, designed by MAGNUS ISÆUS the architect, the designs being rewarded by the Industrial Association in Stockholm, the silversmith's work done by A. BERGMAN, and chiseling by Messrs. LUNDMARK and MALMBERG.

Prev. aw.: Copenhagen, 1872, bronze medal; Bogota, 1874, silver medal.

The company was established 1870, by Messrs. A. AMBROSIUS, G. TH. FOLCKER, E. PETTERSON and P. F. PALMGREN, and was changed to a limited company in 1875, Mr. E. PETTERSON being its general manager. In the factory, which has a steam-engine of 6 H. P., there are employed 45 men and 30 women, the wages of whom, in 1874, amounted to $11,000 gold. A sick-fund has been established for the benefit of the working people; the support for each sick person being $2.20 gold a week, and from the same fund $20.83 gold are paid for their funeral.

During the last business year, 1,600 lbs. work-silver, 170 lbs. fine silver, 0.70 lbs. gold, and $5,000 worth of nickel-silver-ware were used. The manufactures were silver-ware to the value of $30,300 gold, and silver-plated nickel silver-ware to the same value, the total, $60,600 gold, being 150 per cent. more than the value of the entire production five years earlier. Agents in Norrköping, Linköping, Piteå, Umeå, Hernösand, Gefle, Falun, Uppsala, Westerås, Göteborg, Kalmar, Karlskrona, Karlshamn, Ronneby, Malmö, and Wisby. 15–17 per cent. discount is granted at wholesale.

103. Gustafsbergs Fabriks Intressenter.
Table china. (See Cl. 210).

104. Reymyra Glasbruk. (See Cl. 215).
Table glass.

105. Rörstrands Aktiebolag. (See Cl. 210).
Table china.

CLASS 220.

106. Petterson, C. E. Stockholm.

Gilt frame with embroidered portrait of General WASHINGTON.

Table in renaissance-style, with glass-slab, all richly ornamented and gilt.

CLASS 222.

	Import-Duty in United States.	Import-Duty in Sweden.
IRON STOVES and STOVE-PLATES, cast,	per lb. 1½ cts.	per lb. 1 öre.

107. J. & C. G. Bolinder's Mekaniska Verk-Stads Aktiebolag. *J. & C. G. Bolinder, Machine Manufacturing Co., Lim.* Stockholm.

Various **Heating apparatus.**
(**Sawing Machines**—Cl. 510).
(**Emery wheels**—Cl. 514).

Prev. aw.: Stockholm, 1847 and 1851, silver medals; London, 1851, bronze medal; Paris, 1855, 1 silver and 1 bronze medal; Paris, 1857, gold medal; London, 1861, 2 prize medals, Stockholm, 1866, 3 silver medals and 1 bronze medal; Paris, 1867, 4 bronze medals; Stockholm, 1868, 1 gold and 2 silver medals; Copenhagen, 1872, 2 silver medals; Vienna, 1873, diploma of honor and medal of merit. Altogether 2 gold medals, 10 silver medals, 7 bronze medals, 3 other prize medals, and 1 diploma of honor.

The manufacture was commenced in 1845.

In the shops are employed 522 men; $101,-153, gold, were paid them in wages during the year 1874.

One steam engine of 40 H. P., and 3 steam engines of 16 H. P. each, supply the power required for the establishment.

The production, which in 1869 amounted to $181,075, gold, had in 1874, increased to $430,106, gold, the annual taxes on this production being $474, gold, to the government, and $2,368, gold, to the community.

The raw materials used for the production consisted of cast-iron 50,400 cwt., wrought iron 5,974 cwt., steel 1,797 cwt., band-iron 396 cwt., sheetcopper 315 cwt., refined copper 402 cwt., tin 46 cwt., zinc 96 cwt., lead 19 cwt., antimony 228 lbs., borax 272 lbs., rosin 424 lbs., rolled sheet-iron 6,300 lbs., fireproof brick 8,575 pieces, fireproof clay 1,200 cubic feet, linseed oil 438 gallons, red lead 500 lbs., white lead 489 lbs., zinc white 15 cwt., machine-oil 1,250 gallons, tallow 10 cwt., coke 114,000 lbs., forge coal 3,200 bbls., steamboat coal 7,800 cwt., charcoal 320 lasts.

During last 25 years, cooking-stoves have been exported to the Cape of Good Hope.

The company provides suitable dwellings for its employees.

For the benefit of the workmen, a sick and burial fund has been established.

108. Hedengran, A. F. & Son. Eskilstuna.

Stove sets.

109. Eriksson, G. Eskilstuna.

Brass doors for stoves.

110. Kallinge Bruk. (See Cl. 224.)

Kitchen utensils of iron and steel-sheet.

111. Mobergs Gjuteri och Mekaniska Werkstad. *Moberg's Iron Foundry and Machine Factory.* Stockholm.

(**Fire engine** with carriage, to be drawn by one or two horses, is worked by 20 men, and gives 75 gallons of water per minute, throws the stream 150 feet from the engine.—See Cl. 664).

Cooking stove with round revolving top.

In the factory 90 men are employed.

The power required, is supplied by a steam engine of 10 H. P.

During 1874, were manufactured:

164 fire engines and 64 cooking stoves, with a value of 12,000, gold. Castings to the value of $24,000, gold, and sundry other works, to the value of $8,200, gold, or altogether $44,700, gold, for which $21, gold, were paid in taxes to the government, and $100, gold to the community.

For the benefit of the workmen, a sick and burial fund, and a savings fund are established.

112. Rörstrands Aktiebolag. Stockholm.

Stoves. (See Cl. 210.)

113. Wiberg, M., *P. D.* Stockholm.

Kitchen range.

114. Wiman & Co. Stockholm.

Ventilation stoves.

These stoves of faience, cause a circulation of air in the room, store and gradually emit and equally distribute the heat and prevent the discomfort of cold floors.

115. Åkerlinds Aktiebolag. *Åkerlind Co. Limited.* Stockholm.

Stoves.

116. Elfving, C. E. Stockholm.

Lamp-wick-cleaner invented and made only for home consumption; is therefore not in the market, and not patented. The lamp-wick-cleaner consists of an iron or brass cylinder with a bottom made fast to it, and provided with a loose cover. Outside of a small hole on the middle of the cylinder, a conical scraper is fastened. With this scraper the burned part of the wick is scraped into the cleaner, by turning the cylinder around, inside the burner of the lamp.

The lamp-wick-cleaner was first manufactured in 1871.

Price: from 7 cents to 28 cents according to finish.

CLASS 224.

	Import-Duty in United States.		Sweden.	
IRON VESSELS, cast,	per lb.	1 ½ cts.	per lb.	1 öre.
IRON HOLLOW-WARE, glazed or tinned,	" "	3½ "	" "	1 "
IRON FRYING PANS, etc., wrought and tinned,	" "	35 per cent.	" "	10 "
" " " " galvanized with metal,	" "	2½ cts.	" "	10 "
JAPANNED-WARE, n. o. p. f.,	" "	40 per cent.	" "	15 "

117. Kallinge Bruk. *Kallinge Manufactory;* by F. H. Kockum. Ronneby.

Tin-lined and **enamelled, blocked-out,** and **handworked household vessels** of iron and steel-plates.

(**Wrought** and **cut nails.** See Cl. 284.)

(**Galvanized** iron vessels. See Cl. 291.)

(**Dairy-vessels.** See Cl. 675.)

Prev. aw. for vessels: at the industrial exhibitions in Stockholm, 1866; Copenhagen, 1872; Malmö, 1895 and 1875; Göteborg, 1871, and Mariestad, 1875. For the cut nails: Malmö, 1865; Göteborg, 1871, and the industrial exhibition in Copenhagen, 1872.

(For the wrought nails, as yet, no awards have been received, as they have not before been exhibited.)

Agencies in Stockholm, Göteborg, Malmö and Kristiana.

The manufacture of vessels was commenced in 1869, of cut-nails in 1856, and of wrought iron in 1873.

In the manufactory are employed 78 men, 29 women, 48 boys, and 13 girls under 15 years of age.

The power required is supplied by water-engines of the following aggregate capacities:

For vessels,	30 H. P.
" cut-nails,	35 "
" wrought-nails,	30 "
	95 H. P.

The production during 1874 consisted of

Vessels,	2,475 cwt
Cut nails,	12,700 "
Wrought nails,	11,000 "

The value of which were:

Vessels,	$47,000 gold.
Cut nails,	97,000 "
Wrought nails,	5,000 "
Total,	$149,700 gold.

for which the government taxes were $79, gold, and the community taxes $177, gold.

The raw materials used were:

For vessels:	Iron- and steel-plates,	3,300 cwt.
	Iron and iron-wire,	326 "
	English tin,	135 "
	Zinc,	30 "
For cut-nails:	Band-iron,	14,300 "
	Brass plates,	71 "
	Copper- and zinc-plates,	81 "
For wrought nails:	Band-iron,	15,000 "

The refuse cuttings are resmelted.

The exports go to Norway, Finland, Denmark and Germany.

For the benefit of the employees are established an evening and primary school, and a sick fund.

118. Kuntze & Co. Eskilstuna.

Water-filters, refrigerators.

CLASS 225.

119. Bolinder's, J. & C. G. Mekaniska Verkstads Aktiebolag. (See Class 222).

Stove for smoothing Irons.

120. Lafquist, J. A. Eskilstuna.

Smoothing irons.

CLASS 227.

	Import-Duty in United States.	Sweden.
TIMBER, hewn, or sawed for buildings,	20 per cent.	free.
" squared or sided, n. o. p. f.,	pr. cub. ft. 1 ct.	free.
SAWED BOARDS, plank, deals and other lumber of hemlock, whitewood, sycamore and basswood.	$1 pr. 1,000 ft. board meas.	free.
ALL OTHER varieties of rough, sawed lumber,	$5 pr. 1,000 ft. board meas.	free.

	Import-Duty in United States.	Sweden.
Provided, That when lumber of any sort is planed or finished, in addition to the rates herein provided, there shall be levied and paid for each side so planed or finished, 50 cents per 1,000 feet; and if planed on one side and tongued and grooved, $1 per 1,000 feet; and if planed on two sides and tongued and grooved, $1.50 per 1,000 feet.		
SHINGLES,	35 cts. pr. 1,000.	free
MANUFACTURES OF WOOD, n. o. p. f.,	35 per cent.	See Cl. 218.
LOCKS of brass or iron,	35 per cent.	See Cl. 218.
" others,	45 per cent.	
HINGES and BUTTS of copper,	45 per cent.	
" " " of brass,	35 per cent.	
" " " of gold, silver, or German-silver,	40 per cent.	
" " " of iron,	2½ cts. pr. lb.	

121. Björk, J. O. Eskilstuna.

Hardware of molified iron.

122. Dickson, James & Co. Sandarne.

Specimens of various kinds of plain and ornamental carpenters' work.

Prev. aw.: Göteborg, 1871, silver medal; Copenhagen, 1872, silver medal; Moscow, 1872, gold medal; Vienna, 1873, medal for progress.

Agents in Stockholm, Duisburg, Antwerp, Copenhagen and London.

In the "mechanical carpenter's work-shop" of Sandarne, situated seven miles south of Söderhamn, all sorts of frame-work for houses and interior finish are manufactured. The workshops were built 1870, the manufacturing partly begun in 1871, and in 1872 the whole factory was in full running order. At present 250 men and boys are employed in this factory, which has steam engines with a total capacity of 120 H. P.

During the last business year 575,000 cubic feet lumber of various descriptions, were used for the manufacturing of 25,000 doors, 6,000,000 feet of moulding, 3,000,000 feet of planed board, etc.

The lumber is dried by hot air, in drying-rooms capable of containing 235,000 cubic feet.

The value of the whole production in 1874, amounted to $139,000 gold, and most of it was exported to England, Egypt, Germany and Russia.

The children of the working-men receive their education in schools, which are supported by the proprietors. A fund for the poor and sick, an association for furnishing provisions at cost price, or so-called co-operative society, circulating library, bath-house and hospital have been established for the benefit of the working-men. Moreover, the latter have free lodging, full medical attendance and medicine. A church has also been built on the grounds, the company paying the minister's salary.

A special steamboat and railway furnish connection with the shipping port at the Baltic.

123. Essen, H. H. von, *Baron.* Tidaholm.

Various frameworks, doors, sashes, panels, fences, etc.

(**Iron for turning veneer.** See Cl. 510).

(**Pair of pruning-shears.** See Cl. 720).

Prev. aw.: Göteborg, 1871, 2 silver medals; Mariestad, 1874, giving employment to 32 men and 4 boys.

In the iron manufactories and nail shops 14 men and 2 boys are employed.

The machinery is worked by water power of about 90 H. P.

As materials were used in the factories during 1874, 1,000,000 cubic feet boards and 160,000 lbs. of iron; the following being the fabrics produced during said year: 2,140 dozen planks, 5,830 dozen boards, 4,530 dozen mouldings, 1,400 doors, 1,400 bay windows, 1,400 double bay windows, 600 bay doors, 136,000 lbs. of locksmith's and other hardware, 23,000 lbs. of nails. The value of said products being:

Frame-works,	gold, $33,300
Smiths-works,	" 1,300
Nails,	" 1,600
Total,	$43,200

The drying of the timber is effected by means of a caloric-engine, which throws a blast of heated air through the drying-room and draws it out again when saturated with moisture, in this manner the highest possible degree of dryness is obtained.

The refuse wood is used for fences, shingles, wood-pulp for the paper-mills, established at the same place, and as fuel in the workmen's lodgings, and in the just mentioned caloric engine.

Government taxes, $30 gold; community taxes, $60 gold.

A savings fund for the workmen is just being arranged.

124. Hedlund, J. Eskilstuna.

Metal-work for buildings.

125. Wengström, J. O. Stockholm.

Manufactured parts of buildings.

E.—YARNS AND WOVEN GOODS OF VEGETABLE OR MINERAL MATERIALS.

CLASS 228.

	Import-Duty in United States.	Import-Duty in Sweden.
WIRE, brass,	35 per cent.	free.
" copper,	45 "	free.
" iron, not over ¼ inch diameter, not thinner than No. 16 W. G.,	$2 pr. 100 lbs. & 15 pr. ct.	free.
" " over No. 16, not over No. 25 W. G.,	$3.50 pr. 100 lbs. & 15 pr. ct.	free.
" " over or finer than No. 25 W. G.,	$4 pr. 100 lbs. & 15 pr. ct.	free.
" " over ¼ inch diameter,	35 per cent.	free.
" steel, less ¼ in. diam., not less than No. 16 W. G.	2½ cts. pr. lb. & 20 pr. ct.	free.
" " less or finer than No. 16 W. G.,	3 cts. pr. lb. & 20 pr. ct.	free.

126. Anderson, J. Kjärdingagärde, Gnosjö.

Brass netting.

Tinned iron wire netting.

Plain iron wire netting.

Fine iron wire.

Brass rings.

Cow bell. Sheep bells.

Prev. aw.: Mariestad, 1874, bronze medal.

During the last few years the annual value of the production has amounted to about $5,500 gold.

At wholesale the discount is 10 per cent.

The manufactures are sold in Sweden, Norway and Denmark.

CLASS 330.

	Import-Duty in United States.	Import-Duty in Sweden.
COTTON-YARN, not wound upon spools, according to value,	10 to 40 cts. pr. lb. and 20 pr. ct.	pr. lb. 8 öre.
COTTON FABRICS, n. o. p. f., unbleached,	5 cents per square yard.	" 25 "
" " " " bleached,	5½ cents per square yard.	" 40 "
THE SAME, finer, unbleached,	5 cents per square yard.	pr. lb. to 1 Kr. 75 "
" " bleached,	5½ cents per square yard.	pr. lb. to 1 Kr. 25 "
COTTON CANVAS,	35 per cent.	pr. lb. 6 "

127. Berg, J. T. Nääs, Floda.

Unbleached, bleached, (and **dyed,** see Class 231), **cotton yarn** of different numbers, **twilled yarn** and other articles therefrom, showing the manufacture in its different stages, from the raw materials to the finished yarn.

Prev. aw.: Medals in Paris 1855, London 1862, Stockholm 1866, Borås 1870, and Wenersborg 1872; diploma of merit in Vienna, 1873.

Agency in Göteborg.

Nääs Manufactory (18 miles from Göteborg) was established in 1833, and the spinning was commenced in June, 1834. The dye-works were erected in 1836.

In the cotton mills are employed 33 men, 106 women, 26 boys and 38 girls under 15 years of age.

In the outside works, the workshop, the

dyeworks and the bleachery are employed 38 men, and 3 women.

The power required is supplied by 4 turbines, of together 204 H. P.

The manufactory consists of two cotton mills, dye works, and bleachery.

During 1874 were manufactured 96,876 hanks of cotton yarn, weighing 1,035,703 lbs., part warp, partly woof of different fineness, from No. 4 to No. 40, of which 13,540 hanks were dyed and 5,844 hanks bleached. At wholesale a discount of 2½ to 5 per cent. is made.

The production has amounted to :

Year.	No. of Hanks.	Weight: lbs.	Value, $ gcld.
1865,	57,578	617,838	287,900
1870,	95,783	1,024,768	288,900
1871,	93,357	998,913	263,200
1872,	93,300	095,248	271,100
1873,	94,465	1,080,775	264,300
1874,	90,976	1,035,703	252,900

In 1874, the government taxes were $420, gold, and the community taxes $505, gold.

The raw materials consist of American and East India cotton. During 1874, 2,288 bales American cotton, weighing 994,530 lbs., and 631 bales Madras, weighing 201,920 lbs., were used.

The refuse generally amounts to about 13 per cent. In 1874, it amounted to 160,740 lbs., of which about 35,000 lbs. were manufactured into wadding. The rest is partly tangle, for wiping machinery, and oakum, partly dirt, sand, and dust.

Among the measures adopted for the benefit of the laborers, may be mentioned that most of them have a free dwelling near the factory, with fuel and a garden plot, that the so-called co-operative society, formed among the workmen, is provided with a store and residence for the manager of the business, by which arrangement the members of the society get the necessities of life at the lowest possible price. With this society is also connected a savings and burial fund. A large school house erected by a former owner of Nääs, at his own expense, is situated close by the factories, and is frequented by the children of the workmen, who have also access to the parish library kept at the school.

128. Malmö Manufaktur Aktiebolag. *Malmö Cotton Manufacturing Co.* Malmö.

Samples of the Company's manufactures.

Prev. aw.: Medals in Stockholm an Malmö

Agency in Stockholm.

The manufacture was eommenced in 1856.

In the manufactory are employed 26 men, 124 women, 2 boys and 8 girls under 15 years of age; altogether 160 employees. They are mostly paid by the piece.

The power required is supplied by a steam-engine of 35 H. P.

The annual production consists of about 3,425,000 feet of sundry kinds of unbleached, bleached and dyed cotton goods.

Ten per cent. discount is allowed at wholesale.

The value of the manufacture during 1874 amounted to $122,200, gold, showing an increase since 1869, of $39,900, gold.

The government taxes in 1874,, were $160, gold, and the community taxes $636.

The raw materials consist principally of Swedish cotton-yarns, and some English yarns.

The twist refuse is used for wiping off the machinery.

The manufactures are sold mainly in Sweden, but a small part is also exported to Denmark.

129. Rosenlunds Spinneri Aktiebolag. *Rosenlund Cotton Manufacturing Co. Lim.* Göteborg.

Cotton-yarns, unbleached and bleached.

Cotton-yarns for fishing nets, all kinds.

Cotton-yarns for stockings.

Cotton-cloths, unbleached and bleached.

Cotton-canvas for sail-making.

Lamp-wicks.

Dyed cotton-yarns and fabrics. (See Cl. 231).

Prev. aw.: Silver and gold medals in Paris, 1855 and 1867; London, 1862 and 1872; Stockholm, 1866; Copenhagen, 1872; Moscow, 1872, and Vienna, 1873.

The company's works consist of the Rosenlund and Gammelstad factories, both in Göteborg, and the Anderstorp factory in Lindome, Halland.

Agencies in Stockholm, Copenhagen, Kristiania and Bergen.

The two first-named factories commenced operations in 1848, with 28,900 spindles, and the last-named, in 1874, with 20,000 spindles.

The number of persons employed at these three factories is 928, consisting of:

Men,	232
Women,	539
Boys under 15,	76
Girls under 15,	81

The power required is supplied by steam engines of 240 H. P.; 60 H. P. for the factory, commenced in 1875, being included.

The production in 1874, consisted of:

Cotton-yarns,	197,268 hanks.
Cotton cloths,	47,877 pieces.
Cotton-canvas,	1,172 pieces.
Lampwicks,	2,500 pounds.

To this production will be added in 1875, about 100,000 hanks, through the operations of the new mills.

The value of the manufacture during 1874, amounted to $539,000, gold, on which the government taxes were $850 and the community taxes, $3,010, gold.

The raw materials used during 1874, were 6,250 bales of cotton; in 1875, 9,950.

The refuse in 1874, was 233,000 lbs., which was sold partly for oakum, partly for filling in bedding and furniture, and also for paper-making.

The exports go to Norway and Denmark, and during the last two years also to Finland.

The workmen sustain two sick funds, established by the company.

At Rosenlund a bath-house is erected for the workmen, and a library with a reading-room and meeting-rooms are provided. A co-operative society is established by the workmen and is provided with a store, fitted up by the company. The workmen also receive free medical attendance and medicines in case of sickness.

CLASS 231.

	Import-Duty in United States.	Sweden.
DYED COTTON-FABRICS, n. o. p. f.,	5½ cts. pr. sq. yard and 10 pr. ct. per lb.	40-50 öre.
THE SAME, " " finer,	5½ cts. pr. sq. yard and 20 pr. ct. "	75 öre to 1 Kr. 25 öre.

130. Berg, J. Th. (See Cl. 230.)

Dyed cotton-yarns.

131. Malmö Bomulls Väfveri Aktiebolag. *Malmö Cotton Weaving Co., Lim.* Malmö.

Dyed cotton fabrics.

132. Rosenlund's Spinneri Aktiebolag. (See Cl. 230.)

Dyed cotton fabrics.

CLASS 232.

133. Johansson & Carlander. Göteborg. **Calicoes, etc.**

CLASS 233.

	Import-Duty in United States.	Sweden.
LINEN, Damask,	35 to 40 per ct.	pr. lb. 65 öre.

134. Stenberg's, G. Enka., (*Widow.*) Jönköping. **Diaper and damask linen fabrics.**

F.—WOVEN AND FELTED GOODS OF WOOL AND MIXTURES OF WOOL.

CLASS 235.

	Import-Duty in United States.	Sweden.
WOLLENS, n. o. p. f.,	20 to 50 cents pr. lb. and 35 pr. ct.	pr. lb. 25 to 75 öre.

135. Bergsbro Aktiebolag. *Bergsbro Co. Lim.* Norrköping.

Worsted and **woolen goods.**

Prev. aw.: Malmö, 1865, silver medal; Stockholm, 1866, silver medal; Paris, 1867, silver medal; Norrköping, 1869, silver medal

London, 1871, Diploma of Honour; Copenhagen, 1872, silver medal; Vienna, 1873, Medal of Merit.

Agencies in Stockholm and Borås.

Factories were founded in 1864. Water- and steam-power 90 H. P.; 152 men, 137 women, 51 boys and 39 girls employed.—7 assortments spinnings with 2,545 spindles, 110 looms, the required number of appreture machines, and a dye-house. In 1874, 231,144 lbs. washed wool, and 216,078 lbs. unwashed wool were used for making:

2,497 pieces of broadcloth, containing 73,007 yards,	value	$161,532 gold.
2,086 pieces of fancy broadcloth containing 60,051 yards,	"	187,895 "
Total, . . .		$349,427 "

The total value of the fabrics manufactured in 1870 amounted to about $170,000 gold, thus showing an increase of about 100 per cent. during the last 5 years.

Government taxes for 1874, .	$339 gold.
Community " " " .	186 "

Pension fund for aged and infirm, a sick and burial fund are established.

136. Drags Aktiebolag. *Drag Manufacturing Co., Lim.;* Norrköping.

Sundry fulled Woolens, plain and figured.

Prev. Aw. London 1862, first prize; Stockholm, 1866, second prize; Paris 1867, London, 1872, and Copenhagen, 1872, first prize; Vienna, 1873, Diploma of Honor and Medal of Merit; besides first prizes at several smaller exhibitions in Sweden.

The manufacture was commenced in 1854.

The power required for the operation of the mills is supplied by water engines of 220 H. P.

The annual production of the mills consists of 550,426 feet of woolens.

The value of the production amounted to:

in 1870, . . .	$251,000 gold.
" 1874, ...	485,000 "

The taxes on the production are, 1 per cent of the net income to the government, and, 5 per cent. of the same to the community.

The raw materials are 567,000 lbs. of wool.

No export.

For the benefit of the operators, sick and burial-funds have been established, and dwellings and bath houses are provided.

137. Landskrona Fabriks Aktiebolag. *Landskrona Manufacturing Co. Lim.;* Landskrona.

Woolen cloths, worsted coatings, etc.

Prev. aw.: Honorable mention: Copenhagen, 1872.

This factory, founded 1861, used last year 96,000 lbs. wool, and 56,000 lbs. shoddy for the manufacturing of 190,000 ft. cloths and coatings, at a value of $0.40 to $1.05 gold, per foot, all sold to the home-trade. The value of the whole production during 1868, amounted to $90,000 gold, and in 1873, to $122,000 gold. The machinery is worked by a steam engine of 35 H. P., and about 230 prisoners, sentenced for life, superintended by 9 foremen, are employed in the workshops.

138. Malmö Yllefabriks Aktiebolag. *Malmö Wool Manufacturing Co. Lim.;* Malmö.

Cardwool-fabrics.

139. Stockholm's Yllefabriks Aktiebolag. *Stockholm Woolen Manufacturing Co. Lim.* Reimersholm, Stockholm.

Woven and felted goods of wool.

Prev. aw: Copenhagen, 1872, (medal of second class), Vienna, 1873, (medal of merit).

The manufactory was established in 1868.

In the manufacture are employed: 37 men, 104 women, 12 boys and 10 girls, under 15, Besides these, the company employs 150 prisoners from the state's-prison, at Långholmen, and 60 female prisoners, from the prison on Norrmalm, Stockholm.

The power required is supplied by steam-engines of 100 H. P.

The company manufactures cloths, corduroys, doeskins, and all other qualities of goods pertaining to the woolen industry.

In the year 1874, the production consisted of:

Cloths, Doeskins, Corduroys—323,304 feet, .	value	$224,300 gold.
Blankets and shawls—15,033 pieces, . .	"	51,700 "
Total value, . .		$276000 "

In 1868, the value of the production was $141,500 gold.

The government taxes in 1874, were $169 gold, and the community taxes $274 gold.

All the refuse from the spindles is used in the factory, and that from the cutting-machine, is sold and used in the manufacture of coffins and wall paper.

Eight buildings are being erected on the Reimersholm estate, containing sufficient accommodations for the families of 50 workmen, and a large bathing-house will be built during the ensuing summer. Savings, and sick funds are about to be formed, but their by-laws have not yet been definitely adopted.

G.—SILKS.

CLASS 245.

	Import-Duty in United States.	Import-Duty in Sweden.
SILKS, plain, woven,	60 per cent.	pr. lb. 1 Kr. to 1 Kr. 50 öre.

140. Almgren, K. A. Stockholm. **Plain woven silks.**

H—CLOTHING, JEWELRY, AND ORNAMENTS, TRAVELING EQUIPMENTS.

CLASS 250.

	Import-Duty in United States.	Import-Duty in Sweden.
CLOTHING, ready-made, and wearing apparel, Dutiable according to material; all n. o. p. f.,	35 per cent.	20 per ct. additional duty to duty on the chief material.

141. Ek. J. A. Stockholm.
Military Equipments.

142. Fernlund, E. F. Stockholm.
Military and Civil Clothing.

143. Heurlin, G. U. & Co. Stockholm.
Military Clothing.

144. Kongl. Krigs Ministeriets Intendents Departement. *Roy. War-Office, Department of Investment.* Stockholm.

Complete equipment of a foot soldier.

Complete equipment of a mounted soldier.

Specimens of cloth, linens, etc., used in soldiers' uniforms.

145. Swedmark, G. Malmö.
Kidskin-jacket.

146. Wallgren, A. R. Stockholm.
Military Clothing.

CLASS 251.

	Import-Duty in United States.	Import-Duty in Sweden.
HATS, BONNETS AND HOODS, n. o. p. f.,	40 per cent.	per piece 40 öre.
" " " " of silk,	60 " "	" " 1 Kr. 50 "
GLOVES, Kid or Leather,	50 " "	per lb. 1 Kr.
BOOTS AND SHOES, Leather,	35 " "	" " 40 öre.
BOOTS, Leather, Sea, or Hunting,	35 " "	per pair 50 "

147. Forsell, D. & Co. Stockholm.
Hats and Caps. (See Cl. 256).

148. Jacobson & Andersson. Malmö.
Gloves.

149. C. E. Svanberg. Jönköping.
Hand-made shoes.
Machine-made shoes.

Prev. aw.: Malmö, 1865, medal; Copenhagen, 1872, medal; Vienna, 1873, medal; Mariestad, 1874, medal.

The manufacture of hand-made shoes was commenced in 1859, that of machine made in 1874.

Agencies in Stockholm, Kalmar, Wexiö, and Linköping.

From 20 to 50 workmen are employed.

150. Swedmark, G. Malmö.

Gloves.

151. O. Tornberg. Göteborg.

Boots and Shoes.

Prev. Aw. Copenhagen, 1872, silver medal, Vienna, 1875, medal of progress, Mariestad, 1874. silver medal.

Workshops opened 1870, employ 36 men, and 2 women.

Government taxes $17 gold, community taxes $58.

152. Ödberg, C. R. Stockholm.

Hunting-boots.

CLASS 252.

	Import-Duty in United States.	Import-Duty in Sweden.
EMBROIDERIES, n. o. p. f., ...	35 per cent.	20 per ct. additional duty to duty on the chief material.

153. Petterson, C. E. Stockholm. **Embroidered Portrait of** WASHINGTON.

CLASS 253.

154. Klintberg, J. W., & Co. Wisby. **Jewelry made of Petrifactions.**

CLASS 254.

	Import-Duty in United States.	Import-Duty in Sweden.
PINS, ...	35 per cent.	per lb. 25 öre.
HUMAN HAIR, Manufactures, ...	40 " "	" " 50 "

155. Anderson, J. Kjärdingagärde, Gnosjö.

Pins.

156. Berg, F. J. Göteborg.

Wigs, braids, and **chignons.**

Prev. aw.: Vienna, 1873; Mariefred, 1874; Uddevalla, 1875.

CLASS 256.

	Import-Duty in United States.	Import-Duty in Sweden.
FURS, of kid, reindeer, seal, moose, deer, kangaroo and hare, dressed, ... ,	20 per cent.	pr. lb. 10 öre.
MANUFACTURES of same, ...	35 " "	1 öre pr. lb. and 40 per cent.
FURS, of beaver, weasel, chinchilla, marten, sable, bluefox, otter, etc., dressed, ...	20 per cent.	1 Kr. pr. lb. and 20 per cent.
MANUFACTURES of same, , ...	35 per cent.	1 Kr. pr. lb. and 40 per cent.

157. Bergström, P. N. Stockholm.

Furs, a special catalogue of which will be found in the exhibition.

Agencies in 16 Swedish cities.

Prev. aw.: Silver medals in Stockholm, 1866; Paris, 1867; London, 1862, and at several local exhibitions.

In this factory, which was founded 1844.

there are at present employed 12 men, 12 women, and 2 children.

158. Forsell, D. & Co. Stockholm.

Furs.

CLASS 257.

159. Royal Swedish Commission. 29 life size figures, dressed in national costumes.

I.—PAPER, BLANK-BOOKS, AND STATIONERY.

CLASS 258.

	Import-Duty in United States.	Sweden.
PENHOLDERS, ...	35 per cent.	pr. lb. 25 öre.

160. Berggrén, A. N. Stockholm.

Penholders of cork. These penholders, being made of cork, are very light and elastic. The hand therefore never tires by their use, and in consequence of their thickness they enable the muscles to rest, which in the use of common penholders are under constant strain.

Prev. aw: Vienna, 1871, (medal of merit).

These penholders were first manufactured in 1870, at present being made only by hand.

For sale by book-sellers and stationers throughout Sweden. Wholesale price $0.83 gold, per dozen, $8.33 gold, per gross, retail price, 10 cents a-piece.

The penholders have been exported to Copenhagen, Kristiania, Helsingfors, Vienna and other places. Every penholder is marked, "A. N. BERGGRÉN, Skriflärare, Stockholm."

161. Brunell, J. E. Stockholm.

Penholders, made of the common reed (*Phragmites communis*).

A piece of cork is glued inside the reed, in which socket holder the pen is fastened; in this reed a stopper of cork is inserted, a cut is made with a cutting drill, and in the cut the pen is inserted, or inside the reed another reed is glued, between these two reeds a piece of cottonweed is fastened, and between this and the inner reed, room is made for the pen.

The principal virtues of these penholders are that they are the lightest penholders made, can be made of different sizes, and therefore are well adopted for all writers, especially for those who suffer from writers cramp. Manufacture commenced in 1875.

162. Klintberg, J. W., & Co. Wisby.

Letter-presses of petrifactions.

163. Kullgren's, C. A., Enka (*Widow*). Uddevalla.

Letter-presses of polished granite.

164. Nyström, M. S. Stockholm.

Stamps of Cork for marking Linen and paper.

These stamps give a clearer impression than those of wood or metal.

CLASS 259.

	Import-Duty in United States.	Sweden.
WRITING-PAPER and ENVELOPES, ...	35 per cent.	pr. lb. 8 öre.

165. Bock, Chr. A. Klippan, Åby.

Samples of different kinds of paper, manufactured at the mills of Klippan.

(**Wood-pulp.**—See Cl. 360).

Prev. aw. At exhibitions in Sweden and London.

The manufacture of paper was commenced about 1650. In the manufactory 94 men, and 72 women are employed, and besides these 250 rag-pickers.

The annual production is about 2,800,000 lbs. of paper, with a value of $317,300 gold.

Sick fund, etc., are established.

166. Litografiska Aktiebolaget, *Lithographical Co. Lim.;* Norrköping.

Envelopes.

167. Munktell, J. H. Grycksbo, Falun.

Filtering papers of different qualities.

(**Wood pulp**, see Class 250.)

Prev. aw.: Paris, 1867, bronze medal; Copenhagen, 1872, silver medal.

Agents: A. PETRÉ & Co., Stockholm.

These filtering papers are handmade, from the finest linen rags, the two best kinds are made during the coldest part of the winter season, a very low temperature being required in order to obtain a paper of superior quality.

In the filtering-paper factories of Grycksbo, are employed 40 men, and 60 women and children. The necessary force is supplied by water-engines of 60 H. P.

The annual production has during the last ten years, amounted to $40,000 to 60,000 gold, according to the supply of water. The taxes for this production paid to the government being $416 gold, and to the community $277 gold per annum.

A school and a prayer chapel are established at the factory, and the savings of the operators are deposited in the savings bank of the county.

CLASS 260.

	Import-Duty in United States.	Import-Duty in Sweden.
WOODPULP, dried,	20 per cent.	pr. lb. 2 öre.
PASTEBOARD,	35 " "	" " " "
PAPER, printing,	20 " "	" " " "
" wrapping,	10 " "	" " " "
" others, n. o. p. f,	35 " "	" " " "

168. Bock, Ch. A. Klippan, Åby.

Wood-pulp. (See Cl. 259).

169. Ekman, C. D. Bergvik.

Wood-pulp, chemically prepared.

170. Lewenhaupt, Sten, *Count.* Wermbohl. Katrineholm.

Chemical wood-pulp.

171. Mamlö Trämassefabriks Aktiebolag. *Malmö Wood-pulp Manufacturing Co. Lim.* Elmhult, Delary.

Chemically manufactured wood-pulp for paper-making.

The manufacture was commenced in 1872.

In the manufactory are employed 60 men, 40 women, and 10 children under 15 years of age.

The necessary power is furnished by water-engines of 100 H. P.

The annual production is about 1,500,000 lbs. wood-pulp, with a value of $5.56, gold, per 100 lbs

The raw materials used for this production are: 200,000 lbs. caustic soda, 600,000 lbs. calcined soda, 216,000 cubic feet pine-wood, 100,000 lbs. lime, besides 4,000,000 peat-bricks used for fuel.

The refuse, filtered soda-lime, is used for agricultural purposes.

The production is exported to England, Germany and France.

For the benefit of the employees, there is a school and bath-house at the factory. Savings-bank has been established at Elmhult, the nearest railroad station.

172. Munkedals Aktiebolag. *Munkedal Manufacturing Co.;* by Ivar, Kullgren, Munkedal, Uddevalla.

Wrapping-paper and **Bagging-paper**, finer and coarser, of different colors.

Paste-board for **walls**, nearly water-proof.

(**Tarred Paste-board**, for ground floors and outerwalls of wooden houses.—See Cl. 263).

(**Wall-paper**, in different colors.—See Cl. 264).

Stretching-paper, for ceilings.

Bagging-paper, etc. The manufactures are from wood, and distinguish themselves for strength, density, impenetrability to air and water, and in comparison with others, for cheapness.

Prev. aw. Uddevalla, 1874, gold medal, Mariestad, 1874, silver medal.

The manufacture was commenced in 1874.

The power required is supplied by water engines of 1000 H. P., by a fall of 137 feet.

As the manufactory has not yet gotten fully into operation, the amount and value of production so far received, and the taxes paid thereon do not show the real capacity of the factory and are therefore not included in this statement.

The raw materials used are, wood, colorings, glue, and fuel.

The production is exported to England, Germany, Denmark and Africa.

A sick-fund has been formed, by monthly contributions, from the workmen.

Price List of paper and pasteboard, from Munkedal Manufacturing Co., Uddevalla, Sweden.

	Price in pence pr. Engl. lb.
Paper for wall-paper manufacture (Long Elephant)	2½ d.
Wrapping-paper, fine and thin	3 d.
" fine, ordinary thick,	2 ½d.
Wrapping paper, less fine	2¼ d.
Pasteboard for wall-sheathing in rolls, waterproof	2¼ d.
Bagging-paper, thick, waterproof	2½ d.

173. Munksjö Pappersbruk. *Munksjö Paper-mills*; by O. Ljungquist, Jönköping.

Samples of **wrapping-paper.**

Building-paper. (See Cl. 263).

Prev. aw: Karlstad, 1762; Malmö, 1864; Stockholm, 1866 and 1868; Copenhagen and Moscow, 1872; Vienna, 1873 (all silver medals); and Paris, 1867 (honorable mention).

The manufacture was commenced in May, 1862.

In the mills are employed about 80 to 100 men, and 20 to 25 women, all above 20 years of age.

The power required is supplied by:

1 steam-engine, with condensor, of 75 H. P.
1 " " " " 50 "
1 " without " " 10 "
1 " " " " 5 "

N. B.—All nominal horse-power, but which experiment has shown to be more than double.

The production during 1874, consisted of:

Wrapping-paper from straw, etc., about . . .	15,000 cwt.
Mixed straw and rags—paste-board and unmixed rag-board, .	27,000 "
Asphalted and tar-soaked pasteboards for the outside covering of roofs and walls, about	12,000 "

The value of the production in 1874, amounted to $257,000 gold, during the quinquennium 1869-74, to $881,000 gold, and during the quinquennium 1864-69, to $42,700 gold.

The taxes during 1874, were $286 gold, to the government, and $1,112 gold, to the community.

The raw materials for the same production, consisted of rye-straw 36-40,000 cwt., rags, about 20,000 cwt., tar from coal-gasworks, about 3,500 barrels.

Of wrapping-paper, 30,000 to 50,000 reams are yearly exported to England, and South America, via Hamburg. The paste-board goes mainly to the Scandinavian countries, also to Finland and Russia.

Several savings funds, established for the benefit of the workmen, are managed by themselves, and a larger one is managed by the office of the manufactory. Library, reading-room and bath-rooms, with hot and cold water, are established at the mills, and are free to be used by the employees. Dwellings for the workmen, with water and a garden, are already designed in a park on the grounds of the manufactory.

174. Munktell, J. H. Grycksbo, Falun.

Woodpulp. (See Cl. 259.)

175. Nynäs Kartonfabrik. *Nynäs Pasteboard Factory;* by W. Almquist. Nynäs, Mavlda.

Paste-board of various kinds.

CLASS 262.

	Import-Duty in United States.	Import-Duty in Sweden.
PLAYING CARDS, ...	25 to 35 cents per pack.	pr. gr. 18 Kr.

176. Djupafors Fabriks Aktiebolag. *Djupafors Manufacturing Co. Lim.;* by T. Palander. Djupafors, Ronneby.

Pasteboard and carton, manufactured from wood-pulp, assorted with from 50 to 400 sheets per cwt. Dimensions 22 by 32 inches.

Air-dried wood-pulp, prime quality from pine (in pasteboard-form).

Prev. aw: Copenhagen, 1872, silver medal; Moscow, 1872, silver medal; Vienna, 1873, diploma of merit.

The manufacture commenced in 1869. In the manufactory are employed 40–50 men, with wages from 30 to 85 cents per day; 10 to 15 women, with wages from 20 to 25 cents per day; 10 to 12 boys, with wages from 15 to 20 cents per day.

The power required is supplied by water-engines of 265 H. P.

The annual production is about 13,000 cwt., consisting of air-dried wood-pulp, paste-board and carton, polished sheathing-board in form of slates, for roofing, and asphaltum-paper, for sheathing walls. For this manufacture are used 308,000 cubic feet of selected pine-wood, besides asphaltum-tar, etc.

The value of the production is about $25,-000 gold. At wholesale, a discount of 20 to 25 per cent. is given.

In the manufacture of the wood-pulp, it is collected on pasteboard cylinders in thick sheets and then air-dried, no pressing whatever being employed. In consequence thereof, the pulp is very soluble, white, and even.

All the wood-pulp, and most of the pasteboard is exported to England, Denmark, France, and Belgium.

177. Köhler & Co. Malmö.

Playing-cards.

178. Litografiska Aktiebolaget. *The Lithographical Co., Lim.* Norrköping.

Playing-cards.

CLASS 263.

	Import-Duty in United States.	Import-Duty in Sweden.
WALL PAPER, ...	35 per cent.	per lb. 8 öre.
PASTEBOARD FOR WALLS, ...	35 " "	Free.

179. Djupafors Fabriks Aktiebolag. (See Cl. 252).

Pasteboard for Walls, building-paper and method for using it.

180. Munkedals Aktiebolag. (See Cl. 260).

Building paper.

181. Munksjö Pappersbruk. (See Cl. 260).

Building paper.

CLASS 264.

182. Edgren, J., (late L. W. Norling.) Jönköping.

Wall Papers, from the plainest, one colored, machine printed on ordinary ground and gloss, to hand-printed on ordinary ground and finer gloss and fine, dull ground, part in color only, part in gold leaf and gold dust, varnished, machine and hand printed, and hand made wall-paper.

Borders, Corners, etc.

The products have not before been exhibited.

The manufacture was commenced by the former owner in 1853, transferred to present owner in 1871.

The number of workmen employed varies between 30 and 40, consisting of 15 men, 10 women and 10 to 15 boys under 15 years of age. Their wages have during late years, averaged 14,160 gold per annum.

Only hand-power is employed.

The production amounted to:

in 1871, 200,000 rolls of wallpaper and 4,000 rolls of border.

in 1872, 240,000 rolls of wallpaper and 4,000 rolls of border.

in 1873, 230,000 rolls of wallpaper and 6,000 rolls of border.
in 1874, 240,000 rolls of wallpaper and 6,000 rolls of border.
besides some friezes, etc.

At wholesale the discount varies between 10 and 20 per cent, with from 30 to 180 days credit.

The value of the production was:

In 1871, ...	$19,000 gold
In 1872, ...	25,000 "
In 1873, ...	26,100 "
In 1874, ...	27,100 "

The government taxes are one per cent of income, the community taxes 4½ per cent.

The rawmaterials consist of:

Paper, ...	$1,300 gold.
Colors, Glue and Glue-gloss, Varnishes, Dusts, etc.	$3,300 gold.

The refuse, paper-cuttings, is sold to paper-mills

Hitherto wall-paper has only been exported to Norway, to the value of from $1,600 to $2,200 gold per annum.

Deposits in the savings-bank, are made from a fund, formed through a certain percentage of extra allowance for the industry of the workmen and is paid them semi-annually.

183. Kåberg, C. A. Stockholm.
Wallpaper.

184. Mineur, C. G. Stockholm.

Wallpaper, imitation of leather and **ornaments in wood-pulp**—the exhibitor's invention, patented in Sweden. Patent in United States applied for.

185. Munkedals Aktiebolag. (See Cl. 260)
Wallpaper.

186. Rosell, P. A. & Co. Jönköping.
Wallpaper.

In the manufacture of wallpaper 3 ingeniously constructed machines are used, by means of which several different colors can be printed at once; also, hand-printing machines, a goffering machine, and 2 rolling machines.

Prev. aw.: At the exhibition for western Sweden, 1872, medal of gratification, Mariestad, 1874, silver medal.

The manufactory was established in 1857, and purchased by the present firm in 1868; it employs 30 men, who receive from $2.77 to $3.33 gold per week, and 20 boys who receive from $0.83 to $1,66 gold per week.

At present only hand-power is employed.

In 1874, 600,000 rolls of wall-paper, with a value of 155,600 per cent. gold were produced.

From 15 to 20 per cent. discount is allowed at wholesale.

The government taxes are 1.47 per cent. of the net income.

The community taxes are 5.16 per cent. of the net income.

The raw materials consisted of paper 210,000 lbs.; color, varnishes, gold, silver, glue, etc., 750 cwt.

Most of the forms and rollers of different patterns, are produced at the factory, which is done nowhere else in the country.

The paper refuse is sold to the paper mills.

The annual export to Norway amounts to about $5,500 gold.

There is a savings-bank in the community, and a sick-fund sustained by the workmen.

J.—MILITARY AND NAVAL ARMAMENTS, ORDNANCE, FIRE-ARMS, AND HUNTING-APPARATUS.

CLASS 265.

	Import-Duty in United States.	Import-Duty in Sweden.
FIRE-ARMS, all kinds, ...	35 per cent.	per lb. 20 öre.
IRON SHOTS, cast, ...	20 " "	per lb. 25 "

187. Husquarna Wapenfabriks Aktiebolag. *Husqvarna Arms Manufacturing Co. Lim.;* by Emil Ankarcrona, Musquarna, Jönköping.

Rifles, Carbines, Single and Double-Barrelled Shot-Guns, after REMINGTON'S model.

Sporting-Arms, single and double barreled, breech loading and central ignition.

Revolvers and **Pistols.**

Machine made guns.

(**Tools.** See Cl. 280.)

Sewing-Machines, and **parts** thereof. See Cl. 531.)

Prev. aw.: London, 1862, Honorable Mention; Stockholm, 1866, silver medal; Copenhagen, 1872, bronze medal; Moscow, 1872, one gold and one silver medal; Vienna, 1873, medal of merit; Mariestad, 1874, silver medal.

There are employed 350 men, 35 boys and girls. Their wages vary from $0.30 to $0.80 gold per day.

The power required is supplied by three turbines of about 200 H. P.

The annual production consists of 15,516 guns, 3,000 gun locks, etc., 230 sewing machines, and sundry casts.

The value of the production amounts to $178,000 gold, on which the government taxes were $275 gold and the community taxes $222 gold.

The raw materials used were:

Steel,	2,744 cwt.
Iron,	1,456 "
Steel-barrels,	776 "
Coal,	13,740 cub. ft.
Unfinished gun-stocks,	15,516 pieces.
Pig-iron,	1,400 cwt.

The production of arms is partly for the Swedish Army, and partly sold within the country.

For the workmen are erected 23 dwellings partly of wood, partly of stone.

The married workmen have garden-plots to their dwellings and have permission to erect their own houses, of which 15 have availed themselves.

The workmen have a sick and burial-fund of their own, to which the company contributes about $115 gold per annum, and the same amount to a pension institution for old workmen and their widows.

The company has besides given the workmen a large 4 story house to be used for a restaurant and grocery store. The company supports its own gas works, bath-house with hot and cold water, and a flour mill, where the workmen have their grain ground free.

188. Kongl. Krigs-Ministeriets Artilleri-Departement. *Roy. War-Office, Artillery Department.* Stockholm.

Military small arms, from the Royal Factory at Karl Gustafs Stad.

The work-shops of the royal gun factory at Karl Gustafs Stad, are contained in 3 buildings, viz.: The ram-house, the main building, and the stockmakers shops, occupying an aggregate area of 21,600 sq. feet.

Water-power is employed in 3 motors, with a minimum of 105 H. P., and this power is transmitted by 900 feet of shafting and 8,000 feet of belting to 187 machines, mounted in the shops.

These machines are:—

7 rams, 2 trip-hammers, 4 excenter-presses, 57 millings-machines, 4 rifle-machines, 1 barrel-polishing (emery) machine, 5 barrel-boring machines, 2 lead-finishing machines, 7 screw-machines, 4 screw-nut machines, 14 boring machines, 32 grinding and polishing (emery) machines, 8 profiling- and engraving-machines, 9 machines for cutting gun-stocks, 1 centring machine, 13 turn-benches, 7 plaining machines, 10 sundry other machines. Total, 187 machines.

The number of workmen varies from 150 to 400. Officers are: Chief Manager, Superintending Artillery-Officer, Boss, Cashier and Paymaster, 2 Clerks, 1 Inspector of Ordnances. The annual production can amount to 20,000 guns; the value of each gun, last year, was $8.33 gold.

No workmen are by contract bound to work at the factory any length of time.

CLASS 266.

189. Kongl. Krigs-Ministeriets Artilleri-Departement. *Roy. War-Office, Artillery Department.* Stockholm.

Field-gun with carriage.

Ammunition-carriage.

Field-forge.

Fusees, time and percussion, in different stages of fabrication.

190. Motala Mekaniska Verkstads Aktiebolag. *Motala Mechanical Works Co., Lim.* Motala.

Hoops for heavy guns.

191. Palmcrantz, Helge. Stockholm.

Mitrailleuse.

CLASS 267.

192. Ekman, Carl, Finspong, and **De Maré, A.** Ankarsrum.

Steel-guns and **shots.**

193. Kongl. Krigs-Ministeriets Artilleri Department. *Royal War-Office, Artillery Department.* Stockholm.

Fortification-ordnance with **carriage** and **shots.**

CLASS 268.

	Import-Duty in United States.	Import-Duty in Sweden.
SWORDS AND KNIVES, with handles, ...	40 to 50 pr. ct.	pr. lb. 10 to 50 öre according to material of handle.
THE SAME, blades only, polished, . - - -	35 per cent.	pr. lb. 25 öre.

194. Eskilstuna Jernmanufaktur Aktiebolag. *Eskilstuna Iron Manufacturing Co., Lim.;* by Jacob Svengren. Eskilstuna.*

Swords, Blades, Sabres, Foils, and Hunting knives.

Prev. aw.: Stockholm, 1851, and 1856; Paris, 1855 and 1867; Copenhagen, 1872; Moscow, 1872; Vienna, 1873.

This manufacturing began about 1820, MR. CHR. ZETTERBERG being at that time owner and manager of the works. At present the said company manufactures all sorts of cutlery, hardware for buildings, etc. The quantity of sword-blades manufactured varies according to orders issued from the regiments. The value of the entire production in 1866, amounted to $13,800 gold, and in 1875 to $16,300 gold, whereof only 41 per cent. ($7,500) for sword-blades. For this manufacturing were used:

7,400	lbs of various kinds of	steel.
41,100	" " " "	iron.
17,400	" " " "	iron- and steel-plates
5,500	" " " "	other materials.

* The town of Eskilstuna was founded in 1606, by King KARL IX, whose practical eye had already detected the advantages which the situation of the place and its plentiful supply of water-power offered for manufacturing purposes. Iron-workers and engineers were encouraged to settle there, and were promised munificent privileges as well as exemption from tithes and taxes. The settlement, however, progressed but slowly until 1654, when REINHOLD RADEMACHER, a Livonian, whose large iron-works had been ruined by the war between Sweden and Poland, was induced to remove to Eskilstuna with all his workmen. King KARL X GUSTAF (Charles Gustavus X), who was extremely anxious to advance the manufacturing interests of Sweden, which was then in its infancy, and shared the common belief of his age in the beneficial effects of monopolies, endowed Rademacher and his followers with great immunities and special privileges. They were granted as much land as they wanted for building purposes, and as pasture for their cattle. Dwelling-houses were erected for them at the expense of the Crown, sufficient water-power was assigned to them, and coal and wood were supplied by the Crown. Moreover, Rademacher was entitled to have a large amount of copper coined yearly, without paying any seignorage, and a high protective duty was imposed on an article, which the new factories were to produce.

Still, in spite of all these privileges, the works did not thrive. The principal difficulty seems to have been the want of workmen. Numerous complaints were soon made, that the apprentices did not serve out their time, and, although the Orphan asylum, at Stockholm, was directed to supply Rademacher with thirty apprentices yearly, and exemption from military service promised all persons, who, after having served out their apprenticeship of three years would stay five years longer. These advantages seem to have been insufficient to procure sufficient laborers. At Rademacher's death the works were found to be bankrupt, and were sequestrated by the Crown, which, however, a few years later ceded them back to his son-in-law. Still very little activity was displayed at Eskilstuna during the following eighty years.

After a second sequestration by the Crown and several subsequent changes of owners, the land, on which the old works had been erected, was finally in 1771 bought back by the government, which then decided upon trying another system. That which monopoly and privileges had failed to perform *liberty* was called on to accomplish. Eskilstuna was declared a free town, and immunity from all personal taxes granted, not as before to one man and his followers, but to all who chose to settle in the town for the purpose of engaging in the iron and steel trades. Transports to Eskilstuna were freed from all custom duties, and perfect liberty allowed the manufacturers in carrying on their work and disposing of their goods, a boon of no slight importance in this age of regulations and restrictions, when all over Europe the strictest rules interfered in even the most minute details of every trade. Events proved the liberal spirit which had dictated these exemptions from the petty tyranny of trade guilds and corporations to have been wise in its policy. No more privileges were needed to attract working-men to the town, which, under the Rademacher monopoly, could not find hands enough. Competition and freedom from artificial restraint were all that was wanted to make industry prosper,, until now, after a period of over 100 years, its products have attained a world wide renown and the Eskilstuna steel has found its way to all the principal markets of the world.

600 cubic feet of coals and coaks, (the quantity of charcoal not being kept account of).

Power: 63 men, 2 women, 5 boys; grinding-works with two water wheels of altogether 15 H. P.

The company carries on business with its own and other's products, last years sales amounted to $123,000 gold. 19 per cent. were sold to Finland and Russia, 2 per cent. to Norway, ⅔ per cent. to Denmark—the rest in Sweden.

The factory keeps a library of its own, open to the workmen. A Sunday- and evening-school, free bath-house, a sick- and burying-fund, savings-bank, etc., are established in the town for the benefit of the workmen at the various factories.

A large factory is being built by the company at Tunafors, close to the town.

K.—MEDICINE, SURGERY, PROTHESIS.

CLASS 272.

	Import-Duty in United States.	Import-Duty in Sweden.
MEDICINAL PREPARATIONS, n. o. p. f.,	40 per cent.	free.
" " patent,	50 " "	importation prohibited.

195. Piltz, G. Stockholm.

Gelatinæ medicatæ in lamellis; thin laminas of gelatine containing different kinds of medicines, invented by Professor A. ALMÉN of Uppsala, prepared by the exhibitor.

Prev. aw.: Paris, Geogr. Congr., 1875.

196. Lamm, Axel, *M. D.* Stockholm.

Galvano Caustic apparatus, Price $330 gold.

Uterine-rheophore. " 21 "

CLASS 276.

	Import-Duty in United-States.	Import-Duty in Sweden.
SURGEONS' INSTRUMENTS, not cutlery,	according to material.	pr. lb. 15 öre.
" " cutlery,	35 per cent.	" " " "

197. Kongl. Krigsministeriets Fältläkare-Kontor. *Royal War Office Sanitary Department,*. Stockholm.

Set of Surgical Instruments for military use.

198. Stille Alb. Stockholm.

Surgical Instruments.

Cutlery for **Naturalists.**

199. Zander, G. *M. D.* Stockholm.

Apparatus for Mechanical Gymnastics.

See Cl. 340.

L.—HARDWARE, EDGE-TOOLS, CUTLERY, AND METALLIC PRODUCTS.

CLASS 280.

	Import-Duty in United States.	Import-Duty in Sweden.
STEEL, manufactures of n. o. p. f.,	45 per cent.	pr. lb. 10 to 25 öre.
CUTLERY, all kinds, but pen, pocket, and jack-knives,	35 "	See cl. 268.
" pen-, pocket-, and jack-knives,	50 "	See cl. 268.
IRON, manufactures of n. o. p. f.,	35 "	per lb. 1½ to 6 öre.
" nails, spikes, etc., cut,	pr. lb. 1½ cts.	per lb. 1½ to 6 öre.
" " " " wrought,	" 2½ "	per lb. 1½ to 6 öre.
" screws, n. o. p. f.,	35 per cent.	per lb. 1½ to 6 öre.
BRASS, lead, tin, etc., manufactures of n. o. p. f.,	35 "	per lb. 15 öre.
TOOLS, hand, and for factories,		50 per cent.
BRASS NAILS and YELLOW METAL for sheating,		free.

200. Eskilstuna Jernmanufaktur Aktiebolag.
Screw-plates. (See Cl. 260.)

201. Fagersta Bruks Aktiebolag. (See Cl. 111.)
Saws.

202. Liberg, B. & O. Rosenfors.
Edge-tools. (See Cl. 281.)

203. Nya Filfabriken. *New File Factory*, by C. M. Looström & Co. Eskilstuna.
Files.

204. Uddeholms Aktiebolag.
Hand-tools.

205. Öberg, C. O. & Co. Eskilstuna.
Files.

CLASS 281.

206. Engström, Joh. Eskilstuna.
Razors.

207. Gustafsson, G. Eskilstuna.
Knives.

208. Halling, A. Eskilstuna.
Knives.

209. Heljestrand, Chr. Eskilstuna.
Razors, Knives, and Cork-screws.

210. Liberg, B. O. *Rosenfors.*

Scissors, Skates, Plane-irons, Chisels and Cork-screws.

The manufacturing commenced in 1863, and gives employment to 60 men.

The power required is supplied by water-engines of 24 H. P.

The production during 1864, amounted to $1,300 gold, and during 1874, to $33,000 gold, for which latter production $55 gold, were paid in taxes to the government, and $138 gold to the community.

The exports are principally to Norway, Finland and Denmark.

211. Ståhlberg, L. F. Ståhlfors.

Table-Knives, Carving-Knives, Kitchen and Bread-Knives, Chopping-Knives, Butcher, Pocket, Shoemaker's, and several other kinds of knives.

Prev aw. Stockholm, 1858 and 1866, Paris, 1855 and 1867, Malmö, 1865, Lysekil, 1868, Copenhagen, 1872, Vienna, 1873.

Ståhlfors manufactory was established in 1847, and commenced operation in 1848.

For the manufactory are employed:

Assistants	2.
Workmen over 18 years of age	29.
" under 18 " " "	8.

altogether 39 persons.

The power required for running the manufactory is supplied by two water engines of 12 H. P. each, and in case of necessity a steam engine of 6 H. P.

The value of the manufacture in 1869, amounted to $5,500 gold, and in 1874, to $15,300 gold, on this latter sum the taxes to the government were $40 gold, to the community $127 gold, and to the pastor $26 gold.

In 1874, the following rawmaterials were used:

Bessemer-steel,	338 cwt.
Ebony, .	178 "
Charcoal, .	1200 barrels.

For the forging, mechanical hammers are employed; thus giving quicker and better work at less cost.

The refuse, steelcuttings, are sold to Iron-works.

The largest part of the manufacture is sold in Sweden, the next largest amount in Norway, and smaller quantities in Denmark and Finland.

Deposits for the children of the workmen, have been made in the Life-annuity and Capital Assurance Institution of Stockholm.

212. Svalling, E. M. Eskilstuna.
Knives.

213. Söderen, F. M. Eskilstuna.
Knives.

CLASS 284.

214. Fagersta Bruks Aktiebolag.
Nails. (See Cl. 111.)

215. Eskilstuna Jern Manufaktur Aktiebolag. Eskilstuna.
Hinges. (See Cl. 268.)

216. Hedlund, Joh. Eskilstuna.
Locks.

217. Jernbergh, S. Eskilstuna.
Latches.

218. Johnson, A, & Co. Stockholm.
Cart-spring.

219. Kallinge Bruk.
Nails. (See Cl. 210.)

220. Lafquist, J. A, Eskilstuna.
Hinges.

221. Lagerbeck, H. Eskilstuna.
Locks.

222. Lindström, J. F. Eskilstuna.
Hardware.

223. New Gellivara Co. Lim. (See Cl. 111.)
Nails.

224. Robson, Albert. Aspa, Askersund.

Oak spikes, wrought by water hammer, from bars drawn from pig-iron of exhibitor's own manufacture, from ores from the mines of Striberg, Pershytte, Klacka, in Nora, mining districts, and from ores from the Sanna mine, in Lekeberg mining-district.

Prev. aw.: for oak spikes, London, 1862, medal; Paris, 1861, honorable mention.

The power required is supplied by water-engines.

The raw materials annually used are:

Ores from the exhibitor's own mines,	66,579	cwt.
Pig-iron,	33,729	"
Bar-iron,	20,201	"

The refuse, scrap-iron, is exported.

The bar-iron is exported to England and America.

The principal brand is:

CK LANCASH GASWD SWEDISH

225. Stenman, F. A. Eskilstuna.
Locks.

226. Strandberg, J. Eskilstuna.
Brass.

227. Strandell, A. L. Eskilstuna.

228. Sundström, F. O. Charlottenberg.
Nails.

229. Udderholms Aktiebolag.
Springs.—(See Cl. 111).
Hardware.

230. Walén, Joh. Eskilstuna.
Locks.

231. Wiklund, W. Stockholm.
Brass-hardware.

20 per cent. discount allowed at wholesale.

M.—FABRICS OF VEGETABLE, ANIMAL, OR MINERAL MATERIALS.

CLASS 285.

	Import-Duty in United States.	Import-Duty in Sweden.
MANUFACTURERS OF INDIA RUBBER mixed with cotton, etc.,	35 per cent.	per lb. 75 öre.

232. Tuxen, Louis von. Stockholm.

"Technical Patent Leather."

This leather is manufactured from new and old leather, which is ground and then condensed by chemicals, and used for Tarpaulins, Sun-tents, Floor-mats, Wall-covering, Machine-belts, Gas-, Water-, and other kinds of Pipes, Press- and Machine-packings, etc.

The manufacture was commenced in 1865, and gives employment to 9 men, 3 women, and 2 boys, with wages aggregating $70 gold per week.

The power required is supplied by a steam engine of 4 horse-power, of TANGYÉ'S Patent, Birmingham.

The raw material used are leather-refuse, india rubber and chemicals.

The india-rubber is dissolved in turpentine, benzine, or bisulphide of carbon, in the manufactory.

CLASS 286.

	Import-Duty in United States.	Import-Duty in Sweden.
BRUSHES,	40 per cent.	per lb. 5 to 20 öre, according to material of handle.

233. Stocklassa, F. Stockholm, **Brushes.**

CLASS 289.

	Import-Duty in United States.	Import-Duty in Sweden.
ARTICLES MADE OF WILLOW, finer,	35 per cent.	per lb. 25 öre.

234. Olsson, M., Deaf and Dumb. W. Årnäs, Lima.

Flower-stand, willow-chair and **basket.**

Prev. aw. Stockholm and Vienna.

CLASS 291.

	Import-Duty in United States.	Import-Duty in Sweden.
IRON-WARE, GALVANIZED,	per lb. 2½ cts.	30 öre.

235. Galvaniserings Aktiebolaget Kariskrona, *Karlskrona Galvanizing Co.* Karlskrona.

Zinc-plated Swedish Sheet-iron, which by the plating has not lost its flexibility, but can be bent or worked into any object desired, the zinc-plating still remaining intact.

Prev. aw: Moscow, 1172, bronze medal; Vienna, 1173, medal of merit; Mariestad, 1874, large silver medal.

Agencies in Stockholm, Göteborg, Malmö, Norrköping, Landskrona, Wisby, Copenhagen, Kristiania, and Nystad.

The manufacture was commenced in 1870.

The plating process, secret.

236. Kallinge Bruk. (See Class 224.)
Galvanized Vessels.

DEPARTMENT III.

EDUCATION AND SCIENCE.

A —Educational Systems, Methods, and Libraries.

	Import-Duty in United States.	Sweden.
All printed matter, engravings bound or unbound, illustrated books and papers, maps and charts, n. o. p. f.,	25 per cent.	free.
Books, printed abroad in the Swedish language and n. o. p. f.,	free.	per lb. 15 öre.
Philosophical apparatus and instruments, n. o. p. f.,	40 per cent.	per lb. 15 öre.

CLASS 300.

237. Abrahamson, August. Nääs, Floda.

Works by the pupils to the Nääs Mechanic's School.

Prev. aw. Agricultural Exhibition at Venersborg, 1872, silver medal, at Mariestad, 1874, silver medal.

The school was opened by its present director, in 1872, for boys, with two teachers and twelve pupils, who are paid respectively 50 cts. and 12 cts. gold per day.

About 40 per cent of the earnings of the boys is deposited in a savings bank.

The subjects taught are elementary mathematics, physics, drawing, and all subjects taught in "common schools," together with handiwork.

A class for girls was formed in 1874, with 16 pupils.

Subjects: Women's handiwork, housekeeping and such as are taught in the "common schools."

238. Alard, A. F. Simtuna, Enköping.

Musical Staff Table, $2.00 gold.

Favorable opinion expressed by the R. Swed. Academy of Music.

239. Anderson, N. J., with assistance from Erdmann, Holmgren, Johanson, Kinman, and Lovén. Stockholm.

Specimens of evertebrate animals, plants and minerals. $400.00.

240. Bagge, G. B. Paris, France.

Geographical Maps.

241. Berggren, A. N. Stockholm.

Method of Penmanship. $6.50.

242. Brunell, J. E. Stockholm.

A set of Penholders. $1.00.

243. Cervin, C. G. Hesselby, Stockholm.

Model of a School-house.

Mr. Cervin, late owner of Hesselby estate, situated in the parish of Spånga, nine Eng. miles from Stockholm, established, in 1873, a school for the benefit of his tenants. The cost of the building was $3000 gold. At present sixty children receive daily instruction. The building contains, besides a large school-room, four rooms and two kitchens for the master and the governess of the school, It is sourrounded by a garden in which every pupil has his own little plot to cultivate. The scholars are instructed in reading, writing, religion, history, geography and arithmetic, besides which a tailor, a shomaker and a cooper teach the children, at times, their different professions. The girls receive lessons in sewing from the governess.

244. Collective Exhibition of the R. Swedish Commission.

(Partakers in the Collective Exhibition; Anderberg, Ida; Anderson, N. J.; Arrhenius, J.; Askerberg, F. C.; Beckman, J.; Beijer, F.; Berg, F. J.; Bonnier, Alb.; Borgman, Hilda;

Burman, Conny; Carlsson, Mathilda; Dalström, J. G.; Ekberg, H.; Ekman, P. J.; Erdmann, Edv.; Ewerlöf, F.; Fritze, C. E.; Gernandt, C. E.; Hartelius, F. J.; Hasselgren, L. C.; Hedlund, S. A.; Huldberg, P. A.; Hübenette, A.; Hübenette, F.; Hörnsten, Jenny; Klemming & Co.; Lindblad, J.; Lindström, H.; Ling, H.; Lithografiska Atiebolaget, Norrköping; Lovén, N. H.; Lundh, L. A.; Lundholm, Pr,: Lundholm, T.; Lundin, F.; Lundström, Laura: Lyth, G. W.; Mentzer, F. A. von; Norstedt, P. A. & Sons; Olafson, J.; Peterson, H.; Petterson, Lotten; Samson & Wallin; Sandström, Andr.; Siljeström, P.; Sjölander, C. O.; Sjöström, Th.; Smitt, F. A.; Smitt, J. W.; Stille, Alb.; the Economical Survey of Sweden; the Primary School at Finspong; the Primary Schools in Stockholm; the Society for the Promoting of Useful Knowledges; the Topographical Survey of Sweden; Wadner, L. A.; Wallberg, M. V.; Wallberg, Octavia; Wallquist, A. L.; Östling, G.)

A Primary Country school-house with accessories of furniture, books, maps and apparatus for instruction. Architects, ISÆUS and JACOBSON. Size 40 feet by 50 feet. Situated in the exhibition grounds, north of the Main building. A one-story frame house, containing schoolrooms and the interior arrangements of a Swedish school-house. The frame-work for the building was imported from Sweden, and is on exhibition by G. O. WENGSTRÖM, of Stockholm.

Model of an elementary school-house.

Swedish common school material.

(ALL PRICES IN DOLLARS GOLD.)

RELIGION.

1. The Holy Bible: Swedish Bible Society's edition. (0.75).
2. The Holy Bible, Illustrated. (3.35).
3. The New Testament, (larger). (0.25).
4. " " " (smaller). (0.20).
5. Bible Manual, by BERG. (0.60).
6. Short Bible Manual, by EKEBORG. (0.10).
7. Introduction to Old and New Testament, by BRODÉN. (0.50).
8. The hymnal and prayer-book. (0.90).
9. " " with chorals. (0.65).
10. LUTHER'S Small Catechism, with explanations, by LINDBLOM. (0.07).
11. LUTHER'S Small Catechism, with explanations, by HULTKRANTZ. (0.07).
12. Catechism, by FLODMAN. (0.25).
13. " " LINDBERG. (0.10).
14. " " BERGQUIST. (0.25).
15. " " ÖSTBERG. (0.07).
16. The Revised Catechism. (0.25).
17. Revised Catechism, by BJÖRLING.
18. Biblical History, by HALLBERG. (0.25).
19. " " " ROOS. (0.07).
20. " " " HOLMGREN. (0.30).
21. " " " KURTZ. (0.45).
22. " " " SANDBERG. (0.10).
23. " " " HÜBNER. (0.30).
24. " " " PETTERSSON. (0.10).
25. " " " STEINMETZ. (0.07).
26. " " " ÅKERBLOM. (0.07).
27. " " " EKEBORGH. (0.07).
28. " " " SONDÉN. (0.07).
29. " " " BOHM. (0.07).
30. " " " LANDGREN. (0.07).
31. " " " WELANDER. (0.30).
32. " " " LUNDGREN. (0.07).
33. " " " BÄCKMAN. (0.07).
34. History of the Swedish Church, by ANJOU. (0.60).
35. Bible-Atlas, by WADNER. (0.30).
36. Map of Palestine, by STEINMETZ. (0.10).
37. Map of Palestine, by MENTZER and WADNER. (1.25).
38. Biblical pictures. (2.80).

THE SWEDISH LANGUAGE.

39. Vocabulary, by the SWEDISH ACADEMY. (1.25).
40. Swedish Dictionary, by DALIN. (2.00).
41. Swedish Synonymes, by DALIN. (0.85).

42. Word-families of the Swedish Language, by DALIN. (0.85).
43. Foreign words, by DALIN. (2.75).
44. Swedish Grammar for elementary schools, by SUNDÉN. (0.75).
45. Swedish Grammar for common schools, by SUNDÉN. (0.15).
46. Swedish Grammar for common schools, by UPPMARK. (0.25).
47. Swedish Grammar for common schools, by BRODÉN. (0.30).
48. Swedish ortography, by SUNDÉN. (0.15).
49. " " " ALMQVIST. (0.15).
50. READER for the common school. (0.45).
51. Swedish reader, by SUNDÉN & MODIN. (0.65).
52. Reader, by BJURSTEN. (1.10).
53. " " SVEDBOM. (0.85).
54. " " SILJESTRÖM. (0.15).
55. " " BÄCKMAN. (0.50).
56. " " LANDGREN. (0.35).
57. " " GLASELL. (0.85).
58. " " KYHLBERG. (0.15).
59. " " CNATTINGIUS. (0.30).
60. " " VINGE. (0.25).
61. Poetic reader, by ÖMAN. (0.15).
62. Historic-poetical reader, by LINDBLAD. (0.75).
63. Patriotic reader, by HAZELIUS. (0.85).
64. History of the Swedish language and literature, by CLAESSON. (0.35).
65. History of the Norwegian and Danish literature, by UPPMARK. (0.35).
66. Reader for children, by TOPELIUS. (2.75).
67. Reader for the primary school, by KASTMAN. (0.20).
68. Reader for the primary school, by SANDBERG. (0.15).
69. Primmer for the primary school, by SANDBERG. (0.20).
70. New Primmer, by RANCKEN. (0.15).
71. Box containing alphabet. (1.15).

ARITHMETIC AND GEOMETRY.

72. Arithmetic (larger) by SILJESTRÖM. (0.12).
73. " (smaller) " " (0.10).
74. " " BÄCKMAN. (0.30).
75. " " NYSTRÖM. (0.60).
76. Elementary course in Arithmetic, by BERGIUS. (0.45).
77. Arithmetic, by SIEVERS. (0.25).
78. " " LANDGREN. (0.52).
79. " " PIHLSTRAND. (0.35).
80. Exercises in Calculation, by SILJESTRÖM. (0.15).
81. " " by NORDLUND. (0.25).
82. Arithmetic Problems, by SEGERSTEDT. (1.10).
83. Mental Arithmetic, by SEGERSTEDT. (0.30).
84. Formulas and book-keeping, by SEGERSTEDT. (0.10).
85. Geometry for the Common School, by LILJESTRÖM. (0.12).
86. Elementary Geometry, by BERGIUS. (0.65).
87. Geometry and linear drawing, by BERGIUS. (0.45).
88. Geometry for the Common School, by BÄCKMAN. (0.20).
89. Geometry, by SEGERSTEDT. (0.15).
90. Geometry, by BJÖRKMAN. (0.15).
91. Table of Swedish measures, weights, etc. (0.15).
92. Calculating-staffs. (0.25).
93. Abacus, (larger). (0.75).
94 " (smaller). (1.75).
95. Apparatus for instruction in Arithmetic, by NORDLUND. (12.50).
96. Calculating cube. (5.00).
97. Box with smaller calculating cubes. (1 00).
98. Stereometrical figures. (7.00).
99. Conical sections. (1.00).
100. Compasses and protractor. (3.50).

HISTORY AND GEOGRAPHY.

101. Textbook of Swedish History, by STARBÄCK. (0.15).
102. Narratives from Swedish History, by STARBÄCK. (5.50).
103. Swedish Historical Reader, by STARBÄCK. (0.50).
104. Swedish Historical Text-book (larger), by ODHNER. (0.85).
105. Swedish Historical Text-book (medium), by ODHNER. (0.45).
106. Swedish Historical Text-book (smaller), by ODHNER. (0.15).
107. Pictures and narratives from Swedish history, by SANDBERG. (0.30).
108. Text-book of Swedish history, by KASTMAN and BRUNIUS. (0.15).
109. Pictures from the universal history, by KASTMAN and BRUNIUS. (0.40).
110. Text-book of universal history, by PALIN. (0.60).
111. The History of the Middle Ages, by PALIN. (0.50).
112. Text-book of universal history, by WENNERSTRÖM. (0.20).
113. Historical Reader, by SJÖGREN. (1.15).
114. Historical Reader, by SPILHAMMAR. (1.75).
115. Text-book of Geography, by ERSLEV. (0.15).
116. Geography for the Common School, by ERSLEV. (0.15).
117. Text-book of Geogrphy, by BÄCKMAN. (0.25).
118. " " " " ÅLUND. (0.15).
119. Geographical Pictures, by KASTMAN & BRUNIUS. (0.50).
120. Notable places in Sweden, by STARBÄCK. (0.15).
121. Sweden, Illustrated. (1.85).
122. The Swedish people, by WALLANDER. (5.60).
123. Our country and people, by SCHÜCK. (1.40).
124. Geographic-historic Reader, by HOFBERG & LJUNGSTEDT. (0.45).
125. The Regents of Sweden. (0.85).
126. Atlas to the Swedish history, by WIBERG & MENTZER. (2.10).
127. Map of the Middle and Southern parts Sweden, by HAHR. (5.00).
128. Map of the Northern part of Sweden, by HAHR. (1.40).
129. Country maps, by LARSSON. (0.85).
130. Atlas for the school and home (printed in Gotha), by ROTH. (0.30).
131. Map of Sweden, Norway, and Denmark, by ROTH. (1.85).
132. County Atlas of Sweden, by VON MENTZER. (3.50).
133. School-Atlas, by VON MENTZER. (0.60).
134. Atlas for Common Schools. (0.25).
135. Political wall-map of Sweden and Norway, by VON MENTZER. (4.50).
136. Physical wall-map of Sweden and Norway, by VON MENTZER. (4.50).
137. Map of Scandinavia, by VON MENTZER. (1.70).
138. The Scandinavian North, by VON MENTZER. (0.35).
139. Historical Period of the Scandinavian North, by VON MENTZER. (0.60).
140. Increase of the Swedish Power, by VON MENTZER. (0.20).
141. Illustrated Statistics, by VON MENTZER. (2.50).
142. Map of Europe, by VON MENTZER. (0.30).
143. Map of America, by VON MENTZER. (0.45).
144. Map of Asia, by VON MENTZER. (0.45).
145. Map of the World, by VON MENTZER. (0.60).
146. Maps of the Economical Survey. (0.60).
147. Geographical tables (edited by the Society for popular instruction) (0.70).
148. For geographical intuitive instruction and map-drawing, by ÅBERGH. (0.05).
149. Terrestrial globe (larger). (17.00).
" " (smaller). (3.40).
150. Celestial globe. (8.50).
151. Tellurion and lunary. (9.80).
152. Black-board map for elementary geographical instruction. (8.50).

NATURAL SCIENCE.

153. Natural History reader, by BERLIN. (0.45).
154. Text-book of Natural History, by BERLIN. (0.25).
155. Text-book of Natural History, by CELANDER. (0.30).
156. Natural History, by SEGERSTEDT. (0.25).
157. Text-book of Natural History, by PAYKULL. (0.20).
158. Outlines of zoological study, by TORIN. (1.15).
159. Zoology, by TORIN. (1.15).
160. Text-book of zoology, by MILNE-EDWARD & THORELL. (0.80).
161. Manual of zoology, by HOLMGREN. (4.85).
162. Useful and injurious insects, by HOLMGREN. (0.35).
163. Natural History, by BACKMAN. (0.30).
164. Short review of the natural history of animals. (0.10).
165. Charts of the human body. (4.25).
166. Charts of the animal kingdom. (8.50).
167. Atlas of the Scandinavian Mammals, by MEVES. (5.25).
168. Zoological walltable, by SCHUMBURG. (1.75).
169. Swedish Birds, by VON WRIGHT. (35.00).
170. Scandinavian Fishes, by VON WRIGHT & FRIES. (15.00).
171. Useful wild animals, by ARRHENIUS. (0.15).
172. Elementary course in Botany, by ARRHENIUS. (1.20).
173. First principles of Botany, by ARRHENIUS. (0.25).
174. Esculent Mushrooms of the North, by ARRHENIUS. (0.60).
175. Natural families of plants, by THORIN. (0.30).
176. Pictures from the vegetable kingdom, by FRIES. (0.60).
177. Excursion Fauna, by WAHLSTRÖM. (0.30).
178. Directions for collecting and arranging objects from the vegetable kingdom. (0.10).
179. Botanical wall-tables, by ANDERSSON. (4.50).
180. School Herbarium, by WINSLOW, (5.00).
181. Chemical composition of the Fodder-plants, by MÜLLER. (0.45).
182. Swedish Woods. (5.60).
183. Our best esculent Lichens. (0.10).
184. The esculent and poisonous mushrooms of Scandinavia (with engraved tables), by SMITH. (2.80).
185. Outlines of general Physics, by FOCK. (1.00).
186. Textbook of Physics, by FOCK and DAHLANDER. (3.10).
187. Textbook of Geology, by BERGSTRAND. (1.40).
188. Intuition in Mineralogy, by ANDERSON. (0.24).
189. The Mineral Kingdom, by PAYKULL. (0.15).
190. Textbook of Mineralogy and Geology, by PAYKULL. (0.35).
191. Geological wall-tables, by ERDMANN. (2.80).
192. Collection of Minerals, by ANDERBERG. (12.50).
193. Atlas of Natural History, by OHLSSON. (0.50).
194. Brehm's Life of Mammals, Illustrated. by SMITH and LINDAHL. (3.50).
195. Pictures for the school and home, by SANDBERG. (2.20).
196. Map of Zones. (1.70).
197. Astronomical Diagrams. (3.50).
198. Agricultural Wall-tables. (1.40).
199. Physical Apparatus.
    - Lampstand with BERZELIUS' alcohol-lamp. (3.60).
    - Glassblower's lamp with table. (8.40).
    - Balance with Sp. Grav. apparatus. (5.60).
    - Hydrostatic apparatus. (1.10).
    - Air-pump used for both attenuation and compression. (11.00).

Waterpump, suction and force-pump. (5.60).
Lever. (0.85).
Pendulumstand with two pendulums. (1.40).
Elasticity, bars of iron and steel. (0.30).
Barometer. (3.50).
Thermometer. (0.30).
Bar-Magnets. (1.10).
Compass. (2.20).
3 Glass Lenses. (1.40).
Telescope, (astronomical and terrestrial). (2.80).
Microscope. (4.20).
Glass-prism. (0.30).
Concave Mirror. (1.60).
Convex " (1.60).
Electrical Machine. (7.50).
Leyden Jar. (0.60).
Electric Pile, (2 elements). (2.25).
Electro-magnet. (2.80).
Centrifugal machine. (8.40).
Incline plane. (5.60).
Pulley. (3.50).
Parallelogram of forces. (4.00).
Adhesive plates. (1.75).
Pyrometer. (6.25).
Apparatus to show the condition of heat by solids. (0.70).
Apparatus for showing the upward pressure of liquids. (6.25).
Magdeburg-hemispheres. (4.20)
Glass bell. (0.60).
Fall tube. (4.20)
Globe, for weighing air. (3.50).
Sound plate, on a foot. (2.25).
Tuning Fork. (0.45)
Fiddle bow. (0.60)
Etc., etc.

CALLIGRAPHY.

200. Course in writing for trade-schools. (0.60).
201. Course in writing, by MEIJERBERG. (0.10).
202. " " " by SANDBERG. (0.15).
203. Copy book, by VON MENTZER. (0.25).
204. " " ENGDAHL. (0.10).
205. " " CROOMARD. (0.60).

DRAWING.

206. Wall-tables for drawing, I. and II. (4.20).
207. Course in drawing, by NYBERG. (1.40).
208. " " " BURMAN. (0.80).
209. " " " SALOMAN. (8.40).
210. Course in drawing. (0.80).
211. Lessons in drawing, by MESSMAN. (4.20).
212. Elementary course in geometrical forms and drawing, by J. E. B. (0.70).
213. Blocks for instruction in drawing (6.75).

MUSIC AND SINGING.

214. Book of chorals of the Swedish church, by HAEFFNER. (2.20).
215. Book of chorals of the Swedish church, for the home and school, by HAEFFNER. (0.70).
216. The Swedish book of hymns, with chorals and other religious songs, by MANKELL. (1.40).
217. The choral melodies of the Swedish church, by RYDGREN. (0.20).
218. The choral melodies, by TÖRNVALL. (0.10).
219. Singing book for the schools, by TÖRNVALL. (0.15).
220. Schoolsongs, by JOSEPHSON. (0.70).
221. Singing book for the common school, by SANDBERG. (0.25).
222. Singing book for schools, by SANDBERG.
223. Book of melodies, by SANDBERG. (0.15).
224. Art of singing, by CRONHAMN. (0.60).
225. Vocal music, by SANDBERG. (0.10).
226. Harmonics, by LUNDH. (0.60).
227. Tone hitting, by LUNDH. (0.25).
228. Preludes for organ, by LUNDH. (1.40).
229. Singing-tables in *Sol. Fa.*, by SANDBERG.
230. Monochord. (0.15).

GYMNASTICS AND MANUAL OF ARMS.

231. Regulations for gymnastics, by LING. (0.15).
232. Direction for instruction in gymnastics, by NYBLAEUS. (0.15).
233. Gymnastics for girls, by SANTESSON. (0.30).
234. Manual of gymnastics, by HARTELIUS.

HORTICULTURE.

235. Horticultural manual, by DAHLBERG. (0.35).
236. Textbook of horticulture, by LINDGREN. (0.15).
237. " " " " HOLM. (0.90).
238. " " " " ENEROTH. (0.10).

PEDAGOGY AND METHODIC.

239. Contributions to pedagogy and methodic, by ANJOU & KASTMAN. (0.85).
240. Pedagogy and methodic, by OLDBERG (0 60).
241. " for teachers of common schools, by WALLIN. (0.40).
242. Schoolmaster's art, by DAHM. (0.65).
243. Pedagogical directions, by SANDBERG. (0.30).
244. Art of instruction, by SANDBERG. (0.60).
245. The infant school, I—IV., by SANDBERG. (1.50).
246. On religious instruction, by TORÉN. (0.30).
247. Instruction in the mother tongue, by KASTMAN. (0.25).
248. Geometry in the common school, by SEGERSTEDT. (0.15).
249. Directions regarding calculating staffs, for the common schools, by STEINMETZ. (0.25).
250. Thoughts about the history of the fatherland in the common school, by STARBÄCK. (0.05).
251. Methodic for calligraphy, by CROOMARD. (0.60).
252. The *Sol-Fa* method, by SANDBERG. (0.10).
253. Something about gymnastics and manual of arms as a means of general education, by NYBLAEUS. (0.15).
254. On schoolgardens, by ENEROTH. (0.15).
255. The history of the Swedish school-systems, by BRODÉN. (0.25).
256. The Swedish common school, by RUDENSCHÖLD. (0.40).
256. The common school in Sweden, by ENEROTH. (1.00).
257. History of the popular instruction in Sweden, by POULSSON. (1.25).
259. Childhood's Paradise. (1.00).
260. The last reports of the Inspectors of the common schools.
261. The Common School Journal. (0.80).
262. The Pedagogical Magazine. (1.50).

SCHOOL-HOUSES, SCHOOL-FURNITURE, Etc.

263. Drawings of school-houses with descriptions. (0.80).
265. Ventilating "calorifere" for schools, constructed by BOLINDER.
266. Airpurifying apparatus, constructed by STILLE. (2.25).
267. School desks. (4.00).
268. Chathedra with chair. (20.00).
269. Map case. (10.00).
270. Slates. (0.15).
271. Slatewiper. (0.20).
272. Maphook, ruler and pointer. (0.70).
273. Bell and signal whistle. (0.50).

SCHOOL AND PARISH LIBRARY,

consisting of about 1000 volumes on religion, history, geography, natural history, travels, poetry, etc., of which a special catalogue will be found in the school house.

245. Erdmann, Edw. Stockholm.

6 Geographical diagrams for schools.

Models illustrating common geological phenomena. $5.00.

Prev. aw.: The original drawings of the diagrams were exhibited in Vienna, 1873, and rewarded with honorable mention; the first printed edition was published in the beginning of 1873, the second edition was exhibited at the geographical congress of Paris, 1875, and rewarded with honorable mention. The models are freshly executed, never before exhibited.

246. Glömsta Fabrik. *Glömsta Carpenters' Work.* Huddinge.

Universal school-form.

247. Lewenhaupt, Cl. M., *Count;* Claestorp. Katrineholm.

Toys, Split Shavings for mats, etc.

The objects exhibited are manufactured in an industrial school, established in the year 1872, on the Claestorp estate, owned by the exhibitor. This school is superintended by two teachers practiced in carpenter-work, turning, basket-making, brush-making and several other trades. These two persons, instruct boys from 7 to 15 years of age, on all week days, from 6 A. M. to 6 P. M.; there is neither tuition, nor any set hours for the coming and going of the pupils. A strict record is kept of the number of hours each boy works, and every 10 hours reckoned as a day. The work done by the children is inspected every Saturday, and they are paid for all work that is delivered in a finished condition. As an example of how much a boy can earn in this manner, it may be stated that a 14 year old boy earned in 143 days, 75.32 Kr., another 13 years old, in 215 days, 88.76 Kr. This method has been found to be much more advantageous, than that of giving instruction alone, as the immediate reward for their work is their strongest incentive to industry.

It is of course necessary to choose such work, as will enable even 7 year old children, with their inferior strength, to get some small earnings. When the children have learned a certain kind of work, as for instance, to carve certain kinds of toys, animals or the like, they only make the rough outlines in the schools, and complete the details at home by the fireside, during the long winter evenings.

As the intention has been to introduce some new kind of home industry in the neighborhood, as for instance, the manufacture of straw-shoes, straw-wrappings for bottles, door and floor mats of rush, covering of bottles with rush, plaiting of slippers from lists, etc., a lady has been induced to learn how to do this kind of work, and to undertake the instruction of others. All articles thus manufactured are bought by the owner of the estate, at a fixed price, which is regulated by the market price of the article. The latter, which always exceeds the former, by so much as will cover the interest and risk on the capital invested, is always communicated to the operatives, whereby it is sought to impress upon them the fact, that employers and employees, if the interests of both are to be promoted, are mutually dependent upon each other. To rightly engraft this on the minds of the rising generation is the principal aim of these schools, as the only means of preventing strikes, equally ruinous to both parties.

248. Lindblad, M. A. Stockholm.

About 100 dried plants, to demonstrate the morphology of vegetable types, $15.00 gold.

Cryptogamic types, 25,00 "

249. Lundholm, C. A. V. Stockholm.

An organ, $65.00 gold.
An organ, 36.00 "

250. Nordlund, K. Gefle.

Apparatus for instruction in Arithmetic, $40.00 gold.

251. Schlyter, G. R., *P. D.* Karlskrona.

Roman Garbs, with illustrations and description.

Tunica (laticlava), $2.00 gold.
Toga (prætexta), 7.00 "
Chlamys, 1.50 "

252. Svensson, A. Stockholm.

Stuffed mammals, birds and fishes, $100.00 gold.

253. Wiman & Co. Stockholm.

A stove, $55.00 gold.
Model of a stove, 14.00 "

254. Winslow, A. P., *P. D.* Göteborg.

Herbarium for schools, $5.00 gold.

The Herbarium contains the most common and important Swedish trees and shrubs, fodder, medicinal, and poisonous plants, weeds, lichens, used as bread-surrogate in times of need, and several other plants of economical importance in other respects.

The herbariums were first made in 1868.

London, 1871, diploma; Moscow, 1872, silver medal; Göteborg, 1871, silver medal; Vienna, 1873, medal of merit.

255. Vrana Folkhögskola. *Vrana National High-School;* by W. Nauckhoff. Vrana.

Samples of pupils works.

256. Zanders, H. Norrköping.

Drawings of gymnastical apparatus.

yearly. The wools are mostly from Germany, the Cape, Buenos Ayres, Australia, and other places, and are generally bought in the European wool markets and at wool sales; of late, however, some has been imported direct from transatlantic ports.

The manufacture of articles of carded wool has its principal seat at Norrköping, where abundant waterfalls offer a good impellant power. In 1873 thirty-eight *Cloth Manufactories* were in operation, at which, in all, 3,301,000 feet of woolen cloth were manufactured, at a value of $2,-445,000 gold, the greater portion of which was produced by the large factories of Drags & Ströms Joint Stock Companies. Besides the woolen-cloth manufactories at Norrköping, there are several of importance in the towns of Halmstad, (with a production in 1873 valued at $498,000), Stockholm (two of which, one near the town, with a production worth about $280,000 gold), Malmö and Landskrona, so that in the above-mentioned year, there were, in the whole Kingdom, fifty-two cloth manufactories, distributed in seven towns, one borough, and in seven country places, in which 4,900 workmen manufactured as follows: 920 feet fine cloth, 45,550 feet middling fine, and 947,980 feet coarse cloth, and 4,469,740 feet besides 17,120 pieces of various textile fabrics, with a total value of $37,500,000 gold. The manufacture of broad-cloth has been continuously increasing of late years. Thus, in the year 1869, the value of the manufacture was only $2,183,000 gold.

Among the cloth manufactories, are not included six *manufactories for woolen and mixed fabrics*, to which the so-called stuff-manufactories, or the manufactories for flannel and bunting are reckoned. In 1873, the value of the manufacture at these was $210,500 gold.

Besides, there are a great many (46 in the year 1873,) smaller mills for the spinning of *carded wool*, which are spread all over the country, where the greater part of the wool produced is spun into yarn, chiefly for the country people, which afterwards like the woolen yarn spun on their own distaffs, is manufactured by domestic industry into wadmaal, which is used by the peasentry for wearing apparel.

The woolen fabrics manufactured in Sweden, are chiefly sold in the country itself, and only a small portion is exported to Norway and Denmark. The import of such articles on the other hand is very considerable, and amounted in the year 1873, to 3,935,400 Swedish pounds, valued at $4,671,600 gold, an amount that it never came to before. In the same year, 839,400 pounds dyed, and 315,200 pounds undyed mohair and woolen yarn, valued at $1,194,500 gold, were imported.

SILK, AND SILK FABRICS, AND MIXTURES IN WHICH SILK IS THE PREDOMINATING MATERIAL.

[CLASS 242-249]. **Silk Culture.** As early as in the middle of last century, trials were made in the culture of silkworms in Sweden, and also encouraged by the Diet, and supported by pecuniary grants. These were, however, soon withdrawn, and hence not only all the breeding of silkworms gradually ceased, but very considerable plantations of mulberry-trees were either lost, or intentionally destroyed, and it was a long time before new trials were made. The Swedish Society for the Breeding of Silk-worms, under the protection of the then Crown-Princess JOSEPHINE, was not founded until the year 1830, when some interest was again taken in this branch of culture. Since that time, the Society, whose endeavors are supported by the State, has annually distributed seeds, and plants of the mulberry-tree, gratis as well as eggs of the silk-moth, and have tried to spread the knowledge of, and to create an interest in the culture of the silk-worm, by publishing papers and annual reports, though as yet without any noteworthy result. Of late years trials have been made

CLASS 305.

272. Kongl. Statistiska Central-Byrån, *Roy. Statistical Central Bureau;* Stockholm.

Statistical diagrams.

273. Sidenbladh, Elis, *P. D.* Stockholm.

Statistical Accounts of Sweden.

CLASS 306.

274. Aktiebolaget Klemmings Antiquariat och Sortiment. *Klemmings Antiquarian and Modern Library Co. Lim;* Stockholm.

Old Books.

Books, printed in Sweden in the sixteenth, seventeenth, and eighteenth centuries, with accounts of the earliest Swedish settlements in America, by ACHRÆLIUS, CAMPANIUS HOLM, HEMMERSAM, KÖPING, SCHOOTEN, USSELINX, etc.

275. Central-Tryckeriets Aktiebolag. *The Central Printing Co., Lim.;* by *Dr.* C. J. Fahlcrantz, Stockholm.

Typographical productions.

This company, which was established in 1873, with the purpose of carrying on a "printing business, and auxiliary industries," took possession of the Lithographical Institute of Messrs. SCHLACHTER & SEEDORF on June 1st of the same year, and erected a building 186 feet long, 51 feet wide, and four stories high, besides attic and basement. The company commenced, during the summer and fall of 1874, operations in the other branches of the business. The Central Printing Establishment at present embraces book-binding, and cartoon shop, type and stereotype foundry, lithographical and galvanoplastic establishments, book publishing and stationery business.

The company uses 12 typographical lightning steam presses of different constructions, 4 lithographical lightning steam presses, 23 hand presses, 3 satineer presses, 2 hydraulic presses, and 4 type founding presses, besides stone polishing, guilloche, perforating, lineation, numbering, and other machines. The lightning presses, satineer presses, and two elevators, by means of which all transports between the different stories are made, are run by a steam engine of twenty-five horse power, from the boiler of which the steam, for the heating of the entire building, is furnished.

There are about 200 persons employed in all the departments, the majority of which are men, women being, with two or three exceptions, employed only in the bindery and on the satineer presses.

The value of the production for 1875, the first year during which all the branches of the business have been in uninterrupted operation, cannot at the present writing be stated, but will probably exceed $140,000 gold.

Previous awards to the Lithographical Department, Copenhagen, 1872, silver medal; Vienna, 1873, medal of merit.

For the benefit of the workmen are established a sick and burial fund, and in the basement of the building a restaurant.

276. Gumælius Arvid. Örebro.

Allehanda for Folket, — "The Workmen's Magazine," an illustrated weekly.

This publication was started in 1873, with an average edition of 4,500, which was doubled in 1874, and quadrupled the following year.

Terms of subscriptions:

For one year, . 40 cts. gold.
For three months . 13 cts. "

Manager: ARVID GUMÆLIUS.

Editors: Arvid Gumælius, V. E. Öman, Otto Serrander.

Contributors:

Poetry and General Literature: Böttiger, Gumælius, Gödecke, Hedberg, Hermelin, Jolin, "Onkel Adam", Sander.

Agriculture: Arrhenius, Bergstrand, Henning, Spaak.

Mining and Geology: O. Gumælius, Erdmann.

Archeology: Montelius, Hofberg.

Miscellany: Gyldén (Astronomy), Nordenskiöld (Mineralogy and Arctic Explorations), Wrangel (Sport), and others.

An able corps of artists, and also home and foreign correspondents—a special one for the Centennial—are employed.

The illustrations consist mostly of illustrious and public men, noteworthy places and events, natural objects, &c.

277. Key Axel. *Prof. of Medicine,* Stockholm.

Nordiskt Medicinskt Archiv, a medical periodical paper, edited by the exhibitor, with contributions from all the leading medical authors of Sweden, Norway, Denmark, and Finland.

This paper was started 1869, and is published quarterly. Since 1873 each number is provided with a *summary in French* of all the original articles contained in that number. Present edition, 1,050 copies. The price, which varies according to size and number of illustrations, averages $2.80 gold a year.

278. Key Axel and **Retzius, Gustaf,** *Professors of Medicine,* Stockholm.

Studies in the Anatomy of the Nervous System and Connective Tissue, (in the German language), 1st part, with 39 plates. Folio. $44.00 gold. Agent for America, WESTERMAN, New York.

"Ur Vår Tids Forskning," a periodical paper upon popular science.

279. The Roy. Swedish Commission.

Collection of all newspapers at present published in Sweden.

B.—INSTITUTIONS AND ORGANIZATIONS.

	Import-Duty in United States.	Import-Duty in Sweden.
ALL ARTICLES for the use of any society or institution for philosophical, educational, scientific or literary purposes, or encouragement of the fine arts, and not intended for sale, ...	free.	free.

CLASS 312.

280. Hammer's Museum. Stockholm.

Photographs, Descriptions, and **Catalogues of the Museum.**

281. Nordenskiöld, A. E., *Prof. R. Ac. Science,* Stockholm.

Meteorite from the Isle of Disco, Greenland, discovered by the exhibitor, 1870; descriptions published by DAUBRÉE, LINDSTRÖM, NAUCKHOFF, NORDENSKIÖLD, STEENSTRUP, VON TSCHERMAK, WÖHLER, etc.; a summary of all these descriptions being published by W. FLIGHT in the Geol Magazine, 1875.

282. Norrbottens Läns Kongl, Hushållnings-Sällskap. *Roy. Economical Society of the Län of Norrbotten,* Luleå.

Lapplanders' Costumes and Utensils.

C.—SCIENTIFIC AND PHILOSOPHICAL INSTRUMENTS AND METHODS.

*CLASS 320.**

283. Göteborgs & Bohus Läns Kongl Hushållnings Sällskap, *Roy. Agricultural Society of the Län of Göteborg & Bohus,* by Professor F. L. Ekman.

Deep Water Drawer.

Marine Evaporimeters.

Prev. aw. Geographical Congress, Paris, 1875, silver medals.

*The apparatus used in deep sea dredging, and soundings, were greatly improved by Prof. S. LOVÉN, and later by Prof. O. TORELL, who may be said to have been the first to have produced positive proofs of abundant animal life at greater ocean depths, when in 1859 in Greenland, and in 1861 off Spitzbergen, he dredged up numbers of well developed specimens of vertebrates from depths varying from 300 to 1500 fathoms, thus exploding the Forbesian theory of a life limit at about 300 fathoms. The instruments used by the Swedish Naturalists have been further improved and adapted for deep-sea researches by the English, and especially by J. GWYN JEFFREYS, F. R. S., in the amply outfitted expedi-

The Deep Water Drawer is so constructed as to enable one to obtain a specimen of sea water from any desirable depth, for which it is only necessary to sink the instrument to the required depth; as soon as its downward movement is arrested, encloses a quantity of water which can then be brought to the surface without being mixed with water from a lesser depth, and free from air except that which is contained in the water at that depth. The articles exhibited are accompanied with printed descriptions.

The drawings exhibited, show the means by which the yearly evaporation over the Skager-Rack coast is determined.

Upon the suggestion of Count A. EHRENSWÄRD, Governor of Bohus Lãn, the Agricultural Society established an observatory in 1874, for the observation of the evaporation and all phenomena connected with it, also the height of the water currents, changes in the quantity of salt in the water and temperature at different seasons. The Society predicts that these data will be of great value, especially to such as are dependent upon the production of the sea as the chief source of their livelihood.

284. Gundberg, J. W. L. Stockholm.

Sieves and **vessels** for cleaning and preserving zoological specimens.

285 Leja Joseph. Stockholm.

Thermometer.

286. Lindahl, Josua. *P. D.* Lund.

Apparatus for Scientific explorations of the sea, viz: dredges, conical seive, seive-box, seive-scoop, towing-nets, sets of copper- and glass-vessels, etc.

Current Drag, being a modification of the Current-Drag invented by Capt. CALVER, R. Engl. N., for the deep-sea exploring expedition in H. M. S. Porcupine, 1870.

287. Ljungström, J. P. Stockholm.

Surveyor's Tripod; distinguished from others in the manner of the leg attachment, in a special contrivance for accurate adjustment by means of an eccentric disc, and in the plane-table.

Distance Telescope, with self-regulating scale of distances, giving Cosines' square of the distances read in the inclined telescope, or reducing them to horizontal distances.

Circular Planimeter, which gives the area of any plane figure from 5 square millimètres to upwards of six square mètres in size in a single operation and with great accuracy.

Mirror-graphometer, intended for graphically measuring angles in the field without the use of the tripod, to be used in reconnoitering, in off-hand surveying and in the graphical solving of the *Pothenot-problem.*

Graphical Theodolite, for graphic surveyings and triangulations of the fourth order; the instrument is provided with distance telescope and scale of distance for Cosine-square as well as scale of height, both of them for direct reading.

Pantograph, for direct copying of maps.

Pr. Aw. Paris, Geogr. Congress, 1875, 1st medal, for the distance telescope.

The three first mentioned instruments are the property of the Public Surveying Bureau, in Stockholm, the other three being new inventions are manufactured at the cost of the Swedish Government, and they belong to the State.

288. Rose, J. L. Uppsala.

Mining Magnetometer.

2 Mining Compasses.

Prev. Aw. 1st prize-medal of the Kongl Hushåilnings Säliskapet in Uppsala.

289. Theorell, A. G., *P. D.*, and **Sörensen, P.** Stockholm.

tions in Her Majesty's Ships *Lightning* and *Porcupine*, 1869—70. Many of these improvements, and some purely English apparatus, were introduced into Sweden again by J. LINDAHL, assistant zoologist to the English Expedition of 1870, and used by him in the expedition of 1871, to Greenland and Newfoundland, and by Prof. NORDENSKIÖLD and his companions in the expeditions to Spitzbergen, 1872—3, and to Nova Zembla, 1875, as well as by several other Swedish Zoologists off the coast of Sweden. Among the English apparatus may especially be mentioned Captain CALVER'S, (F. R. S.,) "Hempen Tangle." All the apparatus was modified a little for use on smaller steamers and sailing vessels. A very important step in the investigation of sea waters from different depths was gained by Prof. F. L. EKMAN, who, a few years ago, invented an apparatus for obtaining samples of water from any required depth; this apparatus, which suggested to Dr. H. A. MEYER the idea of his "Wasserschöpfapparat," used in the Scientific Exploration of the German Ocean, an improvement of questionable value, has been further improved by the inventor during the last year. Among the various apparatuses used for bringing up ooze, etc., from the sea bottom, should be mentioned those of Capt. F. A. ARVIDSON, R. N., Chief of the Hydrographical office, and that of Lieut. C. H. RAMSTEN, R. N. Both of these apparatus are distinguished for great simplicity and practicableness. The latest Swedish invention of this class is Dr. M. VIBERG'S "Botttenhuggare," being a so-called Bull-dog Machine attached to a buoy which lifts the apparatus to the surface as soon as the weight is detached, by striking the bottom of the sea. It was invented on the application of Prof. NORDENSKIÖLD, for the expedition to Nova Zembla and Kara Sea, 1875, and was used with great success. A great part of this apparatus is exhibited at the Centennial.

Theorell's Printing Meteorograph.
($7,000 gold.)

Meteorological observations are shown by this instrument on tables printed on a slip of paper.

The registration takes place by means of electrical currents, which are closed in the barometer and both the thermometers by contact between the quicksilver and steel wires that descend into their tubes, and at the weather-cock and anemometer by contact between a metal knob, which is put into motion by the current, and a wheel, which is in a direct mechanic combination with each of these instruments.

The interval between the observations is a quarter of an hour.

A meteorgraph of this construction has now been used at Uppsala observatory for 2 years, and during that time it has made 4 observations every hour without causing any perceptible change in the surface either of the quicksilver or the steel wires, that could in any way affect either the free efficiency of the instrument or its degree of accuracy, which, throughout the whole time, has been found to be as above stated.

As the clock, which determines the times of the observations, does not require winding up, the instrument itself restoring the tension of the mainspring every quarter of an hour, it continues going as long as the impellent force, i. e. the electric current is maintained; and as the slip of paper applied lasts for fully 3 months, it is clear that that is the period for which the instrument may be left to itself. The work then requisite is little more than taking out, cutting, and sewing up, in order, the paper of observations, and replacing it by another slip. Thus, this instrument requires but very little time and labor from the person who takes charge of it.

A printing Meteorograph differing from this only so far that the latter has been improved and perfected in several details, has been constructed by the same mechanician Mr. Sörensen for the Imperial Central Establishment for meteorology in Vienna, where it has been in daily use since September, 1874; and during that time it has given exact and true observations. A description of this Meteorograph is inserted in "Zeitschrift der Österreichischen Gesellschaft für Meterologie, redigirt von C.Jelinek und J. Hann." Volume X, Nis. 16 and 17.

The principle on which this instrument has been constructed, may be adopted with the same advantage for observing the particulars of any other phenomenon, provided they can be indicated by an index which produces a galvanic contact.

290. Wiberg, M. *P. D.* Stockholm.

Bottenhuggare, or "Bulldog apparatus" for deep sea soundings.

Agent in Philadelphia, Dr. H. A. W. LINDEHN.

CLASS 321.

291. Brehmer, E. F. A. Stockholm.

Ticket Registering apparatus with **date stamp,** such as used on the railroads of the Swedish Government.

Guillotine Stamps.

Drill Press.

Levelling Instrument, water-level of iron.

(**Paper-cutting machine.**—See Cl. 546).

Prev. aw.: Vienna, 1873, diploma of honor.

292. Petterson, C. J. Karlshamn.

Calculating machine.

293. Unge, V. T., *R. A.* Stockholm.

Distance-watch, for military use.

294. Wiberg, M., *P. D.* Stockholm.

Logarithmical tables, calculated and printed by a counting machine, invented by the exhibitor.

CLASS 323.

295. Linderoth, G. W. Stockholm. **Pendulum Clock.**

CLASS 326.

296. Otter, C. G. von, *Baron, Captain R. N.* Stockholm.

Signal Lantern with registering apparatus, Controller, invented by the exhibitor, manufactured by G. W. LYTH.

The Lantern is intended for transmitting signals at night, both at sea and on land, and at distances not exceeding eight to ten miles; *the Controller* for registering given or received signals, its aim being principally to prevent errors.

The system used in telegraphing is the same which has lately been tried and partly adopted in several countries; but *the means* are different.

Morses' telegraphic lines and dots are represented by *long and short flashes, letters and figures,* by various *groups of flashes.* Flashes belonging to the same group are separated by dark intervals of *short* duration, groups and sentences by dark intervals of *longer* duration (pauses), the extent of the latter being limited by the skill and of the operators.

Two strings are suspended from the lantern and passed through the controller. By pulling *the one* of these strings *long flashes* (lines) are produced, and by pulling *the other, short flashes* (dots). By pulling a third string, hanging down from the controller, between the two strings from the lantern, a *pause* will be produced, and the signalized letters or figures is impressed on a self-acting forthcoming strip of paper.

The strings should be pulled with even force and to their full extent, but without jerking.

Signalling between two or more places is effected in the most convenient and sure manner, by each receiver of a signal repeating on his lantern and controller the signs conveyed. The communication is thereby printed on the above mentioned strip of paper, without it being necessary for the receiver to understand the telegraphic characters.

The lantern may also be employed independently of the controller *in transmitting signals* and vice-versa., the controller used independently of the lantern *in receiving signals.* In the latter case, three keys, attached to the upper part of the controller should be used instead of the corresponding strings.

A suitable weight attached to the block under the lantern brings into action a proposed new method of distinguishing lights from each other, rendered necessary by their increasing number. It is proposed that each light, on the principle of the above signals, shall describe its name every alternate or every third minute, by combinations of long and short flashes; for the exact reading of which a simple and easily-worked apparatus is annexed.

These lights may be either revolving or fixed. In the former case the flashes will be produced by lenses, in the latter by Venetian blinds as shown in the model.

The lantern exhibited gives the signal:

— —— —— — —— —

which signifies P. N. (Pater Noster, a rock with lighthouse off the west coast of Sweden).

297. Kuntze & Co. Stockholm.

Air Telegraph.

CLASS 327.

	Import-Duty in United States.	Sweden.
INSTRUMENTS, MUSICAL, n. o. p. f.,	30 per cent.	per piece, 1 krona.
PIANOS,	" "	" " 60 kr.
ORGANS AND HARMONIUMS,	" "	5 per cent.

298. Ahlberg & Ohlson, by L. Ohlson. Stockholm.

Brass Instruments, cornet in A flat, cornet in E flat, cornet in B flat, alto-horn in E flat, tenor, horn in B flat, tenor, bassoon in B flat, bombardon in F, bass-tuba in F. The instruments are all hand-made, and munufactured from brass and german silver.

Pr. aw.: Stockholm, 1851, silver medal; London, 1851, bronze medal; Stockholm, 1866, silver medal; Paris, 1867, silver medal.

Manufacture commenced in 1850.

15 to 20 workmen are employed, with wages from $4.50 to $8.50 gold, per week.

The annual production amounts to $8,500 to $12,000 gold, on which a tax of $12 gold is paid to the government and $47 gold is paid to the community.

The annual exports are about 30 instruments to Finland and Norway, and occasional instruments to America and Melbourne.

299. Lundholm, C. A. V. Stockholm.

School-Organs and **Harmoniums.**

The manufacturing began in 1874, giving employment to 17 men and women. Value of production during the first year about $7,000 gold. Agencies in Umeå, Sundsvall, Gefle, Norrköping, etc. 10 to 15 per cent. discount at wholesale.

300. Malmsjö, J. G. Göteborg.

Pianos.

Prev. aw. in Copenhagen, Göteborg, Karlstad, London, Malmö, Paris, Rugby (Engl.), Stockholm, Uddewalla, Venersborg and Vienna.

The pianos are mostly sold in Sweden, or exported to England and Finland.

The factory was founded in 1845, and gives employment to 40 workmen, with an average pay of $11 gold per week; the steam-engine used has a capacity of 8 H. P.

CLASS 333.

301. Norrman, C. G. V., *Captain, R. A.* Stockholm.

Model of a **Pontoon-Bridge,** with a printed description.

D.—ENGINEERING, ARCHITECTURE, CHARTS, MAPS, AND GRAPHIC REPRESENTATIONS.

CLASS 335.

302. Bagge, G. P., *Captain.* Paris, France.

Geographical Map.

303. Erdmann, E. Stockholm.

Geological Maps and **Models.**

304. Kongl-Svenska General-Staben, *Roy. Swedish Staff-General;* by Baron Hugo Raab. Stockholm.

Topographical Maps.

305. Nordenskiöld, A. E, *Professor.*

Map of the route followed by the Swedish expedition, 1875, to *Kara Sea* and *Jenisey.*

306. Roth, Magn., *P. D.* Stockolm.

Geographical Maps.

307. Sahlbom, W. Stockholm.

Maps, showing the yearly development of the Swedish **Railroads** from 1845 to 1875, incl.

Prev. aw.: Moscow, 1872, silver medal; Vienna, 1873, diploma of honor.

308. Sveriges Ekonomiska Kartverk. *The Economical Survey of Sweden.* Stockholm.

Economical and Agronomical Maps.

309. Sveriges Geologiska Undersökning. *The Geological Survey of Sweden* by Professor OTTO MARTIN TORELL. Stockholm.

Geological Maps of Sweden, illustrated with **printed descriptions** (and **collections** of minerals, rocks, and soils. See cl. 100.)

The institution was started by the Swedish government 1858, the late Professor A. ERDMANN being its first Director. At present the scientific staff consists of (except the chief) 11 geologists constantly employed, and a varying number of assistants in the field works during the summers. The appropriation for 1876 is $195,00 gold.

E.—PHYSICAL, SOCIAL AND MORAL CONDITION OF MAN.

CLASS 340.

310. Zander Gustaf, *M. D.* Stockholm.

Apparatus for Mechanical Gymnastics.

Photographs representing the interior of the Mechanico-Therapeutical Institute in Stockholm, with the apparatus.

The apparatus exhibited consists of 12 different machines, of which 7 are intended for active movements and 5, which are worked by steam, for passive ones. The whole set forms a part of the gymnastic apparatus used in the *Mechanico-Therapeutic Institute of Stockholm.*

This institution was established in 1865 by a chartered corporation under the direction and management of Dr. ZANDER, who is the inventor of all its apparatus. Gymnastics have long been honored in Sweden. Professors LING and BRANTING were the first to apply scientific principles to this art, which aims at developing the organs of the human body by appropriate and well-defined movements of the muscular system. While athletics tend to develope one particular power, gymnastics produce the harmonious development of all. Moreover gymnastics are brought to bear on the human body as a curative agent. It requires for that purpose a greater precision and regularity of movement as well as a slow and gradual increase in the use of the muscular power. Before Dr. ZANDER's inventions, *manual* gymnastics were considered the best calculated to insure the necessary precision. The patient was placed in charge of an experienced gymnast by whom he was put through all the different exercises. Of these some, called *active* movements, were performed partly by the patient himself, the gymnast moderating it by offering a certain resistance to it, partly by the gymnast, the patient being made to resist his action. Others called *passive* movements consisted of certain mechanical operations by the gymnast on the whole or a part of the body of the patient, such as shaking, chopping, rubbing, etc.

DR. ZANDER, during his experience as a gymnast, was struck by the difficulty of adapting the amount of force to be used by the gymnast exactly to the strength of the patient. Too much would cause a strain, too little would be useless. To remedy this defect it occurred to him to replace the gymnast by machines, as the movement of these would always be the same and their effects could be regulated to a nicety to suit all constitutions. It is this idea which has been carried out by the Mechanico-Therapeutical Institution. No less than 50 different machines are now in use in this establishment, of which a great number are worked by steam. These latter are intended for passive movements. All have numbered scales or other contrivances, which enable the patient to regulate their force and gradually to increase the action of his muscular system, as well as to ascertain exactly how much he may have gained in power.

The success of Dr. ZANDER's invention is best demonstratad by the fact that since the opening of this institute the number of patients has steadily increased from 132 in 1865 to 900 in 1876. Of these latter 200 were ladies. The establishment is largely attended, not only by those who seek in gymnastics a cure for some particular disease, especially heart disease, but also by those who want to find in it a preventive against the evils engendered by a sedentary life and the seclusion of office. The movements being performed with the aid of machines, which never tire, never need rest, and are not subject to illness, as is unfortunately the case with gymnasts, the establishment is able to receive a much larger number of patients than any gymnastic institute could accommodate. It has thus popularized the science and placed its beneficial influence within the reach of very moderate means.

The machines exhibited are used for the following movements:

No.	Movement	
1.	Arm-twisting,	Active movement of the arms.
2.	Hand-flexion and extension,	
3.	Arm-abduction,	
4.	Leg-flexion,	Active movement of the legs.
5.	Leg-abduction,	
6.	Foot-rolling,	
7.	Trunk-back-flexion,	Active movement of the trunk.
8.	Shaking or vibrating,	Passive movements.
9.	Chopping,	
10.	Foot-rubbing,	
11.	Trunk-rolling,	
12.	Chest-spanning,	

This set of machines can be sold at a price of $3,300 gold. A complete system, consisting of 30 machines for active movements and 18 for passive movements, will be delivered on board in Stockholm for $15,000 gold.

Beside this Institution in Stockholm, Dr. ZANDER has supplied 5 other towns with similar establishments.

311. Roy. Swedish Commission.

Collection of Swedish Bank-Notes, comprising all kinds at present in use as well as those of the last three decenniums.

Collection of the Swedish Gold-, Silver-, and Bronze-coins at present in use.

312. Lindehn, H. A. W., *P. D.* Stockholm, (present addr., Swedish Commission, Philadelphia.)

Swedish Patent Letter-Box, invented by Dr. MARTIN WIBERG, Stockholm.

Description:—

The Swedish Patent Letter-Box, is so constructed that a letter-carrier may collect the letters from several letter-boxes in one bag without having any means of access to the letters collected. To effect this object, the fixed letter-boxes are constructed so that their bottoms open downwards, and the bag of the letter-carrier is fitted at the shop with an iron frame in which there is a door opening downwards, or towards the interior of the bag. This bag slides under the fixed letter-box in such manner that the lock-bolts of the bag press upwards against those of the letter-box, by which means the bag and the letter-box become locked together, and afterwards open, so that the letters fall down out of the letter-box into the bag. By a lever, fitted to the door of the bag, both the doors are again lifted up, upon which, the bag and the letter-box become re-locked and the bag is detached. The letter-carrier then takes the bag to the next box, when the same process is repeated.

(Signed) M. WIBERG.

DEPARTMENT IV.

ART.

	Import-Duty in United States.	Sweden.
STATUES of marble or wood, carved, . .	10 per cent.	free.
" " bronze, ...	35 "	"
" " plaster and terra cotta, cast, . .	40 "	"
PAINTINGS, all n. o. p. f., ...	10 "	"
PHOTOGRAPHIC PICTURES OR VIEWS, . .	20 "	"

(Works of art, etc., imported for museums, etc., see page 65.)

A.—SCULPTURE.

CLASS 400.

ALL PRICES IN DOLLARS GOLD.

313. Börjeson, J. Rome.

a. **Naiads,** group in plaster, $ 500.
(The same in marble, $7000.)

b. **Psyche,** statue in plaster, $ 500.
(The same in marble, $3500.)

CLASS 405.

314. Lundmark, A. Stockholm.

Carved implements for the writing-desk. $1.67.

315. Östergren, Johan Peter. Westerås.

Woodcarvings, representing scenes from the second Article of Faith, carved in two divisions, each from a single block, without any gluing whatever. The lower division represents the birth of Christ, his resurrection, ascension, and suffering in the garden of Gethsemane. The upper division shows the taking down of Christ, from the cross.

Chess-board with carved pieces, which are symbolical of the struggle now going on between ultramontanism and the modern spirit in Germany. On one side of the board appear the Emperor WILLIAM and the Empress AUGUSTA as *King* and *Queen*, Prince BISMARCK and the Minister FALK as *Bishops;* the *Knights* are Prussian Uhlans and the *Pawns* are soldiers and recruits. On the other side stands PIO IX. as *King*, while the *Queen* is an Abbess holding a waxen taper well-nigh burned out. The *Bishops* are Cardinals, the *Knights* are Monks riding on asses and the *Pawns* are Monks on foot.

316. Wästfelt, Carl C: son. Kölingsholm.

Carvings in Wood.

B.—PAINTING.

CLASS 410.

317. Adelsköld, C. Stockholm.

a. **Preparing for dinner,** $800.

b. **A gale on the coast of Sweden,** 480.

318. Ankarkrona, H., *Assoc. Ac. F. Arts.* Stockholm.

a. Evening Prayer in the desert, $400.
b. View from the boundaries of Algiers and Morocco, $400.

319. Arborelius, O. P. U. *Assoc. Ac. F. Arts.* Stockholm.
a. View from Mora, Dalarne, $300.
b. Winter Landscape, $200.

320. Arsenius, Joh. *Assoc. Ac. F. Arts.* Stockholm.
On the Ice, $230.

321. Bennet, C., *Baron.* Stockholm.
Royal Palace, Stockholm, $220.

322. Berg, Albert. *Assoc. Ac. F. Arts.* Stockholm.
a. Marine. $280.
b. View from Stockholm Skärgård. $280.
c. Winter in the Skärgård. $280.
d. Moonlight. $280.

323. Berg, Edv. *K. N. S., Professor Ac. F. Arts.* Stockholm.
a. Fishing-harbor on the coast of Bohus Län. $1,400.
b. Birch-forest. $1,400.
c. Waterfall in Småland, (N. M.)
d. Interior view of Pine-forest, (N. M.)
Prev. aw., Medals in Paris, Hague, London, Copenhagen and Vienna.

324. Bergman, Elizabeth, *Miss.* Stockholm.
Landscape in Vermland. $55.

325. Bergstedt, Amanda. Stockholm.
Returned lesson. $175.

326. Billing, Th., *Memb. Ac. F. Arts.* Stockholm.
Landscape in North Sweden. $350.

327. Boklund, J. Chr., *Director of the Roy. Academy of Fine Arts, K. N. S.* Stockholm.
a. Marauder pursuing his prey. $580.
b. Consultation, GUSTAF II ADOLF and three warriors, (N. M.)

328. Brandelius, P., *Lieutenant R. A., Memb. Ac. F. Arts.* Stockholm.
Dangerous Excursion. $1,000.

329. Börjesson, Agnes, *Miss, Memb. Acad. F. Arts.* Rome, Italy.
a. Farewell. $900.
b. A happy finding, $300.
Prev. aw.: Medal in Vienna, 1873.

330. Cantzler, H.,† *late Assoc. Ac. F. Arts.*
a. Northern Landscape. $300.
b. Reaping in Italy. $300.

331. Cedergren, P. N. Stockholm.
View of Stockholm. $280.

332. Cederström, G., *Baron. Assoc. Ac. F. Arts.* Stockholm.
Dark moments, $1.000

333. Dietrichson, M., *Mrs.* Kristiania, Norway.
The recovered document. $400.

334. Ekström, P. Stockholm.
Summer Evening. $800 gold.

335. Engström, V. O. Düsseldorf, Germany.
a. Good Morning! $200.
b. Bird of prey catching a rabbit. $400.

336. Fagerlin, F. *K. N. L.; Memb. Ac. F. Arts.* Düsseldorf, Germany.
a. Smoking Boys, (N. M.)
b. Jealousy, (N. M.)
Prev. aw.: Medals in Paris, 1867, and Vienna, 1873.

337. Fahlgren, C. A. Stockholm.
Landscape. $300.

338. Hafström, A. G. Düsseldorf, Germany.
A Captured Frenchman. $360.

339. Hermelin, O. *Baron, Assoc. Ac. F. Arts, Commissioner for the Swedish Art-Department.* Stockholm.
a. Winter-Day, neighborhood of Stockholm. $1000.
b. Poor People's Grave-yard, near Stockholm, $1000.
c. The First Snow. $600.
d. Fishing-place, near Stockholm. $400.
e. Spring-day on Mont Martre. $320.

f. **Sunny day on Mont Martre.** $120.

g. **In a Stockholm Suburb.** $250.

h. **Church of St. Pierre,** Paris. $250.

i. **Returning Home.** $120.

k. **Landscape,** in Södermanland, $120.

l. **Birch-forest.** $120.

m. **Autumn-day at Djurgården,** Stockholm. $120.

n. **Fishing-harbor,** near Stockholm. $280.

340. Hertzberg, A. G. *Assoc. Ac. F. Arts.* Stockholm.

Going to Confirmation, (N. M.)

341. Holm, P. D., *Professor Ac. F. Arts.* Stockholm.

a. **In the Mining-districts of Wermland,** (N. M.)

b. **In the Forest.** $525.

342. Holmlund, Josefina, *Miss.* Stockholm.

Fredrika Bremer's First and Last Home. $250.

343. Holst, F. G., von, *Captain, R. A.* Stockholm.

a. **Sheep on the Pasture,** $350

b. **A Fruitless Attempt.** $350

344. Höckert, J., *late Professor R. Sw. Ac. F. Arts, K. Leg. Hon.* Stockholm. (Ob. 1866.)

Burning of the Royal Palace, Stockholm, 1697. $2,500

Prev. aw.: Medals in Paris, etc.

345. Jernberg, A., *Painter to the R. Sw. Court, Memb. Ac. F. Arts.* Düsseldorf, Germany.

a. **Marketday in Düsseldorf.** $3,500

b. **The broken Pipe.** (N. M.)

c. **Preparations to Festivals.** $1,350

d **Visitors in the Amsterdam Museum regarding Rembrandt's "Night-Watch."** $1,000

Prev. aw.: Medal in Vienna, 1873.

346. Jernberg Olof. Düsseldorf, Germany.

Swedish Landscape. $500

347. Kallenberg, And., *Assoc. Ac. F. Arts.* Stockholm.

a. **Cattle in Skåne.** $800.

b. **Beech Forest.** $550.

c. **Farmhouse in Skåne,** (N. M.)

348. Kiörboe, C. F., *Memb. Ac. F. Arts; K. V.; K. Leg. Hon.* Dijon, France.

Dogs attacking a fox, (N. M.)

Prev. aw.: Several medals in Paris.

349. Koskull, A. G. B., *Baron; Memb. Ac. F. Arts.* Stockholm.

The Boy and Wolves. $280.

350. Kulle, Jacob. Stockholm.

Bridal attendance in Skåne. $680.

351. Lindegren, Amalia, *Miss, Memb. Ac. F. Arts.* Stockholm.

a. **Father returned from market,** (N. M.)

b. **Merriment at home,** (N. M.)

c. **Girl with an orange,** (N. M.)

352. Lindman, A. Stockholm.

Evening at the west coast of Sweden, $500.

353. Lindström, A.

Landscape, autumn, (N. M).

354. Löfgren, Klara, *Miss.* Stockholm.

Sorrow, $110.

355. Lönnroth, F., *Captain, R. A.* Södrakulla, Borås.

Norwegian Horses, $280.

356. Malmström, J. A., *Professor Ac. F. Arts.* Stockholm.

Dance of Elves, (N. M).

357. Nilson, Severin. Paris, France.

a. **Sigurd Ring.** $800.

SIGURD RING, king of Scandinavia and England, asked two petty-kings in Bohus, to give him their young sister, ALFSOL for wife. At their refusal on account of his age, they were challenged to a battle. As they saw that they were to loose, they gave their sister poison. When, after the battle, King Ring found Alfsol dead, he loaded his draggon ship with the killed warriors, put fire to it and shaped for the ocean with his dead bride in his arms.

b. **The King of the Children.** $400.

c. **Brother and Sister.** $280.

358. Nordenberg, Bengt. *Painter to the R. Sw. Court, Memb. Ac. F. Arts.* Düsseldorf, Germany.

a. Dalecarlians put to flight by a Fire in the Forest. $850.

b. Wedding in a Country Church. $850.

c. Rest in a "Säter" (alpine dairy house) in Dalarne. (N. M.)

d. The killed Sheep.

Prev. aw.: Paris, 1863, honorable mention; Lyon, 1866, and Vienna, 1873, medals.

359. Nordgren, Anna, *Miss.* Paris, France.

a. Italian Girl. $150.

b. Genre. $60.

360. Nordgren, Axel. *Memb. Sw. Ac. F. Arts.* Düsseldorf, Germany.

a. View at the Promontory Kullen. Skåne. $725.

b. Coast Scenery. $440.

361. Nordlander, Anna, *Miss.* Stockholm.

The Toilet of the Favorite. $170.

362. Palm, G. W. *Memb. Sw. Ac. F. Arts.* Stockholm. $660.

View of Stockholm.

363. Perseus, Edward. Stockholm.

Parisian Maid. $350.

364. Post, Christine, von, *Miss.* Paris, France.

The Five Foolish Virgins at the Locked Door. $4,000 gold.

365. Ribbing, Sophie. London, England.

a. Girl with Grapes. $150

b. Girl at the Säter, (alpine dairy-house.) $100.

c. The Gardener's Children. $900.

d. Girl with Eggs. $150.

366. Rosen, George, von, *Count, Memb. Ac. F. Arts.* Stockholm.

Portrait of Count E. VON ROSEN, the Founder of the Sweedish Railroads. (N. M.)

367. Rydberg, G. F. *Memb. Ac. F. Arts.* Stockholm.

a. Winter—Landscape. (N. M.)

b. Spring—Landscape. (N. M.)

c. Landscape in Blekinge. (N. M.)

368. Salmson, V. *Assoc. Ac. F. Arts.* Paris, France.

Odalisque.

369. Saloman, Geskel, *Memb. Ac. F. Arts.* Stockholm.

a. Maid with an open letter. (N. M.)

b. At the letter-box. $250.

c. Religious ceremony on the coast of Algiers. $250.

370. Schwerin, A. von, *Miss.* Düsseldorf.

a. Landscape with Cattle. $300.

b. Landscape with Cattle. $450.

371. Sidwall, A., *Miss.* Paris.

Mulatto-woman. $180.

372. Skånberg, C. E. Paris, France.

In the Spring—Interior of Beech Forest at Fontainebleau. $1,000 gold.

373. Svensson, Fr. Stockholm.

H. Sw. M. Frigate "Vanadis." $300.

374. Södergren, Sophie, *Miss.* Paris, France.

French Coast—Landscape. $200.

375. Törnå, Oscar. Paris, France.

a. Pine Forest, Sweden. $300.

b. Moonlight, Sweden. $200.

c. Birch Forest, Sweden. $300,

376. Wahlberg, Alfred, *Memb. Sw. Ac. F. Arts. K. W.; K. Leg. Hon.* Paris, France.

Landscape in Moonlight. (N. M.)

Prev. aw.: Medals in Paris, Vienna. Lyon, Copenhagen, etc.

377. Wahlquist, E. Stockholm.

a. Hunting Party. $300.

b. The Fortress Kronoborg. $300.

c. Smugglers. $300.

378. Wallander, V. *Memb. Ac. F. Arts.* Stockholm.

Forge in the Forest, Dalarne. $300.

379. Wallander, V., *Memb. Ac. F. Arts* and **Torslow, H.,** *Assoc. Ac. F. Arts.* Stockholm.

a. Norrland Scene. Shepherd making fire, the smoke of which keeps off the mosquitos from the cattle. Landscape by TORSLOW, figures by WALLANDER. $800.

b. **Saturday Night on the Alpine Pastures,** Delsbo, Helsingland. Landscape by TORSLOW, figures by WALLANDER. $550.

380. Werner, Gotthard. Naples, Italy.

The Salamander, Christian Slave attending at a Heathen Orgie in Rome. $550.

Prev. aw.: Medal at the Exhib. of Christian Art in Rome, 1870.

381. Winge, Hanna, *Mrs.* Stockholm.

a. **Sunday Morning at the Church of Rättvik,** Dalarne. $200.

b. **Before Service.** $200.

382. Winge, M. E., *K. W., Professor, Ac. F. Arts.* Stockholm.

a. **Signe and Hagbard.**

HAGBARD, a Sea-King from Trondhjem, Norway, and SIGNE, daughter of King SIGURD, had sworn for one another true love for ever. The sons of SIGURD, however, having killed HAGBARD'S brothers, he, HAGBARD, claimed vengeance, and killed them, Once when in disguise, he ventured to call on Signe, he was discovered, captured and sentenced to be hung. When this execution was being performed, SIGNE put fire to her "maidens-house" and followed her bridegroom in death. $1600.

b. **Viking-fleet.** $650.

Prev. aw.: Stockholm, 1866, Diploma of Honor; Vienna, 1873, Medal for F. Arts.

383. Virgin, A. J. G. *Assoc. Ac. F. Arts.* Stockholm.

a. **Letter-Box,** Rättvik, Dalarne. $200.

b. **On the Meadow,** Orsa, Dalarne, $150.

384. Zetterström, A., *Mrs.* Paris, France.

"What does she think of?" $400.

CLASS 411.

385. Ahrenberg, J. Stockholm.

City-Gate of Rouen.

386. Blackstadius, J. L. *Assoc. Ac. F. Arts.* Stockholm.

a. **Miller's Cottage at Alvastra,** $70.

b. **Utö in Stockholm's Skärgård,** $70.

387. Gardell, Anna. Stockholm.

a. **Views from Skåne.** $110.

b. **A Spring-Day.** $110.

388. Hellquist, H. Paris, France.

Genre. $175.

389. Hägg, J. *Lieutenant R. N.* Stockholm.

a. **On the River at Stockholm.** $90.

b. **Man of War.** $90.

390. Kylberg, Regina. Stockholm.

The Halsfors in Norway.

391. Larson, Virginia. Stockholm.

a. **Peasant Girl from Dalarne.** $145.

b. **Swedish Landscape.** $90.

C.—ENGRAVING AND LITHOGRAPHY.

CLASS 422.

392. Meyer, Wilhelm. Stockholm. **Autographical Specimens.**

CLASS 423.

393. Cardon, J. Stockholm.

Lithographs.

394. Centraltryckeriets Aktiebolag. (See Lithograpical Products.

395. Huldberg, Fr. Stockholm.

Lithographs

D.—PHOTOGRAPHY.

CLASS 430.

396. Florman, G. Stockholm.

Photographs.

a. H. R. M. OSCAR II., King of Sweden and Norway.

b. H. R. M. SOPHIA, Queen or Sweden and Norway.

c. The Royal Palace in Stockholm.

397. Huldberg, Fr. Stockholm.

Photographs.

398. Lindahl, Axel. Göteborg.

Photographic Views of Stockholm, Göteborg and Trollhättan.

399. Lundberg, W. A. Stockholm.

Photograps on paper and glass.

400. Löfström, Sophie, *Miss.* Uppsala.

Photographic Portraits.

Atelier opened, 1872. Prize medal obtained in Uppsala, 1873.

401. Osti, Henri. Uppsala.

Photographs.

Prev. aw.: Uppsala, 1873, silver medal; Vienna, 1873, diploma of merit.

402. Roesler, Rob. Stockholm.

Photographic views of Stockholm, and environs; **Photographs for Xylography, photographic printing plates of copper for Heliography, and Photo-typography.**

Prev. aw.: Stockholm, 1866, diploma of honor.

403. Wiklund, O. Westerås.

Photographic views and portraits.

Prev. aw.: Vienna, 1873, diploma of merit; London, 1874, bronze medal.

The atelier opened 1869; all the winter views taken in a car, especially constructed for the purpose, and in a temperature of 5° to 14° F.

CLASS 431.

404. Carleman, J. G. V. Stockholm.

Specimens of the exhibitor's invention to transfer photographs from nature to metal plate, and to etch this plate for being used either in a common printing press or in a lithographic press.

Prev. aw.: London, Moscow and Vienna.

The engravings made in this way, cost at least 50 per cent. less than wood cuts, which they supercede in correctness.

DEPARTMENT V.

MACHINERY.

A.—Machines, Tools, and Apparatus of Mining, Metallurgy, Chemistry, and the Extractive Arts.

	Import-Duty in United States.	Sweden.
Machinery, Drawings and models of, and of other inventions,	free.	free.
Iron, wrought, for ships, steam-engines, locomotives, or parts thereof, n. o. p. f.,	per lb. 2 cts.	free.
" axles, or parts thereof,	" " 2½ "	free.
" locomotive-tire, or parts of,	" " 3 "	free.
Steel, railway bars,	" " 1¼ "	free.
" manufactures, n. o. p. f.	45 per cent.	free.

(Compare Class III.)

CLASS 503.

407. Nilson, G. Eskilstuna. **Jacks.**

CLASS 504.

408. Wiklund, W. Stockholm. **Centrifugal pump.**

CLASS 505.

409. Alsing, J. R. Stockholm.

Model of Pulverizing-Cylinder, with samples of powders of hard substances.

Prev. aw.: Stockholm, 1868, large silver medal. The only exhibition in which it has participated.

Agents: C. P. Möller, St. Petersburg, Russia; H. W. Konow, Paris, France; Messrs. A. W. Schmidt & Co., Hamburg, Germany.

The manufacture was commenced in 1868.

The cylinders are made of different sizes, and have been introduced into all the principal porcelain manufactories of Europe.

Testimonials:

St. Petersburg, Feb. 24, 1869.

(No. 93.)

The Imperial Bureau of Technology hereby certifies that the pulverizing cylinder of Mr. J. R. Alsing, has been tested by the Bureau with highly satisfactory results; the cylinder pulverizing the hardest subtances quickly and well, with a greater degree of economy, both of money and labor, than any other machine known to it. Therefore the Imperial Bureau, by order of his majesty, the Emperor of Russia, delivers the present certificate.

Signed,

W. Benjenkanof,

Director of the Imperial Bureau of Technology.

To Mesrs. A. W. Schmidt & Co.,

Brandenburger Strasse.

(No. 45 E. V.)

Dear Sirs: I have had one of Mr. Alsing's "pulverizing cylinders" in constant use since last October; it gives perfect satisfaction in every respect. In a day of 10 hours, it has pulverized as many as 7 cwts. of feldspar, so finely that it was fit for immediate use without sieving.

Signed,

Möller,

Director of the Royal Porcelain Manufactures

410. Samuelson, S. H. Töskefors.
(**Peat.**—see Cl. 101).

Machine for the manufacture of **Tube-Peat.**

The Tube-peat was invented by the exhibitor in 1863. In 1875 letters patent were granted on the improved machine now exhibited, for 7 years. By the use of the tube form a much easier and *more complete* drying of the peat is obtained, so that by air-drying alone its percentage of water can be reduced to from 10 to 12 per cent. The combustion of the peat is also greatly facilitated. By the use of pistons in the pressing out of the tubes, the peats are of even thickness, which is not the case when a screw is used, as this, by wet and fat peat, is nearly inactive. For the working of the peat mass, the screw is excellent; while the use of the knives for such purposes necessitates constant cleanings.

The manufacture of the machines was commenced in 1864.

About 200 machines are at present in use in Sweden, Norway, Denmark and Finland.

B.—MACHINES AND TOOLS FOR WORKING METAL, WOOD, AND STONE.

CLASS 510.

411. Bergström, J. W. Stockholm.

Universal screw-cutting machine.

412. J. & C. G. Bolinders Mekaniska Verkstads Aktiebolag. (See Cl. 222).

Sawing Machines.

413. Stridsberg & Biörk; by Ernst Stridsberg. Holmen, Torshälla.

Blades for Frame-saws, Circular-saws, Timber-saws, Wood-saws, Pit-saws, etc.; Machine-knives, Trowels, Ship-scrapers, Machine-plane-irons, and Mowing-machine-knives, etc.

Thin-sheet-iron.

Prev. aw.: Stockholm, 1868, 1st prize; Göteborg, 1871, small gold medal; Moscow, 1872, large gold medal.

Agencies in Stockholm, Göteborg and Kristiania.

The manufacture was commenced in 1869, and employs at present, 63 men and 7 boys.

The power required for the grinding works, is supplied by a water-wheel of 15 H. P.

The power for running the rolling-mills for sheet-steel and iron, is supplied by a steam-engine of about 30 H. P.

The raw materials annually used are:

Steel, about 1,900 cwt.
Iron, " 4,800 "
Wood, " 600 cub. feet.

The refuse, scrap from sheet-iron and steel, is sold for remelting.

The exports go to Finland and Norway.

The working men deposit from 10 to 15 per cent. of their earnings every pay-day, and are besides obliged to belong to a sick- and burial-fund, established among the workmen of this and other factories in the town.

414. Fagersta Bruk. (See Cl. 111.)

Saw Blades.

CLASS 514.

415. Sandvikens Jernverks Aktiebolag. (See Cl. 111.) **Piston-Rod for a Steam-Hammer.**

CLASS 514.

416. Bolinders, J. & C. G., Mekaniska Verkstads Aktiebolag. (See Cl. 222.)

Machine for making Metal Cartridges.
Emery Wheels.

417. Köpings Mekaniska Verkstads Aktiebolag. *Köping Mechanical Works Co. Lim.* By O. Hallström, Köping.

Turning Machine.

D.—MACHINES, APPARATUS, AND IMPLEMENTS USED IN SEWING AND MAKING CLOTHING AND ORNAMENTAL OBJECTS.

CLASS 531.

418. Hedlund, Joh. Eskilstuna.

Twelve Sewing Machines.

419. Husquarna Vapen Fabriks Aktiebolag. (See Cl. 265.)

Sewing Machines.

E.—MACHINES AND APPARATUS FOR TYPE SETTING, PRINTING, STAMPING, EMBOSSING, AND FOR MAKING BOOKS, AND PAPER WORKING.

CLASS 546.

420. Brehmer, E. F. A. Stockholm.

Paper Cutting Machine, with a printed description of its use; **Paging Machine,** printing 4 columns of figures; **Ticket Counting Machine,** together with a **Date Stamp,** such as used on the railroads of the Swedish Government; **Drill Press, Leveling Instrument, Water Lever of Iron, Guilottine Stamp.**

Prev. aw.: Vienna, 1873, diploma of honor.

The manufacture of the paper cutting machines commenced in 1870.

F.—MOTORS AND APPARATUS FOR THE GENERATION AND TRANSMISSION OF POWER.

CLASS 551.

421. Atterberg, A. J. Råda, Hagforsen.

Drawing of a Double Axial Turbine of 130 H. P. by a fall of 26 feet.

Two such run the saw mill at Munkfors, owned by the Uddeholm Manufacturing Co.

Drawing of a Radial Turbine without guide bars.

This turbine of 70 H. P., by a fall of 45 feet, runs a rolling mill for Bessemer castings at Langhanshyttan, owned by the Leejöfors Manufacturing Co.

Drawings of Two Radial Turbines of 19 H. P. each.

By a fall of 45 feet supplies the power required for the machine shop and iron foundry at Hagforsen.

Drawing of a Double Axial Turbine of 1000 H. P., by a fall of 80 feet intended to run the Bessemer blast engines at Hagforsen.

Drawing of a Rapid Running Blast Engine, for Bessemer works, with slide and valve.

422. Wenström, W. Örebro.

Profile and Plan of a Turbine.

This turbine was invented by the exhibitor in 1867, and patented in 1868; 40 specimens, with a total capacity of 2,700 H. P. are now in use in Sweden, also a few in Finland.

Prev. aws.: The inventor obtained the Wallmark medal of the Royal Swedish Academy of Sciences, in Stockholm, 1871, and a medal at the International Exhibition in Moscow, 1873.

CLASS 552.

423. Kockum's Mekaniska Verkstads Aktiebolag. *Kockum Machine Manufacturing Co. Lim.* Malmö.

Two Steam Engines. One of these engines of about 25 nominal H. P. is provided with a safety valve of the exhibitors own system, besides; this machine has a surface condensor. The other engine of 3–4 nominal H. P. is intended for dairy use.

Ship Models. Four models of vessels built during the year 1874, one of these is that of a transport steamer, of about 1,000 tons burden; two are smaller tug and passenger boats, and one is intended for the laying of torpedoes off the coast.

The business of the company embraces, machine shops and ship yard, iron foundry and manufacture of railroad cars.

The manufacture was commenced in 1842.

The company employs 900 men with wages amounting to $240,000 gold annually.

The power required is supplied by steam engines of about 100 nominal H. P.

The value of the manufacture during 1874, amounted to 600,000 gold and for the last year shows an increase of about $70,000 gold.

The government taxes for 1874 were $365 gold and the community taxes $1,650 gold.

The raw materials used during the same year consisted of:

Steel, - - -	122 cwt.
Wrought Iron, - -	23,800 "
Sheet Iron, - - -	11,111 "
Pig Iron, - - -	30,000 "
Sundry Metals - - -	620 "
Anthracite Coal, -	150,000 cub. feet.
Timber, - -	20,0000 "

Sundry materials to the value of $100,000 gold.

For the benefit of the workmen, are established, a sick fund, and a baking association. The company provides dwellings for them.

424. Kristinehamns Mekaniska Verkstad. *Kristinehamn Machine Manufacturing Co.*, by H. Asplund. Kristinehamn.

Marine Steam Engine, of WOOLF's system, about 20 nominal H. P., with two cylinders one inside the other.

Tank Engine, for 3 feet gauge, of new construction, patented in Sweden and England by Engineer Asplund.

Railway Car Wheels. (See Cl. 573.) Has not before participated in any exhibition.

The manufacture was commenced in 1865, although then on a very small scale.

In the machine shops are employed 200 men, whose average wages are about $0.65 gold per day.

The power required is supplied by 2 high-pressure steam engines of together 25 H. P.

During 1874, were manufactured:

Marine Engines of 30 H. P. Woolf's system,	4
Locomotives, - - - -	5
Passenger Cars, - - -	16
Baggage Cars, - - - -	5
Freight Cars, - - - -	117
Switches and Turn-tables, - -	119
Car Wheels, - - - -	164
Car Wheel Boxes, - - -	124

And sundry cuttings and works for neighboring works, etc., altogether with a value of $140,000 gold, on which the government taxes were $280 and the community taxes $640 gold. During 1870, the value of the productions amounted to only $23,800 gold.

The raw materials used in 1874, consisted of:

Cast Iron, - - -	8,500 cwt.
Wrought and Sheet Iron, -	2,500 "
Steel, - - -	800 "
Copper and Brass, - -	140 "

Wood and sundry materials, to the value of $19,000 gold.

There is a sick and burial fund established by the company and supported by the workmen, who pay 2 per cent. of their earnings to the fund, and receive in case of sickness 50 per cent. of their daily wages.

The machine shops, which have a very advantageous situation, close by the government railroad station, Kristinehamn, with tracks to the docks of the port, will be considerably extended for the manufacture of locomotives and other railroad material.

425. Köpings, Mekaniska Verkstads Aktiebolag. Köping.

(See Cl. 515.)

Cast-Iron Cylinders for 60 H. P. propeller steam engine.

CLASS 553.

426. Sandvikens Jernverks Aktiebolag (See Cl. 111.) **Axles for Propellers.**

CLASS 555.

427. Runquist, C. R. Stockholm.
Oscillating Governors for running machinery, and **Oscillating Governors** for steam engines, with printed description.

G.—HYDRAULIC AND PNEUMATIC APPARATUS, PUMPING, HOISTING, AND LIFTING.

CLASS 560.

428. Wiklund, W, Stockholm. **Centrifugal Pump.**

CLASS 562.

429. Atterberg, A. J. Hagforssen, Råda. **Drawings of Blowing Engine.**

H.—RAILWAY PLANT, ROLLING STOCK, AND APPARATUS.

CLASS 570.

Björkman, C. R. Kristinehamn.
Design of a Narrow Gauge Locomotive.

430. Kristinehamns Mekaniska Verkstads Aktiebolag. *Kristinehamn Machine Manufacturing Co. Lim.*, by H. ASPLUND. Kristinehamn.

431. Locomotive, patented for engineer H. ASPLUND, in Sweden and England.

The object of the construction of this species of locomotives is to produce, irrespective of the rail-gauge, sufficiently powerful engines, that is to say, to obtain space for an adequately large steam-boiler and fire-box. This object is accomplished by arranging in front and immediately adjacency of the fire-box, a transverse plate, which will operate a connection between the foremost frame-plates, running longitudinally inside the drag-wheels, and the aft-plates, which are lying outside of the leader-wheels.

With a view of utilising the increased engine-power, thus obtained, without increasing the pressure on the wheels and rails, the weight of the locomotive is spread over several coupled wheels, placed as close to one another as possible, in order to prevent the locomotive from wrenching and cranking, at curves, with comparatively short radius.

The constructor has further had in view, by adapting so called radial axel-boxes, of his own invention, on the foremost or aftermost axle of the leader-wheels, entirely to counteract the consequences of the increased distance between the axles, produced by the adaptation of these wheels, that is to say, to prevent the aforesaid wrenchings and crankings, consequent thereon, at curves, with short radius.

These radial axel-boxes are acting in such a manner, that the axle, on which they rest, at any curve, and whatever be its radius, takes the exact direction of that radius, producing, at the same time, the side-motion that is requisite, to prevent the wrenching. These radial axle-boxes will, moreover, become self-acting, from the circumstance, that the under-side of the steer-block, lying on the rollers, is provided, at both ends, with a downward bend.

When the wheel-axle, with its radial boxes is forced, at a curve, to move sideways and consequently must work against the inclined planes, at the extremities of the Steer-block, then the axles and their boxes are forced back, by the same inclined planes, and will resume their former position, at the same moment that the side, pressure, at the end of the curve, ceases. By this means, the wheel-axle will always remain parallel with the other axles, when the locomotive goes on a straight road: but will commence sliding sidewise, whenever the locomotive enters into a curve.

CLASS 573.

432. Adelsköld, C. Stockholm.

Radial Journal-Boxes.

Prev. aw.: Copenhagen, 1872, medal of 2nd clas; Moscow, 1872, silver medal.

The invention consists, in the journal having a flange, moving circularly in a corresponding excavation in the journal-box, whereby the axle, through the pressure of the wheel-flange against the outer rail on curves of the road, is placed radially.

The boxes are used on the Uddevalla-Wenersborg-Herljunga Railroad, for locomotives; on the Pålsboda-Finspong R. R., for locomotives and cars; on the Uppsala-Gefle R. R., for locomotives and cars; on the east Vermland R. R., and on the Lenna-Näs R. R., for locomotives.

The advantages of the invention are: that the cars can have longer axle-boxes, whereby they run steadier; that the wear and the tear of the rails in curves, and of the tires is lessened; and that the cars run nearly as easily on the curves, as on the straight road.

433. Arboga Gjuteri och Mekaniska Verkstad. *Arboga foundry and iron-works.* Arboga.

Wheels for Railroad-, tramway, and mine-cars, etc.

Prev. aw. Stockholm, 1866, bronze medal Copenhagen, 1872, bronze medal.

The works have two turbines of 30 H. P. 160 men and 12 boys are constantly at work. Annual production about 2,500 wheels of chilled cast-iron. The street car wheels are used on the tramways of Copenhagen, Edinburgh, Glasgow, London, Moscow and Petersburg.

434. Ekman, Carl. (See Cl. 111.)

Railway Wheels.

435. Fagersta Bruks Aktiebolag. (See Cl. 111.)

Axles.

436. Kristinehamns Mekaniska Verkstad. (See Cl. 552.)

Railway Wheels.

437. Köpings Mekaniska Verkstads Aktiebolag. *Köping Machine Manufacturing Co. Lim.*, by O. Hallström. Köping.

Axles.

438. Sandvikens Jerwerks Aktiebolag. Sandviken. See Cl. 111.

Railway-wheels and axles.

CLASS 574.

439. Ankarsrums Bruk. (See Cl. 111.)

Chilled Railway Switches.

440. Östrand, Herrman. Helsingborg.

Design of Chilled Railway Switch.

Many of these switches have been laid at the more important railway stations in Sweden.

Aerial, Pneumatic, and Water Transportation.

CLASS 591.

441. Lesjöfors Aktiebolag. (See Cl. 111.) **Wire Cables.**

CLASS 594.

442. Kockums Mekaniska Verkstad. (See Cl. 552.)

Models of Steamers and of a **Torpedo Boat.**

443. Royal Swedish Commission.

Models of Fishing Boats. (See Cl. 647).

CLASS 595.

444. Motala Mekaniska Verkstads Aktiebolag. *Motala Iron and Steel Works.*

Compound Marine Engine of about 35 nominal, or 100 indicated H. P.

DEPARTMENT VI.

AGRICULTURE.

A.—ARBORICULTURE AND FOREST PRODUCTS.

CLASS 600.

(For the Import-Duty compare class 227).

New Gellivara Co. Lim.; by J. A. Wikström. Luleå. See Cl. 111.

Sections of fir-timber, grown at 67° N. lat.

Specimens of lumber from steam and water-power saw mills at the bay of Bothnia.

C.—AGRICULTURAL PRODUCTS.

CLASS 620.

	Import-Duty in United States.	Sweden.
WHEAT,	per bushel of 60 lbs., 20 cts.	Free.
RYE,	" 56 " 15 "	"
BARLEY,	" 48 " 15 "	"
OATS,	" 32 " 10 "	"
SEEDS, flax or linseed,	" 59 " 20 "	"
" oil seeds, excepting flax or linseed,	per lb. ½ ct.	"
" agricultural, all n. o. p. f.,	20 per cent.	"

445. Björkegren, E. Källtorp, Örebo.

Samples of cereals.

446. Fogelmark, Sixten. Ava, Luleå.

Wheat, rye and barley raised at Ava, the northernmost agricultural school on the earth, being located only *48 Eng. miles south of the North Polar Circle.*

Prev. aw.: Paris, 1867, bronze medal, and, 1872, silver medal; Vienna, 1873, diploma of honor.

447. Hagendahl, C. A. Örebro.

Cereals and **seeds.**

448. Hofmeister, Chr. Ingelstad, Kristianstad.

Samples of **wheat and barley.**

449. Hultenberg, C. A. Borgholm.

Barley.

450. Kalmar Läns Norra Hushållnings Sällskap. *Agricultural Society of N. Kalmar.* Westervik.

Cereals.

451. New Gellivara Co. Lim.; by J. A. Wikström. Luleå. See Cl. 111.

Agricultural products, specimens of wheat, rye, barley and oats, from Svartå and Milderstien.

452 Norrbottens Läns Hushållnings Sällskap. *The Agricultural Society of the Län of Norrbotten*; by H. A. Widmark. Luleå.

Specimens of agricultural products of the Län.

Potatoes from different parts of the Län.

Rye, Barley, Oats and **Flax** from the following places:

	Latitude North.	Longitude fr. Stockholm, + E., — W.	Height above the lev. of sea	
Pite, Öjebyn,	65°22′	+3°20′	50	R.B.O.H
Arvidsjaur,	65°35′	+1°20′	1230	B.
Arjeploug,	66°8′	—0°22′	1440	B.
Neder-Lule,	65°39′	+3°55′	50	B.
Öfver-Lule,	65°49′	+3°38′	50	R. B.
Quikkjokk,	66°57′	—0°18′	1065	B.
Neder-Kalix	65°51′	+5° 5′	45	R. B.
Öfver-Kalix,	66°19′17″	+4°49′	135	R.
"	66°23′	+4°40′	140	B.
Gellivare,	67°7′	+2°36′	1233	B.
Haapakylä,	66°23′11″	+5°37′	216	R.
Turtula,	66°41′	+5°48′	278	R.
Ruskola,	66°22′	+5°36′	200	B.
Pajala,	66°57′	+5°47′	340	B.
Wittangi,	67°40′20″	+3°35′	860	B.

R.,—Rye; B.,—Barley; O.,—Oats; H.,—Hemp.

453. Platen, Carl von, *Count.* Örbyhus.

Cereals and seeds of foragers plants.

454. Scheele, G. von. Kilanda, Göteborg.

Cereals and seeds.

455. Stenström, O. E. Gårdsjö, Karlstad.

Cereals.

Prev. aw. in Copenhagen, Paris, Stockholm and Vienna.

456. Uppsala Läns Hushållnings Sällskap. *Agricultural Society of the Län of Uppsala.*

Cereals, seeds of forage plants and other **agricultural products.**

457. Westerbottens Läns Hushällnings Säll-skay. *The Agricultural Society of the Län of Westerbotten;* by Dr. F. Unander, Umeå.

458. Westmanlands Läns Hushållnings Säll-skap. *Agricultural Society of the Län of Westmanland;* by J. W. Broberg, Stenby, Strömsholm.

Cereals and other **seeds.**

459. Örebro Läns Hushållnings Sällskap. *Agricultural Society of the Län of Örebro;* by A. G. Löwenhielm, (Nora), Örebro.

Cereals.

CLASS 621.

	Import-Duty in United States.	Sweden.
BEANS, PEAS and VETCHES, dried for food, . . .	10 per cent.	free.
THE SAME for seed, ...	20 per cent.	free.

640. Hofmeister, Chr. Ingelstad, Kristianstad. **Samples of Peas.**

CLASS 623.

	Import-Duty in United States.	Sweden.
TOBACCO, unmanufactured, n. o. p. f., ...	30 per cent.	per lb. 29 öre.
" " stems, ...	per lb. 15 cts.	per lb. 29 öre.
" manufactured, of all descriptions, . . .	per lb. 50 cts. (and int. rev. tax of 20 cts. per lb.)	per lb. 35 öre. to 1 Kr. 30 öre.

461. Beggren, D. & J. Stockholm.

Tobacco, grown near Stockholm.

Prev. aw.: London, 1865.

The tobacco raising was started in 1856. During the planting and gathering seasons, 10 men, 40 women and 14 children are employed.

462. Dahl, P. Karlshamn.

Samples of **Snuff.**

Prev. aw.: Blekinge silver medal. Manufacture commenced 1848; employ: 7 men, wages, 41 to 59 cents per day; 8 boys, wages 12 to 14 cents per day. Steam engine 6 H. P.

In 1874 189,145 lbs. of Clarksville tobacco were used for making 283,394 lbs. of snuff, sold at a rate of $16.11 gold per 100 lbs., showing an increase in the total value of the production of about $5,555 gold in 5 years.

About 5,000 lbs. exported to Denmark.

Government taxes $85 gold. Community $150 gold.

463. Hennig & Papenhagen. Kalmar.

Chickory, raw and prepared.

E.—MARINE ANIMALS, FISH CULTURE, AND APPARATUS.

CLASS 641.

464. The Royal Swedish Commission. Collection of Swedish Fishes preserved in Alcohol.

CLASS 642.

	Import-Duty in United States.	Sweden.
HERRINGS, pickled or salted,	$1 per bbl. or 0.50 per 100 lbs.	
SALMON, pickled,	$3 per bbl.	free.
MACKEREL,	$2 per bbl.	"
FISH, all kinds, *in oil,*	30 per cent.	"
" " " otherwise prepared,	35 per cent.	"

465. Amundson, C. M., *Mrs.* Uddevalla.

Oyster-Anchovies.

The oyster-anchovies, unlike the common anchovies, are twice packed with spices.

The anchovies have not before been exhibited at any International Exhibition.

Agencies in all larger towns of Sweden.

The manufacture was commenced in 1845.

For the packing no steady force of workmen is employed, as the time of the catch proper extends only over a short period in Spring and Autumn.

The packing is all done by hand, and for the manufacture of packing boxes the usual tinsmiths' machines are used.

The prices are :

For 1 tin box of anchovies, $0.35 gold.
" ½ " " " 0.20 "

To agents, or at wholesale, 10 per cent. discount is allowed.

The anchovies are exported to Denmark, Germany, Russia and Finland.

466. Andersson, Gustaf. Fjellbacka.

Anchovies, Dainty-Herrings and **Swedish Sardines.**

Prev. aw.: Malmö, 1865; Bergen, 1865; Stockholm, 1866; Boulogne, 1866; Moscow, 1872; Vienna, 1873; Berlin, 1873; Mariestad, 1874.

Agencies in Stockholm and Örebro.

The manufacture was commenced in 1845 and employs 2 or 3 men at 30 cents per day, and 10 to 12 women at 15 to 17 cents per day.

The prices are :

For ½ barrel of anchovies,			$4.17 gold.
" ¼ " "			2.22 "
" ⅛ " "			1.11 "
" 1 keg of anchovies of	0.60 gallon,		0.42 "
" ½ " "	" 0.30	"	0.23 "
" 1 box of "	" 0.30	"	0.23 "
" ½ " "	" 0.15	"	0.14 "
" 1 glass jar of "	" 0.30	"	0.28 "
" ½ " " "	" 0.15	"	0.19 "
" 1 china jar of "	" 0.30	"	0.35 "
" ½ " " "	" 0.15	"	0.21 "
" 1 box of dainty herring,			0.25 "
" ½ " " "			0.17 "
" 1 " " skin and boneless,			0.22 "
" ½ " " "	"		0.17 "

The production, during 1874, amounted to $1,670 gold.

The raw materials used for the production, during 1874, were 6,000 firkins of sprats.

The refuse, skin and bones, is composted, and used as a fertilizer.

The manufactures are exported to Russia, England, France, Germany, America, Egypt and Denmark.

467. Bergström, H. C. Lysekil.

Anchovies and "**Skin- and Bone-less Appetite" Herrings.** The anchovies are packed in whole and half cans, the herrings in whole and half boxes.

Prev. aws., three medals.

The manufacture was commenced in 1867, and employs 15 persons, with wages aggregating $2,800 gold per annum.

The tin cans and boxes are all made in the factory, on 7 machines worked by hand.

The prices are, cash, in Göteborg or Uddevalla:

For	1 tin box of anchovies,	$0.35.
"	½ " " "	0.20.
"	1 " " appetite herrings,	0.35.
"	½ " " " "	0.20.

Ten per cent. discount at wholesale.

Chief Agent, Mr. H. A. BÜRGER, Göteborg.

468. Ericsson. N. O. Tången, Lysekil.

Anchovies, and **Skin and Boneless Delicacy Herring.** The anchovies are packed in well-made tin vessels.

Agencies in Stockholm aud Göteborg. The manufacture was commenced in 1874. Six workmen are employed with wages averaging 36 cents per day. The annual production amounts to about $3,300 gold, for which the taxes are about $14 gold.

The prices are: per 100 whole cans,		$30.55	gold.
" " "	½ "	18.05	"
" " "	whole boxes,	30.55	"
" " "	½ "	18.05	"

with 15 per cent. discount, when at least 100 cans of each kind are ordered.

The raw material used in the manufacture consist of about 1000 firkins of sprats. The refuse is mixed with muck and sold as a fertilizer.

The production is, in part, exported to England, Germany, Denmark, and Russia, in varying quantities.

469. Hallgren, J. J. Gullholmen, Oroust.

Delicacy Anchovies, and **Skin- and Boneless Delicacy Herrings,** put up in tin cans, holding about 50, 25, and 15 cub. inches, and also in small tin boxes.

Prev. aw.: 1st prizes at the exhibitions at Moscow, Copenhagen, Kongelf, Lysekil, Göteborg, Wenersborg, Vienna, Berlin, Wiborg, altogether 11 medals, beside diplomas.

The products are sold exclusively through Mr. PAUL CARAVELLO, in Göteborg.

The manufacture was commenced in 1865, and employs 9 men, with wages aggregating about $100 gold per month, and 10 women, whose wages aggregate $70 per month.

In the manufacture of tin vessels, machines run by hand power are used.

The annual value of the production is about $16,600 gold; per annum government taxes are $10, and the community taxes about $15 gold.

The price of the products are:

For	1 can of anchovies,	$0.35	gold.
"	½ " "	0.20	"
"	¼ " "	0.13	"
"	1 box of skin & boneless herring,	0.35	"
"	½ " " "	0.20	"

with 10 per cent. discount at 30 days at wholesale.

The materials used. consist of sprats, salt, sugar, spices, etc., quantity uncertain.

The refuse from the manufacture are used as fertilizers.

The products are sold in Sweden, Norway, Denmark, Germany, France, Russia, England and several other countries.

470. Lundgren, P. W. Stockholm.

Preserved fish.

471. Lysell, Aug. Lysekil.

"Delikatess anjovis" and **"skinn och benfri-anjovis"** (dainty anchovies, skin and boneless anchovies).

Factories started 1872, employ 20 men, 10 women, 10 boys, and 5 girls, their wages amounting to about $700, gold.

Materials used: 2,000 bushels of sprats.

Prices:

Delikatess anjovis,	100 large boxes,	$35.00	gold.
" "	" small "	20.00	"
Aptit, "	" large "	35.00	"
" "	" small "	20.00	"

Prices calculated for 3 months; cash 10 per cent. discount.

472. Nilsson, Edv. Grebbestad, Göteborg.

Preserved mackerel.

Mackerels of the fattest and best quality are cleaned as usual, and all the bones taken out, then covered with a mixture of sugar, salt, and white pepper, in which mixture they are allowed to remain for a certain time, after which time they are smoked in the smoke from juniper sprigs until they have acquired a light brown color; and then cut up in small slices and packed in tin boxes with sweet oil, the boxes being soldered up when filled.

Prev. aw.: Wenersborg, silver medal and diploma of honor; Mariestad, bronze medal, and Viborg, diploma of honor.

Agency at Göteborg.

The manufacture was commenced in 1872.

During the fishing season, 1875, were employed 22 women with wages of $0.21 per day, and 2 men who were paid $0.56 for every hundred boxes soldered up, their day's work being usually 125 to 150 boxes.

The production during 1872 was between 8000—10,000 boxes, at a price of $0.28 per box. At wholesale a discount of 10 per cent. is given.

As yet no separate taxes have been paid for this business, but they have been assessed together with the taxes for the mercantile business of the firm.

That part of the refuse which is useful for food, such as heads, fins, roes, milts, etc., are sold cheaply to the poorer population, the rest of the refuse (the intestines of the fish) has not yet been made use of, but as this part is a very valuable fertilizer, it will in the future be composted.

Formerly the boxes were of two sizes, whole and half boxes, but at present only one size, as mentioned before, is put up.

Letters patent, for five years in Sweden, was granted, in 1875.

473. Roy. Swedish Commission; by H. WIDEGREN, *P. D., Intendent of Fisheries.* Stockholm.

Contributions from A. ANDERSSON, Motala; P. ANDERSSON, Helsingborg; J. VON BERGEN, Karlshamn; O. BERNSON, Marstrand; R. LUNDBERG, Stockholm; A. J. LYTH, Hemse, Gottland; N. MARTIN, Kivik; A. MATTSON, Karlshamn; J. OSTERMAN, Skillinge; SVENSKA FISKEREDSKAPS AKTIEBOLAGET, Stockholm; SPIEGELBERG Stockholm; W. WAHLBERG, Wermdön; and J. P. ÅKERVALL, Leckö.

a. **Collection of fishes**, from the fresh-waters and coasts of Sweden, being important to the living of the inhabitants in said country—altogether 77 species, preserved in glass jars and spirits of wine.

b. **Fishing-gear**:

10 Herring-nets of the Gottland model 5, white, 5 brown—the most common in Gottland.

6 herring-nets of the Blekinge-model.

5 " " Skåne-model.

2 " " Norrland-model.

6 mackerel-nets.

2 flounder-nets of the South-Sweden model.

2 " " Bohuslän-model.

1 seine of the Vettern-model.

12 nets for salmon and lake fishing.

5 salmon-nets, as used off the coast of Blekinge.

4 salmon-lines, as used in the Baltic Sea.

3 cod- and flounder-lines, as used in the Baltic sea.

A complete collection of hook-fishing gear, and its accessories of grapnels, buoys, etc., as used by the Swedish fishers, when fishing on the North Sea- and Kattegat-banks.

A collection of fish-gigs, fishing lines and smaller hook fishing gear, as used in the inner sounds and fresh waters of Sweden.

Samples of white net-work.

c. **Models of fishing-crafts, viz.**:

Bank-fishing vessel, as used on the bank of the North Sea.

Mackerel-boat, as used in Bohuslän.

Herring-boat, as used in Skåne.

" " Blekinge.

" " Gottland.

" " Norrland.

Boat, as used in Dalarne.

Boat used for fishing and traveling on the Lappland rivers.

"Eka," Skiff, for fishing in smaller lakes.

" " transport of living fish in Stockholm.

d. **Products of fishing**:

1 sample of salted Gottland-herring.

1 " " Blekinge-herring.

1 " " " -eel.

1 " dried cod.

1 " salt cod.

1 " dried ling.

1 " pickled sprat, ("anchovy")

474. Leidesdorffska Fiske-redskaps Fabriken. *Leidesdorff Fishing Implement Manufactory,*" by Edw. Leidesdorff. Stockholm.

Fishing implements.

Prev. aw.: Malmö, 1865, silver medal; Aarhus, 1875, silver-medal; Bergen, 1856, honorable mention; Vienna, 1873, medal of merit.

Agency in Göteborg.

The manufacturing was started in 1861, Only 4 men, 3 women and 2 boys are employed, the greatest part of the goods being made by home-work.

During the last business year 1,000 lbs. German silver, 2,000 lbs. linen yarns, not twisted; 800 lbs, twisted linen yarns, and 100 lbs. raw silk were used for the following production:

15,000 pieces squids, at a value of	$6,000 gold.
8,000 coarse linen fishing lines,	1,400 "
500 set lines with hooks,	420 "
500 hand-made nets for fishing,	600 "
2,000 lbs. linen yarns, and lines for long-reefs, at a value of	840 "

The total production amounted to $10,000 gold, being twice that of 1870, and three times that of 1865. The production has not as yet been sufficient to supply the home demand.

A discount of 25 to 33⅓ per cent. is permitted in wholesale dealing.

F.—ANIMAL AND VEGETABLE PRODUCTS.

CLASS 651.

475. Wästfelt, Carl Carlsson. Kölingsholm, Mullsjö. **Rennet.**

CLASS 652.

476. Ericsson, Anders. Stockholm.

Calfskins, used for making fine shoes.

Prev. aw.: London, prize medal.

The manufacture was commenced in 1872, and gives occupation to 5 men with wages of 90 cents per day. The power required is supplied by a steam engine, 2 H. P.

In 1874, the value of the productions amounted to $6,000, for which the government taxes were $9, and the community taxes $10.

List of prices:

Calfskins, Brand	A,	$26.66	gold, per doz.
" "	A 1,	30.00	" "
" "	A 2,	33.33	" "
" "	A 3,	36.66	" "
" "	B,	40.00	" "
" "	B 1,	43.33	" "
" "	B 2,	46.66	" "
" "	B 3,	50.00	" "

" of corresponding brands of medium kind, 5 per cent. discount.

All per cash.

The raw materials used for the production are 2,500 calfskins per annum.

The refuse consists of glue-leather used for making glue; calfshair used for making horse blankets.

The skins are exported to London. This manufacture is however, yet new and consequently the trade little developed.

477. Johannesson, C. S. Stockholm.

Leather, Cow-Leather, Oil-Leather Wax-Leather, Horse-Leather, Wax-Leather-Skins, Patent Sleek-Leather-Leggings, Patent Leather-Uppers.

Prev. aw.: Moscow, 1872, bronze medal; Vienna, 1873, honorable mention.

The manufactory was established in 1802, the present owner took possession in 1867.

In the manufactory are employed 10 men.

The bark-mill is driven by a horse. The manufacture in 1874, amounted to about $25,000 gold, in 1868, to only $11,000 gold. The government and community taxes for 1874, were together $56 gold.

The prices are:

For Sole-Leather,	$0.43	gold, per lb.
" Cow-Leather,	0.43	" "
" Oil-Leather,	0.49	" "
" Wax-Leather,	0.54	" "
" Horse-Leather,	0.70	" "
" Wax Leather-Skins,	0.97	" "
" Sleek-Leather-Leggins,	12.50	" per doz.
" Sleek-Leather-Uppers,	10.00	" "

The manufactures are all sold through a travelling agent, who receives two per cent. commission on his sales.

The raw materials used are: Buenos Ayres, Para, Pernambuco and Swedish hides, kid, calf, goat and sheep-skins.

In the manufacture are used catechu, valonia, oak-bark, etc.

The leather cuttings obtained as refuse are used for a new manufacture of artificial leather. The rest of the refuse is used for fuel.

The exports go to Germany, Silesia, and the Netherlands.

The workmen deposit their savings in the saving banks of Stockholm.

CLASS 656.

	Import-Duty in United States.	Import-Duty in Sweden.
PREPARED fish, game, meats, and vegetables, n. o. p. f.,	35 per cent.	free.
CONFECTIONERY, and preserved fruit, n. o. p. f.,	per lb. 15 cts.	per lb. 20 öre.

478. Frommel, C. J. Göteborg.

Confections and Preserved Fruits.

479. Vikström, Zacharias. Stockholm.

Preserved Vegetables.

CLASS 657.

480. Landskrona Franska Ångqvarn. *The French Steam Flour Mill.* Landskrona.

Samples of Flour and Grit.

Prev. aw.: Göteborg and Malmö, silver medals; Copenhagen, 1872, and Vienna, 1873; diploma of merit.

Mill built 1870; steam engine 25 H. P. 15 men employed.

Cereals prepared last year: wheat, 76,780 cubic feet; rye, 65,730 cubic feet; barley 853 cubic feet. Value of preparations last year, $165,800 gold. About one-tenth is exported to Norway, nine-tenths are sold in Sweden.

481. Schéele, Götrick von. Kilanda.

Samples of Seeds and Grain, whole and manufactured into grits and flour.

Prev. aw.: At exhibitions in Göteborg, Wenersborg, and Copenhagen. Medals for merit at Vienna, 1873.

Agents in Göteborg, Karlstad, Norrköping, and Kristiania.

The manufacturing, which begun in 1867, is worked by nine men and a water-power of 36 H. P. Last year the materials used were, oats, 9,000 cubic feet; barley, 500 cubic feet; wheat, 1,500 cubic feet, and rye, 2,000 cubic feet. In manufacturing oat grits, the oats are previous to grinding steam-boiled and kiln-dried. After the whole process a residue of 50 per cent. is left, which, mixed with roots, furnishes a very valuable food for cattle. The annual proceeds of the "Grinding Mill" are estimated at $450 gold, and the value of the whole manufacture, which in the beginning was about $1,500 gold, has during the last years amounted to $9,000 gold per annum. As to the exports, only a quantity of about 20,000 pounds goes to Norway.

Within the community of Kilanda there is an excellent common school, and also a library that is freely availed of.

482. Ystads Franska Ångqvarn. *The French Steam Flour Mill;* by G. Schönbeck & Joh. Borg, Ystad.

Flour and Grits.

Prev. aw. Stockholm, 1856; Skåne's Economical Society, 1865 & 1867, silver medals; Malmö, 1865, silver medal; Paris, 1867, Copenhagen and Leipsic, 1869; Göteborg, 1871, and Vienna, 1873, medal of merit.

Agents in Stockholm, Göteborg, Gefle, Sundswall, Kristiania, Bergen, Trondhjem, and Drammen.

The mill was built in 1864. The motive power is supplied by a steam engine of 25 H. P. There are employed,

1 manager at . . .	$35	gold per month.
2 engineers at . . .	$20	" " "
1 " " . . .	$14	" " "
13 workmen and apprentices at . .	$7 to $14	" " "

The amount of grain ground yearly is wheat, 132,254 cubic feet; rye, 74,982 cubic feet, and barley, 11,27 cubic feet; the value of the annual manufacture being about $226,000 gold. All the residue is sold to the neighboring farmers as feed. The superiority of the manufacture is to a high degree owing to the method of kiln-drying the grain by steam, and fanning it by a centrifugal apparatus. The government taxes are $85 gold, and the community taxes $397 gold per annum. One-third of the wheat and rye flour manufactured is sold to Norway, and the demand is greater than can be supplied. Commission at wholesale 1 per cent.

CLASS 660.

	Import-Duty in United States.	Sweden.
LIQUORS, *malt* in bottles, duty on bottles included,	35 cts. per gallon.	20 to 40 öre per kanna.
" " not in bottles, . , .	20 " "	" "
" *spirituous*, n. o. p. f., exclusive of duty on bottles, ...	$2.00 per gallon.	1 Kr. 30 öre, to 2 Kr. per kanna.

483. Berg, C. G. Karlshamn.

Swedish Punch and refined **Whiskey** ("Brånvin.")

Prev. aw. Malmö, 1865, silver medal; Stockholm, 1867, silver medal; Paris, 1867, bronze medal; Copenhagen, 1875, silver medal; Vienna, 1873, silver medal; London, 1873, bronze medal, no silver medals awarded.

The manufacture was commenced in 1873.

The working force (consisting of men, women, boys and girls) can not be stated for the punch manufacture separately, as this one is principally managed by the same force as the distillation.

Only hand-power is employed. The manufacture of punch in 1874 amounted to $45,000 gold, and of refined Swedish whiskies to about $125,000 gold.

At wholesale a deduction of from 3 to 5 per cent. is made.

In 1874, 15,000 bottles of punch were exported to Denmark and Germany. Their export increased in 1875.

484. Bergen, J. N. von, & Son. *Karlshamm.*

Swedish Punch.

Prev. aw.: Copenhagen, 1872, silver medal; Vienna, 1873, medal of progress; London, 1873, medal.

Agencies in Berlin, Hamburg, and Copenhagen.

The manufacture was commenced about 1844, and employs 6 men and 2 women, whose yearly wages aggregate about $1275 gold.

The annual production is about 70,000 bottles, with a value during 1874 of $0.35 gold per bottle. At wholesale 3 per cent. discount is allowed.

The annual value of the production thus amounts to about $19,500 gold, which, however, is an increase over that of 5 or ten years ago with about 40 per cent.

The custom duties paid to the government during 1874 amounted to $8,750 gold, and the community taxes $280 gold.

The article is consumed principally within the country, but some is exported to Germany, Denmark, Norway, Brazil, and the Southern states of North America.

The workmen deposit their weekly surplus earnings in the savings-bank of the town.

485. Broddelius & Åkerman. Göteborg.

"Militär-Punch."

Pr. aw.: Vienna, 1873.

Manufacture began 1849.

486. Cederlund's J. Söner, (*Sons.*) Stockholm.

"Genuine Caloric Punch."

Pr. aw.: Medals in London, 1862; Stockholm, 1867; Paris, 1867; Moscow, 1872; Copenhagen, 1872; Vienna, 1873; and London, 1873.

Price: $4.50 gold per dozen bottles, packing included, in cases of 1, 2, or 4½ dozen bottles, delivered on the vessel at Stockholm free of charge.

The manufacturing began 1823. Products exported to Germany, France, England, Austria, Russia, Denmark, Italy, North and South America.

Agencies in Paris, London, Hamburg, and Copenhagen.

487. Creutz, A. Mariefred.

Swedish Punch, manufactured from best *arrack*, and put up in white glass bottles, provided with label and a yellow metal cap over the neck of the bottle, both marked: "Gripsholms Pounsch, A. Creutz, Mariefred."

The manufacture was commenced in 1871. Branch factory in Strengnäs.

During 1874 the production amounted to 4035 gallons, with a value of $8,750 gold.

The price of the punch is 42 cents per bottle, and $2.17 gold per gallon. At wholesale, when at least 100 bottles or 20 gallons are ordered a discount, of 6 per cent. is allowed.

Exportation to Denmark.

488. Dahlheim & Engström. Stockholm.

Arrac Punch.

Prev. aw.: Moscow, 1872; Vienna, 1873, medal of merit; London, 1873, medal.

The business began 1870. Products exported to England, Germany, France and Russia.

489. Högstedt & Co. Stockholm.

Arrac Punch.

Prev. aw.: Medals in London, Paris and Vienna.

The manufacture of punch has been carried on by this firm, on a large scale since 1842, and has doubled itself during the last few years.

Exports to Denmark, England, Germany, France and America.

490. Moboda Fabriks Bolag. *Moboda Manufacturing Co.;* by C. A. Hagendahl. Moboda.

Spirits manufactured from Lichens.

Manufacture commenced in 1868.

In the distillery are employed 20 men, with wages from 45 cents to 55 cents per day.

The steam required is supplied by two small boilers.

The productions last year was 43,204 gallons of 50 per cent. proof-spirits, on which the tax is $38.61 gold per 100 hundred gallons.

Some years, when two distilleries have been used, the production has amounted to 86,408 gallons of 50 per cent. proof spirits. The wholesale price is $77.72 gold, per 100 gallons.

The raw materials used were 1,200,000 lbs. of lichens.

Origin of this manufacture:

It has long been known that the cellular tissue of plants, by being boiled with certain acids, may be changed into starch, gum or dextrin and finally into grape-sugar, from which by the usual methods alcohol may be obtained. It has also been tried to turn this property of the cellular tissue, to practical use in the manufacture of alcohol; but these attempts have hitherto not met with the success expected, as it was found that the quantity of alcohol obtained in this manner, did not compensate for the costs and trouble expended on its production. In the autumn of 1867, when occupied with researches on the lichens, Professor STENBERG, of Stockholm, found that the cellular tissue of the cryptogams, embraced under the general name of Lichens, differs from the common cellular tissue in that, that upon being boiled with diluted acids, it is changed much more easily and more completely into grape-sugar than the latter; so that, from lichens which contain little or no starch, there may be obtained without any difficulty and with but a small expenditure of acid,—from 65 to 70 parts of sugar, from 100 parts of dried lichens. On this fact is founded the manufacture of alcohol from reindeer "moss," (*Cladonia Rangiferina*). This lichen, which in the northern countries grows in immense quantities, contains only an exceedingly small quantity of starch, and without the above-named peculiarity of its cellular tissue, the aforesaid manufacture would not be possible. By a series of experiments, made by Professor STENBERG in the year 1868, and described by him in a treatise entitled "Om tillverkning af lafbrännvin" ("On the manufacture of spirits from lichens") Stockholm, 1868, it was further proved, that the production of alcohol from reindeer moss, could be managed profitably even on a large scale, and several manufactories for this production were then established in Sweden and Norway, Finland and Russia, in which last-named country, as well as in the United States, the process of the manufacture of spirits, from lichens is patented by Professor STENBERG.

491. Petterson, Otto. Stockholm.

Swedish Punch.

The manufacture was commenced in 1870.

The price of the punch is $0.56 gold per bottle.

492. Platin, C. G. & Co. Göteborg.

Punch strong, red brand, price per bottle $0.35.

Punch, less strong, blue brand, price per bottle, $0.35.

Mandarin punch, white brand, price per bottle, $0.42.

The manufacturing began in 1847. Raw materials used in 1875 were about 100,000 lbs. and 12,000 gallons of Dutch arrack.

Export to Germany, Denmark, England, Spain and Australia.

493. Thålin, W. Nyköping.

Arrac-punch.

The business was commenced in 1856, and during the last years the annual production has amounted to 7,000 gallons, with an average value of $2, gold, per gallon. When sold in bottles of 1-7 gallon's capacity, at a price of $0.30 to $0.45.

5 per cent, discount is allowed at wholesale.

494. Tulldahl, A. H. Landskrona.

Pale Ale.

Price per 1 bottle, $0.15.

Price per ½ bottle, $0.08.

495. Ullander, Ad. Uppsala.

Punch.

496. Wallis, A. B. Dybeck, Malmö.

Ale in bottles.

Prev. aw.: Malmö, 1865; Ystad, 1867: Copenhagen, 1872; Vienna, 1873; London, 1873.

Motive power steam-engine, 6 H. P. Employs 10 men.

Production last year, 120,500 gallons at 18½ cts.

Materials used, 12,080 kubic ft. barley, 3,314 lbs. hops.

Government taxes $58 gold.

Community taxes $70.

CLASS 661.

497. Feith, H. J. & Son. Uppsala.

Biscuits, which can be kept for ½ a year without changing. These biscuits are recommended as a fine and palatable cake to be eaten with coffee, tea, chocolate, wines, liquors, etc.

Hard Rye- and Rusk-Bread.

Ships-bread, (Italian bread).

Prev. aw.: London, 1873, large medal; Vienna, 1873, diploma of honor; Uppsala, 1874, two silver medals; Mariestad, 1874, one silver, and one bronze-medal.

Agencies in all parts of Sweden and Norway, also in Copenhagen and London.

The bakery was commenced in 1848; the biscuit- and cracker-manufactory in 1872.

In the manufacture are employed about 37 men, 15 boys and 8 women, altogether 60 employees, with wages aggregating 15,560 gold per annum.

Only hand-power is employed, together with auxiliary machines.

In the bakery, are baked about 100 different kinds of bread; in the confectionery, many kinds of fancy cakes; in the cracker-manufactory, about 200 kinds of crackers; and in the biscuit-manufactory, about 50 kinds of biscuits. At wholesale 10 to 15 per cent. discount is allowed. Several kinds of hard rye- and rusk-bread are also sold at wholesale. The value of the production in 1871, amounted to $21,000 gold, and in 1874, to $55,000 gold.

The firm was in 1874, assessed for an income of $1,400 gold, besides the real estate.

The raw materials consumed during 1874, were:

Wheat flour, ...	5,000 cwt.
Rye flour, ...	2,000 "
Sugar, ...	50,000 lbs.
Butter, ...	40,000 "
Eggs, ...	10,000 doz.
Milk, ...	23,041 gals.

besides spices, etc.

By the manufacture quite a large amount of refuse is obtained, which is sold at ½ or ¼ of its cost value.

The exports in 1874, were: to Norway, 10,000 lbs. of biscuits; to Denmark, 1,000 lbs. of biscuits, the high duty, 17 öre per lb., preventing a larger export to that country; to London, about 1,000 lbs of biscuits.

A new manufactory for steam-machinery is under erection.

498. R. Swedish Commission.

Hard Rye Bread.

H.—MACHINES, IMPLEMENTS AND PROCESSES OF MANUFACTURE.

(For Import-Duties see page 78).

CLASS 670.

499. Eklundh, L. P. Hjelmafors, Ulricehamn.

Patent Steel Ploughs.

Prev. aw.: 2 gold medals, 11 silver medals, 4 bronze medals, 2 diplomas of honor, and 1100 crowns.

The manufacturing was started 1860 at Westlandaholm, and moved to Hjelmafors, 1874, where the work is done by water power and 52 workmen, all full-grown, to whom $8,600, gold, a year are paid, as wages.

Plough No.	weight	lbs., price	$	gold.
1A.		160	12	
" 2	"	150	" 11	"
" 3	"	140	" 10.50	"
" 3A.	"	100	" 8.50	"

500. Göteborgs Mekaniska Werkstads Aktiebolag. *Göteborg Machine Manufacturing Co. Lim.* Göteborg.

Plows, with mould boards and shares of steel; coulters sheeted.

Prev. aw.: 5 gold medals, 50 silver and bronze medals, 14 diplomas of honor, and a large number of money awards.

Agencies in nearly all the towns of Sweden, and in Kristiania, Trondhjem, Stavanger, Åbo, Helsingfors, St. Petersburg, Riga, Capetown, Bogota in Columbia, and other places.

The manufacture was commenced in 1843, and employs about 800 men.

The power required is supplied by steam engines of 85 H. P. The manufacture consists of Iron Steamers, Steam Engines, and Steam Boilers, Railroad Cars, Farming Implements and Machines, Machines and Tools for Factories, etc.

At wholesale 10 per cent. discount is allowed.

The value of the manufacture during 1874 amounted to $600,000, gold.

The raw materials are: Pig-Iron, Bar-Iron, Sheet and Rolled Iron, Steel, Copper, Tin, Zinc, etc.; Anthracite Coal, Charcoal, Coke, and Peat. Timber: Oak, Pine, etc.

The exports go to the above mentioned countries.

For the benefit of the workmen are established pension and sick-funds. Workmen's dwellings are being erected.

CLASS 672.

501. Palmcrantz, Helge. Stockholm.
Mower.

502. Petterson, C. E. Långö, Elfdalen.

18 Scythes of different models, viz:

2 No. 1 Wira-model,
2 No. 3 Nerike,
2 No. 4 Hedemora,
2 No. 6 Åsele,
2 No. 8c. Småland,
2 No. 6 Skåne,
2 No. 10 Bohus,
2 No. 19 Danish,
2 No. 20 Russian.

Prev. aw.: Göteborg, 1871, bronze medal; Copenhagen, 1872, bronze medal; Moscow, 1873, silver medal; London, 1873, gilt medal; Mariestad, 1874, silver medal; Vienna, 1873, diploma of honor.

Agencies in Stockholm, Göteborg, Karlstad, Kristiania, and Trondhjem.

The works were established 1805, and have during the last few years been occupied in the manufacture of scythes exclusively. 18 able smiths and 16 apprentices are employed in the works. The water power is not less than 100 H. P. The production has been doubled in the last few years. During the last year 8,000 dozen scythes were made at a value of $3.44 to $10.20 per dozen, and sold with 5 and 6 per cent. discount at wholesale.

As raw material were used last year 500 cwts. Bessemer steel, 500 cwts. Bessemer pig iron, 1,000 cwts. of wrought iron, and 2,000 "läster" of charcoal.

The scythes are mostly sold in Sweden and Norway, and have just begun to be exported to Denmark and Finland.

Government taxes, $209; community taxes, $195; church taxes, $42.

A school for the workingmen's children, a savings bank, and a sick fund raised by weekly deposits in the bank for workingmen as well as of the widows.

CLASS 675.

503. Andersson J., Kjärdingagärde, Örebro.

Cow-Bells, Sheep-Bells.

504. Atterling, Carl. Örebro.

Dairy Apparatus constructed in such a manner that it can be set upon the open ground, and easily transported from one place to another.

Prev. aws., Stockholm, Paris, Göteborg, Moscow and Vienna.

The manufacture was commenced in 1857, and gives employment to 40 men with wages of $100, gold, per day, and 10 boys with wages of 30 cents, gold, per day.

The power required is supplied by a steam engine of 4 H. P.

The productions consists of Gas, Water and Heating Conduits, Apparatus for drug stores, distilleries, sugar refineries, dairies, soda-water, manufactories, breweries, dye-works, bathing and laundry establishments, steam-boilers, fire engines, and pump works, suction and forcing pumps, iron furniture, lightning rods and electrical bells, etc.

The annual value of the production is about $22,000 gold.

The raw materials used are:

Copper,	350 cwt.
Zinc,	100 "
Lead,	60 "
Tin,	50 "
Brass,	200 "
Bar Iron,	400 "
Castings,	varying.

The exports go to Finland, Russia, and Denmark.

A savings fund is being formed.

The common schools of the town are frequented by the children of the workmen. The rooms of the working men's society are used as reading rooms. A bath house is provided for the workmen at the manufactory.

505. Kallinge Bruk. See Class 224. Malmö.

Dairy Utensils of iron and pewter.

506. Rehnström, M. Tibble, Köping.

Drawings of dairy-houses and **utensils**.

I.—AGRICULTURAL ENGINEERING AND ADMINISTRATION.

CLASS 681.

507. Friestedt, A. W. See Cl. 200.

Commercial Fertilizers.

508. In de Betou. *P. D.* Stockholm.

A collection of all the **Artificial Manures** prepared in Sweden and their raw materials.

509. Stockholm's Superfosfat Aktiebolag.

Fertilizers, prepared, and raw materials.

CLASS 683.

510. Löfvenskiöld, Ch. Im. Bergatorp, Mariestad.

A collection of Drawings with directions in the text for the construction of suitable, simple and cheap **peasant cottages** and other **dwellings for workingmen, farm houses** and **barns, dairies, stables, pig-sties, sheep-folds, tool-houses, kilns** for threshed and unthreshed grain, smaller farm **dwellings, privies**, etc., all with detail drawings of **building parts, crib arrangements, joinings** and simple **ornaments,** even for **brick ornamented granite, ventilation, brick making,** etc., and directions for planting trees around the dwellings.

Prev. aw.: The large and small gold medal. of the Royal Agricultural Academy. Silver medal for useful work, by the Skaraborg Län agricultural Society. Stockholm, 1866, diploma of honor. Stockholm, 1868, large silver medals Göteborg, 1871, small silver medal. Mariestad, 1874, large silver medal, etc.

These works were commenced in 1836. In 1874, 751 drawings, with descriptions were executed, besides several thousand directions for building purposes. Of the drawings about 361 are already printed, or ready to be printed. In these drawings are represented a mass of simple, practical and popular arrangements, in order to facilitate and cheapen the erection of farm buildings, all systematically arranged with regard to the saving of labor and time, in all departments of farming.

The works of the exhibitor embrace a new literature, heretofore, totally unknown in Sweden which aims to create a *more moral* and *industrious homelife*, for the farmers, to procure better accommodations for the *domestic animals*, and a more careful attention to *the crops*.

DEPARTMENT VII.

HORTICULTURE.

GARDEN TOOLS.

CLASS 720.

511. Essen, H H. von, *Baron.* Tidaholm. See cl. 227. **Gardeners Scissors.**

DEPARTMENT VIII.

WOMAN'S WORK.

---

512. **Andersdotter, Margaretha.** Lättarp, Forserum.

Two Carpets.

513. **Andersson, Amanda,** *Mrs.* Stockholm.

Oil Paintings.

a. Dalkulla (Dalecarlia woman).

b. Lapplander girl.

c. Copy of "Valkyria." by ARBO.

514. **Bagge, Charlotta,** *Mrs.* Kramfors Vermland.

Frames, painted pillows.

515. **Billström, A.** *Miss.* Stockholm.

Artificial Flowers.

516. **Engdahl, Agnes,** *Miss.* Stockholm.

Writing Utensils.

517. **Fürst, Betty,** *Mrs.* Uppsala.

Portfolio, designed and made by the exhibitor.

518. **Handarbetets Wänner.** *The society "Friends of Handiwork."* Stockholm.

Women's Work in old North Patterns, made by peasant women and art-seamstresses, working under the guidance of the society, after ancient Swedish patterns, arranged and applied to the wants of the present time by artists and connoisseurs.

The embroidered exhibits are manufactured by Mrs. Friberger and Misses L. and M. Bonde, M. Friberger, Hedblad, Hedenblad, Nyman, Oxehufvud Rogberg and Schröder.

The lace-works by Mätta and Kjersti Dahlsjö, Bengta Gudmunds, Elna Hägg, Hanna Larsdotter, Ingeborg Lars Nils, Kjersti Måns Svens, and Silja Persdotter.

The tissues by Baroness Hermelin, Anna Andersson, Fina Bellman, Carlson, Maria Eskelund, Fröjd, Sophie Jonson, Chr. Lundin, O. Nilsson, and Mina Wulf.

Prev. aw.: The president and foundress of the society received a medal of merit at the international exhibition in Vienna, 1873. Its working-women have received several medals at provincial fairs in Sweden, besides rewards from the Swedish "Royal Patriotic Society."

The society did not properly commence its work until October, 1874.

The society, which works only for a principle, not for pecuniary gain, has its headquarters in Stockholm, but also employs working-women in different parts of the country, as in Skåne Blekinge, Småland, Dalarne, etc.

Through the impulse of the Swedish society a similar one is formed in Finland.

The society, which commenced its operations with *one* weaver-woman and *one* art-seamstress, now cannot get as many as it wants for the effectuation of the orders received during the last quarter-year, and is therefore, going to establish a school for ancient Swedish handiwork.

For further information, see the appendix to Part I.

519. **Hansdotter, Anna.** Lumsheden, Svärdsjö.

Linen Yarn, 1-10 Swedish mile (3,600 sw. feet long) weighing 5.5 ort. (0.055 sw. lbs).

Prev. aw.: Paris, 1867, bronze medal.

520. **Klinghammer, Gerda.** Landskrona.

Flowers and articles of dress and ornaments, made from fish scales.

521. **Nilsson, Alma,** *Miss.* Landskrona.

Artificial Flowers of fish scales, for ladies ornament.

522. **Petersén, Otto,** *Lieutenant, R. N.* Karlskrona.

Embroidery, made in Sweden about 150 years ago.

523. **Påhlman, S.,** *Miss.* Vexiö.

Embroidery.

524. Segebaden, Hermina. Grimethon.

Embroidered Pocket-Handkerchief, Cushion, Pin Cushion, Collar and Cuffs.

Prev. aw.: medals in Birmingham and Manchester.

525. Söderberg, Maria. Visby.

Lady's Top-coat of artificial fur (imitation).

526. Weidenhayn, Carolina. Stockholm.

Print from Wood Engraving, framed.

Prev. aw.: medals in Stockholm and Vienna; diploma in Moscow.

No. 7, Price $1.40 gold.

No. 8, Price $0.90 gold.

No. 3, Price $1.40 gold.

No. 9, Price $0.90 gold.

No. 12, Price $0.50 gold.

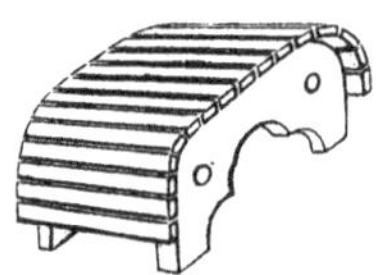

No. 13, Price $0.20 gold.

No. 10, Price $0.85 gold.

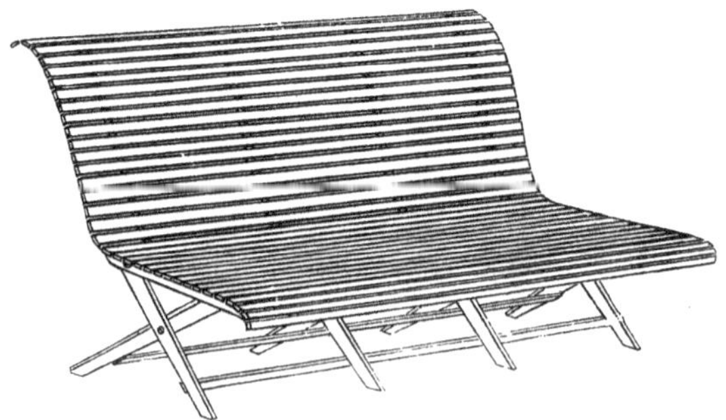

No. 2, Price $2.65 gold.

Glömsta Fabriks Bolag.

(*See page 33*).

www.ingramcontent.com/pod-product-compliance
Lightning Source LLC
LaVergne TN
LVHW010149110826
845151LV00002B/467

* 9 7 8 1 4 2 5 5 3 7 6 9 2 *